Content Literacy for Today's Adolescents

Honoring Diversity and Building Competence

Fifth Edition

William G. Brozo
George Mason University

Michele L. Simpson
University of Georgia

PEARSON

Merrill
Prentice Hall

Upper Saddle River, New Jersey
Columbus, Ohio

Library of Congress Cataloging-in-Publication Data
Brozo, William G.
   Content literacy for today's adolescents : honoring diversity and building competence / William G. Brozo, Michele L. Simpson.— 5th ed.
   p. cm.
   Rev. ed. of : Readers, teachers, learners.
   ISBN 0-13-228671-8
   1. Reading (Secondary)—United States. 2. Language arts (Secondary)—United States. I. Simpson, Michele L. II. Brozo,
William G. Readers, teachers, learners. III. Title.

LB1632B7 2007
428.4071'273—dc22   2006006783

Vice President and Executive Publisher: Jeffery W. Johnston
Senior Editor: Linda Ashe Bishop
Senior Production Editor: Mary M. Irvin
Design Coordinator: Diane C. Lorenzo
Senior Editorial Assistant: Laura Weaver
Text Design: Candace Rowley
Cover Designer: Janna Thomson Chordas
Cover Image: SuperStock
Photo Coordinator: Maria Vonada
Production Manager: Pamela D. Bennett
Director of Marketing: David Gesell
Marketing Manager: Darcy Betts Prybella
Marketing Coordinator: Brian Mounts

This book was set in Souvenir by Carlisle Publishing Services. It was printed and bound by Von Hoffmann Press, Inc. The cover was printed by Phoenix Color Corp.

Photo Credits: Silver Burdett Ginn, 2; Ken Karp (Prentice Hall School Division) 22; Anthony Magnacca/Merrill, 42, 168, 252; Scott Cunningham/Merrill, 86; Anne Vega/Merrill, 130, 208, 372; 2003, Trish Gant © Dorling Kindersley, 292; Liz Modre/Merrill, 330.

Pearson Education Ltd.
Pearson Education Singapore Pte. Ltd.
Pearson Education Canada, Ltd.
Pearson Education—Japan

Pearson Education Australia Pty. Limited
Pearson Education North Asia Ltd.
Pearson Educación de Mexico, S.A. de C. V.
Pearson Education Malaysia Pte. Ltd.

10 9 8 7 6 5 4 3 2 1
ISBN: 0-13-228671-8

For Carol, Hannah, and Genevieve
— *William G. Brozo*

For Tom
—*Michele L. Simpson*

Preface

In every case, it is the reader who reads the sense, it is the reader who grants or recognizes in an object, place or event a certain possible readability; it is the reader who must attribute meaning to a system of signs, and then decipher it. We all read ourselves and the world around us in order to glimpse what and where we are. We read to understand, or to begin to understand. We cannot do but read. Reading, almost as much as breathing, is our essential function.

Alberto Manguel (1996)

*T*hose of us who "cannot do but read" are part of a culture of letters dating from the first Sumerian tablets of the fifth millennium B.C. to Greek scrolls; from the codices of St. Augustine to the quartos of Shakespeare; from graphic novels to CD-ROMs. Every word read is part of a history of language and sense filled with tales of anarchy, censorship, triumph, and passion. To read and write, then, is to become part of that history and, moreover, to learn from the voices of the past.

Just as the printing press and mass production of books, plays, and pamphlets revolutionized conceptions of literacy in the Renaissance, today new information and communications technologies are changing the ways we think about what it means to be literate. At the same time, researchers are calling attention to social, cultural, and political dimensions of literacy, leading many to assert that literacy should no longer be defined as mere reading and writing of print but something much more complex, fluid, and multifaceted.

Drawing significant inspiration from current theorizing about multiple literacies, we are pleased to introduce the fifth edition of our book *Content Literacy for Today's Adolescents: Honoring Diversity and Building Competence.* Those of you familiar with previous editions will immediately notice the first significant change—a new title. Formerly called *Readers, Teachers, Learners: Expanding Literacy Across the Content Areas*, the revised title reflects the most current thinking in the field of adolescent and content area literacy. But a new book edition must have more than a name change to be able to boast that it's genuinely new. Users of *Content Literacy for Today's Adolescents* will become aware of the breadth of updating in this book upon perusing the Table of Contents: two new introductory chapters, a new chapter on motivation for reading and learning, a new chapter on reading from multiple sources, and a new chapter on ways of increasing engagement and literacy achievement for striving readers. Although these changes are substantial, the core theme of the book has not changed. *Content Literacy for Today's Adolescents* continues to show deference to the life-worlds of middle and secondary school teachers while supporting their daily struggle to make instruction more responsive to the needs of an increasingly diverse population.

The Philosophical Message of This Text

As the book's new title suggests, we have chosen in this edition to foreground the research and practice that honor the academic and cultural diversity of today's youth. Numerous scenes of teaching and instructional approaches are described that demonstrate how youth can be taught to bridge their literate practices outside of school with the literacies required in academic settings. The evidence clearly shows that as youths' discourse flexibility and critical thinking skills expand, confidence in their ability to succeed in life and in the workplace expands as well. And, although many of today's adolescents continue to find entry points to literacy in traditional print texts, a growing number have their first exciting learning experiences with digital media. This phenomenon has profound implications for teaching and learning in middle and secondary schools. In order to take full advantage of the resources all youth bring to the classroom, teachers will need to employ innovative practices that value the literate activity "*NetGen*" youth engage in with these new media while building their competence to perform academic literacy tasks. In this fifth edition, we greatly expand the position taken in previous editions that guiding youth to be critical readers of new media and traditional print as well as a range of alternative information sources can be complementary and mutually supportive.

Included in this text are overarching, guiding principles. These evidence-based principles contextualize the practices we advocate and help disciplinary teachers appreciate that strategies-based teaching is most effective when there is a clear understanding of learning goals and the needs of the students. These principles are not intended to prescribe a specific set of practices, but are offered to help teachers envision instructional possibilities within their own school and classroom milieu. With fresh and exciting reading, writing, and literacy research as a backdrop, we have tried in a collaborative spirit to empower teachers with the confidence to make their own best decisions about the learning that goes on in their classrooms.

Another vital message of the book has been made more vivid in this fifth edition: teachers inform us as much as we inform them, and our students are the ultimate curricular informants. In a very real sense, the growth and improvement of adolescents' language processes and disciplinary knowledge will depend on the strength of the interactions between teachers in higher education and teachers in middle and secondary schools, as well as the strength of the relationships between students and their teachers.

Being an active reader can expand young people's life and career options and enlarge their sense of self. This edition, as with each of its predecessors, is about widening life and career options for youth in the middle and upper grades through literacy. We are confident *Content Literacy for Today's Adolescents* will continue to be used as a resource by teachers in every discipline to create engaging and constructive learning environments where youth use literacy for personal pleasure, as a tool for academic achievement, to expand self-efficacy, and to envision new possible futures for themselves.

Organization of the Text

This text is designed to help you teach disciplinary content more effectively and to develop independent learners who can think about information and ideas in competent and critical ways. This text is also designed to help you envision the possibilities for exciting teaching and learning in your classroom. To this end, we have filled *Content Literacy for Today's Adolescents* with practical examples, teaching scenarios, and classroom dialogues. We want to reiterate that the strategies and practices in this book should always be regarded as suggestions instead of prescriptions, which in the hands of innovative and caring teachers can be adapted to meet the needs of every learner.

Chapters 1 and 2 provide important foundational and contextual information about adolescents and content literacy. Chapter 1, *Adolescent Identities and Literacies*, paints in broad strokes the character and culture of today's adolescents. You will quickly come to learn that adolescence is multifaceted and that each individual youth brings to school a set of unique and valuable experiences. When viewed as a resource, adolescent experience with literacy and language provides a connection to academic literacy and disciplinary knowledge. In Chapter 2, *Principled Practices for Effective Reading and Learning*, we present six essential principles to guide content literacy. These principles frame the discussion of theory, research, and practice in all subsequent chapters. We strongly recommend that you read these first two chapters before reading the others, because the remaining chapters build on the foundations established in Chapters 1 and 2.

Sequencing chapters for a book on content literacy is never easy. Regardless of the content that you teach or plan to teach, each chapter can provide you with insights into effective classroom interactions and practical examples of teaching strategies. Chapters 3 through 7 are filled with strategies and ideas for classroom implementation. Chapter 3, *Principled Practices for Expanding Comprehension*, reflects the most current ideas about how to foster meaningful reading and critical thinking. *Classroom Assessment of Literacy Growth and Content Learning*, Chapter 4, presents a range of useful assessment strategies to inform teachers' instructional decisions and students' self-awareness as learners. A revised Chapter 5, *Creating Motivating Contexts for Literacy and Learning*, has been significantly expanded to include much more than readiness to read and learn new material. In this chapter revision, strategies and practices for motivating youth to read and learn content at any phase of instruction are presented. Chapters 6, *Developing General and Content-Area Vocabulary Knowledge,* and 7, *Writing as a Tool for Active Learning*, discuss new and exciting practices for expanding youths' word knowledge as well as engaging adolescents in content-area writing.

A thoroughly revised Chapter 8, *Reading and Learning from Multiple Sources*, formerly devoted to ways of linking textbooks and trade books, now provides principles and practices related to an increasingly commonplace expectation in disciplinary classrooms that students read and learn from a variety of sources in addition to or other than a core textbook. To maximize the benefits of using multiple sources, we describe numerous strategies that have been found to be effective for increasing literacy abilities and content knowledge. Chapter 9, *Learning Strategies,* focuses on ways of developing independent, strategic readers and thinkers, while Chapter 10, *Expanding Literacy and Content Learning Through Information and Communication Technologies*, is filled with outstanding new ways teachers in the content areas are employing digital technology to increase student motivation, expand opportunities for language development, and make learning more accessible and memorable.

Finally, a new Chapter 11, *Honoring Diversity and Building Competence: Supporting Striving Adolescent Readers Across the Disciplines,* has been included because disciplinary teachers everywhere struggle to find appropriate ways of meeting the needs of youth who have difficulty with reading and writing assignments and who come from disparate backgrounds. By using the term *striving reader* instead of *struggling reader* or even *reading disabled*, we hope to promote positive perceptions of what these youth are capable of doing when provided effective instruction. The practices described in this chapter are guided by all six principles, since striving adolescent readers deserve our best strategies and approaches.

Case Studies. With this fifth edition, all eleven chapters include case studies. After each chapter introduction, you will be asked to consider a particular problem or issue from an actual teaching scenario related to the content of the chapter. At the conclusion of the chapter, the case study is revisited, and you are invited to offer teaching or problem-solving suggestions. This process makes your reading and studying more interactive, and it is hoped you will become better able to envision the potential applications of the strategies in genuine classroom environments. We urge you to take full advantage of the case studies as you read and reflect on chapter information.

Text Features and Important Updates

Those readers familiar with our previous editions will immediately notice some major revisions in this book in both format and content.

- **Anticipation Guides**—Each chapter opens with interactive guides that ask readers to activate their prior knowledge and foreshadow the important concepts in each chapter. Readers are then asked to return to the guides after reading and studying each chapter to self-assess their learning. The use of anticipation guides is a strategy we strongly advocate teachers use with their own students.

NEW!
- **Guiding Principles**—Six overarching principles are introduced in new Chapter 2 to highlight the most critical elements of content-area literacy. These principles are meant to serve as guiding themes for the strategies and practices presented in each chapter.

- **More Actual Teaching Vignettes**—Again in this edition, we provide numerous scenes of teaching woven into the description of content literacy strategies and practices. This feature has been touted by readers of previous editions as one of the most appreciated. By reading actual teaching situations and scenarios in the form of vignettes, readers find it easier to envision application of the strategies we present. The scenarios demonstrate the valuable lessons to be learned from content-area teachers struggling and succeeding as they implement stimulating reading, writing, and learning strategies. Guiding principles frame these vignettes and examples, which offer glimpses of teachers making literacy and content learning work.

NEW!
- *Teacher as Learner* **Boxes**—New to this edition and appearing throughout every chapter are special boxed features entitled "Teacher as Learner." This boxed material offers readers an opportunity to extend their understanding of key concepts and practices in an interactive format. Prompts direct readers to brainstorm ideas, connect material to their own experiences, and think critically about personally held beliefs and attitudes. To get the most out of each chapter, be sure to take the time to complete the "Teacher as Learner" boxes.

NEW!
- *The Role of the Teacher Leader* **Boxes**—Another new feature of this edition are segments in every chapter that describe how teacher leaders can and have supported their colleagues in implementing best practices with youth. If you already serve in a teacher-leader role or may envision that role for yourself in the future, material in these boxes will be extremely helpful in providing realistic models of *effective* literacy leadership for disciplinary teachers.

NEW!
- *Honoring Diversity and Building Competence in the Content Classroom* **Segments**—New to this edition and appearing in Chapters 1 through 10 are special boxed features entitled "Honoring Diversity and Building

Competence in the Content Classroom." This boxed material describes content-area teachers working with students who deserve extra learning support. Our goal with this approach is to help reinforce the idea that all adolescent readers/learners, regardless of ability level or linguistic/cultural background, are deserving of responsive instruction in *every* classroom. In addition to these segments in the first ten chapters, Chapter 11 focuses entirely on the reading and learning needs of these youth.

- **Expanded Marginal Notes**—Notes in the margins that signal important content and ideas are richer and have been improved upon by the addition of references to the book's Companion Website. At this site, readers will find a variety of supporting information, such as useful Internet sites. These notes now include references to other relevant professional literature.

- **Companion Website**—Accompanying this edition is an improved, user-friendly Companion Website that provides readers a variety of helpful resources. Within each chapter, marginal notes direct readers to the Website where chapter objectives, multiple-choice review questions, links to other helpful Internet sites, and other relevant links may be accessed.

Assumptions Underlying the Literacy Strategies in the Fifth Edition

As with the previous editions, a major theme of this book is that teachers who employ practices based on sound and supportable principles are more likely to engender active learning and expand literacy for youth in the middle and upper grades. Throughout *Content Literacy for Today's Adolescents* we describe strategies that exploit adolescents' beliefs, abilities, and backgrounds and provide new, imaginative experiences for helping them find reasons to learn. The strategies we discuss demonstrate how disciplinary teachers can support youth's efforts to become independent, active learners. Above all, the strategies and practices in this book are intended to make learning engaging and accessible for all.

Our selection of strategies for this fifth edition was guided by our belief that students can become engaged and purposeful learners when provided opportunities for sustained experiences in constructing meaning from and with text and when they are made to feel welcome as active participants in content classrooms. Youth are likely to become active members of a classroom community when teachers create learning experiences that are positive and authentic, when they make learning meaning centered, when they work with youth to shape the nature of learning, and when they give youth personally relevant reasons to learn.

The following assumptions form the foundation on which our ideas for teaching and learning rest.

1. **Teaching is more than dispensing information, because learning is more than receiving and remembering information.** Learning is the construction of meaning, an active process on the part of the learner. Teaching is creating classroom contexts that support the knowledge construction process.

2. **A major goal of education should be the development of critical thinkers and active, independent learners.** Youth should be provided opportunities to play active roles in the meaning-making process. Students should be engaged in learning experiences that help them critically evaluate their worlds and participate in active problem solving of real-world concerns.

3. **To be literate is to use literacy as a tool for learning.** In supportive learning environments adolescents can learn to use literacy as a tool for meaningful and functional learning.

4. **Content and process should be taught simultaneously.** Youth should be led to see that *what* is learned is inextricably tied to *how* one learns. Furthermore, youth should come to see that content learning and content literacy are essentially one and the same.

5. **Content-area teachers need to develop students' will to learn.** Literacy and learning skills are of little help if youth are unmotivated to learn. Motivation results when teachers create interesting learning environments and help students develop their own personally relevant reasons for learning.

Acknowledgments

This preface would be incomplete without recognizing the supporting role of the Merrill editorial and production staff. A very special thanks to Linda Bishop, our editor and friend, who walked with us every interesting step of the way down the sometimes bumpy, sometimes smooth, road to this revision. Without her generosity of time and advice and faith in the power of our message about content-area literacy this fifth edition would never have been transformed into a new and better resource for teachers. Thanks as well go out to our production editor Mary Irvin and our production coordinator Jolynn Kilburg for their specific assistance in ensuring each word in our book was accessible to readers. Thanks also to our media editor Dan Parker for his patience and wizardry in guiding us in our mapping and content planning for our Companion Website.

We are, of course, extremely indebted to our diligent reviewers whose helpful insights made this fifth edition an even better text than its predecessors. They are: Deanna Birdyshaw, University of Michigan; Katrina Hunter-Mintz, Berry College; Gay Ivey, James Madison University; Steve Wellinski, Illinois State University. Finally, we thank all the students, teachers, and colleagues whose experiences inspired us and continue to influence our work.

In physics, the term "butterfly effect"—small influences that create dramatic effects—is derived from the idea that the mere flap of an insect's wing in your backyard might ignite a chain of meteorological events leading to a hurricane on the other side of the globe. This book is dedicated to small influences that bring about big changes in the way adolescents and teachers in middle and secondary schools interact to enhance the quality and ensure equity in youth learning.

Bill Brozo
Michele Simpson

References

Copper-Mullin, A., & Coye, J.M. (1998). *Once upon a heroine: 400 books for girls to love.* Chicago, IL: Contemporary Books.

Manguel, A. (1996). *A history of reading.* New York: Viking.

About the Authors

William G. Brozo is a professor of language and literacy at George Mason University. He earned his bachelor's degree from the University of North Carolina and his master's and doctorate from the University of South Carolina. He has taught reading and language arts in junior and senior high school in the Carolinas. He is the author of numerous articles on literacy development for young adults as well as *To Be a Boy, To Be a Reader* (International Reading Association), a book of strategies for helping teen and preteen males become active readers. Dr. Brozo serves on the editorial review boards of the *Reading Research Quarterly* and *Reading Research and Instruction* and the editorial advisory board of the *Journal of Adolescent & Adult Literacy*. He is also a member of the Commission on Adolescent Literacy. Dr. Brozo regularly speaks at professional meetings around the country and consults with teachers and administrators to discuss ways of enriching the literacy culture of middle and secondary schools and making teaching more responsive to student needs.

Bill lives in Vienna, Virginia, with his wife and daughter and their standard poodle, Teddy. He is an aficionado of opera and Renaissance music and drama. He runs daily to stay fit.

Michele L. Simpson is a professor of reading at the University of Georgia, where she teaches learning strategy courses to undergraduates, conducted research, and mentored doctoral students, in addition, she has served as coordinator of a program for new professors representing a wide spectrum of academic disciplines such as chemistry, biology, history, and mathematics. After receiving her bachelor's and master's degrees from the University of Northern Iowa, she taught speech, reading, and language arts to students in junior and senior highs in Illinois, Iowa, and Michigan. In Iowa she was recognized as the Reading Teacher of the Year, the first secondary teacher to win such an award. Michele has co-authored two textbooks on learning strategies and vocabulary development and has contributed numerous chapters to edited books such as the *Handbook of Reading Research* (Vol. 3). In addition to making presentations at national and international conferences, she has published more than 60 articles in journals such as the *Journal of Adolescent & Adult Literacy*, the *Journal of Literacy Research*, and *The Journal of Educational Psychology."*

Michele lives in Athens, Georgia, with her husband and Siamese cat named Red Chief (if you know O'Henry, the author, you understand the cat's name). When she is not teaching or writing, she enjoys biking, traveling, and maintaining her Hatha Yoga regime.

Teacher Preparation Classroom

TEACHER PREP

MERRILL
PRENTICE HALL

See a demo at
www.prenhall.com/teacherprep/demo

Your Class. Their Careers. Our Future. Will your students be prepared?

We invite you to explore our new, innovative and engaging website and all that it has to offer you, your course, and tomorrow's educators! Organized around the major courses pre-service teachers take, the Teacher Preparation site provides media, student/teacher artifacts, strategies, research articles, and other resources to equip your students with the quality tools needed to excel in their courses and prepare them for their first classroom.

This ultimate on-line education resource is available at no cost, when packaged with a Merrill text, and will provide you and your students access to:

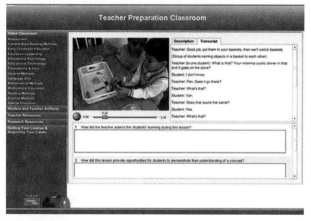

Online Video Library. More than 150 video clips—each tied to a course topic and framed by learning goals and Praxis-type questions—capture real teachers and students working in real classrooms, as well as in-depth interviews with both students and educators.

Student and Teacher Artifacts. More than 200 student and teacher classroom artifacts—each tied to a course topic and framed by learning goals and application questions—provide a wealth of materials and experiences to help make your study to become a professional teacher more concrete and hands-on.

Research Articles. Over 500 articles from ASCD's renowned journal *Educational Leadership*. The site also includes Research Navigator, a searchable database of additional educational journals.

Teaching Strategies. Over 500 strategies and lesson plans for you to use when you become a practicing professional.

Licensure and Career Tools. Resources devoted to helping you pass your licensure exam; learn standards, law, and public policies; plan a teaching portfolio; and succeed in your first year of teaching.

How to ORDER *Teacher Prep* for you and your students:
For students to receive a *Teacher Prep* Access Code with this text, instructors **must** provide a special value pack ISBN number on their textbook order form. To receive this special ISBN, please email **Merrill.marketing@pearsoned.com** and provide the following information:
- Name and Affiliation
- Author/Title/Edition of Merrill text

Upon ordering *Teacher Prep* for their students, instructors will be given a lifetime *Teacher Prep* Access Code.

Contents

Special Features

Honoring Diversity and Building Competence in the Content Classroom

chapter 1

Adolescent Identities and Literacies

Anticipation Guide

Directions: Read each statement carefully and decide whether you agree or disagree with it, placing a check mark in the appropriate *Before Reading* column. When you have finished reading and studying the chapter, return to the guide and decide whether your anticipations need to be changed by placing a check mark in the appropriate *After Reading* column.

	Before Reading		After Reading	
	Agree	*Disagree*	*Agree*	*Disagree*
1. "Raging hormones" is the best way to describe the period known as adolescence.	____	____	____	____
2. The negative behaviors youth exhibit mirror the behaviors of the adults around them.	____	____	____	____
3. Adolescent literacy can be defined as reading and writing text.	____	____	____	____
4. Youth bring a range of competencies to any learning experience.	____	____	____	____
5. Adolescent identity is tied directly to discourse practices and language competencies.	____	____	____	____
6. Nearly any practice is justifiable if it's done in the service of developing academic literacy.	____	____	____	____

To know one child you have to swallow the world.

—Rushdie (1991)

*U*nderstanding today's youth requires an attitude of openness to their unique and diverse nature. As the lead quote to the chapter implies, it is perhaps only through an appreciation of the lifeworlds of adolescents and how they shape and are shaped by their worlds that we can ever really come to know them. Popular stereotypes about adolescence are conveniences that belie the multidimensionality and complexity of this stage in human development (Hersch, 1998). As some would have it, adolescents, at best, are merely imperfect adults in transition (Serafini, Bean, & Readence, 2004); at worst, they're a bundle of raging hormones, callow and self-centered, and even menacing (Lesko, 2001). Stoking these stereotypes are media that sensationalize, teen violence and sexual promiscuity (Barbour, 1999), as well as myths about young adults' poor reading habits (Aronson, 2001) and academic shortcomings. Males (2001) responds to these characterizations of teenagers by insisting that adults raise a mirror to themselves when passing harsh judgment on youth behavior:

> Adolescents behave like the adult society that raises them. They did not land on a meteorite. We raised them. They share our values. They act like us. . . . If teenagers behave like the adult society that raises them, their evil is the same as ours, and it is not curable by aiming increasingly absurd, cosmetic panaceas at the young. (p. 40)

Like Males, Aronson (2000) sees a kind of dual standard in play for many adults who allow themselves a great deal of latitude in their search for self while narrowing expectations for adolescents' identity experimentation. He says "Adults keep expanding the psychological space they need for self-expression. . . . But at the very same time . . . want their adolescent progeny to behave like children. . . . What they are exploring in themselves is exactly what they want to prevent in their children" (p. 7).

This chapter is devoted to discussing various facets of youth culture and the part literacy plays in adolescent identity formation. By opening the lens wide to view the ever-shifting and multifarious nature of adolescence, we hope to make clear just how important it is to increase our understanding of the individuals for whom all the strategies and ideas contained in this book are intended. We believe that it is only with a disposition of openness toward newer conceptions of today's youth and the literacies they use and need can we become better teachers of subject matter as well as more responsive teachers of students (Moje, 1996; Moje, Young, Readence, & Moore, 2000).

Go to *http://www. prenhall.com/brozo,* select Chapter 1, then click on Chapter Objectives to provide a focus for your reading.

Go to Web Resources for Chapter 1 at *http://www. prenhall.com/brozo,* and look for Mike Males Web site.

CASE STUDY

Bridging her students' culture and personal interests with the content of her high school business classes is the only way Marta knows how to teach. Some topics, however, have been more difficult to link to students' lifeworlds than others. One such topic, writing business contracts, created unique challenges for Marta because most of her students were from financially strapped homes with parents employed part-time. Few if any had ever seen an actual business contract before or had any experience at all with the workworld.

Case studies in this textbook provide an opportunity to apply principles and practices to new contexts.

To the Reader:

In this chapter we raise several important issues about adolescent literacies and identities. One overarching theme is that adolescents are more likely to remain engaged readers and learners if their everyday experiences and discourses are honored and made to enrich the classroom culture. As you read, consider how a teacher like Marta might capitalize on what her students bring to the business class as a link to understanding the topic of business contracts.

The Multidimensionality of Youth Culture

A growing body of research into youth culture has expanded our understanding of what it means to be an adolescent while challenging our traditional constructions of adolescence (Finders, 1998/1999; Larson, Richards, & Moneta, 1996; McDonald, 1999; Moje, 2002). A fruitful place to begin our discussion, then, is to evaluate our own opinions about adolescents. In the following Teacher as Learner box, decide where you stand relative to each statement about America's teens. Afterward, read the statements in the next box entitled *Facts About Adolescents* and compare them with your own opinions.

Popular constructions of adolescence do not adequately account for the complexity of youth.

We believe it is productive to deconstruct stereotypes about American teens by exposing the worst myths that have built up around them. The 10 statements in the opinionnaire activity come from sociologist and youth advocate Mike Males's (2001)

TEACHER AS LEARNER

AN OPINIONNAIRE ACTIVITY ABOUT AMERICAN TEENS

Directions: Consider carefully each of the following 10 statements and then write a sentence stating your own opinion about each statement. Afterward, look at the *Facts About Adolescents* box and compare your opinions with the facts.

1. *Teenagers are uniquely violent and crime-prone.*
   Your Opinion: _____
   _____

2. *The worst danger to youth is children killing children.*
   Your Opinion: _____
   _____

3. *Youth violent crime is skyrocketing while adult violence is declining.*
   Your Opinion: _____
   _____

4. *Teenagers are innately prone to reckless behavior and are stimulated to violence primarily by media images, impulsiveness, and gun availability.*
   Your Opinion: _____
   _____

5. *Today's schools are cauldrons of violence.*
   Your Opinion: _____
   _____

6. *Teenage birth rates are out of control.*
   Your Opinion: _____
   _____

7. *Teenagers are the most at-risk for AIDS.*
   Your Opinion: _____
   _____

8. *Teenagers have high risk for suicide.*
   Your Opinion: _____
   _____

9. *Teenagers are the group most at-risk of drug abuse.*
   Your Opinion: _____
   _____

10. *Teenagers smoke because of immaturity, peer pressure, and tobacco ads.*
    Your Opinion: _____
    _____

top-10 myths about adolescents, as do the statements of actual facts about teens. This exercise highlights the need among those of us involved in the care and education of youth to reject the glib and largely groundless accusations about their behavior. Instead, we should recognize that teens are more likely than not to mimic the adults around them. Thus, as we come to appreciate how adult and teen behaviors are interconnected, the chances grow for improving dialog, understanding, cooperation, and learning.

FACTS ABOUT ADOLESCENTS

1. *Youth and adults commit crimes at roughly equal rates.*
2. *The great majority of children 17 years and younger who are killed are killed by adults.*
3. *An increase in violent crime for youth and adults has been identical.*
4. *U.S. society as a whole has a violence problem. Senior citizens in the United States are more likely to kill someone than a European teenager.*
5. *Risks of murder and being victim to other crimes of violence are extremely low in schools as compared with neighborhoods and homes.*
6. *Teenage birth rates are identical to those of the adults around them. Three-quarters of babies born to teenagers are fathered by adult men.*
7. *Teens rank third by age group in studies of when HIV infection was acquired. Nearly all HIV transmission to teens is from adults.*
8. *Suicide rates for high school age youths are half those of adults.*
9. *Teens are the least at-risk of drug abuse, whereas there have been record levels of middle-aged drug abuse.*
10. *Youths from homes where parents smoke or from social groups with high proportions of adults who smoke are three times more likely to smoke than others.*

As we have suggested, the search for tidy, all-inclusive definitions of youth is doomed to failure because of the complex nature of adolescent life. Due in large part to persistent stereotypes and rigid perceptions of adolescence, it is only relatively recently that youth culture has been the focus of scholarship by the psychological, sociological, and anthropological communities. These new perspectives on youth offer a more complete and nuanced view of the shared experiences and values of adolescents. Before discussing these perspectives, however, let's begin with a look at some important demographic considerations.

The Demographics of Youth Culture in America

So who are the individuals and groups that comprise youth culture in the United States at the outset of the 21st century? One way to answer this question is by looking at the most recent census data available (U.S. Census Bureau, 2003). The adolescent population today, ages 10 to 19, totals over 40 million and is growing. While White youth make up over 60% of this segment of our society, it is more racially and ethnically diverse than ever before and more so than the general population. Hispanic youth now represent a greater percentage (15.6%) than African American youth (14.5%), and this trend is expected to continue for the foreseeable future as Hispanic immigration increases. Asian/Pacific Islanders at the present time represent less than 4% of youth, but are projected to double in size by 2020. Over half of all adolescents, mostly White, live in suburban settings; and more than a quarter live in central city areas, where there are much higher concentrations of African American and Hispanic youth.

As youth culture becomes more diverse the need for teachers trained to work with them will grow.

The expected increase in the numbers of Hispanics and Asian/Pacific Islanders comes as a result of an unprecedented wave of immigration we are experiencing nationwide. The decade of the 1990s saw immigration population growth that has rivaled any period in our history (Rong & Preissle, 1998; U.S. Census Bureau, 2002). This unparalleled level of transnational migration has introduced into our middle and secondary schools ever-growing numbers of students with limited English skills. The United States Department of Education estimates that over 5 million school-aged children and youth occupy this category, two times the number of just one decade ago (Hawkins, 2004). Though the growing number of immigrants has enriched the racial, ethnic, cultural, and linguistic diversity within the United States, the increased diversity in population challenges long-held beliefs about what it means to be "American" (Miron, Inda, & Aguirre, 1998). At the same time, data point to a shortage of teachers across the nation who are qualified or trained to teach these new immigrant children, with claims of as few as 1 qualified teacher available for every 100 English language learners (ELLs) (Zhoa, 2002). Furthermore, it has been estimated that only 2.5% of teachers with ELL students in their classes have any special preparation to work with them (Ruiz-de-Velasco, Fix, & Clewell, 2001).

Go to Web Resources for Chapter 1 at *http://www. prenhall.com/brozo,* and look for Kids Count 2005 Data Book and U.S. Census Bureau.

What other important demographic data do we have for these young adults? The good news is that overall child well-being has improved nationally. Eight of 10 critical indicators such as the rate of teen deaths by accident, homicide, and suicide; teen birth rate; high school dropouts; and number of children living in poverty all moved in a positive direction during the period from 1996 to 2001 (Kids Count, 2004). About two-thirds of all teens are growing up in households with both parents, and most have demonstrated reading and math levels at the basic level or higher.

Despite these positive indicators, it's helpful to put into perspective the facts and figures compiled on youth in order to underscore the very real perils of adolescent life in America. For instance, on a typical day in 2001, the following could be said (Kids Count, 2004):

- 18 teens died from accidents
- 5 teens died from homicide
- 4 teens committed suicide
- Nearly 400 children were born to females ages 15 to 17
- 750 children were added to the poverty ranks
- 1.5 million children had parents behind bars
- 3,000 students dropped out of high school

Holding in mind the myths about youth (noted in *Facts About Adolescents*) and realizing that there have been improvements in the overall quality of life for teens, these facts remind us, nonetheless, that our work is never done concerning improving the living and learning conditions for every young person. We know from research that caring, engaged teachers who actively seek to form supportive relationships with adolescents can help sustain student effort, increase achievement, and improve students' life and career options (Ancess, 2003). Given the galaxy of potentially harmful influences in the lives of many teens, it becomes all the more critical that their learning and relational needs do not go unaddressed at school (Davidson, 1996).

▌*Conceptualizing Adolescent Identity*

If there is one safe assertion we might make about this period of development, it's that adolescence is marked by an active and self-conscious process of identity construction. Indeed, shaping one's sense of self is considered by many to be the primary developmental task for adolescents (Erikson, 1980; Gee, 2001; Markus & Nurius, 1986). Teen and preteen youth struggle with concerns and questions about how they're perceived by others, how they define themselves, and what they are to become. At the same time, adolescents develop a growing awareness of their membership in various discourse communities, which they help define and which serve as funds of knowledge in their burgeoning awareness of the world and of themselves (Moje et al., 2004). Family, friends, school, work, and virtual worlds contribute to a multifaceted self that defies stereotypes and simple categories. Hannah, a 15-year-old 10th grader, offers these insights into the complex nature of adolescent identity during this crucial period in her life:

Go to Web Resources for Chapter 1 at *http://www.prenhall.com/brozo,* and look for Adolescents.

> It's difficult fitting in. It's difficult to be your own person and be accepted. There's a lot of pressure to conform and become someone you may not be or do something you don't normally do or feel. It's like personalities going everywhere. (Brozo, 2003, p. 7)

Identity, Engagement, and Literacy Competencies

Linked closely to the process of identity construction is what it means for young adults to be competent and literate learners in both academic and out-of-school contexts. A body of evidence (Alvermann, 2002a; Bandura, 1993; Bean, 2000; Pajares, 1996; Phelps & Hanley-Maxwell, 1997) makes clear that youth are more likely to succeed academically and go on to be successful in adulthood when they see themselves as able and authorized members of learning communities (Cook-Sather, 2002; Edwards, 2001; Sturtevant et al., in press). Yet, many adolescents who possess talent, energy, and intelligence find themselves in school settings where these competencies may go untapped (Hinchman, Alvermann, Boyd, Brozo, & Vacca, 2003/2004; Nelson, 2004). The results of failing to align school curricula with students' interests and outside-of-school competencies are not inconsequential.

The so-called "Fourth-grade slump" (Cummins, 2001; McCray, Vaughn, & Neal, 2001; Snow, 2002), a period during the intermediate and early middle school years when motivation to engage in school-related behaviors begins to wane, has been well-documented in the literature (Eccles, Wigfield, Midgley, Reaman, MacIver, & Feldlaufer, 1993; McPhail, Pierson, Freeman, Goodman, & Ayappa, 2000) and bemoaned by parents and teachers. Why is it that so many youngsters as they begin formal schooling are full of enthusiasm for the day's activities, only to find school laborious and detached from their desires and goals by the time they reach preteen years? This motivational crisis might be explained as arising from a mismatch between the competency and identity needs of adolescents and conventional curricular schemes of middle and secondary schools (Gee, 2001; McCarthey & Moje, 2002). Alvermann and her colleagues (Alvermann et al., 2001) assert that:

> . . . our nation's schools have not always recognized and made use of the very real but widely disparate abilities of our nation's adolescents. Their diversity, the result of individual differences and life trajectories, as well as community differences and

cultural backgrounds, are too often seen as liabilities rather than as the helpful opportunities for education they can be. In spite of a growing body of scholarship on the intellectual, emotional, and social needs of teenagers, most schools have not employed the curricula and instructional methods this work suggests. (p. 6)

As young adolescents become more cognitively astute and self-aware they seek contexts that support their growing sense of autonomy, desire for social networking, and identity development (Holland, Lachicotte, Skinner, & Cain, 1998; Lesko, 2001). If they encounter traditional, teacher-centered instructional practices in middle and secondary schools, positive affect for learning diminishes and a psychological distance from school-related activities increases (Serafini et al., 2004). On the other hand, when offered a curriculum that is responsive to the interests and abilities they bring to school, and pays attention to who they are as individuals, young people will sustain their engagement in learning (Ancess, 2003; Brozo, 2002; Heron, 2003).

The Danger of Disengagement

Ensuring adolescents remained engaged learners and stay the course in school is crucial for success in adulthood. Despite signs that the overall well-being of youth has improved nationally over the past decade, there is a growing number of "disconnected" adolescents who seem to have foreclosed on their futures (Sawatzki, 2004). It is estimated that nearly 5 million young people ages 16 to 24 are living their difficult lives below the radar screens of most shapers of public policy (Herbert, 2001). According to Herbert:

Most lack basic job skills as well as solid literacy . . . they are neither working nor looking for jobs. They are not in vocational training. They are not in manufacturing. They are not part of the information age. They are not included in the American conversation. (p. 15)

Being consigned to a life of invisibility may be in part the legacy of school practices and content that failed to engage these youths' imaginations, provide safe boundaries for identity construction, and nurture competencies within and beyond the school walls (Duncan, 2000; Flores-Gonzalez, 2002; Rymes, 2001). As you'll see in the next section, literacy can be a powerful tool in the lives of youth for exploring, expressing, and constructing healthy identities.

Language, Culture, and Identity

Who we are is inextricably tied to the ways we express ourselves. Dat, a senior in high school whose second language is English, explains how the full breadth of his personality goes unrecognized for those who only know his English persona: "Even though my English is pretty good, I don't feel like myself unless I'm speaking Vietnamese." Indeed, Dat's awareness of the connection between language and identity must be shared by countless numbers of immigrant youth in schools and communities across the land struggling daily to meet the linguistic expectations of school and the dominant culture (Leander, 2002). Census data reveal that over 35 million people in the United States speak a language other than English at home (Morrell, 2002). As noted in this chapter, Latinos are the fastest-growing minority group, with 50%

of the total minority population being Spanish speakers. These Spanish speakers comprise over 70% of the ELL population, while the number of Vietnamese students, like Dat, totals nearly 5%. Combined, then, these two groups account for over 75% of the total linguistic minority population (Ruiz-de-Velasco et al., 2001).

As you can see, for most language minority students like Dat who are entering our secondary schools in larger and larger numbers, many issues of identity are at stake. Although most ELL students acquire English language proficiency at varying levels, many of them have problems with adjustment and identity that may go unaddressed in school. It's critical to point out that immigration issues for people of color have been unfairly and inappropriately compared to those of previous waves of immigrants of European descent. Unlike earlier, largely White immigration, immigrant youth of color are confronted by unfounded social stereotypes and generalizations about achievement and behavior that act as barriers to personal and academic advancement. Hones (2002) argues that the vast majority of students of color, particularly Latino and Asian youth, who fail to live out the "American Dream" begin to fix blame for their failure on themselves, their parents, and their racial or cultural group. Our secondary schools could and should be sites of critical self-exploration for these students where identity construction, language development, and academic success occur within supportive and caring learning environments.

Go to Web Resources for Chapter 1 at *http://www. prenhall.com/brozo,* and look for English Language Learners.

Academic Literacy and Language Identity Disjunctures in Secondary Schools

We would like to stress that challenges of identity arising out of linguistic differences between students and school are not restricted to immigrant populations (Ogbu, 1998; Tatum, 2005). Speakers of any dialect at variance from that of the school and dominant culture are often made to feel incompetent and must cope with stereotypes others have for them based on their language difference (Richardson, 2003; Willis, Garcia, Barrera, & Harris, 2003). This idea shouldn't be that difficult to understand for any of us who travel abroad or spend time as a dialect-different speaker in monolingual cultures here at home. And because our identity matters a great deal to us, so too must our language. Consequently, ignoring, denying, or demeaning the language of identity of a young person is in a very real sense devaluing the individual him or herself.

Few teachers are guilty of intentionally demeaning the language identity of students, yet a dispiriting message is received daily by many youth who bring to school literacy and language tools different from those expected in academic contexts (Labov, 2003). Morrell (2002) posits that one of the biggest challenges facing literacy educators in the United States today is finding effective ways to teach an increasingly diverse student population. At the heart of the challenge is the struggle to develop academic literacies through curricula and strategies that are inclusive and affirm the cultural value and individual identities of every adolescent. Indeed, this is the challenge we take up in this book.

When we use the expression *academic literacy* we are referring to ways of engaging with, producing, and talking about texts that are valued in school, on standardized assessments, and lead to career and professional opportunities highly regarded in the dominant culture (Harris & Hodges, 1995; Street, 2003; Venezky, Wagner, & Ciliberti, 1990). Middle and secondary school students and teachers need to possess sophisticated language tools to explore information and concepts in content-area subjects such as history, mathematics, science, and literature (Borasi & Siegel, 2000; Crawford, Kelly, & Brown, 2000; Echevarria, 2003; Hinchman &

Honoring adolescent diversity means viewing youth as a resource of language abilities and experiences rife with curricular connections.

The Role of the Teacher Leader

Given the complexity of today's youth culture, meeting the literacy and learning needs of every youth will require a total commitment on the part of administrators, teachers, parents, and any concerned adult whose life intersects with adolescents. All across the United States, one professional being asked to take on more and more responsibility for the overall academic welfare of middle and secondary students is the *literacy specialist* or *coach*. The literacy coach is a master teacher who provides vital leadership for the overall secondary literacy program (Sturtevant, 2003). As the embodiment of a district's or school's commitment to maximizing the literate potential of all youth, the literacy coach must assume some heady challenges. Among these include leading literacy teams (Anders, 2002), guiding teachers in using appropriate teaching strategies, liaising with teachers and administrators, and modeling expert teaching (Bean, Swan, & Knaub, 2003).

In the critical role as expert teacher, the literacy coach can demonstrate for content-area teachers numerous ways of making instruction more responsive to the cultural, language, and learning uniqueness of each young person (Tatum, 2004). For example, the coach could demonstrate how history and government teachers might take advantage of the funds of knowledge recent immigrant youth bring with them to the study of America's colonial past or ways urban youth might form or participate in community action projects to resist the expansion of waste sites in their communities. The literacy coach can support teachers in organizing cross-age tutoring or mentoring programs for ELL students and striving readers as an alternative to pull-out, remedial reading classes (Sturtevant et al., 2006). Woven into each of these initiatives are numerous opportunities for youth to practice and extend traditional print literacy skills as well as employ familiar information and communication technology tools.

In each subsequent chapter of this book we include highlighted information about the role of the teacher-leader in furthering the development of particular literacy and learning strategies for youth.

Zalewski, 1996). Students who come from backgrounds in which the discourse of home and community is similar to academic discourse are more likely to experience success in school contexts. For many students, however, their knowledge of subject matter and language as well as their literacy tools may compete with those of their peers and teachers (Moje, Callazo, Carrillo, & Marx, 2001). Where integration and accommodation of inside- and outside-of-school discourse practices occur for these students, literacy and learning benefits can accrue (Brozo, 2006). In the case study in this chapter and in others throughout the chapters that follow, we demonstrate numerous ways in which teachers help youth find connections from the language and knowledge resources they bring to school to the content and concepts under consideration in the classroom. This is an essential guiding premise of our book.

❚ *Literacy in the Everyday Lives of Youth*

If understanding adolescence in today's society requires a large degree of openness, the same might be said about coming to know and learning to value adolescents' literacies. Their discourses pose new challenges for teachers, especially those who hold to traditional notions about reading and writing. The very definition of what it means to be literate is undergoing perpetual revision in this age of digitized media, rapidly evolving vernacular, language hybrids, and global communication. And youth are the purveyors of these new literacy practices, even though some view them as banal and corruptible (Males, 1996; Washburn & Thornton, 1996). Notice in the following excerpt from a contemporary scholar in sociolinguistics (Hawkins, 2004) how the boundaries of literacy have been stretched to take in many new assumptions about language and communication:

> Just as "language" is not simply the ability to manipulate words in correct grammatical structures, "literacy" is not simply the ability to encode and decode print. The "new literacy studies" propose a view of "literacies" as the requisite knowledge and skills to send and interpret messages through multiple media and modes in (rapidly changing) local and global contexts, and to align meanings within situated social practices (New London Group, 1996). A variety of scholars from a variety of fields are pointing out the rapid changes in communication design, function, and mode in our rapidly changing world. As we move toward ever-more-global economies, and constant re-design of our means and methods of local and distance communications, we need to re-think what communicative (language and discourse) skills it will take to participate successfully in that world, and how our school practices do or don't provide access to those skills and forms of participation. (p. 19)

New media youth use and create are forcing literacy professionals to rethink what counts for reading.

Youth Literacies and Traditional Print Literacy

As youth begin to use more naturally and develop more expansively these new, multiple forms of communication and expression, concerns are being raised about whether traditional print literacy, the kind of literacy most valued in academic contexts and privileged on standardized tests of achievement, will become a dying skill (Birkerts, 1994; Oppenheimer, 2003). Though there are indications that less reading of literary books (National Endowment for the Arts, 2004) and newspapers (Ahrens, 2005) is occurring among young people and adults, there are other signs suggesting youth today are navigating the print world at least as well as their predecessors (Aronson, 2001). To illustrate, American fourth graders were ranked ninth in overall reading/literacy on the Progress in International Reading Literacy Study (PIRLS), as compared with 34 other countries across the globe (Mullis, Martin, Gonzalez, & Kennedy, 2003). On a similar international assessment for 15-year-olds, reading achievement scores place American youth about in the middle of the participating countries (Organisation for Economic Co-Operation and Development, 2001). Furthermore, many argue that youth are not eschewing traditional literacy but developing new, unique forms of literacy that are nonetheless print based, such as instant messaging, e-zines, and the like (c.f., Alvermann, 2002b).

Although American youth have fared well on international assessments of reading, here at home concern about their literacy abilities often coincides with the publication of the results from the newest National Assessment of Educational Progress (NAEP). For the past 30 years a consistent pattern has emerged from these NAEP data. While most middle and high school students can read and comprehend text at basic levels, fewer have demonstrated competencies on more challenging comprehension tasks (Campbell, Hombo, & Mazzeo, 2000). Furthermore, in the most recent national assessment, nearly 26% of 13-year-olds were considered to be struggling readers (Donahue, Daane, & Grigg, 2003). Confirming this pattern are data reported in *The Nation's Report Card: U.S. History 2001*. According to the report over 80% of middle school students were below the proficient level in reading comprehension. In addition, there were significant achievement gaps favoring White students over students of color, students from rural and suburban schools over those from urban schools, and students from high-income homes over low-income homes (Lapp, Grigg, & Tay-Lin, 2002).

Secondary educators are laboring over ways to meet the literacy needs of these learners who, as middle-and upper-grade students, face increasingly difficult texts as well as greater content-learning expectations (Biancarosa & Snow, 2004). Federal

Go to Web Resources for Chapter 1 at *http://www. prenhall.com/brozo,* and look for National Assessment of Educational Progress.

Teacher as Learner

WORD GRID ACTIVITY—MATCHING YOUTH LITERACIES WITH TRADITIONAL LITERACY

For many disciplinary teachers it is challenging to accept that literacy can include many practices that extend well beyond reading print on a page. And yet, most of what scholars are referring to as "new literacies" also involve traditional forms of reading and writing, not to mention significant language skills. Below is a word grid of everyday youth literacy practices listed on the left side. Match them with a more traditional form of literacy listed along the top by placing a check in the corresponding square. Afterward, add additional everyday literacy activities youth engage in and match them with the traditional forms of literacy.

	Reading	Writing	Speaking	Listening
Instant Messaging				
Using the Internet to Buy a Guitar				
Playing a Computer Game				
Creating a Menu of Songs from MP3 Downloads				

initiatives have brought renewed interest in adolescent literacy, too. Proposed legislation such as "Pathways for All Students to Succeed" (PASS) would fund literacy reforms in high schools by placing trained adolescent reading specialists and coaches in every school or district. The No Child Left Behind Act, originally passed as a program to boost reading achievement for children in the elementary grades, has been expanded to include support for high school "striving" readers. Whether these attempts at addressing the needs of striving adolescent readers will bear fruit is still uncertain. One thing is certain, however: Concern for the literacy development of students beyond the elementary years is not likely to fade any time soon as our nation continues to compete in an ever-more-fierce global economy. But programs and initiatives at the national, state, or local levels are destined to failure if they do not honor the unique cultural experiences and personal needs of youth (Neuman & Rao, 2005).

Only within the past two decades have researchers begun to focus on the variety of ways youth learn literacies, the interconnecting contexts in which literacies are learned, and their multiple purposes for engaging literate practices. This scholarship has emphasized the role of multimodal forms of representation and meaning making in the lives of young people (Cope & Kalantzis, 2000; O'Brien & Bauer, 2005). Those on the vanguard of new multiliteracies (c.f., Street, 2003) argue that "literacy pedagogy must now account for the burgeoning variety of text forms associated with information and multimedia technologies" (New London Group, 1996, p. 60). Many (Alvermann, 2002b; Goodman, 2003; Kress & Van Leeuwen, 2001; Love, 2004; Schofield & Rogers, 2004) urge that schools must make room in language and disciplinary curricula for students' different experiences and outside-of-school discourses that are expressed through a variety of media.

Youth Literacies in the Mediasphere

Calls for secondary schools to honor the literacies and discourses of youth derive from the realization that we live in a "mediasphere" (O'Brien, 2001), "a world saturated by inescapable, ever-evolving, and competing media that both flow through us and are altered and created by us" (Brozo, 2005, p. 534). Adolescents are the most active participants in the mediasphere, creating forms of discourse that should be acknowledged and appreciated in school settings because competency in these new forms of communication will serve youth well in the ever-evolving global reach of the digital age (Lankshear & Knobel, 2002). We believe the discourse worlds most teens inhabit offer them a kind of "language of intimacy" (Dowdy, 2002, p. 4), which could increase engagement in literacy and content learning if validated in the public sphere of schools and classrooms. Formal secondary education is the setting where youths' multiple literacies—digital, graphic, aural—could find expression in the understanding, critical analysis, and reinterpretation of concepts and content.

> Mediasphere is a useful term that captures the digital, information saturated, image-rich world of today's youth.

As we have stated, one of the biggest challenges confronting teachers of youth is coming to terms with what counts as literacy in their lives and in the worlds they inhabit. It is essential that content-area teachers in middle and secondary schools remain ever mindful of the material uses and practices of youth as they prepare them to assume their roles as literate individuals in society (Kinzer & Leander, 2003). This will entail exploiting the multiple literacy competencies adolescents bring to school (Knobel, 1998), such as the ability to (a) communicate through digital means (e.g., e-mail and instant messaging); (b) create hypertext documents; (c) interpret and think critically about music CDs, video/computer games, Web sites, and videos; (d) construct Web pages and e-zines; and (e) engage in identity construction using digital technologies. In secondary school settings, alongside traditional reading and language arts schemes, room will need to be made for demonstrations of students' semiotic competencies and for valuing students' out-of-school literacies in order for teachers to learn from their students and help them fulfill their goals in our ever-expanding digital world (Leu, Kinzer, Coiro, & Cammack, 2004).

Another reason literacy scholars and teachers urge that room be created in the secondary curriculum for students' out-of-school competencies with new literacies and media has to do with building on students' strengths for developing academic knowledge and skills (Holmes, 2005; Hull & Schultz, 2002). For example Goodman (2003) found that by helping a group of high school students in New York City create their own documentary about gun violence in their neighborhoods, he could expand the teens' literacy and thinking skills while building confidence in learning. "Unlike so many of their other experiences at home and at school, which (end) in disappointment and failure," Goodman says, their video production experiences "yielded tangible evidence that they can succeed" (p. 99). He goes on to describe the experience for the students in this way:

> In translating the familiar to the unfamiliar, the students are asked to reflect more deeply on their own taken-for-granted language and culture. They are asked to identify and define the commonsense folk terms and concepts that emerge from the interviews in the community. They are also asked to identify gaps in information

between the familiar and unfamiliar domains and formulate specific questions for obtaining the missing information. (p. 59)

It's clear that those responsible for providing adolescent and content literacy instruction need to know more about the funds of knowledge and discourse competencies youth bring with them to middle and secondary school classrooms (Jetton & Dole, 2004; Strickland, & Alvermann, 2004). Coming to know students in this way will lead to more responsive instruction that integrates in- and beyond-school literacy and learning practices (Lee, 1997; Moje et al., 2004; Schultz, 2002). In subsequent chapters, particularly Chapters 8 and 11, we describe numerous enactments of such a curriculum.

Disciplinary teachers can engage youth in reading and learning by tapping into their vast funds of knowledge about life and language.

Before writing your suggestions for Marta in the case study, go to *http://www.pren/hall.com/ brozo*, select Chapter 1, then click on Chapter Review Questions to check your understanding of the material.

CASE STUDY REVISITED

Recall Marta, the business teacher. She was trying to generate ways of linking classroom topics to the real-world interests and cultural values of her students. Now that you have read Chapter 1, write your suggestions for how Marta might accomplish this goal.

As Marta observed her business students enter the classroom one day, she became inspired by an obvious way the topic of writing business contracts could be linked to their real-world interests and desires. Many had Tejano music pulsing from their headsets, which led Marta to consider how her students' love of this Mexican American musical hybrid could form the basis of a fun and meaningful lesson.

She began by inviting students to play their favorite Tejano music CDs for the class. With the music playing quietly in the background, Marta initiated a discussion about Tejano music artists and their recording companies. She asked questions about the agreements and contracts that need to be signed and formalized in order that the musicians get paid for the sale of their CDs. She described the familiar life story of the late performer Selena and what business contracts meant to her short but illustrious career. Marta then went on to inform the class that the topic for the day was business contracts and that by studying recording agreements and then negotiating and writing their own agreements, the class would have a much better appreciation for the importance of these business instruments.

With her students' interest piqued, Marta asked them to form pairs so that one could represent a recording artist and another a record company. She then handed each group a set of directions for completing their in-class assignment. First, they had to write out on a formatted sheet a fictitious name for both the company and the artist. Next, groups were asked to access helpful Internet sites from a list provided to obtain background on the language and format of contracts in the music recording business.

Sylvia, representing a recording artist she called "Baby Sister," and Juan, representing a recording company he called "Sanchez Records," went to the computer lab and acquired information on music industry contracts from Web sites such as Mo's *Music Management Recording Agreement* (**http://www.planmagic. com/mmm/recdeal.htm**), *Record Contract Basics* (**http://www.music-law. com/ contractbasics.html**), and *Recording Agreements* (**http://www**

musicianunion. org.uk/files/recording.html). Sylvia and Juan took notes on relevant pages printed from the sites as they answered key questions given to each group: What are the most important issues addressed in a music recording contract? How can the rights of both the record company and recording artists be protected in a contract?

When students returned to the classroom after completing the Internet research, Marta engaged them in a discussion about the answers to the key questions. As comments were made, Marta wrote important points on the board. She then posed a couple of typical problems in contract disputes: (a) when a band is wrongfully denied payment for services and (b) when a band is in breech of contract. Groups were asked to explore these issues in a short passage Marta gave them entitled *When Someone Refuses to Pay the Band* (**http://www.music-law.com/payrefusal.html**). Lively discussion emerged out of this exercise, particularly between students representing the two parties in such an agreement. Juan wondered whether his partner's Tejano singer, "Baby Sister," could claim "lack of creativity" as a legitimate reason for failing to record a certain number of original songs for an upcoming CD. Marta explained that such an excuse could be acceptable if provided for in the record contract and that these provisions are not uncommon.

Johnny, who represented a Tejano band, suggested that a "sickness and injury clause" be included in a contract to protect his musicians from ill-timed health problems or accidents that might occur just before a recording date. This comment led to a variety of exaggerations and jokes from both sides. Marta allowed the class its fun because she knew they were beginning to develop critical understandings of contract law by connecting it to their interest in music and by role-playing the principle parties in a Tejano music recording agreement.

In the last phase of the lesson, Marta asked her student pairs to reflect on the important points that emerged from their research and class discussion and, based on these points, write an actual recording contract. To guide their negotiations, the groups used standard clauses from authentic music industry contracts (**http://www.musiccontracts.com/**). So others could observe the role-plays, Marta employed a fishbowl discussion strategy (see Chapter 3). While one pair of students hammered out a contract, other pairs of students looked on; then the roles were switched. At regular intervals, student observers were given the opportunity to share reactions to and ask questions of the pair of negotiators they were observing.

When Sylvia and Juan finally hashed out the fine points of an agreement, they signed their contract and shook hands. Marta then urged comments and questions from the observers. Manolo asked Sylvia why she didn't include a clause that would protect "Baby Sister" from liability if she was irresponsible and missed a recording deadline. While some snickered, Marta assured the class that if such a provision could be agreed upon by both parties, it and numerous other "wild" protections could be written into a record contract.

Marta requested that, when finished, students place the final drafts of their contracts on the class Web site, which was linked to the school site. In this way, other students could refer to them as examples for help in completing a similar assignment.

Her students accumulated many such products at the site as source material to select from when compiling a professional portfolio.

Looking Back, Looking Forward

The goal of this chapter has been to dispel myths and deconstruct stereotypes of adolescents while stressing the need for middle and secondary school teachers to embrace youth in all their dimensions as a valued resource in content-area learning and literacy. When youth are portrayed by popular cultural media and education systems as "irresponsible" and "out of control" because of hormones or some other nonspecific developmental etiology, attention is drawn away from the role of instruction and texts in promoting and sustaining engaged learning and community. Like the adults who influence them, adolescents are never one way, either in behavior or discourse. Instead, as youth studies have revealed, they are individuals in search of agency and autonomy with multiple identities formed within the various worlds they inhabit as well as by the different texts they encounter and create both in and beyond school. To throw off rigid constructions of adolescence is to see youths as constantly creating and re-creating new selves that are hybrids drawn from all the text experiences and funds of knowledge in their daily lives.

As you progress through this book, we hope you will come to appreciate the exciting possibilities for crafting and supporting responsive content-area and adolescent literacy experiences for youth. In the next chapter, we outline the principles that undergird the literacy and learning practices we advocate in all subsequent chapters. These principles derive from the view expressed in this opening chapter, that the potential and resourcefulness of youth be given expression in the classroom in order to honor adolescents' identities, engage them as learners, and expand their range of literate competencies.

References

Ahrens, F. (2005). Hard news: Daily papers face unprecedented competition. *The Washington Post*, February 20, F1, F5.

Alvermann, D. (2002a). Effective literacy instruction for adolescents: Executive summary and paper commissioned by the National Reading Conference. *Journal of Literacy Research, 34,* 189–208.

Alvermann, D. (2002b). *Adolescents and literacies in a digital world.* New York: Peter Lang.

Alvermann, D., Boyd, F., Brozo, W., Hinchman, K., Moore, D., & Sturtevant, E. (2001). *Principled practices for a literate America: A framework for literacy and learning in the upper grades.* New York: Carnegie Corporation.

Ancess, J. (2003). *Beating the odds: High schools as communities of practice.* New York: Teachers College Press.

Anders, P. (2002). Secondary reading programs: A story of what was. In D. Schallert, C. Fairbanks, J. Worthy, B. Maloch, & J. Hoffman (Eds.), *51st Yearbook of the National Reading Conference.* Oak Creek, WI: National Reading Conference.

Aronson, M. (2000). The myth of teenage readers. *Publishing Research Quarterly, 16,* 4–9.

Aronson, M. (2001). *Exploding the myths: The truth about teenagers and reading.* Lanham, MD: Scarecrow Press.

Bandura, A. (1993). Perceived self-efficacy in cognitive development and functioning. *Educational Psychologist, 28,* 117–148.

Barbour, S. (1999). *Teens at risk: Opposing viewpoints.* San Diego, CA: Greenhaven Press.

Bean, R., Swan, A., & Knaub, R. (2003). Reading specialists in schools with exemplary reading programs: Functional, versatile, and prepared. *The Reading Teacher, 56,* 446–454.

Bean, T. (2000). Reading in the content areas: Social constructivist dimensions. In M. L. Kamil, P. D. Pearson, & R. Barr (Eds.), *Handbook of reading research* (Vol. 3, pp. 631–644). Mahwah, NJ: Erlbaum.

Biancarosa, G., & Snow. C. (2004). *Reading next: A vision for action and research in middle and high school literacy.* New York/Washington, DC: Carnegie Corporation/Alliance for Excellent Education. Retrieved February 10, 2005, from http://www.all4ed.org.

Birkerts, S. (1994). *The Gutenberg elegies.* New York: Ballentine Books.

Borasi, R., & Siegel, M. (2000). *Reading counts: Expanding the role of reading in mathematics classrooms*. New York: Teachers College Press.

Brozo, W. G. (2002). *To be a boy, to be a reader: Engaging teen and preteen boys in active literacy*. Newark, DE: International Reading Association.

Brozo, W. G. (2003). "It's like personalities going everywhere": Listening to youths' stories of life and literacy in a suburban high school. Unpublished manuscript.

Brozo, W. G. (2005). Book review: Adolescents and literacies in a digital world. *Journal of Literacy Research, 36*, 533–538.

Brozo, W. G. (2006). Authentic contexts for developing language tools in vocational education. In J. Flood, D. Lapp, & Farnan, N. (Eds.), *Content area reading and learning: Instructional strategies*. Mahwah, NJ: Erlbaum.

Campbell, J. R., Hombo, C. M., & Mazzeo, J. (2000). *NAEP 1999 trends in academic progress: Three decades of student performance*. Washington, DC: National Center for Education Statistics.

Cook-Sather, A. (2002). Authorizing students' perspectives: Toward trust, dialogue, and change in education. *Educational Researcher, 31*, 3–14.

Cope, B., & Kalantzis, M. (2000). *Multiliteracies: Literacy learning and the design of social futures*. London: Routledge.

Crawford, T., Kelly, G. J., & Brown, C. (2000). Ways of knowing beyond facts and laws of science: An ethnographic investigation of student engagement in scientific practices. *Journal of Research in Science Teaching, 37*, 237–258.

Cummins, J. (2001). Magic bullets and the grade 4 slump: Solutions from technology? *NABE News, 25*, 4–6.

Davidson, A. L. (1996). *Making and molding identity in schools*. Albany, NY: SUNY Press.

Donahue, P., Daane, M., & Grigg, W. (2003). *The nation's report card: Reading highlights 2003*. Washington, DC: National Center for Education Statistics.

Dowdy, J. K. (2002). Ovuh Dyuh. In L. Delpit & J. K. Dowdy (Eds.), *The skin that we speak: Thoughts on language and culture in the classroom* (pp. 3–13) New York: The New Press.

Duncan, G. A. (2000). Urban pedagogies and the ceiling of adolescents of color. *Social Justice, 27*, 29–42.

Eccles, J. S., Wigfield, A., Midgley, C., Reaman, D., MacIver, D., & Feldlaufer, H. (1993). Negative effects of traditional middle schools on students' motivation. *Elementary School Journal, 93*, 553–573.

Echevarria, M. (2003). Anomalies as a catalyst for middle school students' knowledge construction and scientific reasoning during science inquiry. *Journal of Educational Psychology, 95*, 357–374.

Edwards, S. (2001). Bridging the gap: Connecting school and community with service learning. *English Journal, 90*, 39–44.

Erikson, E. (1980). *Identity and the life cycle*. New York: W.W. Norton.

Finders, M. J. (1998/1999). Raging hormones: Stories of adolescence and the implications for teacher preparation. *Journal of Adolescent & Adult Literacy, 42*, 252–265.

Flores-Gonzalez, N. (2002). School kids/Street kids: Identity development in Latino students. New York: Teachers College Press.

Gee, J. P. (2001). Reading as situated language: A sociocognitive perspective. *Journal of Adolescent & Adult Literacy, 44*, 714–725.

Goodman, S. (2003). *Teaching youth media: A critical guide to literacy, video production, and social change*. New York: Teachers College Press.

Harris, T. L., & Hodges, R. E. (1995). *The literacy dictionary: The vocabulary of reading and writing*. Newark, DE: International Reading Association.

Hawkins, M. R. (2004). Researching English language and literacy development in schools. *Educational Researcher, 33*, 14–25.

Herbert, B. (2001, September 3). In America: On the way to nowhere. *The New York Times*, p. A15.

Heron, A. H. (2003). A study of agency: Multiple constructions of choice and decision making in an inquiry-based summer school program for struggling readers. *Journal of Adolescent & Adult Literacy, 46*, 568–579.

Hersch, P. (1998). *A tribe apart: A journey into the heart of American adolescence*. New York: Ballantine.

Hinchman, K., Alvermann, D., Boyd, F., Brozo, W., & Vacca, R. (2003-2004). Supporting older students' in- and out-of-school literacies. *Journal of Adolescent & Adult Literacy, 47*, 304–310.

Hinchman, K., & Zalewski, P. (1996). Reading for success in a tenth-grade global-studies class: A qualitative study. *Journal of Literacy Research, 28*, 91–106.

Holland, D., Lachicotte, W., Skinner, D., & Cain, C. (1998). *Identity and agency in cultural worlds*. Cambridge, MA: Harvard University Press.

Holmes, K. P. (2005). *Engaging reluctant readers through foreign films*. Lanham, MD: ScarecrowEducation.

Hones, D. F. (2002). In quest of freedom: Towards critical pedagogy in the education of bilingual youth. *Teachers College Record, 104*, 1163–1186.

Hull G., & Schultz, K. (2002). *School's out! Bridging out-of-school literacies with classroom practice.* New York: Teachers College Press.

Jetton, T. L., & Dole, J. A. (Eds.). (2004). *Adolescent literacy research and practice.* New York: Guilford.

Kids Count. (2004). *Kids Count 2004 data book online.* Retrieved January 6, 2005, from http://www.aecf.org/cgi-bin/kc.cgi?action=profile&area=United+States.

Kinzer, C. K., & Leander, K. (2003). Technology and the language arts: Implications of an expanded definition of literacy. In J. Flood, D. Lapp, J. R. Squire, & J. M. Jensen (Eds.), *Handbook of research and teaching the English language arts* (pp. 546–566). Mahwah, NJ: Erlbaum.

Knobel, M. (1998). *Everyday literacies: Students, discourse, and social practice.* New York: Peter Lang.

Kress, G., & Van Leeuwen, T. (2001). *Multimodal discourse: The modes and media of contemporary communication.* New York: Oxford University Press.

Labov, W. (2003). When ordinary children fail to read. *Reading Research Quarterly, 38,* 128–131.

Lankshear, C., & Knobel, M. (2002). Do we have your attention? New literacies, digital technologies, and the education of adolescents. In D. Alvermann (Ed.), *Adolescents and literacies in a digital world.* New York: Peter Lang.

Lapp, M., Grigg, W. S., & Tay-Lin, B. (2002). *The nation's report card: U.S. history 2001.* National Center for Education Statistics Publication No. NCES-2002-483. Washington, DC: U.S. Department of Education, Education Publications Center.

Larson, R., Richards, M., & Moneta, G. (1996). Changes in adolescents' daily interactions with their families from ages 10 to 18: Disengagement and transformation. *Developmental Psychology, 32,* 744–754.

Leander, K. (2002). Locating Latanya: The situated production of identity artifacts in classroom interaction. *Research in the Teaching of English, 37,* 198–250.

Lee, C. D. (1997). Bridging home and school literacies: Models for culturally responsive teaching, a case for African American English. In J. Flood, S. B. Heath, & D. Lapp (Eds.), *Handbook of research on teaching literacy through the communicative and visual arts* (pp. 334–345). New York: Macmillan.

Lesko, N. (2001). *Act your age! A cultural construction of adolescence.* New York: Routledge Falmer.

Leu, D., Kinzer, C., Coiro, J., Cammack, D. (2004). Toward a theory of new literacies emerging from the Internet and other information and communication technologies (ICT). In R. Ruddell & N. Unrau (Eds.), *Theoretical models and processes of reading* (5th ed.). Newark, DE: International Reading Association.

Love, M. S. (2004). Multimodality of learning through anchored instruction. *Journal of Adolescent & Adult Literacy, 48,* 300–310.

Males, M. (2001). Debunking the 10 worst myths about America's teens. *Teacher Librarian, 28,* 40–41.

Males, M. A. (1996). *The scapegoat generation.* Monroe, ME: Common Courage Press.

Markus, H., & Nurius, P. (1986). Possible selves. *American Psychologist, 41,* 954–969.

McCarthey, S. J., & Moje, E. B. (2002). Identity matters. *Reading Research Quarterly, 37,* 228–238.

McCray, A. D., Vaughn, S., & Neal, L. I. (2001). Not all students learn to read by third grade: Middle school students speak out about their reading disabilities. *Journal of Special Education, 35,* 17–30.

McDonald, K. (1999). *Struggles for subjectivity: Identity, action and youth experiences.* New York: Cambridge University Press.

McPhail, J. C., Pierson, J. M., Freeman, J. G., Goodman, J., & Ayappa, A. (2000). The role of interest in fostering sixth grade students' identities as competent learners. *Curriculum Inquiry, 30,* 43–70.

Miron, L. F., Inda, J. X., & Aguirre, J. K. (1998). Transnational migrants, cultural citizenship, and the politics of language in California. *Educational Policy, 12,* 659–682.

Moje, E. B. (1996). "I teach students, not subjects": Teacher-student relationships as contexts for secondary literacy. *Reading Research Quarterly, 31,* 172–195.

Moje, E. B. (2002). Re-framing adolescent literacy research for new times: Studying youth as a resource. *Reading Research and Instruction, 41,* 211–228.

Moje, E. B., Callazo, T., Carrillo, R., & Marx, R. (2001). Maestro, what is "quality"?: Language, literacy, and discourse in project-based science. *Journal of Science Teaching, 38,* 469–496.

Moje, E. B., McIntosh, Ciechanowski, K., Kramer, K., Ellis, L., Carrillo, R., & Collazo, T. (2004). Working toward third space in content area literacy: An examination of everyday funds of knowledge and discourse. *Reading Research Quarterly, 39,* 38–70.

Moje, E. B., Young, J. P., Readence, J. E., & Moore, D. W. (2000). Reinventing adolescent literacy for new times: Perennial and millennial issues. *Journal of Adolescent & Adult Literacy, 43,* 400–410.

Morrell, E. (2002). Toward a critical pedagogy of popular culture: Literacy development among urban youth. *Journal of Adolescent & Adult Literacy, 46,* 72–77.

Mullis, I., Martin, M., Gonzalez, E., & Kennedy, A. (2003). *PIRLS 2001 international report: IEA's study of reading literacy achievement in primary schools in 35 countries*. Boston: International Study Center, Boston College.

National Endowment for the Arts. (2004). *Reading at risk: A survey of literacy reading in America*. Washington, DC: National Endowment for the Arts.

Nelson, D. W. (2004). *Remarks made at the 2004 KIDS COUNT Youth Summit*. Baltimore, MD: Annie E. Casey Foundation.

Neuman, M., & Rao, S. (2005). Adolescent literacy: Beyond English class, beyond decoding text. *SEDL Letter, 27*(2), 18–21.

New London Group. (1996). A pedagogy of multiliteracies: Designing social futures. *Harvard Educational Review, 66*, 60–92.

O'Brien, D. G. (2001). "At-risk" adolescents: Redefining competence through the multiliteracies of intermediality, visual arts, and representation. *Reading Online, 4*(11). Available online at: http://www.readingonline.org/newliteracies/lit_Index.asp?HREF=/newliteracies/obrien/index.html.

O'Brien, D. G., & Bauer, E. B. (2005). New literacies and the institution of old learning. *Reading Research Quarterly, 40*, 120–131.

Ogbu, J. U. (1998). Voluntary and involuntary minorities: A cultural-ecological theory of school performance with some implications for education. *Anthropology and Education Quarterly, 29*, 155–188.

Oppenheimer, T. (2003). *The flickering mind: The false promise of technology in the classroom and how learning can be saved*. New York: Random House.

Organisation for Economic Co-Operation and Development. (2001). *Knowledge and skills for life: First results from PISA 2000*. Paris: OECD.

Pajares, F. (1996). Self-efficacy beliefs in academic settings. *Review of Educational Research, 66*, 543–578.

Phelps, L. A., & Hanley-Maxwell, C. (1997). School-to-work transitions for youth with disabilities: A review of outcomes and practices. *Review of Educational Research, 67*, 197–226.

Richardson, E. (2003). *African American literacies*. New York: Routledge.

Rong, X. L., & Preissle, J. (1998). *Educating immigrant students: What we need to know to meet the challenges*. Thousand Oaks, CA: Corwin Press.

Ruiz-de-Velasco, J., Fix, M., & Clewell, B. C. (2001). *Overlooked and underserved—immigrant students in U.S. secondary schools: Core findings and conclusions*. Retrieved February 15, 2002, from http://www.urban.org/pdfs/overlooked.pdf.

Rushdie, S. (1991). *Midnight's Children* NY: Penguin Books.

Rymes, B. (2001). *Conversational border lands: Language and identity in an alternative urban high school*. New York: Teachers College Press.

Sawatzki, D. (2004). *4 million youth face tough road to adulthood success*. Baltimore, MD: Kids Count.

Schofield, A., & Rogers, T. (2004). At play in fields of ideas. *Journal of Adolescent & Adult Literacy, 48*, 238–248.

Schultz, K. (2002). Looking across space and time: Reconceptualizing literacy learning in and out of school. *Research in the Teaching of English, 36*, 356–390.

Serafini, F., Bean, T. W., & Readence, J. E. (2004). Reconceptualizing adolescent identities. *Reading Research Quarterly, 39*, 482–489.

Snow, C. (2002). *Reading for understanding: Toward an R&D program in reading comprehension*. Santa Monica, CA: Rand Education.

Street, B. V. (2003). What's new in new literacy studies? Critical approaches to literacy in theory and practice. *Current Issues in Contemporary Education, 5*, 1–14.

Strickland, D., & Alvermann, D. E. (Eds.). (2004). *Bridging the literacy achievement gap, grades 4–12*. New York: Teachers College Press.

Sturtevant, E. (2003). *The literacy coach: A key to improving teaching and learning in secondary schools*. Washington, DC: Alliance for Excellent Education.

Sturtevant, E., Boyd, F., Brozo, W. G., Hinchman, K., Alvermann, D., & Moore, D. (2006). *Principled practices for adolescent literacy. A framework for instruction and policy*. Mahwah, NJ: Erlbaum.

Tatum, A. (2004). A road map for reading specialists entering schools without exemplary reading programs: Seven quick lessons. *The Reading Teacher, 58*, 28–39.

Tatum, A. (2005). *Teaching reading to Black adolescent males: Closing the achievement gap*. Portland, ME: Stenhouse.

U.S. Census Bureau. (2002). *Census 2000*. Available online at http://www.census.gov.

U.S. Census Bureau. (2003). *American factfinder, cenus 2000 summary file 1*. Washington, DC: Author.

Venezky, R. L. Wagner, D.A., & Ciliberti, B.S. (1990). *Towards defining literacy*. Newark, DE: International Reading Association.

Washburn, K., & Thornton, J. F. (1996). *Dumbing down: Essays on the strip mining of American culture*. New York: W.W. Norton.

Willis, A. I., Garcia, G. E., Barrera, R., & Harris, V. J. (2003). *Multicultural issues in literacy research and practice*. Mahwah, NJ: Erlbaum.

Zhoa, Y. (2002, August 5). Wave of pupils lacking English strains schools. *The New York Times*, p. A1.

chapter 2

Principled Practices for Effective Reading and Learning

Anticipation Guide

Directions: Read each statement carefully and decide whether you agree or disagree with it, placing a check mark in the appropriate *Before Reading* column. When you have finished reading and studying the chapter, return to the guide and decide whether your anticipations need to be changed by placing a check mark in the appropriate *After Reading* column.

	Before Reading		After Reading	
	Agree	*Disagree*	*Agree*	*Disagree*
1. Principles of instruction specify the strategies content-area teachers should use.	_____	_____	_____	_____
2. Sound principles guide the use of contextually appropriate strategies.	_____	_____	_____	_____
3. Adolescents' funds of knowledge are the books they have read in the past.	_____	_____	_____	_____
4. Principle-based instruction suggests that only informal assessments provide useful information.	_____	_____	_____	_____
5. Principled instruction in the disciplines makes room for a variety of student responses to the topics under study.	_____	_____	_____	_____

6. Learning the content of various disciplines is as much about learning to read, write, and think as it is about learning concepts and facts.

_____   _____   _____   _____

*W*hat drives your instructional decision making? Do you employ certain strategies and cover particular content because it is how you have done it in the past? Because it is written in curriculum guides? Because it is what other teachers are doing? Or do the ways you teach and the topics you deem important derive from a clear, supportable set of principles about teaching, learning, and adolescent development? For obvious reasons, we hope you answered yes to this last question. If you didn't, however, you are not alone. Many adolescent literacy and content-area teachers find it difficult to rationalize their instructional approaches on the basis of foundational principles. And yet, we know that effective teaching is principled teaching (Smagorinski, 2001). This means that practices are grounded in evidence and ever-present in the thinking and planning of teachers for supporting content literacy and learning development for youth (Sturtevant et al., 2006).

In this chapter we present six principles to guide effective teaching for today's youth. Within the explanation of each principle are numerous references to supporting research literature as well as examples and vignettes of teachers enacting principled practices in a variety of content areas and literacy-learning contexts. We believe these principles are so important that we have foregrounded them at the opening of each of the remaining chapters of this book in a boxed section entitled "Chapter Principle." You will find these principles expressed directly and indirectly throughout the entire book. For some chapters a principle will serve as the framework for the ideas and strategies presented. For others, these principles will be invoked as support for acts of teaching that are innovative, student-centered, and responsive to the needs of middle and secondary school learners.

To be clear, principles are not directives or injunctions that must be adhered to strictly. Instead they inform effective practices that have myriad permutations depending upon students and teachers in particular learning contexts. The many scenes of teaching we share are taken from actual school settings and are meant to demonstrate this last point: Literacy and content-area learning strategies are effective only when they are applied in appropriate ways and not as a "one-size-fits-all" approach. With this point in mind, we describe what can be accomplished—given the unique circumstances and available resources—by teachers and students who engage in practices based on research-supportable principles.

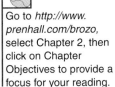

Go to *http://www. prenhall.com/brozo,* select Chapter 2, then click on Chapter Objectives to provide a focus for your reading.

Principles serve as guidelines for content area teachers that allow a wide range of practices within their unique instructional contexts.

 CASE STUDY

As a high school building trades teacher, Chauncey is always looking for opportunities to move his students out of the shop and into the field. He knows that his lessons on engineering principles, design concepts, and drafting techniques only become meaningful to youth when applied to authentic projects. Finding such projects and working out the arrangements to have his class participate in them has been a challenge, but it has always been worth the effort. Chauncey has seen how real-world applications of students' knowledge and skills have proven invaluable in increasing their levels of engagement, problem-solving abilities, and critical thinking. After hearing an announcement on the radio for local labor to help with a Habitat for Humanity project about to begin in the area, Chauncey telephoned the project foreman and offered the services of his class. Every student was interested in volunteering and promptly returned parent permission and insurance forms.

Case studies in this textbook provide an opportunity to apply principles and practices to new contexts.

To the Reader:
As with the case study in Chapter 1 and all of the case studies in this book, we will revisit Chauncey and his building trades students at the end of the chapter. Before you return to the case study, however, you will read about essential principles for content-area instructional practices. Keep these principles in mind when you read the rest of the description of Chauncey's activities, both inside and outside the classroom, for his students.

Principles That Promote Engaged Reading and Learning

When teachers' instructional decision making is guided by the following sound, evidence-based principles, they create supportive content-area classrooms that help students from diverse cultures, language backgrounds, and abilities:

1. Connect *everyday literacies* and *funds of knowledge* with academic literacy and learning.
2. Use assessment as a tool for learning and future growth.
3. Engage and sustain effort in reading, writing, and thinking.
4. Express critical perspectives and interpretations.

Go to Web Resources for Chapter 2 at *http://www. prenhall.com/brozo,* and look for Evidence-Based Practices.

5. Gather and organize print and nonprint sources for increasing understanding of information and ideas.

6. Expand and generate new understandings using information and communication technologies.

Principle 1: Connect Everyday Literacies and Funds of Knowledge with Academic Literacy and Learning

The key elements of this principle have already been given considerable attention in Chapter 1. As you recall, we proposed that in honoring student's outside-of-school literacies, interests, and competencies, we help them see how what they learn in school relates to their lifeworlds beyond the classroom walls. Concern for relevance in secondary school teaching and learning has been renewed in recent years (Gates, 2005; Legter, Balfanz, & McPartland, 2002; McPartland, Legter, Jordan, & McDill, 1996). This is because many cite the disjuncture between the experiences and goals youth bring to educational contexts and how they're expected to perform in those contexts (Balfanz, McPartland, & Shaw, 2002; Chen, Stevenson, Hayward, & Burgess, 1995). This lack of fit is seen as the primary reason why many adolescents seem to lack interest in school-based learning and, for far too many, find themselves failing and even dropping out (Ruiz-de-Velasco, Fix, & Clewell, 2001; Valdés, 1998).

This principle has its roots in cognitive and social constructivist notions of reading and learning. From a cognitive perspective, we have known for some time that what learners take from a text, discussion, or other classroom discourse depends on how much they bring to it (Bransford & Johnson, 1972; Pressley, 2000; Wilson & Anderson, 1986). The social constructivist dimension accounts for the ways new understandings emerge for learners as a result of interactions with the teacher and students during text study, discussions, and all other forms of classroom discourse (Bean, 2000). For example, students living in an arid climate may encounter a passage in their science textbook about the water cycle for which they might think they have little prior knowledge or that would seem to have little connection to their concerns as youth. If denied opportunities to discover how this topic relates to their own lives, as well as opportunities to interact with the teacher, peers, and others who could enlarge their understandings, then comprehension of the text will depend solely on each individual student's own cognition and prior knowledge. On the other hand, if students are asked to consider how the water cycle relates to the cost of finding and purifying potable water, how the scarcity of clean water limits their use of community swimming pools and restricts how often they can wash their cars, and how they themselves might imagine possible solutions to local and regional water shortages, then any individual student's comprehension of the text will be supported by the various interesting activities experienced in the classroom. This is the difference a more active social constructivist classroom environment can achieve.

Adolescents in secondary content classrooms make meaning of and create written and spoken texts based on the various discourse communities they inhabit, such as homes, peer groups, sports teams, and even the neighborhood hair salon (Hull & Schultz, 2002; Kelly & Green, 1998). Viewed as funds of knowledge (Valdés, 1998), these networks of relationships shape ways of talking, reading, writing, and knowing (Gee, 2000). Space can be made in content classrooms for students to explore how their many different funds of knowledge and literate practices might inform, connect to, and be integrated with the knowledge of the academic disciplines (Alvermann, Young, Green, & Wisenbaker, 1999; Thernstrom & Thernstrom, 2003).

Go to Web Resources for Chapter 2 at *http://www. prenhall.com/brozo,* and look for Constructivism.

Consider all the different experiences and discourse communities that have informed and continue to contribute to your understanding of your discipline—these are funds of knowledge.

Principle-Based Instruction in Math

Alonzo makes certain his ninth-grade math students are always fully aware of the ways in which mathematical principles and calculations are braided into their daily lives.

For example, when covering a unit on statistics, a topic that students can easily tune out, Alonzo floods the classroom with statistical artifacts the students have encountered within their communities, neighborhoods, and homes. Students are asked to bring in such items as copies of utility bills, newspaper sports pages, and pamphlets from community health centers. They're also given an assignment to listen for and document every time they hear a family member, friend, shop owner, clergy, or any other person with whom they interact invoke some form of statistics in daily discourse.

With the artifacts, Alonzo demonstrates examples of how statistics are used. For example, he draws the class's attention to a graph on an electric bill charting kilowatt consumption for the previous 12 months that was used to establish a statistically average monthly payment. He then distributes the various other items to small groups of students and asks them to locate as many applications of and references to statistics as possible. One group finds numerous statistics in a health center brochure on sexually transmitted diseases, while another points out how statistics are applied to establishing field goal percentages and rebound averages for basketball players. Phrases such as "They ain't never going to win" in reference to one of the city's baseball teams from habitués of a local barbershop, and "That girl always gettin' into trouble" from gatherers in front of the neighborhood fruit market were analyzed and linked to statistical averages by another group.

The variety of everyday statistical references in the artifacts Alonzo and his students bring to class are arranged on murals by the class with colorful drawings of familiar locations and people interspersed. These serve as regular reminders of and experiential referents for the juncture between the study of mathematics in a school-based context and students' knowledge of mathematical principles and applications in their worlds outside.

Instead of hearing complaints of "This doesn't have anything to do with me" or "Why do we have to learn this stuff" Alonzo's students are able to make direct connections from the content of his class to the activities and experiences in their daily lives. And in this way, the math content is made more meaningful and memorable.

Like Moje and her colleagues (2004) we believe *content learning* and *content literacy learning* are one in the same. Learning the content of the disciplines, such as history, science, literature, and math, is as much about learning to read, write, and talk about the content as it is learning the concepts and facts. In other words, academic literacy and disciplinary knowledge are, in essence, inseparable. Therefore, teaching reading, writing, and thinking skills in the disciplines *is* teaching the disciplines (Braunger, Donahue, Evans, & Galguera, 2005). Knowing this provides teachers of youth even greater opportunities to build on the literacy and language skills as well as the prior experiences and knowledge they bring to disciplinary study. To provide appropriate scaffolding for learning, teachers of content subjects will need to have a keen understanding of the funds of knowledge influencing students' skills and attitudes as well as the demands their texts place on them. Only then is it possible to offer literacy strategies and processes most suited to the comprehension and critical thinking of developing students (Best, Rowe, Ozuru, & McNamara, 2005; Caccamise, 2005; Greenleaf & Schoenbach, 2004; Kintsch, 2005).

Youth must be shown that literacy cannot be separated from content; to understand content means youth can also communicate clearly about what they understand.

Teacher as Learner

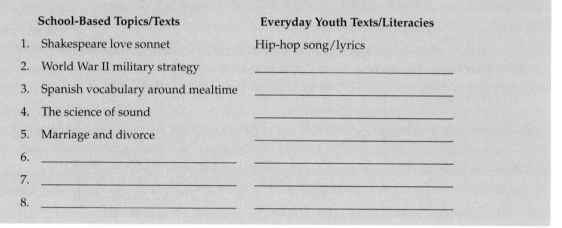

CONNECTING SCHOOL-BASED TOPICS AND TEXTS WITH EVERYDAY YOUTH LITERACIES

Principle 1 stresses the need to make connections for youth between everyday and school-based literacy and learning. For each school-based topic/text below, think of a text adolescents encounter or literacy practice they engage in every day that could be linked to it. Then, identify your own topics and possible real-world texts from the lives of youth you teach or may teach in the future. Remember to think of text and literacy practices beyond just the printed word. An example is supplied.

School-Based Topics/Texts	Everyday Youth Texts/Literacies
1. Shakespeare love sonnet	Hip-hop song/lyrics
2. World War II military strategy	_____
3. Spanish vocabulary around mealtime	_____
4. The science of sound	_____
5. Marriage and divorce	_____
6. _____	_____
7. _____	_____
8. _____	_____

Principle 2: Use Assessment as a Tool for Learning and Future Growth

Constructivist approaches to schooling stress the need for students to be authors of their own understanding and assessors of their own learning (Cook-Sather, 2002). From this perspective assessment is seen as a tool for promoting critical thinking, metacognitive awareness, and self-efficacy (Dweck, 1999). The goal of constructivist assessment is to help students and teachers reflect upon new understandings and become empowered, rather than victimized, by the assessment process (Tierney, 2000). Empowerment through assessment comes in the form of teachers having a broad and deep understanding of students' abilities, needs, and learning potential— and students having an equally full understanding of their own abilities, needs, and potential.

As we explained in Chapter 1, as youth get older their overall self-awareness increases. At the same time, they should also be gaining greater awareness of their academic identities. Assessment practices in content classrooms that offer students ongoing reflections of their literacy processes (Clark, Chow-Hoy, Herter, & Moss, 2001), are appropriate to their needs (Bauer, 1999), and are embedded within meaningful and engaging learning experiences (Shavelson, Baxter, & Pine, 1992) will help youth become more knowledgeable about what they know, how they learn best, and what they need to reach their academic and personal goals (Pajares, 1996).

Principle-Based Instruction in Biology

Maria, an experienced 10th-grade biology teacher, began to realize her class textbook was becoming less and less useful to many of her students. Some were

Go to Web Resources for Chapter 2 at *http://www.prenhall.com/brozo*, and look for Alternative Assessments.

refusing to read it and consequently couldn't do many of the assignments, and others were racing through sections, chapters, and the assignments so quickly they found themselves with little left to do during much of the 90-minute block. In consultation with the school's literacy coach she decided it would be important to determine whether a mismatch existed between the reading abilities of her students and the readability of the textbook.

Maria and her colleague used the readability tool available in Microsoft Word to peg the overall difficulty of the biology class text at the 9.2 grade level. They then assessed each of her students with a standardized reading achievement test and discovered something quite remarkable. Within Maria's class she had an ability spread of 12 grade levels. On the low side, an inclusion student with a learning disabilities label was reading at the fifth-grade level; on the top end a student had achieved a grade-level score of 17. Initially, Maria was stunned by this revelation. Once recovered, however, she realized how these results helped explain the student behavior she was observing, especially for those who were disengaged either because they were turning the textbook away due to its difficulty or were gliding through it effortlessly.

Armed with these low-stakes test results and with the support of the literacy coach, Maria held brief individual conferences with each student to review the results and gather their input on ways to make learning the biology content more interesting. Her instructional modifications were designed to ensure all students had opportunities to be active learners in her classroom. For example, to accommodate the low reading ability levels of some students she made available to them a range of alternative texts, including easier readings from helpful Web sites, newspaper and magazine articles, informational books, and even graphic novels. To keep the exceptional readers in class challenged, Maria gave them options for crafting alternative projects, allowed them to read popular adult novels with science and biology connections (e.g., Michael Crichton's Congo, 2003), and had them research and compile lists of Internet sites with related readings more in keeping with their own high ability levels.

Maria's use of low-stakes reading achievement tests made it possible for her to bring all students into the flow of instruction, increase their self-knowledge as learners, and elevate their overall level of engagement.

Secondary content teachers who employ assessment strategies based on this principle know that assessment is best when it improves student learning (Stiggins, 2002) and increases students' awareness of their academic identities (Johnston & Costello, 2005; Wiggins, 1998). This leaves open the possibility for a range of assessment approaches, such as everyday informal checks for understanding, interviews and conferences, portfolios, performances and demonstrations, and, yes, even standardized achievement testing (Jackson & Davis, 2000). In working with high school teachers in various disciplines we discovered that in spite of the avalanche of negative sentiment toward achievement testing found in the literature today (Kohn, 2000; Miller, 2001; Pearson, 2001; Popham, 2001), a place can be made for it at the secondary level, if the context and purposes are appropriate (Brozo & Hargis, 2003). Finally, in an increasingly multicultural and multilingual world where the boundaries between print and other media are disappearing, content teachers operating with this principle as their guide are also mindful that new and emerging literacies will require new forms of assessment (Johnston, 2005). Along with clear guidelines for completion and evaluation, these new assessments ought to include demonstrations of understanding through role-plays, actual and virtual constructions, map making, model building, applications to hobbies, song writing, and much more. The key is that information coming from either standardized or contextualized means can be translated into more responsive instructional practices for teachers and meaningful self-reflections of learning for students.

Principle 3: Engage and Sustain Effort in Reading, Writing, and Thinking

Content teachers engage and sustain students' efforts in reading, writing, and critical thinking when they create educational environments and implement classroom practices with students' interests, needs, and goals foremost in their thinking and planning. These teachers know that engagement must remain connected to academic literacy and learning processes in order to give energy and direction to them (Eccles, Wigfield, & Schiefele, 1998; Guthrie & Humenick, 2004). Thus, a science teacher who shares a graphic novel with his class about Nicola Tessla, the inventor of alternating current, knows this type of engaging text not only encourages his students to read but also delivers important scientific information in an easily digestible and fun way. Teachers who embrace this principle are also keenly aware of the influence of family, community, and peers on adolescents' academic motivation and regard them as resources to help sustain student effort (Valdés, 1998).

Youth, like the adults in their worlds, are motivated by and enjoy activities and pastimes of their own choosing (Csikszentmihalyi, 1990; Ryan & Deci, 2000). Secondary teachers can take advantage of the power of choice by expanding what counts as learning, by allowing students options for demonstrating new understandings, by giving students freedom to co-construct knowledge with friends and classmates, and by accepting the everyday multiliteracies youth bring to the learning environment.

Engaging practices needs to be incorporated into disciplinary teachers' daily instruction in order to ensure all students are active participants in learning.

Principle-Based Instruction in History

When the principal of Barbara's school announced that students could no longer wear shirts and other apparel containing references to Southern flags, Southern heritage, the Confederacy, or Rebels, the response from students was greater than expected. Barbara's third-block American history class had a variety of complaints about the new dress policy, including: "It's my right to wear anything I please," "That's violating my freedom of speech," and "I'm not a racist; that's just my heritage." The strength of the students' feelings on the matter seemed an ideal source of energy for introducing the upcoming unit on the Bill of Rights in the American Constitution.

To ensure all students were actively engaged in studying the topic, Barbara created a lesson around a role-play activity derived from the dress code controversy in her school. First, she had students draw cards that required them to assume the role of either a supporter of the new dress policy, a nonsupporter, or a scriptor. She issued each of the nonsupporters a clip-on badge with a Confederate emblem or slogan to wear during the activity. Barbara then asked one supporter, one nonsupporter, and one scriptor to form a team. Once all students were in their groups, she asked them to prepare a short skit that reproduced the conflict in some way and presented a positive resolution. While the two opposing students worked on their skits, the scriptor documented and summarized their arguments and resolution on a poster.

Felicia, an African American student, and Brittany, a White student, performed their skit by recreating a conversation while in the lunch room. Their conversation included these exchanges:

Felicia: Brittany, I really wish you wouldn't wear that, because, you know, it reminds me of a time when my people were slaves.

Brittany: Give me a break, Felicia, I'm not wearing it for that reason. You know, like, Dixie is part of our history and our heritage. It's the South; it's where we live.

Felicia: *I'm cool with that, but, like, you know, if it hurts people like me, you need to understand that. Like, I'm supposed to be your friend, right?*

Brittany: *So what do you want me to do?*

Felicia: *Like, maybe you should just wear it at home and not at school or in public.*

Brittany: *Well I guess if you feel that way about it . . .*

Felicia: *So you'll leave it at home?*

Brittany: *Yeah, okay.*

Felicia: *Sweet!*

Jasmine's and all the other scriptors' posters were attached to the classroom walls. The class participated enthusiastically in the skits. Some skits were more confrontational and thus more difficult to resolve, but all students played an active role and had the psychological and attitudinal disposition to begin an exploration of protections of personal freedoms in the U.S. Bill of Rights.

By taking advantage of a local issue that had captured the attention of the students in her school, Barbara was able to sustain their engagement in the issue and segue into a more formal exploration of an important topic in American history.

It is critical to keep in mind that youth are not passive receptacles of facts and information. Instead, as has already been emphasized, within classroom discourse communities, they are active co-constructors of meaning (Ruddell & Unrau, 2004). To regard adolescent learners in this way leads to exploring how to create learning conditions that drive engagement (Alexander & Fox, 2004; Lepper & Henderlong, 2000). We know that motivation for learning, though linked to individual identities and interest, appears to trend downward as students progress through the grades (Guthrie & Wigfield, 2000; Organization for Economic Cooperation and Development, 2001). Discovering ways of tapping interest to motivate youth to develop active learning strategies and acquire concepts and information in the content areas is an omnipresent challenge for secondary teachers (Ainley, Hidi, & Berndorff, 2002; Deci, Koestner, & Ryan, 2001; Watkins & Coffey, 2004).

Principle 4: Express Critical Perspectives and Interpretations

Politicians and pundits make what seem to be daily pronouncements about the inadequacies of secondary education in America (Alliance for Excellent Education, 2005; Center for Workforce Preparation, 2004). We hear that youth aren't developing the knowledge and skills necessary to compete in a global economy (Forgione, 1999). We are told youth need flexible learning and problem-solving strategies and critical thinking skills in order to maneuver with competence through an increasingly complex information-based society (Brozo, in press). Although we reject the characterization that our middle and high schools are in a state of "crisis," we do embrace the importance of imbuing youth with a critical consciousness that makes them wiser consumers *and* creators of print, visual, and aural texts (Alvermann, 2002; Goodman, 2003; Ridgeway, Peters & Tracy, 2002; Sturtevant et al., 2006). Creating conditions for students to develop and extend their abilities to express critical understandings of concepts and information as well as their experiences inside and beyond the classroom walls is at the heart of this principle.

The literacy and learning practices associated with this principle will promote youths' abilities to discuss, write, and use digital media to create texts that demonstrate

Helping youth explore disciplinary content from various critical perspectives will better prepare them for the challenges of navigating their information-laden and media-saturated worlds.

Teacher as Learner

GENERATING PRINCIPLE-BASED STRATEGIES TO ENGAGE READERS AND WRITERS

Read the following three short scenarios. After each one, propose instructional practices that could be employed to gain and sustain student participation in learning. Use the principle of engagement (Principle 3) we just described as a guide to your strategies.

Scenario 1

Terrell is a Black 16-year-old 11th-grader who has no time for Shakespeare's *Romeo and Juliet*. He has difficulty with Elizabethan language as well as visualizing the action of the play. Above all, he cannot see the relevance of the play to concerns and issues in his own life.

Your Instructional Suggestions:_____

_____

_____

_____

Scenario 2

It seems that everything Maita reads in her ninth-grade U.S. history book is by or about, in her words, "dead white men." As a Latina, she rarely finds the perspective of her people represented in the description of major events of the past. This cultural disconnection often leaves Maita with a "so what?" attitude. Her class is about to read and study a chapter on America's Westward expansion during the middle of the 19th century.

Your Instructional Suggestions: _____

_____

_____

_____

Scenario 3

Sixth-grader Troy often finds himself dreaming of a new strategy for playing his favorite computer game while right in the middle of science class. As his teacher lectures, he stares in her direction to give the impression he's listening. He wishes he could show her how good he is with his computer games, but doesn't think that would matter to her, so he keeps on dreaming. He catches a word or two as his science teacher begins to talk about the scientific method, then he drifts off again.

Your Instructional Suggestions: _____

_____

_____

_____

deep and meaningful understandings, critique the ideas and assertions of others, and explore their school-based learning and lifeworlds outside of school.

Principle-Based Instruction in Music

Phineas was having a difficult time getting his brass players to express themselves with more feeling. His high school band had talent and most members were skillful, but their playing was mechanical and they were uneasy about creating their own compositions. Then he attended a recital of a renowned trombonist, and an idea struck him. The musician played a piece entitled "Eight Poems by William Carlos Williams." In the piece, the trombonist read a poem, and then played an interpretation. Phineas realized how the poem had inspired the music and thought his students might be equally inspired if they could find a text that reached them.

Phineas asked his horn players to bring in a favorite book, poem, or other material. He also had on hand several different newspapers and magazines. Once they had found something of interest, he told them to read a few sentences or lines and, holding their instruments to their lips, let their imaginations go and play anything they felt. The room quickly filled with the cacophonous sounds of trumpets, french horns, sousaphones, and trombones playing random notes and meandering melodies. After several minutes, Phineas asked the students to pair up and read the poem or other piece to their partners, then play their interpretations. There was plenty of grinning and chuckling, but soon the students surprised themselves with their own abilities to capture an inner feeling through music inspired by a poem or other text.

Phineas invited volunteers to give demonstrations. Mondo read an excerpt from some hip-hop lyrics about violence between rival Latino and African American gangs, then blew loud, dissonant notes that resolved into Taps. He explained afterward that he first tried to capture the fighting that was going on in the 'hood, then he saw death and played notes universally associated with funerals. Tameka recited some lines from Martin Luther King's "I Have a Dream" speech, which she said her mother had read to her when she was a little girl, then slid her trombone as low as she could, applying tremolo. This, she explained, represented the power she felt in King's words.

Phineas could see after these free-form sessions that his student musicians were more willing to explore interpretations instead of coldly reproducing notes of manuscript. By helping them find their own source of inspiration in written words and then allowing them complete freedom of expression, Phineas's class was developing a new sense of awareness of how music can be a voice in making sense of the world around them.

For example, a pair of urban youth doing a report on AIDS in a high school health class would take video and audio equipment into their own neighborhood to explore the impact of the disease on the local community, interview victims, convene and moderate a panel comprised of public health personnel and social workers for their classmates, and produce a script for a video documentary of their research. In another example, a class of seventh graders living near a coastal water system that is becoming increasingly polluted would take on the role of "Water Landlords" responsible for overseeing the cleansing of the marine environment and maintaining its health. Students would analyze data gathered along the coast to identify high-pollution areas and determine possible causes. They would create two written products: (1) an informative notice to swimmers and fishers, and (2) a letter to a local representative and the state environmental protection agency using the data the class acquired to urge actions to be taken to address the problem. In both cases, teachers crafted instruction consistent with the guidelines of Principle 4 in order to support students in their efforts to critically investigate issues of relevance and generate thoughtful texts with real-world applications.

The Role of the Teacher Leader

No one in a middle or secondary school is perhaps more important to ensuring content-area teachers' instructional practices are guided by effective evidence-based principles than the literacy specialist or coach (McAndrew, 2005; West & Staub, 2003). As a teacher leader, the literacy coach is ideally positioned to help teachers recognize how much they already know about teaching and learning and how their practices might be extended to be even more responsive to the academic and personal needs of youths (Toll, 2005).

Changing teaching practices is rarely easy, however. Even when policy makers enact the laws, administrators supply the pressure, and staff developers present the innovative strategies, teachers themselves make the decision to change or not change the ways they teach. Coaches are there to support teachers, not to "fix" them or demand change from them. Only in this kind of professional relationship can content-area teachers take the necessary risks and accept collegial input that leads to effective principled practices.

When Judith became a secondary reading specialist she quickly realized that not only was she expected to be an expert teacher, knowledgeable of current research and strategies and capable of putting this knowledge and ability to practice, but also an effective collaborator. Collaborating with high school disciplinary teachers meant Judith had to understand their change-process needs, appreciate the depth and complexity of their various curricula, and build on their strengths. For example, when teaming with Dennis, a world geography teacher, on assisting the English language learners and inclusion students in his class, she began by becoming familiar with the course syllabus and textbook and getting acquainted with the students and classroom dynamic. Next, she conducted strategy demonstrations designed to accommodate the different levels of ability and then met with Dennis afterward to debrief and discuss modifications. This stage was followed by co-instructional lessons that included strategic teaching as well as flexible delivery of content. Finally, Judith observed Dennis as he tried out new strategies and practices and then offered helpful comments to improve upon them.

Dennis told a history department colleague, "If she had come to me with all these do's and don'ts, I would have tuned her right out. But it was obvious she really wanted to help, and she really knew what she was doing, so I felt more comfortable accepting her advice and suggestions." Dennis's comment about his experiences with Judith strongly suggests that teacher leaders, such as literacy coaches, can help other teachers become more aware of the importance of principle-guided practice through the very ways they interact with and scaffold change for them (Bean, 2004).

Principle 5: Gather and Organize Print and Nonprint Sources for Increasing Understanding of Information and Ideas

Go to Web Resources for Chapter 2 at *http://www. prenhall.com/brozo*, and look for Teaching Students to Do Online Research.

Adolescents often enter middle and high school content classrooms without the ability to gather relevant information from a variety of sources and organize information and concepts into useful forms for review or application. These skills are becoming increasingly vital for youth given the sheer volume of information available on every imaginable topic as well as the variety of both print and nonprint media at their disposal. To sort through and organize information from multiple sources, students need to develop a range of sophisticated study strategies for reading. This principle is concerned with endowing youth with these study strategies.

Notetaking, summarization, and graphic organization skills have supported student learning for many years but serve today's adolescent learners especially well. Flexibility with these study strategies and others like them makes it possible for students to determine the relative importance of information and ideas, condense information and ideas into essential bits of meaning, and group and arrange various source material into manageable forms.

Teachers guided by this principle know that students need multiple opportunities to develop skill with and find applications for study reading strategies in order to reach an appropriate level of ownership and expertise (Alexander & Jetton, 2000; Nist & Simpson, 2000). Thus, content teachers apprentice youth in these strategies through modeling, practice, reflection, and, above all, meaningful application with class assignments and projects.

Principle-Based Instruction in English Literature

Pride and Prejudice was Nell's most treasured novel. As a brand new teacher assigned to English 10, she couldn't believe her good fortune when she discovered it was part of the sophomore literature curriculum. The book had been a favorite since childhood, and she knew it on every level, so teaching it would be a snap . . . or so she thought. The novel failed to do much for her students that first year primarily because, as they told her, it was difficult keeping track of the motives and behavior of all the characters. The students also had difficulty relating to the early-19th-century time period in which the novel is set.

The following year, Nell was determined to make the novel a more enjoyable experience for her class. To achieve this goal, however, she would need to do more than exude her own sincere enthusiasm for the book. Nell realized her students needed strategies for organizing their understanding of the characters as well as ways of expanding their understanding of the time and transcendent themes of the book.

After consulting with the district reading specialist, Nell was given some useful resources that explained and exemplified study reading strategies. The specialist also gave her suggestions for helping students relate to the time period and themes of the novel. A summer's worth of planning resulted in a new and improved curriculum for reading and studying Jane Austen's vaunted novel.

- *Charting (see Chapter 9) was the strategy Nell decided to teach her students, because it is designed to facilitate the summarizing and organizing of vital information while showing uniquenesses and relationships. A chart would also be an important study tool for class discussion or test preparation.*

- *To help students better appreciate the setting for Jane Austen's novel, an early-19th-century country parsonage in England, Nell structured assignments around Internet searches for period pictures, historical accounts, literary criticism, and primary documents. Installments of the humorous British public television series The Vicar of Dibley were also included as another view into the novel's setting. Finally, at regular intervals and especially after critical episodes in the novel, she showed the film version of each.*

- *After reading Herz and Gallo's (1996) book From Hinton to Hamlet: Building Bridges Between Young Adult Literature and the Classics, Nell was convinced her students could come to appreciate how the themes and characters' motives relate to their adolescent lives today. First she chose a contemporary young adult novel with similar issues. Among the countless books involving teen romance, Nell settled on Charms for the Easy Life by Kaye Gibbons Putnam (1993). Putnam's novel for youth traces three generations of Southern women in a lively story about how, in spite of their feminist views, they each manage to "get their man."*

Nell's multidimensional approach to the study of Pride and Prejudice proved much more successful in her second year of teaching 10-grade English. Students were given tools for organizing critical information about the characters from the novel, which improved their class discussions and test performance.

Exploring multiple sources allowed Nell's students to better understand the historical and physical contexts for the novel's plot. And after reading Putnam's young adult novel as a prelude to Austen's classic, students made far more frequent connections between the behavior of the Bennet daughters and their suitors, Darcy and Bingley, and adolescent relationships today.

Expression of Principle 5 will take many forms. For instance, a recent émigré from Bosnia was asked to report on the Balkan Wars in a ninth-grade history class. She compiled sources ranging from Joe Saco's graphic novels to transcripts of interviews with her parents and relatives. To organize the information while obtaining it, she used a split-page notetaking procedure designed to cluster big ideas with supporting details. To collapse the volume of information, she wrote summaries of the content in each source. To organize the information in a way that would assist her in seeing how the summarized information and ideas were related, she would create a map. Finally, from the map, summaries, and notes, she would write her report.

Principle 6: Expand and Generate New Understandings Using Information and Communication Technologies

We asserted in Chapter 1 that today's youth are active participants in a mediasphere of ever-evolving print, digital, visual, and aural information competing for their attention and shifting to meet their desires. Studies continue to reveal how print-based and digitally mediated literacy practices permeate the daily lives of many adolescents (Bean, Bean, & Bean, 2000; Chandler-Olcott & Mahar, 2003; Lewis & Fabbos, 1999). In a recent survey (Lenhart, Simon, & Graziano, 2001), over 70% of teens in the United States said they use the Internet as the primary source for their school reports. Internet Web browsers have made available a convergence of information and communications technologies (ICTs) including print, images, databases, instant messaging, e-mail, fax, radio and video conferencing, interactive programs, and virtual reality. These new technologies are both easily consumed and produced. And youth from all areas of the world are quick to take advantage of them (Bruce, 2004).

Our wired and increasingly wireless world presents unparalleled challenges and opportunities for teachers of youth. Teachers guided by this principle appreciate that ICTs with which adolescents have developed such facility need not conflict with school-based learning. Instead, ICTs can be embraced as a resource for expanding students' content knowledge, learning strategies, and critical thinking. Bruce (2002) puts it this way:

> Whatever else new technologies have done, it is difficult to make the case that they diminish literate practices or fully replace old forms of meaning-making with new ones. Instead, as they are assimilated they simply enrich a growing matrix of multiple genres and media. (p. 12)

This principle also implies that teachers must understand the importance of ensuring that all adolescents, regardless of background or ability, are able to read and manipulate a range of ICTs (Alvermann & Hagood, 2000; Smith & Wilhelm, 2004; Tatum, 2000). To realize this principle, content-area teachers—on a regular and frequent basis—will need to create the space and opportunity, as well as in some cases advocate for resources that allow students access to numerous types of digital technology, such as hypertexts (Bolter, 1998) and multimedia (Eken, 2002). They will need to rethink the authority and primacy of traditional print as the exclusive information source for classroom learning and restructure assignments and activities to encompass a variety of ICTs.

Using ICTs in the disciplinary classroom offers youth engaging ways to bridge outside- and inside-of-school literacies.

Go to Web Resources for Chapter 2 at *http://www. prenhall.com/brozo*, and look for ICT Tools in the Classroom.

Principle-Based Instruction in Culinary Arts

Micah believes it's important for his culinary arts students to develop effective communication skills. He does this by incorporating into class activities authentic opportunities for reading and writing, such as reading and applying guidelines for proper food handling and sanitation of equipment and surfaces in OSHA pamphlets, using newspapers and the Internet for restaurant reviews, and reviewing health department sanitation ratings of teens' favorite eateries. After receiving several humorous but helpful reviews from his students, he talked with the class about making them available to a larger audience outside of school. Micah and the students tossed around several ideas, including a monthly magazine and a Web site. But it wasn't until the suggestion of a restaurant guide in the form of an e-zine that the students became really enthusiastic.

E-zine is shorthand for electronic magazine, and there are hundreds of these Web creations focused on every possible topic. Youth in increasing numbers are responsible for creating and maintaining e-zines. The idea became even more appealing after Micah talked with the technical support staff and learned the school had the software and infrastructure to support Internet publishing. (See Chapter 10 for a fuller explanation of e-zines and additional examples.)

To make progress as quickly as possible on the project, Micah formed three teams of students to work on content, technology, and promotional and advertising issues. Because there were already several good restaurant reviews completed by classmates, the content team set about selecting the best ones, editing them, writing introductory and filler material, and planning future installments, such as healthy eating tips and information about careers in the restaurant industry. The technology team worked closely with the technology teacher to create and design the e-zine. Adobe PageMaker was the supported software in the school and so was chosen to format the restaurant reviews and other pieces. To find the right logos and colors, the group experimented with various on-screen palettes. Soon they had a visually appealing presentation. The advertising group was responsible for the e-zine name and a plan to ensure as many potential readers as possible. They also worked with the technology team to devise a counter to monitor visitors to the Web site.

"Teen Bites Dog: A Guide to Local Fare, Healthy Eating, and Careers in the Culinary Arts" was launched a month after its conception. Micah and his students were broadcast on the school's closed-circuit TV and were featured on a local television's newscast. They explained the history of their new electronic publication, gave a brief demonstration, and encouraged suggestions and contributions.

Blending print and nonprint media, Micah's students were able to create and sustain a real-world project that served as a vehicle for improving their language and communication skills as well as applying their growing knowledge of the culinary arts and the restaurant industry.

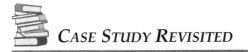

CASE STUDY REVISITED

Now that you have read and thought critically about the six principles of effective reading and learning in the content areas, consider all the ways Chauncey's decision making about how to maximize student learning through involvement in the Habitat project can be framed by these principles. Write your ideas now.

continued

Before writing your suggestions for Chauncey in the case study, go to *http://www. pren/hall.com/ brozo,* select Chapter 2, then click on Chapter Review Questions to check your understanding of the material.

First, Chauncey invited the Habitat for Humanity project architect to talk to his building trades class about the work to be done and how the students might contribute. The architect was especially interested in ideas students had for improving room design. He explained that four houses would be built around town, and that each one would follow a common general plan, with small variability depending on the size and grade of the lot. He distributed copies of blueprints of the small houses and asked students to look for ways of improving room flow that would maximize living areas. Chauncey expanded on this request from the architect by asking students to work in design groups to (a) research the history and mission of Habitat for Humanity; (b) make structural drawings to scale using appropriate terms and symbols; and (c) identify an architectural problem in the challenge given by the Habitat's architect, devise a plan for solving the problem and blueprints for executing the solution, and write and present a brief PowerPoint™ on the problem and solution.

While Chauncey's students worked on this assignment, they also donated a few hours a week assisting in the construction of the houses. He was able to use a school van to take students to and from the building sites where they donned their hardhats and goggles and joined other volunteers in the various tasks the foremen assigned. At each site Chauncey's students were able to give their suggestions about room flow and living space to the architect, as well as ask questions about important architectural features and techniques. The architect was invited back to class to observe the students' PowerPoint™ presentations and offer additional helpful comments on their ideas and methods.

A digital scrapbook was compiled by the students and placed on their class Web site. It included a brief history of Habitat for Humanity, statements of its mission, and descriptions of the project accompanied by plans and blueprints from the PowerPoint™ presentations, photos and video clips of the progression of the Habitat homes under various stages of construction, and photos of themselves, their teacher, and the architect and foremen.

Looking Back, Looking Forward

In this chapter we have described what it means for teachers of youth to support skillful and thoughtful literacy as well as expand ways of thinking about content-area information and concepts. As adolescents grow in literacy and disciplinary knowledge, life and career options widen for them as well. The research literature and anecdotal evidence make clear that expanding options for youth can be achieved when teachers, guided by evidence-based principles, braid meaningful literacy instruction into the curriculum of each subject area, strive to make learning relevant to all students, help establish a climate of cultural sensitivity, and form personal connections with youth.

Principle-based literacy instruction at the middle and secondary levels is multidimensional. It includes using reading and writing to bring pleasure and expand one's sense of self. It means using literacy to become a more fully realized and participatory citizen in a democratic society such as ours. It means being able to use reading, writing, speaking, and listening to acquire and apply knowledge in content-area classrooms. And it also means using multiple literacies, including technological literacy, to access and critically evaluate information.

It is important to remind ourselves that the six principles described and exemplified in this chapter should not be viewed as mutually exclusive of one another. Indeed, principle-based teaching means that teachers are employing practices associated with one, some, or all of these principles depending upon the time, resources, and other local constraints. Remember the purpose of the principles: they're not prescriptions for instant success, but guidelines for effective practice with an enormous variety of permutations depending upon the teaching and learning context.

It is equally important to bear in mind that rhetorical knowledge of effective instructional principles is not enough if the principles are never put into practice. At the same time, engaging in innovative, student-centered teaching often happens without full knowledge of broader principles. Yet, as teachers become more aware of evidence-based principles, inevitably their practices become more effective.

In the following chapter, Principled Practices for Expanding Comprehension, the first principle outlined here concerned with linking outside- and inside-school literacies is invoked again as a guideline for crafting learning environments that maximize student meaning making. With the best and most current research evidence and actual classroom examples we present a range of possibilities for building students' competencies as comprehenders and critical thinkers of disciplinary texts.

References

Ainley, M., Hidi, S., & Berndorff, D. (2002). Interest, learning, and the psychological processes that mediate their relationship. *Journal of Educational Psychology, 94*, 545–561.

Alexander, P. A., & Fox, E. (2004). A historical perspective on reading research and practice. In R. Ruddell & N. Unrau (Eds.), *Theoretical models and processes of reading* (5th ed., pp. 33–68). Newark, DE: International Reading Association.

Alexander, P. A., & Jetton, T. (2000). Learning from text: A multidimensional and developmental perspective. In M. Kamil, P. Mosenthal, P. D. Pearson, & R. Barr (Eds.), *Handbook of reading research* (Vol. III). Mahwah, NJ: Erlbaum.

Alliance for Excellent Education. (2005, September 6). Americans on high schools: "In need of improvement!" *Straight As, 5*, 1–2.

Alvermann, D. (2002). *Adolescents and literacies in a digital world.* New York: Peter Lang.

Alvermann, D. E., & Hagood, M. C. (2000). Fandom and critical media literacy. *Journal of Adolescent & Adult Literacy, 43*, 436–446.

Alvermann, D. E., Young, J. P., Green, C., & Wisenbaker, J. M. (1999). Adolescents' perceptions and negotiations of literacy practices in after-school read and talk clubs. *American Educational Research Journal, 36*, 221–264.

Balfanz, R., McPartland, J., & Shaw, A. (2002). *Re-conceptualizing extra help for high school students in a high standards era.*

Washington, DC: Office of Vocational and Adult Education.

Bauer, E. G. (1999). The promise of alternative literacy assessments in the classroom: A review of empirical studies. *Reading Research and Instruction, 38*, 153–168.

Bean, R. (2004). *Reading specialist: Leadership for the classroom, school, and community.* New York: Guilford Press.

Bean, T. (2000). Reading in the content areas: Social constructivist dimensions. In M. Kamil, P. Mosenthal, P. D. Pearson, & R. Barr (Eds.), *Handbook of reading research* (Vol. III). Mahwah, NJ: Erlbaum.

Bean, T. W., Bean, S. K., & Bean, K. F. (2000). Intergenerational conversations and two adolescents' multiple literacies: Implications for redefining content area literacy. *Journal of Adolescent & Adult Literacy, 42*, 438–449.

Best, R., Rowe., M., Ozuru, Y., & McNamara, D. (2005). Deep-level comprehension of science texts: The role of the reader and the text. *Topics in Language Disorders, 25*, 65–83.

Bolter, J. D. (1998). Hypertext and the question of visual literacy. In D. Reinking, M. C. McKenna, L. D. Labbo, & R. D. Kieffer (Eds.), *Handbook of literacy and technology.* Mahwah, NJ: Lawrence Erlbaum Associates.

Bransford, J., & Johnson, M. (1972). Contextual prerequisites for understanding: Some interesting investigations of comprehension and recall. *Journal of Verbal Learning and Verbal Behavior, 11,* 717–726.

Braunger, J., Donahue, D., Evans, K., & Galguera, T. (2005). *Rethinking preparation for content area teaching: The reading apprenticeship approach.* San Francisco: Jossey-Bass.

Brozo, W. G. (in press). Authentic contexts for developing language tools in vocational education. In J. Flood, D. Lapp, & N. Farnan (Eds), *Content area reading and learning: Instructional strategies.* Mahwah, NJ: Erlbaum.

Brozo, W. G., & Hargis, C. (2003). Using low-stakes reading assessment. *Educational Leadership, 61,* 60–64.

Bruce, B. (2002). Diversity and critical social engagement: How changing technologies enable new modes of literacy in changing circumstances. In D. Alvermann (Ed.), *Adolescents and literacies in a digital world.* New York: Peter Lang.

Bruce, B. (2004). New technologies and social change: Learning in the global cyberage. In L. Bresler & A. Ardichvili (Eds.), *Research in international education.* New York: Peter Lang.

Caccamise, D. (2005). Theory and pedagogical practices of text comprehension. *Topics in Language Disorders, 25,* 5–20.

Center for Workforce Preparation. (2004). *A chamber guide to improving workplace literacy.* Washington, DC: U.S. Chamber of Commerce.

Chandler-Olcott, K., & Mahar, D. (2003). "Tech-savviness" meets multiliteracies: Exploring adolescent girls' technology-related literacy practices. *Reading Research Quarterly, 38,* 356–385.

Chen, C. S., Stevenson, H. W., Hayward, C., & Burgess, S. (1995). Culture and achievement: Ethnic and cross-cultural differences. In M. L. Maehr & P. R. Pintrich (Eds.), *Advances in motivation and achievement* (Vol. 9, pp. 119–151). Greenwich, CT: JAI Press.

Clark, C., Chow-Hoy, T. K., Herter, R. J., & Moss, P. A. (2001). Portfolios as sites of learning: Reconceptualizing the connections to motivation and engagement. *Journal of Literacy Research, 33,* 211–241.

Cook-Sather, A. (2002). Authorizing students' perspectives: Toward trust, dialogue, and change in education. *Educational Researcher, 31,* 3–14.

Crichton, M. (2003). *Congo.* New York: Avon Books.

Csikszentmihalyi, M. (1990). Literacy and intrinsic motivation. *Daedalus, 119,* 115–140.

Deci, E. L., Koestner, R., & Ryan, R. M. (2001). Extrinsic rewards and intrinsic motivation in education: Reconsidered once again. *Review of Educational Research, 71,* 1–27.

Dweck, C. S. (1999). *Self-theories: Their role in motivation, personality, and development.* Philadelphia: Psychology Press.

Eccles, J., Wigfield, A., & Schiefele, U. (1998). Motivation to succeed. In W. Damon (Series Ed.) & N. Eisenberg (Vol. Ed.), *Handbook of child psychology: Vol. 3. Social, emotional, and personality development* (5th ed., pp. 1017–1095). New York: Wiley.

Eken, A. N. (2002). The third eye. *Journal of Adolescent & Adult Literacy, 46,* 220–230.

Forgione, P. (1999). *Achievement in the United States: Are students performing better?* Washington, DC: National Center for Education Statistics.

Gates, B. (2005). *National education summit on high schools: Prepared remarks.* Retrieved April 29, 2005, from http://www.gatesfoundation.org/MediaCenter/speeches/BGSpeechNGA.050226.htm.

Gee, J. P. (2000). Discourse and sociocultural studies in reading. In M. Kamil, P. Mosenthal, P. D. Pearson, & R. Barr (Eds.), *Handbook of reading research* (Vol. III). Mahwah, NJ: Erlbaum.

Goodman, S. (2003). *Teaching youth media: A critical guide to literacy, video production, and social change.* New York: Teachers College Press.

Greenleaf, C., & Schoenbach, R. (2004). Building capacity for the responsive teaching of reading in the academic disciplines: Strategic inquiry designs for middle and high school teachers' professional development. In D. Strickland & M. Kamil (Eds.), *Improving reading achievement through professional development.* Norwood, MA: Christopher Gordon.

Guthrie, J. T., & Humenick, N. M. (2004). Motivating students to read: Evidence for classroom practices that increase reading motivation and achievement. In P. McCardle & V. Chhabra (Eds.), *The voice of evidence in reading research.* Baltimore: Brookes Publishing.

Guthrie J., & Wigfield, A. (2000). Engagement and motivation in reading. In M. Kamil, P. Mosenthal, P. D. Pearson, & R. Barr (Eds.), *Handbook of reading research* (Vol. III). Mahwah, NJ: Erlbaum.

Herz, S., & Gallo, D. (1996). *From Hinton to Hamlet: Building bridges between young adult literature and the classics.* Westport, CT: Greenwood Press.

Hull G., & Schultz, K. (2002). *School's out! Bridging out-of-school literacies with class room practice.* New York: Teachers College Press.

Jackson, A. W., & Davis, G. A. (2000). *Turning points 2000: Educating adolescents in the 21st century.* New York: Teachers College Press.

Johnston, P. (2005). Literacy assessment and the future. *The Reading Teacher, 58,* 684–686.

Johnston, P., & Costello, P. (2005). Theory and research into practice: Principles for literacy assessment. *Reading Research Quarterly, 40,* 256–267.

Kelly, G., & Green, J. (1998). The social nature of knowing: Toward a sociocultural perspective on conceptual change and knowledge construction. In B. Guzzetti & C. Hynd (Eds.), *Perspectives on conceptual change: Multiple ways to understand knowing and learning in a complex world* (pp. 145–182). Mahwah, NJ: Erlbaum.

Kintsch, E. (2005). Comprehension theory as a guide for the design of thoughtful questions. *Topics in Language Disorders, 25,* 51–65.

Kohn, A. (2000). *The case against standardized testing: Raising the scores, ruining the schools.* Portsmouth, NH: Heinemann.

Legter, N., Balfanz, R., & McPartland, J. (2002). *Solutions for failing high schools: Converging visions and promising models.* Washington, DC: Office of Vocational and Adult Education.

Lenhart, A., Simon, M., & Graziano, M. (2001, September 1). *The Internet and education: Findings from the Pew Internet & American Life Project.* Available: online at http://www.perinternet.org.

Lepper, M. R., & Henderlong, J. (2000). Turning "play" into "work" and "work" into "play": 25 years of research on intrinsic and extrinsic motivation. In C. Sansone & J. M. Harackiewicz (Eds.), *Intrinsic and extrinsic motivation: The search for optimal motivation and performance* (pp. 257–307). San Diego, CA: Academic Press.

Lewis, C., & Fabbos, B. (1999, December). Chatting on-line: Uses of instant message communication among adolescent girls. Paper presented at the annual meeting of the National Reading Conference, Orlando, Fl.

McAndrew, D. A. (2005). *Literacy leadership: Six strategies for peoplework.* Newark, DE: International Reading Association.

McPartland, J., Legter, N., Jordan, W., & McDill, E. (1996). *The talent development high school: Early evidence of impact on school climate, attendance and student promotion.* Washington, DC: Center for Research on the Education of Students Placed at Risk.

Miller, D. W. (2001, March 2). Scholars say high-stakes tests deserve a failing grade. *The Chronicle of Higher Education, 47,* A14–A16.

Moje, E. B., McIntosh-Ciechanowski, K., Kramer, K., Ellis, L., Carrillo, R., & Collazo, T. (2004). Working toward third space in content area literacy: An examination of everyday funds of knowledge and discourse. *Reading Research Quarterly, 39,* 38–70.

Nist, S., & Simpson, M. L. (2000). College studying. In M. Kamil, P. Mosenthal, P. D. Pearson, & R. Barr (Eds.), *Handbook of reading research* (Vol. III). Mahwah, NJ: Erlbaum.

Organization for Economic Cooperation and Development. (2001). *Knowledge and skills for life: First results from PISA 2000.* Paris: OECD.

Pajares, F. (1996). Self-efficacy beliefs in academic settings. *Review of Educational Research, 66,* 543–578.

Pearson, P. D. (2001). Making our way through the assessment and accountability maze: Where do we go from here? *The Clearing House, 74,* 175–182.

Popham, W. J. (2001). Uses and misues of standardized tests. *NASSP Bulletin, 85,* 24–31.

Pressley, M. (2000). What should comprehension instruction be the instruction of? In M. Kamil, P. Mosenthal, P. D. Pearson, & R. Barr (Eds.), *Handbook of reading research* (Vol. III). Mahwah, NJ: Erlbaum.

Ridgeway, V., Peters, C., & Tracy, T. (2002). Out of this world: Cyberspace, literacy, and learning. In C. C. Block, L. Gambrell, & M. Pressley (Eds.), *Improving comprehension instruction: Rethinking research, theory, and classroom practice.* San Francisco: Jossey-Bass.

Ruddell, R., & Unrau, N. (2004). *Theoretical models and processes of reading* (Vol. 3). Newark, DE: International Reading Association.

Ruiz-de-Velasco, J., Fix, M., & Clewell, B. C. (2001). *Overlooked and underserved— Immigrant students in U.S. secondary schools: Core findings and conclusions.* Retrieved February 15, 2002, from http://www.urban.org/pdfs/overlooked.pdf.

Ryan, R. M., & Deci, E. L. (2000). Self-determination theory and the facilitation of intrinsic motivation, social development, and well-being. *American Psychologist, 55,* 68–78.

Shavelson, R., Baxter, G. P., & Pine, J. (1992). Performance assessment: Political rhetoric and measurement reality. *Educational Researcher, 21,* 22–27.

Smagorinsky, P. (2001). *Teaching English through principled practice.* Upper Saddle River, NJ: Prentice Hall.

Smith, M., & Wilhelm, J. D. (2004). I just like being good at it: The importance of competence in the literate lives of young men. *Journal of Adolescent & Adult Literacy, 47,* 454–461.

Stiggins, R. (2002). Assessment crisis: The absence of assessment for learning. *Phi Delta Kappan, 85,* 758–765.

Sturtevant, E., Boyd, F., Brozo, W. G., Hinchman, K., Alvermann, D., & Moore, D. (2006). *Principled practices for adolescent literacy: A framework for instruction and policy*. Mahwah, NJ: Erlbaum.

Tatum, A. W. (2000). Against marginalization and criminal reading curriculum. *Journal of Adolescent & Adult Literacy, 43*, 570–572.

Thernstrom, A., & Thernstrom, S. (2003). *No excuses: Closing the racial gap in learning*. New York: Simon & Shuster.

Tierney, R. (2000). Literacy assessment reform: Shifting beliefs, principled possibilities, and emerging practices. In R. Robinson, M. McKenna, & J. Wedman (Eds.), *Issues and trends in literacy education*. Boston: Allyn and Bacon.

Toll, C. A. (2005). *The literacy coach's survival guide: Essential questions and practical answers*. Newark, DE: International Reading Association.

Valdés, G. (1998). The world outside and inside schools: Language and immigrant children. *Educational Researcher, 27*, 4–18.

Watkins, M. W., & Coffey, D. Y. (2004). Reading motivation: Multidimensional and indeterminate. *Journal of Educational Psychology, 96*(1), 110–118.

West, L., & Staub, F. (2003). *Content-focused coaching*. Portsmouth, NH: Heinemann.

Wiggins, G. (1998). *Educative assessment: Designing assessments to inform and improve student performance*. San Francisco: Jossey-Bass.

Wilson, P. T., & Anderson, R. C. (1986). What they don't know will hurt them: The role of prior knowledge in comprehension. In J. Orasanu (Ed.), *Reading comprehension: From research to practice*. Hillsdale, NJ: Erlbaum.

chapter 3

Principled Practices for Expanding Comprehension

Anticipation Guide

Directions: Read each statement carefully and decide whether you agree or disagree with it, placing a check mark in the appropriate *Before Reading* column. When you have finished reading and studying the chapter, return to the guide and decide whether your anticipations need to be changed by placing a check mark in the appropriate *After Reading* column.

	Before Reading		After Reading	
	Agree	*Disagree*	*Agree*	*Disagree*
1. Once students develop reading comprehension skills in elementary school, they are set for life.	_____	_____	_____	_____
2. Comprehension is a complex, multidimensional process.	_____	_____	_____	_____
3. Teachers should focus on developing youths' cognitive skills if they want them to be good readers.	_____	_____	_____	_____
4. Personal and social aspects of comprehension are equally important as other aspects.	_____	_____	_____	_____
5. Better readers are better students in all the disciplines.	_____	_____	_____	_____
6. Comprehension is a meaning-making rather than a meaning-using process.	_____	_____	_____	_____

7. Adolescents should be taught to use the text and their prior knowledge to expand comprehension.

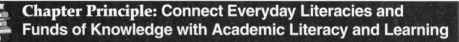

📚 Chapter Principle: Connect Everyday Literacies and Funds of Knowledge with Academic Literacy and Learning

In the previous chapter we laid out six critical guiding principles for successful content-area literacy practices. The research literature makes clear that when disciplinary teachers base their interactions with youth on these principles, instruction and learning improve (Sturtevant et al., 2006). In this chapter we invoke the first of these guiding principles to address a ubiquitous concern among middle and secondary school teachers: how to increase youths' comprehension abilities while honoring their outside-of-school literacies, interests, and competencies.

*W*hen 15-year-old Aurora reads aloud to her father an article from a Spanish-language newspaper about their favorite soccer team in Mexico then discusses the implications for postseason play, she is demonstrating her ability to comprehend. When Hillary instant messages her friend Maya with a terse description of a movie she saw over the weekend and her personal reactions to it, she is demonstrating her ability to comprehend. When Fareed downloads a "cheat sheet" of shortcuts and consults it for solving a popular computer game, he is demonstrating his ability to comprehend. And when Tony uses an owner's manual to adjust the idle speed on his motorcycle, he, too, is demonstrating his ability to comprehend.

Go to *http://www. prenhall.com/brozo,* select Chapter 3, then click on Chapter Objectives to provide a focus for your reading.

These examples of everyday acts of meaning making from and with text that adolescents like Aurora, Hillary, Fareed, and Tony engage in for authentic purposes speak to the resources youth bring with them to disciplinary classrooms. Although the demands of academic literacy and learning are considerable, teachers have adolescents' experiences with communication, problem solving, and critical thinking to build upon (Behrman, 2003). We asserted in Chapter 1 and again in relation to our discussion of principled practices in content literacy in Chapter 2 that secondary teachers should be ever mindful of ways to capitalize on youths' outside-of-school literacies as bridges to academic, disciplinary text reading and learning. This is especially important for today's youth who live in a world saturated by attention-competing media where conceptions of what counts as text are continually evolving (Kinzer, 2003; Lankshear & Knobel, 2002). In this new world, we are being asked to think of text not as a mere sequence of alphabetic characters on a piece of paper (Bruce, 2002; Gee, 2001), but as "any configuration of signs that provides a potential for meaning" (Smagorinsky, 2001, p. 135). According to this definition, many things can be "read" as text, such as clothing, graffiti, buildings, sports, and new technologies (King & O'Brien, 2002). A preservice teacher put it this way: "If you are deriving a message from it, you are reading it" (Alvermann, 2002, p. 73). It's easy to see, then, how youth are routinely reading the signs in their worlds (Friere, 1987).

Exploring ways of apprenticing and scaffolding youths' acts of meaning making with print and other texts so as to increase academic literacy in school is the focus of this chapter. We believe it is the teacher's role to recognize how thinking, reading, and communicating are inseparable from the content of the disciplines, and therefore must become part of the instructional practices in science, history, math, and all the other subjects. Here is why we believe this notion is so important. A seventh grader who is knowledgeable in science also possesses excellent science literacy skills, enabling her to read, comprehend, critically consider, and write and talk about science information and concepts. Even if it were the case that the seventh grader developed these literacy skills on her own, that does not diminish the need for them to be taught in systematic and routine ways in order to make it possible for all students to become highly competent in science. It is helpful at this point to restate an assertion we made in the previous chapter: We believe *content learning* and *content literacy learning* are one in the same. Thus, effective teachers of the disciplines cannot help but be *effective* teachers of processes for reading and communicating about the disciplines.

Remember an important premise from Chapter 2, content knowledge and content literacy are inseparable and this made clear to youth when literacy practices are braided into daily instruction.

This chapter is dedicated to practices for expanding comprehension in the content areas. The practices we share emerge from our understanding of youth as well as the principles that guide effective literacy teaching and learning. We begin with a discussion of four dimensions of text comprehension as a practice for learning in the disciplines. This is followed by descriptions and examples of several principle-based strategies that account for the multidimensional nature of text processing and promote purposeful, thoughtful, and skillful reading.

CASE STUDY

Case studies in this
textbook provides an
opportunity to apply
principles and practices to
new contexts.

Charles teaches 10th-grade general biology in a large consolidated high school in the Midwest. After 3 years of teaching, he has noticed that many of his students (1) generally have a difficult time understanding the textbook, (2) do not complete homework reading assignments, and (3) seem to be trying to memorize information while failing to learn to observe and think about scientific phenomena. Charles is highly interested in discovering ways to help his students become more enthusiastic about science learning and better able to deal with and benefit from textbook reading.

Midway through the first semester of the new school year, Charles has begun a 2-week unit on genetics. Within the unit he wants to emphasize students' understanding of genetic engineering and the implications of this technology for their personal lives. In the preceding 2 months, his students studied the scientific method, the cell, and classification of living things, including the life cycle and basic requirements of life.

To the Reader:

As you read and work through this chapter on comprehension strategies, think about and be prepared to generate some strategies that could help Charles accomplish his goals. Consider how the strategies described in this chapter and those generated from your own experience and imagination could be adapted to the teaching and learning of science material.

The Dimensions of Comprehension

Comprehension is a complex developmental and contextual process. It is developmental in that one's ability to understand text continues to increase throughout life. It is contextual in that meaning making is bounded by place, history, social interaction, and function. Eileen Kintsch (2005) captures the essence of this complexity when she says:

> Comprehension is no longer considered to be a single, monolithic process, but rather multiple processes that occur simultaneously at different levels, and each level of processing leaves a memory trace. Thus, what the reader remembers after reading is a multilayered mental representation that may includes some of the surface features of the text, its meaning at the local sentence level, the overall gist of the passage, as well as an interpretation of the text meaning in the light of his or her own experiences, knowledge, goals, and so on. (pp. 62–63)

Because comprehension
is multidimensional,
youths' reading and
literacy skills must be
further developed and
refined across and
throughout the grades.

In light of this complexity, it can never be assumed that once students are taught to read in elementary school they are set for life. It is well recognized that mastering foundational skills in the early grades may be an important first step (National Reading Panel, 2000), but not nearly enough for a lifetime of successful comprehension. There is plenty of evidence that skills and abilities for text comprehension developed in the elementary years are not adequate for the challenges of increasingly complex text students find in middle school and beyond (Duke, Pressley, & Hilden, 2004; Underwood & Pearson, 2004). Every new text and reading situation requires a refined application of literacy skills and abilities. This is especially true of content-area literacy. Findings from the National Assessment of Educational Progress (NAEP) (Campbell, Hombo, & Mazzeo, 2000; Grigg, Daane, Ying, & Campbell, 2003) reveal a very close relationship between adolescents' overall reading achievement on the NAEP reading assessment and academic achievement in school. In other words, youth who can comprehend complex prose are better students in all the subject areas as compared with their peers who struggle to understand what they read.

The complexity of comprehension makes it difficult to define in simple terms. Nonetheless, a helpful definition consistent with our own views comes from the RAND Reading Study Group (RRSG), a special team of literacy scholars commissioned by the Rand Corporation to analyze the state of reading for children and youth. The RRSG spoke of reading comprehension as "the process of simultaneously extracting and constructing meaning through interaction and involvement with written language" (2002, p. 11). Building on the RRSG definition, we offer our own definition:

> Comprehension of print and other forms of text is a *meaning-making* and *meaning-using* process. Meaning is constructed through the interaction of the learner (in all of her or his complexities) and the text (in all of its complexity and all of its various forms of representation) within sociocultural contexts. Meaning is used in direct relation to the level of interest in the learner and the level of functionality of the learning. The degree of interaction and use varies depending upon factors such as (a) the learner's culture, funds of knowledge, strategies, engagement, interests, identity, and agency; (b) the considerateness and type of text; and (c) the classroom environment, instructional strategies, and meaningfulness of the comprehension experiences.

Notice in this definition that our overall goal as comprehenders is to use literate practices to make sense of and act on our worlds. Like all good thinkers, your ability to make meaningful interpretations of this book and use what you learn from it is directly related to:

- How much you already know about the topic of content literacy
- How much experience you have with the organization and discourse of textbook prose
- How interested and engaged you are in reading this text
- What strategies you employ for studying and retaining the ideas and information
- The extent to which comprehension of the ideas and information reinforces a positive literate and professional identity
- The extent to which comprehension of the ideas and information lead to a greater sense of agency
- How the instructor uses the book, structures the literacy context, and provides classroom experiences for learning the concepts and strategies in the book
- How well we as authors have been considerate of you, the reader, in structuring and communicating our message

The various factors inherent in acts of meaning making and meaning using can be framed around what we consider to be four critical, interrelated dimensions: *cognitive*, *textual*, *personal*, and *social*.

Go to Web Resources for Chapter 3 at *http://www. prenhall.com/brozo,* and look for RAND Reading Study Group.

It's helpful for you as a reader to reflect on all of the factors that are involved in successful comprehension so you can design instruction that takes these factors into account for youth.

Cognitive Dimension

Comprehension as a cognitive process is concerned with the skills, strategies, and background knowledge of the reader. All of a youth's cognitive abilities must come into play when trying to understand such varied texts as a chapter on the bicameral nature of our legislature in a U.S. government textbook, an informational book in biology about prey/predator relationships, or an explanation of a balance sheet on a small business Web site.

We have known for some time that active readers and learners use their prior knowledge as they interact with text to enhance comprehension (Afflerbach, 1986; Chiesi, Spilich, & Voss, 1979; Pressley, 2000; Snow & Sweet, 2003; Spires & Donley, 1998). Youth who have been the beneficiaries of rich and varied funds of knowledge are likely to possess well-developed knowledge structures or schemas that allow them to comprehend texts at deep levels (Best, Rowe, Ozuru, & McNamara, 2005; Kintsch, 1998; Nassaji, 2002).

Teacher as Learner
A PRIOR KNOWLEDGE ACTIVITY

To demonstrate the importance of relevant prior knowledge for successful reading and learning, we have an assignment for you. Read the following passage and be prepared to discuss the main points, the supporting details, and the relationships between the themes in the passage and other related passages you have read.

> It is highly unsettling for some to come into close contact with them. Far worse to gain control over them and to deliberately inflict pain on them. The revulsion caused by this punishment is so strong that many will not take part in it at all. Thus there exists a group of people who seem to revel in the contact and the punishment as well as the rewards associated with both. Then there is another group of people who shun the whole enterprise: contact, punishment, and rewards alike.
>
> Members of the first group share modes of talk, dress, and deportment. Members of the second group, however, are as varied as all humanity.
>
> Then there is a group of others, not previously mentioned, for the sake of whose attention all this activity is undertaken. They too harm the victims, though they do it without intention of cruelty. They simply follow their own necessities. And though they may inflict the cruelest punishment of all, sometimes—but not always—they themselves suffer as a result. (Gillet & Temple, 1986, p. 4)

Do you have any idea what this passage is about? Every time we ask our students to read it, they first try desperately to impose a sensible interpretation on the words, offer possibilities that leave them uncomfortable, and finally give up, resorting to protests that sound all too familiar to any classroom teacher: "This is too hard." Most complain that this reading exercise is unfair because the passage has too many unclear referents or is without a title, which makes it impossible to understand with any certainty. The typical guesses at meaning and subject matter we get vary widely from *parents and children* to *concentration camps* to *corporal punishment* to *teachers and students*.

This passage helps us simulate for you the essential nature of schema or relevant prior knowledge for understanding text. By the way, the title is "Fishing Worms." Does that help? Go back and reread the passage now, and notice as you read how all the ideas seem to fit together, how meaning jumps automatically into consciousness. The title acts as an organizer, a unifying theme, and brings to mind your schema—or prior experiences, memories, and knowledge—related to fishing and worms.

We also know that in order to construct and use meaning youth must possess a repertoire of strategies (RRSG, 2002; Ruddell & Unrau, 2004). Good comprehenders summarize and organize as they interact with text (Thiede & Anderson, 2001), think critically and generate new understandings (McNamara, 2004; Paris & Stahl, 2005), and are metacognitively aware (Palincsar & Brown, 1984; Pressley & Hilden, 2004). They set purposes for reading and learning and actively monitor whether they meet them (Kintsch & Kintsch, 2005). During the meaning-making process, good comprehenders notice when something does not fit with what they already know or is unclear, then engage in appropriate strategies to clarify understanding, which might include rereading, seeking help from an expert, creating a visual aid, asking questions and searching for answers, or a host of other possible actions (Caccamise & Snyder, 2005).

The implications from current research for developing cognition for comprehension are many. Not only should teachers have a thorough understanding of their discipline and be capable of deep and meaningful thinking about text, they should also possess the skills to make the processes involved in maximizing meaning making and meaning using obvious for youth (Bransford, Brown, & Cocking, 2000; Fournier & Graves, 2002). Later in this chapter, we'll describe and exemplify comprehension strategies that foster these thinking skills.

Go to Web Resources for Chapter 3 at http://www.prenhall.com/brozo, and look for Constructivism and Cognitivism.

Textual Dimension

The textual dimension of comprehension requires us to consider how the structure and properties of prose and other texts interact with and stimulate a reader's capacity for constructing and using meaning. As noted, textual aspects of comprehension as well as the other dimensions are linked together and cannot be analyzed in isolation from one another. This is particularly true of textual dimensions, because a text, it is theorized, has little inherent meaning but is given meaning by a reader, listener, or interpreter (Smagorinsky, 2001). In other words, a person's cognition and motivation, as well as contextual and relational factors, influence the degree to which a text is comprehensible. Stated another way, a text is not difficult or easy but rather difficult or easy relative to a person's abilities, enthusiasm, perseverance, and level of scaffolding from an expert.

At the same time, a text is not a featureless collection of letters, words, and punctuation. The way it is written as well as other lexical and formatting characteristics can have a significant effect on comprehension (Musheno & Lawson, 1999; RRSG, 2002), especially for those readers who have underdeveloped relevant prior knowledge (Best et al., 2005). For example, an eighth grader may have limited knowledge of science facts and concepts but may achieve a moderate degree of success with the class textbook if the author included structures and features designed to support novice readers of science. These might include helpful *microstructure* features that signal the relationships between and among information and ideas, such as connectives, conjunctions, pronouns, and overlapping sentences (Graesser, McNamara, Louwerse, & Cai, 2004), as well as *macrostructure* features that tie the overall text together, such as titles and subheadings, advance organizers, outlines, summaries, and logical patterns of organization (Hartley, 2002; Sadoski, Goetz, & Rodriguez, 2000). Figure 3.1 shows a list of additional textual characteristics that are "considerate" of intended audiences and, consequently, make for more readable prose.

Though teachers can't be expected to rewrite textbooks, they can familiarize adolescent readers with the organizational structures and other features of a text that can be used to improve comprehension (Meyer et al., 2002). Middle and high school students can also be shown how to make logical connections through inferencing

Figure 3.1   Characteristics of Considerate Text

Though textbooks will never be perfect, there are characteristics that make some more *considerate* (Armbruster & Anderson, 1995) than others. Text is considerate when it is written and formatted in ways to help intended readers follow the ideas easily. Considerate text is achieved when authors (Alexander & Jetton, 2000):

- Effectively communicate their purpose or aim

- Consider the audience of their textbook and provide sufficient background information, a judicious use of well-defined technical words, and referents for any figurative or literary allusions (e.g., myths)

- Have a focus and share that focus with the readers via an overall organization or macrostructure (e.g., headings, subheadings, main ideas that are linked to each other, etc.)

- Have a focus and share that with the readers via a microstructure that provides development via examples, anecdotes, supporting details, explanations, and quotations from primary sources

- Use a style of writing that is clear and explicit

Because good readers use their inferencing abilities to fill in gaps in text in order for it to be processed in a coherent way, practices that help adolescents make inference about text will improve their comprehension.

when navigating text that lacks cohesion or a well-organized format. Ways of helping students capitalize on these text features and make inferences will be presented later in this chapter.

Personal Dimension

Issues of engagement, identity, agency, and goals comprise the personal dimension of comprehension. As you learned in reading Chapters 1 and 2, these aspects of literacy are highly complex, which might explain why they are so often overlooked in the instructional planning of many teachers of youth. Ignoring the personal dimension of adolescent learners when setting expectations for reading often leads to disappointment and frustration for both teacher and students. This is because individual personal attitudes play a vital role in the reading, learning, and remembering process, as researchers have confirmed (Eagly, Chen, Chaiken, & Shaw-Barnes, 1999).

Consider the case of Keshawn, an African American ninth grader and member of Mary Kay's history class. Bright and energetic, he possessed adequate reading skill to comprehend the information and concepts in the textbook, but lacked the will or desire to read it. Mary Kay was unsure how to work with Keshawn and tended to blame his low test grades on laziness. After observing the class and discussing the concern with Mary Kay, we helped her develop motivational readiness activities for upcoming chapters, demonstrated how alternative texts by and about African American historical figures could be incorporated into lessons, and explored ways of expanding Keshawn's choices for reading and responding to the content. These strategies along with Mary Kay's efforts to create closer ties with Keshawn to help her better understand his personal and career goals brought about a significant improvement in his performance.

Students, like Keshawn, need experiences in content classrooms that turn interest into engagement (Schiefele, 1999) and cultivate their desires for autonomy and control (Behrman, 2003). Offering students choices of texts and options for responding to them encourages investment in their own learning, which has been shown to improve comprehension (Ainley, Hidi, & Berndorff, 2002; Flowerday & Schraw, 2000). Improving comprehension of text can, in turn, serve as conduit for increasing students' agency. In learning environments where youths' cognitive and personal learning needs are supported, they are more likely to persevere with academic texts and expend the energy to understand them (Greenleaf, Schoenbach, Cziko, & Mueller, 2001).

In addition to helping students increase their independence and control over the meaning-making process, teachers mindful of the importance of the personal dimension will also find ways of building youths' literate identities (Moore, 2002). We made clear in Chapter 1 that adolescents' sense of themselves as readers is bound up in their identities in and out of school. The more content teachers do to make text engaging and comprehension possible for youth, the more confident they become in their identities as capable readers and meaning makers (Guthrie & Humenick, 2004; Langer, 2001). This confidence then translates into greater effort to understand text and apply new knowledge in meaningful ways.

> The personal dimension of reading may be especially important to exploit for youth because it places value on their interests and experiences which leads to engaged learning.

Social Dimension

The social dimension of comprehension takes into account that making, extracting, and using meaning is a social process (Green, 1990; Myers, 1992; Turner, 1995). Social processes fashion social languages, according to Gee (2001), that are "used to enact, recognize, and negotiate different socially situated identities and to carry out different socially situated activities" (p. 413). From this point of view, an individual's meaning making is understandable only when it is viewed in relation to others. For instance, when Monica, a 10th grader, confides in her English journal that her boyfriend has been unfaithful, she might write: "I'm feeling really angry today because Jack, my boyfriend, or should I say my ex-boyfriend, is seeing someone else." After school, on the walk home with her best friend, Tara, Monica tells her: "I found out today that Jack's goin' out with Kristi. That scumbag is dead!" For her English teacher, Monica uses socially agreed-upon discourse conventions; when talking with her friend away from school space, she uses another culturally distinctive language form that defines herself and her friend as socially intimate partners.

To be a meaning maker, then, is to be part of a social context. Even when you curl up with a book in the "private" act of reading, you are not alone—you are interacting with an author who holds other ideas, points of view, styles of expression, and so on. In this way, writers are literally "speaking" to you through a printed text that provides a potential for shared and unique meanings to be realized by you and other readers (Smagorinsky, 2001). Adolescent learners' construction and use of meaning for any given text depends on other meanings acquired through interaction in the various discourse communities they inhabit and the funds of knowledge upon which they can draw (Kelly & Green, 1998; Valdés, 1998). It has been demonstrated that acts of meaning making and meaning using increase when teachers exploit the social world of the classroom and solicit socially derived texts from their students (Bloome & Egan-Robertson, 1993; Marshall, 2000; Unrau & Ruddell, 1995).

The instructional implications of the social nature of text comprehension are many and varied. On a general level, youth in disciplinary classrooms should be encouraged to build shared meanings of information and concepts through numerous formal and informal interactions with peers and teachers. The meanings of texts can be analyzed through various cultural lenses for their universality, bias, and relevance. Within a community of learners, teachers can apprentice youth in the practices of content literacy through modeling, reciprocal teaching, and a host of other collaborative experiences. On a practical level, the classroom itself should be arranged to encourage social interaction among the teacher and student meaning makers. Instead

> Go to Web Resources for Chapter 3 at *http://www. prenhall.com/brozo,* and look for Social-Cognitive Theory.

of organizing desks in rows, for instance, with the lines of communication moving from the teacher to individual students, we recommend a more flexible seating arrangement and flexible grouping patterns that encourage student-student discussion and problem solving. In the next section of this chapter we offer more detailed suggestions for promoting meaningful comprehension of classroom texts within dynamic social contexts.

Multidimensional Approaches to Developing Text Comprehension

Teachers who are mindful of the complex and overlapping network of obvious and sometimes not so obvious factors at play in the meaning-making process are better able to support their students' comprehension of content texts (Braunger, Donahue, Evans, & Galguera, 2005). Although the strategies we are about to share have been aligned with one particular dimension of comprehension, in the hands of the knowledgeable and responsive teachers spotlighted in the vignettes, you will see how they can be expanded to account for the multidimensional nature of text comprehension in order to meet the needs of all learners.

Cognitive Dimension Strategies

Developing a Language of Process About Text

Disciplinary teachers need to create multiple opportunities for students to eavesdrop on their thinking while negotiating text so they can model the process of constructing and extracting meaning. Too often classroom text talk remains focused on the content while rarely including conversation about the processes involved in understanding the content. For example, a teacher might state a main idea for a paragraph or passage, but not take that next step and explain to her students how she determined the main idea. Failure to apprentice youth in the ways of thinking about text that lead to comprehension leaves them without the cognitive tools to construct and apply meaning independently. On the other hand, by ensuring that classroom discussion around text always includes process comments in addition to content statements, teachers will be providing students a language for describing *how* they're thinking (Kymes, 2004; Wilhelm, 2001) to go along with the language they use to describe *what* they're thinking. In this way youth not only increase their knowledge of disciplinary content but also increase their abilities to learn from text. See Figure 3.2 for a description and examples of common content statements and process comments.

Go to Web Resources for Chapter 3 at *http://www. prenhall.com/brozo,* and look for Think Alouds.

Manolo scaffolds his sixth-grade science students' thinking about text by teaching them to divide their mental focus into both processing activities and comprehension-monitoring activities. He does this through a model-elicit teaching approach. First he models a way of thinking about text, then elicits the same thinking behaviors from his students. By repeatedly demonstrating and gathering demonstrations of certain comprehension processes, Manolo is able to foster understanding of science material while elevating his class to higher levels of metacognitive awareness.

In the following excerpt, Manolo and his students are engaged in a discussion about lightning from a chapter in the class textbook. He and his students are taking turns commenting about the information in the chapter *and* using a language of process to label how they are monitoring their understanding of the material. Students are sitting in clusters of four around small tables with their books open to the

Figure 3.2 A Language of Process

A language of process refers to the labels we use to describe thinking processes while constructing meaning from text. Content statements, on the other hand, are those that are made about specific information and ideas in a text. To illustrate, look at the examples below of process comments and content statements. You will notice that content statements derive directly from the words and ideas in the text, whereas process statements are a reflection of metacognitive thinking about these words and ideas.

- **Making and Checking Predictions**

  <u>Content Statement</u>

  Okay, it says here "Where Have All the Nurses Gone?" so I think the author is going to explain in this next section why the number of nurses is declining.

  <u>Process Comments</u>

  What I'm doing now is *predicting* what the text is going to be about based on the title and subheading. As I read further I can check to see if my predictions are correct or need to be changed. This will help me concentrate more closely on the information.

- **Using Contextual Strategies for Word Learning**

  <u>Content Statement</u>

  It says here that the Romans had *agrarian* laws giving all citizens equal shares of land . . . so *agrarian* probably refers to land or agriculture.

  <u>Process Comments</u>

  See how I'm using the *context clues* right within this sentence—the words before and after *agrarian* . . . to figure out what *agrarian* means. When you're trying to figure out the meaning of a word, you can do the same thing.

- **Imaging**

  <u>Content Statement</u>

  I can just picture this guy, Ian, trapped in a mine shaft, with no light, and not knowing which way to turn.

  <u>Process Comments</u>

  By creating an *image* in my mind of the events of the story, I can almost see them happening and the story becomes more understandable. Do this when you read; try to create a little movie scene in your mind of the characters, scenes, and action.

- **Linking Prior Knowledge to Text**

  <u>Content Statement</u>

  They're really in trouble now, aren't they? See, their truck broke down on the way to California. That reminds me of the time I was driving to Michigan in the middle of the winter and my car overheated on this back road in the middle of nowhere . . .

  <u>Process Comments</u>

  I'm thinking about my *prior knowledge,* something from my past, an experience that I can relate to the text so I can understand it better. As you try to make sense of text, see if you can think about what you already know because you've read about it, seen it, or actually had a similar experience. When you do this, text doesn't seem so separate from your own life and you'll find it easier to comprehend.

continued

Figure 3.2 *(Continued)*

- **Summarizing and Paraphrasing**

  <u>Content Statement</u>

  What the author is getting at on this page is that Native Americans made many positive contributions in the United States' effort to defeat the Germans in World War II.

  <u>Process Comments</u>

  Do you see how I've *created a summary*? I've taken all of these positive words the author used in reference to Native Americans, like "helped" in the first paragraph, "served honorably and bravely" in the next one, and "valuable asset" in the last paragraph, and grouped them together around "important roles." That's how I *make a summary,* I look for things that are emphasized with bold print or italics, or ideas that are repeated. In this case these positive terms are repeated. Then I come up with a straightforward, general statement without including all the details and examples.

- **Verbalizing Points of Confusion and Demonstrating Fix-Up Strategies**

  <u>Content Statement</u>

  The text says that the sun is actually slightly closer to the earth during the winter than it is during the summer. So when the sun is closer to the earth it's colder, and when it's farther away, it's warmer on earth.

  <u>Process Comments</u>

  This is very confusing to me . . . is it confusing to you, too? Doesn't it make more sense to think about it just the opposite way? What I'm doing now is *talking about the stuff that's confusing,* or if I were reading this alone I'd be *thinking about how this makes me confused.* When I do this, I can either work through the confusion or do something else to *fix the problem I'm having with comprehension.* One thing I can do is reread this section or I can read further to get more explanation. I might also look at the illustrations more closely or even ask a friend or look through another book for clarification.

---

chapter on lightning. Manolo makes both a content statement and process comment after reading the first short paragraph.

Content Statement

Okay, this chapter starts out by saying that up until very recently we haven't known much about lightning, but now things are changing. I'd guess that we'll probably read about the technology we're using to figure out how lightning occurs.

Process Comment

You see how I'm using the information to make a prediction about what the author will say next about lightning. I may be wrong, but by making a prediction and then checking to see if I'm right, I'll pay closer attention to the information and ideas. Do you see what I mean? Okay, at your tables talk about how you can make and check a prediction for the next couple of paragraphs, and I'll call on someone to talk us through how you did it.

Later in the chapter, Manolo modeled another important comprehension-monitoring strategy, gave it a process label, and elicited similar verbalizing of cognitive behavior from his students.

Content Statement

. . . this bit about how it's a folklore to seek shelter under trees during a thunderstorm is something I found out when I was playing golf last summer. I was with a couple of buddies and when it started to rain we ran for cover in this stand of tall oak trees. We were all huddled around a tree when all of a sudden there was a really loud boom, and just 50 feet away or so lightning had struck a tree and a giant branch crashed to the ground.

Process Comment

By linking textual information to prior experiences I've had, I'm able to make more sense of this because I see how it fits with real life. You can do the same thing when you read, even if your experiences aren't exactly the same as what the author is describing. After you read the next short section on page 103, see if anyone in your group can come up with a way of relating it to prior experience or something you already know about the topic.

Nicola volunteered to share content statements and process comments related to prior knowledge she and her group generated for the next section in their chapter.

Content Statement

It says here that lightning strikes between positive and negative particles in cumulonimbus clouds.

Process Comment

We related this to something we learned last year about magnets. Opposite charges attract, just like how lightning bolts go from one charged particle to the opposite charged particle. It made it easier for us to see how lightning happens when we think about it this way.

When the class finished the entire section on lightning, Manolo modeled a third important cognitive process, summarizing.

Content Statement

Overall it's talking about how technology is helping us to better understand lightning so that we can figure out how to protect ourselves from it.

Process Comment

Okay, to summarize what we've just read, the first thing is, I'm going over it and skimming through the section again so I can remember where I saw the important things. The important information is highlighted for us in bold print and italics. Be sure to look for these signals from authors of what's important. If it isn't in italics or bold print, it might be repeated words or phrases or even use of the words "important," "critical," "necessary," and words like that. Okay, so then I thought of how the important things fit together, and I came up with technology and safety because it's mentioning all these high-tech ways we're learning about lightning and it's also giving examples of poor and wise decisions when there's a lightning storm.

Manolo then asked his students to continue working with the groups at their tables and find either an information book of their choosing from among those he had brought into the classroom or a Web site that addressed the topic of weather and lightning. With this material students were to prepare a summary and a spokesperson from the group was to share the summary with the class along with an explanation of the thinking processes involved in generating it.

Notice how this approach to teaching comprehension of text brings into play virtually all the dimensions we discussed earlier. The cognitive dimension is accounted for by modeling and eliciting thinking processes and metacognition while making meaning of the material on lightning. The textual dimension is foregrounded by drawing students' attention to text features that signal important information in the development of their summaries. The personal dimension is taken into account when Manolo gives his students choices for identifying texts related to the topic of study for creating summaries. And, finally, the social dimension is embodied in the interactions Rob has with his class during modeling and eliciting of meaning-making processes, as well as the student-student interaction in their groups.

Generating Understandings of Text

Modeling and eliciting comprehension processes, as we have stated, is a great way to help youth develop thinking strategies they can use on their own with virtually any text. Another way to promote independence is to encourage adolescents to become generative readers and learners. Too often students are in passive roles in secondary classrooms, responding only to the teacher's or the text's prompts. Yet, we know that students learn best when they are actively engaged in meaning-constructing processes. Generative learning theory (Wittrock, 1990) holds that students learn best when they are taught how to create or generate their own learning prompts and demonstrations (Nist & Simpson, 2000; Pressley, 2000).

Disciplinary teachers can increase engagement and promote long-term recall of newly learned information and ideas by teaching students how to generate their own comprehension prompts and aids. Through scaffolding and guided practice, students can learn to transform any text- or teacher-provided prompt they normally receive into a generative learning aid (see Figure 3.3).

> Modeling and eliciting comprehension processes is the best way to apprentice youth to successful disciplinary reading and thinking.

Figure 3.3   Generative Text Comprehension Prompts and Aids

If the text or teacher provides . . .	Then the learner should be taught to:
Headings and subheadings	Compose headings and subheadings
Titles	Compose titles
Highlighted words or phrases	Highlight important words and phrases
Questions	Develop questions
Objectives	Write objectives
Summaries	Produce oral and/or written summaries
Marginal glossaries	Create marginal glossaries
Analogies	Give analogies
Examples	Provide examples
Graphs and tables	Prepare graphs and tables
Maps	Draw maps
Problems to be solved	Create problems to be solved
Graphic overviews	Make graphic overviews

Snikta has taught her 11th-grade keyboarding students to become generative learners by insisting they not wait for questions and other prompts from her but create them on their own to challenge themselves and their peers. In Snikta's class, students learn keyboarding with word-processing and other text-formatting programs. She uses a textbook, additional online supporting materials and activities, as well as her own questions and directives as examples of prompts, and then guides her class in the development of their own prompts. For example, students encounter a series of requests online requiring the application of keyboarding and word-processing techniques to fulfill, such as *Demonstrate as many ways as you can to frame or box text*, and *Reproduce this paragraph, then edit it so that it matches the original*. Students are asked to create similar prompts then post them with their names attached on the class Blackboard Web site so everyone can access them. As individual students complete the requested tasks, they check the site again for the suggested response supplied by the author of the prompt. Where there are significant discrepancies, students instant message with one another to reconcile them. In this way, Snikta is able to combine regular and meaningful keyboarding practice with generative thinking activities.

In another example, Snikta projects from the computer screen a new section from the textbook that has been scanned, with the headings and subheadings deleted. She goes over the section as students follow along from their terminals. Next, working with a partner, students type in what they believe to be appropriate headings and subheadings. Snikta then supplies the author's headings and subheadings, and these are compared and contrasted with those generated by the class. A similar approach is used when generating summaries, graphic overviews, and other comprehension aids.

Not only do Snikta's teaching practices develop students' cognition for text comprehension, they also improve extracting and meaning-construction abilities by accounting for the other dimensions of comprehension as well. Her approach to generative learning includes students working together while focusing on and generating critical text features. These activities are accomplished within an engaging and supportive classroom context. It doesn't surprise us, therefore, that Snikta reports since adopting these generative strategies, her students have become more effective independent comprehenders of text information and ideas. She has also heard from colleagues that her students are applying the generative thinking strategies learned in the keyboarding class to their other disciplinary subjects.

> The research evidence is clear that adolescents who are independent, generative readers and thinkers have greater academic success than passive learners.

Processing Text at Different Levels of Understanding

One important way you can encourage your students to think deeply and meaningfully about disciplinary texts is through a strategy that sensitizes them to the fact that comprehension is more than understanding just the surface or verbatim message of the author. Text comprehension also involves inferencing, application, and other critical cognitive abilities that create meanings beyond the directly stated words.

Youth can be shown that comprehension falls along a continuum that is text-based at one end and reader-based at the other (see Figure 3.4). Text-based processing is literal-level comprehension, or in the kid-friendly parlance of cognitive researchers Taffy Raphael and P. David Pearson (1985), *right there* thinking. *Right*

Figure 3.4 Comprehension Continuum

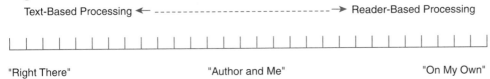

Text-Based Processing ← - → Reader-Based Processing

"Right There"   "Author and Me"   "On My Own"

there thinking means the information and ideas can be found nearly word-for-word in the text. As we progress along the continuum we enter a realm of comprehension that relies increasingly on the inferencing abilities of the meaning maker. Raphael and Pearson refer to this type of text processing as *author and me*. In other words, the author's words are combined with the ideas of the person processing the text to create interpretations, generalizations, and other implied understandings. Finally, at the other end of the comprehension continuum is a form of thinking that is far removed from a dependency on individual printed or spoken words. This kind of processing, known as *on my own* thinking (Raphael & Pearson, 1985), requires that learners possess relevant prior knowledge for the topic sufficient to create sophisticated understandings based on minimal print cues.

Teacher as Learner
A COMPREHENSION CONTINUUM ACTIVITY

To provide you with firsthand experience in identifying the different levels of processing, read the following short passage and the questions and answers that follow. In the space next to each question and answer, fill in the type of thinking required (*right there, author and me, on my own*). The experience will give you a much better grasp of the processing requirements placed on students in a typical text-comprehension exercise.

The Story of Buck Billings

"Buck" Billings left Teddy's Rough Riders the very day peace was signed with the Spanish. There were wild stories about gold in the Klondike, and he couldn't wait to claim his stake. In the port of Havana he planned to pick up a boat to Tampa, then head north by train. After 3 days' trek through mosquito-infested swamps, he found that all the boats were packed with soldiers and civilians leaving for the States. He hopped aboard a ship bound for Venezuela. From there he found passage on a banana boat heading for South Carolina. The boat was turned back by a hurricane and forced to dock in Santiago Harbor. On a small sailing vessel he was finally able to reach the southern coast of Florida. He walked for 2 days to a train depot. After several weeks, he made it through the southern plains and eventually arrived in Denver, the town of his birth. Since it was already November, he moved back into his Aunt Dolly's boarding house, where he planned to stay for the next 4 months. During that winter, however, his yellow fever returned, and he succumbed to it on the first day of the new year.

Questions and Answers

1. Why was the boat forced to turn back? (Because of a hurricane) _____

2. Where is Aunt Dolly's boarding house? (Denver)_____

3. Where is the Klondike? (In Alaska)_____

4. Where was Buck's ship forced to dock after the hurricane? (In Santiago Harbor)_____

5. If Buck intended to head back to the States, why did he take a boat to Venezuela? (Because all the boats heading for the States were packed, and he thought he could get back to the States from Venezuela) _____

6. Where did Buck get yellow fever? (Cuba) _____

7. What was the boat carrying that was heading for South Carolina? (Bananas) _____

8. Did Buck make it to the coast of South Carolina? (No, the boat was forced back by a storm.) _____

9. Where was Buck the day peace was signed with the Spanish? (Cuba) _____

10. Who is Teddy? (Teddy Roosevelt) _____

Explanation

Think about how you categorized these questions and answers as you read our categorization and rationales. We placed questions 1 and 4 in the *right there* category because these questions cue the reader to the answers with words taken directly from the relevant sentence in the text.

Questions 2, 5, 7, and 8 we identified as *author and me* questions. Question 2 requires the reader to combine ideas from two sentences—the one stating that Buck arrived in Denver and the next one stating that Buck moved back with his aunt. The inference is that Buck is from Denver and has lived with his aunt before. To answer question 5 also requires some inferential reasoning. Buck was unable to go directly north to the States because all the ships were filled. By heading south first, he hoped to get there from Venezuela by avoiding Cuba altogether. Unfortunately, he found himself back in Cuba anyway. Question 7 asks the reader to make a low-level inference that connects the words in the question "What was the boat carrying?" to the sentence in the text that refers to the boat heading for South Carolina as a "banana boat." To answer question 8, the reader must combine information from two sentences—one stating that Buck was on a boat bound for South Carolina and the next one stating that the boat was forced to dock in Santiago Harbor. To answer "no" to this question requires more inferencing than may initially meet the eye. Notice that the reader must realize that Santiago Harbor is not in South Carolina, and because no other mention of South Carolina is made in the passage, it can be assumed that Buck never arrived there.

We grouped questions 3, 6, 9, and 10 in the *on my own* category. Certainly, to answer question 3, the reader must already know the geographical location of the Klondike. The text provides no clue. If the reader also realizes that peace with the Spanish over Cuba was signed at around the turn of the century, this knowledge could reinforce the time frame for the Alaskan gold rush. To know that Buck probably contracted yellow fever in Cuba (question 6) means that the reader has prior knowledge that yellow fever is a tropical disease and that many soldiers suffered and died from it as a result of their experiences in the war with Spain over Cuba. To answer question 9, the reader must integrate several bits of textual information with a great deal of prior knowledge. The reader must possess knowledge

continued

Teacher as Learner *(continued)*

about the Rough Riders and Teddy Roosevelt and know that they fought the Spanish in Cuba. Question 10 requires prior knowledge related to question 9; certainly, the reader must know that it was Teddy Roosevelt who commanded the Rough Riders.

Go to Web Resources for Chapter 3 at *http://www. prenhall.com/brozo,* and look for Content Literacy Strategies.

The ultimate goal of teaching levels of understanding is to move adolescent learners further along the comprehension continuum beyond text-based processing by sensitizing them to the idea that there are various ways of thinking about a text. The classroom description that follows demonstrates how a science teacher was able to help her students recognize that effective comprehension occurs when they are able to move flexibly from text-based to reader-based processing.

Beth, an eighth-grade science teacher, exploits the social dimension of comprehension by allowing her students to work in cooperative groups throughout the school year with nearly every topic she and her class explore. Students in this class develop a deeper understanding of science content through interactions with their peers by speaking, listening, reading, and writing. All students are provided greater opportunities to articulate and reinterpret text concepts and vocabulary, raise questions, discuss answers, and become more active class members.

The topic the class was considering was "What Makes Ice Ages?" Beth first asked students to form into their study reading groups, three to a group. Her students were used to many different grouping arrangements that allow them to move in and out of groups, interacting with different students, depending on the purpose of the group. For instance, two other common grouping patterns in Beth's classroom were interest groups and research groups. Beth briefly rehearsed the "Rules for Group Membership," which students had in their notes and which were also written in bold letters on the side wall bulletin board.

Go to Web Resources for Chapter 3 at *http://www. prenhall.com/brozo,* and look for Literature Circles.

- Each member must be strongly committed to doing the work and carrying out his or her specific role within the group.
- Each member should understand and follow the directions for completing assigned work.
- Each member should respect other members' input.
- A member who disagrees with another member should defend his or her own point of view, giving specific reasons based on the text or on personal experience.
- No member should dominate or withdraw; every member should add something to the discussion.
- Each member should be positive and encourage other members.

Beth then introduced the idea of levels of processing text using PowerPoint slides to focus the discussion. She discussed with the students how becoming more sensitive to *right there, author and me,* and *on my own* thinking can improve their ability to get more out of their textbook reading. She explained each of the levels of thinking and provided a handout with the labels and explanations. Beth asked students to open their science textbooks to the beginning of the section on ice ages. Using the computer projector, she presented a series of questions accompanied by answers covering the first page of this section. In their groups, students discussed among themselves what level of processing was required to answer each question.

Afterward, students shared their responses and rationales with the whole class. Beth allowed students to debate their answers, providing support, feedback, and demonstrations of her own processing-level designations for her answers.

In the next phase she assigned responsibilities to each of the three group members. Beth asked each student in the groups to generate questions with answers for one of the three levels of thinking. The groups then went over their questions, helping each other focus on the appropriate question for the assigned level. Beth then asked groups to exchange questions, emphasizing that the questions not be labeled. The groups worked with their new questions, determining levels of thinking required and rationales. During this time, Beth sat in on each group's discussion, answering questions, providing necessary input, and reinforcing group efforts. Questions were given back to their authors with comments so students could rework them.

To get a better idea of the kinds of group discussions students had as they worked cooperatively on identifying levels of understanding, here is a short excerpt. This discussion took place between three students trying to determine whether a question required *author and me* or *on my own* processing.

Student 1: The question is, "If the greenhouse effect is true, what kind of climate will Chicago have in 50 years?"

Student 2: What's the answer?

Student 1: It says "6 to 12 degrees warmer." Like Florida.

Student 3: How are we supposed to know that?

Student 1: We can figure it out. We have to look in the book first to make sure it doesn't tell us about Chicago.

Student 3: I don't remember anything about Chicago.

Student 2: It doesn't, I'm looking right now. I can't find anything about it.

Student 1: It does say that if carbon dioxide keeps getting worse, the world temperature is going to go up. You see where I am, on page 128.

Student 3: It's for sure not a *right there* or in-the-book question.

Student 1: Does it say by how many degrees? I'm looking down here. Yeah, here it is. It says that "if carbon dioxide levels continue to increase at the present rate, in 40 to 50 years the greenhouse effect will cause temperatures worldwide to increase by about 6 to 12 degrees centigrade."

Student 2: So, big deal, that doesn't sound like very much. How could that make us as warm as Florida?

(Students attend to the text.)

Student 3: Look, I found this part up here that says that a 100 million years ago the earth was a lot warmer even at the poles. So maybe if the poles were warm, we would be really warm too. What do you think?

Student 1: I like it. This is a hard one.

Student 2: So we're saying it's what, *on my own* or *author and me*?

(They ponder.)

Student 3: I think it's sorta like both. You can find some of the information in the book, but you have to figure it out by yourself when it comes to the part about Chicago.

Student 1: Don't we have to say one or the other?

Student 3: I don't think so. She said they could be one or the other or anywhere in between.

(Student 1, designated as the recorder, writes down the group's rationale. They move on to the next question.)

Levels of understanding training promotes sensitivity to various ways of thinking about text while constructing and applying meaning. Levels of processing practices should be designed to refute the common misconception held by students that the text tells all. Reliance on the text as the sole source of information limits students' interactions with text and consequently their depth of understanding. If students are only required to process information at the *right there* level, they will likely form only a superficial understanding of text. On the other hand, if students are taught to extend their thinking along the comprehension continuum, they will come away from text encounters with more meaningful and critical understandings.

Using a question-and-answer-generating strategy was helpful to Beth and her students. Because Beth's approach integrates multiple dimensions of the meaning-making process, her students are able to think about text in a more elaborative fashion and move toward greater independence in comprehension.

Process Guides

Process guides like the other cognitive strategies we have shared emphasize helping youth develop ways of thinking about text as opposed to delivering content to be memorized.

Process guides provide students with models and suggestions on how they should summarize and organize key content-area concepts. These guides, however, are written suggestions that "walk" students through the processes involved in reading, as would, for example, an expert in biology or an expert in history. The process guide is a particularly effective and efficient way to begin a semester because it provides students the necessary assistance and scaffolding as they adjust their reading approaches to a particular content area.

You can provide a variety of suggestions in a process guide. Some of these suggestions might guide students in how to read their assignment (e.g., skim, slow down, notice the graph) and some suggestions might point out an important idea or relationship that students must understand. The following are examples taken from a variety of content areas:

1. Page 93, paragraphs 3–6: Pay special attention to this section. Make sure you identify three reasons for Hunter's actions.
2. Page 145: Notice the three subtopics under the boldface heading titled "Involvement in Vietnam." These three subtopics represent three reasons for our involvement. What are those three reasons?
3. Page 22: Study the graph. Be prepared to explain the processes represented in the graph. HINT: Read the graph from top to bottom.
4. Read the summary on page 223 BEFORE you begin to read. Why? The section's key ideas are highlighted for you.
5. Page 99: Skim the first three paragraphs. Then slow down and read very carefully about the two hormonal control systems. Make sure you can explain the two systems using your own words.
6. Page 11, paragraph 4: This paragraph explains why settlers chose this spot for their homes. There are three reasons why—the authors cue these reasons with words like "first" and "furthermore." Make sure you know the three reasons.

As you can see, the process guide can accomplish a variety of goals. One marine biology teacher we know, Christina, described the process guide as being a "personal tutor for each of my students." Christina was concerned that a majority of her students were trying to memorize all the details when they were reading. Some of her students seemed to give up on their reading or chose not to read, hoping she would summarize the information for them. Christina wisely decided not to lecture on the information contained in the book. Rather, she decided she would help her students learn the concepts in her course while modeling the processes involved in reading biology material. Her solution was the process guide.

To prepare the process guides, Christina began by asking herself what she wanted her students to know when they finished reading a chapter. Once she identified those major concepts and ideas, she then read the chapter carefully so she could identify potential problems her students might have as they read. As she read, she realized that many of them would skip the important charts and graphs, some of which illustrated important information not contained in the written presentation. She also realized that they needed to focus on key ideas and summarize those ideas, using their own words. Armed with that diagnostic information, Christina wrote her suggestions, cued to certain pages and paragraphs for the chapter on the sea floor. As illustrated in Figure 3.5, her guide offered specific reading suggestions and asked the students to jot down brief responses to her probes.

Christina introduced the guide to her students with an explanation as to its purpose. After demonstrating how to answer the first two questions, she gave her students 10 minutes at the end of the period to begin their reading and thinking. As the students read the text and their process guide, she circulated the room, guiding and

Figure 3.5 Reading and Process Guide for Marine Biology

READING AND PROCESS GUIDE FOR CHAPTER TWO

Directions: The purpose of this guide is to help you with the processes of reading like a "scientist." Read the suggestions and answer the questions AS YOU READ pages 33 and 34. Remember that reading science material is very different from reading a newspaper or short story—you will need to read more deliberately and focus on definitions, examples, characteristics, and processes.

1. Begin your reading by examining Figure 2.17. Read the caption. You should now know the 3 parts to a continental margin.

2. Now focus on the first major boldface heading titled "Continental Margins." Read the first paragraph and be prepared to write a description of a continental margin and the 3 parts to a continental margin.

    Description of a continental margin:

    3 parts:

3. The first subheading on page 33 is titled "The Continental Shelf." Read the two paragraphs in this section. Be prepared to list below the characteristics of a continental shelf.

    Characteristics of the continental shelf:

    • The shallowest part of the continental margin
    • Biologically very rich
    •
    •
    •

continued

Figure 3.5 *(continued)*

---

4. Did your characteristics of the continental shelf include the following key terms: *submarine canyons* and *shelf breaks?* If you have not examined Figure 2.18, DO THIS NOW! Remember that figures and graphs are very important in science and often present information NOT in the text. What do you learn from Figure 2.18? (HINT: You will obtain an example of a concept.)

5. The second subheading on page 33 is titled "The Continental Slope." Read this paragraph and then write a description of the continental slope, the second part of the continental margin.

   Description of the continental slope:

6. The third subheading on page 33 is titled the "The Continental Rise." Read this paragraph and then write a description of HOW a continental rise is formed.

   Steps in forming a continental rise:

7. Read the italicized summary on page 33. Does this information make sense to you? It should.

8. On page 34 you will find another boldface heading—"Active and Passive Margins." Before reading these 3 paragraphs, examine Figure 2.19. Read the caption. Again, an example is provided. What country is given as an example of active and passive margins? _____

9. Read the first 2 paragraphs under the boldface heading—"Active and Passive Margins." These paragraphs explain how continental margins and habitats are influenced by plate tectonic processes. Obviously, you will need to be able to explain an active and passive margin and how they are formed. Make sure you stop to read Figure 2.20 when the authors ask you to do so.

   How active margins are formed:

   Characteristics of active margins:
   • Steep, rocky shorelines
   •
   •

   Examples of active margins:

10. Now, read the last paragraph for this section. What do you predict this paragraph will describe? _____
   _____ What should you know when you finish this paragraph? (HINT: Look above at what you had to know for active margins.)

   Write the key idea for this paragraph:

---

prompting. Before the bell rang, she assigned her students to finish their reading and hinted at the possibility of a pop quiz over the material. As she informed us, her announcement that students could use their completed process guide if there were a quiz motivated most of her students to do the reading.

Of course, Christina is not planning on writing process guides for all her chapters because she is hoping that the students will soon "figure out" how to read the biology materials. To the critics in her department who suggest she is telling her students too much, she responds that she is merely guiding her students in how to read and think and encouraging many of them to open their books.

Endowing youth with cognitive strategies to improve their comprehension is the responsibility of all disciplinary teachers. As expert thinkers and readers, content-area

The Role of the Teacher Leader

In order to learn the comprehension abilities of youth, teacher leaders have multiple roles to play in support of individual students, classrooms, and the entire school community. At the individual student level, teacher leaders can devise creative practices that reverse cycles of reading failure. Programs such as cross-age tutoring might be employed as an alternative to the remedial reading or learning disabilities classroom. Teacher leaders can demonstrate practices that ensure struggling students have opportunities for success so as to promote positive identities as readers and learners.

In the classroom, the teacher leader can model for colleagues effective meaning-making and meaning-using practices. In close collaboration with content-area teachers, teacher leaders can craft activities and experiences around readings, lectures, video, ITCs, and other information sources that increase student engagement, comprehension, and critical thinking. Teacher leaders can co-teach lessons with disciplinary teachers to demonstrate how comprehension strategies can be woven into the fabric of daily instruction.

At the school level, teacher leaders should promote practices that elevate the overall literate culture. With the understanding that youths' comprehension abilities improve the more they engage in meaning-making and meaning-using processes, teacher leaders can initiate school-wide programs that make interesting, personally meaningful texts accessible as well as provide time and space to engage with those texts. The teacher leader can play an instrumental role in stocking school and classroom libraries with print sources adolescents will find pleasurable and functional. They can also support the ICT infrastructure of the school to ensure students have access to new digital media for meaning-making and meaning-using purposes.

teachers can model for youth the ways in which they make, extract, and use meaning from text. Scaffolding can be provided for youth as they navigate the complexities of expository prose in order to promote text-based and reader-based processing. And youth should be nudged out of passive roles during the comprehension process and taught how to generate their own prompts and aids to understanding.

Textual Dimension Strategies

As you have been reading, you have been using the structure or organization of this chapter to help you identify and summarize important ideas. That is, you may have focused on boxed content and ideas marked by typographical features such as bold-face headings, or you may have noted information that we cued using words such as *furthermore* or *in summary*. We know from the research that skilled readers use text organization to aid their understanding, especially when they find the material they are reading unfamiliar or somewhat challenging (Goldman & Rakestraw, 2000). More specifically, skilled readers use all of these signals to organize what they read:

Go to Web Resources for Chapter 3 at *http://www. prenhall.com/brozo,* and look for How to Read a Textbook.

- previews or introductory statements
- summary statements
- typographic clues such as underlining, italics, and boldface print or headings
- pointer words and phrases, such as "the most important reason why"
- enumeration devices (e.g., first, furthermore, finally)
- connectives (e.g., because, the reasons why, however, the consequences)

You might find it surprising that a majority of adolescents do not understand and capitalize on these signals that authors use to explain and organize their ideas (Chambliss, 1995). Among the many explanations for this situation is that secondary students have had far more experiences with the narrative or story format of writing than they have had with the expository or explanatory format of writing. In fact, we teach children to read with stories because they are already familiar with the structure of stories and their narrative styles most closely approximate oral language patterns.

Stories or narrative text have predictable structures or patterns, called story grammars (Mandler, 1987). For instance, stories have settings; they have characters; the main character is usually en route to a goal; to reach his or her goal, the main character must confront obstacles, essentially conflict; and the conflict is resolved in some way. Apparently, as readers or listeners receive constant exposure to well-structured stories, they internalize these grammars in the form of a story schema, which assists them in understanding and writing stories.

Because most of us prefer the narrative structure, interest in stories rarely wanes throughout our lives. However, most textbooks and classroom presentations do not typically use a narrative structure. Rather, most learning situations in school are organized around an expository or explanatory structure that is more formal and demanding than our oral language. Try to recall the last time you relished the opportunity to crack open one of your textbooks before going to bed. Most of us rarely do, and the same is true of students.

We have observed students plowing through their assigned government and science reading, eager to finish so that they can put down the book. Students in middle and secondary school must learn to deal with the formal expository styles of writing and speaking if they are to be successful readers and learners. By helping them develop an understanding of how writers organize expository text, we can improve their comprehension (Goldman & Rakestraw, 2000). Thankfully, the research shows that almost any approach to teaching youth about the structure of disciplinary texts improves comprehension and recall of information and ideas (Duke & Pearson, 2002).

Bridging Text Ideas

We spoke earlier about the need to supply youth with considerate texts. One important feature of considerate text is cohesiveness (Caccamise & Snyder, 2005). Cohesive texts provide ample cues that help readers link information presented in different sentences. Authors of cohesive texts do this by continuously adding and integrating newly introduced information with previously cited information. They also achieve cohesion through the liberal use of logical connectors, such as conjunctions. Unfortunately, many of the texts adolescents encounter in their disciplinary classes may lack appropriate cohesive ties. Consequently, youth need to (a) recognize and take advantage of cohesive ties that appear in text, and (b) learn how to use information stated previously to infer a logical connection with information that comes after when connectors aren't supplied. Using and inferring logical connectives is a microstructure strategy.

Rita teaches 9th- and 10th-grade history in a large suburban high school, where she has developed a method for helping her students use connectives in comprehending their history textbook. For a list of common connectives used to join ideas see Figure 3.6.

In groups of three to four, students were asked to generate a couple of statements about the Civil War to reflect what they already know about the topic. Afterward, the groups read their statements to the whole class. Rita copied the statements on the board. She studied the list for a moment, and then placed stars next to six of the sentences:

The Civil War was fought for many reasons.

The major reason for the Civil War was to free slaves.

The Civil War was not with a foreign country.

Because connecting words are so common in text they offer disciplinary teachers opportunities to teach reading comprehension in virtually every lesson.

Figure 3.6 A List of Common Connecting Words and What They Signal

Time Words
- then
- presently
- now
- thereupon
- somewhat later
- hereafter
- finally
- since
- as soon as
- when
- meanwhile
- at the same time
- at last
- eventually
- now

Illustration Words
- for example
- for instance

Order of Sequence Words
- next
- secondly
- first
- finally
- to begin with
- in conclusion

Conclusion Words
- hence
- therefore
- so
- thus
- it follows that
- for this reason
- since
- to sum up
- accordingly
- in conclusion
- in other words
- in general terms
- as a result
- because

Restatement Words
- in fact
- that is to say
- indeed
- in other words
- briefly

Additional Thought Words
- and
- again
- next
- in the same way
- also
- besides
- furthermore
- similarly
- too
- moreover
- in addition
- further
- most of all
- further
- in like manner

Contrast Words
- but
- in spite of
- yet
- conversely
- rather
- even though
- instead
- nevertheless
- still
- however
- on the other hand
- notwithstanding
- on the contrary

Teacher as Learner

A BRIDGING ACTIVITY

Directions: Using the list of connecting words from Figure 3.6, insert one that makes logical sense in each of the spaces in this passage. Compare your entries with those of a classmate. Entries may vary, because multiple connectors have similar meanings.

An Odd Incident at Antietam Creek

America was well into the Civil War, (1)_____many battles had been fought between North and South. (2)_____no battle was bloodier nor more puzzling than the Battle of Antietam Creek. General George McClellan was chasing General Robert E. Lee's Confederate Army in Maryland, when on September 13th, an odd thing happened. McClellan's army was near Frederick, Maryland, (3)_____one of his soldiers found three cigars wrapped in a piece of paper lying in a field. The paper turned out to be an order signed by General Lee instructing his generals to split their army into four parts. Generals almost never split up their army in the face of the enemy (4)_____each part is small and weak by itself. (5)_____the order must have seemed unusual to McClellan, (6)_____he chose to take it seriously and revised his battle plans accordingly.

Suggested Answers

1.

2.

3.

4.

5.

6.

American fought American in the Civil War.

Abraham Lincoln was president during the Civil War.

Many soldiers from both sides died.

In addition to laying the foundation for manipulating connectives, Rita provided students with a stimulus for prior knowledge activation with this activity. Plenty of interesting discussion ensued as groups of students offered their statements. For instance, when the statement "The major reason for the Civil War was to free slaves" was read, another student quickly commented that she didn't think that was quite true, and a small debate commenced over the issue. The students finally agreed that the slave issue was one of the significant reasons for the war. During this discussion, Rita did all she could to facilitate by prodding and asking open-ended questions.

Rita then passed around a list of connecting words (see Figure 3.6). She provided information about the significance of the words and modeled how she would use them in her speaking and writing. She then asked students to remain in their small groups and write a paragraph using the connecting words to join together the statements the class generated about the Civil War. Afterward, a spokesperson from each group was invited to read while the rest of the class was asked to listen carefully for whether or not the connectives used signaled the correct relationships among the sentences. Here is the way one group connected the statements:

> **Although** the Civil War was fought for many reasons, the major reason it was fought was to free slaves. The Civil War was not fought with a foreign country; **rather,** American fought American, **and** many soldiers from both sides died. **At that time,** Abraham Lincoln was president.

Rita takes some time within every unit to reinforce students' knowledge of how connectives and other bridging structures operate within the various class texts. For instance, she distributes passages with connectives removed and expects students to supply these missing links. When she reads aloud, the class is asked to listen closely for connectives and overlapping words and phrases, jot them down, and share what they heard during a pause at the end of a sentence or paragraph.

Rita regularly reminds the students to keep a watchful eye out for cohesive ties provided by the authors of the other texts they read as well as encourages them to use cohesive structures in their writing to help explain how their ideas are related. Rita has found that when students are sensitized to the role of connectives in text, they not only improve their comprehension by becoming better able to compensate for disconnected text, but they also compose better-organized written work.

Text Mapping: Scaffolding Understanding of Textbook Features and Organization

If you are a student taking a class for which this textbook is required, or if you have purchased this book on your own to increase your knowledge and skills in content-area literacy, you have probably made numerous markings in the book already. Most of us highlight, underline, or write notes in the margin to aid our comprehension and recall of information and ideas we think are important or that we intend to use. Unlike university students who purchase their own books, middle and secondary school students cannot mark in their books because they do not own them. In fact, students are regularly warned against making extraneous marks in school textbooks. This situation presents a potential problem for teachers trying to help students learn to mark text as a strategy to improve comprehension. Working with copies of selected textbook pages, however, we can help youth learn to identify important organizational features that facilitate meaning making. One such strategy that is excellent for sensitizing students to both micro- and macrostructures of expository and informational prose is *text mapping*.

When Matt teaches text mapping to his 7th-grade history students he follows these steps:

1. At the beginning of the year he identifies pages from the class textbook that contain important organizational features, such as table of contents pages for the first chapter; introductory pages of the first chapter with title, headings, and subheadings; pages with highlighted terms; pages with graphs and charts; glossary and index pages.

2. He then photocopies these pages into class sets with one set per group of three to four students.

3. Matt organizes the pages from table of contents through index pages edge to edge and tapes them together into a long scroll (see illustration in Figure 3.7).

Figure 3.7 A Text-Mapping Scroll

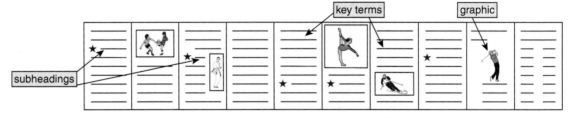

4. He tapes one of the scrolls to the board and distributes one to each of several groups of students. Students spread the scrolls out at their tables.

5. Finally, he distributes markers to students.

Go to Web Resources for Chapter 3 at *http://www. prenhall.com/brozo,* and look for Text Mapping.

Once each group has a scroll and markers, Matt begins by talking about the purpose of the activity. He explains to his students how the process of mapping the scrolled text will help them see more explicitly its structure and organization. He explains further the importance of recognizing and using textual cues and formatting features to guide reading comprehension.

Next, Matt draws the class's attention to various cues and features on the scrolled pages and begins marking them at the board while asking students in their groups to make the same marks on their scrolled pages. For instance, he draws a circle around the hierarchical diagram that serves as a graphic organizer at the opening of the first chapter and writes next to it "visual outline of the chapter." In another case, Matt highlights the words "first," "second," and "third" that appear over two pages and talks about how authors signal the organization of their exposition with enumerative words. He goes on to mark (scribblings, diagrams, pictures, circles, arrows, and other notations), highlight, circle, and make marginal notes for several other format and organizational features, encouraging students to note the same features on their scrolls. Finally, he asks each group to highlight and mark on their own scrolls other organizational cues they can find on the remaining pages. Matt then solicits input from students and requests they also describe how the feature contributes to better understanding of chapter or book content.

Matt tapes the marked scrolls to the wall as reminders to students to be ever vigilant while previewing a chapter or reading a section of important cues to organizing their thinking of expository prose. Early in the school year, the scrolls are referred to often, and when new or unique features show up, copied and marked pages are added to the scrolls. Eventually, as Matt's students demonstrate increasing competence with mentally mapping the organization of chapters based on the author's cues, the scrolls are rolled up and stored.

Charting

Charting is another helpful tool that helps students summarize key ideas and visually sense the interrelationships between these ideas in text. The chart in Figure 3.8 is one that Omar, a biology teacher, used to help his sophomores understand a film they had watched about recent research and experiments involving the pituitary gland. Omar first distributed the partially completed chart and described how the act of creating a chart can help improve understanding and recall. He then told his students to complete the chart after viewing the film. The next day in class, he asked his students to work in small groups to check and discuss the information in their charts. After allowing students to work in small groups, he brought the class together for a discussion of the function and location of the pituitary gland. During the rest

Figure 3.8 Sample Chart for Biology Chapter

The Pituitary Gland				
Hormone	Function	Location	Scientific Name	Chemical Composition
TSH	influences the thyroid by negative feedback	anterior lobe; 1 of 4 tropic hormones	thyroid-stimulating hormone	glycoprotein
FSH	stimulates ovarian follicle	anterior lobe; 1 of 4 tropic hormones	follicle-stimulating hormone	glycoprotein
ACTH				
LH				
Growth				

of the unit entitled "Hormones, Nerves, and Muscles," he created a variety of charting formats so that his students could see their versatility. Omar's long-term plan was to require his students to work in pairs to create their own charts for the next unit of study.

Omar relied on the structure of his supplementary materials and the textbook to organize the charts for his units of study. Although this organizational structure suited his instructional objectives and his students, you may have to make some adjustments, depending on the extent to which the information in your units of study is explicitly organized. Charting then becomes one way of imposing order on information that may not be organized in a suitable way for your students.

Reena, a math instructor, uses charting to improve her students' skills in solving word problems. The following motion problem is typical:

> *The speed of a stream is 4 miles per hour. A boat travels 6 miles per hour upstream in the same time it takes to travel 12 miles downstream. What is the speed of the boat in still water?*

To help her students achieve the reading precision necessary for motion problems, Reena asks them to organize the data in a chart with the headings t, r, and d, representing time, rate, and distance. She explains her lesson this way:

> *My students already know that* $r \times t = d$. *I also have them represent rate downstream as* $b + c$, *where* b *is the rate of the boat,* c *is the rate of the current or stream, and* $b - c$ *is the rate upstream. I point out how the boat and current work together downstream, hence* $b + c$, *and against each other upstream,*

Disciplinary teachers tell us charting is one of the best ways to help students organize complex and detailed information, especially for their visual learners.

hence b − c. Therefore, before looking at the specifics of the problems, the student can make a chart as follows:

	t	*r*	*d*
upstream		$b - c$	
downstream		$b + c$	

My students then can read further and fill in the appropriate information, so the chart looks like this:

	t	*r*	*d*
upstream		$b - c$	
downstream		$b + c$	

Here is the process they follow. Four is substituted for the stream speed. Six and 12 are substituted for distance up- and downstream, and the time is represented as distance divided by rate. To set up an equation, students must look for a relationship, and hopefully they read "same time," so they set the representations for time equal to each other. In other words, the equation is:

$$\frac{6}{b-4} = \frac{12}{b+4}$$

My students seem to catch on to these motion problems much quicker with the charting technique.

Reena knows that she needs to maximize the interactions between her students and their math textbook by employing a variety of strategies that help them focus on key ideas and organize those ideas in a meaningful manner. Organizing formats like Reena's and Omar's can be found elsewhere in this textbook, so we urge you to note them in subsequent chapters (i.e., Chapters 7 and 9).

Middle- and secondary-level teachers should never assume adolescents know about and take advantage of text-structure cues. Drawing youths' attention to how authors signal relationships in text and organize the development of information and ideas should occur regularly in formal and informal ways. What's more, youth should be taught how to organize their thinking about text and infer cohesive ties to make it more comprehensible.

Personal Dimension Strategies

For each of the strategies already described, the teachers using the strategies have accounted for the personal dimension of comprehension in some way. Those that follow are particularly designed to foreground critical personal variables in the meaning-making and meaning-using process. They create spaces for youth to engage in identity work. They exploit youths' desire to have choices and to feel a sense of urgency about their reading and learning. And they are meant to involve youth in active learning experiences.

Opinionnaires

Every adolescent has an opinion on something, whether it's about a teacher, a class, a classmate, a team, parents, musical artist, or current event. The opinionnaire

Figure 3.9 What Are Your Opinions About Health?

Directions: After each statement, write SA (strongly agree), A (agree), D (disagree), or SD (strongly disagree). Be prepared to explain your opinions.

1. Only doctors can heal you when you are unhealthy._____

2. I can help a friend get healthy by just being supportive._____

3. Each of us should take care of our own health needs._____

4. It is important to know how to make yourself healthy._____

5. If I had a serious disease like cancer, I could only get healthy with medical treatment._____

6. When each of us takes care of our health, our whole society is healthier._____

7. Being healthy means more than being physically fit._____

8. Health is a state of mind._____

9. Drugs and medicine are necessary to maintain health._____

10. Home remedies are not as effective as treatment from doctors._____

---

strategy capitalizes on adolescents' propensity to form opinions by asking them to take a stand on declarative statements centered on critical concepts and issues related to the content. White and Johnson (2001) discovered that opinionniares are highly beneficial in promoting deep and meaningful understandings of content-area topics by activating and building relevant prior knowledge and building interest in and motivation to learn more about particular topics. Opinionnaires also promote self-examination, value youth's points of view, and provide a vehicle for influencing others with their ideas.

Opinionnaires are developed by generating statements about a topic that force students to take positions and defend them. The emphasis is on students' points of view and not the "correctness" of their opinions. Virtually every disciplinary topic lends itself to opinionating, even topics traditionally regarded as fact-based and objective. For example, Olga, a health teacher, used an opinionniare (see Figure 3.9) to elicit attitudes and feelings from her students about the nature of health and the role of personal responsibility in maintaining good health. Though there is a science of health and medicine, there is also room for challenging traditionally held views about health. Olga purposely did not include a "maybe" or "not sure" option because she had found many of her students chose it as an easy way out of the discussion.

Olga's students eagerly dug into her opinionniare statements, questioning many of the assumptions about what it means to be healthy and maintain good health. To take full advantage of the strategy, Olga separated supporters from nonsupporters of each statement and facilitated brief but sometimes charged exchanges among her students. By taking a stand on health issues and engaging in critical discussion about those issues, Olga's students not only heightened their expectation of the content to follow but also made many new connections from their opinions and ideas to those of their classmates.

In another case, Julian employed the opinionniare strategy to instigate critical thinking of personally held beliefs about his students' place in the natural world as an introduction to the study of ecosystems in science. For the particular topic of rainforests, Julian asked his students to locate themselves relative to statements in Figure 3.10. He constructed statements youth could relate to their own experiences with people and animals. The discussion the statements inspired then served as a bridge to information and ideas in the science textbook and other class readings.

Youth are particularly engaged by strategies that allow them to express and explore their opinions of and attitudes toward content area topics.

Figure 3.10 Where Do You Fit into the World Around You?

Directions: Read each statement carefully and decide whether it "Describes Me," "Sort of Describes Me," or "Doesn't Describe Me." Write your responses in the spaces provided. Be ready to defend your position.

1. No one else is affected by what I do._____

2. I don't care if forests are cut down if it's to make room to build houses for people.
_____

3. My needs as a human being are more important than those of other living things.
_____

4. I believe it's important to live and let live._____

5. There is a lot we can learn from nature that can help improve our lives. _____

6. Variety in people, animals, and plants makes for a better world. _____

7. Everybody and everything is connected in some way. _____

8. There is a lot I can do to help improve the natural world. _____

9. Things like droughts and famine are beyond our control. _____

10. The natural world should be used to make the lives of humans easier. _____

Opinionnaires, as we have seen, privilege students' personal insights, feelings, and ideas while catalyzing them to think deeply and critically about content-area topics. Tapping the personal dimension in comprehension teaching and learning is necessary in order to ensure youth are engaged, find relevance, and feel valued as members of the classroom culture.

Honoring Diversity and Building Competence in the Content Classroom

Many of Lee's students in her ninth-grade English class are recent immigrants. She employs unique practices to help them build their English vocabularies and develop comprehension abilities. One such practice is the use of movies. Films provide visual context for learning new words, and scenes can be viewed many times over for in-depth analysis and to gain deeper understanding (Holmes, 2005).

A popular film with Lee's class is *Crouching Tiger, Hidden Dragon*. Set in 19th-century China in and around Peking during the later part of the Ch'ing Dynasty, this action fantasy chronicles the stories of martial arts warriors who possess superhuman qualities including the ability to defy gravity. Her students can't get enough of the remarkable special effects and nonstop action, but they also come to appreciate the film's symbolism, character motivation, and themes. It's also a film that has strong appeal to both her boys and girls, since the four main characters include two men and two women with equal fighting prowess.

Before the movie, Lee provides her class a list of the characters and goes over the spellings and pronunciation of their Chinese names. Lee's three students from Taiwan, whose mother tongue is Mandarin, are especially helpful to the rest of the class in pronouncing the character's names correctly, as their

continued

native language is the same as the language of the film. Lee also encourages the students to make connections to the main plotline of the film by reflecting on their own experiences. She asks them to think of a time when someone close to them might have been *vengeful.* This word, along with several others that appear in the subtitles, such as *manipulative, invincible, defeated foe,* and *deep meditation,* are studied. Students put them in a vocabulary notebook with pronunciation guides and brief definitional information. As the words appear in the subtitles, Lee stops the film and engages students in a discussion about how context shapes their meanings. Then, students include a brief description of the context and the actual sentence from the film in their vocabulary notebooks.

As they view the film, Lee and her class pay particular attention to the roles of the lead male and female characters. The movie depicts women who do not want to take on the traditional roles their families have arranged for them. She uses this issue to explore gender stereotypes and the importance of honor and responsibility in her students' families and cultures. For example, students write short themes and conduct role-plays to demonstrate how conflicts might occur based on traditional gender expectations in their cultures and societal norms in their new home in the United States.

While structuring learning experiences around the film, Lee makes certain to stock the classroom with related fiction and nonfiction resources. These materials are sometimes read aloud or used by students during independent reading time. Favorites include *The Legend of Mu Lan: A Heroine of Ancient China* (Jiang), *Chinese Cinderella: The True Story of an Unwanted Daughter* (Yen Mah), and *Eyewitness: Ancient China* (Cotterell).

Throughout the film, Lee has her class focus on particular scenes for in-depth analysis. She models and has students conduct visual scans for different levels of meaning. For instance, a scene is frozen while students name all the immediately recognizable information, such as sword, Shu Lien (a female warrior), village, and so on. This information is at the surface or literal level. Next, they scan the scene thinking about what the literal information means or suggests. Students during this phase of analysis will offer ideas and interpretations related to characters' motives or symbolic meanings of objects. Finally, Lee asks her students to consider broader themes related to the pivotal scenes under analysis. She prompts them to think of ways the meaning might relate to current events or ways people behave today.

Lee has seen the powerful influence viewing and studying films has had on the language abilities and comprehension of her students, many of whom are English learners. Films are instantly motivating and provide a rich visual context for authentic communication. When combined with other meaning-making activities, films serve Lee and her students as an ideal source for expanding vocabularies and building comprehension abilities that transfer to print literacy.

Alternative Texts in the Content Classroom

Engaging youth in disciplinary text reading is not the easiest of tasks, especially for reluctant and struggling readers. Yet, we know that in order to improve comprehension abilities, adolescents need to have frequent, sustained print encounters. In the disciplines, these print encounters should be with texts that are thematically or topically related to the content under study. Making a variety of accessible, content-focused texts available in the classroom, allowing self-selection of reading choices, and linking the texts to instructional activities will help students find personal connections to disciplinary topics. The following are recommendations derived from the work of secondary teachers we have observed who use a variety of texts to engage students in reading and learning about the subject matter.

Go to Web Resources for Chapter 3 at *http://www. prenhall.com/brozo,* and look for Graphic Novels.

Use Information Books and Graphic Novels to Research Class Topics. When Terri teaches about the world wars of the 20th century in American history, she fills the classroom with related books and graphic novels to encourage further reading and promote research skills. Students are given time out of every 90-minute class block to work on individual research assignments that offer wide latitude with respect to particular topics for research and modes of expression. For example, Gino investigated World War I fighter pilots and used the graphic novel *Enemy Ace: War Idyll* (Pratt, 1992) as one of his sources. Gino was transfixed by this book that provides a remarkably vivid and emotive pictorial and written account of the horrors of the World War I, from the perspective of flying aces.

Make Available Less Difficult/Modified Texts. Evidence can be found in the literature (Brozo & Hargis, 2003a, 2003b) that clearly supports the approach of matching adolescents with content-based texts that are commensurate with students' ability levels. Youths' identities as readers and learners get a boost when they find themselves able to access comprehensible text in science, social studies, math, and other disciplines. Furthermore, these kinds of texts provide sorely needed reading practice for reluctant readers and can build their schema of disciplinary topics at the same time. Garrison's science students benefit from his dynamic, activity-based lessons, but they also benefit from the readings he makes available to them that are easier to comprehend than the textbook. Garrison has discovered several useful Web sites with explanations and passages covering many different science topics. One of his favorite sites, **http://www.chem4kids.com/,** has material that even his lowest-performing readers can use profitably. Garrison has compiled an organized guide to the readings from the site geared to the topics he covers in class. After learning about the physical structure of atoms, his students were told they could explore the various print resources in the classroom to answer questions about atoms. Erin, a special education inclusion student, made her way to one of three computers and went directly to the chem4kids Web site. After consulting Garrison's guide to the site, she found several short, colorful readings with easy-to-follow diagrams and illustrations detailing the makeup and function of atomic particles. Erin proudly offered information she gleaned from the site to help answer the questions about atoms Garrison had posed to the class.

Go to Web Resources for Chapter 3 at *http://www. prenhall.com/brozo,* and look for Text Sets.

Read Articles from Popular Magazines and Newspapers. Helping youth personalize understandings of text topics is an achievable goal if students are allowed to find links from the everyday texts in their environments to the ideas and information under study in the content classroom. For Leyla's geometry class, students are asked to find anything in the magazines and newspapers they read or are around the house that relates to geometry and share it with their classmates. Joey brings in a PowerPoint™ slide show of his favorite e-zine on skateboarding. He displays photos of stunts by professionals from the Web site courtesy of *Thrasher,* a print skateboard magazine, and talks about angles, parabolas, and trajectories.

Accounting for the personal dimension of comprehension is vital to keeping youth engaged in meaning-making and meaning-using processes. This concern for the personal side of readers reminds us of a self-styled maxim from a high-school teacher friend of ours who would say "You can lead a kid to a book, but you can't make him take a look." To ensure youth are looking at and thinking about the information and ideas in books and other texts, we need to engage their imaginations, find ways of linking the meaning-making process to their identity construction, and help them discover applications of new understandings to their daily lives.

Social Dimension Strategies

Virtually every comprehension strategy presented thus far has had a social learning element associated with it. As stated before, this is because comprehension is comprised of several dimensions, and teaching it effectively requires the orchestration of strategies and approaches that bring more than one or all of the dimensions into play. Skillful disciplinary teachers understand that the meaning-making and meaning-using process occurs more readily within supportive social contexts. Thus, they create numerous opportunities for youth to learn from and with each other in the classroom.

Reciprocal Teaching

In secondary content classrooms where reciprocal teaching takes place, the teacher and student take turns generating questions and summaries and leading a discussion about sections of a text. Initially, the teacher models questioning, summarizing, clarifying, and predicting activities while encouraging students to participate at whatever level they can manage. Gradually, students become more capable of contributing to such discussions and assume more responsibility for their own learning.

In the following exchange, Rob, a high school study skills teacher, and his students were reading and discussing paragraphs from their social studies textbooks. They took turns asking questions about the topic and summarizing. The first paragraph they discussed was about Commander Peary and his quest for the North Pole. On finishing reading of the short text segment, students immediately responded:

Student 1: I have a question about this. What year did Peary write his diary?

Rob: Not a bad beginning, but I would consider that a question about details. Try to avoid the kind of question you can answer by looking word for word in the paragraph. See if next time you can ask a main idea question, and begin your question with a question word like *how*, *why*, *when*. Go ahead, try that.

Student 2: What if I ask, "Why is Peary's diary important?"

Rob: A very good question. Notice how your question seems to be getting at the most important idea in the paragraph.

Student 3: And you can't answer it by just looking at the words.

Rob: Right. Very good work! Now, can anyone give me a summary statement for the paragraph?

Student 4: Well, the only way we really know if Peary got to the North Pole is from his diary.

Rob: And why is that?

Student 4: Because there was no one else around who knew for sure where they were.

Student 5: You can't bring back any proof you were there.

> **Rob:** Okay, that explains why some think Peary may not have made it to the Pole first. Isn't that an important part of the summary? (Several students agree.)
>
> **Rob:** Let me try to make a summary for you. The most important thing we have learned is that we have to take Peary at his word when he said that he reached the North Pole because we don't have any other evidence to support that he did. Does that make sense? Have I left out anything important? Those are important questions to always ask yourself.

Reciprocal teaching is an ideal constructivist practice for developing shared understandings of content and building discourse communities in the disciplines.

Rob's reciprocal teaching approach seems to be successful because it forces the students to respond, which allows him to evaluate their understanding and provide appropriate feedback. Also, by responding orally, the students are given the opportunity to self-diagnose their understanding and improve their ability to self-question, summarize, clarify, and predict—cognitive processes active comprehenders use. Rob does not merely talk to his students about how to read and then tell them to open their texts and read that way. Instead, he demonstrates how he constructs meaning and, through interactions with students, gives them greater responsibility for learning from text.

Class Discussion

We draw the distinction throughout this book between the obvious difference in classrooms where students are expected to be passive receivers of information and ideas and classrooms where students are active participants in the learning process. Being a good lecturer in the middle and upper grades is not enough; students learn and remember best when they participate in a dialog about class topics (Barton, 1995; Parker, 2001). Samuel Johnson put it best more than 200 years ago when he said; "The seeds of knowledge may be planted in solitude, but must be cultivated in public" (Boswell, 1979, p. 121).

Providing young adults plenty of opportunities to engage in public discourse is often a goal of middle and secondary school teachers, but it presents dilemmas that act to limit the extent to which discussion techniques are employed in content-area classrooms (Larson, 1999). For example, in spite of our numerous demonstrations of ways to conduct class discussions, teachers often respond that it's never as easy for them as we make it appear. They are often hesitant to plan discussions because some of their students act immaturely. Yet, they believe that immature discussants need to engage in discussions if they are ever to become skillful at it. And they are right. The reluctance is based on the fear that students will get out of control. One teacher told us flatly, "A Friday afternoon discussion, forget it!"

Nonetheless, teachers can take measures to increase the likelihood of successful classroom discussions. For instance, Patty, a seventh-grade language arts teacher, spends a considerable amount of time at the beginning of each school year teaching her students about respect and about listening. She stresses that it is important to her that each student in her class has a voice, but of equal importance is that students allow others to have a voice as well. Building community at the front end of a new year pays rich dividends during the remainder of the year in the form of students who are more considerate of one another, who are more willing and comfortable risk takers, and who appreciate the importance of the social construction of knowledge (Larson, 1999).

Teachers who desire to exploit the learning potential of class discussion often tend to undermine it by doing most of the talking and asking most of the questions (Alvermann, O'Brien, & Dillon, 1990; Barton, 1995). These practices inhibit rather

Figure 3.11   11 Strategies for Increasing Student
Engagement in Class Discussions

- *Make a declarative or factual statement*
- *Make a reflective statement*
- *Describe the student's state of mind*
- *Invite the student to elaborate on a statement*
- *Encourage the student to ask a question*
- *Encourage students to ask questions of one another*
- *Maintain a deliberate silence*
- *Encourage other students to answer questions posed to you*
- *Help students link new information to their prior knowledge*
- *Model good listening strategies*
- *Allow for small-group brainstorming first before whole-group*

than foster the enrichment of understanding through the exchange of viewpoints. The goal is to encourage and orchestrate discussions that result in more student–student interaction patterns rather than student–teacher patterns (Guzzetti & Williams, 1996; Wyatt & Willis, 2000). Figure 3.11 presents alternatives to questioning and teacher-dominated discussions that have been shown to increase student involvement in class talk and discussion.

Middle and secondary school teachers can use many other simple discussion techniques to energize the content-area classroom and heighten enthusiasm for learning (Green, 2000). Here are some of the best that we have witnessed.

Turn-to-Your-Neighbor-and-Discuss. This strategy is simple to implement. Before beginning an exploration of new content, ask students to consider a problem or question or make a prediction, and then turn to the classmate sitting next to them and discuss a response. Limit the time for a response so students will start thinking quickly and stay on task. Thirty seconds to a minute may be best, though with weightier questions and problems, more time may be needed. As students are discussing, move around the room to monitor their conversations and encourage equal participation. After the brief discussions, you can ask students to share their ideas without necessarily revealing the exact nature of the content to be presented. We have seen this strategy used successfully to overcome the problem of only the effusive students answering a whole-class discussion question. When all students are given even a brief opportunity to think and say something about a topic with one another, they seem to be better prepared to offer their comments afterward to the whole class.

Think-Pair-Square-Share. This discussion strategy is very similar to the one just described. After being given an issue, problem, or question, ask students to think alone for a short period of time, then pair up with someone to share their thoughts. Then have pairs of students share with other pairs, forming, in effect, small groups of four students. Again, your role as teacher is to monitor the brief discussions and elicit responses afterward. Be sure to encourage student pairs not to automatically adopt the ideas and solutions of their partners. These short-term discussion strategies actually work best when a diversity of perspectives is expressed.

Round Robin. After placing students in or forming groups of three to five, pose a problem or question and have each student around the circle quickly share ideas

Go to Web Resources for Chapter 3 at *http://www. prenhall.com/brozo,* and look for Constructing Knowledge in the Classroom.

or solutions. You can give students one opportunity to "pass" on a response, but eventually *every* student must respond. This technique is used most effectively when, after initial clockwise sharing, students are asked to write down on a single piece of paper each of their responses. This allows all opinions and ideas of the groups to be brought to the teacher's and the rest of their classmates' attention. It also provides a record of the group's thinking, which might be used in grading.

Inside-Outside Circles. We have immensely enjoyed participating in this discussion strategy, so much so that we use it often in our own university classes. It offers a novel format and can bring about face-to-face discussion between students who might never have the opportunity otherwise.

Students stand and face each other in two concentric circles. The inside circle faces out and the outside circle faces in. After posing a readiness problem or question, ask students to discuss ideas and answers with the person standing most directly in front of them. The interesting aspect of this technique is that at any time you can ask the inner or outer circle to rotate until you say "stop." Then the discussion can begin anew. After a few rotations, we randomly ask individual students to share their own ideas or those of the person(s) with whom they have been discussing. The advantage of this strategy is the variety of inputs possible through simply rotating the circles of students. Be sure to make enough space in the room for this discussion activity, and move about the circle to listen in on students' brainstorming.

A variation on the inside-outside circles technique is one called *line-ups.* When classroom space is too limited for two concentric circles, you can get essentially the same benefits of this approach by forming two lines of students close enough together so that they can face each other and discuss. Instead of rotating circles as in the previous technique, have one of the lines move down. When this happens, students on the ends will not have someone directly in front of them, so they can walk around to the end of the other line to begin a conversation with a new student.

Value Lines. This approach to discussion is especially useful when preparing to present students with content that evokes strong responses and controversy or when you want students to take a stand on an issue. You can begin by creating an imaginary line or symbolic line in the classroom. We have seen teachers isolate a row of desks in the middle of the room to create a line. A long strip of colored paper or even a piece of yarn can work. Next, you read a statement or make an assertion and ask students to move to one side of the line reserved for those who agree with it and the other side for those who disagree. Then have the students turn to another person on their side of the line and discuss why they agree or disagree with the statement. After a short while, have students converse with someone across the line to share why they believe the way they do. At any time, you can ask pairs of opposing conversants to give their opinions and ideas. As you monitor discussion, encourage respectful disagreements and polite arguing.

Fishbowl Discussions. With this technique, a small group of students is asked to discuss an issue or problem while another group of students looks on. The idea of the fishbowl is that the outside group must listen but not contribute to the deliberations of the students "in the fishbowl." At some point during the discussion, those looking in should be given an opportunity to discuss among themselves their reactions to the

Go to Web Resources for Chapter 3 at *http://www. prenhall.com/brozo,* and look for The Knowledge Loom.

conversation they observed. Then you can ask both groups to share with the entire class the nature of their discussions. This approach to discussion allows the outside group to assess and critique the ideas of the fishbowl discussants.

Before writing your suggestions for Charles in the case study, go to *http://www.prenhall.com/ brozo,* select Chapter 3, then click on Chapter Review Questions to check your understanding of the material.

Strategies for expanding comprehension are more effective when youth are able to interact with peers to explain and extend new understandings. Accounting for the social dimension of comprehension involves shifts in the physical arrangement of the classroom as well as shifts in the patterns of interaction among class members. We have spotlighted reciprocal teaching and discussion as representative strategies of teaching to the social dimension of comprehension, and we have also demonstrated how the other strategies in this chapter can be extended to involve students in group and peer-to-peer activities.

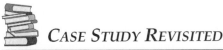

CASE STUDY REVISITED

Charles, the biology teacher introduced at the beginning of this chapter, was searching for ways to engage his students in more meaningful interactions with his course content. Now that you have read this chapter, propose strategies that may help Charles move his students toward more elaborative and meaningful processing of text material related to the topic of genetic engineering.

Charles decided to use a variety of readiness strategies to introduce his students to the new content and gain their interest. He began by exposing them to alternative source material for exploration of the topic. He captured his students' interest by reading aloud daily from a science fiction novel, Hayford Peirce's (2003) *Phylum Monsters*, about a genetic engineer called a "life-stylist." The novel helped motivate the class to dig deeper into the content.

Charles also presented examples of exciting experiments done by genetic researchers. For example, he read to students about researchers at the University of California, San Diego, who in 1986 took the gene that makes fireflies glow and inserted it into the DNA of tobacco. The researchers were then able to raise tobacco plants that glowed in the dark.

Charles asked his students to read articles on genetic engineering in news magazines and to summarize the key ideas on index cards. He reminded the students to include in their summaries the advantages and disadvantages for this technology. Using the discussion web strategy, students met in pairs and groups of four to discuss and prepare what they would say to the whole class on the central question of whether genetic engineering was morally responsible.

When he assigned a section on genetics from the textbook for all the students to read, Charles took class time to carefully front-load the assignment. Then, on the next day, he gave the students a pop quiz with an index card to make sure they were reading and thinking about the key ideas. Finally, Charles helped his students write to the Food and Drug Administration explaining their views on the subject of genetically engineered food.

As a result of these efforts to prepare students for and introduce them to their new learning, Charles saw his students become active learners. They read and participated with enthusiasm and were motivated to work together in small groups and as a class to explore further the topic of genetic engineering.

Looking Back, Looking Forward

In Chapter 2 we outlined six overarching principles to guide teaching and learning for youth. Those guiding principles can be seen in the comprehension strategies described and the teacher vignettes presented in this chapter. To develop youths' meaning-making and meaning-using abilities, teachers in the vignettes executed practices that connected everyday literacies with academic literacy, engaged and sustained students' efforts to think and read, created opportunities for expression of critical perspectives and interpretations of text, and employed print and nonprint sources as well as information and communications technologies to increase comprehension.

Content-area teachers can use a variety of strategies consistent with the multidimensional nature of comprehension. To help students move toward a more sophisticated level of thinking about text, you, as an expert reader, can model processes of thinking, scaffold strategies for comprehension, and engage youth in interactive experiences that require them to go beyond mere memorization. Along with your apprenticing role, you should also be challenging students to accept more and more responsibility for their own critical and elaborative thinking. Many different comprehension strategies were presented in this chapter; we want to remind you that throughout this textbook you will find descriptions of numerous practices that challenge students to become active meaning makers and meaning users.

In the next chapter, Assessment of Literacy Growth and Content Learning, you will see how assessment and instruction in the disciplines can be flip sides of the same coin. Assessment for learning involves strategies that give both the teacher greater insight into the reading and learning needs of students, and students greater insight into their own ways of knowing.

References

Afflerbach, P. (1986). The influence of prior knowledge on expert readers' importance assignment processes. In J. A. Niles & R. V. Lalik (Eds.), *National reading conference yearbook. Vol. 35: Solving problems in literacy: Learners, teachers and researchers.* Rochester, NY: National Reading Conference.

Ainley, M., Hidi, S., & Berndorff, D. (2002). Interest, learning, and the psychological processes that mediate their relationship. *Journal of Educational Psychology, 94,* 545–561.

Alexander, P., & Jetton, T. (2000). Learning from text: A multidimensional and developmental perspective. In M. Kamil, P. Mosenthal, P. D. Pearson, & R. Barr (Eds.), *Handbook of reading research* (Vol. 3). Mahwah, NJ: Lawrence Erlbaum Associates.

Alvermann, D. (2002). *Adolescents and literacies in a digital world.* New York: Peter Lang.

Alvermann, D., O'Brien, D., & Dillon, D. (1990). What teachers do when they say they're having discussions of content area reading assignments: A qualitative analysis. *Reading Research Quarterly, 25,* 296–322.

Armbruster, B., & Anderson, T. (1995). Producing "considerate" expository text: Or easy reading is damned hard writing. *Journal of Curriculum Studies, 17,* 247–274.

Barton, J. (1995). Conducting effective classroom discussions. *Journal of Reading, 38,* 346–350.

Behrman, E. (2003). Reconciling content literacy with adolescent literacy: Expanding literacy opportunities in a community-focused biology class. *Reading Research and Instruction, 43,* 1–30.

Best, R., Rowe., M., Ozuru, Y., & McNamara, D. (2005). Deep-level comprehension of science texts: The role of the reader and the text. *Topics in Language Disorders, 25,* 65–83.

Bloome, D., & Egan-Robertson, A. (1993). The social construction of intertextuality in classroom reading and writing lessons. *Reading Research Quarterly, 28,* 304–333.

Boswell, J. (1979). *The life of Samuel Johnson.* New York: Viking Press.

Bransford, J., Brown, A., & Cocking, R. (2000). *How people learn: Brain, mind, experience, and school* (expanded edition). Washington, DC: National Academy Press.

Braunger, J., Donahue, D., Evans, K., & Galguera, T. (2005). *Rethinking preparation for content area teaching: The reading apprenticeship approach.* San Francisco: Jossey-Bass.

Brozo, W. G., & Hargis, C. (2003a). Taking seriously the idea of reform: One school's efforts to make reading more responsive to all students. *Journal of Adolescent & Adult Literacy, 43,* 14–23.

Brozo, W. G., & Hargis, C. (2003b). Use it or lose it: Three strategies to increase time spent reading. *Principal Leadership, 4,* 36–40.

Bruce, B. (2002). Diversity and critical social engagement: How changing technologies enable new modes of literacy in changing circumstances. In D. Alvermann (Ed.), *Adolescents and literacies in a digital world.* New York: Peter Lang.

Caccamise, D., & Snyder, L. (2005). Theory and pedagogical practices of text comprehension. *Topics in Language Disorders, 25,* 5–20.

Campbell, J. R., Hombo, C. M., & Mazzeo, J. (2000). *NAEP 1999 trends in academic progress: Three decades of student performance.* Washington, DC: National Center for Education Statistics.

Chambliss, M. (1995). Text cues and strategies successful readers use to construct the gist of lengthy written arguments. *Reading Research Quarterly, 30,* 778–807.

Chiesi, H., Spilich, G., & Voss, J. (1979). Acquisition of domain-related information in relation to high and low domain knowledge. *Journal of Verbal Learning and Verbal Behavior, 18,* 275–290.

Duke, N., & Pearson, P. D. (2002). Effective practices for developing reading comprehension. In A. Farstrup & S. J. Samuels (Eds.), *What research has to say about reading instruction* (3rd ed.). Newark, DE: International Reading Association.

Duke, N., Pressley, M., & Hilden, K. (2004). Difficulties with reading comprehension. In C. Stone, E. Silverman, B. Ehren, & K. Apel (Eds.), *Handbook of language and literacy.* New York: Guilford Press.

Eagly, A., Chen, S., Chagiken, S., & Shaw-Barnes, K. (1999). The impact of attitudes on memory: An affair to remember. *Pscyhological Bulletin, 125,* 64–89.

Flowerday, T., & Schraw, G. (2000). Teacher beliefs about instructional choice: A phenomenological study. *Journal of Educational Pscyhology, 92,* 634–645.

Fournier, D., & Graves, M. (2002). Scaffolding adolescents' comprehension of short stories. *Journal of Adolescent & Adult Literacy, 48,* 30–39.

Friere, P. (1987). *Literacy: Reading the word and the world.* South Hadley, MA: Bergin & Garvey.

Gee, J. P., (2001). Teenagers in new times: A new literacy studies perspective. *Journal of Adolescent & Adult Literacy, 43,* 412–420.

Gillet, J. W., & Temple, C. A. (1986). Understanding reading problems: Assessment and instruction. Boston, MA: Allyn and Bacon.

Goldman, S. R., & Rakestraw, J. A. (2000). Structural aspects of constructing meaning from text. In M. Kamil, P. Mosenthal, P. D. Pearson, & R. Barr (Eds.), Handbook of reading research (pp. 311–336). Mahwah, NJ: Lawrence Erlbaum Associates.

Graesser, A., McNamara, D., Louwerse, M., & Cai, Z. (2004). Coh-Metrix: Analysis of text on cohesion and language. *Behavioral Research Methods, Instruments and Computers, 36,* 193–202.

Green, T. (2000). Responding and sharing: Techniques for energizing classroom discussions. *The Clearing House, 73,* 331–334.

Greenleaf, C., Schoenbach, R., Cziko, C., & Mueller, F. (2001). Apprenticing adolescent readers to academic literacy. *Harvard Educational Review, 71,* 79–127.

Grigg, W., Daane, M., Ying, J., & Campbell, J. (2003). *The nation's report card: Reading 2003, National Assessment of Educational Progress.* Washington, DC:National Center for Education Statistics.

Guthrie, J., & Humenick, N. (2004). Motivating students to read: Evidence for classroom practices that increase reading motivation and achievement. In P. McCardle & V. Chhabra (Eds.), *The voice of evidence in reading research.* Baltimore, MD: Brookes Publishing.

Guzzetti, B., & Williams, W. (1996). Changing the pattern of gendered discussion: Lessons from science classrooms. *Journal of Adolescent & Adult Literacy, 40,* 38–47.

Hartley, J. (2002). Designing instructional and informational text. Retrieved June 1, 2005, from http://aect-members.org/m/research_handbook/Chapters/34.pdf.

Holmes, K. P. (2005). *Engaging reluctant readers through foreign films.* Lanham, MD: Scarecrow Education.

Kelly, G., & Green, J. (1998). The social nature of knowing: Toward a sociocultural perspective on conceptual change and knowledge construction. In B. Guzzetti & C. Hynd (Eds.), *Perspectives on conceptual change: Multiple ways to understand knowing and learning in a complex world* (pp. 145–182). Mahwah, NJ: Lawrence Erlbaum Associates.

King, J., & O'Brien, D. (2002). Adolescents' multiliteracies and their teachers' need to know: Toward a digital détente. In D. Alevermann (Ed.), *Adolescents and literacies in a digital world.* New York: Peter Lang.

Kintsch, E. (2005). Comprehension theory as a guide for the design of thoughtful questions. *Topics in Language Disorders, 25,* 51–65.

Kintsch, W. (1998). *Comprehension: A paradigm for cognition.* Cambridge: University Press.

Kintsch, W., & Kintsch, E. (2005). Comprehension. In S. Paris & S. Stahl (Eds.), *Current issues on reading comprehension and assessment.* Mahwah, NJ: Lawrence Erlbaum Associates.

Kinzer, C. (2003 June). The importance of recognizing and expanding boundaries of literacy. *Reading Online, 6.* Available online at http://www.readingonline.org/electronic/elec_index.asp?HREF=/electronic/kinzer/index/.html.

Kymes, A. (2004). Teaching online comprehension strategies using think-alouds. *Journal of Adolescent & Adult Literacy, 48,* 492–500.

Langer, J. (2001). Beating the odds: Teaching middle and high school students to read and write well. *American Educational Research Journal, 38,* 837–880.

Lankshear, C., & Knobel, M. (2002). Do we have your attention? New literacies, digital technologies and the education of adolescents. In D. Alvermann (Ed.), *Adolescents and literacies in a digital world.* New York: Peter Lang.

Larson, B. (1999). Influence on social studies teachers' use of classroom discussion. *The social studies, 90,* 125–132.

Mandler, J. (1987). On the psychological reality of story structure. *Discourse Processing, 10,* 1–29.

Marshall, J. (2000). Research on response to literature. In M. Kamil, P. Mosenthal, P. D. Pearson, & R. Barr (Eds.), *Handbook of reading research* (Vol. III). Mahwah, NJ: Lawrence Erlbaum Associates.

McNamara, D. (2004). SERT: Self explanation reading training. *Discourse Processes, 38,* 1–30.

Meyer, B., Middlemiss, W., Theodorou, E., Brezinski, K., McDougall, J., & Bartlett, B. (2002). Effects of structure strategy instruction delivered to fifth-grade children using the Internet with and without the aid of older adult tutors. *Journal of Educational Psychology, 94,* 486–519.

Moore, D. (2002). Adolescent literacy for all means forming literate identities. In C. Roller (Ed.), *Comprehensive reading instruction across the grade levels: A collection of papers from the reading research 2001 conference.* Newark, DE: International Reading Association.

Musheno, B., & Lawson, A. (1999). Effects of learning cycle and traditional text on comprehension of science concepts by students at differing reasoning levels. *Journal of Research in Science Teaching, 36,* 23–37.

Myers, J. (1992). The social contexts of school and personal literacy. *Reading Research Quarterly, 27,* 297–333.

Nassaji, H. (2002). Schema theory and knowledge-based processes in second language reading comprehension: A need for alternative perspectives. *Language Learning, 52,* 439–481.

National Reading Panel. (2000). Teaching children to read: An evidence-based assessment of the scientific research literature on reading and its implifications for reading instruction. Washington, D.C.: National Institute of Child Health and Human Development.

Nist, S., & Simpson, M. (2000). College studying. In M. Kamil, P. Mosenthal, P. D. Pearson, & R. Barr (Eds.), *Handbook of reading research* (Vol. 3). Mahwah, NJ: Lawrence Erlbaum Associates.

Palincsar, A. M., & Brown, A. (1984). Reciprocal teaching of comprehension fostering and monitoring activities. *Cognition and Instruction, 12,* 117–175.

Paris, S., & Stahl, S. (2005). *Current issues on reading comprehension and assessment.* Mahwah, NJ: Lawrence Erlbaum Associates.

Parker, W. (2001). Classroom discussion: Models for leading seminars and deliberations. *Social Education, 65,* 11–15.

Pratt, G. (1992). *Enemy ace: War idyll.* New York: Warner Books.

Pressley, M. (2000). What should comprehension instruction be the instruction of? In M. Kamil, P. Mosenthal, P. D. Pearson, & R. Barr (Eds.), *Handbook of reading research* (Vol. 3). Mahwah, NJ: Lawrence Erlbaum Associates.

Pressley, M., & Hilden, K. (2004). Toward more ambitious comprehension instruction. In E. Silliman & L. Wilkinson (Eds.), *Language and literacy learning in schools.* New York: Guilford.

RAND Reading Study Group (RRSG). (2002). *Reading for understanding: Toward an R&D program in reading comprehension.* Santa Monica, CA: RAND, 2002.

Raphael, T., & Pearson, P. D. (1985). Increasing students' awareness of sources of information for answering questions. *American Educational Research Journal, 22,* 217–236.

Ruddell, R., & Unrau, N. (2004). Reading as a meaning-construction process: The reader, the text, and the teacher. In R. Ruddell & N. Unrau (Eds.), *Theoretical models and processes of reading* (Vol. III). Newark, DE: International Reading Association.

Sadoski, M., Goetz, E., & Rodriguez, M. (2000). Engaging texts: Effects of concreteness comprehensibility, interest, and recall in four text types. *Journal of Educational Psychology, 92,* 85–95.

Schiefele, U. (1999). Interest and learning from text. *Scientific Studies of Reading, 3,* 257–279.

Smagorinsky, P. (2001). If meaning is constructed, what is it made from? Toward a cultural theory of reading. *Review of Educational Research, 71,* 133–169.

Snow, C., & Sweet, A. (2003). Reading for comprehension. In A. Sweet & C. Snow (Eds.), *Rethinking reading comprehension.* New York: Guilford.

Spires, H., & Donley, J. (1998). Prior knowledge activation: Inducing engagement with informational texts. *Journal of Educational Psychology, 90,* 249–260.

Sturtevant, E., Boyd, F., Brozo, W. G., Hinchman, K., Alvermann, D., & Moore, D. (2006). Principled practices for adolescent literacy: A framework for instruction and policy.

Thiede, K., & Anderson, M. (2001). Summarizing can improve metacomprehension accuracy. Paper presented at the meeting of the American Educational Research Association.

Turner, J. (1995). The influence of classroom contexts on young children's motivation for literacy. *Reading Research Quarterly, 30,* 410–441.

Underwood, T., & Pearson, P. D. (2004). Teaching struggling adolescent readers to comprehend what they read. In T. Jetton & J. Dole (Eds.), *Adolescent literacy research and practice.* New York: Guilford.

Unrau, N., & Ruddell, R. (1995). Interpreting texts in classroom context. *Journal of Adolescent & Adult Literacy, 39,* 16–27.

Valdés, G. (1998). The world outside and inside schools: Language and immigrant children. *Educational Researcher, 27,* 4–18.

White, B., & Johnson, T. S. (2001). We really do mean it: Implementing language arts standard #3 with opinionniares. *The Clearing House, 74,* 119–123.

Wilhelm, J. (2001). *Improving comprehension with think-aloud strategies.* New York: Scholastic.

Wittrock, M. (1990). Generative processes of comprehension. *Educational Pscyhologist, 24,* 345–376.

Wyatt, C., & Willis, C. (2000). Students make the grade. *The Science Teacher, 67,* 40–43.

chapter 4

Classroom Assessment of Literacy Growth and Content Learning

Anticipation Guide

Directions: Read each statement carefully and decide whether you agree or disagree with it, placing a check mark in the appropriate *Before Reading* column. When you have finished reading and studying the chapter, return to the guide and decide whether your anticipations need to be changed by placing a check mark in the appropriate *After Reading* column.

	Before Reading		After Reading	
	Agree	*Disagree*	*Agree*	*Disagree*
1. Standardized tests have more disadvantages than advantages.	____	____	____	____
2. Assessment is an activity that occurs primarily at the beginning of the school year.	____	____	____	____
3. Reading specialists should be the ones to assess students' literacy strengths and needs.	____	____	____	____
4. Assessment should focus only on students' reading and writing weaknesses.	____	____	____	____
5. Students should be involved in assessment activities.	____	____	____	____
6. Assessment can inform teaching and learning.	____	____	____	____

85

In Chapter 2 we described the six guiding principles for enhancing students' learning across the content areas. As you can probably surmise, this chapter focuses on the second guideline and the importance of assessment. Assessment, as defined by Stiggins (2005), is the "process of gathering evidence of student learning to inform instructional decisions" (p. 5). Accordingly, we will examine ways in which classroom teachers can plan, gather, and interpret the data they collect about their students.

*M*ore than 20 years of theory development and research has characterized literacy as an interactive, context-bound, purposeful process of meaning construction (Bissex, 1980; Clay, 1975; Gee, 2000). During the same time, we have progressed in our understanding of what literacy behaviors should be assessed, how that assessment should be represented, and which participants or stakeholders should be involved. At the middle and high school levels, these changes have translated into an emphasis on teachers defining what it means to be literate and knowledgeable in their classrooms and designing a variety of performance-based activities and authentic opportunities to assess their students as they interact with content-area concepts (Frey & Hiebert, 2003).

In this chapter issues and assessment techniques are presented relative to one basic assumption: The goal of literacy assessment is to provide teachers with knowledge about how best to improve and support learning and self-knowledge for students so that they will become more reflective, active, and purposeful learners. We demonstrate how your assessments can reveal to you and your students important information about students' thinking, language processes, and content knowledge. Because assessment guides and informs instruction and can be integrated into the daily flow of instructional events in the classroom, this chapter provides a foundation for assessment strategies that appear in later chapters.

Go to *http://www. prenhall.com/brozo*, select Chapter 4, then click on Chapter Objectives to provide a focus for your reading.

CASE STUDY

Selma is a seventh-grade general science teacher interested in discovering more about her students' ability to comprehend textbook information. After attending in-service workshops on content-area assessment procedures, she began to recognize the need for alternative assessments to the chapter check tests in her science textbook. After 5 years of teaching, she discovered that she was relying more and more on these tests for grading purposes and less and less on other "views" of her students as learners and knowledge seekers. Moreover, the results of these tests were not providing Selma with information about why students performed the way they did. She had no way of discovering whether success or failure was tied in any way to students' study processes or to their ability to understand the science text.

The in-service presenter emphasized the need to tie content material to the processes for learning it effectively. Suggestions were made concerning ways teachers could teach and assess at the same time using the class textbook. Selma decided to use this information to develop teaching strategies for improving students' thinking about text structure.

To the Reader:
Think about Selma concern as you read this chapter, and be prepared by the end of this chapter to suggest possible assessment/teaching solutions for her.

Guidelines for Literacy Assessment

The following five guidelines are based on a synthesis of current research and theory about assessment of literacy and learning. These guidelines should assist you as you plan your instructional units and determine the ways in which you hope to assess and evaluate the students in your content area.

Content-Area Assessment Is a Continuous Process of Becoming Informed About Students' Learning

For learning to occur, assessments should be rooted in activities that have genuine purposes (Avery, Carmichael-Tanaka, Kunze, & Kouneski, 2000; Frey & Hiebert, 2003). In this way, acquiring information about student learning does not become an end in

Effective assessment
procedures should
account for all dimensions
of student learning.

itself but is an evolving process of gathering feedback for the teacher and student so that instruction can become more engaging, more tied to real-world issues and concerns, and more personally meaningful.

What do we want to know about students that requires us to assess them? We want to know under what conditions they learn best, what instructional strategies we can employ to facilitate their learning, and how to encourage independent, active reading and learning. In other words, as teachers we need to know more about our students' prior knowledge, their beliefs, their interests or attitudes, and how they process information and why they choose to do so. We also want students to discover more about themselves as learners so that they can expand their abilities as literate knowledge seekers. Middle school and high school teachers want to know whether or not their students are likely to profit from textbook reading, daily instruction, process writing, research projects, and so on.

The assessment tools we use for these purposes should therefore be designed to provide insights into students' reading, writing, and thinking strategies with the actual texts they must use daily and in the actual, authentic contexts of their use. In this way, the information gained from assessment can be immediately translated into action.

Not only should assessment be authentic, but it also should occur over time (Reutzel & Cooter, 2003; William, 2000). As we have noted previously, learning is a continuous and dynamic process that takes place over time and changes with each new instructional situation. Therefore, to obtain more useful and meaningful information about your students' literacy and learning abilities, we recommend that you base instructional decisions on long-term observations and assessments done on a daily basis. Later in this chapter, we discuss specific assessment formats that use day-to-day information gained from observing students and gathering reflections of their progress. Only with such important assessment data can we expect to build a supportive learning environment in the classroom.

Assessment of Literacy and Content Learning Should Use Multiple Data Sources Across Multiple Contexts

Since learning is a
dynamic process, the best
assessments occur over
time, using a variety of
data sources.

A basketball coach who wants to find out how well new recruits can play the game does not give a paper-and-pencil test. The players are required to perform various tasks on the court, and their ability is assessed while being directly observed. By making multiple assessments of situated performances, a coach can learn the most about a player's true ability and potential. So it is with the assessment of literacy and learning in content-area classrooms. That is, no single standardized test, teacher-made quiz, or written task can provide teachers the information they need to know to promote student learning (Stiggins, 2005).

Rather than relying on one source of information about students, teachers need information from multiple and overlapping sources in order to plan appropriate instruction. Such a perspective, of course, requires careful planning on the part of teachers, but planning is an integral part of the assessment process (Frey & Hiebert, 2003). For example, a science teacher's assessment plan for the first semester could include three different data sources: (a) her students' ability to process and understand the textbook information, (b) her observations of the students' problem-solving abilities, and (c) her interpretation of their learning logs. The advantage of determining students' progress and understanding with the actual materials used in the science class is that the teacher would then have a much clearer idea about how to modify her instruction to improve students' learning.

This example reinforces the point that students' literacy skills are context bound. No single test can adequately reflect the teaching and learning process. As a former student of ours said, the old "clump theory" of literacy no longer makes sense. Traditional views of literacy held that all of us possess a given, measurable quantity, or clump, of literacy ability and that reading tests could accurately weigh our clumps. As our conceptions of what it means to be literate have changed to include the social, dynamic, generative, and idiosyncratic nature of literacy, we have begun to realize that the process of assessment must be expanded to include multiple demonstrations of ability in situated contexts of authentic teaching and learning.

Effective Assessment Involves Students

Traditionally, assessment has been interpreted as a professional activity that teachers "do to students." However, many who believe that assessment is an ongoing activity that involves both students and teachers in the improvement of instruction have challenged this traditional view (e.g., Conley & Hinchman, 2004). Stiggins (2005) eloquently explained the rationale for this differing perspective: "The instructional decisions that contribute the most to student success are, in fact, not made by the adults. Rather the decisions that contribute the most to determining student success or failure in learning are made by students themselves" (p. 18).

Teachers can use students as curricular informants to make instruction more responsive to their needs.

This equal partnership means that students are involved in a variety of ways. For example, they can (a) recommend possible assessment activities, (b) assist in the creation of rubrics and checklists, (c) apply rubrics and checklists to their own work, and (d) participate in self-reflection and evaluation activities that encourage them to relate their performances to the strategies they have used.

When students participate in the assessment and evaluation of their own strengths and needs, over time you will notice differences in their behaviors (e.g., motivation, metacognitive awareness) and in their performances and products (Cleary & Zimmerman, 2004; Graham, 2005). For example, in one long-term study the students who wrote journal entries that encouraged them to self-reflect and evaluate about the strategies they used were the ones who earned As and Bs in a history course (Hubbard & Simpson, 2003).

In addition to self-evaluation journal writing activities, rubrics are also a powerful way to involve students in assessment (Reutzel & Cooter, 2003). Simply defined, rubrics are scoring guides or rating systems that inform students in advance "what the teacher wants in a particular product." Rubrics generally include the quality features or characteristics that designate a targeted assignment, the criteria that students must meet, and a range of possible points. Although we will discuss rubrics and all their variations in Chapter 7, the example in Figure 4.1 should help clarify their appearance. This particular rubric was designed by a vocal music teacher who asked her students to find a current article in a magazine or newspaper that critiqued some type of musical performance. Notice that she informed the students on how the total points for the assignment would be awarded. She also asks her students to use this rubric as a way of evaluating and monitoring their own work before they hand it in to her.

Effective Assessment Requires Planning, Interpreting, and Managing a Variety of Data

This fourth guideline reiterates the importance of viewing assessment in a comprehensive manner. As noted by Cronbach (1960) over 40 years ago, effective informal assessment involves teachers in careful observations, a variety of data collection

Figure 4.1 Library Project Rubric

> *Directions:* Use this checklist to evaluate your assignment before you hand it in to me. The criteria listed below should help you locate strengths and weaknesses in your work. I will also be using the checklist to evaluate your assignment.
>
> _____ 1. The references were listed on the index card correctly and completely. (WORTH 6 POINTS)
> _____ 2. The two articles were appropriate to the assignment. (WORTH 4 POINTS)
> _____ 3. There was a complete and accurate summary of the key ideas of the two articles you read. (WORTH 10 POINTS)
>
> **TOTAL POINTS:**
>
> **COMMENTS:**

Effective assessment, according to Angelo (1998), "closes the loop" because the data we collect is also the data we use to plan lessons and teach.

methods, and the integration of the information. Frey and Hiebert (2003) slightly modified Cronbach's suggestions to include these elements of assessment: planning goals and purposes, collecting data using a variety of techniques, and interpreting the data (i.e., the products that students create and the processes that students engage in during learning). They also stressed the importance of viewing assessment as a recursive process rather than a linear process. That is, once teachers reflect upon and interpret their data, they should eventually integrate the information into their classroom routine, modifying when essential and setting the scene for future assessment opportunities.

Thus far, we have emphasized the importance of collecting data using a variety of methods. However, we must also address the importance of the other two assessment elements—planning and interpreting. Planning involves teachers in a reflection of their curricular goals and their views of literacy, especially what it means to be a successful learner in their content area. The assessment methods and activities they choose should reflect these views and goals. Interpreting involves teachers during all phases of the instructional process, not just at the end of the lesson or assessment activity. Goodman (2003) labels this on-the-spot diagnosis as "interpretative evaluation" because teachers are simultaneously involved in explicating the nature of learning and teaching at the same time they are collecting data and making decisions. The interpretation of data also implies that teachers have a variety of ways to record, manage, and summarize the information they collect, whether that be in the form of field notes, memos written scribbled on index cards, checklists, or charts that reveal class trends. Later in the chapter we will examine how content-area teachers have managed this potentially information overload into meaningful trends.

Assessment Should Include Students' Interests, Attitudes, and Belief Systems

Obtaining information about students' real-world needs and interests can be very useful in planning ways to teach and reach your students. Interest is one of the most potent motivators for students, and teachers can take full advantage of this fact in a number of ways (Ainley, Hidi, & Berndorff, 2002; Brophy, 1998). One obvious strategy is to introduce students to reading materials related to their interests. These materials may be tied to the topic of study in your classroom or may simply be relevant to students on a personal level. In Chapter 8 we explain how teachers can take full advantage of young adult literature to help meet students' needs.

Honoring Diversity and Building Competence in the Content Classroom

Carmen, who teaches a sheltered language arts class to eighth graders, knows the importance of delineating her students' interests and attitudes and employs a variety of intriguing techniques to do so. She begins every school year with an activity called "My Bag." Carmen and her students bring in bags filled with objects and items that represent who they are.

Carmen asks students not to do a show-and-tell but to use an item to elicit questions. For example, Juanita took an onyx ring out of her bag and passed it around for her group members to inspect. Soon students were asking her questions: "Where'd you get it?" "Was it your mom's?" "What kind of stone is that?" Juanita revealed that the ring belonged to her *tia*, her *aunt*, with whom she had a very close and friendly relationship; she said the ring was given to her just before her aunt died. In another case, Carlos showed his group a model car and a screwdriver. Before long, he was responding to questions that allowed him to go into great detail about his interest in fixing cars with his older brother and his plan to be an auto mechanic.

While students go through the My Bag activity, Carmen circulates throughout the room, taking note of students' interests, desires, needs, and concerns, such as Juanita's relationship with her aunt and Carlos's interest in auto repair. Armed with this knowledge, Carmen tailors certain writing, reading, and group projects to her students' needs and desires. She alludes to particular characteristics of students revealed through the My Bag exercise during class activities, which helps demonstrate her interest in and concern for her students and builds a caring atmosphere in the classroom. In the end, Carmen, too, shares her bag, allowing students to get to know their teacher as a real person who has goals, desires, and interests, just as they do. Carmen has found that in being part of the My Bag activity herself, she can establish an initial foundation on which trust and cooperative problem solving can be built. Through the use of the My Bag strategy, Carmen gathers invaluable assessment information about her students' interests and beliefs in a highly personal, unique, and enjoyable way.

In addition to assessing students' interests, teachers need to identify their beliefs systems about learning and how they view themselves as learners (Schommer-Atkins, 2002). Students with naive conceptions about learning and how knowledge is acquired tend to believe that learning is something that is simple and happens quickly, with very little effort (Hofer, 2004). As a result, they are less likely to use strategies that engage them in elaborative levels of thinking, choosing instead to use rote-level strategies emphasizing the memorization of facts. For example, because many students believe that knowledge about science is simply the memorization of isolated

Students with mature
views of learning
perceive it as complex,
involving them in a
persistent effort over a
sustained period of time.

facts, they tend to focus on those facts without thinking about the interrelationships between them and the concepts they represent. This type of learning is obviously something that students can do in a rather superficial fashion rather than by investing any mental effort.

These implicit beliefs about learning have a subtle impact on how students comprehend what they read, problem solve, and persist when assigned difficult tasks by their teachers. In addition, Schommer (1994) found an association between students' grades and their naive conceptions of learning. In her study of 1,000 high school students, a regression analysis that controlled for general intelligence indicated that the more students believed in quick learning, the more likely they were to have a low overall grade point average. Later in this chapter and in Chapter 9 we will present some assessment activities that will help you identify students' interests and beliefs about reading and learning and discuss how you can use that information to inform your teaching.

Before we describe authentic assessment procedures that reflect these five guidelines, we address the important issue of standardized tests.

Our Standardized Testing Culture

What are standardized reading achievement tests? They are objective measurements, simple to administer and score, with comprehensive tables and charts for deriving a variety of scores. And with more than 100 reading tests on the market, they are accessible and widely discussed in the media. Although reading tests have been around since the beginning of the last century, only since the 1930s has the question format become the most popular method of assessing comprehension and the basis for current standardized tests of reading achievement (Readence & Moore, 1983). Educators over the past 50 years have regarded the question-answering format as the most convenient, objective, and cost-effective means of comprehension assessment.

The term *standardized* means that the test was administered and scored under standard and uniform testing procedures. Measurement specialists working with curriculum experts and teachers typically construct these tests. Following is a representative "objective" question written by these experts:

Question

Audrey strained to see the people who were coming through the crowd. Somewhere down there her parents were waiting to welcome her after her voyage.

   a. Audrey is standing in a crowd, waiting to meet a plane.
   b. Audrey is in a crowd, walking toward her parents.
   c. Audrey is on a ship, looking out at a crowd waiting for the ship.
   d. Audrey is looking at a ship on which her parents are arriving. (Reading Yardsticks, Form B, 1981, p. 11)

Before a standardized test is made available to schools and teachers, it is given to a large number of students, who represent the group for whom the test was intended. This representative group of students is called the **norm** group. The norm group's scores on the test are transformed statistically into standard scores, which are usually made available in tabular form in the test's users manual. These standard scores allow teachers and schools to compare their students with a national group of students or with other similar students in their state. The most common standard scores used by schools to interpret student performance on reading achievement tests are **grade equivalents** and **percentiles.** A grade-equivalent interpretation of a student's reading achievement test score is indicated in terms of years and months— for instance, 10.6, or 10th grade, 6th month. When interpreting reading test performance in terms of a percentile, we describe a student's score as a point at or below which a given percentage of other scores falls. For example, a student who scored at the 80th percentile scored as well as or better than 80% of the students in the norm group.

The norm group of the standardized tests you use should be similar to the students in your classes.

Two other characteristics of standardized tests are particularly important to understand: reliability and validity. When a test has **reliability** it means that it will consistently measure what it purports to measure, no matter how many times it is administered. That is, a student who took the Iowa Basic Skills Test on a Friday should score similarly if he were to take the test a week later. A test with strong **validity** measures what the authors claim it will measure. As you can surmise, a test must be valid to be useful to classroom teachers. For example, if a test claims that it measures students' abilities to read critically, but really measures their abilities to skim short passages and answer factual questions, a red flag should be raised. That is why it is always important to read the testing manual to discover whether the authors provide a theoretical rationale and evidence for their conceptions. If the authors do not provide a rationale or their questions do not match the stated purposes, you know that the test probably lacks strong validity.

The Uses and Potential Limitations of Standardized Tests

What are the potential uses of standardized tests? At the district level, principals and superintendents can use a standardized test as one way to evaluate a special program or intervention in order to determine its effectiveness. For example, if a school district has been using a particular reading program that encourages students to read widely and frequently, the administration might choose a standardized test that measures students' reading fluency and comprehension to determine the success of the program.

The trends from a standardized test can be an excellent starting point for further diagnosis and assessment.

In addition, the data from a standardized test can often inform administrators and teachers about large-scale trends at the district level. These trends can reflect the skills that are being taught effectively and those that need more emphasis. For example, we know of one school district where the middle school teachers and administrators examined the results of the Iowa Basic Skills Exam for the sixth graders' strengths and weaknesses. As a result of their analysis, they identified vocabulary as a goal for the next school year because the sixth graders scored much too low on this subtest.

Standardized test results can also be used by classroom teachers. Some teachers use these scores as a large-scale screening device to determine possible groupings or skills that need emphasis for the class and for individual students. For example, when Maria examined the test results for Joseph, an incoming sixth grader, she saw these scores:

vocabulary	5.1	grade equivalent
comprehension	2.8	grade equivalent

Joseph's scores suggest that he needs work on reading comprehension but that his vocabulary background is not a contributing factor to his low score on comprehension. Maria hypothesized that Joseph may need help with active reading for main ideas to improve his comprehension. Of course, Maria used that information as a preliminary hunch. She verified that hunch with her own assessment activities to learn more about the strengths and skill needs of Joseph and the other students in her sixth-grade language arts classes.

Standardized tests, however, have received considerable criticism. Many of the criticisms of standardized tests focus on how the test scores will be used. Teachers and parents, for example, worry that students will be placed in classes on the basis of one standardized test. What needs to be remembered, however, is that standardized tests, like any other assessment instrument, are only one data source or sample of students' behaviors, skills, and strategies. As the assessment guidelines have suggested, any instructional decision about a student is best made using a variety of sources of information.

> Reading tasks that appear on standardized tests are vastly different from the reading tasks content area teachers assign their students on a daily basis.

Other criticisms or limitations have focused on the fact that the passages, problems, and questions on standardized tests do not reflect the specific goals and curriculum of a school or a classroom. For example, a 10th-grade health education teacher may wonder what the percentiles and grade equivalents she received about her students have to do with their reading and learning in her class. Perhaps very little, and for obvious reasons. First, the comprehension passages on a test like the Iowa Basic Skills Test may not cover health issues such as nutrition or exercise. Second, the kind of reading demanded by reading comprehension tests is significantly different from the way a student would read and study a health education textbook. For example, on the test, a student reads one or two paragraphs under strict time limitations. In contrast, the reading assignment in the health education class may require the student to spend an entire week reading and discussing a 20- to 30-page chapter, allowing enough time to learn the material. Finally, the Iowa Basic Skills Test measures reading performance with multiple-choice questions. The health education teacher may require students to write out answers to short and long essay-type questions.

In addition to these potential limitations, experts have suggested that standardized tests are only a gross estimate of a student's reading ability (Stiggins, 2005). In fact, it is quite possible that you will have students in your class who scored high on a standardized reading test yet have substantial difficulties in processing information in your class. Such a phenomenon occurs because standardized tests cannot possibly measure students' background knowledge, their depth of engagement with the material, their metacognitive awareness, or the strategies they employ while they read (Conley & Hinchman, 2004; Unrau, 2004).

Many of these limitations, of course, can apply to any teacher-designed assessment instrument or activity. Hence, sensitivity to the uses and limitations of standardized tests should help you in planning your own assessment activities.

Communicating with Parents and Students About Standardized Reading Test Results

School districts have an obligation to inform students and parents of reading achievement test results. It is their right to know. Whereas some testing experts have argued that the distribution of assessment results should be limited to those who are prepared to use them, classroom teachers in science, math, history, and language arts may be given printouts of their homeroom students' reading test scores. Furthermore, it is not uncommon for the classroom teacher to be asked by students and parents to explain test scores. These facts point to the need for all teachers to become informed about what these scores mean and how they can be used. Following are several suggestions for reporting and explaining standardized reading test results to students and/or parents. These suggestions come from our own experience as middle school and high school teachers as well as the experience of others.

1. Put parents at ease. Welcome them and make sure that they are comfortable. If possible, meet where there is good lighting and privacy.

2. Before presenting information to parents, find out what information they have already received from other teachers, counselors, or administrators. Failure to do so may put you in the uncomfortable position of contradicting a colleague, having to change your position, or reporting redundant information.

3. Before presenting information, determine exactly what kind of information the parent wants.

4. If assessment information is inadequate or contradictory, be willing to admit the weaknesses of evaluation based on these data.

5. Urge parents not to fixate on standard scores but instead pay close attention to a variety of data sources, such as the student's previous work and the teacher's evaluations.

6. If necessary, explain the limitations of grade equivalents. They are too easily misinterpreted to be given to parents indiscriminately. These norms are often extrapolated; that is, they are often estimates based on trends in scores established by the norm group. In other words, if a 10th grader obtains a grade equivalent of 5.5 (5th grade, 5th month) on a reading achievement test appropriate for 10th graders, it is unlikely that students at the 5.5 grade level were actually in the norming group for the 10th-grade test. Therefore, this grade equivalent is merely an estimate based on the hypothetical performance of students at the 5.5 grade level if they had taken the 10th-grade test. As you can tell from this explanation, grade equivalents are very difficult to explain and interpret properly. Another limitation of grade equivalents is that the amount of error may be anywhere from half a year to a full year and a half. So a score of 10.0 could be as low as 8.5 or as high as 11.5—we simply do not know for sure.

7. When explaining percentile scores, make it clear that they are not to be confused with percentages of questions answered correctly. It might be best to say, "In comparison with 10th graders throughout the United States, John is in the upper 10 to 15%, as measured by the Iowa Silent Reading Test when this test was taken last October."

Because reading grade equivalents can be confusing to parents and students, be prepared to explain what they mean and their limitations.

There is no need for classroom teachers to become test and measurement experts simply because occasionally they may be asked to administer and interpret the scores of standardized reading tests. By combining some basic knowledge about these tests with common sense, you can improve your chances of communicating effectively with students and parents.

Because there are viable alternatives to formal assessment procedures, we now turn our attention to a variety of informal assessment measures that should assist content-area teachers in their quest to improve students' learning.

The Role of the Teacher Leader

Given the recent expansion of the No Child Left Behind Act to adolescents who are "striving" readers, assessment is probably a high-profile issue for many content-area teachers. Teacher leaders can capitalize on the uncertainty and concern that many of their colleagues feel by mentoring and sharing pertinent information. Of course, the process should begin with teacher leaders delineating their own assessment plans and goals, authentic assessment opportunities, and methods of recordkeeping and interpretation.

In terms of mentoring, teacher leaders can share with their colleagues their assessment plans and invite them to visit their classrooms to observe some of the authentic assessment activities. For example, it might be appropriate for a new teacher to see how a rubric could be created or introduced to students. Alternatively, the teacher leader might share her Content-Area Reading Inventory (discussed later in the chapter) with a veteran teacher, asking for input and suggestions. We know of one teacher leader who asked his colleague to take the Inventory in order to determine whether students could finish it within the class period. Such collaboration serves two purposes: it assists the teacher leader in editing the final product and it subtly educates a colleague about authentic assessment possibilities at the secondary level.

At the departmental level teacher leaders can serve as a mentor by explaining and sharing authentic assessment opportunities and activities that the department may have overlooked. For example, it is quite possible that an English department, in its frenzy to meet state mandated performance exams, overlooked the importance of assessing students' attitudes and interests. Alternatively, it could also be that the department does not coordinate assessment activities across the grade levels, a prerequisite for avoiding lost data. For example, if students are given a study skills inventory in 9th grade, that information should be passed on to the 10th-grade teacher in the same way that reading profiles and writing samples are exchanged and shared. The teacher leader can initiate these discussions and suggest possible solutions (e.g., a folder for each student).

At the school level, the teacher leader can volunteer to work with administrators as they analyze and prepare testing reports for parents and the community. For example, because the reports from standardized tests or state-mandated assessments are often shared on a school's Web site or at parent-teacher conferences, they should be edited for jargon. In addition to editing jargon, teacher leaders may wish to offer clarifying statements about issues that incite parents to anger and concern, such as whether their students are reading at "grade level." A concise and clear statement about what constitutes a grade-level equivalent would be very useful and could be crafted by a teacher leader.

Finally, teacher leaders can become active members of literacy teams or study groups at their school, suggesting possible books and recent articles about authentic assessment or the "striving adolescent reader."

Informal, Authentic Assessments of Students

One of the key principles of reading assessment discussed earlier is to embed assessment in the contexts of actual literacy and learning activities so that the results of assessment will have direct and immediate instructional implications. To this end, middle school and high school teachers need to devise their own approaches to assessment to determine the extent to which their students can read and learn from the various materials used in the classroom and use this new learning in functional and purposeful ways. The approaches teachers have employed to accomplish this goal have taken a number of forms, but all have these four critical characteristics in common:

1. They assess literacy and learning processes with the materials used in the classroom and in the actual contexts of their use.
2. They are so closely related to instruction that assessment and instruction become virtually indistinguishable.
3. They reflect the essential role of the teacher's judgment in student evaluation.
4. They develop students' abilities to think metacognitively and self-reflect.

In the following section, we will examine successful authentic assessment procedures that middle school and high school content-area teachers are using with their students. Some of these assessment opportunities involve students in reading and thinking about content-area concepts, some involve students in writing, and some involve students in completing self-report instruments.

Using Classroom Activities to Assess and Evaluate

As we mentioned earlier in the guidelines, when teachers employ effective assessment procedures they are not only keeping track of their students' learning, but they are also assisting their students to learn more (Stiggins, 2005). Such an outlook suggests that content-area teachers should capture appropriate assessment moments before a lesson begins, anytime during that lesson, and once a lesson ends. For example, a culinary arts teacher wanting to identify at the beginning of a unit her students' background knowledge about herbs and spices might administer a quick true/false quiz, much like the quizzes many of us take in popular magazines.

Of course, exemplary teachers have been automatic information gatherers for quite some time. They have noted their students' facial expressions and body language, answered their content-based questions, and evaluated their products, delineating quality and mediocre work. What is different, however, is that some teachers collect these data in an implicit and subconscious fashion, whereas others collect and interpret these data in an explicit and reflective manner (Angelo, 1998). The latter approach is what we all are striving for, whether it is called "diagnostic teaching" or "snapshot diagnosis" (Angelo, 1998; Unrau, 2004). It is the difference between collecting information, as did the culinary arts teacher, and collecting the information and reflecting upon it in order to improve instruction. In order to clarify the nuances of this distinction, let's examine some examples of how content-area teachers have used their classroom activities as opportunities for assessment.

Phillip, an eighth-grade science teacher, uses a technique called **word fluency** or **focused listing** (Angelo, 1998) to help him gather information about his students' processing. He begins the activity by asking his students to meet in pairs and list all the words they can recall about a topic, such as the six different kinds of forces. With this activity, one student talks as the other student writes down the words that his or her partner says. After 2 minutes, the roles are switched and the process begins again. To increase the interest in the activity, Phillip sets a kitchen timer, which clicks away as he walks about the room listening to what the students are saying and watching what they are writing.

Phillip tells us that this activity helps him determine rather quickly which students seem to understand the key terminology, which ones have misconceptions about the content, and which ones are already sensing connections between the concepts. Sometimes he asks the students to work individually and create their own lists on a piece of paper that he collects and analyzes. Before he meets the students again he quickly sorts through their answers, placing them in piles he labels as "exemplary," "appropriate," or "insufficient." With this diagnostic information, Phillip knows which concepts he needs to reinforce and where to direct his next lesson.

In addition to the word fluency activity, many other classroom activities can be used to assess students' strengths and needs. To illustrate this point, we turn to an astronomy classroom. In order to measure his students' connected knowledge of astronomy, Jerome uses a fill-in concept map. This strategy entails creating a partially completed graphic that depicts networks of related concepts and requesting students complete the graphic by supplying the appropriate missing terms in their correct

We will examine six informal, authentic assessment procedures that will help teachers learn more about their students while insuring that their students as much content as possible.

Using concept maps as a teaching and assessment tool helps students make critical knowledge connections.

places in the graphic. In Figure 4.2, Jerome's students are asked to use the word list at the top to complete the map. You will observe in this example 10 blank bubbles with only 7 key terms, which means some terms will be used more than once. Jerome scores the concept map based on the percentage of correct responses to the total number of blank bubbles.

Because Jerome's approach to teaching astronomy and all his science subjects is to facilitate knowledge connections, his use of concept maps for assessing his students' abilities to demonstrate critical links in their new knowledge lends further authenticity to his efforts. An added benefit is that his students like completing the maps, especially students with lower levels of communication skills.

Assessments conducted as students interact with text and complete daily assignments, engage in class discussions, or work cooperatively to solve problems can provide a rich source of information about students' relative strengths and needs, as well as how instruction can be modified to facilitate learning. Throughout this textbook you will encounter numerous other strategies and activities that can be used to assess your students while improving their learning.

Kidwatching and Observational Checklists

Suggesting to teachers that they assess through observation is like asking them to breathe or walk; it comes so naturally to most of them that its importance and power as an assessment strategy is often overlooked. Goodman (2003) has referred to

Figure 4.2   Science Bubble Map

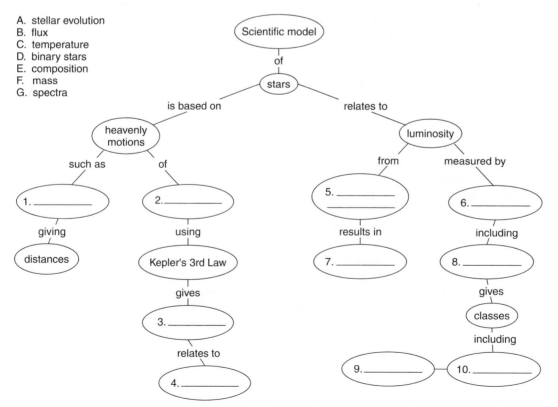

observation and the explicit decision-making processes that accompany observation as **kidwatching**. Regardless of the label used, observational assessment provides teachers a vast amount of information, especially when combined with other data sources such as samples of student work (Frey & Hiebert, 2003).

Assessing through observation requires that teachers become more sensitive to the entire instructional situation: the reader, the text, the tasks required of the reader, the processes needed to complete the tasks, and the environment in which the tasks occur. Observing students over time in a variety of classroom situations can provide teachers with an objective, unbiased view of students. Earlier, we discussed the limitations of making instructional decisions based on a single assessment at one point in time—specifically, that single assessments are not reliable measures of a student's true reading and learning ability. In contrast, observational assessments are ongoing and occur within the context of normal classroom activities while students are engaged in learning content-area concepts.

In addition to capitalizing on teachable moments, teachers can structure their observations with the use of a checklist. These observations and checklists can focus on students as they (a) read for enjoyment, (b) read from textbooks or other content-area sources, (c) write, (d) take tests, (e) read aloud (plays, poems), (f) discuss and present ideas, and (g) follow written and oral directions. For example, Phillip created an observation checklist (Figure 4.3) in order to collect information on which students were having difficulty reading the textbook and laboratory activity booklet. With this checklist, he can screen and identify which individuals may need special assistance.

Another teacher created her observation checklist (see Figure 4.4) based on what she believed to be characteristics of effective readers in her classroom. Notice that she has designed her checklist so she can summarize the trends across the classroom.

Because these observations occur as a natural part of the content-area lesson, students can demonstrate their true ability. Teachers can obtain highly relevant and

> Checklists formalize the processes involved in "kidwatching" and provide teachers valuable information on their students, especially those needing special assistance.

Figure 4.3   Observational Checklist to Screen for Struggling Readers

---

Student:

1. Avoids eye contact with me, especially when I'm asking questions of the class over the reading assignment.

2. May create the impression that he or she knows the answer to my question by looking intently and flagging his or her hand.

3. During oral reading of the textbook, tries to be the first one to read to get it over with.

4. During oral reading, tries to be the last one to read or tries to avoid being called on to read.

5. Frequently forgets to bring to class books and other materials that may be used for oral reading or needed to do in-class work.

6. Twists and turns restlessly in seat, often talking with neighbor.

7. Attempts to disrupt class.

8. Uses manipulative techniques within and outside of class to try to create a positive perception of his or her ability in spite of poor performance.

9. Uses neighbor for information about assignments and answers to questions.

Figure 4.4   Sample Items for Observation Checklist

Maria   Jade   Josh   Heather   Andres   Keidra

Comprehension Behaviors
1. Establishes purposes for reading
2. Identifies and understands key ideas
3. Follows the chapter's organizational structure
4. Summarizes important ideas, using own words
5. Monitors understanding
6. Adjusts reading rate to material being read
7. Concentrates and begins tasks appropriately
8. Has a variety of ways to determine the meaning of new words

Study Behaviors
1. Utilizes book parts
2. Knows how to skim, preview, and scan
3. Interprets visual aids correctly and appropriately
4. Takes effective class notes
5. Knows how to prepare for tests
6. Organizes information
7. Identifies useful sources for research
8. Understands how to critique research sources

Attitude and Interest
1. Chooses material for personal reading
2. Demonstrates enjoyment of reading
3. Has varied reading interests

KEY: 1=**Excellent (consistently)**
2=**Good (usually)**
3=**Average (sometimes)**
4=**Below average (seldom)**
5=**Poor (never)**

useful data by measuring what they choose to measure in the classroom context where students perform actual reading, writing, and learning tasks.

Assessment Activities Using Students' Writing

Writing is a powerful communication tool because it mirrors what we understand and think about certain ideas. Writing is also permanent, allowing us to reflect upon the

Teacher as Learner

THE ONE-SENTENCE SUMMARY

Your task is to summarize the five guidelines about assessment that we discussed at the beginning of the chapter. To facilitate your summary, we have provided you an outline and answered the first two questions:

Who?   content-area teachers

Do What?   assess

To What or Whom?

When?

Where?

How?

Why:

In sentence form, your summary: _____

_____

_____

meanings that we attempted to construct on paper or on a computer screen. Hence, it is logical to use writing activities as one way to assess students' comprehension of a text (Tovani, 2004). In this section, we will explain the one-sentence summary, an assessment activity with advantages for both students and teachers. Summary writing and other exploratory writing tasks such as the double-entry journal and learning log also capitalize on the power of writing and are found in Chapter 7.

One-Sentence Summary

The one-sentence summary assessment technique asks students to answer the questions of "Who does what to whom, when, where, how, and why" and then to synthesize that information into one long, meaningful sentence (Angelo, 1998). By requiring students to summarize a large amount of information into a concise statement, students are encouraged to think about important ideas and condense that information using their own words. Teachers, on the other hand, gain the advantage in that they have a set of summaries that will take relatively little time to skim and analyze. Moreover, these one-sentence summaries can be used across the content areas, whether it is to summarize historical events, the plots of stories, mechanical processes, or chemical reactions.

> In addition to one-sentence summaries, students can write lengthier summaries and place them in a learning log.

In order to understand how the one-sentence summary works, turn to the activity in the accompanying Teacher as Learner feature.

Learner Autobiographies

The **learner autobiography** is an effective method for discovering more about students' interests and belief systems (Gilles et al., 1988). The idea is that students need opportunities to examine their personal histories as readers, writers, and learners both in and out of school. By exploring their past, students might better understand their current approaches and beliefs about learning.

Honoring Diversity and Building Competence in the Content Classroom

Anna, a seventh grade math teacher, has developed a variety of techniques to uncover her students' beliefs and concerns about mathematics. She particularly likes the mathematics autobiography for her students with learning disabilities or severe math anxieties. At the beginning of the year her students make their first entry in their journal, using these directions:

Write your math autobiography. Think and write about the experiences you have had that relate to mathematics. These questions may be used as guides.

1. How did you feel about math in elementary school?
2. What are your experiences with effective and ineffective math teachers?
3. Is there one particular experience that stands out?
4. What were or are the attitudes of your family members toward math?
5. Was there a time when you liked math? Hated it? Why did you feel the way you did?
6. Did you have any special strategies for getting through (or around) math classes? Have these strategies worked for you? Why or why not?
7. Is there one particular experience you feel is responsible for your present feelings about math?

Anna tells us that she quickly learns a great deal of useful information about her students' attitudes, anxieties, and mathematical strategies from these learner autobiographies. She then uses classroom observations of her students, as well as their homework and test performance, to validate these self-reports. One of her students, Zena, is the author of the following entry that provided Anna with some useful insights:

When I was in elementary school I had a little trouble with adding and subtracting. I now have difficulties with my multiplication tables. Story problems really bother me so my mother tries to help me with these. I still am nervous about math, especially if the test is timed. In stores I always make sure they give me the correct change, but I have trouble figuring out the prices on clothes when they have sales.

If I have good teachers I do great, but when I have poor teachers I do bad. I had a teacher who didn't like me and tried her hardest to make me fail her class. My parents told me to just do the best I can and not to worry about how the teacher feels about me. My father and brothers are all good in math, so I am the only math dummy in our house. I like math when I understand it, but if I don't understand it, I don't like it. I usually am afraid to ask questions when I am lost—so please be patient with me.

Of course, the questions Anna posted could be modified to suit any context area. To help your students reflection their past experiences as language users and learners, we recommend the following approach:

1. In small groups, ask students to brainstorm their past as readers, writers, and learners. They should try to remember about a time, person, school year, class, event, assignment, textbook or other book, teacher, friend, relative, or the like.
2. After brainstorming, students should write about that event, time, or person that had a positive or negative impact on their thinking and feeling about literacy and learning.

3. Be sure students focus on two questions: What happened that influenced the way you presently read, write, and learn? How do you feel about that influence now?

4. Students should be allowed to write as much as necessary to describe and reflect fully on their past influences and experiences related to how they currently think about themselves as readers, writers, and learners.

5. After thinking and writing, students could be allowed to exchange their drafts with members of their brainstorm group for comment, questions, and feedback.

6. Volunteers could be asked to share their autobiographies.

7. We recommend that you also take part in this activity by writing and sharing your autobiography with the class.

If you feel uncomfortable using these procedures with the learner autobiography, you can ask students to write parts of the autobiography throughout the school year. For example, we know one economics teacher, Hector, who asks his students to write on an index card what they think it means to read, study, and learn in an economics course. He does this activity at the beginning of the class period the first week of classes. After collecting and reading the index cards, Hector discusses with his students his perceptions of what it means to read and learn in economics.

During the school year he follows up this initial assignment by asking students to write on other topics, such as the following:

This week I really liked _____ because _____; what really confused me this week was _____; and I would like to know more about _____ because _____.

These brief assignments on index cards have two advantages. First, students react positively to them because the required amount of writing seems less intimidating. For Hector, the index cards allow him to assess quickly what his students are thinking, learning, and feeling as they study economics.

The information gained from autobiographies and other writing tasks from your students can help you make instructional decisions, deconstruct maladaptive attitudes and beliefs about literacy, target certain activities and projects to particular students, and improve and support healthy attitudes about literacy and learning.

The Content-Area Inventory

The content-area inventory is extremely valuable because it asks students to demonstrate their thinking and learning processes as they read content-area textbooks or any written/oral material teachers may use in their courses (Rakes & Smith, 1992). The results of this type of assessment are far more informative than commercially prepared tests, we believe, because the assessment is based on material students will be using throughout the year. Hence, when teachers use the content-area inventory, they quickly discover which students will have difficulty reading and thinking about the assigned materials used in their course. Moreover, the information gained from a content-area inventory can help teachers identify skills that students will need to be taught to succeed in a particular content area.

Although the content-area inventory can be developed in a variety of ways, traditionally it has had two main sections. The first section usually measures students' skills in using book parts, using reference skills, and reading illustrative materials such as diagrams, tables, and charts. As students answer these questions, they are free to use

In some situations it is useful to share with students the trends that emerge from your assessment procedures.

all the parts of the textbook necessary. For the second section, the students read silently a lengthy excerpt from the textbook and then answer a series of questions with the textbook closed. These questions in the second section measure students' skills in understanding technical and general vocabulary words and comprehending what they have read. Music, art, and physical education teachers may wish to have students complete a listening task in this section rather than a reading task because listening skills are more crucial in these content areas.

To develop your own content-area inventory, use the following steps:

1. Identify the reading, writing, listening, and thinking skills essential to your course.

2. Select a typical excerpt from the textbook or material the class will probably be reading in your course. The selection need not include the entire unit or story, but it should be complete within itself and not dependent on other sections of the chapter. In most cases, two or three pages will provide a sufficient sample of students' behaviors and skills.

3. Read the selection and design at least 25 questions for the first and second sections. These questions should reflect the skills you intend to assess and should be open-ended so that students have to use their recall and writing skills to answer them.

4. To make sure you have created a reliable instrument with no ambiguities, ask a colleague to read the excerpt and answer your questions. Then debrief the experience with the colleague and revise accordingly.

5. Prepare a student answer sheet and a key, noting specific page references for discussion purposes after the testing is completed.

The content-area inventory in Figure 4.5 was developed by a driver's education department in a large metropolitan high school. The teachers had determined that it was important for students to be able to use their textbook effectively, to interpret illustrative materials, to understand technical vocabulary, and to identify and paraphrase the key ideas of what they had read. The driver's education teachers administered this assessment during the first week of class at the beginning of the school year. With the results, they were able to determine to what extent students could use their text as a resource and comprehend and process the textual information at a meaningful level. This knowledge led to specific instructional approaches such as cooperative grouping, direct process instruction in comprehension and concept knowledge, and training in designing and using study aids based on text and lecture information.

The teachers in this department have pointed out that it is important to explain the purposes of the content-area inventory to the students. That is, the students should do their best work because the information from the inventory will help in planning appropriate instruction. In addition, students should be told that they will be reading silently and then answering short-answer questions without the assistance of the textbook.

One ninth-grade team of teachers told us that they observe students as they read during their content-area inventory in order to note any who are demonstrating behaviors indicating frustration. For example, they make anecdotal notes of their students who appear to use excessive lip movements and who seem restless and generally inattentive. These behaviors may identify students who are experiencing difficulty comprehending what they are reading.

You can choose to grade the content-area inventory in class the next day, using that time to discuss the questions and answers with the students, or you can choose to grade the inventory outside of class. Once the content-area inventory has been

Figure 4.5   Content-Area Inventory for a Driver's Education Course

---

Using Book Parts

1. On what page does the unit (section) entitled "When You Are the Driver" begin?
2. On what pages can you find information on smoking and driving?
3. In what part of the book can you find the meaning of *kinetic energy?*

Understanding Graphs and Charts

1. According to the chart on page 61, what is the second most important cause of rural fatal accidents?
2. What does the chart on page 334 imply about the relationship between speed and fuel consumption?
3. Using the chart on page 302 and your own weight, determine what alcohol concentration in your blood would make you legally drunk.

Vocabulary in Context

1. What does the word *converse* mean in the following sentence?
   Do not take your eyes off the road to *converse* with a passenger.
2. What does the word *distracting* mean in the following sentence?
   He should avoid *distracting* the driver.
3. What does the word *enables* mean in the following sentence?
   It *enables* you to carry out your decisions promptly and in just the way you planned.

Summarizing and Sensing Key Ideas

1. Write a one-paragraph summary of the section entitled "A Defensive Driver's Decision Steps" on page 101. Be sure to include the key ideas and any other pertinent information. Use your own words as you write the summary.
2. Using your own words, state the key idea of the following paragraph:

   Not only does a defensive driver have to see all hazards and decide on his defense, he also has to act in time. A defensive driver's thinking shows in his actions as he drives. He anticipates hazards and covers the brake in case a stop is needed. He has both hands on the wheel so that he will be ready to act.

3. Write one or two sentences stating the key idea(s) of Chapter 18, "Controlling Your Emotions and Attitudes."

Creating Study Aids

1. Imagine that you will have a multiple-choice and short-answer test on Chapter 18. Organize the material in that chapter by taking notes on it or by creating some form of study aid.

---

graded, total the number of items each student answered correctly in both sections. Enter that total in your grade book and use the following criteria for interpretation:

80% of the items correct—The student will probably be able to use and comprehend the textbook or materials.

79–65%—The student will need some assistance in the form of teacher-directed strategies.

Below 65%—The student will require significant assistance because the textbook or material is too difficult.

Some teachers like to use a yellow highlighter to note in their grade book which students are finding the content material too difficult.

The content-area inventory will also help you see patterns in the skills for which students will need additional teaching and reinforcement. Rosa, a sixth-grade math teacher, developed a Classroom Summary Form to help her see these patterns. As illustrated in Figure 4.6, Rosa listed one class of students on the vertical axis. On the

Classroom summary forms can help teachers discern patterns in skill deficits that might have gone undetected had the students' answer sheets been filed in a folder.

Figure 4.6 Classroom Summary Form: Content-Area Inventory

Classroom Summary Form: Content-Area Inventory

Names	Using Parts of the Book					Following Directions				Understanding Math Symbols				Understanding Vocabulary				Noting Main Ideas				Drawing Conclusions				
	1	2	3	4	5	6	7	8	9	10	11	12	13	14	15	16	17	18	19	20	21	22	23	24	25	26
Jason	✓					✓	✓	✓		✓	✓	✓		✓		✓	✓	✓	✓	✓	✓	✓	✓	✓	✓	✓
Tamika		✓									✓			✓		✓					✓	✓	✓	✓	✓	✓
Jorge			✓								✓		✓		✓		✓		✓			✓	✓	✓	✓	✓
Michelle		✓	✓	✓		✓	✓	✓		✓	✓	✓	✓	✓	✓	✓						✓	✓	✓	✓	✓
Tyrone	✓			✓	✓					✓	✓			✓	✓	✓		✓	✓	✓		✓	✓	✓		
Gareth						✓				✓	✓			✓	✓	✓		✓	✓	✓				✓		
Avery	✓					✓	✓	✓	✓	✓	✓			✓		✓	✓									
Judd			✓			✓	✓	✓	✓	✓	✓			✓				✓	✓	✓		✓	✓	✓	✓	
Chanda		✓									✓			✓				✓	✓	✓		✓	✓	✓	✓	✓
Jennifer		✓																								

Place a check mark under the number of the question that was missed and alongside the name of the student who missed it.

horizontal axis she listed the reading skills she wants her students to master in her math course. Then she placed a check mark in the appropriate column for the students who missed more than half of the questions on a specific skill. For example, any student who missed three content-area inventory questions about Understanding Math Symbols received a check on the Classroom Summary Form. Rosa believes that this additional analysis helps her identify the reading and problem-solving skills that most of her students will need to be taught to succeed in mathematics. An added advantage of the content-area inventory is that it can be created for any course, regardless of whether you present the objectives and information to your students in written form or in the form of discussions, lectures, labs, and demonstrations.

Self-Report Inventories and Questionnaires

Inventories and questionnaires are the simplest and most direct way of acquiring information about students' skills, interests, attitudes, and belief systems. Although self-report instruments have been criticized because students tend to use the cues embedded in the questions to determine how they should answer in order to be judged competent (Garner, 1987), you can reduce these potential limitations by using a variety of techniques. For example, ask your students to describe what they do, and ask the question in two different ways to validate the consistency of their responses (e.g., Several questions in Figure 4.8 target students' abilities to understand what they read.)

Some inventories and questionnaires, such as the Interest Inventory I (Figure 4.7) and the Survey of Study Strategies (Figure 4.8), require students merely to read and place a check mark in the appropriate place. Other inventories, like the Interest Inventory II (Figure 4.9), ask students to write more elaborate answers to questions regarding their interests. The Writing Strategies Questionnaire in Figure 4.10 has been used by middle school and high school teachers to discover important past experiences their students have had with writing and how they think and feel about writing.

Although your students' attitudes about themselves as learners in your classroom may be difficult to uncover with one simple inventory or questionnaire, they are a starting point for acquiring more in-depth information about your students. The key is that opportunities are provided on a regular basis for students to explore and share their underlying beliefs and attitudes toward literacy and learning. Remember, the examples of inventories and questionnaires we have presented are merely suggestions of the kinds of issues and questions you may find relevant to your teaching situation. We urge you to use these suggestions to develop your own inventories that suit your particular need to know more about your students.

To avoid duplication of efforts and save time, colleagues who teach the same students should share the data that they gather from assessment instruments such as the Survey of Study Strategies or the Writing Strategies Questionnaire.

Figure 4.7   Interest Inventory I

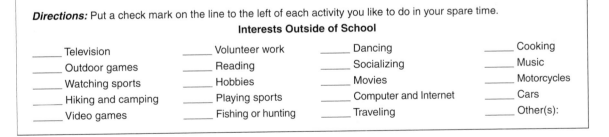

Directions: Put a check mark on the line to the left of each activity you like to do in your spare time.

Interests Outside of School

_____ Television	_____ Volunteer work	_____ Dancing	_____ Cooking
_____ Outdoor games	_____ Reading	_____ Socializing	_____ Music
_____ Watching sports	_____ Hobbies	_____ Movies	_____ Motorcycles
_____ Hiking and camping	_____ Playing sports	_____ Computer and Internet	_____ Cars
_____ Video games	_____ Fishing or hunting	_____ Traveling	_____ Other(s):

Figure 4.8 Survey of Study Strategies

Your Name: _____

Date: _____

SURVEY OF STUDY STRATEGIES

	Strongly Agree	Agree	Neutral	Disagree	Strongly Disagree
Time Management					
1. I put off my homework until the last minute.					
2. I plan regular times to study.					
3. I study less than an hour a day outside class.					
4. I cram for tests the night before the exam.					
5. I study with the radio, stereo, or TV on.					
6. I have a specified and quiet place for study.					
Remembering and Understanding					
1. I examine each of my textbooks for its overall organization.					
2. I look over a chapter before reading it in detail.					
3. I have to read a chapter several times before I understand it.					
4. I'm halfway through a chapter before I understand what it is about.					
5. I do not know which information in a chapter is important and which is not.					
6. My mind wanders to other things while I am reading an assignment.					
7. I have trouble remembering what I read.					
8. I try to set purposes and questions to be answered in my reading assignments.					
9. I find reading difficult because of the big words.					

	Strongly Agree	Agree	Neutral	Disagree	Strongly Disagree
Notetaking and Listening					
1. I take notes on my assigned readings.					
2. My notes on my textbooks are unorganized and messy.					
3. My notes don't make any sense to me.					
4. I don't know what to write down in my notes.					
5. I can't find information in my notes when I need it.					
6. I don't get much out of lectures.					
7. I find myself doodling or writing letters during lectures.					
8. I can't pick out important ideas from a lecture.					
9. I review my lecture notes as soon as possible after class.					
Test Taking and Test Preparation					
1. I study the wrong things for a test.					
2. I do not perform well on tests.					
3. I have mental blocks when I take a test.					
4. I know how to prepare for an essay exam.					
5. I have an effective strategy for approaching my upcoming exams.					
6. I know techniques for memorization.					
Reading Rate Strategies					
1. I hurry through all my assignments as quickly as I can.					
2. My reading speed is fast enough for my assignments.					
3. It takes me a long time to read any assignment.					
4. I can scan for specific information with little difficulty.					
5. I read most material at the same rate.					
6. I read as quickly as most people in my class.					

Figure 4.9 Interest Inventory II

Directions: Finish each sentence so that it tells something about you. You may write as much as you wish to finish each sentence.

1. After school I like to _____

2. On weekends I like to _____

3. _____ is my favorite TV show because _____

4. The kind of music I like is _____

5. When I graduate from high school, I want to _____

6. If I could go anywhere in the world, I'd go to _____ because _____

7. If I could take only one book with me on a trip to Mars, that book would
   be _____ because _____

8. I have seen the movie _____ and wish I could find a book similar to it because
   _____

9. I have reread the book _____ because _____

10. When I read the newspaper or a magazine, I like to read _____
    because _____

Figure 4.10 Writing Strategies Questionnaire

1. If you knew someone was having trouble writing, what would you do to help?

2. What would a teacher do to help that student?

3. If you were told you have to write an essay due in 1 week, what would you do to make sure it is done on time and is well written?

4. Think about someone you know who is a good writer. What makes that person a good writer?

5. What is the best advice you've ever been given about writing?

6. How did you learn to write? When? Who helped you?

7. What would help you improve your writing?

8. Do you think you're a good writer? Why or why not?

9. Why do people write? What are your reasons for writing?

10. Does the writing you do in school interest you? Why or why not?

In the next section we examine portfolio assessment and provide a variety of content-area examples.

Portfolio Assessment: Another Form of Authentic Assessment

Portfolios for instruction and assessment remain popular with teachers in nearly every field. We're sure most of you are by now quite familiar with the term and have, perhaps, even used portfolios in your own teaching. One of the best working definitions of a portfolio we have seen was developed at the Northwest Regional Educational Laboratory (Arter, 1990):

> A portfolio is a purposeful collection of student work that exhibits to the students (and/or others) the student's efforts, progress or achievement in (a) given area(s). This collection must include: (1) student participation in selection of portfolio content; (2) the criteria for selection; (3) the criteria for judging merit; and (4) evidence of student self-reflection. (p. 2)

Portfolios are a relatively recent and unique innovation in the areas of literacy and content learning (Kish, Sheehan, Cole, Struyk, & Kinder, 1997; Lockledge, 1997). Although in fields such as commercial arts, modeling, photography, and journalism, portfolios have been used for some time to showcase artistic and professional achievement (Tierney, Carter, & Desai, 1991), portfolio assessment in writing emerged only in the early 1980s with the work of Judy and Judy (1981) and Elbow and Belanoff (1986) in a first-year writing course. The growth in portfolio assessment in educational circles during the decade of the 1990s was remarkable. However, in recent years, the idealism of using portfolios to document literacy growth and content learning has diminished somewhat as the reality of their implementation has become clearer to measurement specialists (Koretz, 1998) and practitioners (Parsons, 1998; Simon & Forgette-Giroux, 2000) alike.

This is not to say that portfolio assessment is a flawed approach to teaching and documenting student achievement. On the contrary, portfolios offer teachers an excellent vehicle for meeting the calls by education experts for performance-based measures of reading and learning (Bol, Nunnery, Stephenson, & Mogge, 2000). Nonetheless, researchers and practitioners are now taking a more prudent and perhaps a more realistic view of the benefits and difficulties of portfolio assessment and teaching.

Why has the allure of portfolio assessment persisted in spite of the challenges it poses? Put simply, portfolios offer an assessment framework that reflects our current understanding of the process of literacy and content learning. We know, for instance, that:

A portfolio involves content area teachers supporting and students documenting authentic learning over time.

1. Learning takes place over time—portfolios are collections of learning demonstrations at many points during the learning cycle.

2. Learning occurs in multiple contexts—portfolios sample work from a variety of teaching/learning situations.

3. Effective learning occurs when learners are engaged in meaningful, purposeful learning activities—portfolio teaching/assessment provide teachers an ideal way to promote authentic learning.

4. Effective learning requires personal reflection—portfolios have self-reflection built into the process.

Advocates of the portfolio system suggest that the following five questions should be answered during the planning stage.

What Will the Portfolio Look Like?

All portfolios should have a physical structure as well as a conceptual structure. Physically, a portfolio may be structured chronologically, by subject area, or by style of work. Some individuals are even experimenting with electronic portfolios using the Internet and a special Web site. The conceptual structure refers to your goals for student learning. After identifying goals, you should decide the best ways to document students' work relative to the goals.

What Goes in the Portfolio?

To determine what goes in the portfolio, several related questions must be answered first: Who will evaluate the portfolios (parents, administrators, teachers)? What will these individuals want to know about student learning? Will portfolio samples document student growth that test scores cannot capture? Or will they further support the results of test scores? What is the best evidence that can be included in the portfolio to document student progress toward goals? Will students include their best work only, or will the portfolio contain a progressive record of student growth, or both? Will the portfolio include drafts, sketches, and ideas in unfinished as well as finished form?

Because portfolio assessment is authentic in that it represents genuine, meaningful learning activities in the classroom, work samples should come from the variety of daily and weekly assignments and projects in which students are engaged. If you are documenting the literacy progress of a seventh grader, for example, then his portfolio would likely contain samples from a writing folder, excerpts from journals and literature logs, early and final drafts of written reports and themes, and copies of assignments from various content areas that required reading and writing.

A 10th-grade biology student's portfolio might include lab reports documenting her ability to conduct an experiment and analyze and interpret the results, actual project hardware, photographs and logs from field work, and questions and hypotheses for further scientific inquiry.

A math student in the eighth grade might include in his portfolio documentation of his improving ability to understand increasingly complex story problems or algebraic equations, samples of computations, descriptions of certain mathematical properties, explanations of why certain mathematical processes work, and evidence of using math to solve everyday problems.

Jade, a high school physics teacher, requires her students to demonstrate mastery of each objective she hands out at the beginning of a new unit. Typical objectives might ask students to determine the average speed of an object in motion or explain changes in velocity and acceleration of a ball when it is thrown up and returns to the thrower. Students need to provide evidence in their portfolios of ways in which the critical physics concept under investigation reveals itself in the real world. Jade allows evidence such as:

- A written description and analysis of an experiment or demonstration conducted either in class or at home
- A written description and analysis of an article or a picture from a newspaper or magazine that shows the concept in action
- A photograph, graph, or drawing accompanied by an explanation of why it qualifies as evidence of the physics concept
- A digital video or CD-ROM of the concept in action accompanied by audio or written narration explaining it.

In addition to work samples, portfolios should contain reflective records. Vital to the process of learning through portfolio teaching/assessment, reflective records are documentation of students' personal reflections and self-evaluations. Students should study their portfolios at various points throughout the year, focusing on a single work, a set of revisions, evidence of growth in a particular area, or the portfolio materials as a whole. In reflecting on these samples, students should ask themselves questions such as the following:

Why did I select this piece of work?

Is this a sample of my best work?

Go to Web Resources for Chapter 4 at *http://www.prenhall.com/brozo* and look for authentic teaching and assessment in math.

What special strengths are reflected in this work?

What was particularly important to me during the process of completing this work?

What have I learned about (math, science, history, writing, etc.) from working on this piece or project?

If I could continue working on this piece or project, what would I do?

What particular skill or area of interest would I like to try out in future works?

Self-evaluative questions concerned solely with writing might include the following:

How has my writing changed since I wrote this?

If I revised this, what would I change?

What have I learned since I wrote this report that I would include in a follow-up report?

How did drafting and revising help me develop this essay?

How have I used this process to create other essays and reports?

> When students reflect upon and evaluate their products of learning, they are engaging in important processes involved in becoming successful, independent learners.

Answers to these questions in the form of comments and reflections then become part of the student's portfolio. Students should also date their work and comment briefly on why it was included in the portfolio.

You should also include brief notes about why certain samples of students' work were chosen. At the same time, you should keep personal and anecdotal records of students' work and progress based on classroom observations, inspection of portfolio samples, and conferences on the portfolio with students, parents, and other teachers. These records can complement students' reflective records. Given most middle school and high school teachers' severe time constraints, recordkeeping of this kind can often pose the biggest challenge in portfolio assessment.

Jenny, an 11th-grade English teacher, handles recordkeeping by writing brief comments on adhesive name-tag-sized labels from rolls she can hold in her hand. She then affixes her comments to the work sample in the portfolio. Comments on each label include identification of the sample, why the activity was completed, why the sample was included, and brief notes about what the sample shows about a student's progress toward achieving instructional and personal goals. Jenny has found her system to be more manageable than others she has tried, especially because she can also hold the roll of labels during classroom activities and make observational and anecdotal records on them quickly and unobtrusively. Later, these notes, too, can be placed in students' portfolios.

Many teachers have found the use of checklists and questionnaires essential for analyzing portfolios and keeping records on them. A math teacher uses the following set of questions to assess students' math work samples:

- What mathematics did the student learn?
- How does this relate to what the student has learned before?
- Of the math the student has done lately, what areas of strength and confidence are exhibited in this work?
- What aspects of this work reflect a lack of or incomplete understanding?

A seventh-grade history teacher uses an overall checklist such as the one shown in Figure 4.11 to keep track of his students' progress relative to portfolio criteria established in collaboration with his class.

Figure 4.11 Portfolio Criteria Checklist

Name	Project	Self-Evaluation	Reference Skills	Improvement

How and When Will Samples Be Selected?

Both teachers and students will benefit if there is a timeline with due dates for submitting possible items for a portfolio.

It's important to establish a clear and efficient system for selecting materials to go into and come out of the portfolio throughout the school year. Most teachers make these decisions at the end of a unit, grading period, semester, or school year. These are all good times to keep and add work samples that provide the clearest and most compelling evidence of student growth and achievement and, where appropriate, to eliminate other samples. Many teachers have found time lines helpful in making the entire class aware of when portfolio checks, revisions, and new entries will occur. In this way, students are brought into the decision-making process about what to include in their portfolios and further develop the ability to monitor their own progress. As stated, the more students are brought into the teaching-learning process, the more responsibility they take for their own learning.

The physics teacher noted earlier, Jade, schedules at least one day per week for her students to use class time to work on their portfolios. The time is spent talking with individual students about their portfolio evidence, monitoring peer sharing and brainstorming, and assisting students in setting up and photographing experiments that generate data for their objectives. To ensure efficient use of in-class portfolio time, Jade requests that students submit in writing at least a day in advance what they intend to photograph and any special arrangements or supplies that will be needed.

How Will Portfolios Be Evaluated?

It is essential that evaluative criteria be established relative to the learning goals you and your students set up beforehand. We recommend that the greater part of a student's portfolio be evaluated on the basis of growth, in terms of both academic achievement and self-knowledge, instead of on the basis of comparison with other students' work.

The evaluation process typical in most middle school and secondary classrooms or schools where portfolio assessment occurs looks like this:

1. The teacher discusses and negotiates goals of portfolios with students.
2. Teacher and students develop guidelines and procedures for showcasing portfolios.
3. A showcase portfolio is developed by students with assistance and feedback from peers.
4. Students develop self-evaluation comments and present their portfolio.
5. Students evaluate their portfolio according to criteria they help develop with the teacher (e.g., evidence of improvement, evidence of effort, quality of self-evaluation, range of projects, presentation, future goals).
6. The student submits his or her portfolio to the teacher, who reviews it along with the student's self-evaluations and peer criteria scores. A grade is awarded.
7. The portfolio is returned to the student.

Figure 4.12 illustrates a portfolio grade sheet (Krest, 1990) that can be used to record individual grades for each writing sample and portfolio grades for students' progress.

Jade, the physics teacher, gives her students a time line with due dates for submitting possible items to be included in their portfolios and for the final portfolio. She also gives her class two scoring rubrics: one for evaluating the overall portfolio, which counts toward 70% of students' final grades, and another for evaluating peers, worth 30% of the final grade.

About 2 weeks into a new unit, Jade conducts a portfolio preview to check students' progress. She writes comments on the portfolios in progress and returns them to students promptly so they can make necessary changes. Her students appreciate this feedback, and others who might be having difficulty find this deadline motivates them to get to work.

On the day final portfolios are due, Jade assigns students to groups of three to share their work. Students take turns presenting for about 5 minutes and then evaluate the portfolio presentations of their peers. Presenters explain how their portfolio documents support the unit's objectives while the peer reviewers, the other students in the group, listen, peruse, and evaluate. Jade moves about the room constantly to listen in on the presentations, occasionally asking a clarifying question or challenging an assertion, and to monitor group activity. When finished with their presentations, students hand in their portfolios, and Jade grades them according to an evaluation checklist that includes the critical documentation criteria. Evaluating portfolio previews and using a checklist limits Jade's grading time to 10 minutes or so per portfolio. This approach to evaluation has resulted in very few students questioning their grades.

How Can Portfolios Be Passed On?

As many teachers have noted, one of the special advantages of portfolio assessment is that the records of student progress can be passed on to succeeding teachers. In this way, the portfolio process promotes continuity in a student's education and collaboration among teachers at various grade levels. We suggest that as the school year draws to a close, you get together with other teachers at the next grade level to discuss their expectations and to find out what kind of information from portfolios would be most helpful to them in determining student accomplishment. In this process, you can make decisions about what to include or exclude before passing on portfolios. This is also a good time to have a conference with students about their portfolios in

Portfolios create excellent opportunities for teachers to have in-depth conversations with parents, with colleagues who teach the same students, and with colleagues who will be teaching the students in the future.

Figure 4.12 Portfolio Grade Sheet

Due Dates: _____
_____
_____

Name: _____
_____

	Date	Portfolio Grade	Sample	Comments

HP:*
MP:
LP:

HP:
MP:
LP:

HP:
MP:
LP:

HP:
MP:
LP:

_____

*HP = high priority; MP = middle priority; LP = low priority

terms of the kind of work they believe would best reflect their growth and achievement for next year's teacher.

A Study of Portfolio Assessment: What We Learned

We conducted a 6-month-long research project during which we worked with and observed an experienced high school French teacher, Jayne, as she implemented portfolio instruction and assessment (Moje, Brozo, & Haas, 1994). Our goal was to gain insights into the potential effectiveness of the strategy and the teacher-change process itself. Furthermore, we hoped to develop a better understanding of the realities of using portfolios in a secondary school classroom where an individual teacher was attempting to put ideas from the literature into practice.

One of the most important things we learned from this study was how teachers should begin their entry into portfolio assessment. Hence, we share the five principles that emerged from these data.

Start with Simple Activities

We suggest that you begin to use portfolios by asking students to complete simple, short writing activities. The activities can take any form. For example, in an advanced algebra class, students could make journal entries that allow them to reflect on their reasons for taking the advanced class, or they could prepare goal statements or biographies that link the class to their needs and interests. Starting with simple activities with foreseeable deadlines will allow students to work up slowly to more comprehensive projects.

Negotiate Firm Deadlines

When students are not used to the cognitive ambiguity and uncertainty of the portfolio process, it is important to help them set deadlines to keep them focused on their work. Despite the fact that the portfolio is designed to be an ongoing activity as opposed to a finite project, students who are accustomed to due dates may require your guidance in setting deadlines to get work completed and to meet project goals.

Encourage Students to Set Concrete Goals

Rather than expecting all students to be able to generate their own projects and samples for the portfolios, we suggest that you conduct conferences with students to create a plan of action. Such a plan would provide students with short-range goals that could be accomplished according to agreed-on deadlines, giving students a clearer view of their progress toward long-range goals. Plans of action can also provide students with a means of self-assessment because students would be able to evaluate both their progress toward meeting steps in the plan and the wisdom of the steps they chose.

Provide Initial Resources

Providing initial resources is critical in classrooms where portfolios will comprise project materials and samples. Students who are not used to conducting extended research that might require finding contacts, following up leads, making phone calls, and the like will need an initial source of specific information to get them started. These sources can help students sustain their research efforts while helping them learn valuable reference skills in the process.

Integrate Other Classroom Activities with the Portfolios

Many teachers feel the necessity of covering certain concepts that are integral to their content area by means of direct instruction to ensure that the concepts are learned. Jayne, for example, felt it was necessary to continue using the French text and to provide direct instruction in grammar and vocabulary. She understood that students might be unprepared for complete immersion in the portfolio project and consequently moved back and forth between the two types of teaching. The stark contrast, however, between the teacher-led instruction and the student-led portfolios created tension and ambiguity among students.

Although Jayne wanted the portfolio writings to be applications of the book lessons, students didn't readily make the connections on their own. On reflection, Jayne decided that she could have tied together activities in a variety of ways. For example, she could have demonstrated the grammar rules the students read about in the textbook by pointing out the uses of grammatical structures in their portfolio writing samples. Integration helps students see the utility and value of portfolios as an integral part of the learning process in content classrooms.

Perhaps the most outstanding benefit of portfolio assessment is that it invites students and teachers to be allies in the assessment process. When a portfolio culture is established, there is a good chance that students will become more concerned, thoughtful,

Content-area teachers should remember these five research-based guidelines when they begin their first learning portfolio endeavors.

and energetic learners. At the same time, teachers will find renewed enthusiasm for providing support and guidance of others' learning while growing as learners themselves.

Teachers' Grades: A Form of Assessment and Evaluation

Grades are another important assessment issue that teachers address on a daily basis. Some have suggested that most of the time teachers spend on assessment during the school year is for giving grades (Hargis, 1999). Although many of us might not prefer the traditional grading process, grading probably will always be with us. Mindful of this, we offer some thoughts and guidelines based on what we as teachers have done and what we have observed other teachers do when they grade. Most important, the uneasiness and ambiguities connected with grading can be lessened if we place grading in the proper context. That is, grading should only be a minor part of student assessment (McKeachie, 1994; Stiggins, 2005). The major part of assessment and evaluation is the qualitative information we communicate to students and parents on a regular basis. We will, however, examine both aspects of assessment—the quantitative grade we compute and the qualitative information we share.

Our observations and conversations with teachers have helped us develop some basic guidelines that make the quantitative aspects of assessment and evaluation easier.

1. *Make explicit how you will determine a course grade.* Teachers need to make explicit what factors are considered in determining students' course grades. That is, will the course grade be based solely on a student's performance or achievement on tests? Will a student's effort count? How much will homework count? What role will a student's participation in class discussion or a cooperative project play in computing a grade? We cannot answer these questions for you, but you should consider them all carefully and then make sure that students and parents understand at the beginning of the school year the factors that you include when you assign a grade.

2. *Make explicit how you will evaluate an assignment.* Although grading is subjective, it can become more objective if you tell students in advance what you expect from them in their work or assignments. The more information you give them on how you will evaluate a lab report on an experiment or a summary of an article, the more comfortable students will be about the grade they receive. Specifically, students need to know in advance the value of the assignment and what a quality product or performance looks like. If, for example, the assignment is to write a summary of a newspaper article, the students could be told the following:

   > The summary you will write is worth 20 points. Your summary should be at least six sentences in length and should include the author's thesis and an explanation of how the thesis was developed. A summary with these characteristics will receive the full 20 points.

   Other teachers like to use a checklist that specifies the evaluation criteria. As mentioned earlier, there are numerous examples of checklists and rubrics throughout this textbook.

3. *Award credit when students try out new strategies or approaches.* Students will not be risk takers if they realize there is an inherent penalty for trying out

new strategies or approaches. Hence, it is important to acknowledge these risks and award proper credit. If, for example, a student tries to develop a map for a chapter rather than outline it, as he usually does, provide the student with substantive feedback on his first attempts at mapping. If the map is not adequate because it overlooks some key points or interrelationships, still award as much credit as possible or allow the student to revise and modify the strategy before a grade is assigned.

4. *Include grading opportunities for both the process and the product.* Although college professors assign grades only for tests, quizzes, and the papers students write, middle school and high school teachers have the opportunity to include in their grading procedures more than just a final product. Sometimes more important than a product is the process of learning because it acknowledges students' attempts to construct meaning in a particular content area. Those attempts to construct meaning might include strategies to improve recall and understanding, journal entries about difficult concepts, classroom discussions about controversial ideas, or essay revisions.

Teachers also gave us several guidelines on how to communicate qualitative information to students about their performance in a particular content area. The following three guidelines seem particularly pertinent:

5. *Provide students with a variety of qualitative feedback.* The qualitative information connected with assessment and evaluation can occur in many forms. Most common are the comments teachers write on papers, the responses they offer to students' statements or queries, or the checklists they develop to describe the qualities of an activity or strategy that students have completed. The key, however, is to provide students with a variety of feedback in a format that makes sense to them.

6. *Provide students with timely feedback on their work.* We are sure you remember receiving a paper in one of your college writing classes that the professor took 3 weeks to grade. The grade at that point meant little because you had almost forgotten what you had written. Obviously, effective feedback must occur as soon as possible after students have completed a task if they are to improve their performance and learn.

> Students learn more when grades, a quantitative measure, are combined with a variety of qualitative measures that emphasize the thinking processes involved in learning.

Admittedly, this is difficult because middle school and high school teachers might receive work from more than 100 students a day. Grading students' summaries or providing them with information on their progress becomes very time intensive. However, substantive and timely feedback can be provided in a variety of ways (e.g., checklists, rubrics, the use of symbols to expedite the writing of your comments). Chapter 7 provides numerous examples of these.

Some teachers complain that students do not read the qualitative information they are given, but instead focus only on the grades awarded. One middle school language arts teacher told us that she circumvents that difficulty by not writing the letter grade on the assignment until the student writes a response to her comments. Once she reads the student's comments, she places a grade on the paper. Regardless of how it is handled, quick, substantive feedback is important to the learning process.

7. *Involve students in the evaluation process.* Interestingly, all of the qualitative information discussed thus far has emphasized the teacher's responsibility, not the student's responsibility or participation. Assessment, however, should include students in self-reflection and evaluation activities. As we

mentioned in the guidelines and in the section about portfolios, students should play an active role in setting goals and evaluating whether they have reached those goals. When students are involved in evaluating their work in a content area, they are more likely to link their performance with effort rather than ascribe it to luck or chance or the whims of a teacher (Graham, 2005).

Assessing Textbooks in Relationship to Your Students

Most content-area teachers, especially those new to a school system, inherit the textbook they will be using with their students. They begin the school year hoping that this textbook will include the most pertinent and recent information and that their students will find the ideas easy to follow, yet engaging. Unfortunately, this perfect textbook scenario rarely occurs. In fact, there probably is no such thing as a perfect textbook, but we know from the research that some textbooks are more effective or considerate of the reader than others. Hence, it is important to assess the qualities of a considerate textbook because you will be asked several times during your career to make a recommendation for an upcoming textbook adoption. Moreover, it is important for you to assess your students' interactions with that textbook. In order to address these two critical issues, we will examine three techniques: readability formulas, evaluation scales and checklists, and the cloze procedure.

> Content-area inventories are also an excellent way to assess the appropriateness of your textbooks in relationship to your students.

Using Readability Formulas

The readability of printed material has been interpreted to mean that challenging texts are ones that have long sentences and difficult, long words. Conversely, easy materials are those with shorter sentences and shorter words. Readability formulas such as Fry's (1968) use these easily quantifiable indices to yield either a grade level or a score similar to a reading level. Many textbook writers, editors, and publishers have attempted to lower the reading level of their textbooks by asking the authors to use short, simple sentences and fewer multisyllable words. The goal, of course, is to sell more books because school districts want "readable" materials.

The example in the accompanying Teacher as Learner feature demonstrates what happens when authors are asked to rewrite something using readability indices. Before reading further, take a break to complete the activity on p. 121.

More than likely, you answered that Version Two was more considerate because the author explained in detail how changes in light affect plants. You could probably almost visualize what happens as night falls from the author's description. Which version was "easier" according to a readability formula? Version One was "easier" because it contained only 5 sentences, 35 words, and 52 syllables. A quick check on Version Two would reveal that it contained only 4 sentences, more words per sentence, and far more multisyllable words than Version One. In the first version, the author's use of short, simple sentences often obscured the relationships among the ideas in the text. In the second version, the author echoed words that ended the previous sentence by placing them at or near the beginning of the following sentence (e.g., *leaf openings*) and inserted words that tied together the text and made the relationships more obvious (e.g., *consequently*). Those features in Version Two are features of an effective considerate textbook (Alexander & Jetton, 2000).

> Fry's readability formula is one of many formulas for determining a textbook's appropriateness.

Many middle school and secondary textbooks are similar to Version One and have a high degree of inconsiderateness. They contain misleading titles and subtitles,

Teacher as Learner

EVALUATING A TEXT'S CONSIDERATENESS

The two paragraphs that follow provide explanations of why leaf openings close. Which one best explains the concept and is more considerate? Which one is easier according to a formula such as Fry's?

Version One

In the evening, the light fades. Photosynthesis slows down. The amount of carbon dioxide in the air space builds up again. This buildup of carbon dioxide makes the guard cells relax. The openings are closed.

Version Two

The fading light of evening causes photosynthesis to slow down. A plant's ability to "breathe," however, does not depend on light and thus continues to produce carbon dioxide. The carbon dioxide in the air spaces builds up again, which makes the guard cells relax. The relaxing of the guard cells closes the leaf openings. Consequently, the leaf openings close in the evening as photosynthesis slows down. (Anderson & Armbruster, 1984, p. 206)

In your opinion, which version best explained the concept of why leaf openings close? _____

lack explicit main ideas, omit crucial information, contain contradictory information, and are ambiguous. In order to address these substantive textbook qualities that are overlooked by readability formulas, many content-area teachers choose to use an evaluation scale or checklist.

Using Evaluation Scales or Checklists

Content-area teachers can use evaluation scales or checklists to assess and evaluate the appropriateness of a textbook, whether it is one presently being used or one being considered for adoption. Although these scales or checklists probably contain many of the characteristics considered important by teachers, they are particularly advantageous in that they are inclusive and provide a systematic procedure for a department to review materials.

Theresa, a ninth-grade health education teacher, was provided the opportunity to select a new textbook for the upcoming school year. Her department chairperson gave her a checklist (see Figure 4.13) to use in judging the textbooks sent to her and her colleagues from the various publishers. As you can tell from a quick perusal of the checklist, it incorporates characteristics that focus on the understandability of a text and the external and internal organizational features of a text. Theresa found the checklist extremely helpful in reviewing the many textbooks because she had specific characteristics to evaluate that went beyond the mere coverage of content in the field of health. Theresa and her colleagues selected the text they believed would best maximize the learning potential of their students. Admittedly, they had hoped to find the perfect health education textbook but soon realized that such a book did not exist. Rather, they decided to provide supplementary sources for their students on topics they wished to stress that were not contained in the textbook and to use specific comprehension-building strategies to facilitate their struggling readers' understanding of the concepts.

Throughout this text you will find research-based, teacher-proven ideas to help overcome the potential difficulties posed by an inconsiderate content-area textbook.

Figure 4.13 Criteria for Measuring a Textbook's Suitability or Appropriateness

Directions: Check the column that best describes the textbook's use of these characteristics that promote active and successful learning.

	Excellent	Good	Poor
1. Difficult new vocabulary words are highlighted, italicized, underlined, or defined in the margins.	_____	_____	_____
2. Concepts are presented clearly in relatively direct and understandable sentences.	_____	_____	_____
3. The chapter's main idea(s) or purposes for reading are explicitly stated at the beginning.	_____	_____	_____
4. The authors present a list of objectives, questions, or organizational structure to guide the students while reading/studying.	_____	_____	_____
5. The authors use explicit and appropriate words to signal the text's structure and organization (e.g., *on the other hand*).	_____	_____	_____
6. The authors use practical real-life situations, examples, or analogies that students can relate to and in which they have an interest.	_____	_____	_____
7. The authors use boldface headings and subheadings that are logical to the concepts being discussed and useful to students with little or no prior knowledge.	_____	_____	_____
8. The authors internally summarize key concepts and present useful summaries at the end of the chapter.	_____	_____	_____
9. The authors help students use appropriate prior knowledge by reviewing or reminding readers of previously learned concepts (e.g., *in the last chapter we discussed . . .*).	_____	_____	_____
10. The text includes quotations from primary sources and authorities to support and add interest.	_____	_____	_____
11. When there are questions at the end of the chapter, different kinds (e.g., true/false) of questions are supplied that require higher levels of thinking (e.g., on my own) and responses using students' own words.	_____	_____	_____
12. The table of contents shows a logical development of the subject matter.	_____	_____	_____
13. Captions under graphs, tables, diagrams, and pictures are clearly written.	_____	_____	_____
14. Math and science problem examples match the concepts and steps previously discussed.	_____	_____	_____
15. The authors inform the students when information contained in graphs, tables, or diagrams is not also contained in the text.	_____	_____	_____
16. When the text refers to a graph or table, that aid is on the same page as the textual reference.	_____	_____	_____
17. The authors suggest other resources and activities for students motivated to explore the area or for students who have difficulties with specific objectives or specific tasks.	_____	_____	_____

Using the Cloze Procedure

Unlike readability formulas and checklists, the cloze procedure provides content-area teachers feedback about their textbooks in relationship to their students. The cloze procedure is based upon the psychological principle that individuals attempt to complete a familiar but not-quite-finished pattern. Although the procedure was originally developed by Taylor (1953) as a measure of readability, the cloze can also predict how efficiently students can read from a particular text or selection. In the cloze procedure, words are systematically deleted, usually every fifth word. Students' ability to correctly supply the missing words is supposedly indicative of their potential to read and understand the targeted material.

To create a cloze procedure, you should identify a representative piece of text that makes sense on its own and is reasonably complete. Many authorities recommend that you select approximately 300 words for your targeted passage, thus providing 50 deleted words and blanks. However, others point out that struggling readers may find such a task frustrating, so you may wish to reduce the length of the passage and the number of blanks (Alvermann & Phelps, 2005). Leave the first and last sentence intact and begin deleting every fifth word. Carefully type the passage, double-spacing between the lines. Number each blank, leaving a uniform length so you do not unintentionally provide clues about the word deleted.

Before explaining the administration, scoring, and interpretation of the cloze procedure, you might wish to complete the one in the accompanying Teacher as Learner feature taken from Chapter 9 of this textbook (see p. 124). Because the deleted words follow the cloze passage, cover them while you read and fill in the blanks.

Content-area teachers should use the following instructions for administering, scoring, and interpreting their cloze passages.

Administering

1. Provide students with instructions and sample exercises before asking them to complete the actual cloze procedure. The oral instructions may be similar to the following:

   a. On the board is an example of the kind of questions you will be answering. Your job is to determine what word was left out of each space and to write that word in that space.

   Example: Please turn off the _____ before you leave the room.

   What was the word that was deleted?

   b. Before you try to fill in the blanks on your exercise, read through the entire selection. This will help you to guess the correct word.

   c. Write only one word in each space. Spelling does not count. Try to fill every blank and do not be afraid to guess. You may skip blanks and come back to them later.

   d. After you have filled in the blanks, read over the selection to see if the passage makes some sense.

2. There is no time limit to the cloze procedure.

Scoring

1. Count as correct every exact word a student supplies.

2. Determine the percentage of exact word replacements. For example, if you have 50 blanks, multiply the total correct by 2. If, however, you have fewer

Teachers will gather more reliable data from the cloze procedure when they make sure they follow all these administrative steps.

Teacher as Learner

THE CLOZE PROCEDURE

Students' Self-Knowledge

Students with low self-efficacy are more likely to attribute their failures to external factors (e.g., the test was not fair) or to a fixed ability that they cannot change. For example, it is _____ (1) atypical to hear adolescents _____ (2) something like this: "I _____ (3) not good at math _____ (4) never will be." As _____ (5) result, these students decide _____ (6) give up before they _____ (7) enter the classroom or _____ (8) the first setback or _____ (9). Interestingly, you will find _____ (10) students' self-efficacy varies _____ (11) the content areas. For _____, (12) a student may have _____ (13) strong sense of self-_____ (14) in a history course _____ (15) feel totally overwhelmed or _____ (16) in an English course _____ (17) requires her to write _____ (18) or creative responses to _____ (19) she reads. Students' sense of self-efficacy can also vary according to the context in which they are placed.

Deleted Words:

1. not	8. at	15. but
2. say	9. challenge	16. frustrated
3. am	10. that	17. that
4. and	11. across	18. critical
5. a	12. example	19. what
6. to	13. a	
7. even	14. efficacy	

blanks in your cloze, you will need to change that multiplier (e.g., if a student correctly replaced 18 words from a total possible of 25 deleted words, his score would be calculated in this way: 18 times 4 = 72%).

Interpreting

1. Scores above 60% indicate that the students can read and understand the targeted material with ease. Some individuals refer to this as the student's independent level of reading.

2. Scores between 40% and 60% indicate that the passage is on the students' instructional level. In other words, students can read the textbook if they receive direct assistance from the teacher (e.g., preteaching, comprehension strategies).

3. Scores below 40% indicate that students will find the material too difficult to understand. In other words, the text is at their frustrational level.

To maximize students' reading and learning, a text should be on their independent or instructional level.

When scoring these cloze procedures teachers often wonder whether they should count as correct a synonym that is closely related to the deleted word (e.g., *instance* instead of *example*). If you are using the cloze procedure as an instructional tool, the synonyms could be counted as correct. However, to maintain the reliability of the cloze procedure and to maintain objectivity and consistency, it is best to count as correct only the exact word deleted. Given that students can receive a score of 60% and still be functioning at the independent level of reading, this policy is generous and makes considerable sense.

The cloze procedure is one additional tool that will help you assess the considerateness of your textbook. Moreover, it can be used as an initial screening device at the beginning of the school year to highlight students who may have reading difficulties (i.e., those scoring below 40%). Having said that, we should also point out that the cloze procedure is only a rough estimate and should be used in conjunction with other assessment tools. That is, teachers should develop a textbook assessment plan that includes a checklist, the cloze procedure, and the content-area inventory. With such a comprehensive plan, content-area teachers have multiple data sources about their students in relationship to the materials they will be assigning them. Multiple data sources are especially important if you want valid and reliable information.

CASE STUDY REVISITED

Selma, the seventh-grade science teacher introduced in the case study in the beginning of the chapter, wanted to find a classroom-based assessment strategy of her students' ability to understand their science text. Now that you have read about and explored a variety of assessment approaches in this chapter, reflect again on Selma concerns and generate a few suggestions for meeting her assessment needs. Afterward, read about what she actually did to assess her students.

Mindful of the problems students have in thinking like writers, Selma decided to combine some of the suggestions she obtained from an in-service workshop with her own ideas. From the workshop she learned how to construct a content-area inventory using the materials from her course. The excerpt she selected was about rocks, a typical reading assignment that required students to identify types and characteristics as well as similarities and differences. Because Selma wanted to assess how well students could read to determine these writing patterns, her content-area inventory contained many items like the following:

1. According to the paragraphs you have just read, what are two types of igneous rocks?

2. According to the paragraphs you have just read, what are some characteristics of these types of rocks? Name one characteristic of each rock.

3. According to the paragraphs you have just read, how are these types of rock different?

4. What words or phrases did the author use to cue you that the rocks were different in some ways? One such phrase was *very different*. What was the other?

In addition to the information she gained about her students from the content-area inventory, Selma carefully observes her students in a variety of settings.

continued

Before writing your suggestions for Selma, go to *http:www.prenhall. com/brozo*, select Chapter 4, then click on Chapter Review Questions to check your understanding of the material.

CASE STUDY REVISITED (CONTINUED)

For example, she pays special attention to the following signals that her students understand text organization and structure:

- As students are summarizing or discussing an assignment, she determines whether they are using the author's organizational structures as their ideas or comments unfold.
- When students are writing responses to text reading, she looks for indications that they are using text structure knowledge as a framework for developing their writing.

Selma has also found useful a classroom activity that her students really enjoy. She gives her students articles that have been cut up at paragraph boundaries and scrambled and tells them that they will be reading a text that is mixed up. Working in pairs, students are asked to put the article back together in the original fashion. While doing so, they are asked to think out loud and explain their decisions during the text reconstruction process to their partners. Selma moves about the room and listens to each pair of students to monitor their progress and provide assistance through modeling or questioning. She looks for evidence that her students grasp the problem-solution pattern employed by the author. Her evidence comes from students' comments and statements such as these:

Number 5 has to go near the end because it sounds like a summary of the problems with deforestation in developing countries.

By combining text reconstruction activities with the content-area inventory and classroom observations, Selma has learned a lot about her students and why they perform the way they do. This information has helped her realize the importance of using a variety of strategies to help her students understand important concepts in science.

Looking Backward, Looking Forward

Assessment of literacy and content learning is a process of becoming informed about teaching and learning to improve instruction for the teacher and increase self-knowledge for students. In this chapter we emphasized the importance of authentic assessments that integrate process and content and help make the boundary between assessment and teaching nearly indistinguishable. Because content-area teachers need a variety of practical assessment activities and instruments, we described how teachers have created assignment-based assessment strategies, employed portfolio approaches, and used other methods, such as classroom observations during teachable moments, students' writing, checklists, and the content-area inventory.

In this chapter we also made clear the importance of middle and secondary school teachers finding ways to take advantage of standardized testing and make it more meaningful. When results from standardized reading and achievement tests heighten teachers' sensitivity to the needs of struggling readers and learners, then curricular and instructional changes might be made to improve learning progress for these students.

Finally, we stressed that when process assessment of literacy is integrated within the content classroom, the result is that assessment and teaching become nearly indistinguishable. Therefore, throughout this book we discuss strategies in relation to how they can be used to assess and teach particular literacy/learning processes. For example, in Chapter 6 we describe vocabulary strategies that have built-in assessments for the teacher and self-assessment for the student. And in Chapter 7, we demonstrate how students' writing can be used in assessment and development of comprehension. Many of the strategies for teaching with trade literature, developed in Chapter 8, can be used to reveal what students are learning. In Chapter 9, strategies for developing text study processes are interwoven with teacher assessment and self-assessments of these strategies.

References

Ainley, M., Hidi, D., & Berndorff, D. (2002). Interest, learning, and the psychological processes that mediate their relationship. *Journal of Educational Psychology, 94*, 545–561.

Alexander, P., & Jetton, T. (2000). Learning from text: A multidimensional and developmental perspective. In M. Kamil, P. Mosenthal, P. D. Pearson, & R. Barr (Eds.), *Handbook of reading research* (Vol. 3). Mahwah, NJ: Lawrence Erlbaum Associates.

Alvermann, D. E., & Phelps, S. F. (2005). *Content reading and literacy: Succeeding in today's diverse classrooms.* Boston: Pearson.

Anderson, T. H., & Armbruster, B.B. (1984). Content area textbooks. In R. Anderson, J. Osborn, & R. Tierney (Eds.), *Learning to read in American schools: Basal readers and context texts.* Hillsdale, NJ: Erlbaum.

Angelo, T. A. (1998). *Classroom assessment and research: An update on uses, approaches, and research findings.* San Francisco: Jossey-Bass.

Arter, J. (1990). *Using portfolios in instruction and assessment.* Portland, OR: Northwest Regional Educational Laboratory.

Avery, P., Carmichael-Tanaka, D., Kunze, J., & Kouneski, N. (2000). Writing about immigration: Authentic assessment for U.S. history students. *Social Education, 64*, 372–375.

Bissex, G. (1980). *Gyns at work: A child learns to write and read.* Cambridge, MA: Harvard University Press.

Bol, L., Nunnery, J., Stephenson, P., & Mogge, K. (2000). Changes in teachers' assessment practices in the new American schools restructuring models. *Teaching and Change, 7*, 127–146.

Brophy, J. (1998). *Motivating students to learn.* Boston: McGraw-Hill.

Clay, M. (1975). *What did I write?* Auckland, New Zealand: Heinemann.

Cleary, T. J., & Zimmerman, B. J. (2004). Self-regulation empowerment program: A school-wide program to enhance self-regulation and self-motivational cycles of learning. *Psychology in the Schools, 41,* 537–550.

Conley, M., & Hinchman, K. (2004). No Child Left Behind: What it means for U.S. adolescents and what we can do about it. *Journal of Adolescent and Adult Literacy, 48,* 42–50.

Cronbach, L. J. (1960). *Essentials of psychological testing* (3rd ed). New York: Harper & Row.

Elbow, P., & Belanoff, P. (1986). Portfolios as a substitute for proficiency examinations. *College Composition and Communication, 37,* 336–339.

Frey, N. & Hiebert, E. H. (2003). Teacher-based assessment of literacy learning. In J. Flood, D. Lapp, J. Squire, & J. Jensen (Eds.), *Handbook of research on teaching the English language arts* (Vol. 2, pp. 608–618). Mahwah, NJ: Lawrence Erlbaum Associates.

Fry, E. G. (1968). A readability formula that saves time. *Journal of Reading, 11,* 513–516, 575–578.

Garner, R. (1987). *Metacognition and reading comprehension.* Norwood, NJ: Ablex.

Gee, J. P. (2000). Discourse and sociocultural studies in reading. In M. Kamil, P. Mosenthal, P. D. Pearson, & R. Barr (Eds.), *Handbook of reading research* (Vol. 3). Mahwah, NJ: Lawrence Erlbaum Associates.

Gilles, C., Bixby, M., Crowley, P., Crenshaw, S., Henrich, M., Reynolds, F., & Pyle, D. (1988). *Whole language strategies for secondary students.* New York: Richard C. Owen.

Goodman, Y. (2003). Informal methods of evaluation. In J. Flood, D. Lapp, J. Squire, & J. Jensen (Eds.), *Handbook of research on teaching the English language arts* (Vol. 2, pp. 600–607). Mahwah, NJ: Lawrence Erlbaum Associates.

Graham, S. (2005). Writing. In P. Alexander & P. Winne (Eds.), *Handbook of educational psychology*. Mahwah, NJ: Lawrence Erlbaum Associates.

Hargis, C. (1999). *Teaching and testing in reading: A practical guide for teachers and parents*. Springfield, IL: Charles C. Thomas.

Hofer, B. K. (2004). Epistemological understanding as a metacognitive process: Thinking aloud during online searching. *Educational Psychologist, 39,* 43–55.

Hubbard, B. P., & Simpson, M. L. (2003). Developing self-regulated learners: Putting theory into practice. *Reading Research and Instruction, 42,* 62–89.

Judy, S., & Judy, S. (1981). *An introduction to the teaching of writing*. New York: Wiley.

Kish, C., Sheehan, J., Cole, K., Struyk, R., & Kinder, D. (1997). Portfolios in the classroom: A vehicle for developing reflective thinking. *The High School Journal, 80,* 254–260.

Koretz, D. (1998). Large-scale portfolio assessments in the US: Evidence pertaining to the quality of measurement. *Assessment in Education, 5,* 309–334.

Krest, M. (1990). Adapting the portfolio to meet student needs. *English Journal, 79,* 29–34.

Lockledge, A. (1997). Portfolio assessment in middle-school and high-school social studies classrooms. *The Social Studies, 88,* 65–69.

McKeachie, W. J. (1994). *Teaching tips* (9th ed.). Lexington, MA: D. C. Heath.

Moje, W., Brozo, W. G., & Haas, J. (1994). Portfolios in a high school classroom: Challenges to change. *Reading Research and Instruction, 33,* 275–292.

Parsons, J. (1998). Portfolio assessment: Let us proceed with caution. *Adult Learning, 9,* 28–30.

Rakes, T. A., & Smith, L. J. (1992). Assessing reading skills in the content areas. In E. K. Dishner, T. W. Bean, J. E. Readence, & D. W. Moore (Eds.), *Reading in the content areas: Improving*

classroom instruction. Dubuque, IA: Kendall/Hunt.

Readence, J. E., & Moore, D. W. (1983). Why questions? A historical perspective on standardized reading comprehension tests. *Journal of Reading, 26,* 306–313.

Reading yardsticks. (1981). Level 14—Grade 8. Chicago: Riverside.

Reutzel, D. R., & Cooter, R. B. (2003). *Strategies for reading assessment and instruction* (2nd ed). Upper Saddle River, NJ: Merrill/Prentice Hall.

Schommer, M. (1994). An emerging conceptualization of epistemological beliefs and their role in learning. In R. Garner & P. A. Alexander (Eds.), *Beliefs about text and instruction with text*. Hillsdale, NJ: Lawrence Erlbaum Associates.

Schommer-Atkins, M. (2002, April). Personal epistemology: Conflicts and consensus in an emerging area of inquiry. Paper presented at the American Educational Research Association's Annual Meeting, New Orleans, LA.

Simon, M., & Forgette-Giroux, R. (2000). Impact of a content selection framework on portfolio assessment at the classroom level. *Assessment in Education, 7,* 83–101.

Stiggins, R. (2005). *Student-involved assessment for learning*. Upper Saddle River, NJ: Pearson.

Taylor, W. L. (1953). Cloze procedure: A new tool for measuring readability. *Journalism Quarterly, 30,* 415–433.

Tierney, R., Carter, M., & Desai, L. (1991). *Portfolio assessment in the reading-writing classroom*. Norwood, MA: Christopher Gordon.

Tovani, C. (2004). *Do I really have to teach reading?* Portland, ME: Stenhouse Publishers.

Unrau, N. (2004). *Content area reading and writing: Fostering literacies in middle and high school cultures*. Upper Saddle River, NJ: Pearson.

William, D. (2000). Education: The meanings and consequences of educational assessments. *The Critical Quarterly, 42,* 105–127.

chapter 5

Creating Motivating Contexts for Literacy and Learning

Anticipation Guide

Directions: Read each statement carefully and decide whether you agree or disagree with it, placing a check mark in the appropriate *Before Reading* column. When you have finished reading and studying the chapter, return to the guide and decide whether your anticipations need to be changed by placing a check mark in the appropriate *After Reading* column.

	Before Reading		After Reading	
	Agree	*Disagree*	*Agree*	*Disagree*
1. The skill is more important than the will to read and learn.	_____	_____	_____	_____
2. Motivation can be isolated from social contexts.	_____	_____	_____	_____
3. Youth who are engaged readers are higher achievers in all subjects.	_____	_____	_____	_____
4. High reading engagement cannot make up for other typical risk factors.	_____	_____	_____	_____
5. Youth are often unmotivated due to a disconnection between academic learning and their everyday experiences.	_____	_____	_____	_____
6. If youth bring an interest in a topic to the classroom, additional motivational practices are not needed.	_____	_____	_____	_____

![Chapter Principle icon]

Chapter Principle: Engage and Sustain Effort in Reading, Writing, and Thinking

This principle is concerned with the disciplinary practices of teachers that motivate youth by giving energy and direction to their learning. Content-area teachers who plan instruction with this principle as a guide are always seeking ways of making learning interesting and worthwhile. They elicit input from their students and use it to create learning contexts that maximize participation in reading, writing, and thinking. They always account for the dimension of engagement when thinking about youths' classroom experiences. The strategies and activities presented in this chapter demonstrate the importance of engagement in youth's academic lives.

*W*ithin the past 10 years, volumes have been written about student motivation and engagement and countless workshops and conference presentations devoted to the topic. Yet, virtually all the teachers we meet, as well as teachers from across the nation (O'Flahavan, Gambrell, Guthrie, Stahl, & Alvermann, 1992), feel they need more information and strategies to motivate adolescents to read and learn. And there is evidence that justifies this need. In Chapter 1, we noted the well-documented slump in achievement and motivation during the upper-elementary and middle school years. Curiously, this phenomenon is not restricted to the United States. Youth from around the globe exhibit a similar decline in performance and interest as they move from primary to secondary school (Anderman, Maehr, & Midgley, 1999; Brozo, 2005b). Some of our best thinkers and researchers in youth literacy have proposed that this decline in academic motivation results from a disjuncture between adolescents' need for content and learning experiences that are accessible and relevant, on the one hand, and traditional school-related reading, writing, and disciplinary practices, on the other (c.f., Alvermann, 2003; Fecho, 2004).

The critical point here is that motivation cannot be detached from social contexts, such as classrooms, families, and communities. An individual youth's motivation to read and learn is linked closely to the social worlds that are part of that youth's daily life. And while teachers may have little influence on the social worlds youth navigate outside of school, they have a great deal of control over the arrangement of conditions within the classroom that can foster positive academic motivation for adolescents.

Not only should youth engage in interesting experiences related to *what* they learn but, more important, *why* the content is being discussed and studied. To tell students "You must learn this because it's in our curriculum guide" may be the truth, but does little to motivate youth to become active knowledge seekers. Instead, by linking the learning of disciplinary content to students' own needs, issues, concerns, and interests inside and outside of school, we increase engagement while helping them discover real-world purposes for learning (Edwards, 2001). Greenleaf, Jimenez, and Roller (2002) put it this way, "Only when adolescents read material that is important to them will they understand why one uses . . . reading strategies and skills, [and] only if adolescents understand why they might want to use these skills will they master them and use them" (p. 490). Speaking about how reading, learning, and motivation are tied to functionality, purpose, and meaningfulness echoes an important theme in our definition of comprehension from Chapter 3. Simply put, teachers who work with youth must look to students' own reasons to learn as the source for motivational strategies.

Evidence for the benefits of engaged learning is quite compelling. We know from correlational data derived from the National Assessment of Educational Progress (NAEP) that adolescents who identified themselves as being interested in reading not only achieved better scores on the NAEP but had better high school grade point averages than their less interested peers (Donahue, Daane, & Grigg, 2003). Even more convincing are data derived from the Programme for International Student Assessment, or PISA, a global study of reading literacy for 15-year-olds, in which the United States participates (see Figure 5.1). PISA youth from the lowest

Go to *http://www. prenhall.com/brozo,* select Chapter 5, then click on Chapter Objectives to provide a focus for your reading.

Go to Web Resources for Chapter 5 at *http://www. prenhall.com/brozo,* and look for PISA.

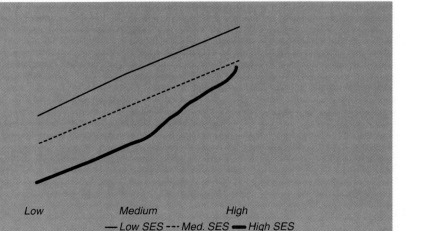

Figure 5.1
Reading Performance and Socioeconomic Background by Level of Reading Engagement for 15-Year-Olds on PISA

socioeconomic status (SES) who were highly engaged readers performed as well on the assessment as youth from the middle-SES group and cut in half the disparity between themselves and their high-SES peers (Organization for Economic Cooperation and Development, 2001). In other words, highly motivated youth made up for low family income and parents' limited educational attainment, two common risk factors in the school lives of adolescents. This should be ground-shaking news, because it strongly suggests that if we can keep students engaged in reading and learning they may be able to overcome what might otherwise be insuperable barriers to academic success.

Because capturing students' imaginations for reading and learning and sustaining engagement is so vital to the academic future of all youths, we put our entire focus in this chapter on strategies and activities secondary teachers can integrate into their instructional practices that increase student motivation. The practices we present of actual middle and secondary school teachers adapting existing strategies or engaging students in creative activities of their own design can all be supported by sound theories of interest and motivation (Bergin, 1999; Guthrie & Davis, 2003; Pintrich & Schunk, 2001; Volet & Jarvela, 2002).

We will begin by drawing from motivational theory several important guidelines for teaching. These will be followed by descriptions of innovative motivational practices and ways teachers have applied them in their particular classroom contexts. Because learning at the middle and secondary school level must occur as a result of exposure to a variety of information sources, we describe strategies that can apply equally effectively to (a) chapters from textbooks, (b) newspapers and popular magazines, (c) novels, (d) guest speakers, (e) videos, (f) experiments, (g) field trips (h) discussions or debates, (i) computer-based learning, activities or (j) lectures. We hope the guidelines for effective motivational instructional practices and the numerous classroom examples described in this chapter will stimulate the development of your own innovative approaches to increasing student engagement in reading and learning.

CASE STUDY

Theresa is an eighth-grade social studies teacher. She has noticed that her students appear to have become increasingly disinterested and passive over the past 10 years. Although she has typically taught units from the textbook, her efforts to enlist students in learning social studies content have been moving further and further from the text—with encouraging results. For instance, early in the school year she employed some new strategies to help students develop a broader sense of community responsibility. To her delight, the class took off with the strategy, exhibiting a level of enthusiasm Theresa hadn't seen for some time.

Theresa is in the process of planning a unit on early Native Americans. Last year was the first year she deviated from the textbook approach to teaching about native peoples by having a member of a local Huron tribe talk to the class about history and customs. He also shared costumes and artifacts. This year she would like to do more to help students develop a better understanding of what is known about the early Native American cultures and how to learn about these cultures. She wants to devise active, hands-on approaches to engage her class in the study of this important topic.

continued

To the Reader:
As you read and work through this chapter, think about possible strategies and teaching approaches Theresa might use to engage her students in learning about early American cultures. Be prepared to offer your suggestions when we revisit this case study at the conclusion of the chapter.

❭ Guidelines for Creating Motivating Contexts for Literacy and Learning

Elevate Self-Efficacy

The research literature makes evident that students with high levels of school-related self-efficacy—the belief and confidence that they have the capacity to accomplish meaningful tasks and produce a desired result in academic settings—are more engaged and motivated than students with low self-efficacy (Pajares, 1996). Content-area teachers can create the conditions for youth that are associated with increased perceptions of competence and, consequently, a willingness to sustain effort to be successful (Schunk & Zimmerman, 1997). These conditions, underpinned by the principles from Chapter 2, include such practices as introducing new content in engaging ways (Brozo, 2004), making a variety of accessible texts available to youth (Brozo & Hargis, 2003a; Ivey & Broaddus, 2001), giving youth choices (Protheroe, 2004), exploiting youths' everyday literacies (Alvermann, 2003), and creating multiple opportunities for collaborative learning (Margolis & McCabe, 2004). These practices are described in more detail within the next few pages and embodied in the strategies presented throughout the chapter.

> Low self-efficacy in academic settings usually means less risk-taking and more passive learning; so helping youth improve academic self-concept should improve behavior and performance.

Engender Interest in New Learning

A self-evident and empirically grounded truth about learning is that students will expend the energy necessary to learn if they are interested in the material (Eccles, Wigfield, Schiefele, 1998; Guthrie & Humenick, 2004; Mosenthal, 1999). This is certainly not a recent revelation. Over 300 years ago, the philosopher Rousseau (1762) made a compelling case for exploiting "present interest" as the single best way to motivate students to read and learn. John Dewey, in the early 20th century, promoted the idea that when students are interested in a topic or activity they will learn "in a whole-hearted way" (1913, p. 65). Today, the desire among educational researchers and practitioners to know more about the influence of student interest on literacy and learning is as strong as ever (Guthrie & Wigfield, 2000; Hidi & Harackiewicz, 2000). The realization that students must have both the skill and the will to learn has led to a variety of instructional practices designed to support the affective as well as the cognitive aspects of literacy development and school achievement.

Unfortunately, although we all pay lip service to this guideline, we often fail to follow it. Perhaps that is what is contributing to a nationwide, and perhaps even a worldwide, decline in youths' interest in print literacy both for pleasure and for school purposes (Baker, 2002; Bintz, 1993; Brozo, 2005b; Dreher, 2003). Disciplinary teachers who understand the importance of interest in acquiring new knowledge do not automatically assume each of their students eagerly desires to learn course content (Brozo, 2005a). Instead, they prepare students for learning by helping them become active participants in the learning process (Moje, 2000), demonstrating how the content can relate to youths' lives and concerns (Bean, 2002), and providing opportunities for youth to enjoy reading and learning (Ogle, 2003).

Generate Local Interest

Even if youth are generally interested in a topic, this does not diminish the need to employ practices that capture their attention and motivate them to read and learn for a particular day and lesson (Brozo, 2005a). For example, a 10th-grader who finds the topic of the American Civil War interesting may not stay focused in class and may not be eager to read on the topic without specific strategies that gain and hold his attention. Even worse, the student's interest might fade if his teacher does little more than lecture or require oral reading from the textbook. Unlike our 10th grader, many of his classmates are going into history, science, math, and other content classrooms without a general interest in any of the topics to be studied. For these students, local, daily strategies for helping them sustain effort are essential.

Thankfully, there are a variety of engaging strategies disciplinary teachers can apply to any content and information source that will often entice even the most reluctant readers and learners to play more active roles in the classroom. If we can spark an interest in learning for just one day, the knowledge gained that day may make it easier to assimilate information and ideas covered the next day (Linnenbrink & Pintrich, 2002). An 11th-grade math teacher explained it to us this way: "I have to get some of my students to learn in spite of themselves. So I have to do things to get them interested in every lesson. Even small things can work. But you have to do something to motivate them."

Connect Outside- with Inside-School Literacies and Learning

Columnist Patrick Clinton (2002) described youth who are disaffected with school in this way:

> They're in the last row, wearing a look that all teachers know, one that says, "I'm invisible. I have nothing to say. Don't call on me." They don't have their books. They didn't read the assignment: They forgot; they had to work; it was just boring. . . . There are kids like these in the back row of almost every high school classroom in America. in some poor schools, they're in all the rows. . . . High school teachers will tell you they can read the words but not the content. (pp. 4–5)

The same students who may be disconnected from academic life and are aliterate within the domain of school-related reading may also be active readers and users of new media at home and in their communities (Alvermann, 2003). Some 20 million strong, youth of the Net Generation (Moore, Bean, Birdyshaw, & Rycik, 1999), many of whom may find little motivation for textbook and other academic reading, are nonetheless engaging in literate practices such as e-mailing, instant messaging, participating in chat rooms and blogs, and consulting computer and video game magazines for strategies. Motivating these students to learn material in content-area classrooms may be possible by tapping into their everyday multiliteracy practices (Hinchman, Alvermann, Boyd, Brozo, & Vacca, 2003/2004; Williams, 2005). Middle and secondary school teachers can create the space for youth to find and make connections between science, math, history, and literature topics and the media they use to know their worlds (Gee, 2003). By exploring innovative ways of motivating youth to become academically engaged by linking everyday literacies with traditional

---

Practices that generate local or situational interest may seem gimmicky but can have a significant payoff in terms of sustaining attention and building knowledge bases.

When the resources youth bring to the classroom are valued, content-area teachers find ways of building on their knowledge and skills with new media for learning new information and concepts.

Teacher as Learner

MAKING SCHOOL-BASED TOPICS RELEVANT FOR YOUTH

Effective disciplinary teachers take an additional step in planning lessons and experiences for youth by making links to life outside the school walls. Virtually any topic can be connected to the real world, resulting in greater student participation, deeper understandings, and more permanent learning. Below is a list of typical content-area topics. After each one, suggest an activity for youth that connects the topic to familiar experiences and contemporary events. Then, add some of your own topics and real-world connections. The first one is completed for you.

Content-Area Topic	Connections to Real-World Experiences/Events
1. covalent bonding—chemistry	1. role-play a marriage ceremony bringing families and property together
2. the American Civil War—history	2.
3. the human brain—science	3.
4. Romeo and Juliet—literature	4.
5. measuring area—math	5.
6.	6.
7.	7.
8.	8.

textbook reading and print media, teachers will also build youths' capacity and efficaciousness as learners (Alvermann, 2001).

Make an Abundance of Interesting Texts Available

When eighth graders across the United States were asked on the National Assessment of Educational Progress (NAEP) how often they read for enjoyment, only 31% reported doing so "a lot" (Donahue et al., 2003). For 12th graders, the figure was about the same, 34%. Of even more concern were the sizable percentages of students who reported reading for fun on only a monthly or yearly basis, or not at all. Why are such large numbers of students turning off to traditional print media? One explanation, of course, is that they are turning to other media with which they engage in alternative literacy practices—activities no less enjoyable than traditional print, but not easily accounted for on surveys like the one used on the NAEP.

Another possible explanation requires a closer look at the types of texts youth encounter in school and how this might influence attitudes toward reading. For example, in separate studies (Ivey & Broaddus, 2001; Worthy, Moorman, & Turner, 1999) it was discovered that the books youth would prefer to read are often scarce to nonexistent in school. When this is the case, students' only print encounters in school may be with the texts they are required to read. Students often find school-related texts difficult and uninspiring, leading to negative attitudes toward reading. These negative feelings may become generalizable to all types of print text, including texts that might otherwise be enjoyable to youth. If reading is seen by many adolescents as unpleasurable, it becomes easier to understand why so many indicated on the NAEP survey that they read for enjoyment so infrequently.

Unfortunately, most of the required reading in middle and secondary schools is with the class textbook (Alexander & Jetton, 2000). If you spend any time working with textbooks, you will soon notice that invariably the prose is abstract, formal, and lifeless (Hartley, 2003; Tyson-Bernstein, 1988). These features of textbook prose are surely contributing to youths' disaffection with school-based reading. It's critical, therefore, that disciplinary teachers make every effort to get students interested in the textbook topic (Sadoski, Goetz, & Rodriguez, 2000; Schiefele, 1999; Wade, Schraw, Buxton, & Hayes, 1993) through the use of alternative texts, such as fictional works and multimedia.

In our own experiences (Brozo & Hargis, 2003a), we have found that when secondary schools and classroom teachers make a total commitment to ensuring every adolescent has readable print within easy access, then motivation for and attitudes toward reading improve. In order to become enthusiastic readers and learners, youth need to see firsthand the value their teachers and other school staff place on reading for personal pleasure and growth. Valuing this type of reading should take the form of strategies and programs that include stocking school and classroom libraries with a variety of interesting texts related to a host of disciplinary topics at a range of difficulty levels, creating opportunities for self-selection of texts, and structuring time for sustained print encounters (Brozo & Hargis, 2003b).

Go to Web Resources for Chapter 5 at *http://www. prenhall.com/brozo,* and look for Motivating Adolescents to Read.

Expand Student Choices and Options

Choice may be one of the most critical elements of motivation (Guthrie & Davis, 2003; Turner, 1995). As students enter preteen and teen years their choices about many things outside of school increase significantly, yet options in school remain limited. For instance, teachers may require students to answer a question in only one way or read just the assigned texts.

Agency in academic settings refers to (a) feeling in control over one's reading and learning performance and (b) the ability to expand and influence others' thinking.

In Chapter 1 we suggested that from a developmental perspective, allowing youth more input into curricular decision making could help increase their sense of autonomy and agency while building academic competence and identities (Williams, 2003). We know from good evidence that students in middle school (Freeman, McPhail, & Berndt, 2002) and high school (Lee, 1999), when given the choice, are quite capable of identifying activities they believe are helpful to their learning. Adolescents from all ability levels can be informants to help bring about more motivating literacy and disciplinary practices (Brozo, 2006). Many have documented the benefits of acquiring students' input into classroom practices and materials and then giving them choices based on this input. Youth feel empowered and motivated to participate constructively in their education when invited to help choose how and what they learn (Cook-Sather, 2002), while teachers gather critical information that helps them better appreciate the lifeworlds of youth and make their teaching more responsive to youths' experiences and perspectives (Cook-Sather, 2003; Wasley, Hampel, & Clark, 1997).

Structure Collaboration for Motivation

We have asserted in previous chapters and once again maintain that learning is, above all, a social process. Thus, when disciplinary teachers create opportunities for students to work together in the pursuit of new knowledge they are taking advantage of the social nature of learning. An added benefit to youth is the sense of belonging that grows out of cooperative and collaborative engagement in the classroom (Anderman, 1999). This sense of belonging for adolescents has been associated with an increase in motivation for reading and learning (Ivey, 1999; Nichols & Miller,

1994; Sumter, 2002). Students can be unmotivated for many reasons, but it seems clear that disengagement is as much a social challenge as it is an educational or other challenge. Consequently, content-area teachers will be more successful in motivating youth if they employ practices consistent with those surveyed by Nolen and Nicholls (1994), who motivated their students by "sit(ting) them with someone who will help them learn"; "putt(ing) them in cooperative learning groups"; and "hav(ing) them choose a project to do with another student" (p. 61).

Another important advantage of creating collaborative contexts for increasing motivation and engagement is that shared experiences become *experiential referents* to which future learning can be linked. Experiential referents as shared motivational experiences bind a community of learners and allow teachers to regularly remind students, as a topic is further explored, that "we have all done this together, we have all witnessed this phenomenon, we have all made this common discovery." Frequent references to shared experiences increase students' chances of making connections between what they learned as a result of the experience and the new information they're encountering.

> Don't underestimate the power of shared motivational experiences for building schema and increasing participatory learning.

A great variety of strategies based on these guidelines have been shown to be useful with adolescents. The balance of this chapter will be devoted to describing successful motivational strategies we have observed middle and high school teachers use with their students. The unexpected benefit of teachers' efforts to develop imaginative, motivational activities is that as they witnessed an increase in engagement among their students, they became more interested in the content and excited about teaching it as well. As you heighten engagement in your classroom, we fully expect this same benefit will accrue to you. And as you know, the more enthusiastic you are about reading and learning, the greater the chance of awakening interest in your students (Powell-Brown, 2003/2004).

Motivating Literacy and Learning in the Content Classroom

The strategies and practices described in this section have all proven to motivate youth to be more actively involved in reading and learning. For convenience, we have organized them according to the particular guideline for creating motivating contexts that is most prominent. However, it's important to recognize that each strategy, whether unique or familiar, can be linked to several of the guidelines. This is because the teachers' motivational practices we describe may have been crafted without any particular guideline in mind. Outstanding strategies to engage youth in reading and learning are, more often than not, generated by disciplinary teachers with an intelligent and caring disposition and a global understanding of the need to motivate their students. So while the guidelines remind us of different aspects of motivation and the range of possible approaches that can be employed to motivate for reading and learning, no single guideline is more important than this simple injunction: *Incorporate motivational practices into every lesson.*

Practices That Elevate Self-Efficacy

Social Studies/English
In our personal experience with eighth-grade Mexican American students from the barrio, we have discovered the crucial role direct experiences can have on their motivation

for learning and their sense of competency as learners (Brozo, Valerio, & Salazar, 1996). Throughout a unit on Hispanic American culture, we had students explore their cultural roots within their families and with the help of community members.

Before the unit began, we took the students on a walking field trip just two blocks away from their school to visit Gracie's garden. Gracie possessed extensive Mexican folk knowledge of the healing powers of plants and herbs. As the eighth graders and we walked through her garden, she explained in a mix of English and Spanish how for generations the native peoples of south Texas, which was once part of Mexico, kept themselves healthy and cured ailments ranging from indigestion to urinary tract infections with "green medicines." Students also went to the local university to participate in Cinco de Mayo ("The Fifth of May," a Mexican American holiday) festivities. There the eighth graders enjoyed a talk and demonstration from a local Mexican American scholar on the curative benefits of herbs and plants. These experiences helped provide the students with a common reference and relevant background information for the stories and books we read about Mexican American folk medicines and culture.

Another way we were able to integrate direct experiences into the unit while taking advantage of community and cultural resources was through Integrated Parent Involvement Packets (IPIPs) (Prouty & Irby, 1995). The IPIPs we used were packaged in a three-ring binder. Introducing the IPIP was a letter to the parents thanking them for taking the time to participate in the unit. On the flip side of the letter was a sign-out chart with a place for the parents' and students' signatures when they completed the IPIP. Next, there was an explanation of what was required to complete the IPIP successfully. This was followed by a story by a Hispanic author along with a short biography of the author. The stories reflected authentic Hispanic cultural experiences and were meant to be read aloud by the parents and the students to one another (Hayden, 1995).

The final component of the IPIP was a hands-on activity for student and parents to share. The activities were typically suggested by the IPIP readings. For example, in one of the stories we included in the IPIPs, Sandra Cisneros's (1990) "Three Wise Guys: Un Cuento de Navidad," a Mexican American family celebrates Christmas with the smell of cinnamon in the holiday air. We then asked parents and students to make cinnamon sticks from the ingredients we provided in a zippered plastic pouch in the IPIP binder. After reading Rudolpho Anaya's (1990) "Salomon's Story," which contains information about brewing traditional teas from local herbs, parents and students were given directions and ingredients for making their own native tea, manzanilla.

Overall, our efforts to involve students directly in learning experiences based in community–school collaboration during the Hispanic culture unit resulted in the eighth graders exhibiting greater enthusiasm for learning, improved literacy behavior, and heightened awareness of their positive cultural identity.

Practices that link pride of culture to classroom learning help build diverse youths' academic self-efficacy.

Practices That Engender Interest in New Learning

History

A class of sophomore history students was failing to comprehend the full significance of Julius Caesar's move to publish the activities of the Roman senate. When students came to class the next day they immediately noticed what Terrell, their teacher, had written on the board "Jay picks his ears," "Myra sniffs glue." Jay and Myra, students in the class who had secretly agreed to participate in the put-on, began protesting vehemently as the others roared. "How many of you would like to have your foolish acts made public? Asked Terrell. "The point is," he went on, "Jay

Interest-generating activities for new units can be more involved than day-to-day motivational strategies devised quickly and applied easily to virtually any disciplinary lesson.

The Role of the Teacher Leader

One of the most important roles a teacher leader can play in middle and secondary schools is to work in concert with disciplinary teachers to buoy youths' academic competence and build positive academic identities (Sturtevant, et al., 2006). The right educational experiences can make the difference between motivated students who sustain commitment to reading and learning and those who fail to become or remain engaged. Teacher leaders are ideally postured to support their content-area colleagues in the development of creative, student-centered motivational practices.

In her position as McArthur High School's reading coach, Bianca spends a good part of each day keeping in touch with teachers who are trying to integrate literacy strategies into their content classrooms. She team teaches, provides lesson demonstrations, and arranges for teachers who are applying certain strategies to observe and debrief with one another. Last year was Inez's first year as a ninth-grade English teacher, so she was quick to take advantage of the support Bianca offered her. Inez thought her students were not focusing closely enough on their readings and wondered if Bianca might have some suggestions. After a couple of classroom observations, Bianca soon recognized that one of the reasons the first-year students were frequently off task or appeared disinterested was the lack of constructivist, interactive teaching strategies. Inez tended to remain near the lectern at the front of the room, from where she called on students to read aloud and interjected questions for the whole class. Bianca could see that Inez's repertoire of teaching strategies was limited and developed a plan for improving her class dynamics.

A simple strategy Bianca introduced was having Inez give students a minute or two to talk with a partner before responding to her whole-class questions. This immediately improved attention and participation. Another strategy to increase motivation was instead of calling on individual students to read aloud from the novel or story having small groups of students to take parts, including the narrator, and read scenes together. After a few pages, a new group would take over. Students were encouraged to read with expression and use simple gestures.

Though these approaches created a more engaging learning atmosphere, some continued to resist participation and remained marginalized from the flow of instruction. Zoran, in particular, a recent immigrant from Eastern Europe, was uninvolved in spite of the new class dynamics, but because he was diffident by nature and nondisruptive, Inez tended to tolerate his behavior, though she was unsure of how to get him more involved. Bianca urged Inez to conference with Zoran to find out if he had any ideas for how he might become a more active member of the classroom community. Inez did this and listened to Zoran talk about how he felt uncomfortable speaking English with his strong accent. She also learned about his carpentry and painting skills, which his father taught him in his native country.

Inez and Bianca decided to find a way to showcase Zoran's talent as a carpenter by asking him to create a set for a classroom reading of Ambrose Bierce's (1988) "Incident at Owl Creek Bridge." Bianca borrowed material from the drama teacher, and got permission from the industrial arts teacher to allow Zoran use of the shop during his study period to construct the props for the scenes in the story. Zoran's skill and imagination resulted in sets for the two main scenes in the story, one of the bridge and one of the antebellum mansion. Zoran was so pleased with this assignment and the compliments he received from his classmates that he also finally agreed to participate in the reading of the story. Bianca and Inez invited other teachers and parents to observe the delivery of the story. All were impressed with Zoran's sets, which helped increase the verisimilitude of the classes' presentation.

Finding a reason for Zoran to be involved based on his out-of-school expertise and identity turned out to be the critical experience for transforming his attitude toward English class. With his increased level of participation in Inez's classroom, he was also remaking his academic identity from one of limited confidence in his own ability to read and comprehend to a growing sense of competence and agency.

and Myra do not want their private acts made public, nor do you—and neither did the Roman senators." Caesar felt that the senators were behaving without decorum, Terrell went on to explain, and believed that having their behavior posted for all to read would pressure them into changing their ways. Terrell then apologized to Myra and Jay for libeling them. By using information gained from what we might call on-the-spot assessment, Terrell modified his instruction to include a concrete example to make his point clearer. He was able to motivate his students to learn by linking new information from a historical study of 2,000 years ago—a disparate culture and time—with the experiences and attitudes of adolescents today.

Chemistry

Brian introduced the study of carbon bonding to his chemistry class through one of the cleverest activities we have ever seen. With the desks moved to the walls, leaving a large open area in the middle, Brian asked his students to stand. He distributed paper bag vests that were labeled with a large, colorful H, C, or O (for hydrogen, carbon, and oxygen). After students donned the vests, he gave a fellow teacher a printed square dance call. He then pulled out a fiddle from its case, and with everyone set, he started to play the "Carbon Bonding Hoedown" as the square dance caller called the moves. Meanwhile, students moved around the room searching for partners; by the conclusion of the square dance, all carbon atoms had bonded appropriately, as represented by the students and their vests. Everyone had fun and it formed a meaningful and motivating introduction to the exploration of the topic. It also provided the class with a memorable experience to which Brian could refer as they progressed through the study of carbon atoms and carbon bonding.

Foreign Language

Engaging her French I students in a study of French history, Marie scoured her imagination and came up with a way of transforming the classroom into the Lascaux Cave of southwest France. In the 1940s a group of boys stumbled upon the caves, which were later found to have great caverns decorated with some of the oldest known cave drawings in the world. Because Marie knew she couldn't take her students to the actual caves, she created a virtual field trip to Lascaux right in the classroom.

The day before, Marie prepared the classroom to simulate the darkness of a cave. To block out as much light as possible, she drew the blinds and taped black paper over the windows. She also taped to the walls large sheets of white and brown butcher paper on which were drawn pictures of animals, hands, and people in the style of prehistoric cave dwellers, as well as some of the French terms associated with caves, the discovery of the Lascaux cave, and exploration. The desks were pushed snug against the walls of the classroom, making a large open area in the middle.

The next day Marie waited outside the room for her students to arrive. When everyone had gathered, she explained that they were going on a virtual fieldtrip for class that day, and that they would need to be equipped with the proper gear. Most of her students remembered to bring flashlights, though she had a few extras for students who had forgotten. With flashlights on, she opened the door and asked everyone to proceed to the center of the room and have a seat on the floor.

Once they were seated, Marie asked them to turn their flashlights off, resulting in total darkness. She then asked them to take a moment to think about things that are permanent, that last forever and don't go away. She told students to position their flashlights under their chins so as to be recognized when they responded. Answers included things like paint, permanent markers, graffiti, death, tattoos, and even school.

To form pairs of student explorers, Marie instructed one student at a time to find a partner by randomly shining her/his flashlight at a classmate. Once grouped, Marie handed out paper and pencils for taking field notes, and invited students to shine their lights around the room to learn about their surroundings. Students were asked to

Honoring Diversity and Building Competence in the Content Classroom

Jamal's role as a special education teacher has changed recently. Once, all students were pulled out of their general classes and provided separate modified instruction in math, science, history, and English in a self-contained environment. Today, Jamal's special education students attend all general classes, where he provides instructional and classroom management assistance to teachers and direct help for his students. His goal is to sensitize the regular general education teacher to the need to modify ways information is disseminated and to help create a learning environment that will hold the attention of his special learners.

In a 10th-grade history class, for example, Jamal worked with the teacher on a readiness activity that had been successful in his self-contained setting. One of his main objectives for a unit on how the American colonies gained their freedom is to develop an understanding of the concept of taxation without representation. Jamal knew that in the past his students were excited about the topic, but he found in his assessments that they failed to grasp the significance of the essential concepts leading to a full understanding of the antecedents and consequences of the American Revolution. Jamal also knew that the more he transformed lifeless textual information into something tangible and personal, the greater the students' involvement and the more they seemed to learn.

As a motivator, and to personalize, the concept, Jamal and the history teacher had the class participate in a simulation activity. They called it a government experiment as they handed out directions and guided the class through them. The students were divided into two groups: one called the "Oros" and the other the "Bindus." Jamal named himself the king of the Oros; the history teacher joined the Bindus. Each group was given directions for electing representatives to make laws or rules. The Bindus were told they could make rules that applied only to themselves, whereas the Oros could impose rules on the Bindus. Each group also was given a lump sum of 1,000 play dollars for its treasury.

Jamal, as king of the Oros, immediately began imposing laws on the Bindus that roughly paralleled the Stamp Act and the Tea Act. The "Paper and Pencil Rule" taxed every Bindu $5 for every pencil, pen, and piece of paper used; the "Pop Rule" taxed the Bindus $10 for having a soda or any other drink in class (the history teacher permitted his students to have soft drinks in the classroom). Interestingly, the turn of events in the history classroom resembled what had happened between the British and the American colonies. Complaining fell on deaf ears, so at first the Bindus gave in to the Oros's rules. Soon, however, the Bindus began to protest—first by not bringing paper or pencils to class and then by simply ignoring the rule and using as many sheets of paper and pencils as they wished. The same thing happened with their soda drinking. Soon the Bindus were challenging the Oros's authority by drinking without paying taxes. By week's end, the Oros were debating as to whether they should drop the taxes or impose penalties and stiffer taxes, while the Bindus were prepared to resist at all costs.

Jamal then asked the class to analyze the situation. The history teacher and the Bindus argued that it was unfair for a separate group to tell them what to do. They said they were able to take care of themselves. One student put it

> succinctly to the Oros; "What gives you the right to tax us?" The Oros had never considered this question. They behaved as though there was only one way to behave. Jamal and the history teacher took advantage of the students' self-discovery about what can happen when one group imposes rules on another against its will by having the students draw parallels to the conditions that led to war between the British and the colonies. They asked students to divide a sheet of paper in half. On one side, they listed the rules imposed on the Oros and the Bindus' reactions to those rules. Then, as they read and studied the chapter, they listed on the other side the events that took place in colonial America just before the Revolutionary War.

record on paper any words or symbols they found on the walls. Student pairs analyzed these recordings and wrote an explanation of what they thought they meant.

Finally, Marie turned on the lights, and while students waited for their eyes to reacclimatize to the brightness of the room, Marie invited them to select markers and create their own "cave drawings" on the butcher paper. While drawing, the class listened to Marie as she described in French the Lascaux Cave and its archeological significance. She concluded the lesson by reminding her students that French history as well as the history of Europe really begins with the drawings and symbols left behind by the ancient peoples who inhabited caves such as Lascaux.

With this approach, Marie introduced the topic in such an engaging way that she had little difficulty keeping her students' attention for the remainder of the unit on French history. Often they would refer back to "Lascaux" as though they had actually been there. The cave experience helped bring about shared understandings of the new content and reinforced a sense of community the students were feeling about the class.

Practices That Generate Local Interest

Journalism

As you'll see, some of the best motivational strategies capitalize on youths' natural curiosities and propensities to form hunches, make guesses, and predict.

A wonderful example of a *prediction* strategy that was used to gain and hold students' attention for a daily lesson was provided by Ty, a senior high journalism teacher. Ty was instructing students in editorial writing by sharing examples of editorials and analyzing them. He handed out a sheet of paper with the title "A No-Lose Proposition," by Stanley J. Lieberman, and the first paragraph, which read:

> *America is the most litigious society in the world. We are suing each other at an alarming and increasing rate, and we have more lawyers per capita than any other nation. Since 1950 the number of lawyers in America has increased 250 percent. We have well over half a million lawyers—one for every 450 people. In New York state the ratio is one lawyer per 18. By contrast, the ratio in West Germany is one lawyer per 2,000.*

After reading this material, the students worked in small groups and discussed the possible directions the editorial might take. Each group was to make two predictions. Ty moved around the room, listening in on each group, assisting when asked. Next, each group's predictions were presented to the whole class while the teacher wrote them on the board. A lengthy and immensely beneficial discussion then ensued, which included a class-derived definition of *litigious* and an impassioned defense of lawyers by a student whose father and mother were attorneys. An impressive amount of background and related knowledge poured out, as did the exchange and exploration of biases, opinions, and beliefs. Ty played a facilitative role during the discussion. He prodded when necessary, refocused the conversation when it seemed to stray too far from the task of determining what the author was likely to say in the passage, and clarified points and details.

When the debate over which predictions were likely to be verified wound down, the students were eager to finish reading the editorial. Three agreed-on predictions remained on the board, and the students were reminded to read and discover to what extent, if any, the text supported them. After reading, the class discussed the accuracy of their predictions. No one had foreseen that the author would make a pitch for mediation as a way to unblock a clogged court system, although one prediction anticipated some kind of workable solution based on the editorial's title.

Reflect on how the preceding scene differs from a typical reading assignment — with little or no preparation or direction. By the time these students were ready to read the editorial, they had developed an interest in the topic through small-group and whole-class discussions that challenged beliefs and biases and piqued curiosity. As a result, attention to the text and comprehension could not help but improve.

Geography

To motivate her eighth graders to focus on the day's lesson, Keitha used the *KWL* strategy (Carr & Ogle, 1987; Ogle, 1992). A perennial favorite among teachers at all levels, KWL uses students' own questions to sustain attention to a text, lecture, video, or other information source (Marchand-Martella, Wasta, Martella, 1996; Sampson, 2002; Santa, 2004). Keitha's geography class was about to begin study of how mountain ranges are formed. First, she had students form groups of three and gave them 3 minutes to brainstorm everything they knew about mountains. When time was up, one student from each group reported the brainstormed information to the whole class. This resulted in a liberal exchange of ideas, until it was decided the class knew two to three facts about mountains for

Go to Web Resources for Chapter 5 at *http://www. prenhall.com/brozo,* and look for KWL.

Figure 5.2 An Eighth Grader's KWL Chart for the Formation of Mountains

K	W	L
Volcanoes help form mountains.	Do mountains grow?	Mountains form when heat within the earth pushes up bedrock.
The Rocky Mountains are very tall.	How do they erode?	Lava forces its way up and hardens into rock, causing mountains to grow bigger.
	Why are the Rockies taller than the Smokies?	Rain and wind wear them down.
		Mountains are part of a cycle—ocean sediment to solid rock pushed up to form mountains, then worn down into the sea again.
		Mountains in the eastern U.S. are very old.
		Mountains in the West are not as old.

certain. Keitha wrote these on the board in the "K" column, which stands for *What I Know* (see Figure 5.2). Her students had individual blank KWL charts on which they wrote the same information.

Keitha then asked the groups to reconvene and take a couple of more minutes to generate three questions they would like answered about the topic of mountains. As students talked among themselves, she moved around the room to listen in, clarify, and answer any questions. Once the time was up, Keitha invited group spokespersons to share their questions with the class. When an agreed-upon list was ultimately derived, these were written in the "W" column of the KWL chart. This column represents what learners *want* to know.

At this point, Keitha's students were poised to receive and seek the information sources to answer their questions. Completing the "K" and "W" processes of the KWL strategy hadn't exactly transformed the class into a group of mountain enthusiasts, but it did accomplish the goal of impelling students to attend more closely to the immediate task of finding answers to their own KWL-generated questions. While listening to Keitha read aloud and share the remarkable photographs from Bredeson's (2001) *Mount Saint Helens Volcano*, students were to stop her when information was provided to help answer a question from the KWL chart. Keitha could see most were listening attentively and freely interrupted her throughout the read-aloud. At the conclusion of the book, at least two questions remained unanswered, so groups were asked to select another book on mountains and volcanoes from the collection Keitha had stacked on a table in the classroom. With the books, such as VanRose's (2000) *Volcano and Earthquakes* and Claybourne's (2000) *Read About Volcanoes*, students worked in their groups until answers were found to the lingering questions.

Health

Dimitrius has found he can motivate his health students to engage more meaningfully with class topics by using *anticipation guides* (Duffelmeyer & Baum, 1992; White & Johnson, 2001). You should be somewhat familiar with the anticipation guide strategy already, as you have been asked to complete one for each chapter of this book.

First, Dimitrius looks over the information sources his students will receive for the day's topic, in this case on diet and nutrition. Based on his lecture notes, the related textbook chapter, and Web sites, he comes up with several statements. He makes sure his guide statements are: (1) related to the major ideas and information students would encounter; (2) representative of the content Dimitrius wanted students to be sure to learn; (3) alluring or challenging; and (4) an appropriate blend of text- and reader-based focus. In addition, he goes over his statements another time to ensure some are written to appear correct but incompatible with the information students will encounter and others seem incorrect yet compatible with the information to follow.

Dimitrius formats his anticipation guides in a way that makes it simple for him to present them to his students without having to create a formal, typed, and photocopied guide (see Figure 5.3). Often, he simply writes the statements on the board, including a *before* and *after* column with *true* and *false* as response options. His students copy the statements into their notebooks with the date and title, so they can hand in their completed guides for a grade.

Dimitrius designs his anticipation guides in ways that do not require students to write extended answers to prompts that resemble discussion or essay questions. Instead, he has students respond with simple check marks. But, to guard against students making random responses without careful thinking as they encounter new content related to the guide, he adds a feature that requires them to verify the information used to corroborate or amend their initial responses (see Figure 5.3).

Figure 5.3 Anticipation Guide for Diet and Nutrition

Part I

Directions: Read each statement. If you believe that a statement is true, place a check mark in the *Agree* column. If you believe the statement is false, place a check mark in the *Disagree* column. Be ready to explain your choices.

Agree   **Disagree**

_____   _____   1. About 45% of the total food dollar is spent on food away from home.

_____   _____   2. More cookbooks are being purchased today than ever before.

_____   _____   3. Soft drinks are essentially sugar.

_____   _____   4. The average person's diet consists of between 60% and 70% fat and sugar.

_____   _____   5. People are eating fewer fruits today than in the 1940s.

_____   _____   6. Many so-called primitive cultures have more nutritious diets than many affluent Americans.

_____   _____   7. Vitamin C has been used effectively to treat mental diseases.

Part II

Directions: Now you will be reading and listening to information related to each of the statements in Part I of this guide. If the information supports your choices in Part I, place a check mark in the *Support* column. If the information does not support your choices, place a check mark in the *No Support* column. Write in your own words the relevant text and/or lecture information for your answer.

	Support	**No Support**	**Text/Lecture Information**
1.	_____	_____	_____
2.	_____	_____	_____
3.	_____	_____	_____
4.	_____	_____	_____
5.	_____	_____	_____
6.	_____	_____	_____
7.	_____	_____	_____

Dimitrius uses anticipation guides not only as a motivator to learn, but also as a vehicle for clearing up misconceptions about the topic. This function seems especially important given research evidence indicating that students' existing prior knowledge and biases will be superimposed on the information sources when the two are at odds (Eagly, Chen, Chaiken, & Shaw-Barnes, 1999).

Environmental Science

A more formal anticipation guide was given to students by Paula, their environmental science teacher, to motivate them to think critically about the topic of pollution (see Figure 5.4). Although this guide required a good deal more planning and time to complete than the health guide created by Dimitrius, it nonetheless possesses the same essential features as the simpler guide.

Figure 5.4 Anticipation Guide for the Topic of Environmental Pollution

Part I

Directions: Below are statements and situations related to the environment. If you agree with the statement, place a check mark in the *Agree* column. If you disagree with the statement, place a check mark in the *Disagree* column. Be prepared to explain your responses.

Agree   Disagree

_____   _____ 1. A poor landowner wants to sell his land to a large chemical refinery. The environmentalists say there is an endangered species on the land. The court says he can't sell the land. Do you agree with the court ruling?

_____   _____ 2. It doesn't matter if I recycle my aluminum cans or not. One person doesn't make a difference.

_____   _____ 3. A small business garage owner goes to a vacant lot to empty motor oil into the ground. The police pick him up for suspicious behavior and find out what he has been doing. He is fined $50,000, which ruins his business and forces him into bankruptcy. Do you agree with the judgment? He says everybody else does it, so what difference does it make?

_____   _____ 4. Your next-door neighbor has a beautiful yard. He sprays the plants almost every day. He never seems to be picking weeds; instead, he sprays his lawn with poison. Do you agree with his technique?

_____   _____ 5. A man and his family saved for years to buy the home of their dreams. After they moved in, the younger child became very ill. He had headaches most of the time. The man eventually found out that he had bought a house on top of an old landfill. He sued the real estate agent and lost the case. Do you agree with the court ruling?

_____   _____ 6. The richest and most diverse terrestrial ecosystems on earth are the tropical forests. Some people want to develop this land for cattle grazing. Do you think that would be a good idea?

Part II

Directions: Now that we have studied facts and issues related to environmental pollution, look back at your responses to the statements in Part I. If you found support for your response, check the *Support* column below; if you didn't find support for your response, check the *No Support* column. Regardless of what column you check, write a sentence in your own words explaining your response.

	Support	No Support	Your Explanation
1.	_____	_____	_____
2.	_____	_____	_____
3.	_____	_____	_____
4.	_____	_____	_____
5.	_____	_____	_____
6.	_____	_____	_____

Common to both guides is the all-important accountability feature. As students encounter text, lecture, or multimedia on the topic, they must find information that either reinforces and verifies existing beliefs, forces them to be altered or modified, or requires completely rejecting them. This process motivates students to focus closely on new content. As relevant information is found it can be written in the form of terse statements with page numbers, URLs, or as lecture note entries. This should include corroborative as well as amended statements that correct unanticipated information.

Another common feature of the two guides is how the teachers used them with students. In both classrooms, students were presented with the anticipation guide statements and asked to pair up to discuss them. Next, a discussion over the statements was opened up to the entire class, wherein students could debate and defend responses. Then, the class was given the opportunity to revise initial responses to the guide statements. At this point, students were provided with the information sources. Periodically as students explored these sources they were stopped and asked to refer back to a particular guide statement about which information was supplied. This was followed by student pairs and then the whole class discussing the statement's veracity. The process continued until all guide statements had been considered and reconsidered in light of the information sources.

Working with anticipation guides helps create the urge in students to know more and sustains interest in topics, at least within the context of a single day's lesson. Guides motivate students to confront the topic ideas and information purposefully and enthusiastically (Hurst, 2001; Strange & Wyant, 1999) and facilitate assimilation of new information into existing schemata (Merkley, 1996/97).

Reading/Language Arts

Renard, an eighth-grade reading/language arts teacher, employs the *lesson impression* strategy to motivate his students to focus more closely on the reading material for any given day. This strategy helps students develop an impression of what the forthcoming lesson will cover, which impels them to read, listen, and observe the lesson content with heightened attentiveness in order to discover whether their predictions are correct. It can be used before exposing students to content regardless of how information and ideas are delivered. In other words, it is equally effective for engendering an immediate and local interest with the variety of typical information sources in middle and secondary schools, such as reading material, a lecture, a guest speaker, a video, a CD-ROM, and a field trip. Lesson impressions can increase motivation by heightening anticipation and providing a meaningful purpose for learning.

Renard conducted a lesson impression by first presenting students a list of words and phrases taken directly from the material to be covered. Renard put the following words and phrases on the overhead:

> *CDs, penny, music, club, hidden commitments, contract, monthly selections, "return to sender," rip-off*

He then asked students to write what they think they were about to read by creating a short description or narrative in which all of the words are used. Renard asked his students to write the words in their notebooks and directed them to craft short compositions on what they thought the lesson would be about, making sure to use all the words.

When his students finished writing, they were given the opportunity to exchange their written impressions with a peer. In this way, they could compare and contrast one another's predictions about the content to be covered in the forthcoming lesson, which acted to heighten their anticipation. After students read one another's impression writing, Renard invited several to share what they had written with the entire class. His goal is to gather a variety of impressions so that students are left with a sense that theirs or any one of their classmates' may be the most accurate.

In response to the lesson impression words Renard gave his students, Juwon created a kind of personal story about the topic. He read to the class:

> *I saw an ad in a magazine that said I could buy 10* **CDs** *for a* **penny** *if I joined this* **music club.** *They had all this cool music so I decided to join. After getting my first 10 choices, I received a* **contract** *that had all these* **hidden commitments,** *like I had to pick out so many* **monthly selections** *or I'd have to*

The lesson impression strategy can be accomplished just as effectively with students sharing oral texts based on the impression words given them in advance of the information source.

*pay for those CDs that were only a penny. By then I knew this was a **rip-off**, so I packed everything back up in the box and wrote **"return to sender."***

At this point in the strategy process, Renard's students were ready to receive the information. As Renard passed out copies of the article entitled "Ten CDs for a Penny? If It's Too Good to Be True, It Probably Isn't," he stressed that he now wanted the class to pay very close attention to determine whether the content jibed with their written impressions—though he hardly had to remind them they were so eager to read. Renard also required his students to keep a record of the similarities and differences between their impressions and the actual content by creating a Venn diagram or a compare/contrast chart. We recommend such practices because they add an accountability feature that raises the level of assurance that students are remaining engaged throughout the lesson.

Students paired up and read sections of the short article aloud together, trading off reading paragraphs. Renard stopped them at regular intervals to ask questions and get responses based on their predictions in the lesson impressions.

Science

Tammy, an eighth-grade science teacher, presented her students with the following words by writing them on the board:

> *breathing oxygen inhale exhale mucus*
> *nose carbon dioxide vocal cords lungs*

Next, she asked her students to write for 5 to 7 minutes using as many of these words as possible in their short compositions. Tammy said they could write what they expected to hear during the upcoming presentation on the human respiratory system. She urged students to be creative, incorporating the words in a song, poem, or story.

Many of the students wrote what they knew about the respiratory system, which helped Tammy discover the extent of their prior knowledge. Others who were more comfortable with the content chose to be creative and were eager to share their work before her presentation began. Tammy found her students paying closer attention during the lesson. Because she had not picked up their compositions, several students corrected their stories with the information they gleaned from the presentation. It was clear that the lesson impression strategy had engendered focused listening and heightened motivation to learn due to students' desire to compare their impression texts with the content of Tammy's presentation.

When Tammy asked students after her presentation what they liked or disliked about the strategy, their responses were consistent. They liked the freedom to be creative and to have a default option in case the creative juices weren't flowing. The students further commented that they thought the lesson impression activity helped them focus on information about the respiratory system of which they were unsure. Two examples of the students' readiness compositions are as follows:

Practices that ask students to write or talk about what they know or think they know in advance of the information sources, promotes generative learning.

Student 1:

My breathing takes in air that contains oxygen. It goes through my nose and the mucus cleans the air before it enters my lungs. But first it goes through the vocal cords. After it enters my lungs, I exhale the carbon dioxide that I don't need.

Student 2:

My nose is very big although I'm very small. When I sneeze my mucus goes all over the wall. My lungs are breathing oxygen, that's a proven fact. I exhale

*carbon dioxide and that's all I have to say about that. Please don't ask me to
sing this hour, because with my vocal cords the notes will be awfully sour.*

Biology

Roberta, a 10th-grade biology teacher, is able to get her students highly motivated to
read and learn the daily content through a variety of creative strategies. One of those
strategies is called *Student Questions for Purposeful Learning* or *SQPL*. SQPL
promotes engaged and purposeful exploration of the topic as students search for answers to their own questions.

As a critical first step in preparing to conduct an SQPL lesson, Roberta looked
over the day's reading material and her notes on the topic she was introducing, human genetics, then crafted a short, thought-provoking statement to present to her
class. She wrote it in big letters across the board:

It is Now Possible to Clone Human Beings

She knew that even though the statement wasn't necessarily factually true, it would
instigate lively conversation among her students and stimulate plenty of good questions in preparation for reading an article on genetic engineering.

For the next phase of the lesson, Roberta allowed her students to pair up and
brainstorm questions they would like to have answered based on the statement.
While students worked together on their questions, Roberta moved throughout the
room to monitor their progress and help clarify the task.

When finished, Roberta went around the room and gathered questions from each
of the student pairs, writing them on the board. The goal here was to gather a variety of
questions by making sure each student pair contributed at least one of its questions. After
every student had an opportunity to add a question to the total, Roberta drew the class's
attention to those questions that were essentially the same, and added stars next to
those questions. Some questions, such as *How do you clone someone?* had five stars,
since at least five separate pairs of students came up with the same or highly similar
question. Another question, *Who will get cloned?* was repeated four times, and *How
much does it cost?* had three stars. Like Roberta, we recommend that you highlight or
star questions asked by more than one pair of students; these become class consensus
questions. You can also consolidate questions by combining similar ones.

At this stage, Roberta's students were more than ready to get answers to their
questions, and immediately began reading just as soon as Roberta handed them the
article entitled, "Can Humans Be Cloned Like Sheep?" Like all of the strategies discussed in this section and chapter, SQPL is adaptable to virtually any information
source, such as reading material, lecture, discussion, video, and the Internet. Students
should be directed to pay close attention to information that answers the questions
the class generated, especially class consensus questions.

Roberta alerted the class that as information is encountered that answers one of
the readiness questions, the information should be written in their notebooks.
Throughout the reading of the article, Roberta stopped students periodically to discuss the piece in general and answers to student questions in particular.

SQPL motivates Roberta's students to invest in the learning process because they
become gatherers of information based on their own inquiry and not on prompts given
to them by her or the textbook. Nonetheless, it is important to point out that student-
generated questions do not necessarily have to comprise the only questions for a given
reading or topic. This is especially true when students are first learning the strategy,
and may fail to derive questions that cover critical information. For instance, if Roberta
notices certain vital questions missing but necessary to direct attention to important
aspects of the topic, she will contribute her own questions to the list, in a tactful way.

SQPL is an effective generative learning strategy since students are prompted to ask and answer their own questions about the content.

Teacher as Learner

AN SQPL ACTIVITY

As you just learned, the key to an effective SQPL lesson is how well the thought-provoking statement given to students in advance of new information stimulates meaningful queries. Following are typical topics covered in content classrooms using print, visual texts, and lectures. For each of these topics, generate possible SQPL statements to prompt good questions before students in disciplinary classrooms are provided information sources on these topics. A suggestion for the first topic is provided as an example.

Content-Area Topics	SQPL Statements
1. The Aging Process	1. *Age is just a state of mind: Even you can live to be a hundred.*
2. The Atom Bomb	2.
3. Asteroids	3.
4. The Civil Rights Movement	4.
5. Symbolism in Poetry	5.

Many highly effective classroom strategies can be employed to increase motivation for reading and learning for a particular day's lesson or topic. In this section, we demonstrated how five useful strategies—prediction, KWL, anticipation guides, lesson impressions, and SQPL—can be used to increase student engagement by generating local interest in various content-area topics. These strategies increase engagement by inducing students to establish purposes for reading and learning, which leads to active exploration of the content to answer their own questions and satisfy their own curiosities. When youth attend to topics more closely, interact with them in more meaningful ways, and combine their world knowledge with new information, higher level thinking and broader understandings are the result.

Practices That Connect Outside- with Inside-School Literacies and Learning

Science

Judy, a sixth-grade science teacher, borrowed her school's old home economics room with its four ovens for a class experiment. She arranged several food items, mixing bowls, and pizza tins on a table at the front of the room. She told her students that they were home alone and were hungry for pizza; however, without money to buy a pizza and no pizzas in the freezer, they would have to create one with the ingredients on the table. Judy divided the class into groups of three, gave each group a sheet for recording the steps involved in their pizza-making adventure, and told them to get started. Under her watchful eye, the groups discussed and gathered, mixed, poured, stirred, baked, and laughed their way through this discovery process. After the fun, Judy asked each group to show off its "pizza," identify its ingredients, and describe the steps taken to create it. Brave volunteers stepped forward to taste test the pizzas. After the class cleaned up and resettled, Judy gave the groups a handout with a detailed description of the five steps of the scientific method. On a posterboard with the same

Motivational theorists and researchers are unanimous in their endorsement of school-based practices that allow youth to find connections to their outside-of-school experiences and competencies.

five steps listed, she and the students wrote out how the steps they took to create their pizzas corresponded with the steps in the scientific method.

Judy's hands-on class experience satisfied several guidelines of motivational teaching. First, it immediately generated a great deal of enthusiasm on the part of the class. Second, students were allowed to work together as they searched for the best possible ingredients and steps to create pizzas from scratch. Third, situating learning within a familiar, home-like context helped Judy's students bridge everyday experiences with school subjects. Finally, the pizza-making activity provided students with an experiential referent for their ongoing study of the scientific method. In fact, throughout the next several days and weeks, Judy constantly referred back to the pizza-making adventure to remind students of a related aspect of the scientific method they were studying.

Chemistry

Angelina used students' everyday experiences as links to classroom topics to create a more engaging context for learning about covalent bonding. To help them better understand this concept and generate interest, Angelina exploited the class's knowledge of marriage, reasoning that just as the bonding of two people in matrimony has certain conditions, so too does the bonding of atoms.

Angelina split her class into two groups, telling one they represented the Doe family and the other, the Smith family. The Does were asked to select a groom for a marriage ceremony, and the Smiths were asked to select a bride. Angelina gave each family an index card with background information to establish a context for forging a successful marriage contract between the two families. As it happens, the two families have had a long-standing dispute, the resolution of which depends upon the terms of the marriage agreement being acceptable to both groups. The Does own land whereas the Smiths own seeds. The groups then appointed negotiators to meet and work out the contract. Once both families agreed to the terms, the happy couple was joined in matrimony amid a festive class atmosphere. Angelina even brought out a cake for the occasion.

While the class settled down to enjoy the confection, Angelina put the activity in chemical terms. Using a graphic display, (see Figure 5.5) she explained that all atoms strive to become noble gases by having eight valence electrons. Two atoms will come

> An experience as common as a marriage ceremony becomes the link to chemistry content in the hands of an innovative-thinking disciplinary teacher.

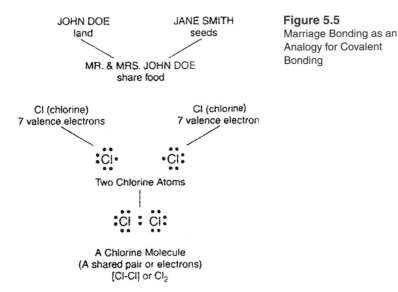

Figure 5.5
Marriage Bonding as an Analogy for Covalent Bonding

together and share a bond to reach this goal. She went on to ask the students to imagine the Doe and Smith families are atoms and the seeds and lands are electrons. As long as the couple stays married and share that bond, they will share the seeds and land between the families. Both families will have food and will prosper together. At the atomic level, when atoms share electrons and form a noble gas, the result is covalent bonding.

U.S. History

A group of Alamo battle reenactors tumbled into Hector's eighth-grade history classroom, including a Mexican soldier, a Tennessee volunteer, and a Texas frontiersman. Outfitted in authentic attire, carrying authentic weaponry, and remaining in character for the entire class period, these three performers talked about their lives and the events at the Alamo as though the battle had happened yesterday. Thus, Hector's students began the study of the Alamo with the help of these memorable guests. Not only did the reenactors create an engaging atmosphere for learning in Hector's classroom, they also helped breath life into the ideas and information in the history textbook by helping students see a connection to real people and events.

Ecology

We watched the eyes of a group of seventh graders grow to saucer proportions as a local ornithologist walked into the classroom with a great horned owl on one arm and an osprey on the other—both nearly 2 feet tall! The guest speaker explained the life habits of these birds of prey and gave demonstrations. Students asked questions and were nearly able to touch the birds as they gathered around the speaker. It was a memorable day for Diane's science class, especially when the osprey unexpectedly let out a loud whistling call. Thus began Diane's unit on birds of prey.

In both of these cases, Diane, the science teacher, and Hector, the history teacher, were clever enough to recognize the power of bringing into class members of the community with expert knowledge. Students began their study of the topics with increased anticipation, excitement, and a store of useful, new knowledge to help them better negotiate the texts and ideas to follow. Furthermore, by inviting people and animals from outside the classroom into the classroom, students had unique, real-world experiences to which they could link new learning.

We believe guest speakers and performers are perhaps the most underused resources teachers can employ to increase student motivation for reading and learning. Even in the remotest communities there is a wealth of knowledge to be tapped—individuals who lived through critical times in history, local authors and artists, and members of the political, industrial, and scientific worlds. Often local municipalities have information services about local experts. Colleges and universities have public information offices with names and addresses of professors and notes on their areas of expertise. We recently contacted a city office for information about local Native American groups and were put in touch with a couple of organizations that supplied guest speakers to a ninth-grade teacher's classroom.

We agree with those (Hoss, 1991; Poling, 2000) who advise that to get the most out of guest speakers and performers, students and guests should be prepared. Students should be given time to generate questions, and guests should know in advance your expectations for their visit, how much time they will have, and any special requests. These preparation procedures can avoid potential problems such as embarrassing comments, rambling, or information unrelated to the topic.

Lindy Poling (2000), a high school social studies teacher, has found that guest speakers in her classroom motivate students to think more critically and provide them a real-world perspective on the curriculum. Being prepared, however, is critical, and she recommends:

- Contacting local organizations that provide effective guest speakers (e.g., local universities, public information offices of local municipalities, veterans and civic organizations)
- Screening guests beforehand to make certain their backgrounds truly match the objectives of the classroom content
- Preparing guests by informing them about what students have been studying in relation to the topic of their expertise and what particular aspects of their expertise you would like emphasized in the presentation
- Establishing a careful question-and-answer plan that requires students to generate questions in advance and submit them to you for screening and possible forwarding to the guest speaker

Youth get the most out of the experience of having guest speakers and performers in their classroom when the guests and the students are prepared for the visit.

Chemistry

Toni, a high school chemistry teacher, invited to her class a friend who was an organic chemist in the research and development (R&D) department of a large local company. She had her students spend a couple of class periods preparing for the guest speaker by first brainstorming their areas of interest about which the guest would likely have information; these included original discoveries and patents, new and future uses of polymers, employment opportunities for women in chemistry, and the day-to-day operation of an R&D department. Toni then asked her students to form small groups based on their interests and generate a set of 10 questions each that they would like answered by the guest chemist. Toni looked over the questions and helped each group refine its list to five good questions. Meanwhile, Toni contacted her friend and told her what the students were most interested in learning. This information made it possible for the chemist to prepare effectively for the classroom visit.

When the day arrived, the school newspaper and science club wanted to cover the presentation, so a video camera was set up to record the event. The chemist gave a brief overview and then asked for questions. Each group was given the opportunity to ask all five of its questions in a set to avoid forcing the guest speaker to jump from topic to topic in a disjointed way. She brought in examples of products developed by her center, and diagrams, notes, and computer graphics on future developments. She talked from experience about her interest and schooling in chemistry and the process of gaining employment in the company. She described how patents are obtained and showed the class some of the patented products for which she was responsible. Finally, using a CD-ROM presentation, she took the class through a computer-simulated field trip of her R&D center.

Practices That Make an Abundance of Interesting Texts Available

Social Studies

Walking down the hall one morning of large suburban middle school where we were providing year-long consulting, Marcus, a second-year, seventh-grade social studies teacher, approached us and invited us into his classroom for a chat. He explained that he had been taught in his university methods classes to teach history using a textbook, but came to realize that he was losing his students to boredom because topics were treated so lifelessly in the class text. He wondered how he could get his students more interested in reading and learning history. Our reply was to create frequent opportunities for engaged reading using alternative texts, and if he were willing to give this approach a try, we would support him in every way possible.

Marcus was excited to get started and began by building a classroom library of interesting trade books and magazines with connections to many of the history topics he covered in his class. He visited second-hand bookstores, thriftshops, and garage sales, checked out discards from public libraries, sought donations of "irregulars" from bookstore chains, and made purchases from online discount sellers. He found a couple of old but solid metal bookcases and a magazine display case in the school district's furniture warehouse, covered them with a fresh coat of paint, and put them in the corner of his classroom. In the same corner, he added a couple of bean bags and inexpensive outdoor folding chairs to create a reading space for his students.

At our urging, Marcus met with the school librarian to enlist her help in finding relevant books and magazines she had that he could add to his class collection. These are texts Marcus would keep in his room during the exploration of certain units and return to the school library when the unit concluded. The librarian was more than willing to assist him, so he gave her his syllabus with topics and dates to help her organize relevant collections ahead of time.

As Marcus gathered new books and reading material he found a renewed interest in reading for his own personal pleasure and growth. Though many of the historical novels, biography, and information books Marcus found were written for youth, he was pleasantly surprised to discover that the quality of writing was often first rate. This discovery made him all the more eager to get these materials into the hands of his students. How to do that was the focus of our next conversation with Marcus.

Informally, Marcus's students were already picking out books and magazines from his classroom collection to browse, and though he was happy with this development, he was also interested in planned approaches to exposing students to these alternative texts. We brainstormed a variety of possible ways of creating opportunities for engaged reading in Marcus's classroom, including:

- Using information books to research history topics
- Reading novels related to class topics
- Making time for sustained silent reading of student self-selected material over any topic related to the class
- Reading aloud from a novel or information book related to a class topic

Next, we asked Marcus to think ahead and identify an upcoming unit that would lend itself to a multiple-text approach. With little hesitation, Marcus suggested the American Civil War, because he had been especially successful finding a range of books and other reading material on that topic. The outstanding sources Marcus had collected included:

- Pinkney's (2001) *Abraham Lincoln: Letter from a Slave Girl*, a fictional correspondence between a 12-year-old slave and President Lincoln. Although the letters are fictional, the information contained in the letters is based on historical facts, giving the reader a sense of the times and emotions of the day.
- Carson's (2005) *The Underground Railroad for Kids: From Slavery to Freedom with 21 Activities*, which powerfully depicts the heroic struggles of thousands of slaves who sought freedom through the Underground Railroad. The book contains eight firsthand narratives from escaped slaves and abolitionists and 30 biographies of passengers and conductors. It contains excellent reference materials for teachers and students along with activities that reinforce the themes of the book.

> One disciplinary teacher made a total commitment to making a variety of texts available to his students and was rewarded by heightened involvement and higher achievement.

- Lester and Brown's *From Slave Ship to Freedom Road* (1999). This selection is comprised of 24 paintings with accompanying text depicting the course of slavery, beginning with the ships sailing from Africa and continuing through the Civil War. The illustrations convey a wide range of the slave experience from the terrifying journey to America to an angry mammy tending her White charges.
- Carpenter's (1999) "Belle Boyd: Confederate Spy," an article from *Cobblestone*, an American history magazine written for middle-grade students. This is an excellent source for enlightening students on the roles played by women and children in the war effort.
- Bordewich's "Free at Last" (2004), which appeared in the *Smithsonian* magazine, is about a new museum in Ohio that celebrates the Underground Railroad. This article shows middle school students the efforts to preserve evidence from the historical period they are studying. The article provides very helpful background information on the Underground Railroad.
- The Web site at **http://bensguide.gpo.gov/.** This URL contains numerous passages for lower-achieving readers on American history topics, including a wide assortment focusing on the Civil War. The Web site is colorful, animated, and user-friendly.

With these sources, Marcus decided to read aloud to his class *Abraham Lincoln: Letters from a Slave Girl*. At the same time, he formed several cooperative groups of students and allowed them to select a source from the other materials to research the topic of slavery and the Underground Railroad. As these topics were encountered in the class textbook, students responsible for gathering information from the other texts were asked to share with their classmates. Students were also given dedicated time each day throughout the unit to browse the bookshelves and magazine rack for self-selected reading of any material related to the topic. They could also lounge in the bean bags or on the floor while reading. In this way, most students obtained multiple exposures to varying perspectives from the material Marcus had collected on slavery and the Civil War. By using interesting alternative sources, Marcus was able to inspire his students to levels of engaged learning he had not seen before. Plus, the feedback he received from his class was that the Civil War unit was the most interesting and fun up to that point in the school year. Furthermore, student test scores were among the highest Marcus received for any unit.

Biology

Loy, who taught 10th-grade biology in a high school in the same district as Marcus, used Farley Mowat's *Never Cry Wolf* (1979) in conjunction with a unit on food chains. His students seemed to become increasingly unmotivated and listless as the school year progressed. He noticed, however, that when he read aloud from virtually any source, their attention improved. Out of desperation, he decided to incorporate a novel into his food chain unit and observed the kind of heightened involvement and sustained effort he had hoped to see.

During one class period, after employing a short PowerPoint presentation that defined and characterized causes and effects of population crashes in the natural world, Loy asked students to work in pairs to seek out as much evidence and as many examples as they could find of such population crashes using the print and nonprint resources available to them. Students were given a recording sheet to document their research. Many began by thumbing back through the novel, *Never Cry Wolf*, and

Another teacher simply added a novel to the textbook in his content classroom and increased learning and motivation significantly.

wrote down information related to Mowat's description of what happened to the vole population when too many wolves were killed or relocated.

Afterward, Loy organized a review of the last chapter read in the novel. The review was in a "popcorn" format whereby Loy gave the class the first critical event of the chapter, then waited for other students to stand up and supply a statement about what happened next. Using this approach, the class was able to cover most of the chapter plot within 5 minutes.

Loy then asked for volunteers to come to the front of the room and take parts reading the next chapter aloud. In this chapter, a bush pilot and a party of hunters make camp near to where Farley is conducting his research of a wolf pack. He and the hunters have a threatening encounter. Loy took the role of narrator while the others read parts for Farley and members of the hunting party. Students participated eagerly, and after a couple of pages a new set of students went up to continue the read-aloud. Loy was patient with all students and waited until one asked for help with a word before he or a classmate provided it. At several points in the action, Loy invited class members who were not reading aloud to ask questions of the students who were. This seemed to keep everyone focused on the plot.

Earlier in the year, we helped Loy discover that his biology book was written at a level too difficult for several of his students. By allowing his students to read from sources that were easier for them, such as young adult novels, he found they tended to read the assigned pages and stay on task. (See Chapter 8 for a comprehensive discussion of strategies for using trade books in the content classroom.)

Practices That Expand Student Choices and Options

Math

Jaqui is the kind of teacher who proves the skeptics wrong. In spite of the odds she always seems to bring her first-year general math students into the flow of instruction. She knows many enter her class with negative attitudes toward math, often the result of years of failure and struggle, but instead of viewing their dispositions as detractors from learning, she sees them as starting points for change.

Transforming dispirited youth into risk takers begins by discovering who they are and what they value. Using the My Bag strategy discussed in Chapter 4, Jaqui is able to find something unique about each of her students. In one class of 32 students, for instance, all but 2 were living with their biological fathers and mothers, but each one possessed an interest or desire that defined them as special in her eyes. For instance, 12 were born outside of the United States. One was the daughter of refugees of the war in Kosovo. One played jazz trumpet. One worked with his uncle as a farm worker during the summers. And three were on the junior varsity football team.

The My Bag strategy can be equally effective when students are given the option of drawing or cutting out pictures from magazines in place of actual items from home to share about themselves.

With information gleaned from the *My Bag* activity, Jaqui was quick to demonstrate how much she valued her students' diversity and wanted to connect mathematics to their histories and experiences. She discussed with the class an upcoming unit on basic statistics—finding averages, compiling and organizing data, determining trends—and invited their suggestions for how they could learn it together. This act of using youth as curricular informants helps Jaqui create learning environments and activities that are responsive to students' actual needs. In this way, she builds math curriculum around students instead of imposing it on them. Examples of the kinds of suggestions her students offered to make learning statistics worthwhile are as follows:

- **Jesús:** "Keep it real."
- **Benita:** "Don't embarrass us."

- **Corey:** "Let us use our hands and stuff."
- **Mondelique:** "What can we do with it?"

From here, Jaqui pooled My Bag information and student suggestions, then conferenced with small groups and individual students to discuss possible projects for using statistics that related to their lives. For example, in consultation with the three football players in class, she helped them decide to maintain a statistics scrapbook on the team's performance throughout the fall season. The student from Kosovo wanted to explore the numbers behind the war and the ethnic cleansing her parents were fortunate enough to escape. The youth who played the trumpet thought it would be "cool" to study how many times he played certain notes while improvising by taping his improvisations then tallying frequencies and percentages. Other groups of students agreed to work together to research statistics related to recent immigrants in their neighborhoods and apartment complexes.

Jaqui met with students on a regular basis to get progress reports, provide additional resources, clarify the assignment, and take advantage of the myriad teaching moments that arose during these face-to-face encounters. Jaqui also helped students put their project work into presentable form, such as PowerPoints, graphs and charts on poster paper, or video. When projects were completed, she organized a celebration forum for sharing students' discoveries with statistics. Parents, relatives, neighbors, other teachers, community members, and administrators were invited to join the forum, which was well-attended. Cake and punch were served, as students, some in lab coats, talked about why they chose to do their projects, their data gathering techniques, the findings of their research, and what the projects meant to them.

The power of student choice and student input in learning is epitomized in the words of Mondelique, who was insistent that Jaqui teach statistics in a way that made it apparent to her why it was important. When wrapping up her presentation, she told the audience: "I was never good in math. And I didn't want to be in this class. But our teacher made it easy because she let us do something we wanted to do with math. I understand it better and feel more confident because she let us do it our way."

Practices That Structure Collaboration

History

As part of an excellent simulation experience designed to maximize student engagement in learning about Westward expansion, Aurora had her sixth graders work together to set up a wagon master election. After asking four students to join her, she formed groups of three with the rest of the class. The groups were given a scenario describing that they were pioneers in the 1850s about to go on an adventure to the West. Before they took their trip, however, they needed to select the best possible wagon master for the job. Groups were given rating sheets with critical criteria for a good wagon master, such as being experienced in dealing with Indians, knowledgeable about the best water sources and smoothest trails, and so on. Meanwhile, the four students Aurora had chosen were to be the individuals vying for the job of wagon master. Each was given a name, a brief biography, and a few minutes to prepare a pitch for the pioneers. When ready, characters like "Calico Katie" and "Buck Duke" told the groups in impassioned tones why they were the best suited for the job, given the many successful wagon trains they had led back and forth across Indian territories. After all wagon master candidates presented themselves, the pioneers checked their ratings and voted on their top choice.

Role plays and simulations are great ways to motivate youth to read and learn because they involve small groups and the entire class in a shared and often fun experience.

This activity and the discussion that followed served as a highly motivating and instructive way to involve Aurora's students in the study of the topic.

Business

To motivate student-centered discussion on the topic of the effects of a recession on the economy, Kish, the business teacher, wrote the word "recession" in large letters on the board. Without saying anything, he waited for students to react, question, and elaborate. In no time, students began to make associations with the word. These initial associations with the concept provided students the opportunity to find connections to their prior knowledge and experiences. As students commented, Kish wrote their responses on the board while purposely avoiding reacting to every response. Responses such as "inflation" and "higher gas prices" were typical, but everyone was surprised to hear the word "grounded" shouted out by a student in the corner. Instead of asking a question himself, Kish looked around the room and asked if anyone had a question for this student. Students were eager to find out what "grounded" had to do with recession and pressed the student for an explanation. She explained that she had inflated her parents' already whopping cell phone bill during a financially tight period that she said was caused by a recession. Her parents punished her by taking away her mobile phone privileges and restricting her after-school activity for a couple of weeks. By using discussion as a readiness-to-learn activity, Kish helped students develop an awareness of their network of associations and allowed them to listen to one another and weigh, reject, revise, and integrate ideas in their own minds. The grounded student's contribution turned out to be profitable because the textbook chapter they were assigned to read devoted a major section to the everyday, personal effects of a recessionary economy.

After the discussion, Kish restated students' initial associations with the concept. This allowed students to reflect on their own thinking and offer any new ideas about the concept of recession. They could verbalize associations that had been elaborated or changed through the discussion and probe their memories to expand on their prior knowledge. Interestingly, several other personal connections with the topic were discovered. One student talked about having to limit his "cruising" because he couldn't afford to waste gas. Another mentioned that his brother had to put off buying a house because he felt his job as a salesman was not secure. By participating more actively in class discussion, students had a better idea when the class ended of how much they knew about the topic. Kish, who created the conditions for an effective student-centered discussion, knew his class was motivated to learn more about the topic as a result of the experience.

Literature

A much more elaborate debate strategy as compared with the one just described in a business class is conducting a mock trial (Beck, 1999). Ya Pin's seventh-grade class was poised to read the breathtaking courtroom chapters in Harper Lee's (1960) English-curriculum stalwart, *To Kill a Mockingbird*. Instead of a teacher-led oral review to bring students to the point of this new episode in the novel, Ya Pin heightened motivation for reading by organizing a simulated court scene with parallels to themes from the novel. Here was the premise for the defense:

> *You are lawyers representing 18-year-old Michael Soo in a court case. Michael, a Korean American, along with his father and brother are being charged with theft of a motorcycle owned by 19-year-old John Adams.*
>
> *Here are the facts presented to you by Michael Soo:*
> *On the morning of Thursday, October 12, 2000, Michael met Mr. Adams in Mr. Adams's driveway to look at a Suzuki motorcycle John was selling. Michael test-rode the bike and then negotiated a purchase price with John of $2,000. Because his father was going to help pay for the motorcycle, Michael hoped he would return the following day, Friday, to buy the motorcycle.*

Michael went home, and when his father returned from work at 6:00 P.M., he talked with him about buying the motorcycle. Michael's father said before he would help pay for the bike, he would need to see it first.

Michael, his father, and his younger brother drove to John Adams's house around 8:30 P.M. to look at the bike. There were no lights on in the house. Michael rang the doorbell, but no one answered. Michael's father aimed the truck so the headlights would shine on the motorcycle that was parked in the driveway. The three of them then inspected the bike.

Michael's father told Michael he wouldn't pay $2,000 for the motorcycle because he didn't think it was worth that much money. John Adams had not returned by the time Michael, his father, and brother drove home. It was 9:15 P.M. Michael decided he would keep looking for a better deal on a Suzuki motorcycle.

Two days later, Saturday, police officers came to Michael's house asking questions. They explained that John Adams's motorcycle had been stolen and that Michael, his father, and brother had been seen late Thursday evening at the scene of the crime. The Soos denied any involvement, explaining their purpose for being at John Adams's home Thursday evening.

Granting a police request to look around, the officers found in the Soo's garage hundreds of motorcycle parts and two or three partially built motorcycles. Many of the parts had the Suzuki name and logo on them. The Soos explained that motorcycles were their hobby and that they had owned several Suzuki motorcycles in the past. Unfortunately, they could not find receipts of purchase for any of the motorcycles or parts.

Michael, his father, and brother were then issued a warrant for their arrest for stealing John Adams's motorcycle.

It is your job as a legal team to prove the Soos are being falsely accused because they are Korean American.

Ya Pin formed several groups and made certain each student had a role. For instance, there were teams of lawyers representing the Soos and John Adams, witnesses, and a jury. Other individuals played the part of a judge, a bailiff, and Michael and John. Her students performed their roles with flare and feeling, swept up in the moment by an imaginary setting and list of accusations that seemed all too real. When the jury found in favor of the plaintiff, John, the stage was set perfectly for reading about what was to happen to Atticus Bob and Mayella Ewell, and Tom Robinson.

With this motivational activity, Ya Pin had created a context that brought the issue of racial prejudice into the present day, set the debate in a place similar to the one in the novel, and made the fictionalized characters ones the students might recognize from their own communities and neighborhoods. Ya Pin's students brought a heightened level of enthusiasm and interest to the reading of the court scene chapters in *To Kill a Mockingbird* motivated by their desire to find out if Tom Robinson's fate would be similar to Michael's.

CASE STUDY REVISITED

Remember Theresa, the eighth-grade social studies teacher? She was preparing for a unit on the early Americans. Take a moment to write your ideas for Theresa to help motivate her students to study this content and become engaged in learning.

continued

Participatory learning is always likely to increase when collaborative activities bring real-world situations and controversies into the classroom.

Before writing your suggestions for Theresa in the case study, go to *http://www.pren/hall.com/brozo*, select Chapter 5, then click on Chapter Review Questions to check your understanding of the material.

Theresa introduced students to a motivational activity on the first day, that we thought was exceptional. She began by involving the class in a discussion of the role of archaeologists in understanding the relationship of artifacts to past societies. She then explained that one way to understand the past is to relate it to the present, and one way they could do that was by making a time capsule. After defining a time capsule, she asked students to think of objects they felt would be important to include in one that would be buried today and excavated 1,000 years later. Theresa jotted down ideas on the board and asked students to explain why their particular object would help people living 1,000 years later to understand what life was like today. Clearly, the purpose of exploring the idea of a time capsule was to motivate students to learn about the past by making it relevant to their own lives. The students were genuinely enjoying this activity, as reflected in interchanges such as this:

Student 1: Did you see that Coke commercial where this class sometime way in the future is walking through a 20th-century ruin and they find a Coke bottle?

Class: Yeah, I've seen that.

Theresa: What does a bottle of Coke say to these future people about ourselves and our culture?

Student 1: That we like to drink Coke.

Theresa: Would it? How could you be sure? Let's say people aren't drinking Coke a thousand years from now, and let's say these people you're talking about also found a tattered T-shirt with "Madonna" written on it, and a broken television or computer. How would they piece together the way we lived if this is all they found?

Student 2: They might think Madonna was our president or something.

Student 3: They might not even know what a television or computer was. I read a science fiction story about these people who could put this machine on their heads, like a headset, and see images in their heads and feel what you would feel if you were there.

Theresa: That's interesting. So they might not even be able to recognize that it was a television or computer or exactly what it was used for, especially if it was really badly broken up. Do you see now how hard it would be for future people to describe who we were and how we behaved from the few things they might find?

Student 4: Maybe if we put a Coke can in our time capsule, we should tape a piece of paper to it that tells what it is and all about it.

Theresa: If the paper didn't crumble and rot away, that would be very helpful for future people. Good idea. Unfortunately for archaeologists, the original inhabitants of North America didn't leave written directions and explanations with all of their artifacts.

Student 5: Didn't they draw pictures in caves of hunting buffalo and stuff like that?

Theresa: That's right, and those wall paintings help us quite a bit, but they don't tell the whole story. For instance, the wall pictures don't tell whether men and women married like they do today, or whether one man could have several wives. They don't tell us if they were nomadic or whether they lived in one place for long periods of time. Did these people have music or play games, and so on?

Eventually, the class formulated a list of things to put in their time capsule. It was fascinating to listen to the students rationalize why certain items would be appropriate to include. For instance, one young man wanted to contribute his tennis shoes; one was green, the other orange, and both were untied. He argued that they would reflect what young people are like today. The class concluded that his mismatched tennis shoes would give a misleading impression because only a small minority dresses that way. Instead, it was decided that pictures from magazines depicting many different fashions would be better. Another student said the time capsule should have a CD of contemporary music. This didn't seem feasible, the class agreed, because in 1,000 years, probably no means of playing the CD would exist.

The final list included a Coke can, accompanied by a picture of someone drinking from a can of Coke; a copy of *Time* magazine; several photographs of cars, fashions, TVs, computers and other high-tech electronics, and houses, lyrics and sheet music to a couple of popular songs; and a class portrait. The activity culminated at week's end with a ceremonial burial on a section of the school grounds of a time capsule (actually a large plastic canister) containing the items the class had decided on.

Theresa conducted a couple of other motivational activities during the week, including a word scavenger hunt, which involves students in a game for learning key words from their readings (see Chapter 6 for details), and viewing a film that traced the journey of the first people to emigrate from Europe to the area we now call Iowa. Students were also provided with a structured overview of the migration patterns, names, and terms associated with the first Americans.

This case study makes clear how varied and yet how effective creative and meaningful activities for motivating reading and learning can be. It demonstrates how a talented teacher takes her students far beyond the traditional boundaries of a content-area lesson by generating interest in the topic and keeping youth engaged in learning from the moment the topic is introduced until consideration of the topic concludes.

Looking Back, Looking Forward

Over 30 years ago, Illich advocated a curriculum that engendered "self-motivated learning instead of employing teachers to bribe or compel the student to find the time and the will to learn" (1970, p. 104). Three decades later Illich's recommendation is as viable as ever (Deci, Koestner, Ryan, & Cameron, 2001; Guthrie & Wigfield, 2000). Students become independent knowledge seekers when they perceive what they are learning to be personally meaningful and relevant to their lives and futures. On one level, then, we are suggesting that meaningful purposes for learning can be established only when the learning itself is meaningful.

Because we believe that the degree of success with a topic of study in the content areas depends on how motivated students are, we have focused this chapter on a range of classroom practices that teachers in middle and secondary schools have used to increase student engagement. The examples included here represent only a few of the potentially endless possibilities for making learning meaningful and getting students excited about the content to be read and studied. We hope these guidelines and examples help you become more sensitive to the importance of creating motivating learning conditions for virtually every disciplinary lesson and inspire you to expand your notions about the kinds of learning dynamics possible in your classroom.

In the next chapter, you will read about a variety of interesting vocabulary strategies that can motivate youth to expand their word knowledge. As you will see, the more students are engaged in word-learning activities, the better their chances for deeper and more meaningful understanding of disciplinary concepts.

References

Alexander, P., & Jetton, T. (2000). Learning from text: A multidimensional and developmental perspective. In M. Kamil, P. Mosenthal, P. D. Pearson, & R. Barr (Eds.), *Handbook of reading research* (Vol. 3). Mahwah, NJ: Lawrence Erlbaum Associates.

Alvermann, D. (2001). *Effective literacy instruction for adolescents* (Executive summary and paper commissioned by the National Reading Conference). Retrieved August 4, 2005, from http://nrconline.org/documents/2001/alverwhite2.pdf.

Alvermann, D. (2003). *Seeing themselves as capable and engaged readers: Adolescents and remediated instruction.* Naperville, IL: Learning Point Associates.

Anderman, E. M., Maehr, M. L., & Midgley, C. (1999). Declining motivation after the transition to middle school: Schools can make a difference. *Journal of Research and Development in Education, 32,* 131–147.

Anderman, L. H. (1999). Classroom goal orientation, school belonging and social goals as predictors of students' positive and negative affect following the transition to middle school. *Journal of Research and Development in Education, 32,* 89–103.

Baker, M. I. (2002). Reading resistance in middle school: What can be done? *Journal of Adolescent & Adult Literacy, 45,* 364–366.

Bean, T. W. (2002). Making reading relevant for adolescents. *Educational Leadership, 60,* 34–37.

Beck, C. (1999). Francine, Kerplunk, and the Golden Nugget—conducting mock trials and debates in the classroom. *The Social Studies, 90,* 78–84.

Bergin, D. A. (1999). Influences on classroom interest. *Educational Psychologist, 34,* 87–98.

Bintz, W. (1993). Resistant readers in secondary education: Some insights and implications. *Journal of Reading, 36,* 604–615.

Bordewich, F. (2004). Free at last. *Smithsonian, 35,* 64–71.

Brozo, W. G. (2004). Gaining and keeping students' attention. *Thinking Classroom/Peremena, 5,* 38–39.

Brozo, W. G. (2005a). Connecting with students who are disinterested and inexperienced. *Thinking Classroom/Peremena, 6,* 42–43.

Brozo, W. G. (2005b). Avoiding the "fourth-grade slump." *Thinking Classroom/Peremena, 4,* 48–49.

Brozo, W. G. (2006). Tales out of school: Accounting for adolescents in a literacy reform community. *Journal of Adolescent & Adult Literacy, 49,* 410–419.

Brozo, W. G., & Hargis, C. (2003a). Taking seriously the idea of reform: One high school's efforts to make reading more responsive to all students. *Journal of Adolescent & Adult Literacy, 43,* 14–23.

Brozo, W. G., & Hargis, C. (2003b). Use it or lose it: Three strategies to increase time spent reading. *Principal Leadership, 4,* 36–40.

Brozo, W. G., Valerio, P., & Salazar, M. (1996). A walk through Gracie's garden: Literacy and cultural explorations in a Mexican-American junior high school. *Journal of Adolescent & Adult Literacy, 40,* 164–171.

Carr, E., & Ogle, D. (1987). K-W-L Plus: A strategy for comprehension and summarization. *Journal of Reading, 30,* 626–631.

Clinton, P. (2002, September/October). Literacy in America: The crisis you don't know about and what we can do about it. *Book, 24,* 4–9.

Cook-Sather, A. (2002). Authorizing students' perspectives: Toward trust, dialogue, and change in education. *Educational Researcher, 31,* 3–14.

Cook-Sather, A. (2003). Listening to students about learning differences. *Teaching Exceptional Children, 35,* 22–26.

Deci, E., Koestner, R., Ryan, R., & Cameron, J. (2001). Extrinsic rewards and intrinsic motivation in education: Reconsidered once again. *Review of Educational Research, 71,* 1–51.

Dewey, J. (1913). *Interest and effort in education.* Boston: Houghton Mifflin.

Donahue, P., Daane, M., & Grigg, W. (2003). *The nation's report card: Reading highlights 2003.* Washington, DC: National Center for Education Statistics.

Dreher, M. J. (2003). Motivating struggling readers by tapping the potential of information books. *Reading & Writing Quarterly, 19,* 25–38.

Duffelmeyer, R., & Baum, D. (1992). The extended anticipation guide revisited. *Journal of Reading, 35,* 654–656.

Eagly, A., Chen, S., Chaiken, S., & Shaw-Barnes, K. (1999). The impact of attitudes on memory: An affair to remember. *Psychological Bulletin, 125,* 64–89.

Eccles, J. S., Wigfield, A., & Schiefele, U. (1998). Motivation to succeed. In W. Damon (Series Ed.) & N. Eisenberg (Ed.), *Handbook of child psychology: Social, emotional, and personality development* (5th ed., Vol. 3). New York: Wiley.

Edwards, S. (2001). Bridging the gap: Connecting school and community with service learning. *English Journal, 90,* 39–44.

Fecho, B. (2004). *Making English relevant: Promoting literacy and democracy through critical inquiry.* New York: Teachers College Press.

Freeman, J. G., McPhail, J. C., & Berndt, J. A. (2002). Sixth graders' views of activities that do and do not help them to learn. *Elementary School Journal, 102,* 335–347.

Gee, J. P. (2003). *What video games have to teach us about learning and literacy.* New York: Palgrave.

Greenleaf, C. L., Jimenez, R. T., & Roller, C. M. (2002). Reclaiming secondary reading interventions: From limited to rich conceptions, from narrow to broad conversations. *Reading Research Quarterly, 37,* 484–496.

Guthrie, J., & Davis, M. (2003). Motivating struggling readers in middle school through an engagement model of classroom practice. *Reading & Writing Quarterly, 19,* 59–85.

Guthrie, J. T., & Humenick, N. M. (2004). Motivating students to read: Evidence for classroom practices that increase reading motivation and achievement. In P. McCardle & V. Chhabra (Eds.), *The voice of evidence in reading research.* Baltimore: Brookes Publishing.

Guthrie, J., & Wigfield, A. (2000). Engagement and motivation in reading. In M. Kamil, P. Mosenthal, P. D. Pearson, & R. Barr (Eds.), *Handbook of reading research* (Vol. 3). Mahwah, NJ: Lawrence Erlbaum Associates.

Hartley, J. (2003). Designing instructional and informational text. Retrieved June 1, 2005, from http://aect-members.org/m/research_handbook/Chapters/34.pdf.

Hayden, R. (1995). Training parents as reading facilitators. *The Reading Teacher, 49,* 334–336.

Hidi, S., & Harackiewicz, J. (2000). Motivating the academically unmotivated: A critical issue for the 21st century. *Review of Educational Research, 70,* 151–179.

Hinchman, K. A., Alvermann, D. E., Boyd, F. B., Brozo, W. G., & Vacca, R. T. (2003/2004). Supporting older students' in- and out-of-school literacies. *Journal of Adolescent & Adult Literacy, 47,* 304–310.

Hoss, M. (1991). Guest speakers are our favorite inexpensive reference tool. *Illinois Libraries, 73,* 540–542.

Hurst, B. (2001). The ABCs of content area lesson planning: Attention to basics, and comprehension. *Journal of Adolescent & Adult Literacy, 44,* 692–693.

Illich, I. (1970). *Deschooling society.* New York: Harper & Row.

Ivey, G. (1999). A multicase study in the middle school: Complexities among young adolescent readers. *Reading Research Quarterly, 34,* 428–436.

Ivey, G., & Broaddus, K. (2001). "Just plain reading": A survey of what makes students want to read in middle school classrooms. *Reading Research Quarterly, 36,* 350–377.

Lee, P. W. (1999). In their own voices: An ethnographic study of low-achieving students within the context of school reform. *Urban Education, 34,* 214–244.

Linnenbrink, E. A., & Pintrich, P. R. (2002). Motivation as an enabler for academic success. *The Psychological Review, 31,* 313–327.

Marchand-Martella, N., Wasta, S., & Martella, R. (1996). Applying the K-W-L strategy in health education. *Journal of School Health, 66,* 153–154.

Margolis, H., & McCabe, P. P. (2004). Self-efficacy: A key to improving the motivation of struggling learners. *The Clearing House, 77,* 241–249.

Merkley, D. (1996/97). Modified anticipation guide. *The Reading Teacher, 50,* 365–368.

Moje, E. (2000). *"All the stories that we have": Adolescents' insights about literacy and learning in secondary schools.* Newark, DE: International Reading Association.

Moore, D. W., Bean, T. W., Birdyshaw, D., & Rycik, J. A. (1999). *Adolescent literacy: A position statement.* Newark, DE: International Reading Association.

Mosenthal, P. (1999). Understanding engagement: Historical and political contexts. In J. Guthrie & D. Alvermann (Eds.), *Engaged reading: Processes, practices and policy implications.* New York: Teachers College Press.

Nichols, J. D., & Miller, R. B. (1994). Cooperative learning and student motivation. *Contemporary Educational Psychology, 19,* 167–178.

Nolen, S. B., & Nicholls, J. G. (1994). A place to begin (again) in research on student motivation: Teachers' beliefs. *Teaching & Teacher Education, 10,* 57–69.

O'Flahavan, J., Gambrell, L., Guthrie, J., Stahl, S., & Alvermann, D. (1992, April). Poll results guide activities of research center. *Reading Today,* 12.

Ogle, D. (1992). KWL in action: Secondary teachers find applications that work. In E. Dishner, T. Bean, J. Readence, & D. Moore (Eds.), *Reading in the content areas: Improving classroom instruction.* Dubuque, IA: Kendall/Hunt.

Ogle, D. M. (2003). Reading and learning about our wonderful world: Information-rich resources and strategies to engage readers. *The NERA Journal, 39,* 7–10.

Organization for Economic Cooperation and Development. (2001). *Knowledge and skills for life: First results from PISA 2000.* Paris: OECD.

Pajares, F. (1996). Self-efficacy beliefs in academic settings. *Review of Educational Research, 66,* 543–578.

Pintrich, P. R., & Schunk, D. H. (2001). *Motivation in education: Theory, research and applications* (2nd ed.). Englewood Cliffs, NJ: Prentice Hall.

Poling, L. (2000). The real world: Community speakers in the classroom. *Social Education, 64,* 8–10.

Powell-Brown, A. (2003/2004). Can you be a teacher of literacy if you don't love to read? *Journal of Adolescent & Adult Literacy, 47,* 284–288.

Protheroe, N. (2004). Motivating reluctant learners. *Principal, 84,* 46–49.

Prouty, J. L., & Irby, (1995, February). Parent involvement: Integrated packets. Paper presented at the Student/Beginning Teacher Conference, Nacogdoches, TX.

Rousseau, J. J. (1762; 1979). *Emile: Or, on education.* New York: Basic Books.

Sadoski, M., Goetz, E., & Rodriguez, M. (2000). Engaging texts: Effects of concreteness comprehensibility, interest, and recall in four text types. *Journal of Educational Psychology, 92,* 85–95.

Sampson, M. B. (2002). Confirming K-W-L: Considering the source. *The Reading Teacher, 55,* pp. 528–532.

Santa, C. M. (2004). Project CRISS: Evidence of effectiveness. Retrieved June 1, 2005, from http://www.projectcriss.com/research.

Schiefele, U. (1999). Interest and learning from text. *Scientific Studies of Reading, 3,* 257–279.

Schunk, D. H., & Zimmerman, B. J. (1997). Developng efficacious readers and writers: The role of social and self-regulatory processes. In J. T. Guthrie & A. Wigfield (Eds.), *Reading engagement: Motivating readers through integrated instruction* (pp. 125–136). Cresskill, NJ: Hampton Press.

Strange, T., & Wyant, S. (1999). The great American prairie: An integrated fifth-grade unit. *Social Education, 63,* 216–219.

Sturtevant, E., Boyd, F., Brozo, W. G., Hinchman, K., Alvermann, D., & Moore, D. (2006). *Principled practices for adolescent literacy: A framework for instruction and policy.* Mahwah, NJ: Erlbaum.

Sumter, M. T. (2002). The assessment of the relation of climate to adolescent academic motivation. Paper presented at the conference of the American Society for Criminology, Chicago, IIL.

Turner, J. (1995). The influence of classroom contexts on young children's motivation for literacy. *Reading Research Quarterly, 30,* 410–441.

Tyson-Bernstein, H. (1988). *A conspiracy of good intentions.* Washington, DC: Council for Basic Education.

Volet, S., & Jarvela, S. (2002). *Motivation in learning contexts: Theoretical and methodological implications.* Queensland, AU: Elsevier Science Ltd.

Wade, S., Schraw, G., Buxton, W., & Hayes, M. (1993). Seduction of the strategic reader: Effects of interest on strategy and recall. *Reading Research Quarterly, 28,* 92–115.

Wasley, P. A., Hampel, R. L., & Clark, R. W. (1997). *Kids and school reform.* San Francisco: Jossey-Bass.

White, B., & Johnson, T. S. (2001). We really do mean it: Implementing language arts standard #3 with opinionniares. *The Clearing House, 74,* 119–123.

Williams, B. T. (2003). Heoes, rebels, and victims: Student identities in literacy narratives. *Journal of Adolescent & Adult Literacy, 47,* 342–345.

Williams, B. T. (2005). Leading double lives: Literacy and technology in and out of school. *Journal of Adolescent & Adult Literacy, 48,* 702–706.

Worthy, J., Moorman, M., & Turner, M. (1999). What Johnny likes to read is hard to find in school. *Reading Research Quarterly, 34,* 12–27.

Trade Books

Anaya, R. (1990). Salomon's story. In C. Tatum (Ed.), *Mexican-American literature.* Orlando, FL: Harcourt Brace Jovanovich.

Bredeson, C. (2001). *Mount Saint Helens volcano.* New York: Enslow.

Carpenter, S. (December, 1999). Belle Boyd: Confederate spy. *Cobblestone, 20,* 2–3.

Carson, M. K. (2005). *The Underground Railroad for kids: From slavery to freedom with 21 activities.* Chicago: Chicago Review Press.

Cisneros, S. (1990). Three wiseguys: Un cuento de navidad. In C. Tatum (Ed.), *Mexican-American literature.* Orlando, FL: Harcourt Brace Jovanovich.

Claybourne, A. (2000). *Read about volcanoes.* New York: Millbrook Press.

Lee, H. (1960). *To Kill a Mockingbird.* New York: Warner Books.

Lester, J., & Brown, R. (1999). *From slave ship to freedom road.* New York: Penguin Putnam.

Mowat, F. (1979). *Never cry wolf.* New York: Bantam Books.

Pinkney, A. (2001). *Abraham Lincoln: Letters from a slave girl.* New York: Winslow Press.

VanRose, V. (2000). *Volcano and earthquake.* New York: Dorling Kindersley.

chapter 6

Developing General and Content-Area Vocabulary Knowledge

Anticipation Guide

Directions: Read each statement carefully and decide whether you agree or disagree with it, placing a check mark in the appropriate *Before Reading* column. When you have finished reading and studying the chapter, return to the guide and decide whether your anticipations need to be changed by placing a check mark in the appropriate *After Reading* column.

	Before Reading		After Reading	
	Agree	*Disagree*	*Agree*	*Disagree*
1. Only struggling readers need to be taught vocabulary words.	____	____	____	____
2. A student with a deficient vocabulary will probably also have comprehension problems.	____	____	____	____
3. A student who can define a word for the teacher understands the word.	____	____	____	____
4. The dictionary is the best way for students to learn word meanings.	____	____	____	____
5. Teaching students 20 words a week from a list of high-utility words should improve their vocabulary.	____	____	____	____
6. The best format for evaluating students' word knowledge is a multiple-choice test.	____	____	____	____

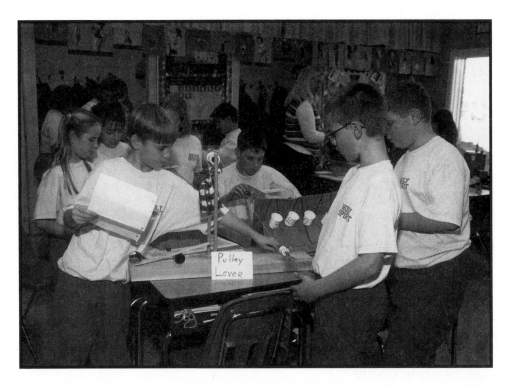

We return to the first principle stated in Chapter 2 and elaborated upon in Chapter 3. We do this because the research literature has consistently indicated that students' understanding of what they read is closely linked to the depth and breadth of their vocabulary knowledge (e.g., National Reading Panel, 2000; RAND Reading Study Group, 2002). These findings, as well as the first principle stated above, provide the framework for our discussion of how content-area teachers can develop their students' general and content-area vocabulary knowledge while enhancing their academic literacies and learning.

7. English teachers are the ones who should develop students' word knowledge.

_____   _____   _____   _____

*W*hat does it mean to "know" a word? That question has been debated for about 50 years, starting with Cronbach (1942), who suggested that word knowledge existed in qualitative dimensions. In the vernacular, to know a word means to be able to define it. But is this an adequate measure of one's word knowledge? When asked what the word *light* meant, 4-year-old Ryan's reply was "It comes from the sun and helps us see things." However, he had no idea what "light as a feather" meant, nor did he know the meaning of *light* in the sentence "I saw the birds light on the tree." Does Ryan really know the word *light*?

One of the primary goals of vocabulary development at the middle and high school levels is not simply to increase the breadth of students' vocabularies (i.e., the number of words for which students have a definition), but also to increase the depth and precision of their word knowledge. In other words, the goal is to help students, like Ryan, develop a full and complete understanding of words. But the goal is much more than improving students' word knowledge. Recent federal reports (e.g., RAND Reading Study Group, 2002) have indicated that vocabulary knowledge is one of the five essential components of reading. Given that most students are expected to read content-area textbooks packed with concepts and technical vocabulary that they need to understand fully if they are to learn, the relationship between vocabulary and comprehension becomes even more significant (Harmon, Hedrick, & Wood, 2005). If too many general or technical words puzzle students, they will read in a halting manner, a behavior that compromises their reading fluency (Joshi, 2005). Moreover, when the processing demands for reading a textbook become elevated because of the vocabulary load, many students will have little, if any, cognitive energy left for thinking about key concepts or monitoring their understanding. As a result of these factors, students become frustrated outsiders to the learning process (Fisher & Blachowicz, 2005).

In this chapter, we present a variety of vocabulary activities and strategies that can be used to expand students' vocabulary knowledge and comprehension of content-area concepts. Throughout the chapter we also reiterate the importance of using effective teaching methods such as demonstrations and modeling, small-group interactions, class discussions, and writing activities in support of the vocabulary-building activities and strategies.

Go to *http://www.prenhall.com/brozo*, select Chapter 6, then click on Chapter Objectives to provide a focus for your reading.

CASE STUDY

Rafalar, Curriculum Director of the Park Forest School District, analyzed the results of the competency-based reading test that was given to 10th graders in the spring. Much to her dismay, the vocabulary scores were again low. She called the principals to highlight her concerns and to recommend that a district committee be formed to investigate the problem and offer some specific solutions. Consequently, a committee was formed of teachers who taught 10th graders across the district. They met regularly during the school year to discuss the problem in more depth, but they could not agree on what should be done. Several committee members thought the language arts teachers should be responsible for improving the vocabulary scores. Other members complained that the additional burden of teaching vocabulary words would rob them of precious instructional time. And three members wanted the school to purchase a computer program promising to teach students 50 words a week. Patience was wearing thin as the school year drew to a close.

To the Reader:

As you read and work through this chapter on expanding vocabulary and concepts across the content areas, consider ways in which the committee could solve this district's problem. Think about the characteristics of effective vocabulary instruction and possible strategies that this school district might incorporate into the curriculum.

Understanding the Nature of Word Knowledge

One of the underlying themes of this chapter is that word-learning strategies should require students to combine new text information with their prior knowledge to yield conceptual understanding of words. The admonitions of our best vocabulary writers and researchers are entirely consistent with this theme (e.g., Scott & Nagy, 2004; Stahl & Stahl, 2004). Earlier in this chapter, we mentioned 4-year-old Ryan, who had partial definitional understanding of the word *light.* But Ryan did not have a full understanding of *light* that would have allowed him to interpret its meaning in a variety of contexts.

Stahl's work (1986, 1999) with vocabulary made the distinction between definitional and contextual word knowledge. Definitional knowledge is essentially knowing a dictionary-like definition for a word. It is important word knowledge, but it limits understanding because students often do not make that connection between the definition of a word and the meaning of the text. When students are not making those connections or inferences, their understanding of the text is usually compromised (Rupley & Nichols, 2005). Contextual knowledge, on the other hand, is meaning gained from the context, whether it be from a picture or graph, an example, an explanatory paragraph, or students' prior knowledge about the topic. Most students use a combination of these meaning-making cues to make sense of their content-area reading assignments.

To help you understand the important distinction between definitional and contextual word knowledge, we have prepared an exercise for you. For the following sentence, two key words have been defined. In the space provided, write what the statement means in your own words.

Surrogate: judge or magistrate

Testator: one making a claim on a will

The learned surrogate has held that an intent to have an apportionment will be imputed to the testator.

In your own words: _____

For the next sentence, the topic area is provided. Given the topic, write in your own words the special definition of the two italicized words in the sentence.

Topic: commodities futures

Live hogs *found* November *unchanged.*

Your definition of *found*: _____

Your definition of *unchanged*: _____

Now that you have finished the exercise, some explanation is in order. In the first sentence, you undoubtedly discovered that even with a couple of the key terms defined, you were still unable to make sense of it. Why? Because the meaning of the sentence is larger than the sum of the definitions of each of its words. To state it another way, to understand this sentence, you must connect individual definitions to a broad context of meaning. You must possess the schema or relevant prior knowledge for these words, for without a schema, the sentence is an unintelligible collection of fragments of definitions. If, however, you were a lawyer of contracts and estate settlements, this sentence would be perfectly understandable.

What about the second sentence? Were you able to supply the appropriate special definitions for the commonly understood words *found* and *unchanged*?

If not, it is likely due to the fact that your schema for the language of commodities futures is not especially well developed. Once again, without the necessary schema, the sentence is as oblique as a line from a surrealistic poem. Of course, if you are a member of the Chicago Board of Trade familiar with hog futures in the commodities market, the expression would make perfect sense to you.

As you now know from your own experience, definitional word knowledge does not imply a deep level of understanding. Hence, the principles and strategies of effective vocabulary instruction discussed in this chapter are not meant to make students experts at reciting definitions. If a strategy or program focuses only on correctly matching a word to a definition, then what is obtained is limited in vision and probably has a low chance of being transferred to students' actual reading, writing, listening, or speaking (Beck, McKeown, & Kucan, 2002). Before examining strategies that content-area teachers can use to help their students understand content-area vocabulary words and concepts, we present six guidelines that should be considered when planning instruction.

> The goal of vocabulary instruction is to insure that students have a deep level of word understanding that permits them to apply this knowledge to real-life situations.

Guidelines for Effective Vocabulary Instruction

Most individuals would agree that no single method, material, or strategy will consistently guarantee that students will improve their word knowledge. Therefore, it seems advantageous for teachers to select a variety of approaches for the general and technical vocabulary words in their content area (Rupley, 2005). In addition, the following seven guidelines, gleaned from a variety of research studies, should be considered when planning vocabulary lessons:

1. Teach vocabulary from a context.
2. Emphasize students' active and informed role in the learning process.
3. Give students tools to expand word knowledge independently.
4. Reinforce word learning with repeated exposures over time.
5. Stimulate students' awareness and interest in words.
6. Build a language-rich environment to support word learning.
7. Encourage students to read widely.

Teach Vocabulary from a Context

Researchers who have reviewed the literature on vocabulary instruction have concluded that vocabulary is best taught in a unifying context (Fisher & Blachowicz, 2004; Stahl & Stahl, 2004). Words taught in the context of a content area such as biology will be learned more effectively than words taught in isolation because context allows students to integrate words with previously acquired knowledge. The implication, of course, is that students will not improve their long-term vocabulary knowledge and understanding by memorizing the definitions of a list of essential words that high school students should know (Joshi, 2005).

Thus, content-area teachers need to select or have students select the targeted words for study from textbooks, newspapers, magazines, or novels. For example, if students are reading a short selection from a speech textbook on words and their meaning, words such as *arbitrary, connotation, denotation,* or *syntax* could be studied. Another alternative is to group general words into themes. An English teacher could organize a lesson around a set of adjectives that negatively describe a person's actions (e.g., *lax, infantile, obsequious, narcissistic*) or a history teacher could organize the targeted words into categories representing individuals, events, or places. Whatever approach is used to provide a context and an organizing schema, remember that lists of words that are introduced on Monday and tested on Friday will probably be forgotten on Saturday.

Emphasize Students' Active and Informed Role in the Learning Process

Although some students may learn a few new words with worksheet type activities, the majority of students need activities that challenge them to think about words and apply them to new situations.

The importance of students' active participation and elaborative processing in learning new words is a consistent theme across the research literature (McKeown & Beck, 2004; Fisher & Blachowicz, 2005; Rupley, 2005). Stahl (1985, 1999) described active involvement of the learner as "generative processing." Generative or elaborative processing engages students in activities such as (1) sensing and inferring relationships between targeted vocabulary and their own background knowledge, (2) recognizing and applying vocabulary words to a variety of contexts, (3) recognizing examples and nonexamples, and (4) generating novel contexts for the targeted word. In contrast, an example of passive involvement related to vocabulary instruction is worksheet-type activities asking students to select definitions, whether in multiple-choice or matching formats, or to fill in empty blanks with a word from a list.

When students have an informed role in vocabulary development, they understand the declarative and procedural requirements of understanding new words (Nagy & Scott, 2000). That is, they have the declarative knowledge that allows them to define a word and the procedural knowledge that allows them to do something with the word in other contexts. Some researchers have determined that students believe vocabulary learning to be a simple and quick task, involving no more than the memorization of a concise one-word definition (Francis & Simpson, 2003). Unfortunately, students who hold such naïve beliefs about words are the ones who do not profit from even the most carefully planned vocabulary instruction and are often the ones who struggle in a content area (Blachowicz & Fisher, 2002). In order to counter students' misconceptions about learning new vocabulary or concepts, teachers should stress on a regular basis that understanding a word involves more than definitional knowledge and that full understanding grows slowly over time. Accordingly, students should also be taught that they can increase their word knowledge and understanding if they use a variety of resources and techniques, all of which have some advantages and disadvantages (e.g., dictionaries, context clues).

Give Students Tools to Expand Word Knowledge Independently

Vocabulary development involves both the "what" and the "how." The "what" focuses on the processes involved in knowing a word. The "how" is equally important because it involves students in learning strategies for unlocking words on their own or independently. Think about it this way: If you teach students some words, they will be able to recognize and add those particular words to their repertoire; but if you teach students some independent word-learning strategies, they will be able to expand their vocabulary continually and read and understand many more texts once they leave your classroom (Edwards, Font, Baumann, & Boland, 2004; Graves, 2004).

We are not suggesting that content-area teachers discontinue their instruction of important words and concepts taken from their units of study. Instead, we make the point that classroom teachers should strike a balance between these two approaches. Students should be exposed to and actively involved in the learning of key terms and concepts related to text topics. In this case, developing broad understanding of a set of critical vocabulary is relevant and purposeful, as it will contribute to greater comprehension of the text. Indeed, we provide many activities and strategies for this purpose in this chapter. Too often, however, word-specific methods for teaching vocabulary involve handing students a list of arbitrarily selected words without demonstrating a clear connection between remembering definitions and meaningful learning. Content-area teachers should also help students become independent consumers and users of new words.

Reinforce Word Learning with Repeated Exposures Over Time

Students' word knowledge takes time to develop and increases in small, incremental steps (Scott & Nagy, 2004). Although it is impossible to identify a specific time frame for all students, we do know from the research literature that word ownership is reinforced when students receive multiple exposures to targeted words in multiple contexts (Beck et al., 2002; Rupley & Nichols, 2005). A math teacher puts this principle into practice by building vocabulary through (1) extensively discussing key terms and symbols and exploring what students already know about them, (2) previewing how the words and symbols are used in their math textbooks, (3) asking students to record the words and symbols in a vocabulary notebook, (4) practicing the words and symbols with a variety of activities and exercises that require students to think and write rather than circle answers, and (5) reviewing and testing in a cumulative fashion. Vocabulary reinforcement approaches such as these ensure students' reading fluency and understanding and hasten their spontaneous use of the words in spoken and written contexts.

Stimulate Students' Awareness of and Interest in Words

As teachers, we all know the role that interest plays in our content-area classrooms. That is, when students are interested in what they hear in class or read about in an assignment, this interest will significantly increase their attention, effort, persistence, thinking processes, and performance. Unfortunately, commercial materials and assignments that ask students to look up 20 words in the dictionary and write sentences using them do not interest or motivate most middle school and high school students. What we need to do as teachers is to increase students' awareness of words and create situations in which learning new words is a valuable knowledge-seeking activity (Graves, 2004; Scott & Nagy, 2004).

For additional ideas on building students' interest in word knowledge, check out this very useful website: *www.reading online.org/newliteracies/ webwatch/vocabulary.*

The best starting point for building word enthusiasm is with you, the teacher. We can hardly expect our students to become sensitive to words and interested in expanding word knowledge if we cannot demonstrate interest in words ourselves. More than 30 years ago Manzo and Sherk stated that "the single most significant factor in improving vocabulary is the excitement about words which teachers can generate" (1971, p. 78). Such a statement still holds true today (Blachowicz & Fisher, 2004). As we emphasized in previous chapters, modeling is a powerful teaching tool. If you want students to learn certain words, then talk about words you recently heard on a television show or read in the newspaper. Show students that you use the dictionary to look up words you do not understand or for definitions you need to clarify so that they realize that vocabulary acquisition is a lifelong goal. During class discussion, in conversation with students, or when responding to journal or other student writing, use words you want them to integrate into their written and spoken vocabularies. Above all, be playful with words and exhibit enthusiasm for words. As pointed out by Fisher and Blachowicz (2005), when teachers encourage students to play with words and manipulate them, students are learning to take a "metalinguistic stand on vocabulary," a stance that builds flexibility and confidence (p. 283). We know a 10th-grade teacher who does just that as she monitors the hallway between periods. As students enter her class she greets them with comments that use their vocabulary words in playful ways (e.g., "Josh, you certainly look disgruntled today. Did the soccer coach yell at you last night?"). The repartee usually continues, with students picking up the word play until class begins.

Numerous school districts use Web sites as a way to enhance students' interest in vocabulary development. These Web sites introduce a new word each day that typically focuses on a weekly theme, such as words relating to Halloween or words of French origin. The entries typically provide a definition, pronunciation guide, a brief explanation of word origin, and a quotation or sentence using the targeted word. Although schools vary in how they incorporate the Web sites into their daily routine, often the words are discussed during homeroom or during an elongated first period. Of course, there are a variety of other ways to build this enthusiasm and interest in words and we will address them later in this chapter.

One example of such a Web site is the following: www.wordcentral.com.

Build a Language-Rich Environment to Support Word Learning

The findings from research studies suggest that students with strong expressive and receptive vocabularies are the ones who are immersed in home and school environments characterized by "massive amounts of rich written and oral language" (Nagy & Scott, 2000, p. 280). Teachers can best promote vocabulary growth by working with students to create an environment where new words are learned, celebrated, and used in authentic communication tasks. Students should be given opportunities to experiment with using words in low-risk situations, to discuss new ideas daily, to talk freely and openly about how text concepts relate to their real-world concerns, to read works

Honoring Diversity and Building Confidence in the Content Classroom

Because there is a gap between students' expressive and receptive vocabularies, teachers should frontload their instruction by emphasizing the oral language use of new words long before students are asked to write about the words (Joshi, 2005). Ricardo practices this principle with his eighth-grade remedial reading class by asking his students, in pairs, to "try out" sentences using a new word After receiving feedback and suggestions from each other, his students then share their sentences orally with the entire class. Hence, after 15 minutes, these students have heard countless examples of how to use a targeted word correctly and how not to use the word. These oral language activities help Richardo's struggling readers to understand the connotative nuances and syntactic rules that govern word knowledge and ensure that they can pronounce the words correctly.

in a variety of text genres related to concepts, and to write purposeful and meaningful texts that employ key words and demonstrate understanding of important concepts (McKeown & Beck, 2004).

Once students become comfortable with a set of new words, teachers can then reinforce and extend their learning by providing regular writing experiences. For example, in order to enhance his students' understanding of the words *egocentric* and *altruistic,* Ricardo asked them to write two different e-mail messages to a close relative, one from an egocentric person and one from an altruistic person. Of course, the revision and editing stages of the writing process become excellent opportunities to engage students in searches for "that one perfect word" that conveys the precise meaning they have in mind.

Encourage Students to Read Widely

As noted by a variety of researchers, students who choose to read widely and frequently have the breadth and depth of word knowledge necessary to understand their content-area textbook assignments (Harmon, et al., 2005; Joshi, 2005). Moreover, findings from comprehensive studies such as the National Assessment of Educational Progress in Reading (Donahue, Voelkl, Campbell, and Mazzeo, 1999) have indicated that students who reported that they read frequently and widely were the ones who also had higher achievement test scores. Although many of these studies are correlational in nature, the trends suggest that students who read frequently have more opportunities to learn new words than students who choose not to read. The implication for content-area teachers is obvious: If we want our students to understand what they read in our courses, we must encourage them to read beyond what they are assigned to read in our classrooms (Graves, 2004). We should also keep in mind that what students read is not as important as the fact that they are reading. Forcing students to read the "important" works or classics will not instill a love of reading and may, in fact, cause negative reactions. Rather than the classics, many teachers like to stimulate recreational reading by encouraging students to read newspapers, magazines, short stories, trade books, and adolescent novels.

Some content-area teachers have discovered that they can hook their students into recreational reading or reading beyond the classroom by bringing into the classroom intriguing supplementary materials. We know a health and fitness teacher who begins each class period by reading aloud a brief selection from a recent magazine or newspaper. He calls it the "reading minute" and uses the brief time to discuss the content (e.g., the death of diet guru Atkins) and to highlight important words that might be problematic or useful to students (e.g., *metabolism*). Surprising as it may seem, adolescents do enjoy hearing these oral interpretations. Researchers have also found that students, especially those with lower vocabulary knowledge, will learn a few new words (Stahl, 1999).

Check Chapter 8 and other chapters throughout this textbook for specific suggestions in how to encourage students' love and interest in reading.

Selecting Key Terms and Concepts

Learning a new word or key concept for a content area is obviously a complex task dependent upon students' prior knowledge and experiences. Graves (1987) has suggested that three tasks are involved in word learning. The first task is learning a new word for a concept when the student understands the concept but has not heard of the label for that concept. For example, most students understand the processes involved in defense mechanisms such as rationalization because they have all rationalized their behaviors in some way. The label, however, will probably be new to them. Words such as these are not as difficult to teach students because they have the experiences to draw upon to understand and learn them.

The second and third tasks involved in word learning are more difficult because students are not as familiar with the underlying concept. With the second task, students are learning a new concept for a known word. In psychology and mathematics, for example, the word *set* has a different meaning from what students understand the word to mean when they talk about having to "set the table for dinner." The third task involves students in learning a new concept for which they have no label and minimal, if any, understanding or background. These tasks challenge both students and teachers. For example, in an ecology unit the concept of *eutrophication* (a gradual and natural process that turns lakes into marshes because of an excess amount of algae) is probably new to most 10th graders, as is the label. Hence, the science teacher would need to spend more time on this word than on others such as *mercury, detergents,* or *biodegradable.* In addition to understanding the three tasks involved in learning a word, it is important to understand the types of vocabulary in a content area.

Types of Vocabulary

If you were to skim a chapter in this textbook, you would probably discover that the vocabulary words could be classified in two ways. The first type are general words that are not particularly associated with any single content area and could be found in any newspaper or weekly magazine. For example, a science teacher who asked his ninth-grade students to read a brief excerpt from Rachel Carson's book *Silent Spring* identified the following general words that he thought should be taught: *maladies, blight, moribund, specter, stark,* and *droned.* A British journalist could have easily used some of these same words to describe a winter day in London because they are common to many communication situations.

The second type are the technical content-area words that are unique to a particular subject such as culinary cooking or ecology. Technical words include general words that are used in a specialized way and words that have only one distinct meaning and application—the second and third tasks involved in word learning. Examples of the former are words such as *table, matter, set,* or *drive,* which take on specialized meanings depending on the content area. Examples of the latter include words such as *alveoli* in science, *sonority* in music, and *matte effect* in art. In addition, symbols that occur in courses such as mathematics, physics, and chemistry are important content-area words that cannot be overlooked by students or teachers.

A Process for Selecting Words to Teach

Because it is impossible to teach all the general and technical words from a content-area reading assignment, an important first step in teaching vocabulary is to decide which terms and concepts should be taught (Fisher & Blachowicz, 2005). Traditionally, teachers have used the textbook as a guide, focusing on the words highlighted in the text. Basing vocabulary instruction on these words alone, however, may not meet your overall goals for teaching the content or unit. Researchers have made it clear that students will learn what is emphasized. If instruction focuses

---

When selecting important vocabulary to emphasize, content area teachers should consider general words, words with multiple meanings, and technical words.

on the important and meaningful details, concepts, and issues, those things will be what students learn and remember. Vocabulary instruction, then, should focus on words related to those important ideas. Sometimes the words the textbook author has chosen to highlight will match the concepts you choose to emphasize; sometimes they will not. It is important, therefore, that you have a system for selecting the appropriate vocabulary terms that help students better understand the key ideas of the unit.

Another issue related to selecting words to teach is that it is impossible to teach students every word they may not fully understand in their texts. Time constraints alone preclude our doing so. Any of you who have tried to identify and teach all the words in a text you think might cause your students difficulty have discovered that your entire lesson can be taken up with vocabulary instruction. It is simply not feasible to attempt to teach every word that might potentially pose trouble for your students. A far more efficient and effective approach is to select the salient terms and concepts, those that carry and represent the most important ideas, and teach them well. A thorough and elaborative understanding of those vocabulary terms will, in turn, contribute to your students' enhanced understanding of the text itself, especially if the targeted words relate to other words or are generative in nature. The criteria listed in the Teacher as Learner feature should help you determine which vocabulary words should be taught as a part of a unit of study.

Teacher as Learner

CRITERIA FOR SELECTING WHICH CONTENT-AREA WORDS TO TEACH

1. Determine what you want your students to learn as a result of reading and studying the content. Your school district or department chair might describe this as the *unit's objectives*. For instance, a music teacher may want students to develop a sense of musical interpretation after covering a unit on opera or an art teacher may wish students to develop a sense of character as a result of reading stories with well-developed characters for a unit on portrait painting.

2. Identify key terms that are related to the unit's objectives. For example, considering the theme of Sparta and its unique political structure, the teacher would likely select technical terms such as *euphors, assembly, council of elders,* and *helots* because they are important words related to the objectives.

3. Decide on appropriate activities or strategies to introduce and reinforce the words. For example, the words related to Sparta could be arranged into a map, a strategy introduced in Chapter 3.

4. Identify the general words that are not necessarily central to the objectives of the unit but that lend themselves to various word-learning strategies that promote independence, such as modeling words in context.

You should not underestimate the importance of these first steps in teaching key terms and concepts related to a unit of study. The more discretionary you are in selecting vocabulary that potentially has the highest payoff regarding comprehension, the greater the likelihood that students will learn the designated content-area material.

❚ *Traditional Approaches to Word Learning*

In this section, we examine three traditional approaches to learning new words—context clues, the dictionary, and morphemic analysis. Although we offer several caveats to each approach, we also outline ways in which content-area teachers can encourage students to use each of them in an effective and efficient manner.

Using Contextual Analysis

Contextual analysis refers to our attempt to understand the meaning of a word by analyzing the meaning of the words that surround it. Put another way, contextual analysis is figuring out a word by the manner in which it is used in a textbook, novel, or magazine. For example, one way in which we figure out the meaning of words is by using extended descriptions or appositives such as the following:

> There was a strange sound emanating from the hood of my car. When I opened the hood, I found a stray cat huddling to keep warm and meowing in fear.
>
> The decadent, or overindulgent, society in which we live spoils children by buying them whatever they see on television.

> On the surface, the idea of learning words from context makes a lot of sense. Logical as it may seem, however, the research on students' incidental learning from context seems to indicate that some learning will occur, but the effect is not very powerful, especially with a single encounter of the targeted word (McKeown, & Beck, 2004).

❚ Learning words from context is not as easy as we imagine, especially for struggling readers.

One reason the utility of contextual analysis is challenged is that previous studies have used contrived, unnatural texts as their materials of study and high-frequency words as their target of study (Nist & Olejnik, 1995). The following examples illustrate the oversimplified exercises that have been used in studies and in workbooks designed to teach students how to use context clues. Can you figure out the meaning of the italicized nonsense words?

> The boys bought their tickets for the brand new outer space movie and entered the theater with mystic expectation all over their *whitors*.
>
> Some even looked alive, though no *fome* flowed beneath the skin.

If you were able to figure out that *whitors* means "face" and *fome* means "blood," congratulations. But is your performance on these sentences indicative of your genuine ability to use contextual analysis? Imagine students who correctly complete 20 sentences similar to those you have just tried. The students may be left with the impression that they have mastered the use of context clues for determining word meanings. Then imagine their enthusiastic attempt to apply their new skills with a real passage from a history or physics textbook. As noted by McKeown and Beck (2004), students may learn a few new history or physics words using contextual analysis, but this vocabulary knowledge develops slowly and is not particularly powerful for those who struggle with reading on a consistent basis.

If real text is not always so generous in providing clues to the meaning of unknown words, should we teach our students to use context clues? The answer to that difficult question is a qualified "yes," if the instruction is explicit. That is, teachers should model, provide students realistic practice and feedback, and emphasize the metacognitive nature of using context clues. Blachowicz and Fisher (2002) recommend that teachers can model and urge students to use these specific four steps: (a) look before, at, and after the word; (b) reason by connecting what you know with what the author has written; (c) predict a possible meaning; and (d) resolve or redo by deciding whether you know enough to proceed or should try again or use another source (p. 27). In addition to these suggestions, let's consider two specific approaches to using context clues that can be incorporated into most content-area lessons: previewing in context and Possible Sentences (Moore & Moore, 1986).

We can help students effectively use context clues with several different teaching techniques.

Previewing in Context

Previewing in context is a teacher-directed activity that relies on modeling and demonstrating to students how word meanings can sometimes be inferred from the context. Modeling how you go about finding clues to word meanings with actual content reading materials allows students to see the practical application of this skill. As an example of how modeling can be used to help students understand some of the key vocabulary in a passage about the Andersonville Raiders, consider these previewing-in-context strategies employed by Keidra, an eighth-grade history teacher.

First, she read the text carefully and identified general and specific key vocabulary and all the words and terms likely to pose difficulty for her students. Her list included the following words:

debilitating	predators
strident	inhumane
depredations	emaciated
retributions	notorious
atrocities	expired

Next, Keidra considered the list and pared it down to those words she felt were essential to the overall understanding of the material and consistent with her unit objectives. She included those words that could be used most instructively for teaching contextual analysis. The reason for this step was both to avoid spending too much valuable class time on teaching vocabulary and to leave several unfamiliar words for the students to analyze independently. Through this process, Keidra's list was limited to the following:

debilitating	emaciated
predator	expired
inhumane	

When Keidra directed students to each word and its surrounding context, she "thought out loud," modeling the use of context clues to determine word meanings. She also questioned students to help them discover a word's probable meaning in the existing context. Some of her specific strategies follow.

1. Keidra spent a considerable amount of time activating students' prior knowledge for the topic. She knew that most of her eighth graders had some information about prison conditions in general. Perhaps they had seen TV documentaries of World War II concentration camps or had read about what it is like to be in prison. Using what her students already knew about the topic, she made it easier for them to figure out many difficult words in this passage, especially the word *emaciated*.

2. She reminded students of what they already knew about syntax and word order in sentences. This clue was helpful in narrowing the contextual definition of

debilitating because it appeared between a modifier (unhealthy) and a noun (conditions).

3. Keidra activated students' prior knowledge acquired in studying other subjects. She thought it likely that the students had encountered the word *predator* in science class as a technical vocabulary word. They were shown how to apply their understanding of the word in science to this context.

4. She impressed on the students the importance of taking advantage of any obvious clues provided. For instance, in the last sentence, the students were given an obvious clue to the meaning of *expired—died*, which was used earlier in the sentence.

5. She alerted students to clues within words—for example, *in* in the word *inhumane*.

6. Keidra made students aware of the idea that context is more than just the few words surrounding an unknown word or the sentence in which the unknown word appears. She helped expand their notion of context to include information and ideas within, before, and after the passage.

7. Finally, she demonstrated checking the dictionary to validate her hunches about the meaning of a word.

Previewing in context is an honest way of demonstrating how challenging it is for readers to employ contextual analysis for determining word meanings in text. Although students' attempts to use context clues may not always produce precise meanings, the use of contextual analysis in conjunction with other sources and approaches should increase their comprehension and understanding.

Possible Sentences

Possible Sentences
involves students in
writing, discussing, and
reading activities.

Possible Sentences is a teacher-directed prereading activity that prepares students for the technical and general vocabulary they will encounter in a reading assignment (Moore & Moore, 1986). During this activity, students make predictions about content, establish connections between words and concepts, write, discuss, and read their assignments carefully to verify their predictions. Notice that the activities involved in Possible Sentences actively engage students in their word learning, an important vocabulary guideline.

The Possible Sentences activity requires minimal advance material preparation but a considerable amount of teacher time in thinking and planning. First, the teacher identifies the general or technical vocabulary that is key to the objective of the unit and is adequately defined by the context. For this activity to succeed, at least five to eight words should be taken from a subsection of a chapter rather than three or four words dispersed across an entire chapter. For example, in the Andersonville Prison excerpt that Keidra used, the following words could be used for part of the lesson:

debilitating   predators   inhumane   expired

Teachers need to select the targeted words carefully because students must be able to verify their predictions by reading the text during the third step.

During the second step, the teacher asks students to select at least two words from the list and generate one sentence that they think might possibly be in the text. Students can either write their sentence before sharing or dictate their sentences to the teacher spontaneously. As students share their predicted sentences, the teacher writes them on the overhead transparency or chalkboard. Moore and Moore (1986) stress that it is important for the teacher to write the sentences just as they are dictated, even if students provide inaccurate information or use the word incorrectly. With the Andersonville Prison excerpt, students might pair the following words in this manner:

> In the Andersonville Prison the predators expired.
>
> During the Civil War the inhumane generals were debilitating.

Note that the second example uses the word *debilitating* in a syntactically incorrect manner, but the teacher recorded it. This sharing of predicted sentences should continue until all the words on the list have been included in at least one sentence.

In step three, the teacher asks the students to read their text to verify the accuracy of the sentences the class created. Once students have finished their reading, during step four they evaluate the predicted sentences. Moore and Moore (1986) recommend that students ask these questions to evaluate the sentences: (1) Which sentences are accurate? (2) Which need further elaboration? (3) Which cannot be validated because the passage did not deal specifically with them? For example, with the first possible sentence cited previously, the teacher would want the students to realize that the predators did die, but not a natural death. The Possible Sentence merely needed more elaboration (i.e., "The predators were caught, tried, and expired as a result of hanging"). With the second Possible Sentence, students will need to discuss the meaning and use of the word *debilitating*, but the context should provide an adequate model for making their evaluations and revisions.

In the fifth and final step of Possible Sentences, students are asked to create new sentences using the targeted words. This activity can be a homework assignment for the next class period, or it can occur during class as students work in pairs or share in the large-group discussion. As students share these sentences, everyone should be involved in checking the text and the agreed-on definitions generated during class discussion. On the plus side, the Possible Sentences activity involves students in the elaborative thinking processes that characterize active learning. However, as with any teacher-directed activity, it will not work with all units of study. This is especially true for units containing a lot of technical vocabulary for which students may not have any prior knowledge.

Previewing in context and Possible Sentences are two teacher-directed strategies for helping students become more comfortable in using contextual analysis to unlock the meaning of difficult words. If students can learn how to use context clues in conjunction with other word-meaning approaches, they will increase their chances of understanding content-area vocabulary (Blachowicz & Fisher, 2002).

Using the Dictionary

If you have ever asked someone the meaning of a word, you were probably told to "look it up in the dictionary." You probably can also recall the frustration you felt as you tried to make sense of the entry once you found the word. Often you were given a definition that would help only someone who already knew the meaning of the word. For example, look up the meaning of the word *conservative* in your dictionary. Did you find a definition similar to this one?

> "of or relating to a philosophy of conservatism" (Webster's Ninth New Collegiate Dictionary)

Did that definition help you? More important, would that definition help your students understand the word *conservative*? Dictionaries are not a panacea for learning the meanings of unknown words (Joshi, 2005).

Interpreting a dictionary entry and identifying an appropriate and useful definition requires sophisticated thinking skills (Beck et al., 2002). Thus, if students are not taught how to use a dictionary, they will have several predictable problems. One such problem is that many students target only a part of the definition, ignoring the rest of the entry. In fact, many students do not read beyond the first definition, even though some dictionaries place the oldest and least used definition first. For example, the first meaning of *excoriate* in *Webster's Collegiate Dictionary* (10th ed.) is to "tear or wear off the skin of." Imagine the difficulty students might have in comprehending text if they had only that definition for *excoriate*. A recent magazine article described how Washington officials were about to excoriate the FBI for the way in which agents conducted an investigation. With only the first definition, students would have a rather grisly interpretation of what the FBI was about to endure. However, had students read the second definition, they would have discovered that the word also means to "denounce or censure strongly."

A second common problem students have with interpreting entries is that they find a familiar word in the definition and attempt to substitute it for the unknown word. Nist and Simpson (2001) cite a good example of this with the word *adamant*. They point out that the dictionary definition of the word is "an extremely hard substance." One of their students who read that definition substituted the familiar word "hard" for *adamant* and wrote the following sentence: "Automobiles are made of *adamant* substances that are not easily damaged."

A third problem students have in using the dictionary is that they cannot construct an adequate and precise meaning from the vague and disjointed fragments provided in the dictionary entries. As Beck et al. (2002) point out, dictionaries give "multiple pieces of information but offer no guidance in how they should be integrated" (p. 34). Nist and Olejnik's research study (1995) provided an excellent illustration of this problem with the word *vacuous*. The dictionary entry for *vacuous* is "devoid of matter, empty, stupid, lacking serious purpose." Unable to synthesize the vague parts of this definition, one of the participants in the study wrote this sentence: "The glass was vacuous because I was thirsty and drank all the Gatorade."

Do these problems that students have with dictionaries mean that we, as teachers, should avoid the dictionary in our classroom? Of course not. What we want to stress is that the dictionary, with all its limitations, can be a tool in building word knowledge. However, it should be used in conjunction with personal experiences and textual context if students are to learn the meanings of unknown words. In short, dictionaries can validate students' hunches about words.

If we want students to construct useful and precise definitions from dictionaries, we should avoid giving them lists of words to look up in the dictionary. Without the context of a sentence or paragraph, students will find it quite difficult to construct an appropriate definition for an unknown word. We can also help students if we teach and reinforce the following ideas about the dictionary:

1. *The format and organization of a dictionary entry.* For example, each dictionary has its own system or hierarchy for arranging definitions. Many dictionaries, such as *Merriam-Webster's Collegiate Dictionary* (10th ed.), list definitions in order of historical usage, thus making their last definition the most current or most widely used. However, others list the most current or widely used definition first. Students need to know that this information can be found by reading the user's guide or introduction.

Many students experience difficulties interpreting dictionary entries, especially if they are given words in a list for which they must define and write meaningful sentences.

2. *The abbreviations and symbols in an entry.* Dictionary entries contain numerous abbreviations and symbols that initially confuse students. These must be mastered so that students can decipher the entries. For example, it is important for students to know that "*n, pl*" stands for the plural noun form of a word.

3. *The etymological information in a typical entry.* Etymological information usually occurs between square brackets [ ] and may appear before the definitions or after them. Inside the brackets are the origins of a word and some interesting stories connected with words such as *meander* or *snafu*. In addition, students may see how the word has changed in meaning over time.

4. *How to select the most appropriate definition for the situation in which they encountered the word.* This is difficult for students for many reasons. One reason is that dictionary entries contain definitions for words used as different parts of speech and for words used in specialized areas. For example, the word *anchors* can be a noun and a verb and can occur in nautical and sports situations.

Most important, we should make sure that our students understand when it is appropriate to use a dictionary and when another source or vocabulary technique would be more effective and efficient (Blachowicz & Fisher, 2002). One of those techniques might be morphemic analysis, the next traditional vocabulary approach we will discuss.

Using Morphemic Analysis

When students use morphemic analysis as a means of unlocking the meaning of unknown words, they are using familiar word parts or morphemes such as prefixes, suffixes, and roots. For example, students who know the meaning of the prefix *in* and the Latin root *cred* should be able to conclude that the meaning of *incredible* is "not to be believed." Because of this logic, morphemic analysis has been a traditional part of vocabulary instruction and has routinely appeared in commercial materials and district-level curriculum guides. Although the research studies have yet to demonstrate on a consistent basis that students can be taught to use morphemic analysis as an independent word-learning strategy, there has been a renewed emphasis on its importance, especially when combined with other techniques such as contextual analysis (Edwards et al., 2004; Graves, 2004). The pairing of contextual analysis with morphemic analysis makes considerable sense given some of the potential limitations of using just morphemic analysis as a word-learning technique. That is, some prefixes, such as *in,* have multiple meanings (i.e., both *not* and *into*). In other situations, word parts that appear to be prefixes are not. For example, if students were to remove the first two letters of *reciprocated* thinking that they have identified a prefix that will unlock meaning, they are left with *-ciprocated,* a base that makes no sense by itself.

Several authorities in vocabulary instruction have outlined guidelines for teaching morphemic analysis, most of which circumvent the possible disadvantages of using morphemic analysis in isolation (Blachowicz & Fisher, 2002; Edwards et al., 2004; Graves, 2004). In general, these guidelines emphasize the following:

> Morphemic analysis is often called structural analysis because students are encouraged to identify and use the structure of a word in order to unlock its meaning.

1. Make sure students understand how morphemic analysis works so they can disassemble words into their parts. For example, they should realize that a word such as *subordinate* consists of the prefix *sub* and the base word, *ordinate*. Adolescents, unless prompted, often do not break longer words into their meaningful parts.

2. Provide explicit instruction and modeling, using words from the students' reading assignments. Content-area teachers should find it relatively easy to locate key terms that use prefixes, suffixes, or roots. Milligan and Ruff (1990) found in their analysis of five social studies textbooks that approximately 71% of the targeted terms contained prefixes or roots. Latin and Greek roots also appear in content-area textbooks such as mathematics (e.g., *pent, oct),* science (e.g., *bio, aqua, photo),* and psychology (e.g., *ego, mania, idio).*

3. When possible, group the instruction by using word families. For example, in an English course where the targeted word is *pseudonym,* it makes a lot of sense to teach the other words using the prefix *pseudo* (e.g., *pseudoin-tellectual, pseuodoscience).* By doing this, students grasp the power of morphemic analysis as an independent word-learning strategy.

4. Select prefixes and roots that are high in utility and consistent in meaning (e.g., the prefix *trans* or the root *graph).*

5. Model situations for students where morphemic analysis does not work and then demonstrate alternative approaches for deriving meaning (e.g., dictionary or glossary, contextual analysis, asking someone).

6. Prompt students to use morphemic analysis as an independent word-learning technique. Some content-area teachers have encouraged students to use morphemic analysis by displaying charts on their walls that contain important words that contain prefixes, roots, and suffixes.

Ideally, students can use the combination of contextual analysis, the dictionary, and morphemic analysis as tools for independently learning the meanings of unknown words. As noted previously, if students are to use these tools efficiently and effectively, content-area teachers will need to introduce the targeted words, model the appropriate techniques in a recursive fashion, and prompt students to use them when they are reading.

Activities That Enhance Students' Vocabulary Knowledge

In this section, we explain four different activities that teachers can use to expand their students' vocabulary knowledge. Some of these activities focus on ways to introduce difficult content-area words and others focus on ways to build students' awareness and interest in their own word knowledge. Using the principle that students will understand and remember more when they experience concepts in a direct and relevant fashion, we begin by discussing the power of demonstrations.

Demonstrations

Because the terminology in content-area textbooks is often sterile, abstract, and lifeless, students are not particularly motivated to read and find it difficult to retain the information. Standing before the class and stating glossary-type definitions of textbook vocabulary merely reinforces students' passivity. As noted in one of the seven guidelines for effective vocabulary instruction, we need to find ways of making key terms and concepts come alive for students so that they are motivated to read and learn.

Ideally, students should be given opportunities to have direct contact with all the words they encounter. Bernardo frequently capitalizes on this truism by providing his

Demonstrations, field trips, exhibits, and dramatized experiences provide students firsthand concept development opportunities and direct ways of experiencing words.

Honoring Diversity and Building Competence in the Content Classroom

Photographed Vocabulary

Another approach providing firsthand and interesting involvement with a word has been labeled *photographed vocabulary* (Stanley, 1971). This approach involves photographing students as they demonstrate the meaning of one word in a tableau. Alicia, a language arts teacher for students who speak English as a second language, uses photographed vocabulary because it capitalizes on her students' "unabashed vanity and love of drama." She told us that she begins the process by selecting a list of 25 "actable" words that the class had previously encountered and discussed. The adjectives the students were to act out or dramatize described people in positive or negative ways and included words such as *studious, timid, sinister,* and *eccentric.* Alicia then used the following steps to introduce the activity:

> Teachers tell us adjectives work best for this vocabulary activity.

1. She told the students that each of them would have responsibility for demonstrating to the class a word from the list. Their demonstration would have to be in a tableau or frozen representation because they would be photographed. While each student was doing his or her tableau, the rest of the class would be writing down the word they felt was being acted out. The entire class would have the list of 25 words, their definitions, and sentences using the words. The students who correctly matched the words to the tableaus would receive 5 extra-credit points.

2. Alicia then asked each student to draw from a hat the word he or she would demonstrate. Students were told to be ready with their tableau in 3 days.

3. The next day, the principal visited the class and modeled how she would do a tableau for the word *exasperated.* Alicia modeled the word *eccentric.*

4. The day before the assignment was due, Alicia checked with all students to make sure they were prepared and offered suggestions for those still groping for ideas.

5. On the day of the photographing, Alicia listed the students' names on the board in the order of presentation. As the students posed, Alicia took the pictures and the rest of the class worked to match the word to the tableau.

As a follow-up to the assignment, Alicia placed all the pictures on the bulletin board. Even 3 weeks later, students still gathered around the board to check the pictures and discuss the words. Alicia told us that this was probably one of the best assignments she had done that year because the students were actually incorporating the words into their writing and speaking, the real touchstone of any vocabulary approach (McKeown & Beck, 2004). Similar to the photographed vocabulary activity are activities focusing on interesting word origins, the next activity we discuss. Both encourage playful moments with words, one of the characteristics of effective vocabulary instruction.

students demonstrations. In one of his lessons on the human memory, he began the class by asking them to write 10 things they did the first day of second grade. Over the initial moans and groans, Bernardo insisted that each student list 10 items within a couple of minutes to "play the game" properly. Eventually, all students were busy working on their lists. When they were finished, Bernardo asked them to read the items on their lists and to talk about how they produced the items they could not recall with certainty. Students read off such things as "met the teacher," "talked with my friends from first grade," "took my seat," "received my books," and so on. Most said they could not remember all the details about what they did the first day of second grade, but they listed the things they assumed they had done. Afterward, Bernardo explained that the students had been "confabulating" by creating their lists on the basis of related experience rather than definite memory.

Defined in the traditional way, with a textbook definition, *confabulation* is a sterile term. When students were allowed to experience confabulation firsthand, however, they had an experience to which they could affix the meaning of the concept in memory. In turn, the textbook chapter on memory should be easier for them to understand. Bernardo said that his students remembered the meaning of *confabulation* and other concepts long after the unit in which they appeared had been completed. The same trend would be true for any content area because demonstrations are a form of firsthand concept development that will encourage students' deeper understanding of the concepts and key terms (Rupley, 2005). Photographed vocabulary, the activity on the previous page also capitalizes on the power of firsthand concept development.

Interesting Word Origins

We know one seventh-grade middle school team that selects and discusses with their students one word each week that has an unusual origin or history. For example, during the first week of school they taught the word *berserk*. This word originated from Norse mythology. Berserk was a fierce man who used no armor and assumed the form of a wild beast in battle. Supposedly, no enemy would touch him. Today, if you are described as *berserk*, you are wild, dangerous, and crazed. The sixth graders had fun with that word, describing their friends, their brothers and sisters, and their first week in a middle school as *berserk*. More important, the sixth-grade teachers discovered that their students remembered and then used those words as they were writing and speaking.

In addition to capitalizing on mythology as a way to build students' interest in word learning, the following are other sources. See how many you already know.

1. **Places.** These are words that owe their meaning to a particular place. Do you know the places and stories connected with words such as *marathon* and *meander*?

2. **Acronyms.** These are words formed from the initial letters of other words. Can you think of any examples? What about the word *laser or scuba?* What do the letters abbreviate?

3. **Portmanteau words.** These are words that are formed by blending portions of one word with another. For example, *Medicaid* is a blend of *medic(al)* with *aid*. Can you think of other examples?

4. **Clips.** These are words formed when they are shortened in length. For example, the word *perks* is a clip of the original word *perquisites.* Can you think of other examples?

5. **Names of people.** Many words owe their heritage to famous individuals. Did you know that the word *maverick* originated from a man named

Samual Maverick who was a Texas rancher in the 1800s? The story behind the word is even more intriguing, as is the story behind the word *gerrymander*, an important word in political science classes.

6. **Borrowed words from other languages.** These are words that we have borrowed from other languages and cultures. For example, the words *gourmet, lariat,* and *pretzel* are borrowed words we use frequently without thinking about their origins. Can you think of other words we have borrowed?

If you had difficulty answering these questions or if you are interested in finding other words with fascinating origins, the sources for these stories can be found in reference books such as Funk's (1950) *Word Origins and Their Romantic Stories.* Other such books that are excellent sources are listed in Figure 6.1.

Students might also be interested in checking the Internet for Web sites that discuss word origins (e.g., World Wide Words at ***www.worldwidewords.org***). As you search for words with intriguing stories, remember the importance of nudging students' awareness, interest, and playfulness with vocabulary, goals that help them become actively engaged and committed to the acquisition of new words (Johnson, Johnson, & Schlichting, 2004).

Go to Web Resources for Chapter 6 at *http://www.prenhall.com/brozo* and look for other websites that discuss word origins.

Knowledge Rating Activity

Content-area teachers can introduce important words from a new unit with an activity called *knowledge rating* (Blachowicz, 1986). Reaffirming the vocabulary guideline that states that it is important for students to have an active and informed role in the learning process, the knowledge rating activity invites students to evaluate their level of knowledge about a set of words. Figure 6.2 illustrates how Jihyun, a 10th-grade geometry teacher, uses the knowledge rating activity with the words *chords, diameter, radius, secant, tangent,* and *point of tangency.* To help students place a check in the appropriate category, Jihyun first described the three self-evaluation categories to the students. That is, if the students had never heard or seen the word, they should check "Don't Know It," if they recognized the word but could not provide any meaning for the word, they should check "Somewhat

Figure 6.1 Books About Interesting Word Origins

Asimov, I. (1961). *Words from the myths.* Boston: Houghton Mifflin.

Asimov, I. (1969). *Words of science and the history behind them.* New York: New American Library.

Asimov, I. (1972). *More words of science.* Boston: Houghton Mifflin.

Funk, C. (1973). *A hog on ice and other curious expressions.* New York: Harper & Row.

Funk, W. (1950). *Word origins and their romantic stories.* New York: Funk & Wagnalls.

Grambs, D. (1986). *Dimboxes, epopts, and other quidams.* New York: Workman.

Jacobson, J. (1990). *Tooposaurus: A humorous treasury of top-o-nyms (familiar words and phrases derived from place names).* New York: Wiley.

Safire, W. (1982). *What's the good word?* New York: Times Books.

Tuleja, T. (1987). *Namesakes: An entertaining guide to the origins of more than 300 words named for people.* New York: McGraw-Hill.

Urdang, L., Hunsinger, W., & LaRoche, N. (1991). *A fine kettle of fish and other figurative expressions.* Detroit: Visible Ink Press.

Figure 6.2 Knowledge Rating Activity for Geometry

	Rating Your Word Knowledge		
TERM	Very familiar(3)	Somewhat familiar(2)	Don't know it(1)
Chords			
Diameter			
Radius			
Secant			
Tangent			
Point of tangency			

Familiar," and if they could define the word or use it meaningfully in a sentence, they should check "Very Familiar." After the students finished their self-evaluation of the words, Jihyun encouraged the students to share their ratings, noting the trends for each word on an overhead transparency. For example, while most of the students evaluated their knowledge of the word *chords, radius,* and *diameter* as "very familiar" or "somewhat familiar," all of them indicated that they did not know the words *secant, tangent,* and *point of tangency.*

By quickly gathering this information Jihyun was now prepared to discuss each of the words, especially the ones with multiple meanings that may have confused her students (e.g., *chords*). After her discussion of the words, Jihyun tied the words to the unit by asking her students to walk through the chapter with her so they could sense the chapter's organization and see the words, in context, once more. As a result of these activities, her students were now more prepared to tackle their reading assignment. Jihyun typically returns to the knowledge rating activity several days later and asks her students to evaluate, again, their level of understanding.

Although these four activities are distinctly different, they share in common the importance of actively involving students in their quest to learn new words and concepts. Admittedly, not all words lend themselves to demonstrations, photographs, or intriguing histories, but these four activities can be used in conjunction with the more traditional approaches we previously discussed (e.g., contextual clues). In the next section we will explain three practical and powerful strategies that any content-area teacher can use to enhance students' word and conceptual knowledge and understanding of what they read.

Strategies for Building Students' Vocabulary and Comprehension Across the Content Areas

In this section we will examine three strategies that encourage students to build connections between words and concepts by using a variety of visual displays.

As we pointed out earlier in this chapter, content-area teachers should be concerned about two vitally important aspects of vocabulary development. One is to enhance students' general vocabulary. The previous sections demonstrated several effective activities that content-area teachers can incorporate into their lessons. Another equally important aspect of vocabulary development is to teach students a variety of strategies for learning words important to their understanding of the content. This section describes three such strategies—word maps, semantic feature analysis, and concept cards—that can be used across the content areas.

The Role of the Teacher Leader

To improve students' vocabulary knowledge and, ultimately, their academic literacies, content-area teachers can interact with their colleagues in a variety of ways. At the departmental level, teachers interested in becoming a leader or literacy coach can discuss with their colleagues the importance of teaching content-area vocabulary words, especially in a judicious manner. For example, if some teachers are asking students to learn words in a list or are requiring students to use a dictionary to define all the targeted words, it might be appropriate to review the research-based guidelines or characteristics of effective vocabulary instruction with the teachers. Alternatively, it might be useful to share with one or two of your colleagues some of the techniques you are using, especially the ones that receive a positive response from your students. If, for instance, you are using the "reading minute" at the beginning of the hour, then share the idea with them as you monitor the halls or eat lunch together. You might also invite a colleague to visit one of your classes as you implement a particular activity (e.g., photographed vocabulary) or strategy (e.g., possible sentences) and ask for their feedback. Change often occurs at the individual level much faster than at the group level.

Beyond your department you can serve as a teacher leader by interacting with teachers from other academic disciplines. We know several English teachers who work in conjunction with science or social science teachers in order to tackle the seemingly unlimited amount of words that students must master. In one instance, a ninth-grade English teacher agreed to teach Latin and Greek prefixes and roots that appeared in the ninth-grade science textbook. In return, the science teacher agreed to include the targeted words on his unit exams. This mutual cooperation between the departments also instilled in the students a belief that vocabulary knowledge is something significant that extends beyond the English classroom.

With a close colleague from another content area, you might also consider the possibility of co-teaching a particular strategy or activity such as the word map or the semantic feature analysis, two of the strategies we explain next. The opportunities for collaboration and learning are limitless.

Word Maps

Students will become more independent in their vocabulary learning if we provide instruction that gradually shifts the responsibility for generating meanings for new words from us to them. One effective way of encouraging this transition is with word maps. Schwartz and Raphael (1985) developed this strategy for helping students establish a concept of definition for content-area words, an important aspect of word learning.

To build a word map, students write the concept being studied, or the word they would like to define, in the center box of a map, such as *quark* in Figure 6.3. Next, in the top box they write a brief answer to the question "What is it?" This question seeks a name for the class or category that includes the concept. In defining *quark*, the category is a "subatomic particle." In responding to the question to the right, "What is it like?" students write critical attributes, characteristics, or properties of the concept or word. In the example, three critical properties of quarks are listed. The question along the bottom, "What are some examples?" can be answered by supplying examples of different kinds of quarks, such as *top* and *charmed*.

Teaching students how to create word maps gives them a strategy for generating word meanings independently. Because of the checking process they go through in asking questions about the context, this strategy also fosters self-monitoring and metacognitive thinking (Schwartz, 1988). The goal, therefore, is to help students internalize this test-questioning process for all of the important words they must learn. All of us ask similar questions when we encounter unfamiliar words in context, though we rarely, if ever, draw (as in the form of a word map) the information we are seeking about the words. Think of the word map as a visual representation of students' thought processes while trying to figure out word meanings in context. Eventually, after they have demonstrated an understanding of the process by creating appropriate

Word maps help students realize that "knowing" a word involves more than just recognizing or reciting a definition.

Figure 6.3 Word Map for Quark

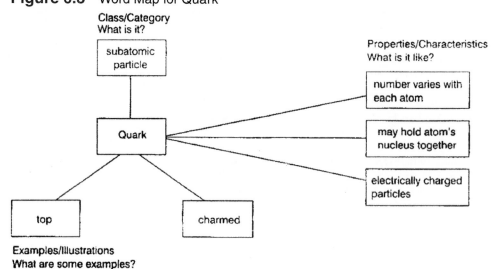

word maps, students should be shown that they do not have to create a map for every word they do not know. Instead, they should go through the questioning process in their heads, as mature readers do.

To help you understand how students can be taught to use word maps in the classroom, we describe the experiences of Tonya, an eighth-grade science teacher. She began her vocabulary lesson by displaying the structure of the word map and introducing it as a visual guide to remind her students of what they needed to know to understand a new and important word or concept. As the components of the map were discussed, she supplied a concept and filled in answers to the questions on the map with information from a recently studied chapter in their science textbook.

Tonya then directed students to the chapter they were about to read and, with their help, identified a key concept occurring in the first few pages: conifer. She asked the students to work in cooperative groups to find information in their texts and in their heads to answer the questions on the word map. As they read about conifers, they discussed the relevant information that helped define the concept and inserted it into the appropriate spaces on the map they were creating. When they completed their maps, Tonya modeled how information about class/category, properties/characteristics, and examples related to the concept could be pulled from the context. She talked about how contexts vary from complete (containing rich information) to partial (containing scanty information). She encouraged students to include their own information and ideas, especially with stingy contexts, to further their understanding of the word. Drawing on the input from groups, the whole class then worked together to create a word map for conifer (see Figure 6.4).

At this point, Tonya asked her students to write a definition for *conifer* based on the word-map activity. Afterward, she asked them to work in their cooperative groups and evaluate each other's definitions to determine if they were complete and, if not, to write down whatever additional information was needed. Definitions were then returned to their owners, who responded to the group's feedback. With their maps and definitions completed, students were shown that their work could serve as excellent study aids for rehearsal and long-term retention of the concept.

Figure 6.4 Word Map for Conifer

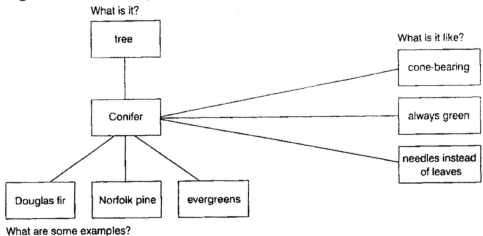

What is it?

What is it like?

What are some examples?

Tonya ended the day's lesson by assigning the students to create word maps for three other key concepts in the chapter. Before leaving, students began their assignment by identifying the possible concepts in the chapter. This procedure of modeling and assigning continued throughout the semester until Tonya was sure that students knew how to apply the word-map strategy independently to their science vocabulary. She also encouraged students to try applying it to their other courses.

Tonya reports, as have others, that word maps have helped her students organize and see connections between ideas, monitor their understanding, and improve their comprehension of what they have studied.

Semantic-Feature Analysis

To read successfully in the content areas, students need to have a deep-level understanding of important concepts and need to sense the relationships among the key concepts and vocabulary. The strategy of semantic-feature analysis is a highly effective visual technique for accomplishing these tasks (Baumann, Kame'enui, & Ash, 2003). Semantic-feature analysis involves building a grid in which essential vocabulary is listed on one axis of the grid and major features, characteristics, or important ideas are listed on the other axis. Students fill in the grid, indicating the extent to which the key words possess the stated features or are related to important ideas. Once the grid is completed, students are led to discover both the shared and unique characteristics of the vocabulary words.

Figure 6.5 is a word grid created by a geometry teacher for a study of polygons. Notice that the vertical axis contains the names of geometric figures, whereas the horizontal axis contains important features or characteristics of these figures.

Shareef, a 10th-grade ecology teacher, introduces the semantic-feature analysis strategy with a simple version that all his students will understand (see Figure 6.6). He begins by asking his class for the names of fruit, writing them on the blackboard in a vertical list as students call them out. After several fruits are listed, he writes a

Semantic feature analysis is also a superb way to reinforce the concepts in a content-area unit.

Figure 6.5 Word Grid for Polygons

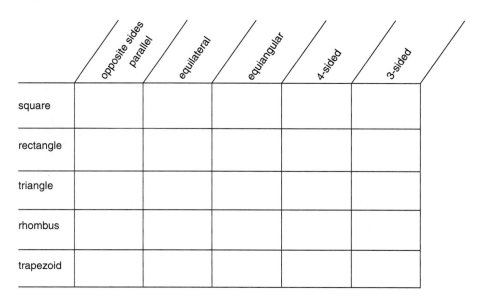

	opposite sides parallel	equilateral	equiangular	4-sided	3-sided	
square						
rectangle						
triangle						
rhombus						
trapezoid						

Figure 6.6 Word Grid for Fruit

	edible skin	tree grown	bunches	citrus	fleshy	
banana	0	2	2	0	2	
peach	2	2	0	0	2	
orange	1	2	0	2	0	
apple	2	2	0	0	2	
grapes	2	0	2	0	2	
grapefruit	0	2	0	2	0	

couple of general features of fruit along the top horizontal axis of the grid, such as "tree grown" and "edible skin"; then he asks for additional features. Finally, he asks the class to consider each type of fruit and whether it possesses any of the listed features. As they go down the list of fruit, they discuss each one relative to the characteristics listed across the top, and Shareef puts a 0, 1, or 2 in the box where the fruit and feature meet on the grid. A 0 indicates that the fruit possesses none of that feature, a 1 indicates that it possesses some of that feature, and a 2 means that it possesses all of the feature. When the grid is entirely filled in, Shareef explains to the students how they can, at a glance, determine the key characteristics of a particular fruit, as well as the similarities and differences between the fruits.

By involving students in the construction of a simple word grid, Shareef has introduced them to the semantic-feature analysis process. He then follows up this demonstration by introducing a word grid appropriate for his ecology unit on biomes. As noted in Figure 6.7, he listed seven key words on the vertical axis, words the students had already encountered in their previous assignments and classroom discussions. Shareef then walks students through the process of deciding on components of the grid, asking them questions and discussing with them the relationships between each major idea and each vocabulary word. Later, as his students improve their ability to design word grids, Shareef gives them increasing responsibility to complete grids on their own. This is accomplished by providing them with partially filled-in grids containing a few key vocabulary words and major ideas or essential features. As students move through the chapter or unit of study, they work in groups to expand the grid so it includes additional vocabulary and features. Once the grids are completed and students have shared their features and key words, Shareef often assigns his students a brief writing assignment that requires them to compare and contrast concepts.

The semantic-feature analysis strategy requires minimal preparation on the part of the teacher while providing students an excellent review for a unit of study. For those teachers who assign narrative or descriptive text, the semantic-feature analysis strategy provides students a visual format for comparing and contrasting themes or characters across several different stories, plays, or novels. Whether the text is narrative or expository, content-area teachers embrace the semantic-feature analysis

Figure 6.7 Characteristics of Biomes

Instructions: Mark an "X" for all features possessed by each of the biomes. Be prepared to discuss your reasoning.						
	H_2O PRESENT	CONIFEROUS	FRESHWATER	HIGH RAINFALL	HIGH SPECIES	DIVERSITY
Desert						
Estuary						
Grasslands						
Temperate deciduous forest						
Taiga						
Tropical rainforest						
Tundra						

strategy because the grid encourages their students to think critically and divergently as they determine the relationships between key vocabulary and major concepts.

Concept Cards

Concept cards are another strategy students can use to learn difficult general or technical vocabulary (Nist & Simpson, 2001). You may have used these in your own studying but probably called them flash cards. Even though concept cards have the same format as flash cards in that they allow students to test themselves, we prefer the term *concept cards* because they involve students in learning more than just a definitions for difficult terminology. Based on the time-honored Frayer Model (Frayer, Frederick, & Klausmeier, 1969), a correctly completed concept card includes important aspects of what is involved in knowing a word or a concept in a deep and full manner. As illustrated in Figure 6.8, on the front of the concept card, students write the targeted word and the superordinate idea for the word. On the back of the card, they provide the following information, when appropriate: (1) definition(s),

Figure 6.8 Content of a Concept Card

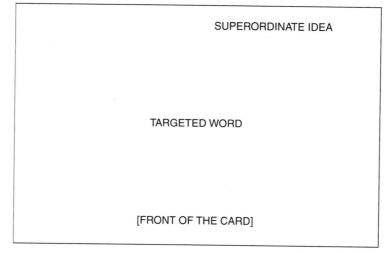

SUPERORDINATE IDEA

TARGETED WORD

[FRONT OF THE CARD]

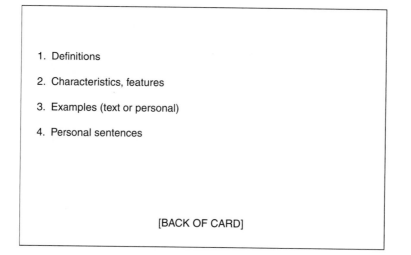

1. Definitions

2. Characteristics, features

3. Examples (text or personal)

4. Personal sentences

[BACK OF CARD]

(2) characteristics or features, (3) examples from the text and/or personal experiences, and (4) personal sentences. Students can also add personal cues, mnemonics, or images to help them understand the targeted word. The card in Figure 6.9 illustrates how one 12th grader used concept cards to study the technical terms for her business course. Notice how she adapted the card to fit her purposes by including in the upper right-hand corner the notation that there are two types of formal organizations, an important fact that she needed to remember.

Students can use either 4 × 6 or 3 × 5 index cards, but it is important that they use cards rather than pieces of notebook paper because the cards encourage students to test themselves rather than to look at the terminology passively. Cards are also more durable and portable, allowing students to study them while standing in line, riding the bus, or waiting for class to begin.

Evelia, a teacher for gifted seventh graders, asks her students to create concept cards for the words she identifies and for the words they choose to learn. The general words she selects for their study come from their integrated history and literature

Figure 6.9 A Concept Card by a 12th Grader for Technical Terms in a Business Course

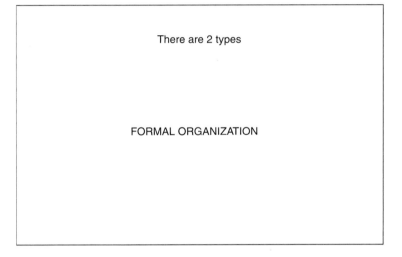

There are 2 types

FORMAL ORGANIZATION

1. Clearly defined relationships, channels of communication, and delegation of authority.

2. Characteristics: clearly defined authority relationships, well-developed communication systems, stable/permanent, capable of expansion.

3. Tools of formal organizations include charts, policy manuals, organization manuals.

4. Example: where my father works (IBM).

units. Each week she also asks her students to select three unfamiliar words from their own reading that they would like to learn. Because she wants her students to understand the original context and to apply the word to new situations, Evelia asks them to write the original sentence on the front of the card and at least one original sentence on the back. Figure 6.10 illustrates a concept card a student made for the word *turgid* that came from a short story.

To determine the students' accuracy in finding the most appropriate dictionary definition and their precision in writing a sentence that uses the words correctly, Evelia usually checks the cards while students are working in groups on another activity. By doing these quick checks of the cards, she knows what words need to be emphasized the next day during discussion. Evelia is a strong believer in taking time to discuss words so students can hear the various definitions and sentences that their classmates have written. She tells us that the nuances and connotations of words are not learned from the dictionary; rather, they are learned from "trying on the words and playing with them" in an environment that invites experimentation.

Figure 6.10 Concept Card for the Word *Turgid*

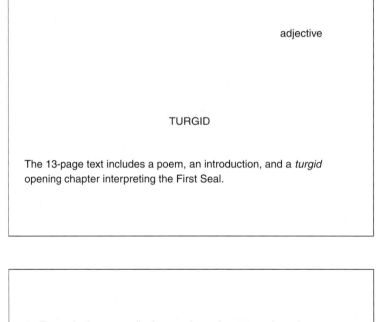

adjective

TURGID

The 13-page text includes a poem, an introduction, and a *turgid* opening chapter interpreting the First Seal.

1. Excessively ornate, flashy, wordy, and pompous in style or language

2. Synonym: *bombastic*   Antonym: *plain, simple language*

The minister's turgid sermon put everyone to sleep on the warm Sunday evening.

Evelia models for the students how they should study their concept cards because she has discovered that many of them merely look at the front of their cards and then at the back without testing themselves or reciting aloud. While modeling, she makes sure that students realize the importance of saying the definitions and sentences aloud. Moreover, she stresses the importance of practicing from front to back and from back to front on the cards and the usefulness of making piles of cards representing the words that are known and the words that need further study. Evelia has been requiring students to make concept cards for about 5 years. She has noticed a substantial improvement in their retention of the words and, more important, their use of the words in their written work.

Word Sorts Using Concept Cards

A word sort is an excellent reinforcement activity that students can use with their concept cards or any list of content-area words. During a word sort, students group their cards into different categories with common features. There are two types of word sorts: closed and open (Gillet & Kita, 1979). With the *closed sort*, students know in advance the categories in which they must place their cards. For example, the students in Evelia's class were asked to sort their concept cards into positive adjectives and negative adjectives. Thus, students sorted words such as *turgid*, *pretentious*, *neurotic*, and *condescending* into the negative adjectives category and words such as *charismatic* and *diligent* into the positive adjectives category. Evelia tells students to do this activity in small groups and then asks each group to explain and justify their groupings. Being able to manipulate the concept cards makes the word-sort activity more interesting and flexible for students.

Open word sorts engage students in higher levels of thinking and processing.

Open sorts require students to determine ways in which their general or technical vocabulary can be grouped. Therefore, students search for relationships that might exist among the words rather than depending on the teacher to provide that structure. In a ninth-grade science class, students were studying pollution and were asked to group their concept cards into one or more categories. The following words share some common categories:

biodegradable	photosynthesis
leaching	surface mining
incineration	acid mine drainage
silting	reclamation projects

Can you group the words into some categories? With open sorts, there are no correct categories. Instead, what is important is that students can explain and justify how they grouped the words. Possible sorts or categories with the preceding words include the broad category of land pollution. On a more specific level of sorting, categories might include causes of land pollution (e.g., silting, acid mine drainage, leaching) and solutions (e.g., biodegradable, reclamation projects). Because open sorts demand more elaborative thinking, they probably should be preceded by several closed-sort activities. Students, however, enjoy both types of activities. More important, teacher preparation for this activity is minimal.

In this section, we have discussed three different practical strategies that focus on helping students master the important words in a content area. These three strategies share in common the goal of enhancing students' abilities to view a content area as more than a linear list of facts to be memorized, an important consideration for any teacher. In the next section, we examine how content-area teachers can reinforce and evaluate students' understanding of words with activities similar to word sorts.

For additional ideas on how to reinforce and evaluate students' vocabulary knowledge, go to *www.readingonline. org/newliteracies/ webwatch/vocabulary* or to Web Resources for Chapter 6 at *http:// www.prenhall.com/brozo.*

Activities for Reinforcing and Evaluating Content-Area Word Knowledge

As mentioned earlier in this chapter, one characteristic of effective vocabulary instruction is that teachers reinforce students' word learning over time. That is, once targeted vocabulary words have been introduced and discussed, students need to practice those words in a variety of new situations. Therefore, fewer words will be taught, and more instructional time will be provided for meaningful reinforcement activities and cumulative review if we want to promote students' understanding of content-area textbooks. The first of the reinforcement strategies discussed, imagery and keywords, can be used across the content areas to help students learn technical and general words.

Imagery and Keywords

Have you ever created a mental picture to remember a difficult word or procedure? Many of us do this routinely because we know that images can be powerful reminders. For example, if the targeted word you need to learn is *acrophobia*, what mental picture could you use to remember that the word means fear of high places? One option would be to focus on the first part of the word, acro, and develop the image of an acrobat who is afraid of heights walking on a tightrope high in the sky. You could follow up with a sentence such as this: "The acrobat, who has always been afraid of high places, suffered from acrophobia." When we make pictures in our minds to help us remember what a word means or how it relates to another word or superordinate concept, we are using the strategy of imagery. Research suggests that imagery can be a powerful tool for reinforcing vocabulary knowledge because students are actively involved in their learning (Hwang & Levin, 2002; Levin, 1993; Scruggs & Mastropieri, 2000).

The keyword strategy differs slightly from imagery in that we think of catchy phrases or sentences related to the word we want to remember. For example, if you were having trouble remembering *amorous,* you might think about a phrase such as "more love for us," which sounds like amorous but has a synonym for the word in it. Although the research findings on the keyword and imagery strategies are positive and promising, they will not work for *every* vocabulary word or for *every* student. In addition, it is important to remember that students' personal images or catchy phrases will always be more powerful than the images or phrases provided by their teacher.

Notice how Martrez encourages Araceli to state the steps of this vocabulary strategy before she applies the strategy independently to another word. Had Araceli not been able to use the strategy after this individual lesson, Martrez would have shown her another strategy to help her keep straight the definitions and functions of the 47 different technical terms in this unit. He tries to present a variety of choices for his students with learning disabilities because he knows that students learn in different ways. With Araceli, however, imagery and keywords worked once she realized the processes involved in them. We should point out, however, that students need not have a learning disability in order to benefit from using imagery or the keyword strategy.

Activities and Test Formats That Reinforce and Evaluate Word Learning

If students are to learn their targeted words at a full and deep level of understanding, the activities and test formats we select for reinforcement and evaluation should

Honoring Diversity and Building Competence in the Content Classroom

Martrez, a 10th-grade biology teacher, uses a combination of imagery and keywords to help his students with learning disabilities remember difficult definitions and relationships between concepts. During his unit on the endocrine system, he modeled the procedures he used in creating images and keywords to remember the functions of the glands and hormones in the endocrine system. One of his students, Araceli, had difficulty applying the strategies, so Martrez met with her during homeroom to help her. The lesson follows.

Martrez: Araceli, let's start with the pituitary gland and the thyrotropic hormone. To remember the definition, we need to think of something memorable from part of the word *thyrotropic.* I'll start first, and then I'll have you help me. When I hear the word *tropic,* I think of the jungles where rain stimulates extreme growth. Thyrotropic hormones stimulate growth in the thyroid, the other part of the word. Do you see what I did, Araceli? I took parts of the word that I could remember because they were already familiar to me. Then I made up a sentence to help me remember the definition. Which word would you like to try next?

Araceli: I missed *prolactin* on the pop quiz. Can we try this one?

Martrez: Okay, Araceli. Let's look at the word carefully—each letter and the parts. Can you divide the word into familiar parts?

Araceli: Well, there is the word *pro,* which means a professional, in the word *prolactin.* There is also the word tin.

Martrez: Okay, Araceli. Will either of them help you remember the definition of prolactin, a hormone that stimulates milk production?

Araceli: No, I don't see how.

Martrez: Okay. Let's see if we can play with the middle part of the word, *lac.* This part of the word sounds like what word in our language, Araceli?

Araceli: *Lack?*

Martrez: That's right! Has your mother ever told you that you lack milk—that you should drink more milk if you hope to be healthy?

Araceli: Yes! And I hate the stuff.

Martrez: Could we use the letters *l-a-c* to remind us of milk? Many people lack the correct amount of milk.

Araceli: Yes, but what about the *pro* part of the word?

Martrez: Good question. Could we use *pro* to remind us in some way that prolactin is a hormone that stimulates milk? Think about this for a moment, Araceli.

Araceli: (a few seconds later) Yes! Professional athletes should not suffer from a lack of milk. Will that work?

Martrez: Will it work for you? That is what makes the difference.

Araceli: Hmm. Yes, I can use that—it makes sense. Professional athletes should not suffer from a lack of milk. Prolactin stimulates milk production.

continued

> ## Honoring Diversity and Building Competence in the Content Classroom (*continued*)
>
> ***Martrez:*** Let's review before we go to the next word. Give me the definitions of *thyrotropic* and *prolactin.*
>
> ***Araceli:*** Prolactin stimulates the production of milk, and the thyrotropic hormone stimulates the thyroid. This is easy.
>
> ***Martrez:*** The next hormone you missed on the quiz is *thyroxine.* Araceli, what are the steps in this process of remembering a definition of a difficult word?

match that level of thinking. Evidence suggests, however, that commercial materials typically use multiple-choice and matching formats as the main method of reinforcement and testing (Joshi, 2005; Simpson and Randall, 2000). We know that these formats do not challenge students to demonstrate their full understanding of words (Blachowicz & Fisher, 2002; McKeown & Beck, 2004). Rather, when students circle letters or draw lines to match a definition to a word, they are passively involved in guesswork. Even asking students to write a definition of a word from memory does not stimulate conceptual understanding. Therefore, alternative reinforcement and evaluation activities are needed.

Constructing creative and appropriate reinforcement and evaluative activities can be challenging. However, several activities and formats can be incorporated into any classroom routine (e.g., bell-work activities), homework assignment. In fact, we know several content-area teachers who begin their class each day with one of these reinforcement activities on the overhead projector. These activities and formats involve students in a variety of elaborative thinking processes. Some of these activities and test formats follow.

> These six reinforcement activities and formats can be easily added to a unit exam or quiz as a way of testing students' mastery of important content-area vocabulary words.

Statement Plus a Request

With the *statement plus a request activity,* students read two related statements, each containing the same targeted word. The second statement, however, asks students to demonstrate their knowledge of the word by exceeding the usual simple definition. In a sophomore history class, a teacher included this question on her unit test:

Directions: Read the first statement carefully. Then read the second statement and answer it. Pay close attention to the italicized word.

1. Statement: Robert LaFollette was a *Progressive* with many ideas on what he wanted changed in Wisconsin.
2. Request: What are some of the *Progressive* ideas that Robert LaFollette had?

Exclusion

Henry (1974) states that excluding is one of the basic operations involved in concept development. When students practice *exclusion,* they discriminate between, negate, and recognize examples and nonexamples. The following example is a sample from an algebra teacher's homework assignment:

Directions: Choose the one equation in each group that does not relate to the others and should be excluded. Write the excluded equation's letter in the blank after "Exclude." In the blank labeled "General Concept," write the concept that describes the remaining words.

Exclusion Activities

1. a. $x^2 - y^2 = (x + y)(x - y)$
    b. $x^2 + 5x + 6 = (x + 3)(x + 2)$
    c. $ax^2 + a^2x = ax(x - a)$
    d. $3x^2 + 4x^2 + 1 = 7x^2 + 1$

Exclude: _____

General Concept: _____

The following example of an exclusion item is from a French teacher's unit test:

1. la glace la moutarde le gâteau la tarte

Exclude: _____

General Concept: _____

Paired Word Questions

The long-term vocabulary study by Beck, Perfetti, and McKeown (1982) employed a question-asking activity that paired two targeted words. To answer these *paired word questions*, students must understand the underlined concepts or words and then determine if any relationships exist between them. The following example is one of several items that an art teacher uses during class when he pairs words for a review. Notice that he tests both technical (*avant-garde*) and general (*incoherent*) vocabulary word knowledge:

> Directions: Answer the following questions as completely as possible, making sure you demonstrate your full knowledge of the underlined words.

> 1. Would an *avant-garde* painting be *incoherent*? Why or why not?

The next example is from a review activity that a ninth-grade physical education teacher included in a unit on nutrition and fitness:

> 1. Would an individual with *hyperlipidemia* be a candidate for *coronary heart disease*? Why or why not?
> 2. Would an individual who had a *calorie deficit* of 3,500 kcal lose 1 pound of *adipose tissue*? Why or why not?

Sensing the Big Picture

With the format called *sensing the big picture*, students are asked to select the word or phrase that subsumes all the other words or phrases. By completing such an item, students demonstrate that they can discriminate the difference between a major concept and a detail or supporting idea. The following example illustrates how a mathematics teacher used the format in one of her review activities:

> Directions: Look at the group of words below and select the one word or phrase that subsumes the other four. Circle it.

> 1. *Distributive properties, axiom, multiplicative inverse, cancellation law, additive identities*

Analogies

Analogies are multifaceted in that they can involve students in knowing the synonyms or antonyms of targeted words or can encourage students to sense the relationships between words in a variety of ways. In fact, there are probably 50 different formats to the analogy. The following example is from a French teacher's homework assignment:

> *Directions: Fill in the blank with the appropriate vocabulary word. You may use each word only once.*

> 1. *beau : mauvais :: froid :* _____

The next analogy is from an 11th-grade art class. The teacher had just finished a unit on film and used items such as this for a review activity:

> 1. *celluloid : film :: matte effect :* _____

Paired Word Sentence Generation

Traditional sentence-writing activities have never been considered particularly creative or productive. However, *paired word sentence generation* forces students to demonstrate their conceptual understanding of both words and to seek out their implied relationship in order to write a sentence that uses the words correctly. The following example illustrates how a history teacher used this format to reinforce important vocabulary words in a class activity.

> *Directions: You will find two words below that I have purposely paired because they have some relationship to each other. Your task is to write one sentence that uses both of the words correctly and clearly demonstrates your understanding of them and their relationship to each other. You will be asked to share your sentence with the class and to explain why you paired the words as you did. The first item has been done for you as an example.*

> 1. *muckrakers,* McClure's Magazine

> *The muckrakers included journalists and novelists who wrote magazines such as* McClure's Magazine *and books such as The* Jungle *to expose the evils and corruption in business and politics.*

> 2. *Wisconsin idea, referendum (you do this one)*

The next example comes from a music teacher's lesson.

> *Directions: Write a sentence using the following word pairs. I have purposely paired the two words because they have some relationship to each other.*

> 1. *cadence, afterphase*
> 2. *binary form, ternary form*

Because these alternative activities and formats may initially confuse or surprise the students, a few important guidelines about their use should be remembered (Nist & Simpson, 2001). First, match the reinforcement or evaluation activity to the unit objectives or goals. Students can demonstrate only the level of conceptual understanding that they have been involved in during the unit. Second, vary the activities and formats across the school year and within the units of study. For example, a culinary arts teacher might include five exclusions, five analogies, and five paired word sentence-generation activities into a unit test to represent the different thinking processes underlying conceptual understanding. Finally, practice and discuss the differing activities and formats with students, especially before they see them on a test. If students are not accustomed to a new activity or test format, their response or score could mask their real understanding. In fact, it is always a good idea to provide a sample item, as did the history teacher for the paired word activity.

Make sure you always provide your students practice and debriefing sessions when you use a different type of evaluation format.

CASE STUDY REVISITED

We now return to the Park Forest School District, where a district-wide committee of teachers has been meeting throughout the school year to solve the problem of extremely low vocabulary scores in the 10th grade. After reading this chapter, you probably have some ideas on how the committee could solve this problem. Take a moment now to write your suggestions.

By the end of the school year, Rafalar, the curriculum director, and the 10th-grade teachers on the committee had reached only one decision. One 10th-grade biology teacher had discussed an article he had read on the characteristics of effective vocabulary instruction, prompting the committee to decide that there were no "quick fixes" and that no single type of commercial material would fully address their vocabulary problems. Perhaps that decision was the most important because it removed as an option the vocabulary computer program that several members were urging the school to adopt. The committee members realized that the computer program expected students to learn the targeted words in lists with no context and that only rote-level definitional knowledge was emphasized on the activities and quizzes. Hence, they were concerned about whether students would learn the words well enough to be able to apply them to new situations.

Although the committee did reach agreement on the use of commercial materials for the students, they still disagreed about the language arts teachers' role in improving students' vocabulary. Some teachers saw the teaching of vocabulary as a time-consuming intrusion into an already hectic teaching schedule. Moreover, they viewed vocabulary instruction as a natural and logical part of a language arts curriculum. Consequently, the curriculum director suggested that the issue be tabled for a while, at least until they had finished their intensive study of vocabulary acquisition.

During the summer, the committee members were provided with a stipend to read and plan further. The curriculum director had the money for the study because expensive commercial materials had not been purchased from the school budget. At their first meeting, she suggested that the committee begin with some general goals rather than adopting commercial materials or another school's approach. With the focus of establishing specific goals for vocabulary instruction at their school, the teachers read intensively about vocabulary development and kept personal learning logs. They chose articles from journals in their own content area, articles from the *Journal of Adolescent & Adult Learning*, and recent books on the topic published by professional organizations such as the International Reading Association. A major breakthrough occurred when one of the more vocal and negative teachers read a review of the literature explaining how vocabulary knowledge was closely related to students' understanding of what they read. She shared that information with the rest of the committee and made a rather compelling case for the importance of vocabulary knowledge to content-area learning. From that point on, very few committee members wanted only the language arts teachers to assume responsibility for vocabulary development.

After considerable reading and discussion, the committee developed the following goals for the school district:

1. The students should develop a long-term interest and enjoyment in developing and refining their vocabulary.

2. The students should learn some independent strategies for learning new technical and general vocabulary words.

Before writing your suggestions for the committee, go to *http://www.prenhall.com/brozo,* select Chapter 6, then click on Chapter Review Questions to check your understanding of the material.

CASE STUDY REVISITED (CONTINUED)

3. The students should become skilled in the use of the dictionary and, when appropriate, contextual analysis.

Pleased with their goals, the committee members decided that their next step was to outline how each goal could be incorporated into their own curriculum and how the departments could reinforce each other. They also decided that these goals should not be limited to the 10th-grade teachers but should involve all grade levels. Their reasoning was that an effective program of vocabulary improvement needed to be comprehensive and cumulative if real growth and change were to occur.

Because the school year was about to begin, the committee decided to implement the first two goals and to evaluate the impact of their unified effort at the end of the school year. They concluded, however, that students' scores on the competency-based reading test would probably not increase suddenly as a result of these small steps toward their unified effort to improve word knowledge and reading comprehension. From their readings and discussions, they realized that their goal of improving students' vocabulary knowledge would involve a long-term commitment by teachers and all others involved.

Looking Back, Looking Forward

In this chapter we have stressed the importance of students having a deep and full understanding of technical and general vocabulary in order to improve their content-area learning. Because simple definitional knowledge of a word is not sufficient for textbook comprehension, teachers need to stress the context links from what students know to what they will learn. This contextual understanding of content-area terms and concepts can be facilitated by a variety of activities (e.g., Possible Sentences).

Teachers need to emphasize the vocabulary of their content area as they encourage students to become independent word learners. We therefore discussed vocabulary strategies such as word maps and concept cards that students can use as they read and study their assignments. Whether they are teacher directed or student initiated, these vocabulary strategies become even more powerful and useful when anchored in content-area lessons that emphasize teachers' demonstrations, modeling, small-group interactions, class discussion, and reciprocal teaching. None of these strategies is mutually exclusive; they can and should be used together. For instance, combining activities such as focusing on word histories with the use of contextual clues will have a stronger and more long-lasting effect than either of these strategies alone.

Like nearly all of the methods presented in this book, the vocabulary strategies discussed here will not always engender immediate enthusiasm for learning words or produce an immediate impact on reading comprehension. Teachers must take time to warm students up to these methods and must allow their students to develop expertise in using the vocabulary strategies.

Finally, remember that any method, regardless of its novelty, will eventually become ineffective if overused. Therefore, it is wise to vary the vocabulary strategies and reinforcement activities often to sustain students' excitement. In the end, however, any vocabulary-development strategies that require students to process terms and concepts in elaborative, meaningful, and unique ways will help them understand words and text more fully and retain important concepts and ideas much longer.

References

Baumann, J. F., Kame'enui, E. J., & Ash, G. W. (2003). Research on vocabulary instruction: Voltaire redux. In J. Flood, D. Lapp, J. Squire, & J. Jensen (Eds.), *Handbook of research on teaching the English language arts* (2nd ed., pp. 752–785), Mahwah, NJ: Lawrence Erlbaum Associates.

Beck, I., McKeown, M., & Kucan, L. (2002). *Bringing words to life: Robust vocabulary instruction.* New York: Guilford Press.

Beck, I., Perfetti, C. A., & McKeown, M. (1982). The effects of long-term vocabulary instruction on lexical access and reading comprehension. *Journal of Educational Psychology, 74,* 506–521.

Blachowicz, C. L. (1986). Making connections: Alternatives to the vocabulary notebook. *Journal of Reading, 29,* 543–549.

Blachowicz, C. L., & Fisher, P. (2002). *Teaching vocabulary in all classrooms.* Columbus, OH: Merrill.

Blachowicz, C. L., & Fisher, P. (2004). Keep the "fun" in fundamental: Encouraging word awareness and incidental word learning in the classroom through word play. In J. F. Baumann & E. J. Kame'enui (Eds.), *Vocabulary instruction: Research to practice* (pp. 218–237). New York: Guilford Press.

Cronbach, L. J. (1942). An analysis of techniques for systematic vocabulary testing. *Journal of Educational Research, 36,* 206–217.

Donahue, P., Voelkl, K., Campbell, J., & Mazzeo, J. (1999). *NAEP 1998 reading report card for the nation.* Washington, DC: National Center for Education Statistics.

Edwards, C. E., Font, G., Baumann, J. F., & Boland, E. (2004). Unlocking word meanings: Strategies and guidelines for teaching morphemic and contextual analysis. In J. F. Baumann & E. J. Kame'enui (Eds.), *Vocabulary instruction: Research to practice* (pp. 159–176.,) New York : Guilford Press.

Fisher, P., & Blachowicz, C. L. (2005). Vocabulary instruction in a remedial setting. *Reading and Writing Quarterly, 21,* 281–300.

Francis, M. A., & Simpson, M. L. (2003). Using theory, our intuitions, and research study to enhance students' vocabulary knowledge. *Journal of Adolescent and Adult Literacy, 47,* 66–78.

Frayer, D. A., Frederick, W. C., & Klausmeier, H. J. (1969). *A schema for testing the level of concept knowledge.* (Working paper No. 16). Madison, WI: University of Wisconsin.

Gillet, J., & Kita, M. J. (1979). Words, kids, and categories. *The Reading Teacher, 32,* 538–542.

Graves, M. F. (1987). The roles of instruction in fostering vocabulary development. In M. McKeown & M.

Curtis (Eds.), *The nature of vocabulary acquisition.* Hillsdale, NJ: Lawrence Erlbaum Associates.

Graves, M. F. (2004). Teaching prefixes: As good as it gets? In J. F. Baumann & E. J. Kame'enui (Eds.), *Vocabulary instruction: Research to practice* (pp. 81–99), New York: Guilford Press.

Harmon, J. M., Hedrick, W. B., & Wood, K. D. (2005). Research on vocabulary instruction in the content areas: Implications for struggling readers. *Reading and Writing Quarterly, 21,* 261–280.

Henry, G. H. (1974). *Teach reading as concept development: Emphasis on affective thinking.* Newark, DE: International Reading Association.

Hwang, Y., & Levin, J. R. (2002). Examination of middle school students' independent use of a complex mnemonic system. *Journal of Experimental Education, 71,* 25–38.

Johnson, D. D., Johnson, B., & Schlichting, K. (2004). Logology: Word and language play. In J. F. Baumann & E. J. Kame'enui (Eds.), *Vocabulary instruction: Research to practice* (pp. 179–200), New York: Guilford Press.

Joshi, R. M. (2005). Vocabulary: A critical component of comprehension. *Reading and Writing Quarterly, 21,* 209–219.

Levin, J. R. (1993). Mnemonic strategies and classroom learning: A twenty-year report card. *Elementary School Journal, 94,* 234–244.

Manzo, A., & Sherk, J. (1971). Some generalizations and strategies to guide vocabulary acquisition. *Journal of Reading Behavior, 4,* 78–89.

McKeown, M. G., & Beck, I. L. (2004). Direct and rich vocabulary instruction. In J. F. Baumann & E. J. Kame'enui (Eds.), *Vocabulary instruction: Research to practice* (pp. 13–27). New York: Guilford Press.

Milligan, J. L., & Ruff, T. P. (1990). A linguistic approach to social studies vocabulary development. *The Social Studies, 81,* 218–220.

Moore, D. W., & Moore, S. A. (1986). Possible sentences. In E. K. Dishner, T. W. Bean, J. E. Readence, & D. W. Moore (Eds.), *Reading in the content areas* (2nd ed.). Dubuque, IA: Kendall/Hunt.

Nagy, W. E., & Scott J. (2000). Vocabulary processes. In M. Kamil, P. Mosenthal, P. D. Pearson, & R. Barr (Eds.), *Handbook of reading research* (Vol. 3, pp. 269–284). Mahwah, NJ: Lawrence Erlbaum Associates.

National Reading Panel. (2000). *Teaching children to read: An evidence-based assessment of the scientific research literature on reading and its implications for reading instruction: Reports of the subgroups.* Washington, DC: National Institute of Child Health and Development.

Nist, S. L., & Olejnik, S. (1995). The role of context and dictionary definitions on varying levels of word knowledge. *Reading Research Quarterly, 30,* 172–193.

Nist, S. L., & Simpson, M. L. (2001). *Developing vocabulary concepts for college thinking.* Needham Heights, MA: Allyn and Bacon.

RAND Reading Study Group. (2002). *Reading for understanding: Toward a research and development program in reading comprehension.* Prepared for the Office of Educational Research and Improvement (OERI), U. S. Department of Education. Santa Monica, CA: RAND Education.

Rupley, W. H. (2005). Vocabulary knowledge: Its contribution to reading growth and development. *Reading and Writing Quarterly, 21,* 203–207.

Rupley, W. H., & Nichols, W. D. (2005). Vocabulary instruction for the struggling reader. *Reading and Writing Quarterly, 21,* 239–260.

Schwartz, R. M. (1988). Learning to learn vocabulary in textbooks. *Journal of Reading, 32,* 108–118.

Schwartz, R. M., & Raphael, T. E. (1985). Concept of definition: A key to improving students' vocabulary. *The Reading Teacher, 39,* 198–205.

Scott, J., & Nagy, W. (2004). Developing word consciousness. In J. F. Baumann & E. J. Kame'enui (Eds.), *Vocabulary instruction: Research to practice* (pp. 201–217). New York: Guilford Press.

Scruggs, T. E., & Mastropieri, M. A. (2000). The effectiveness of mnemonic instruction for students with learning and behavior problems: An update and research synthesis. *Journal of Behavioral Education, 10,* 163–173.

Simpson, M. L., & Randall, S. (2000). Vocabulary development at the college level. In R. Flippo & D. Caverly (Eds.), *Handbook of college reading and study strategy research* (pp. 43–73). Mahwah, NJ: Lawrence Erlbaum Associates.

Stahl, S. A. (1985). To teach a word well: A framework for vocabulary instruction. *Reading World, 24,* 16–27.

Stahl, S. A. (1986). Three principles of effective vocabulary instruction. *Journal of Reading, 29,* 662– 668.

Stahl, S. A. (1999). *Vocabulary development.* Cambridge, MA: Brookline Books.

Stahl, S. A., & Stahl, K. A. (2004). Word wizards all!: Word meanings in preschool and primary education. In J. F. Baumann & E. J. Kame'enui (Eds.), *Vocabulary instruction: Research to practice* (pp. 201–217). New York: Guilford Press.

Stanley, J. (1971). Photographed vocabulary. In M. G. McClosky (Ed.), *Teaching strategies and classroom realities.* Englewood Cliffs, NJ: Prentice Hall.

chapter 7

Writing as a Tool for Active Learning

Anticipation Guide

Directions: Read each statement carefully and decide whether you agree or disagree with it, placing a check mark in the appropriate *Before Reading* column. When you have finished reading and studying the chapter, return to the guide and decide whether your anticipations need to be changed by placing a check mark in the appropriate *After Reading* column.

	Before Reading		After Reading	
	Agree	*Disagree*	*Agree*	*Disagree*
1. Writing assignments should be reserved for English courses.	_____	_____	_____	_____
2. Everything a student writes should be evaluated.	_____	_____	_____	_____
3. Writing tasks are best used after students have read their textbook assignments.	_____	_____	_____	_____
4. Longer writing assignments are better than shorter ones.	_____	_____	_____	_____
5. The best way to respond to students' papers is to write detailed comments on them.	_____	_____	_____	_____

207

Chapter Principle: Express Critical Perspectives and Interpretations

This principle addresses the importance of having students express critical perspectives and interpretations of the texts they read, whether it be a document, a novel, or a recent magazine article. As noted by a variety of experts, one of the best ways to encourage students to think critically and become strategic learners is to incorporate writing activities into every content area in a seamless fashion (Bean, 2001; Graham, 2005). The strategies and activities presented in this chapter will assist content-area teachers with their instructional goals, especially those that focus on higher levels of thinking.

*T*he National Commission on Writing in America's Schools and Colleges (2003) has stressed the importance of having every content-area teacher use writing as a learning tool in the classroom. The Commission eloquently explained their rationale in this manner:

> If students are to make knowledge their own, they must struggle with the details, wrestle with the facts, and rework raw information and dimly understood concepts into language they can communicate to someone else. In short, if students are to learn, they must write. (2003, p. 9)

Such a perspective suggests that writing, when integrated into a content-area classroom, can enhance students' learning and thus is doubly advantageous (Bangert-Drowns, Hurley, & Wilkinson, 2004). For example, a middle school math teacher used writing to help her students with units on multiplication and geometry. The students wrote explanations that described how to do something, defined new words, and explained their errors on quizzes and homework. At the end of the two units, the teacher found that her students who had used writing as a way of learning mathematics scored significantly better on their posttests than did students who had participated in more traditional activities (Jenkinson, 1988).

Thus, it would seem that writing not only facilitates the learning of content-area concepts but also engages students in higher-level thinking and reasoning processes. In this chapter we examine the ways in which content-area teachers can capitalize on the many advantages of writing without sacrificing instructional time or adding another responsibility to their incredibly busy days. Our basic theme is this: Reading and writing are processes that actively involve students in a variety of extremely important cognitive and metacognitive processes. As such, when writing is integrated into the existing curriculum, both teachers and students profit immensely.

CASE STUDY

Dave, a first-year teacher, is a member of the biology department at an urban high school. His students are those who do not plan to attend college, and thus they differ from the students he dealt with during his practice teaching. Dave is a bit frustrated because his first unit did not go well. The students appeared to be bored with the chapters he assigned, and many did not complete any of the homework. In fact, out of his five classes, only 10 students received an A or B on the first unit exam. Dave's department chairperson has urged him to be stricter with the students. Another new teacher in the English department with whom he shares lunch duty has suggested that he incorporate more relevant reading materials and assignments into his units. Dave considers the English teacher's recommendation more intriguing than the chairperson's, but does not know where to begin. He knows he wants to motivate his students to see biology as relevant to their lives, but he needs direction in planning his next unit.

To the Reader:
As you read this chapter, think about how Dave might incorporate writing and any other strategies into his next unit on the environment.

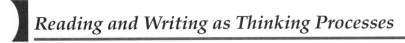

Reading and Writing as Thinking Processes

If your friend observed you reading this book and asked for a synopsis, you probably could provide one with a quick glance at the table of contents. What if, however, you were asked to write a summary? Could you complete this task as quickly and easily? Find out in the accompanying Teacher as Learner activity.

Research and theory suggest that reading and writing are not mirror images of each other but "separate, overlapping processes" that provide students alternative ways of constructing meaning (Shanahan, 1997). When students read an assignment from a textbook or write a paper, they are involved in the active process of building their own text world or internal configuration of meaning. Simply put, when students

Go to *http://www. prenhall.com/brozo*, select Chapter 7, then click on the Chapter Objectives to provide a focus for your reading.

Teacher as Learner

WRITING ABOUT YOUR READING

Write a five-sentence summary of the key ideas of the first six chapters. You are welcome to "peek" at the table of contents if you need to refresh your memory. You can place your summary here:

_____

_____

_____

_____

Did you think about the ideas before you began to write your summary? Did you revise your ideas several times? Are your thoughts about the key ideas presented in this book more focused than when you first started to think about the task? Did you learn anything as a result of your writing? If you answered *yes* to any of these questions, you have experienced the power and permanence of writing. Just as reading is more than moving your eyes across the page, writing is more than "putting ideas" on paper.

grapple with questions such as "How can I factor a polynomial?" or "How can I explain in my own words the relationship between time, velocity, and distance?" they are beginning to construct meaning and create their own text.

The writing process, not unlike the reading process, has overlapping and recursive elements. According to a variety of authorities, when we struggle to put ideas down on paper, much like you did with the previous activity, we move through these processes or phases:

1. *Planning.* Just as active learners use what they already know and set purposes before they begin to read, they also spend extended periods of time before the actual writing to plan, to discover ways of approaching the task, to self-question, and to identify purposes or problems. This phase of the composing process is often ignored because of an inordinate concern for a written product that will be evaluated by the teacher. If students could be provided with more time in class to brainstorm ideas and discuss writing plans with their peers and their teachers, the quality of their writing would significantly increase (Sargent, 1997; Shellard & Protheroe, 2004).

2. *Drafting.* The second phase of the writing process focuses on the initial draft. At this point the writer is engaged in the enormous struggle to get words onto paper and into sentences, paragraphs, and sections. As with the reading process, the writer works to make things cohere and fit between the whole and parts and among the parts. Most writers, however, do not follow an orderly process in this initial drafting. Often teachers do not allow enough time in class for this initial drafting or they allow no time at all. Instead, they assign the writing to be done outside of class, where other classmates and the teacher are not available for support and coaching. If students could write their initial drafts during class, teachers would then gain the timely opportunity to meet with their students to discuss their problems in getting ideas down on paper. Moreover, these mini debriefing sessions can often save teachers considerable evaluation time on the subsequent final product.

3. *Revising.* The third phase of the writing process involves students in revising and reformulating. Just as active readers pause to reflect and monitor and then reread to verify and evaluate, mature writers take the time to read, reflect, and evaluate their writing as another individual would. By taking the role of the reader during this phase of the writing process, students begin to see their "writing" as a piece of "reading."

When students are involved in the revising process, they think about their thesis, modifying it when it is not clear for their anticipated readers. They may also reorganize their papers, adding support and deleting information elsewhere, especially if they have not made their case for their audience. Hence, the recursive nature of the revising process often leads writers back to previous phases and processes (e.g., planning).

Although students are initially resistant to the revision process, there are a variety of techniques that teachers can use to create this expectation and responsibility. We will discuss many of these techniques throughout this chapter.

4. *Editing and polishing.* At this phase writers move from macro-level text concerns to micro-level text concerns. Hence, they examine their sentence structure, search for correct word choices, and proofread for basic errors in spelling, punctuation, or grammar. Because students often believe that the revision phase that emphasizes content and meaning is synonymous with the editing and polishing phase that emphasizes form, teachers will need to stress the differences on numerous occasions.

5. *Postwriting and sharing.* Just as readers use and share the information they have read in some meaningful way, so should writers. That is, writers should share and "make public" their texts. In most situations this sharing typically occurs in a private and limited way because teachers are the sole readers of students' texts. Ideally, however, the audience for students' writing should be more public, whether that means other students, administrators, parents, community members, or individuals outside the community (e.g., politicians, business leaders).

In this chapter content-area teachers will find a variety of activities that will assist their students in understanding the recursive nature of the writing process and in using writing as a way of maximizing their learning.

The intensity and willingness that students devote to any of these phases depend on the two conditions that we, as teachers, can control. First, most students have a naive idea of what it takes to be a good writer, just as they do of what it takes to be a good reader. To them, good writing has correct spelling and grammar, whereas good reading is the accurate pronunciation of words. When teachers share with them the processes of their own writing tasks, students are surprised to discover that professionals or mature writers must evaluate and revise extensively before they concern themselves with the surface features of spelling and grammar. Second, students who have never written for anyone but the teacher often feel that their ideas are not worthy of extended writing and revision or that the teacher already understands the ideas, so there is no need to be explicit and clear. They also have difficulty believing in a real audience because the writing task to them is no more than an occasion for a grade. Teachers can change this misconception by providing their students with real and intriguing audiences for their writing so that the urgency of communicating ideas becomes a passion and a drive. Findings from the research literature suggest that students who know their writing will have an audience other than the teacher are the ones more likely to participate in the revising and editing phases of the writing process (Elbow, 2002; Weber, 2002).

In sum, teachers can help their students understand these recursive and overlapping stages by reserving time in class for brainstorming, planning, drafting, revising, editing, polishing, and sharing. However, we would be amiss if we did not point out that there are many occasions in content-area classrooms where students' writing is exploratory and thus is not revised, edited, or published for a wider audience. Because these kinds of exploratory writing activities have equal value in the content-area classroom, we will devote considerable time to discussing them later in this chapter.

How Can Writing Help the Content-Area Teacher?

Many students are passive learners who expect to be told by their teachers what is important and what they must learn. We know this from our own experiences in the classroom, from what other teachers tell us, and from numerous research studies (e.g., Simpson, Stahl, & Francis, 2004). As a result of this passivity on the part of students, textbook assignments are not read; at best, the ideas are quickly memorized for examinations and then forgotten. In short, many students become sponges soaking up details to pass exams.

The following example from a high school government class demonstrates how the sponge theory operates:

> *Ernesto assigns his 11th graders to read the first part of Chapter 2, which describes the characteristics of public opinion, and to come to class prepared for discussion. In their reading, the students come across one of the characteristics of public opinion, latency, and its corresponding definition—an opinion not yet crystallized or formed.*
>
> *Martrez, an especially diligent student, repeats that definition several times before coming to class, confident that he is prepared for discussion or an unannounced quiz (for which Ernesto is infamous). Ernesto lives up to his reputation. He asks the students to list and define the five characteristics of public opinion and to give an example of each. Martrez, confident of the definition of latency, writes the words "not yet crystallized" but gives no example. In fact, none of the students give examples, and they complain loudly about this aspect of the exam. "There were no examples in the textbook! You are not being fair! We really did read the assignment."*

Was Ernesto unfair? Did Martrez really understand the concept of latency or the words "not yet crystallized"? Should Ernesto's students be expected to create examples of concepts? Although we believe that Ernesto was justified in not accepting rote memorization by his students, we also believe that he could have prevented this minor student revolt by integrating the processes of reading and writing into his lesson plans. The combined use of reading and writing in this government class would have provided the students and Ernesto with several advantages. Before we discuss these advantages, take a moment to complete the activity in the Teacher as Learner box.

Perhaps your lists in the Teacher as Learner activity are similar to the ideas explained next, ideas synthesized from the research literature. Compare and read on because each will be discussed in detail.

1. When students write, at the most simple level they are paraphrasing, summarizing, organizing, and linking new understandings with familiar ones (Casazza, 2003; Friend, 2000).

2. When students write, they are monitoring their comprehension, making it easier for them to identify what they know and what is confusing to them (Bangert-Drowns et al., 2004; El-Hindi, 2004).

3. When students write, they are supported in higher levels of thinking such as elaborating, synthesizing information across texts, and expressing critical perspectives and interpretations (Graham, 2005; Shellard & Protheroe, 2004).

Teacher as Learner

POTENTIAL ADVANTAGES OF USING WRITING ACROSS THE CONTENT AREAS

Reflect on your own experiences as a learner. How have you used writing to assist you in learning some new or difficult concepts? In the spaces that follow, list some of these ways in which writing was advantageous to you.

_____

_____

_____

     Writing is not only advantageous to the learner grappling with new or difficult concepts, but also to the content-area teacher. In the spaces that follow, list some of these ways in which writing can be useful to teachers.

_____

_____

_____

4. When students write, teachers have one more tool to motivate students and to engage them in classroom activities (Bean, 2001; Duffy, 2005).

5. When students write, teachers can readily identify students' misconceptions and lack of conceptual understanding (Angelo & Cross, 1993; Light, 2001).

We now return to Ernesto's classroom in order to examine each of these advantages in more detail.

    Ernesto could have capitalized upon these advantages to writing if he had assigned his students to read the excerpt and then summarize the key ideas, using their own words. In giving the assignment, Ernesto could have modeled how he summarizes and explained how he uses those brief text annotations as a way to monitor his own understanding. The next day students could have compared their summaries while Ernesto circulated the room to eavesdrop on conversations. By doing this he could have gained valuable insights about the students' level of understanding and the problems they were having with the texts. Moreover, he could have used this feedback as a way to open a large-group question-and-answer session.

    Alternatively, Ernesto could have capitalized on the power of writing by frontloading the assignment he gave his students. That is, he could have introduced the chapter and unit by asking the students to take 5 minutes to describe in their journals the typical American's opinion about capital punishment for mass murderers. Then he could have asked them to describe their own opinions. After several students had shared their journal entries with the class, Ernesto could have asked the students to brainstorm reasons why there were so many differences in opinion across the classroom. His students would then have been better prepared and more motivated to read about the five characteristics that influence political opinion, having brainstormed several of them already.

    Finally, Ernesto could have used writing as a way to encourage his students to think critically and creatively. For example, if Ernesto wanted his students to apply the concepts in this chapter to situations in the community, he could have asked his students to work in small groups and poll a representative sample of 25 individuals about a variety of important issues (e.g., bike lanes, zoning regulations). Once they completed their interviews, the groups could have then prepared a written report that summarized their findings and explained the results in light of the characteristics of public opinion presented in the chapter. Ernesto could have also encouraged the students to formulate additional characteristics of public opinion or challenge the authors' interpretations of these characteristics.

In short, writing is valuable to you because students cannot remain passive if they are asked to put their ideas on paper. Writing activities demand participation by every student, not just those who volunteer. More important, writing activities can quickly demonstrate which students understand and where the understanding breaks down so that reteaching can be planned. In the next section we discuss several important guidelines for the use of writing in the content-area classroom.

Guidelines for the Use of Writing Across the Content Areas

You can maximize the potential of writing in your classroom if you remember that writing is a process that may or may not end in a written product that will be handed in for a grade. Admittedly, there are occasions when you will want your students to write answers to essay questions in a biology class or summarize their findings in a lab report for a chemistry class. These are "high-stakes" assignments that are evaluated formally and thoroughly. However, a considerable amount of writing should be informal or "low-stakes" writing (Elbow, 1997). According to Elbow, low-stakes writing assignments are "frequent, informal assignments that make students spend time reflecting in written language on what they are learning from discussions, readings, lectures, and their own thinking" (p. 7). As such, students may complete the writing assignments during class or as homework. These pieces that students write for themselves are considered low stakes because they do not have a major impact on their course grade. In other words, students need not write a formal paper and have you evaluate that paper for them to profit from their writing. In the next section we discuss six guidelines that will assist you as you incorporate writing into your curriculum.

Identify Your Unit's Objectives

Before designing a writing activity, ask yourself what you want your students to learn from a unit of study. Armed with that information, you can then decide if writing is your best alternative or if it would be more appropriate for the students to create a map or chart or complete a study guide. If you determine that a writing activity would be appropriate, then you will need to decide whether that activity will be either low stakes or high stakes. In contrast to the informal and exploratory orientation of low-stakes writing assignments, high-stakes assignments, such as major research papers at the end of a unit of study, adhere to the writing process and involve students in planning, drafting, revising, and editing. Students' final versions of those papers have been crafted to demonstrate their understandings and interpretations and we, as teachers, are judging their knowledge and writing and making suggestions for how to improve both. Obviously, there are many options to consider—options ranging from students creating their own textbook notes to students conducting research in order to inquire about a topic important to them.

Give Effective Writing Assignments

What causes fuzzy thinking and bad writing on the part of your students? Many individuals believe the culprit to be ineffective or unclear assignments. Even though bad writing assignments are never intentional, their effect is the same. Bad writing assignments can become good assignments when certain information is communicated to the students orally and in writing. That information includes these six points: (a) purpose, (b) content and scope, (c) organization and development, (d) audience, (e) suggested steps, and (f) expectations (Shellard & Protheroe, 2004).

A specific statement of *purpose* (e.g., "to understand the impact of words on interpersonal communication") will help students understand why this writing is being done. The *content and scope* for the writing assignment usually originates from the course objectives, but you will need to specify how you want the students to narrow that focus without dictating their thesis. When you provide your students information on the *organization and development* of an assignment, you are providing them the scaffolding that will help them plan and structure their writing. For example, a writing assignment given in an art class that requires students to discuss, in writing, the works of Picasso does not provide them much direction. However, that same assignment becomes more effective when you ask students to debate the contributions of Picasso, the artist.

Whether it be other students in the class, other students in the school, community members, or individuals who support a particular cause in Washington, DC, students need an *audience* for their writing. By having a real and immediate audience, students will be able to decide how to state their position, what information to include, and what format best serves their needs. Students also take more care in choosing their words, explaining their ideas, and proofing their papers when they view their writing as an opportunity to communicate with another individual (Light, 2001; Weber, 2002). In other words, when students write only for their teachers, they will see their audience as someone who "knows it all" already and whose primary reason for reading their work is to give them a grade.

An effective writing assignment should also include information on the recommended *steps* or techniques that a student might use to complete the assignment. Finally, your writing assignment should include information on your *expectations* for (1) length; (2) level of polish; (3) format; (4) grammar, mechanics, and spelling; and (5) method of evaluation.

The following writing assignment was used by Jan, an 11th-grade American history teacher. Notice how she incorporates the six characteristics of effective assignments into the information she shares with her students.

> As with any reading assignment, students will perform better when teachers take the time to make transparent what they want from students in terms of their writing.

We have been studying the Progressive Era for the past week. This assignment will help you summarize the key issues and assess the impact of this intriguing period in our history. I want you to imagine that you are either Dan Rather or Diane Sawyer and you will be interviewing Robert LaFollette or Alice Paul, who have briefly returned from the dead. What would Rather and Sawyer want to ask these individuals? What would the television viewers want to know about these people and this time in history? You are to write out Rather's or Sawyer's questions and LaFollette's or Paul's replies. Then close the interview with a written commentary by Rather or Sawyer that evaluates the impact of LaFollette or Paul and the Progressive Era. Your audience will be television viewers unfamiliar with this historical period.

Your first step in doing this assignment will be to review the relevant readings that we have done this week. You should also watch several news shows so that you can get an idea of the range of questions that could be asked. In class on Wednesday you will have time to brainstorm and role-play with a partner. By Thursday I want you to be prepared for the first draft, which we will write in class.

In grading this assignment I will use these criteria:

1. *Your understanding of the Progressive Era and its impact on history.*
2. *Your creativity and imagination, as demonstrated by your ability to write meaningful and interesting questions, responses, and a commentary.*
3. *Your quality of writing. It should be clear and free of gross mechanical and spelling errors.*

The final draft, which is worth 50 points, will be due at the beginning of class on Tuesday. Please use ink and write on every other line. As for length, the bare minimum is three pages of normal handwriting. These papers will be shared in class.

After assigning this writing activity, Jan also shared some examples of interviews and commentaries from a unit on the Vietnam era so that her students could visualize the finished product. She told us that the time she spends frontloading a writing assignment really pays off in the quality of work she receives from the students.

Vary Formats and Perspectives

If students only summarize what they have read or heard during class, they are not experiencing the full magnitude of writing as a means of learning content-area concepts (Bean, 2001; Graham 2005). Writing is particularly powerful when students are invited to respond or react personally to an idea, event, or issue. When students are asked to think how an issue such as isolationism relates to them or how a story such as "The Lottery" is important to them, they are involved in "constructed knowing" (Belenky, Clinchy, Goldberger, & Tarule, 1986). Writing tasks that encourage students to construct knowledge and become involved in their learning need to be more creative than "summarize the key ideas in this essay or chapter." In fact, an overreliance on "spit back" or data-dumping assignments can discourage many students (Herrington, 1997).

> Content-area teachers do not have to assign term papers or research projects to capitalize on the power of writing.

The options in Figure 7.1 emphasize the many exciting formats or discourse modes for content-area writing assignments. These assignments, such as writing complaints or writing a math problem or math solution, help students feel more com-

Figure 7.1   Possible Writing Formats

Abstracts	Complaints	Jokes and riddles	Protests
Advertisements	Correspondence	Journals, diaries	Rebuttals
Advice columns	Demonstrations	Lab reports	Recipes
Announcements	Dramatic scripts, plays	Letters (personal, public)	Requests for information
Applications	Editorials		Résumés
Biographical sketches	Eulogies	Limericks	Reviews
Brochures	Feature stories	Math word problems	Scripts, skits, puppet shows
Captions for photographs	Forms	Mottoes, slogans	
	Games and puzzles	News stories	Songs, ballads
Cartoons	Guess who/what descriptions	Oral histories	Stories
Case studies		Pamphlets	Tall tales
Character sketches	Historical "you are there" scenes	Parodies	Technical reports
Children's books		Petitions	Telegrams
Coloring books with text	Inquiries	Posters, flyers	Time capsule lists
Commercials	Instructional manuals	Proposals	Word problems

Honoring Diversity and Building Competence in the Content Classroom

We know a teacher who provides a message board inside her classroom for her students with learning disabilities to use as a means of communicating with each other. The message board also provides these struggling students relevant reasons and authentic audiences for their written messages. Rather than pass notes during class, a forbidden activity in most classrooms, the students in Maureen's classroom are allowed to write notes to one another and post them on the board before or after class. Maureen's basic rules for the written messages are that they cannot contain profanity, gossip, ridicule, or inappropriate topics. Students have honored her rules and have used the message board to talk with their friends about content-area concepts, current events, or ideas they have encountered in the media. For example, two of her students carried on this conversation in writing:

Dear Kurt:
Yesterday I was talking with Dean and he told me that extinct animals have been found frozen in ice. I don't believe him, do you?
Neal

Dear Neal:
It's true. I saw a television show about it. They found one of them long-haired elephants. There's a book in the resource center that has pictures of them. Want to see it?
Kurt

The same idea, of course, could be implemented in your classroom if you placed all your students' e-mail addresses on a listserv.

fortable with writing by taking on inviting, engaging, and motivating tasks that facilitate active learning.

In addition to varying the formats you offer your students, it is also productive to vary the perspectives or voices that students can take when they write. For example, Gretel, a 10th-grade biology teacher, asks her students to describe in writing the functions of the endocrine system by taking the perspective of one of the secreted hormones. One student in her class took the perspective of glucose and wrote a letter to his cousin who was recently identified as being a diabetic.

Ideally, your writing assignments should provide students with several choices about possible voices, perspectives, and formats rather than just a single option for the entire class. Even the most reluctant student will become intrigued by writing a letter to the editor of a local newspaper or an imaginary diary. When students have choices, they are more likely to be engaged in their learning.

Ask Students to Write Frequently

This guideline may seem to be in contradiction to the first guideline. However, we want to stress the importance of asking students to write on a regular basis rather than reserving it solely for high-stakes situations such as "the term paper." Consider this analogy to running. If you had a choice of running just one marathon or several different races of shorter duration, what event do you think would provide you the most experience and information to guide you as an athlete? As runners who have run both marathons and shorter races, we know that the 26 miles involved in a marathon truly wear down the body and mind. On the other hand, we have profited from the shorter road races because they have provided us considerable feedback on our running prowess. So it is with writing. Students learn when provided with numerous opportunities and with frequent feedback situations, especially struggling readers and writers (Fisher & Frey, 2003). Frequent informal writing assignments (e.g., journals, logs) in content-area classrooms will ensure that students are "warmed up and more fluent" about a concept and that their formal writing assignments will be "clear" and free from "tangled thinking" (Elbow, 1997, p. 7).

We know a history instructor, Bryant, who has discarded the research paper routine and replaced it with four "one-page" memos that his students write throughout the semester. Bryant is extremely pleased with this change because he and his students have observed growth and improvements in their writing and critical thinking.

Provide Sufficient Time for Prewriting Activities

We believe that frontloading an assignment is the best way to ensure quality thinking and learning from students. When you frontload a writing assignment, you take class time for prewriting activities. Prewriting activities are especially important if you want students to profit from their writing experiences. For example, in one study researchers found that middle school students wrote more persuasive papers after they had the opportunity to role-play their intended audience before they began writing (Wagner, 1987).

In addition to role-playing, there are a variety of other prewriting activities to help students decide on a topic, brainstorm possible ideas, see connections among ideas, and try out the ways in which those ideas could be stated. One such prewriting activity is called the Guided Writing Activity (Smith & Bean, 1980). The Guided Writing Activity is a research-validated instructional strategy that involves students in discussing, listening, reading, and writing about content-area concepts over a 2 or 3-day period. The steps of this strategy are as follows:

1. On the first day, activate the students' prior knowledge on the topic of study by brainstorming and listing ideas on an overhead or chalkboard.
2. Ask the class to organize and label the ideas collectively.
3. Then ask the students to write individually on the topic using this information.
4. In preparation for the second day, have the class read the text and revise their exploratory writing.
5. In class on the second day, give a brief quiz on the material.

Because the steps of the Guided Writing Activity involve students in a variety of expressive and receptive modalities, it appears to be an especially advantageous activity with students who are just developing their English language proficiency and with struggling readers who may lack experience in the more formal modes of academic thinking and expression (Reyes & Molner, 1991).

Publish and Celebrate Your Students' Writing

As we noted earlier, the final phase of the writing process includes publishing. By publishing we mean that when students finish a piece of writing, it is shared and made public. When students realize that their work will be shared with others and not just the teacher, they know they have an audience and thus a reason for working diligently in revising, editing, and proofreading (Weber, 2002). Moreover, when students know

> Just as oral language activities are advantageous to vocabulary and comprehension growth, so they are for helping students write "untangled" prose.

they will be sharing their writing, it is much easier to teach the complex issue of "voice," an important aspect of reading critically (Elbow, 2002). For example, when students are reading other students' work, you can engage them in questions such as these: How does that sound? What kind of person do you hear in those words?

At the most basic level, students can share their work by reading it aloud to their classmates; you too should share your writing with your students. Content-area teachers can also publish their students' work in school literary magazines, newspapers or newsmagazines, or on a school-sponsored Web site. There are also many publications that publish students' writing, poetry, and art. For example, you might investigate the magazine *Merlyn's Pen: Fiction, Essays, and Poems by American Teens* (**http://www.merlynspen.com**). The magazine, which is published annually, has a staff that will respond to every contributor, published or not. The publisher of *Merlyn's Pen,* R. James Stahl, also has a list of other magazines that specialize in publishing work by adolescents (Weber, 2002).

Go to the Web Resources at *http://www. prenhall.com/brozo* and look for additional ideas on how to help students publish and discuss their writing.

Many teachers and students take advantage of the Internet by creating their own Web sites to display and share their writing (see Chapter 10). In addition to these more obvious choices, you might investigate telecommunication networks such as Global Kids: Global Networking for Kids (**http://www.kidlink.org**), a non-profit organization that helps students communicate with each other at a global level. Obviously, the options for sharing and publishing are numerous, so numerous that entire books have been dedicated to the topic (see Weber, 2002 in the reference list).

By adhering to these six guidelines, teachers should be able to enhance their students' mastery of content-area concepts and their skill and fluency in writing. In the next sections we discuss specific writing activities that content-area teachers can use. The first two types are exploratory-based writing activities and thesis-based writing activities.

Exploratory Writing Activities for the Content Areas

Exploratory writing is any type of writing done without revision that encourages students to extend, deepen, generate, monitor, or clarify their thinking and understanding about a content-area concept or process. In this section we explore three types of exploratory writing: Quick Writes, learning logs, and journals.

Quick Writes and "Hot Cards"

Have you ever begun a class by asking the infamous question "Are there any questions about the assigned reading?" If your students are like most adolescents, the result is an uncomfortable silence. Rather than asking a question that rarely will be answered, ask your students to take out a piece of paper and spend a couple of minutes in a Quick Write. Quick Writes have also been called 1-minute papers or admit/exit slips. Regardless of the name or the duration, these informal writing activities are low-stakes assignments completed during class that can stimulate discussion or encourage passive students to reflect and think about a content-area concept. Quick Writes can be used before students read or listen to a class discussion, after they have read, or during a discussion as a way of focusing and summarizing.

You can use a variety of prompts or probes with a Quick Write. We like these two questions because they can be modified for any content-area classroom: (a) What is the big point, the main idea, that you learned from your reading assignment or from class today? (b) What is the muddiest point? What don't you understand from (your reading, the discussion, the lab)? Some teachers, especially in chemistry or physics courses, ask students to list the pages that were confusing to them. What is particularly amazing is to see how many students, especially the shy ones, will ask their questions in writing but never do so during class discussion, even with teacher prompts and encouragement.

The following probes illustrate how Ann, a ninth-grade math teacher, uses the Quick Write at the beginning of her classes. When students enter Ann's classroom, they see a question or probe highlighted on her overhead projector and know that they should immediately sit down to begin their thinking and writing. The Quick Write probes listed next encourage students to state in their own words their understanding of exponents.

Integral Exponents

Rule 7 is in addition to previous ones you have worked with in other chapters. In your own words, explain what this rule means and how you might use it to simplify 2^{-4} and $1/4^{-3}$.

Rational Exponents

1. *Define radical, radicand, index, and principal root. Identify each in an example you supply.*
2. *The cube root of a number means _____.*

We have collected these Quick Write probes from other content-area teachers:

1. Write on the board an interesting quotation from the reading assignment or a statement of opinion (e.g., "The pituitary gland is the most important gland in the endocrine system") and ask the students to explain their stand on the statement.

2. To emphasize a new and important technique that has just been introduced in a science, industrial arts, or home economics class, stop and ask students to write for 5 minutes to describe the technique to another student who was absent from class. This has also been called "Yesterday's News" and can be modified for any content area where you want students to write a summary of the concepts discussed in the previous class (Fisher, 2001).

3. To focus a class discussion that becomes rambling or dominated by just a few students, stop and ask the class to write for 5 minutes. They could respond to the question "What are we trying to explain?" or to the assignment "Restate the key points that have been made thus far."

4. To help students reflect on the key ideas of a specific unit, ask them to review their notes and assigned readings and then begin writing. This activity works best when announced in advance so that students can think and plan for a while. Additionally, you can prime the pump if you provide your students a prompt or question for this type of Quick Write. For example, in a psychology class you might use this probe: During this unit we have examined several theories of personality. What are those theories?

5. To help students predict what might happen next in a lesson or during a lab or demonstration, use the "Crystal Ball" prompt. Students write their predictions and explain why they believe they are right.

These Quick Writes can also be done on note cards and be labeled as *hot cards* (Mitchell, 1996). With this modification of the Quick Write, students are given a note card and asked to respond to a prompt on the card. Of course, there are several advantages to using a note card: they can be sorted into topics or themes, they can be stored for future reference, and they limit the amount of information students need to provide, an important factor for students easily intimidated by writing tasks.

Once the students have completed their Quick Write or "hot card," the next step is for you to decide what you will do with their written work. You have several options. First, you could simply go on with the lesson and hope that the writing has served its purpose in helping students summarize, organize, and monitor their understanding of key concepts. Second, you could give the students an immediate chance to ask questions and clear up any confusion they may have discovered while they were writing. They could pose questions for you to answer or issues to clarify, or they could turn to a neighbor to share their answers and resolve their difficulties together. As the students work, you could circulate around the room to eavesdrop and troubleshoot. Finally, as previously mentioned, you could collect the cards and read them for your own information. The students' writing becomes excellent feedback on whether they learned what you had tried to teach that day.

We know an art appreciation teacher who collects the Quick Writes, reads them, and then shares with her students some of the more pertinent or creative ones at the beginning of the next class session. Sometimes she shares students' interpretations of slides they have viewed (e.g., a comparison of Picasso and Ernst), but she always takes a few minutes to answer the questions they have posed. Of course, she asks permission from the students to do this.

> Quick Writes and "hot cards" are also excellent tools for assessing and evaluating you students' strengths and needs, especially their misconceptions and lack of conceptual understanding.

Quick Writes and the Think-Pair-Share Strategy

When these two activities are used in conjunction with each other, you can be sure that students are constructing meaning from their assignments and monitoring their level of understanding. The Think-Pair-Share strategy was explained in Chapter 3, so you may wish to review it.

You can initiate the activity by asking students to read a selection, either in class or the night before, and to write briefly, using their own words, what they believe to be the main points of the selection (e.g., "After reading, write on your note card the four main points of..."). Then the students work with their partner to discuss and compare their ideas and select the one or two most important points from their Quick Writes. Each student pair then joins another pair and they share their Quick Write ideas, ultimately reaching a consensus on what they believe to be the most important idea. Of course, this is an excellent time for you, the teacher, to circulate the room and eavesdrop on conversations. By doing this you receive valuable insights into the students' difficulties with the concepts.

The teacher then brings the class together and asks each group to share their most important point and their rationales. During this large-class sharing you have an excellent opportunity to clarify any of the students' misconceptions or address some of their "fuzzy" knowledge issues. The next step is totally optional, but requires minimal amounts of time. You can ask the students to either write on the idea receiving the most votes or to write on the idea most of them overlooked. Students can place this brief writing task on the back of their cards or on notepaper. Some teachers collect the Quick Writes for a participation grade, but others continue with the lesson knowing that they have actively engaged their students in thinking and learning.

Learning Logs

Learning logs are more structured than other types of exploratory writing and are very similar to a laboratory notebook that many chemistry and physics teachers assign their students to keep. Students write their log entries in a notebook in order to record ideas, questions, and reactions to what they have read, observed, or listened to in class. Bean (2001) aptly describes learning logs as a "record of the student's intellectual journey through the course" (p. 106). As such, they encourage students to reflect, make connections between different ideas in the course, summarize important ideas or processes, monitor their understanding, and review what they have learned.

A variety of research studies have been conducted on learning logs, especially in math, physics, and biology courses (e.g., Grossman, Smith, & Miller, 1993; McCrindle & Christensen, 1995). The findings from these studies indicate that students profit immensely from the experiences of keeping a learning log. For example, in McCrindle and Christensen's study, biology students who wrote the learning logs scored significantly higher on the biology exams than their counterparts who wrote scientific reports. Moreover, the students who kept logs demonstrated a greater use of learning strategies that required them to think on higher levels and to monitor their understanding.

Clarese, an eighth-grade math teacher, asks her students to write a learning entry for each unit of study. Her students respond to a variety of open-ended probes designed to stimulate their reflection and provide her with valuable assessment information about their knowledge and possible misconceptions concerning a mathematical concept. For a unit on averages, Clarese began the lesson by asking the students to answer the following questions:

1. Where have you heard about averages?
2. Who uses averages and for what?
3. How are averages used?
4. What do you know about forming an average?

As a follow-up to these open-ended probes, Clarese asks her students to share their log entries with their study partner before sharing them with the entire class. Clarese believes that writing activities such as these help her teach more effectively because she learns so much about her students in a short amount of time.

Rosa, a biology teacher, also likes to have her students write in their learning logs before she begins a new unit or lesson. Sometimes she initiates her students' thinking and writing by asking them to preview the next assignment. When students preview a piece of text or selection, they examine the title, headings, subheadings, charts, and summaries. Based on this preview, the biology students then write in the learning logs what they already know or think they know about the topic. After the students read their assignment, Rosa has them write another entry focusing on what they learned, noting any misconceptions in their original log entries.

The following example illustrates one student's learning log entries before and after reading a chapter on common diseases such as strokes and heart attacks.

Learning Log Entry Written Before Reading

In this chapter I'm going to learn about the human brain. I know the brain is split into a right and left half. I think the halves control different things, but I'm not sure what. I also know that when someone has a stroke, blood vessels break in the brain.

Learning logs work especially well in math and science classes.

Learning Log Entry Written After Reading

This chapter mentioned the brain, but it was not the main focus. I learned that the two halves of the brain are called the right and left cerebral hemispheres. But, really, there are four main parts of the brain: the medulla oblongata, the pons, the cerebellum, and the cerebrum. The really important point I learned concerned strokes; they are caused by a blockage in the arteries in the brain. This keeps the brain from getting enough oxygen, and it becomes damaged.

As illustrated in this entry, learning logs help students clarify concepts and monitor their understanding.

As these entries demonstrate, the student was able to use writing as an aid in the process of constructing meaning from the text. The first entry served as a reflection of prior knowledge, whereas the second entry allowed the student to reconsider his initial understandings (e.g., the nature of strokes) and derive new understandings based on his reading of the text.

The research literature suggests that students obtain more benefits from their learning log entries when they are provided specific prompts (Bangert-Drowns et al., 2004). Hence, you might consider using any of the following suggested prompts with your students, especially at the beginning of the year when they are uncertain about what they should "do."

1. List three things important enough to discuss in class.
2. Using your own words, explain two or three important concepts so your younger brother/niece could understand.
3. Why is this important: _____?
4. If you were the teacher, what questions would you ask the students about the ideas in this assignment?
5. How could you use this knowledge in your own life?
6. How do these ideas relate to your other courses or to other parts of this course?
7. What does that equation say in plain English?
8. What makes this problem difficult?
9. Explain how you study for tests. Are these techniques working? Why or why not?
10. What is the most important idea you have learned in class this week? Explain.

If you want your students to respond thoughtfully and elaboratively to these prompts or any of the prompts you provide them, it will be important for you to discuss why you want them to write and what you expect in their entries. Of course, if you share and discuss model entries written by some of your previous students, the quality of the learning logs will improve drastically. Some teachers provide class time for students to write in their logs, whereas other teachers set a specific weekday on which students are expected to write at home.

Journals

Although there are countless variations of the academic journal, we will focus on three types: the reader-response journal, the double-entry journal, and the triple-entry journal.

These three types of academic journals are vastly different from the "journals" students write that are stream-of-consciousness entries or diary entries.

Reader-Response Formats

The reader-response heuristic asks students first to write what they perceive in the text, then to explain how they feel about what they see, and finally to discuss the thoughts and feelings emanating from their perceptions (Petrosky, 1982). This is a personal type of writing that exists for the learner and the reader. Summaries and brief essays require writers to support stances and assertions with public-based information. Conversely, reader-response tasks value the examples, beliefs, and assumptions of the students. Simply put, students are responding to questions that ask them to explain what the selection means to them and to describe the effect the selection has on their own beliefs, goals, and values (Bean, 2001, p. 144). For example, in a genetics class, students might pose these questions about a chapter on hereditary: What does this section about inheritance mean to me? What effect do these theories and concepts about inheritance have on my values, beliefs, goals, or ways of looking at the world?

In addition to the two questions previously mentioned, the following three probes have been proven to be quite successful when used together:

1. What aspect of the text excited or interested you most? Explain.
2. What are your feelings and attitudes about this aspect of text?
3. What experiences have you had that help others understand why you feel the way you do?

The reader-response heuristic can be easily modified for any content area, but you may feel more comfortable with the next two journal formats.

Double-Entry Formats

When students write in a log or journal they can summarize and react to ideas, but they also can reflect on their processes of making sense of what they are reading or learning in a content area. Such journal entries are called double-entry formats (Calkins, 1986). With this format, students use the left-hand column of an evenly divided note page to copy directly from a text quotations, statements, theories, definitions, and other things that are difficult to understand, interesting, of key importance, or require clarification. On the right-hand side, students record whatever thoughts, questions, or comments come to mind as they attempt to make sense of what was copied.

Figure 7.2 is an example of a double-entry format that one ninth-grade student, Chris, created for his reading assignment in a government course. The text he copied on the left-hand side of the paper came from a chapter discussing political opinions and attitudes that Chris found confusing. Notice Chris's comments on the right-hand side. By examining his journal entry, his government teacher was able to determine what concepts were troubling him and what strategies he was using to make sense of his reading. More important, Chris gained some information about himself through his writing. The last comment made by Chris was a very honest and perceptive observation about textbooks that typifies the feelings of some students who are very metacognitively aware. Those comments, however, do not occur as a result of one double-entry journal assignment. Teachers must provide modeling and guidance to develop their students' metacognition.

The double-entry format can also be used in conjunction with mathematical problems or lab experiments. When students write down their thoughts for solving problems, they begin to clearly see the steps and as a result gain immediate feedback and a fresh perspective (Burns, 1995). Moreover, when students write, math and science teachers gain important insights into students' thinking. In order to

Figure 7.2   Entry in a Double-Entry Journal

Text	Responses to Text and Strategy Concerns
Political attitudes may exist merely as potential. They may not have crystallized. But they still can be very important, for they can be evoked by leaders and converted into action. Latent opinions set rough boundaries for leaders. . . . *Source:* From *Government by the people* (p. 175), by J. Burns, J. Peltason, & T. Cronin, 1984, Englewood Cliffs, NJ: Prentice Hall.	I know that this section is supposed to define the key word latent because the boldface heading tells me this. However, I am having problems finding a definition. Help! Okay—I think the second sentence helps me, but I will need to look up the word crystallized. I think, right now, that latent opinions are opinions not formed, but existing as potential for leaders and other people who wish to influence us. Whew! I will read on since our teacher has told us that authors often take several pages to define a word. This is hard work and I think the textbook authors made it even harder for us.

gain that window into students' understanding, math teachers could ask their students to list a difficult problem on the left side of their double-entry journals and to explain, on the right side, the calculations and steps they used to solve the problem, noting any difficulties they were having along the way. During lab experiments in science courses, students could list on the left side their empirical observations or any steps they used; on the right side they could record their conclusions, questions, or reflections.

Bernard's biology teacher asked the students to complete a double-entry journal for their lab session on typing blood. His entry looked like this:

My Steps
My goal is to discover blood types from 2 samples.
I will add Antigen A to both slides

My Conclusions
Because the first slide tended to agglutinate, I think that the blood type was Type A on the first slide. But the second slide did not agglutinate. So it is not Type A.

Triple-Entry Formats

Triple-entry formats (Carroll, 2000) are a modification to the double-entry format. With the triple-entry journal, students divide their notebooks into thirds and use the first two columns just as they did with the double-entry format. However, the third column on the far right-hand side of their paper is reserved for a study partner who reads the entries in the first two columns and then writes a response. That response could be a question, an affirmation, a clarification, a challenge, or a statement that congratulates the partner for his stance on an issue or her explanation of a difficult process.

In order to visualize how a triple-entry format would work, let's return to Bernard's biology class and imagine that Bernard used a triple-entry format rather than a double-entry format. Aricelli, Bernard's study partner in biology, read his journal entry while he read hers. She wrote these comments in the far right-hand column of Bernard's journal:

> **Study Partner's Comments**
> Bernard, you know the blood on
> the second slide is not Type A.
> So, what should you do next?
> I recommend you add Antigen B.

As you can probably surmise, there are a plethora of possibilities for content-area teachers interested in using exploratory writing with their students. These activities can be completed by students outside of class or orchestrated during the class period. They also can be done at the beginning of the class (e.g., bell work), in the middle of class, or near the end of class. In the next sections we examine two more formal types of writing: thesis-based writing and the research paper.

Later in this chapter we will discuss efficient ways in which content-area teachers can respond to students' learning log entries or academic journal entries.

Thesis-Based Writing Activities for the Content Areas

One way we can enhance our students' ability to think critically is to provide them thesis-based writing assignments that challenge them to speculate, reformulate an understanding, or apply a concept to an important issue or problem. An added advantage to such analytical writing assignments is that students find such tasks to be inviting and challenging (Fisher, 2001; Shellard & Protheroe, 2004). Because these writing activities require students to manipulate a smaller number of concepts in more complex ways, they are particularly attractive to content-area teachers who rightfully worry about reading countless pages written by their students. Although no strict rule applies to creating these thesis-based writing activities, we will share five different—but not mutually exclusive—ideas: thesis-support writing, data-provided writing, concept application writing, pro/con writing activities, and framed writing assignments.

Thesis-Support Writing Activities

The thesis-support writing assignment can help students discover issues and develop arguments and stances that are supported with empirical evidence. When writing a thesis-support paper, students must often go beyond the textbook to build a logical, cohesive argument. When students think about and research a particular issue, they actively master the unit's objectives. Most important, they begin to realize that their textbook presents only one point of view and that all content areas are in a constant state of controversy and flux.

An example of a thesis-support writing assignment developed by a seventh-grade general science teacher follows:

Directions: The purpose of this assignment is to provide you with an opportunity to examine an issue in depth by taking a stand and developing a logical argument for that stand. You have two choices, so read the choices below carefully and select one of them. Then determine which side you wish to defend for that issue. For the side you have selected, write a short paper that defends that position. Use evidence and reasoning from your textbook, from our discussion in class, or from the film we watched in class. Class time will be provided for brainstorming, planning, and prewriting. HAVE FUN WITH THIS!

1. *The diversity theory has/has not been proven.*
2. *People do a lot to the environment that encourages/prevents animal extinction.*

After announcing the assignment, the teacher discussed and distributed several examples of thesis-support papers from previous students. Following a discussion of the papers, he invited the class to help him do an analysis of this seemingly simple assignment so that they could plan appropriately. In addition, he provided one class period for the students who had selected the same issues to meet, debate, and brainstorm. Several days later, he set aside a class period for the students to write their initial draft so that he could be available while they wrote. The teacher reported that the students did have fun with this assignment and, more important, did better than usual on their unit exam.

Of course, not all thesis-support writing activities need to be this involved or protracted. Teachers have told us that they have assigned thesis-support writing as homework and that they have asked students to write thesis-support answers during class as a part of the "hot card" routine. Obviously, you will be examining your unit objectives for just the perfect wording of your thesis-support writing task, but it is soothing to know these activities provide significant support to students as they tackle content-area concepts.

Thesis-support and data-provided writing activities can also assist content-area teachers who are searching for ways in which to improve their students' performance on state-mandated writing tests.

Data-Provided Writing Activities

A second type of writing activity is the data-provided paper (Bean, Drenk, & Lee, 1982). With such an assignment students are provided with data in a list of sentences or in a graph, table, or chart. They must arrange the data in a logical order, interpret what they see as trends and patterns, and then offer, in writing, their conclusions or generalizations. This type of writing assignment is especially useful for students who ignore or cannot accurately interpret important visual aids, a typical test item in most state-mandated exams. Of course, the data for this writing activity can come from a variety of sources other than the textbook, sources such as documents, newspapers, magazines, and the Internet.

We know a geography instructor, Deb, who assigns her students several data-provided writing assignments throughout her course rather than the ubiquitous research paper (Martin, 2001, personal communication). She particularly likes the data-provided assignment because it helps her students fully understand important concepts like the population pyramid and the patterns of immigration in the United States. In order to complete the data-provided assignment on these two concepts, Deb provides her students a table that describes the total population of the United States in 1996 and another table that describes the immigrant population in 1996. She then outlines a series of steps that require her students to use the data as they calculate percentages and plot the percentages on two different empty pyramid graphs that she has provided them. Once her students have manipulated the data and drawn their interpretations, Deb then asks them to write about the data with probes and questions such as these: (a) Compare the two pyramids you have created. How is the pyramid for immigrants different from the one for total population? How do you explain these differences? (b) How are immigrants affecting the U.S. population structure? (c) What implications will the Baby Boom generation have for American society in 20 years?

Because students write a limited amount of expository text in response to the data, the evaluation process of these papers moves very quickly for the content-area teacher. However, that "limited amount" of writing is preceded by an immense amount of thinking, planning, and revising on the part of the students so they can explain and defend their interpretations and conclusions.

Concept Application Writing Activities

The third type of writing assignment is the problem posing or concept application paper. With such a writing assignment the content-area teacher asks students to apply important concepts to a different, novel situation or problem not discussed in class or in the textbook. We know from the research literature that students learn concepts at a deeper level of understanding when they are asked to solve problems using what they know and what they have learned (e.g., Elbow, 1997; Unrau, 2004). Although you can organize a concept application writing assignment in a variety of ways, most of them focus on a situation or scenario that you have created.

These situations can be brief, such as this one given by a 12th-grade physics teacher: Write an essay explaining to a 10th-grader why an airplane flies. Assume no knowledge on the part of the student. Hence, you will probably have to discuss the Bernoulli equation that we studied last week in this course (Herrington, 1997). Another such example comes from Lin and Charles, chemistry teachers (Zhu, personal communication, 2005):

> A one-dollar bill is 2.5 inches wide and 6.1 inches long. It takes 60.0 dollar bills stacked flat on top of each other to make a pile of dollars that is 1.0 inch tall. A professional soccer field is 120.0 yards long and 60.0 yards wide. If one billion dollars, $\$1.0 \times 10^9$, were laid evenly on this soccer field, how deep in feet, would the money cover the field?

These situations can also be far more comprehensive, much like cases or scenarios. Deb, the geography instructor, has discovered that her students really enjoy her assignment called "The Geography of Breakfast" (Martin, 2001, personal communication). This writing assignment requires her students to understand and apply the concept of the food chain to their daily breakfast routines. She sets up the assignment guide in this manner:

> *Choose three breakfast items. If the breakfast items are processed food, such as cold pizza, choose the ingredients, such as cheese or tomatoes. For each of these three ingredients or items, answer the following questions:*
>
> *a.* *What is the breakfast item or ingredient?*
>
> *b.* *In what ways is your breakfast regionally or culturally specific? Who else, living where, is likely to eat the same kind of breakfast as you do? Who is unlikely to eat the same kind of breakfast, and why? (HINT: Look for the "made in" or the company's address.)*
>
> *c.* *What does the food's packaging tell you and not tell you about the origin of the ingredients?*
>
> *d.* *For each of the three items or ingredients, use knowledge you already have, the course textbooks and atlas, and as many additional sources of information as you need to describe something about three of the nine elements in the food chain. (EXAMPLE: Wheat used to make the bagel is grown in the Midwest, processed in Texas, and consumed in Georgia. That is approximately a "B" answer—for a higher grade, elaborate on these elements using the descriptions/discussions in the text.)*

When students apply concepts to new situations, they are thinking critically and creatively.

Notice that Deb provides hints to the students and suggestions as to sources they might use to write their paper. As mentioned earlier, you will receive quality written products when you frontload a challenging assignment. That is, you will need to inform students of what you expect, provide them positive and negative examples, suggest possible resources or steps they might take in their thinking and writing, and explain the grading criteria you will use with their papers.

Pro and Con Writing Activities

Although it is an integral component of critical thinking, students often find it difficult to consider an alternative viewpoint on an issue (Hynd-Shanahan, Holschuh, & Hubbard, 2004). That is, for students who believe that a heavier object will fall faster than a lighter one, it is extremely challenging to convince them otherwise, even when they are taught that basic principle of physics. Ultimately, we want students to be able to examine any issue in such a way that they can perceive all viewpoints or positions, and, if needed, argue these positions convincingly. Some individuals have referred to the thinking processes involved in considering alternative viewpoints as "believing and doubting" (Elbow, 1997). Whatever the label employed, we need to encourage and support students in this type of critical thinking.

We can encourage students to examine the pros and cons of an important issue by designing writing activities that elicit that level of thinking and by incorporating discussion opportunities into the classroom routine. The pairing of discussion with writing is especially important because oral language activities, especially those that precede a writing task, seem to improve the fluency, support, and organization of students' writing (Fisher & Frey, 2003; Rubin & Dodd, 1987).

As a way to encourage his students to think critically in his art class, Raymond developed a lesson that involved his students in determining whether or not Picasso was the greatest artist of the modern age. His ultimate goal was for his students to take a position on this question and to explain their rationale in writing. Because he knew many of his students already possessed some firmly entrenched viewpoints about Picasso (e.g., I think anyone could draw the pictures he did), Raymond began his lesson with the Discussion Web (Alvermann, 1992). Discussion Webs encourage students to examine alternative points and offer evidence to support those views. As illustrated in Figure 7.3, the Discussion Web is literally a visual or graphic representation of the thinking processes the students will go through during their discussion. In the center of the Discussion Web is the central issue or question that the students are to discuss in class. The question should be stated so there is more than one point of view. For example, in a driver's education course the question could be this: Should students be required to take a state-approved driver's education course?

On either side of the Discussion Web are spaces for students to list the reasons why they believe that either "yes" or "no" is the answer to the central question. When Raymond used the Discussion Web with his art students, he followed these steps recommended by Alvermann (1992):

1. Prepare students for reading, listening, or viewing by activating their prior knowledge and setting purposes.
2. Have students read the selection, listen to the lecture, or view the video.
3. Introduce the central question and the Discussion Web. Ask students to work in pairs, discussing both points of view. The partners should take turns jotting down their reasons in the two columns. Instruct the partners to allow equal time for both sides of the issue.

Discussion Webs can also be used as an activity to spark students' interest in a content-area reading assignment.

Figure 7.3 Discussion Web for an Art Class

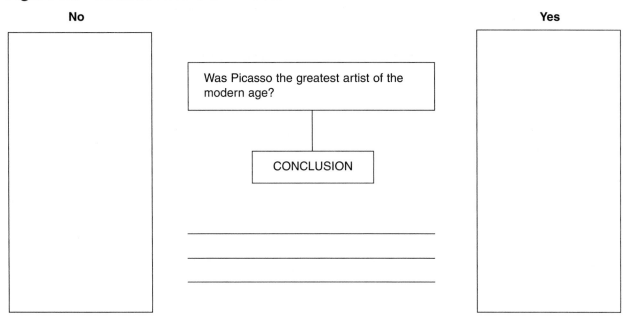

4. After the partners have jotted down a few of their reasons, combine the partners into groups of four. The four students will compare their Discussion Webs, with the ultimate goal of reaching a consensus. Remind the students to keep an open mind and to listen to the members of their group. If they cannot agree on a point of view, they can offer a minority report as well as a majority report.

5. When the groups have reached a consensus or the students' participation seems to be waning, give them a 3-minute warning. Within those 3 minutes they are to decide who will report their views to the large group and what the individual will say.

6. Ask each spokesperson to report what his or her group decided and why.

7. After the whole-class discussion has ended, assign students to write their own responses to the central question in the blanks provided under the Conclusion section of the Discussion Web.

Although Raymond followed these recommended seven steps, he modified and extended the lesson beyond the writing that the students had to do in the Conclusion section of the Web. After instructing his students to state their conclusions in the form of a thesis, he collected the Discussion Webs. The next day in class Raymond returned the Webs to the students, discussed the wordings of their thesis statements, and assigned them to write a one-page memo (he thought "memo" was a less intimidating word) that explained their personal position on the question and their reasons for that position. He gave the students about 15 minutes of class time to begin their assignment and circulated the room as they wrote. The next day the students handed in their memos.

Raymond tells us that he particularly like the Discussion Web because all the students participated actively in class, even the introverted ones who usually were afraid to speak up. Some of the students were even willing to change their minds about Picasso during the discussion. Most important, Raymond noticed that his students defended their positions in a clear, organized fashion rather than the usual ramblings he received from them. We should point out, however, that there are a variety of strategies other than the Discussion Web to stimulate students into examining the pros/cons of an issue (e.g., a chart or map). When you are selecting the strategy that you will use, make sure it involves students in some form of expressive communication before they write.

Framed Assignments

Some students are so intimidated by writing that they cannot seem to begin the process, even if they view the assignment as intriguing and captivating. Hence, framed assignments are an effective way to provide students with guidance and structure so that they can overcome their paralysis when asked to think and write about content-area concepts (Bean, 2001).

Framed assignments are skeletal paragraphs with strategically placed transitions or cue words that signal to students a particular way to think and write about a concept. To complete the framed assignment students must use what they have learned from their reading or classroom participation to fill in the needed generalizations and supporting data. Students can write their framed assignments on note cards, on paper, or in their learning logs or journals.

For students who are struggling readers or who are second language learners, framed assignments are less intimidating and more approachable.

Although there are no set rules for designing a framed assignment, the following two examples are certainly representative:

Psychology Framed Assignment

There are three main theories on why we forget information that we thought we "knew." The first theory is called the decay theory… The second theory is… The third… (make sure you define and give an example for each theory)

Of the three theories, the one with the most support is… (defend your statement)

Business Education Framed Assignment

Businesses use a variety of primary data collection methods, each with their own set of advantages and disadvantages. The first method is… (discuss the second, third, and fourth method, making sure to include advantages and disadvantages)

Framed assignments can also be constructed for narrative text to emphasize the elements of narrative structure such as character, plot, setting, and theme. The narrative framed assignment in Figure 7.4 was written by a seventh-grade teacher to accompany a story that he liked to teach his struggling readers. As you peruse the example, you will note that the teacher provided more text for his students and thus reduced their writing demands. Of course, the teacher started the school year with framed assignments like this one, but gradually throughout the school year decreased the text he provided and increased the text the students needed to write. Students who struggle with reading, writing, or English language proficiencies find assignments such as these less formidable and more approachable (Fisher & Frey, 2003).

If students complete their framed assignment during class, they can share their paragraphs in small groups or with their study partners. Some teachers collect and read them, awarding students participation points for the day. We will discuss efficient, time-saving methods to respond to students' writing later in this chapter.

In the next section we will address the issue of encouraging students' critical thinking and inquiry via the research paper.

Figure 7.4 Framed Paragraph About "La Bamba"

Manuel was a _____ student. He decided to do a pantomime of Ritchie Valens's "La Bamba" at the school's talent show because _____. As he watched the various acts done by his classmates, he was _____. When he went up on stage he felt _____. Once he began dancing and pantomiming, he _____. Then suddenly in the middle of his act, _____. He felt very _____ but decided to keep _____. Once the talent show was over, the audience _____. Manuel was surprised because _____. Ricardo and Manuel's father thought Manuel had _____. That night when Manuel was alone in his room, he decided _____. The irony of this story is _____.

The Research Paper: An Inquiry-Based Task

Research and the processes inherent in research are not reserved just for the classroom. Our students need to know how to become critical consumers of information if they are to thrive in a society saturated with conflicting information. Their employers also expect them to be capable researchers and problem solvers who are comfortable in identifying potential sources of information, analyzing that information in a critical fashion, and making informed decisions. Some content-area teachers choose to use the research paper as a vehicle to teach these important yet demanding thinking skills.

> Research papers have the potential of being positive experiences, involving students in many critical reading and thinking processes.

The Role of the Teacher Leader

More than likely your colleagues, department chair, or principal have been recently discussing the need to improve students' writing skills in your school district. The data that alerted them to this need either emanated from a state-mandated test or from a variety of authorities who have conducted surveys on the status of students' abilities to express themselves in writing. Regardless of the source, you can provide leadership in countless ways.

At the departmental level it might be advantageous to discuss the qualities of effective writing in your content area. For example, what do employers in the area want from their employees in terms of communication skills? What do state-level colleges and universities perceive as necessary writing skills and prerequisites? If your department does not know the answers to these questions, then this is an excellent place to begin, either at the departmental level or at the school level.

You could also initiate a sharing and discussion on the types of writing assignments (e.g., exploratory, thesis-based, other) that students are given or the ways in which writing is evaluated. Perhaps this is the time for you to share one of your more treasured techniques (e.g., the hot card, a rubric) with your colleagues. If you have data about the effectiveness of the technique, this too should be shared (e.g., students' reactions or impressions, recent test scores).

Another way in which you can serve as a leader is to work collaboratively with a colleague outside your department. Find someone who may teach the same students that you do. Perhaps the two of you can teach your students how to write effective thesis statements, an important skill that many students have not mastered. The process could easily begin by asking students to read articles pertinent to your content areas, providing rich opportunities for them to examine how other individuals craft thesis statements. Alternatively, the two of you could work together in teaching students how to conduct credible searches for sources on the Internet.

If you collaborate with someone, consider the possibility of presenting your ideas at a professional conference. For example, the following conferences would be interested in what you have been doing in terms of writing across the content areas: the National Council of Teachers of English, the International Reading Association, and the Association of Supervision and Curriculum Development.

Because of these sophisticated demands inherent in a research paper, students and teachers often become frustrated and disillusioned. Students are frustrated because they do not understand the intricate and time-consuming processes involved in writing from multiple sources. Teachers are frustrated because the products students hand in are not what they have anticipated. Moreover, in some situations students have inadvertently plagiarized ideas because they have copied text rather than paraphrasing and summarizing. What is the solution? Should content-area teachers avoid research papers or written reports? We think a better solution is to define clearly the goals of such assignments and to provide specific mini-lessons that will help students during the processes of researching, reading, planning, and writing. Moreover, we would recommend that students write several brief research papers or memos rather than one lengthy one.

Goals and Stages

The goals of a research paper can vary along a continuum, with one goal emphasizing knowledge telling and the other knowledge transformation (Nelson & Hayes, 1988). *Knowledge telling* requires students to locate and summarize what other individuals have stated about a certain topic. For example, a student in a history course might decide to do a research paper on blacklisting or the Red Scare. *Knowledge transformation* involves students in reading and evaluating information in terms of a specific question or problem they have defined for themselves. A student doing a research paper of this type would selectively read, evaluate, and synthesize information from the sources with the goal of answering a question, such as whether or not the activities and behaviors of people during the Red Scare are in any way characteristic of the present era.

Knowledge telling differs significantly from knowledge transformation in that students must plan, evaluate, and synthesize more with the latter. If teachers want students to do the type of critical thinking and writing involved in knowledge transformation, then they should inform students of that expectation when giving the assignment. Otherwise, students typically will reinterpret the research report as an assignment in which they gather information and then record it in a paper.

In addition to informing students of the goals of a paper, content-area teachers can assist students by guiding them through the recursive processes or stages involved in writing a research paper:

1. Select a problem or issue that interests you.
2. Start with some initial reading and thinking so you can narrow the focus of the topic or issue.
3. Search for more relevant sources and take notes using your own organizational system.
4. Formulate the thesis and structure of the paper.
5. Return to the library or Internet for additional sources to address your thesis.
6. Write the first draft.
7. Evaluate your draft, revising and editing with your audience in mind.
8. Write the final version of the paper.

Students also need to understand the time frame necessary to move from stage 1 to stage 8. Our experience suggests that students often miscalculate the time necessary to find the appropriate sources in the library. More important, they underestimate the time that must be devoted to the stages that follow the research, thinking that the paper can be written the night before the deadline.

Teaching Recommendations

Content-area teachers can use these seven recommendations to help students avoid last-minute efforts and mediocre products while engaged in research projects.

You can help your students progress through the stages of writing a research paper if you follow the seven recommendations discussed next. First, you should provide a reading list or key words that students can use in their library or computer searches. In some situations it might be helpful to teach students how to use search tools if your school does not have a learning specialist with these skills. Second, you should probably review the characteristics of scholarly sources and credible Internet sites in your content area and give students examples. As explained in Chapter 9, students should be taught how to judge the authority and intent of authors and the accuracy and objectivity of their ideas.

Third, you can ask students for progress reports in the form of learning log entries or Quick Writes in which students discuss what they have done and list their concerns or questions. These entries can be shared with the teacher and with other students via group problem-solving sessions during class. Some teachers ask students to hand in writing products as a way of ensuring that students are progressing. For example, students can hand in their initial reference list, outline, or notes to demonstrate that they are on task. Such work, handed in early, also allows you to give your students specific feedback. If you collect the students' first draft of their research paper, as many writing experts would recommend, it is often useful to ask the students to include a brief cover note to their draft (Herrington, 1997). In this brief note the students would indicate what they are most satisfied with at this point (e.g., their thesis statement), what they are still working on or what is still troubling them (e.g., organizing, finding sources), and what they would like feedback on (e.g., am I specific enough in my analysis?). This cover letter could be addressed to you, the teacher, or to a peer who might also read the draft.

Fourth, teachers can help students by demonstrating and providing examples of organizational formats for summarizing and synthesizing ideas from multiple sources. As we mentioned several times, students have significant difficulties in synthesizing from multiple sources. The study sheet and the chart or map are certainly appropriate ways to organize and synthesize ideas for the research paper. In addition to these formats, some teachers have found I-Charts (Hoffman, 1992) to be particularly beneficial for students.

Randall (1996) used a modification of the I-Chart with her eighth graders during an interdisciplinary unit on the wilderness and the environment. She found the organizational strategy to be highly effective, especially with her struggling readers. Her students also raved about the usefulness of the I-Chart, many of them offering testimonials such as "It saved my life" and "I rate it a 10." As illustrated in Figure 7.5, the I-Chart provides students a format to summarize important facts from multiple sources under a topic heading. Such a format assists students in paraphrasing ideas and in sensing patterns across sources. As one student in Randall's class said, "They keep your stuff straight and in order" (Randall, 1996, p. 541).

Fifth, teachers can enhance students' writing by providing them mini-sessions on how to incorporate sources into their papers. This is perhaps one of the most vexing problems that students encounter when they write from multiple sources. They wonder whether they should summarize or whether they should quote and how they should introduce their expert. Unfortunately, they typically choose to quote long blocks of text and lose their own voice in the process. One mini-lesson might focus on phrases that students can use to introduce their evidence, phrases

Figure 7.5 I-Chart Format for Synthesizing Sources

TOPIC: _____

Name:

Subtopic:

What do I already know about this topic?
_____

Source #1   MY NOTES

_____

Source #2   MY NOTES

_____

Source #3   MY NOTES

_____

Facts I find interesting:

Key words:

New questions I should research:

such as these: (a) According to the expert, _____, we need to _____, (b) As pointed out by _____, or (c) _____ concurred with the other authorities in the area when he said this: _____.

Sixth, you can require students to present to the class an oral report of their paper 1 week before the written report is due. In this way, students are forced to think about and organize their ideas for an audience other than the teacher. When students realize that they will be presenting their work to a real audience, they tend to adapt and transform the information they have gathered to meet the needs of their uninformed listeners (Nelson & Hayes, 1988).

Finally, you can help students by giving them in advance the criteria that will be used to grade or evaluate their work. As mentioned earlier in this chapter, explicitly describing writing assignments can prevent bad writing. Students should understand the role of mechanics, organization, content, and writing style in the grading process. Some teachers use a checklist and ask students to attach it to the first page of their paper. The checklist incorporates the grading criteria and helps students evaluate their work before handing it in. We think this is a good idea that can make the grading process somewhat easier.

Following the seven suggestions just discussed should prevent the nightmares that occur for students and teachers when research papers have not been fully thought through and mentored. In the next section we switch gears and address the issue of playful writing tasks.

Teacher as Learner

THE CINQUAIN

A cinquain is a five-line poem that follows a predictable format in which the first line contains two syllables, the second contains four syllables, the third contains six syllables, the fourth contains eight, and the final line contains two syllables. As such, many individuals find it easy and enjoyable to create their own poem. More important, students can write a cinquain as a way to consolidate and review important ideas from a content-area unit of study. For example, this cinquain was written by a student in a culinary arts class:

Planning
Ingredients
Studying recipes
Using different steps and herbs
Sharing

Take some time to reflect on this chapter about writing across the content areas. Then, in the space below, write your own five-line poem to capture some of the chapter's ideas:

_____

_____

_____

_____

_____

_____

Writing Activities that Encourage Playfulness and Creativity

Perhaps this section should have been entitled "writing activities that are not academic, thesis-based papers." Admittedly, students should be able to write papers with well-formulated thesis statements that they have supported with valid evidence and coherent arguments. However, there are occasions when this top-down structure should make room for other types of writing that are a bit more "playful" (Weber, 2002). Moreover, we should remember that there are students in our classrooms who actually enjoy the challenge of writing about a content-area topic but with a twist on the audience, the format, or the perspective. They revel in combining ideas that are not typically associated with each other or in stretching their thinking and ours beyond the typical parameters.

Designing such assignments for these students can be a challenge and sometimes our "creativity" well seems almost dry or empty. Fortunately, two acronyms can guide and stimulate content-area teachers as they design thought-provoking assignments for their students: RAFT (Santa, Havens, & Maycumber, 1996) and SPAWN (Martin, Martin, & O'Brien, 1984).

Content-area teachers tell us that these two acronyms help them develop creative, relevant writing assignments for their students.

Raft

RAFT stands for *role* of the writer (is the author a thing, a concept, a person, an animal?), *audience* (to whom is the author writing?), *form* (what format or discourse mode is the author going to use?), and *topic* (what topic is the author writing about?). Aubrae, a home economics teacher, introduced RAFT during her unit on nutrition because she wanted her students to bring closure to the unit with a creative writing task. After providing her students several examples of how RAFT could be operationalized, one of her students, Chris, decided to use RAFT for his paper. Using RAFT, her writing assignment took on this focus:

    R: I am vitamin D (the concept).

    A: Jack's body (the audience).

    F: I will write a letter (the format).

    T: I will inform Jack what I will do for him (topic).

Chris's letter is illustrated in Figure 7.6.

Spawn

The second way you can design creative writing assignments is by using SPAWN. *SPAWN* stands for *special powers, problem solving, alternative viewpoints, what if,* and *next*. Each is a category of writing assignments that can encourage students to move beyond the memorization of facts. To construct such an assignment, you can select one of the categories from SPAWN and combine it with the most appropriate writing form. (Refer to Figure 7.1 for some examples of writing forms that are creative and nontraditional.)

    RAFT and SPAWN assignments are similar in that they both focus on the importance of having students vary the format, audience, or point of view for their writing tasks. As such, they have the potential of increasing students' motivation to write, especially because the assignments are less conventional. Having said that, it is wise not to overuse such formulaic techniques and to be aware that some students find it difficult and a bit frustrating to write from the point of view of a hormone or a statistic, for example. Hence, it is always wise to give students choices in their writing assignments.

    Before we discuss ways in which to respond to students' writing, it is important to discuss another role of writing in our schools—writing used to evaluate students' mastery of content-area concepts.

Figure 7.6   RAFT Example in Home Economics

Dear Jack,

I would like to introduce myself. I am vitamin D. I am found in many dairy products such as milk and cheese. I promise if you eat me, you will have strong bones and teeth. I can even help you to grow old and be a healthier person. Have you seen the television commercial for milk? That commercial is all about me. I am the reason milk is so good. So, I recommend that you eat foods that contain me. I also recommend that you drink milk. If you do these things, I will do my best to help you.

Sincerely,
Vitamin D

Honoring Diversity and Building Competence in the Content Classroom

Beth is a 10th-grade AP English teacher who decided to use the SPAWN mnemonic to help her construct possible writing topics for the book *Farewell to Manzanar* (Houston & Houston, 1974). The book fit perfectly into the sophomores' unit on prejudice and injustice because it describes the internment of a Japanese girl in an American camp on the West Coast during World War II. Although Beth likes to give her students choices for their writing, she also knows that many of them are so grade conscious that they are not comfortable until they have specific suggestions. Thus, she distributed the following ideas:

Option 1: Special Powers

You have the power to change any event in *Farewell to Manzanar*. You must write and tell what event you changed, how you changed it, why you changed it, and what could happen as a result of the change. For instance, what if Rodine's mother had welcomed Jeanne into the Girl Scouts? Would that affect just that part of the story, or might Jeanne's life have been totally different if she had been accepted right from the first?

After you have completed the written section of this assignment, I will meet in a group with everyone who elected to do this assignment. We will discuss the changes that have been made and the possible consequences.

Option 2: Alternative Viewpoints

We heard Jeanne's viewpoint on her friendship with Rodine. We were told of their experiences as their friendship began to grow through their years at Cabrillo Homes and during junior high school. After entering high school, they began to drift apart. What is Rodine's viewpoint? What happened according to her perspective? How did she feel?

Pretend that you are Rodine. Write several journal entries in which you discuss the beginning of the friendship, a few of the high points, and the time when you finally realized that you were no longer special friends. You will have the chance to share your response with others who do this same assignment.

Option 3: What If?

What if this story took place in Japan after World War II? Rodine's father was in the army as an officer in the occupational forces. He wanted her to become familiar with the Japanese culture, so she attended a Japanese school, where she was the only White person. Jeanne was in her class. Starting with Rodine's first day in class, write a story of the experiences Jeanne and Rodine had. How would life be different now that Rodine is the minority and Jeanne is the majority? You may tell your story from either Jeanne's or Rodine's point of view. You will have the opportunity to meet with others in the class to share your story and discuss the approach that they followed for the same assignment.

Beth reported that the students enjoyed these writing options and that several of them used the SPAWN mnemonic to create their own assignments. More important, this writing assignment measured more completely her students' achievement of unit objectives than any multiple-choice exam she could have created.

Essay and Short-Answer Examinations: Using Writing to Evaluate

Writing can be used to extend students' knowledge, it can be used to assess their knowledge, and it can be used to evaluate what they learned. In this section we address the latter by focusing on two types of evaluative writing that students encounter in school: the essay exam and the short-answer question, formats that are becoming a routine part of most state-mandated tests.

Unlike creative writing assignments, essay and short-answer questions present high stakes for students, especially if the writing tasks are incorporated into state-mandated tests.

Preparing Students for Content-Area Essay Exams

If you have ever used an essay examination in your class as a means of measuring student learning, you probably have shared the reactions of most teachers: "No more essays!" "These students can't write, so why should I waste my time grading these pitiful excuses for essay answers!" or "Did these students even study?" Although the most judicious use of writing is not for testing or evaluating, essay examinations should not be avoided just because students initially are inept with them. As stated in Chapter 4, writing is one of the best means, next to a conference with each student, to assess how well students can think analytically about content. If we expect our students to synthesize, evaluate, and apply course objectives to new contexts, we should design evaluation measures that are sensitive to those objectives. In short, true-false and multiple-choice questions should not be the only examinations students take.

How, then, do we prepare students to be adept at taking essay or short-answer question examinations? One way to help students through their first essay/short-answer test is by teaching them the processes involved in PORPE (predict, organize, rehearse, practice, evaluate), an essay-preparation strategy built on research and theory in writing and metacognition (Simpson, 1986).

PORPE's first step, predict, asks students to generate some potential questions that would make good essays. To help students at this point, teachers should introduce the language used for writing essay or short-answer examinations by providing them with a glossary of commonly used essay-question words such as *explain*, *discuss*, *criticize*, *compare*, and *contrast*. Once students understand the meaning of these essay-word starters, teachers can involve them in brainstorming possible essay questions from a specific chapter. Often the main difficulty students have with essay prediction is that they focus on minute details rather than key ideas. Thus, teachers should instruct them to check the boldface headings and summaries for possible essay topics. Essay prediction is not easy, but all students can learn this important step if given considerable guidance.

The second step in PORPE, organize, involves students in gathering and arranging the information that will answer the self-predicted essay question. This step is very much like brainstorming and prewriting in that students map or outline answers in their own words. Content-area teachers can help students with this step by sharing their own maps or outlines that answer a predicted essay question. Students can also work in pairs to brainstorm their own organizational structure for another predicted essay question. Representatives from each pair could then present and discuss their structure and rationale on the chalkboard. As a final step, students could develop their own map or outline for a different essay question and receive brief written or oral feedback from the teacher. This step encourages students to develop connections among ideas so that the course content becomes reorganized into a coherent structure instead of memorized as a list of unrelated bits of information.

The third step of PORPE, rehearse, engages students in the active self-recitation and self-testing of the key ideas from their maps or outlines. At this point, teachers

To help students rehearse their outlines/maps, many teachers have introduced their students to the strategy explained in Chapter 9 called the talk through.

should stress the difference between the processes of recall and recognition so that students will accept and internalize the need for a rehearsal step in their study. Most of the students we have worked with think that studying is the same as looking at the information, and they see no difference in demands between essays and multiple-choice exams. One of the major reasons students have difficulty writing essay answers is that they have not spent the concentrated time rehearsing information necessary to transfer it to long-term memory.

The fourth step, practice, is the validation step of learning because students must write from recall the answers to their self-predicted essay questions in preparation for the real examination. Teachers can increase students' performance and reduce their anxiety by detailing the procedures for writing an effective answer in an actual testing situation. For example, students should be taught to read each question carefully before they begin to write, underlining key words. Next, they should be encouraged to sketch their outline or map in the margin of their test paper before they begin writing. Once they begin answering the question, they should make sure that their opening sentence rephrases the essay question and/or takes a stand with a thesis statement. Finally, students should reread the essay question to ensure that they have answered it directly.

The final step of PORPE, evaluate, requires students to evaluate the quality of their practice answers. Content-area teachers can introduce this final step by arranging brief sessions where students read, discuss, and evaluate the merits of various essay answers, a process sometimes called "norming." Once students become more accustomed to evaluating essay answers, they can work in pairs to evaluate each other's essays and evaluate their own answers independently.

Even though the steps of PORPE will take some additional class time, it is important to remember that not only will students learn how to prepare for and take an essay exam, they also will learn important course concepts. Thus, the essay test should not be feared by students or teachers but used when appropriate and when students have been taught the "how."

Preparing Students for Short-Answer Questions

Most state-level assessments ask students to write in some manner, but the most common format is the short-answer question. For example, on Florida's state-mandated test students are asked to explain in writing their answers to a mathematical question or problem. Writing an effective paragraph for a short-answer question is very similar to writing an effective answer to an essay question. Unfortunately, many students underestimate the task and provide only a few sentences and no thesis statement. Hence, it is important for every content-area teacher to teach and reinforce the skills involved in writing effective short-answer paragraphs.

When content-area teachers incorporate these four suggestions into their classroom routines, students' performance will improve on state-mandated writing exams that include short-answer questions.

Many of the instructional ideas we discussed in terms of the essay answer can be applied to the short-answer question format. For instance, students need to read the question carefully, underlining key words so they understand what is being asked. Many mistakes are made just because students answered a question that was not asked. They also should begin their answer with a thesis statement and should support that thesis with some type of reasoning or evidence. But how does a content-area teacher provide that type of support and instruction, especially given the time crunch and the number of students seen in a day? To address these questions, we provide the following suggestions taken from a variety of content-area teachers:

1. Provide your students examples of effective short answer paragraphs taken from your content area. Once they internalize the qualities of effective answers, share with them some answers that are not quality, reserving time to

highlight the weaknesses. Remember, however, that students can recognize errors in other individuals' writing, but often have difficulties in avoiding those errors or weaknesses in their own writing.

2. Teach students how to write a thesis statement in response to a question. This could be accomplished via several modeling sessions. In addition, you can assist your students by taking a mediocre thesis statement and, with their input, transferring that statement into a quality one. For the struggling writers and readers, teach them the strategy of turning a question (i.e., the short-answer question) into a thesis statement or topic sentence.

3. Teach students the TIE principle so they can apply to it to own their written answers. According to TIE, each paragraph needs a *Thesis*, one or more *Illustrations*, and some type of *Explanation* as to how the illustrations relate to the thesis. You can also write TIE in the margins of their papers as a reminder of what they need to do to improve their writing.

4. Provide numerous opportunities for students to practice writing short-answer paragraphs. You can assign the paragraphs as a part of students' homework and ask them to time themselves when they write in order to simulate the experience of thinking and writing under a time constraint. Alternatively, you can choose to include one short-answer question on each of your exams. For both situations it is important to debrief the experience with your students. For example, you might explore how they felt writing under a time pressure.

When you take the time to help students write effectively on evaluative tasks such as essay and short-answer questions, you have contributed significantly to their academic success and survival. As the National Commission on Writing in America's Schools and Colleges (2003) has stated, ". . . the problem is not that students do not know how to write, but rather that they do not know how to write with the skills expected of them . . ." (p. 16). Your mini-lessons may well provide your students that knowledge.

> Throughout this textbook you will find many other writing activities, especially the specific teaching suggestions on how to teach summarization in Chapter 9.

Responding to Students' Writing

In a classic study several years ago, a researcher discovered in his interviews with teachers that many were hesitant to incorporate writing into their units of study because of the overwhelming amount of work that would be generated by the 100 or more students they see each day (Pearce, 1983). Over the years, we have collected specific techniques from other teachers and from our own experiences that have made it feasible for students to write and teachers to survive. These techniques acknowledge that teachers have personal lives and thus prefer not to spend the weekend glued to the kitchen table writing comments to students about their written work. All of the techniques are based on the premise that responding is more important than grading in the writing process and in students' mastery of content-area concepts. We begin first with some guidelines for the exploratory writing activities that content-area teachers assign.

Responding to Students' Exploratory Writing

The following are some general guidelines to expedite the process of responding to students' log or journal entries and their Quick Writes or "hot cards." Remember that these types of exploratory writing are what Elbow (1997) describes as "low stakes"

> We will explore a variety of efficient and effective ways that teachers can use to respond to students' exploratory writing tasks and their more formal writing tasks.

writing because they are informal tasks that students write for themselves. In addition, low-stakes assignments typically occur frequently and usually do not have a major impact on students' grades.

General Suggestions

1. Remember the purpose of each writing assignment and keep content the center of your focus. If students write a learning log entry, the purpose is to help them construct meaning or to monitor their understanding of a content-area concept. Moreover, because students do not revise their exploratory writing, your extensive comments are typically a waste of your valuable time. In other words, the evaluation process should reflect their participation and task approximation, and nothing more.

2. Consider using the minus/check/check plus system and quickly skim your students' work. That is, place a minus on the paper if the work is unsatisfactory, a check if the work is satisfactory, and a check plus if the student's work exemplifies high-quality thinking or exploration (Bean, 2001). Many teachers have told us that this system is extremely efficient. At the end of the semester they typically have a system to translate the marks into letter grades and another system to weigh the students' exploratory writing into their grade for the semester.

3. On other occasions, especially with multiple journal entries, some teachers determine in advance the one that they will respond to or ask the students to select their best papers to be evaluated. In this case, you might want to respond to your students' entries by making a comment that focuses not on mechanics, but on content. Praise is always appropriate (e.g., excellent point!).

4. Severely limit the length of some assignments, as with the "hot cards," which are written entirely on an index card. The important criterion should not be length, but rather the students' effectiveness in judiciously selecting the words they will explain or defend. Space limitation not only will save you time, it will also educate your students so that they will not always equate length with quality.

Responding to Students' More Formal Writing Tasks

If, however, the students have worked their way through the processes of writing and class time has been provided for feedback at each stage, evaluate the writing as a final draft. Students should be told in advance the importance of their spelling, grammar, and mechanical errors in the total evaluation process. As discussed earlier, the assignment-making process should be thorough to inform students of your expectations and purposes.

General Suggestions

In addition of these eight general suggestions and a variety of checklists and rubrics, in this section we will explore specific ways to involve students in the evaluation of their formal writing.

1. Avoid zealous error detection as you respond to your students' writing because this type of response can consume huge amounts of your time and energy. Remember that students are more likely to make mechanical errors when they first begin to write on a topic that is unfamiliar or new to them.

2. Write at least one supportive comment or reaction. Sometimes a large "yes!" does the trick or a statement such as "You have provided lively and credible examples." Some content-area teachers like to place wavy lines under ideas that are particularly insightful and straight lines under ideas that are unclear or fuzzy.

3. Use green, purple, or orange pen, or better yet, use a pencil—any color but red, which connotes a highly punitive message.

4. Use abbreviations for comments you frequently make. For example, instead of writing "support your ideas" countless times, write the letter "S." Rather than marking every error, place a check or some other mark next to the line containing an error. Of course, remember to provide students with a list of your abbreviations.

5. When possible, write questions rather than comments (Lunsford, 1997). Questions force students to solve problems and interact with the material. For example, instead of writing the comment "Be specific," you could write a question such as this: "Can you convince me that fitness relates to general health?"

6. Troubleshoot many of the errors that students commonly make by providing them with class time, in advance of the due date, to read and edit their assigned partner's rough draft. This will save you time and provide them with more sensitivity and appreciation for the writing and thinking processes.

7. Stagger your writing assignments across your classes so that you do not require all your students to hand in their work at the same time. For example, your first- and second-period classes could hand in their writing on Mondays, your third- and fourth-period classes on Tuesdays, and your fifth- and sixth-period classes on Wednesdays.

8. Perhaps the most important thing to remember about grading is to think and plan carefully before assigning. Writing tasks do not facilitate all types of course objectives and help all types of students, but are certainly effective in many situations.

Peer Responses to Drafts

Students should be involved in responding to their writing and other students' writing if we want them to gain independence as learners and consumers of print (Graham, 2005; Shellard & Protheroe, 2004). Because many students have been conditioned to respond only on a mechanical level (i.e., "Did I misspell any words?") to their writing, this self-evaluation or peer evaluation takes time to develop. The advantages far outweigh the disadvantages, however, especially in terms of lightening your responsibilities as the sole responder and evaluator. In addition, if students can identify or troubleshoot some common writing problems during class, they can use that information once they begin to revise their final product.

> When students are involved in peer review, they learn a lot about the writing process.

Over the years, we have discovered several activities that help students learn how to evaluate and respond to writing. We have found it best to begin with a whole-class activity that involves students in judging optimal and nonoptimal written models. As noted in Chapter 9, another name for this activity is "The Good, the Bad, and the Ugly" because good writing samples as well as bad ones are shared with the students. It is best not to use actual student work but rather to create samples of student writing that typify what "past students" have written. Usually these samples are combinations of students' work and teachers' concerns about common writing problems.

Students are told to read the samples and then assign a grade to each. After grading each sample, they are to rank the writing samples from best to worst. Once they have completed these tasks, the teacher leads a discussion on the grades, ranks, and students' rationales. From our experiences with this activity, students become highly motivated to participate and defend their judgments.

Once students feel comfortable with the concept of evaluating and responding to their classmates' writing, it is a good idea to pair them for peer evaluation of a writing assignment they have recently drafted. Begin by emphasizing the basic rules for peer evaluation: Be positive and be specific. Then explain the process: One student will read his or her paper while the other student listens, using a set of questions to guide the feedback given to the writer. The questions should vary according to the content area and assignment; the following typify some that can be used:

1. What did you like best about your partner's paper?
2. What could be added to make the paper more interesting?
3. What facts, ideas, and evidence could be added to strengthen your partner's paper?
4. What parts are not clear?
5. What two parts should be changed or revised?

To help students remember what their partner has recommended, it is a good idea to provide students with a form, such as the one in Figure 7.7. After the student reads her paper, the partner shares his ideas and responses to the questions as they talk. It is important that they talk to each other about the writing rather than just exchange forms. After the talking and responding, they switch roles. If the activity is difficult for the students or if they feel uncomfortable initially, you can model the procedure for the class by becoming the partner who responds.

A third activity can be done in small groups. A volunteer in each group reads his paper. Then the other members of the group state ideas from their papers that either were or were not present in the paper just read. Each member of the group must respond. Because all students are required to participate, they profit from hearing how others have interacted with the targeted concepts. This information should assist students in revising their papers once they leave class. Moreover, this activity can serve as an excellent review for an examination.

In addition to these general grading suggestions and the use of students' input and feedback, you can develop some forms (checklists, primary trait evaluation guides, and rubrics) to help decrease the time devoted to providing students with

Figure 7.7   Student Evaluation Form for Working in Pairs

Author's Name: **Peer Reviewer's Name:**

Authors: Read your paper aloud to your reviewer.

Reviewer: Answer the questions below so that the author has a written copy of the comments you will provide orally.

1. This paper is mainly about
2. The best part of the author's paper was
3. These parts of the author's paper were not clear to me:
   a.
   b.
   c.
4. I think the author's paper could be strengthened by:
   a.
   b.
   c.
5. I think the paper could be even more interesting if the author would

Reviewer and Author: Talk to each other about your ideas.

---

quality comments and responses to their written work. These forms, which can be adapted to any content area and any assignment, are discussed next.

Checklists

Checklists contain the general criteria you wish to focus on when you read students' writing, whether it be their thesis statements or their use of support to defend a position. Rather than writing the same comment over and over again (e.g., "Be more specific," "Support your statements"), you merely circle the item on the checklist. In addition, the checklist allows you to indicate the level of competence the student displayed on the checklist's criteria. Figure 7.8 illustrates a type of checklist that Luna, a health education teacher, used when she evaluated her students' papers on heart disease. Notice that it concentrates on content development and organization. You could easily modify such a checklist by adding different criteria.

Primary Trait Evaluations

Much like the checklist, with primary trait evaluations teachers focus on the desired traits they would like expressed in their students' writing. For example, if Luna had done a primary trait evaluation on her students' essays, it probably would resemble Figure 7.9. You have likely constructed something similar and called it your "grading template." We suggest that you write one brief comment for each student and focus on one or two primary traits, especially with students' first efforts in writing about a concept.

Rubrics

A rubric gives content-area teachers more structure for their responses because it summarizes the traits or criteria as well as the characteristics of high-quality and low-quality papers. Using the rubric as a guide, the teacher can quickly read student work and respond specifically and appropriately. For Luna's assignment, the rubric might resemble Figure 7.10.

Students and parents appreciate forms such as the checklist because they provide a specific and organized way of communicating the characteristics you seek in your writing assignments.

Figure 7.8 Checklist for Grading a Health Essay

	Below Average	Average	Above Average
1. The essay has an introduction.	————	————	————
2. The essay answers the question and provides key ideas from the text or lecture.	————	————	————
3. The essay provides support for each of the key ideas.	————	————	————
4. The essay personalizes the information by relating it to situations beyond the text and lecture.	————	————	————
5. The writing is clear and organized.	————	————	————
6. The essay summarizes the findings.	————	————	————

Figure 7.9 Primary Trait Evaluation of Health Essay

1. The essay lists five of the nine factors impacting heart disease.   5 points
   (age, sex, race, genetic factors; cholesterol and triglycerides;
   hypertension; diabetes; obesity; smoking; type A behavior;
   stress; inactivity)
2. The essay explains these five factors with statistics, examples, and   15 points
   support.
3. The essay relates these factors to personal situations (i.e., the   15 points
   author assesses his/her own risk of developing heart disease).
4. The essay is clear and well organized.   5 points

                                                            TOTAL 40 points

Figure 7.10 Scoring Rubric for a Health Essay

An "A" Essay Would Contain

1. An introduction or thesis statement
2. A list of the factors (five minimum) impacting heart disease
3. Explanations, examples, statistics for each of the five factors
4. A personal application or assessment (i.e., the author would assess himself/
   herself about the risk of developing heart disease)
5. An implication statement discussing solutions
6. Very good organization, few mechanical errors

A "B" Essay Would Contain

1. An introduction or thesis statement
2. A list of the factors (five minimum) impacting heart disease
3. Explanations, examples, statistics for four of the factors
4. An attempt of a personal application
5. A summary statement
6. Good organization, few mechanical errors

A "C" Essay Would Contain

1. A list of the factors (five minimum) impacting heart disease
2. Explanations, examples, statistics for three of the factors
3. A conclusion or summary
4. Fair organization, some mechanical errors

A "D" Essay Would Contain

1. A list of the factors (three or four) impacting heart disease
2. Explanations, examples, statistics for two of the factors
3. Below-average organization and many mechanical errors

An "F" Essay Would Contain

1. A list of the factors (fewer than three) impacting heart disease
2. Explanations, examples, statistics for one factor
3. A list of points, poor organization, many mechanical errors

246

Regardless of the form you select, it is a good idea to introduce it with the assignment and ask the students to attach it to their writing assignment. In that way, the form becomes a concrete reminder for students of what the criteria will be for your responses and eventual evaluation.

CASE STUDY REVISITED

At the beginning of this chapter, we described the problems that Dave was experiencing in his first year of teaching biology to non-college-bound students. You probably have some suggestions on how he could motivate his students to become more active participants and learners. Write your suggestions now.

After talking to the English teacher and doing some of his own research and planning, Dave decided to spark his students' interest in the environment unit in several ways. He began the unit with an activity designed to assess his students' present attitudes toward the environment. The students were prepared for a lecture and a textbook assignment when they entered class on the second day of the unit. Instead, they were greeted with Dave's slides of beautiful outdoor scenes and Jethro Tull's "Songs from the Woods" playing in the background. As the song faded, Dave shifted the slides to scenes of human filth and flotsam. Slides of dumps, incinerators, and cities were now shown, and the background music was John Prine's "Paradise." When the slides and song were finished, Dave handed out the following questionnaire:

Directions: Answer as completely as possible. There are no right or wrong answers, so feel free to express yourself.

1. Briefly, tell me how the slide presentation made you feel.
2. What was the message of the second song, "Paradise"?
3. Is there a place outdoors that you especially like to go? Where? Why?
4. Have you ever thought or read or heard about the ideas presented today? If so, tell me about them in more detail. What was the source of those ideas?

Dave read his students' responses and during class the next day initiated a discussion before he revealed the overall objective of the unit. That is, he wanted his students to localize and personalize the issue of endangered species. To develop the unit Dave obtained a list of locally endangered animal and plant species from the Department of Natural Resources and asked each student to select a species from the list. The librarian and the English teacher suggested that he give his students a lot of structure for the assignment, so Dave distributed a handout outlining his expectations:

You are to select one of the species from the list and gather information about its problem of survival. Specifically, I want you to include the following information in your paper: (1) past and present range and population, (2) length of time it has been endangered, (3) reasons for its being endangered, (4) why it is important that this species

continued

Before writing your suggestions for Dave, go to *http://www.prenhall.com/ brozo*, select Chapter 7, then click on Chapter Review Questions to check your understanding of the material.

CASE STUDY REVISITED (CONTINUED)

survives, and (5) actions currently being taken to improve its chances for survival.

You will have 2 weeks to complete this assignment. Your first step in doing the assignment will be to use the classroom library and any resources I have listed for you on the accompanying page. Read extensively and take notes for about 4 days. On the fifth day, begin organizing your ideas into an outline or map, making sure you have answered all five questions. On the sixth day, you will deliver a 3-minute presentation to the class on what you have learned thus far about your endangered species. Rough drafts of your written paper will be due on October 15. I will read them and provide you with feedback. The final paper will be due October 30.

In grading this assignment, I will use these criteria:

1. How well you answered the five questions concerning your species. Were you complete? Accurate? Did you explain yourself clearly so that your best friend could understand? This part is worth 35 points.
2. Your spelling, mechanics, and grammar. This part is worth 15 points. As to length—there are five questions, so I expect three pages as a minimum.

Most of Dave's students attempted to do the assignment, so he was pleased. He realized, however, that he probably should have started on a smaller scale with a less intimidating discourse mode. After chatting with the English teacher during lunch, he decided to try letter writing because it was a less formal type of writing and was closer to talking, something with which his students had lots of experience.

The next week, Dave began his final activity for the unit. The class brainstormed what could be done to stop or slow down the process of environmental degradation. When Dave asked his students what they could do, he received many blank stares. He then suggested to them that education was one answer and that they could be a part of that educational process by becoming informed and involved. Dave explained that involvement can occur in many forms, and that letter writing was one powerful and permanent means of disseminating ideas. With that introduction, he told each student to write a letter to his or her senator or representative asking for support of legislation they considered important for the protection of wildlife. After discussing the proper form for a letter to a government official, the students were given time to begin their rough drafts. Dave provided feedback on all rough drafts, and by the end of the week he had 24 letters to mail to Washington, DC. Many students doubted whether they would receive a response, but within a month, all of Dave's students had received replies from the senators and representatives. Copies of the 24 letters were placed on Dave's bulletin board and on his Web site. Even after 4 months and several other units of study, the students still gathered at the bulletin board to read those letters and discuss the status of their environment.

Dave is still struggling with ways to involve his students with the biology curriculum. He has some good days and some bad ones, but he feels that his students are certainly more involved than they were before, when he taught only from the textbook.

Looking Back, Looking Forward

In this chapter we have made the case that the writing process can be a powerful tool in helping students learn content-area concepts. Writing, like reading, is a constructive process that can stimulate passive learners to become active learners as they grapple with the task of putting their own words on paper.

This chapter was organized on the assumptions that writing can be used to help students (1) prepare for their reading assignments, lectures, demonstrations, and class discussions; (2) summarize and organize concepts and monitor their understanding of those concepts; and (3) think critically and creatively. Using those three assumptions, we presented a variety of exploratory writing activities such as learning logs, Quick Writes, and the double-entry journal. We also examined a variety of thesis-governed activities that all content-area teachers can incorporate in their classrooms. For those teachers wondering how to evaluate or respond to their students' writing, we offered some practical grading guidelines and suggestions to make the task easier and more reasonable.

References

Alvermann, D. E. (1992). The discussion web: A graphic aid for learning across the curriculum. *The Reading Teacher, 45,* 92–99.

Angelo, T. A., & Cross, K. P. (1993). *Classroom assessment techniques* (2nd ed.). San Francisco: Jossey-Bass.

Bangert-Drowns, R. L., Hurley, M., & Wilkinson, B. (2004). The effects of school-based writing-to-learn interventions on academic achievement. *Review of Educational Research, 74,* 29–58.

Bean, J. C. (2001). *Engaging ideas.* San Francisco: Jossey-Bass Publishers.

Bean, J. C., Drenk, D., & Lee, F. D. (1982). Microtheme strategies for developing cognitive skills. In C. W. Griffin (Ed.), *New directions for teaching and learning.* San Francisco: Jossey-Bass.

Belenky, M., Clinchy, B., Goldberger, N., & Tarule, J. (1986). *Women's ways of knowing.* New York: Basic Books.

Burns, J., Peltason, J., & Cronin, T. (1984). *Government by the people.* Englewood Cliffs, NJ: Prentice Hall.

Burns, M. (1995). Writing in math class? Absolutely! *Instructor, 14,* 40–47.

Calkins, L. M. (1986). *The art of teaching writing.* Portsmouth, NH: Heinemann.

Carroll, P. (2000). Journal to the third power. In L. Baines & A. Kunkel (Eds.), *Going Bohemian: Activities that engage adolescents in the art of writing well* (pp. 5–9). Newark, DE: International Reading Association.

Casazza, M. (2003). Using a model of direct instruction to teach summary writing in a college reading class. In N. Stahl & H. Boylan (Eds.), *Teaching developmental reading* (pp. 135–144). Boston: Bedford/St. Martin.

Duffy, S. P. (2005). Writing in political science. In M. Segall and R. Smart (Eds.), *Direct from the disciplines* (pp. 115–124). Portsmouth, NH: Boynton/Cook Heinemann.

Elbow, P. (1997). High stakes and low stakes in assigning and responding to writing. In M. Sorcinelli & P. Elbow (Eds.), *Writing to learn: Strategies for assigning and responding to writing across the disciplines* (pp. 5–13). San Francisco: Jossey-Bass.

Elbow, P. (2002). Writing to publish is for every student. In C. Weber (Ed.), *Publishing with students: A comprehensive guide* (pp. 1–8). Portsmouth, NH: Heinemann.

El-Hindi, A. E. (2004). Connecting reading and writing: College students' metacognitive awareness. In S. Bernstein (Ed.), *Teaching developmental writing* (pp. 79–92). Boston: Bedford/St. Martin's.

Fisher, D. (2001). "We're moving on up": Creating a schoolwide literacy effort in an urban high school. *Journal of Adolescent & Adult Literacy, 45,* 92–101.

Fisher, D., & Frey, N. (2003). Writing instruction for struggling adolescent readers: A gradual release model. *Journal of Adolescent and Adult Literacy, 46,* 396–405.

Friend, R. (2000). Teaching summarization as a content area reading strategy. *Journal of Adolescent and Adult Literacy, 44,* 320–330.

Graham, S. (2005). Writing. In P. Alexander & P. Winne (Eds.), *Handbook of Educational Psychology.* Mahwah, NJ: Lawrence Erlbaum Associates.

Grossman, F., Smith, B., & Miller, C. (1993). Did you say "write" in mathematics class? *Journal of Developmental Education, 17,* 2–6.

Herrington, A. J. (1997). Developing and responding to major writing projects. In M. Sorcinelli & P. Elbow (Eds.), *Writing to learn: Strategies for assigning and responding to writing across the disciplines* (pp. 53–66). San Francisco: Jossey-Bass.

Hoffman, J. V. (1992). Critical reading/thinking across the curriculum: Using I-Charts to support learning. *Language Arts, 69,* 121–127.

Houston, J. W., & Houston, J. (1974). *Farewell to Manzanar.* New York: Bantam.

Hynd-Shanahan, Holschuh, J., & Hubbard, B. (2004). Thinking like a historian: College students' reading of multiple historical documents. *Journal of Literacy Research, 4,* 238–250.

Jenkinson, E. B. (1988). Learning to write/writing to learn. *Phi Delta Kappan, 69,* 712–717.

Light, R. J. (2001). *Making the most of college: Students speak their minds.* Cambridge, MA: Harvard University Press.

Lunsford, R. F. (1997). When less is more: Principles for responding in the disciplines. In M. Sorcinelli & P. Elbow (Eds.), *Writing to learn: Strategies for assigning and responding to writing across the disciplines* (pp. 91–104). San Francisco: Jossey-Bass.

Martin, C. E., Martin, M. A., & O'Brien, D. G. (1984). Spawning ideas for writing in the content areas. *Reading World, 11,* 11–15.

McCrindle, A. R., & Christensen, C. A. (1995). The impact of learning journals on metacognitive and cognitive processes and learning performance. *Learning and Instruction, 5,* 167–185.

Mitchell, D. (1996). Writing to learn across the curriculum and the English teacher. *English Journal, 45,* 93–97.

National Commission on Writing in America's Schools and Colleges. (2003). *The neglected "R": The need for a writing revolution.* New York: The College Board.

Nelson, J., & Hayes, J. R. (1988). *How the writing context shapes college students' strategies for writing from sources* (Tech. Rep. No. 16). Berkeley: Center for the Study of Writing, University of California at Berkeley.

Pearce, D. (1983). Guidelines for the use and evaluation of writing in content classrooms. *Journal of Reading, 27,* 212–216.

Petrosky, A. R. (1982). From story to essay: Reading and writing. *College Composition and Communication, 33,* 19–36.

Randall, S. N. (1996). Information charts: A strategy for organizing student research. *Journal of Adolescent & Adult Literacy, 39,* 536–542.

Reyes, M. L., & Molner, L. A. (1991). Instructional strategies for second-language learners in the content areas. *Journal of Reading, 35,* 96–103.

Rubin, D. L., & Dodd, W. M. (1987). *Talking into writing: Exercises for basic writers.* ERIC Clearinghouse on Reading and Communication Skills. Urbana, IL: National Council of Teachers of English.

Santa, C., Havens, L. & Maycumber, E. (1996). *Project CRISS: Creating independence through student-owned strategies.* Dubuque, IA: Kendall/Hunt.

Sargent, M. E. (1997). Peer response to low stakes writing in a WAC literature classroom. In M. Sorcinelli & P. Elbow (Eds.), *Writing to learn: Strategies for assigning and responding to writing across the disciplines* (pp. 41–52). San Francisco: Jossey-Bass.

Shanahan, T. (1997). Reading-writing relationships, thematic units, inquiry learning: In pursuit of effective integrated literacy instruction. *Reading Teacher, 51,* 12–20.

Shellard, E., & Protheroe, N. (2004). *Writing across the curriculum to increase student learning in middle and high school.* Arlington, VA: Educational Research Service.

Simpson, M. L. (1986). PORPE: A writing strategy for studying and learning in the content areas. *Journal of Reading, 29,* 407–414.

Simpson, M. L., Stahl, N., & Francis, M. (2004). Reading and learning recommendations for the 21st century. *Journal of Developmental Education, 28,* 2–15.

Smith, C. C., & Bean, T. W. (1980). The guided writing procedure: Integrating content reading and writing improvement. *Reading World, 19,* 290–294.

Unrau, N. (2004). *Content area reading and writing: Fostering literacies in middle and high school cultures.* Columbus, OH: Pearson.

Wagner, B. J. (1987). The effects of role playing on written persuasion: An age and channel comparison of fourth and eighth graders. *Dissertation Abstracts International, 47,* 4008A.

Weber, C. (2002). *Publishing with students: A comprehensive guide.* Portsmouth, NH: Heinemann.

chapter 8

Reading and Learning from Multiple Sources

Anticipation Guide

Directions: Read each statement carefully and decide whether you agree or disagree with it, placing a check mark in the appropriate *Before Reading* column. When you have finished reading and studying the chapter, return to the guide and decide whether your anticipations need to be changed by placing a check mark in the appropriate *After Reading* column.

	Before Reading		**After Reading**	
	Agree	*Disagree*	*Agree*	*Disagree*
1. Multiple sources can be successfully implemented into any classroom by following a few simple steps.	_____	_____	_____	_____
2. The textbook is the most common source used in disciplinary teaching.	_____	_____	_____	_____
3. Primary documents refer to the most important texts students read on a topic.	_____	_____	_____	_____
4. Comic books have no place in school or the content classroom.	_____	_____	_____	_____
5. Alternative sources can put a human face on the facts and generalizations in textbooks.	_____	_____	_____	_____
6. Determining unit themes and topics can guide the selection of appropriate multiple sources.	_____	_____	_____	_____

![books icon] **Chapter Principle: Gather and Organize Print and Nonprint Sources for Increasing Understanding of Information and Ideas**

The principle guiding the content of this chapter is concerned with exposing youth to multiple sources in disciplinary classrooms. This means moving away from textbook-centered teaching and infusing classrooms with a range of interesting, authentic texts. These texts can be used as motivators for learning, to develop critical reading and thinking, and as vehicles for improving students' abilities to organize information and concepts from a variety of sources into useful forms for review or application.

*A*lmost from the first word of this book we have proposed that teachers of youth give fresh consideration to what counts as literacy. In this chapter we ask disciplinary teachers to take a new look at the possibilities for teaching using a variety of texts. We do so because in typical upper-grade classrooms today there remain two ever-present, authoritative information sources—the teacher and the textbook (Walker & Bean, 2002). Yet, youth of the digital age have access to and facility with a wide array of richly informative print and multimedia sources. Furthermore, it has been asserted that providing content in a variety of forms of representation increases students' abilities to think and communicate using different symbol systems (Eisner, 1997; Wade & Moje, 2001).

Go to *http://www. prenhall.com/brozo*, select Chapter 8, then click on Chapter Objectives to provide a focus for your reading.

We know from our own experiences and those of our innovative middle and high school colleagues that when alternative sources are given legitimacy in history, science, math, literature, and the other content classrooms, youth benefit from their unique perspectives on topics. These sources, we further maintain, while going largely untapped in traditional school settings, may hold the key to engaging adolescents in meaningful reading and learning as well as elevating their achievement.

Our guiding principle for this chapter informs us that secondary students should receive their first serious look at different cultures, historical eras and events, politics, and scientific advances of the human race through a variety of interesting media in addition to content-area textbooks. Because of the demands of limited space, adoption committees, and readability constraints, textbook publishers often present a distilled version of content-area information. Emphasis is placed on important facts, broad views, pivotal characters, and general effects on whole populations, resulting inevitably in a detached tone and dry material.

At the same time, however, we recognize that for most American middle school and high classes a core textbook is the designated information source. In this chapter we do not advocate suppression of textbooks, but the inclusion of alternative sources to enrich teaching and learning in the content classroom. Such sources as (a) young adult literature; (b) graphic novels; (c) primary documents; (d) newspapers, magazines, and real-world reading material; and (e) a variety of multimedia have the potential to transform bland, textbook-centered learning environments into exciting venues for authentic exploration of disciplinary topics.

CASE STUDY

Linda is a high school teacher who has two junior-level American history classes. In planning a unit on "Immigration to the United States," she established three primary goals. First, she wanted her students to recognize and appreciate that the United States is made up of immigrants from virtually every country of the world who have played a role in the creation of our country and our culture. Second, she wanted her students to recognize, explain, and describe the concept of cultural diversity and determine the advantages and challenges that cultural diversity has brought to this country. Finally, she wanted her students to recognize that immigration is an ongoing part of America's history that contributes to an ever-evolving American identity. During the year, the class discussed immigration several times as it related to various eras of our country's history, from colonial times through global migrations to the United States in the 20th century and continuing today.

To the Reader:
As you read and work through this chapter on the use of multiple sources to improve content learning, consider ways in which Linda could incorporate a variety of print and nonprint texts into her unit in order to meet her goals. Think about how the strategies described and those from your own experience and imagination could be applied to the teaching of a unit on immigration.

Case studies in this textbook provide an opportunity to apply principles and practices to new contexts.

Common Types of Multiple Sources to Enrich the Content Classroom

In this section we describe several common alternative text and media sources disciplinary teachers have made use of in their instruction.

Young Adult Literature

Within textbook treatments of cultures, social movements, historical eras, and scientific advances lie richly detailed stories about the people who made them or who watched them being made and were affected by them. The narrative element—the stories that lie within all human interactions—is often left out of many content-area lessons (Connor, 2003). Yet, it is narrative that can bring the content to life (Bean & Moni, 2003; Galda & Liang, 2003). One rich source of narrative is young adult literature.

According to Donelson and Nilsen (2004), any literature read by young adults is considered young adult literature. This would include a large variety of texts, such as classics, popular adult fare, and bestsellers. For our purposes, young adult literature refers to books written or marketed primarily for teens and preteens. It is literature that deals specifically with issues and themes relevant to their interests and needs. Another distinguishing feature of these books is that the protagonists and other main characters are typically of the same age as the readers for whom the books were written.

There are several major genres or types of young adult books. Indeed, the world of young adult literature is wonderfully rich, with countless high-quality books of fiction and nonfiction that cover a wide range of topics (Bushman & Haas, 2001). Three genres more amenable to disciplinary teaching are historical fiction, science fiction, and nonfiction.

> The variety and volume of young adult literature available to today's content-area teachers make it easier than ever to include this text source in virtually any lesson.

Historical Fiction

Historical fiction allows adolescents to appreciate important historical events in human terms through the eyes of adolescents who lived through them (Spencer, 1994). Because these books deal with events of the near and distant past, they often have a timeless quality that permits their use for many years (Elkassabany, Johnson, & Lucas, 2000).

Science Fiction

Youth who are interested in science are often great fans of science fiction (Westcott & Spell, 1999). By the same token, quality science fiction books can play an important role in developing students' interest in science (Hartwell & Cramer, 1994).

Nonfiction

An important genre of adolescent literature, nonfiction books written for youth draw them into the reading and learning process the way no textbook ever could (Jones, 2001). Nonfiction books, often referred to as informational books, are typically written by authorities who cover topics from dinosaurs to dating using engaging and informative writing styles and writing from the perspectives of their intended readers. According to some (Sullivan, 2001), nonfiction is the most frequently read literature among adolescents.

Using young adult literature in the content classroom has been widely recommended for virtually every subject area (Austin, 1998; Jacobi-Karna, 1995; Lightsey, 1996; Lombard, 1996; Miller-Hewes, 1994; Pappas & Barry, 2001; Royce & Wiley, 1996).

Graphic Novels and Comic Books

It wasn't that long ago when comic books were not to be dignified in libraries, schools, and classrooms. Perhaps it was because they were regarded as the bottom of the literary food chain by librarians, teachers, and parents that many youth spent their outside-of-school leisure time reading exclusively comics. But then in 1992, Art Spiegelman's *Maus* was awarded a Pulitzer Prize and the term "graphic novel," which had been in use among devotees as far back as the 1960s, came into vogue. Since then, the comic book format has changed dramatically. Graphic novels are now being recognized for their literary and artistic merit and their authors and illustrators are taking on everything from the Palestinian-Israeli conflict to growing up with an epileptic sibling (Mui, 2004).

Although we use the terms interchangeably in this chapter, *graphic novel* is commonly used to distinguish certain works from comic books, which for many have juvenile and humorous connotations. It implies a more serious, mature, and literary work than traditional comics. Another distinguishing feature is that the graphic novel generally refers to any long-form comic book or the comic's analogue to a prose novel, novella, or play.

Graphic novels come in numerous genres, including fiction, historical fiction, biography, science fiction, and nonfiction. This variety, along with their enormous popularity with youth, make graphic novels and comic books an engaging and useful additional resource for teaching and learning in any content classroom (Weiner, 2002).

Finally, graphic novels and comic books have been shown to be an invaluable tool for motivating reluctant readers (Schwarz, 2002; White, 2005). The illustrations can provide the needed contextual clues to the meaning of the written narrative, especially for striving and visual learners. And though these materials have been shunned in the past by librarians, many are observing how graphic novels are generating a whole new energy among youth. In asserting the legitimacy of reading material such as comic books in school settings, Stephen Krashen (1993) notes:.

> Perhaps the most powerful way of encouraging children to read is by exposing them to light reading, a kind of reading that schools pretend does not exist and a kind of reading that many children, for economic or ideological reasons, are deprived of. I suspect that light reading is the way that nearly all of us learned to read. (pp. 47–48)

Go to Web Resources for Chapter 8 at *http://www. prenhall.com/brozo*, and look for Graphic Novels.

Primary Documents

A textbook is a distillation of a variety of source material. By their very nature textbooks are at least one and more commonly several times removed from the original sources. Textbooks youth encounter in schools rarely include primary documents, those texts written by and about individuals and groups who experienced the events of history, made or were impacted by the discoveries of science, or logged the development of their own ideas leading to new geometrical principles in math and engineering.

Primary documents are the authentic pieces of evidence historians use to interpret and describe the past. Vivid and personal documents, such as a letter or a

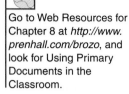

Go to Web Resources for
Chapter 8 at *http://www.
prenhall.com/brozo*, and
look for Using Primary
Documents in the
Classroom.

photograph, when made available to youth will intrigue them and provoke thoughtful and engaged responses (Barton, 2005; Hynd, 1999). This is the case because historical artifacts used by scholars faithfully depict the language, thinking, and behavior of the past without the sanitizing and glossing characteristic of textbook treatments.

Though these texts rarely find their way into most classrooms, it is worth noting that those students who read primary documents on a fairly frequent basis, as often as at least once per week, have higher achievement scores than their peers who see these sources rarely (U.S. Department of Education, 2002). So there's something about primary sources that make them more attractive and engaging to students than traditional textbook treatments of topics and promotes meaningful and long-lasting learning (Lawlor, 2003).

Newspapers, Magazines, and Other Real-World Texts

It almost seems too commonsensical to remind disciplinary teachers of the value of using newspaper and magazine articles and other documents in the everyday lives of youth and adults as teaching resources. And yet, our own informal observations of hundreds of secondary school classrooms along with findings from Larimer and Schleicher (1999) reveal that these alternative, commonsense texts are not being utilized nearly as often as they could be or to the best extent possible.

Teachers who have discovered the benefits of incorporating these types of texts into their instructional practices find students are more engaged and thoughtful learners because the content is more relevant to their lives and experiences (Jarman & McClune, 2001, 2003; McClune & Jarman, 2000). Science teachers can increase involvement by structuring activities that allow students to read and consult popular science magazines, such as *Scientific American* or *Popular Science*, during class time. Government teachers can focus students' attention on the role of government in establishing rules and regulations for the protection of citizens' health by reading and analyzing food preparation and food handling brochures published by the Food and Drug Administration. Economics teachers can elevate student interest by bringing into class credit card forms, bank statements, and other personal finance documents as accompaniments to textbook coverage of the topic.

Virtually every issue that emerges from the study of science, math, history, and literature can be enriched and made more relevant with newspaper and magazine articles and a great variety of other real-world documents (Hammer, 2000). Furthermore, to help youth see the importance and utility of learning disciplinary content, we recommend that teachers bring into the classroom familiar, everyday texts students encounter outside school that link directly to school-based topics. Equally viable, of course, is electronic access to these documents. Every imaginable form from loan applications to drug and health brochures are readily available online, and countless newspapers and magazines can be viewed online as well.

There are many examples of teachers who routinely integrate real-life reading materials into their content instruction to help students see connections between disciplinary content inside the classroom and real-world issues and events outside the classroom boundaries. For example:

- A health teacher has students bring in menus from restaurants and cookbooks from home when working on food preparation and nutrition.
- A business education teacher, for his unit on career explorations, brings in several examples of employment applications. He also urges students who may be applying for part-time jobs to bring in their applications.

- A chemistry teacher asks students to bring in labels from household cleaning products and foods indicating that certain chemicals are being used.
- A government teacher uses popular news magazines to relate text topics to current events.
- An accounting teacher asks students to bring in actual bills and account statements to teach accounting terms and budgeting.
- A math teacher asks students to write/create math problems using tables, maps, and graphs from the local newspaper.

The list could go on and on because the possibilities for integrating everyday reading materials into the content classroom are virtually limitless.

When looking at the variety of different ways disciplinary teachers have used real-world texts, think about how you might do the same in your content-area lessons.

Popular Media and Music

An obvious source for enlivening disciplinary learning is popular media and music (Knabb, 2003; Pailliotet, 2003). Because today's youth live in the "mediasphere," as we explained in Chapter 1, it makes good sense to find as many linkages as possible between the images and music with which they are familiar and topics under study in the classroom. One of the more interesting youth media/literacy phenomena is "fan-fiction"—a text of any genre created about a cartoon or video game character. This new form has been described as coming from fans of mass culture who base their writing on media texts and images (Chandler-Olcott & Mahar, 2003; Jenkins, 1992). Later in this chapter we describe an English teacher who took full advantage of fan-fiction in her classroom.

Frequently in this book we have asserted and exemplified the importance of honoring youths' outside-of-school media and literacies while bridging them to academic concepts and information. Music, as a medium of identity construction for many youth, is also a very viable alternative text form underexploited by most content-area teachers (Newman, 2005; William, 2001). Scaffolding for new understandings means working with what adolescents bring to the classroom, including their interest and knowledge of popular music (Morrell & Duncan-Andrade, 2002).

Of course, the most pervasive popular medium in youth's lives is the computer. Throughout this book we have described how computers can be utilized to increase various aspects of content learning. This chapter, too, will have frequent references to computers and the alternative texts they offer disciplinary teachers. For a thorough discussion of instructional principles and approaches using computer technology, however, see Chapter 10, Expanding Literacy and Content Learning Through Digital Information and Communication Technologies.

Guidelines and Practices for Integrating Multiple Sources into Content Classrooms

The contributions that multiple sources can make to the teaching of disciplinary content are limited only by your own sensibilities. But regardless of whether you tend to plan conservative or more flamboyant lessons, what is of overarching importance is that you strive to take greater advantage of the numerous print and other resources available to you and your students. As we stated in the introduction to this chapter, while advocating for the use of multiple texts, we are not suggesting the traditional textbook has become passé for today's classroom. In fact, you will see in most of the teaching examples described that the textbook serves a helpful role as a reference resource among several resources at students' disposal as they expand their understandings of information and ideas and become more engaged and thoughtful learners.

We urge the use of these alternative texts because we know that youth will quickly turn off to reading if they find texts difficult or boring (McPhail, Pierson, & Freeman, 2000; Pennac, 1994). On the other hand, Guthrie and Wigfield (2000), in reviewing research on the influence of affect in the reading process, observed that when students find reading pleasurable and interesting, their positive attitudes toward reading rapidly become generalized to most other subjects, which leads to a deeper love of reading as a primary source of information and enjoyment. Furthermore, students' reading comprehension has been shown to be greater with high-interest materials because interesting material maintains their attention more effectively (Baker, Afflerbach, & Reinking, 1995; McDaniel, Waddill, & Finstad, 2000).

Each of the multiple sources we have described can be a powerful motivator for reading, writing, and learning, and all are important schema-builders. In earlier chapters you learned that schema theorists posit that the more developed the knowledge structures readers possess about a particular topic, the greater the likelihood they will be successful in dealing with new information related to that topic. The most important instructional implication of schema theory is that teachers should build bridges between new information to be learned and students' prior knowledge (Hartman, 1995). Texts and media familiar and interesting to youth can provide the background information and call to mind related ideas, building the foundation for easier assimilation of new textual information (McMackin, 1998).

The duration and scope of any lesson or series of lessons that integrates multiple sources will depend on the topic and on your judgments and preferences. Throughout this book we have noted the benefits of planning and teaching in units, whereby students experience a series of lessons often lasting up to several weeks that revolve around a unifying theme with related subtopics. The primary benefit of this approach to both you and your students is time—sufficient time to investigate a topic thoroughly through reading, discussion, writing, and research and, therefore, time to get interested in and excited about learning while producing considered responses. The following guidelines and methods are most applicable to unit-based teaching.

Multiple sources are more easily incorporated into the content classroom when disciplinary teachers plan and teach units.

Identify Salient Themes and Concepts

The process of identifying important themes and concepts for a unit of study is essential for integrating appropriate sources. Multiple sources should be bridged by overarching themes and concepts related to the most important information and ideas of the unit. The process involves, first, deciding what you want your students to know as a result of the unit and then using this theme as a guide, identifying the related concepts and subtopics.

Here is where textbooks can prove most helpful, because they are usually organized by units, which makes it easier to identify broad themes for unit plans. As we have recommended before, however, you should develop unit themes that are meaningful to you and your students, regardless of the extent to which the topics are dealt with in the textbook.

Unfortunately, although textbooks are excellent dispensers of facts, they often lack explicit development of important themes. Therefore, you must infer essential ideas from them in order to develop unit themes that are meaningful to you and your students, regardless of the extent to which the topics are dealt with in the textbook.

In this way, you can take advantage of your own and your students' special skills or interests. Try asking yourself the following questions as you look over a textbook unit:

- What are the driving human forces behind the events?
- What phenomena described in the textbook have affected ordinary people (including me and my students) or may do so in the future?
- What universal patterns of behavior related to this reading should be explained?

Answers to these questions will go a long way toward helping you decide what students should know as a result of the unit and thereby will provide direction for selecting appropriate sources to tie in with the theme. For example, when Hahnan, a seventh-grade social studies teacher, applied these questions to the textbook's unit on Australia, she inferred that the geography of a place affects the lives of its inhabitants. This theme seemed particularly apparent in the case of Australia, with its curiously evolved wildlife and bush country lifestyles, so Hahnan believed that this would be an advantageous context in which to teach her unit.

After establishing a theme for a unit of study, we recommend you explore the content further to identify important concepts and subtopics related to the unit's theme. To accomplish this, we suggest you create a visual display or a web (Pappas, Kiefer, & Levstik, 1999). Beginning with the unit topic or theme written in the center of a large piece of paper, you, with help from your students, generate related subtopics and write them around the main topic. These ideas may come directly from the text or from prior knowledge. Figure 8.1 is an example of a web co-constructed by Dora and her ninth-grade science class for their Astronomy unit.

Creating topic/subtopic webs can lead to a more complete exploration of unit themes and the identification of relevant texts.

Teacher as Learner
ESTABLISHING THEMES FROM TEXTBOOK TOPICS

To further illustrate the process of establishing important themes related to textbook topics, consider the following excerpt about the Nazis, the Jews, and the Holocaust taken from an 11th-grade American history book. Indeed, the quoted section is nearly the extent of text related to the Holocaust in this history book. As you read the excerpt, ask yourself the three questions just posed. Then write down a theme you believe would be important to teach in relation to this content.

> When news of the Holocaust—the term later given to the Nazis' extermination of European Jewry—first leaked out in early 1942, many Americans discounted the reports. . . . How much could have been done remains uncertain. . . . The War Refugee Board managed to save the lives of just two hundred thousand Jews and twenty thousand non-Jews. Six million other Jews, about 75 percent of the European Jewish population, were gassed, shot, and incinerated, as were several million gypsies, communists, homosexuals, Polish Catholics, and others deemed unfit to live in the Third Reich. (Boyer, Clark, Kett, Salisbury, Sitkoff, & Woloch, 2004, pp. 807, 810)

Theme: _____

_____

You probably found that this preceding text is like most textbook prose. It covers the facts but offers few ways of identifying the underlying critical themes and concepts. By asking our three recommended questions, however, we believe you can identify one of the most important themes of this content—*the dangers of racial prejudice*—only hinted at in the sweeping, factual account of Nazism and the Holocaust.

Figure 8.1 Web for an Astronomy Unit

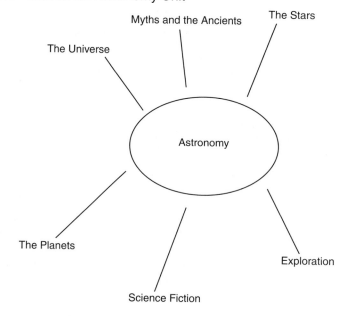

The connections between subtopics (indicated by the lines in Figure 8.1) are indicative of another important benefit of unit teaching: The scope of a unit is broad enough to reveal relationships between different aspects of a topic, thereby helping students knit information together, expand schemata, and improve their overall understanding of the topic. With the completed web, Dora then decided which subtopics were most relevant to the theme of the unit. Rarely is there time to cover every aspect of a topic generated in the webbing process, and some subtopics must be de-emphasized or omitted entirely—even though the information may be covered in the textbook. Finally, under the subtopic headings to be included in the unit, Dora listed related sources (Figure 8.2). We will talk more about how Dora organized instruction with multiple sources later in this chapter.

Identify Appropriate Sources to Help Teach Concepts

Once an important theme for the unit is established and related subtopics and concepts have been identified, the next step is to find multiple sources that are directly and/or thematically related.

Becoming more knowledgeable about the multitude of sources available to teach disciplinary unit themes will seem like a daunting task at first. It can be made easier by the many bibliographies, reference guides, lists, and reviews of current comics, graphic novels, and young adult literature available to all of us on the Web. Another invaluable resource for identifying alternative texts is your school and local librarian. Librarians can do Internet searches to find accessible articles, and our holdings for relevant graphic novels, young adult books, magazine and newspaper articles, and government documents.

Regarding our topic of Jews in Europe during World War II, Keshawn, an eighth-grade history teacher, located a wealth of related sources using electronic references. He also found ideal young adult books right within his neighborhood and school libraries. These included one of our timeless favorites, *Friedrich* (Richter, 1970), and

Your best friends in the quest to infuse content instruction with multiple sources are school and public librarians.

Figure 8.2 Web for an Astronomy Unit, Including Appropriate Sources

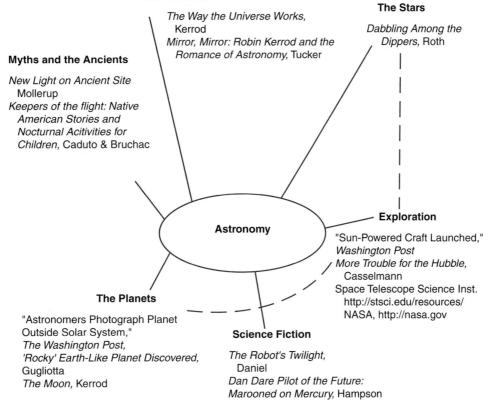

many other fine selections, such as *Hitler Youth: Growing up in Hitler's Shadow* (Campbell-Bartoletti, 2005), *Germany's Black Holocaust* (Carr, 2003), *Holocaust Memorial Museum: Learning About the Holocaust* (http://www.ushmm.org/education/forstudents/), the *Boston Globe* article "A Factory for Death: What Was the Worst Thing *About* Auschwitz?" (Jacoby, 2005), the *Junior Scholastic Article* "Never Again" (McCollum, 1995), and *Maus: A Survivor's Tale* (Spiegelman, 1992). Boundless rewards awaited Keshawn and his students as they approached the unit on the Holocaust that would include this marvelous range of interesting texts. (For a description of each of Keshawn's sources see Figure 8.3.)

Once relevant multiple sources are located, the most enjoyable aspect of this process begins—you get to read them before using them in class. We have found that as teachers become acquainted with multiple sources, they rediscover the joy of reading, they develop fresh perspectives on the topic, and their enthusiasm for teaching grows.

On reading these various texts Keshawn introduced to his students, you will note that the characters and others like them are, first of all, human. You will understand that the effects of distant, large-scale events such as war will become real to students only when translated into terms of what they mean to fictional and factual characters who witnessed it and were victimized by it. After hearing Keshawn read *Friedrich* aloud to the class, one of his eighth-grade student commented, "This book describes

Figure 8.3 Multiple Sources for Teaching a Unit on the Holocaust in
Eighth-Grade Social Studies

Young adult novel. In the young adult novel *Friedrich* the reader meets a German boy and his Jewish playmate and learns how both are gradually victimized by Nazi propaganda and pogrom during the years 1925 to 1942.

Nonfiction memoir. In *Hitler's Youth: Growing up in Hitler's Shadow* we learn about adolescents faced with unbelievable choices during World War II. It includes points of view from adults who had belonged to Hitler's youth and those who resisted.

Nonfiction picture book. *Germany's Black Holocaust* offers readers a highly unique perspective on the plight of Blacks caught in the Nazi web. It includes interviews of an African American female Holocaust victim and an African American officer who liberated Blacks from a concentration camp.

Web site. *The Holocaust Memorial Museum* is an interactive Web site that allows visitors to explore such items as photographs and personal diary excerpts from victims that leave youth with a deep appreciation for the human dimension of the Nazi's ethnic extermination campaign. At this site they also learn how to be vigilant of racial prejudice in their communities and even within themselves.

Newspaper article. In the *Boston Globe* article, "A Factory for Death," the author describes the horror of Auschwitz, the site of the greatest mass murder in recorded history, using his father's memories of surviving this dreadful ordeal.

Magazine article. The *Junior Scholastic* article "Never Again" presents the gripping story of one survivor of the Holocaust who retells his story of liberation 50 years later.

Graphic novel. *Maus* is a saga of the Holocaust, in which Jews are depicted as mice, Germans as cats, and the Polish as pigs; the horrors of ethnic cleansing and persecution are rendered in compelling illustrations and text.

---

the life of these people so well you'd think that *Friedrich* and his mother and father were a part of your own family." Were it not for alternative texts like those Keshawn found and brought into his classroom, most historical events of national and international scope and most notable human achievements and tragedies would remain for many young adults distant or even mythical notions with no emotional connection to their own lives and experiences.

A second notable characteristic of quality alternative sources, such as those Keshawn had his students read, is that unlike a typical textbook they describe the effects of large-scale events on ordinary people. Within the narration of realistic human interaction, concepts can be made understandable and real to youth. Earlier, we referred to prejudice as an important concept to be explored in the study of Nazism and World War II. Excellent passages and activities for exploring the nature of this concept can be found in the multiple sources Keshawn gathered for his students. Consider, for example, the following passage from Richter's *Friedrich*. In it, the 13-year-old Jewish boy is trying to retrieve his clothes from a swimming pool attendant in Germany in 1938.

> "Just take a look at this!" the attendant said. "You won't get to see many more of them." Everyone could hear his explanation: "This is one of the Jewish identification cards. The scoundrel lied to me. He claims his name's Friedrich Schneider—it's Friedrich Israel Schneider, that's what it is—a Jew that's what he is! A Jew in our swimming pool!" He looked disgusted.

All those still waiting for their clothes stared at Friedrich. As if he could no longer bear to touch it, the attendant threw Friedrich's identification card and its case across the counter. "Think of it! Jewish things among the clothes of respectable human beings!" he screamed, flinging the coat hanger holding Friedrich's clothes on the ground so they scattered in all directions. (Richter, 1970, pp. 76–77)

When reading passages such as this, students cannot help but be affected by the injustice and humiliation suffered by this character they come to know as decent, likable, and intelligent. Furthermore, the theme of the dangers of prejudice—its meaning, its effect on people, and its often terrible results—is made startlingly clear. After hearing *Friedrich*, another of Keshawn's eighth-grade students wrote:

> Any youth reading or hearing these lines from *Friedrich* will be able to put a human face on the cold statistics and facts dispensed in textbooks.

The book made you feel how you would have felt if you were Jewish or German at the time. I learned how brave the Jewish family was in the book. I also learned how cruel and unthinking people can be and not caring and thinking that these people are the same as we are—human. Another thing I learned is that war is horrible. I hope, even though I doubt it, that there will be no more wars and discrimination in this world. The book really touched me.

Organize the Content and the Classroom for Multiple Sources

Clearly, alternative sources to the textbook have the potential of affecting young adults deeply; even so, teachers who have never used anything other than the textbook often ask us questions such as "How can I find the time to work multiple sources into my daily plans when I barely have enough time to cover the chapters?" or "I have 20 to 25 students per class. How can I manage my classroom if I use the textbook and other sources?"

Making Time for Multiple Sources

The first concern is easy enough to understand when you consider the fragmented, fact-laden curricula within which so many content-area teachers try to operate. Not only is each content area taught as a separate entity, but each subject is broken down into bits of information that students are required to memorize (Bean, 2000; Brown, Collins, & Duguid, 1989; O'Brien, Stewart, & Moje, 1995). Almost invariably, so much time is spent learning the small details that no time is left to experience holistic treatments of the topic and to understand the big picture. As a result, many students rarely enjoy or see the point in studying history or science facts, forget them, and often have to relearn them the next year. In contrast, time spent exploring various other texts and media can be both efficient and effective because it gets students interested in learning the content and, when the sources are chosen appropriately, can serve as the material for content instruction (Bean, Kile, & Readence, 1996; George & Stix, 2000; Lott & Wasta, 1999).

For example, one of the sources used in Dora's unit on astronomy was Kerrod and Sparrow's (2002) *The Way the Universe Works*. From this book, students learned accurate and current information about the planets, stars, galaxies, and other remarkable phenomena of outer space. Students benefited from the experience of reading a whole, well-written work of nonfiction by astronomers with American and Russian space program experience and a real passion for their subject matter. At the same time the authors reinforced a message Dora sent her students about the importance of continuing space exploration.

We believe the best way to approach the problem of finding time to make use of multiple sources is to choose the most important themes and overarching concepts to be taught and then place instructional emphasis on them. Naturally, some of the textbook content is not as pertinent to the important themes as other content and, consequently, should be given less attention; deciding on a focus thus frees up time that can be spent on relevant, important information. For example, in his unit on the American Revolution, Frank decided to emphasize three important themes: (1) freedom, both for countries and for people, has a price (the heavy toll of war, even on the victor; the responsibilities that accompany self-government and personal independence); (2) war affects all citizens of a country; and (3) alternatives to war exist.

Frank then selected several possible sources that would help to reinforce these themes, finally deciding to use one primary young adult historical novel, *Johnny Tremain* (Forbes, 1945), and to suggest others sources for students' independent reading. *Johnny Tremain* is a classic of accurate and compelling historical fiction. By its copyright, this may seem to be a dated work for today's adolescents, but because its subject matter centers on events in our nation's past more than 200 years ago, it has a timeless quality that makes it as relevant now as ever.

Next, Frank went through the 12 chapters in the text unit and, keeping his salient themes in mind, made decisions about how to teach each chapter (Figure 8.4) and listed potential writing activities for many of the chapters (Figure 8.5).

Managing the Classroom with Multiple Sources

We can address the second concern—how to manage the content classroom with multiple sources—by describing the experiences of three different teachers whose approaches represent three management systems.

Figure 8.4 American Revolution: Teaching Ideas

Chapter	Suggested Activity
1	Life in New England—Students read; compare with trade book; write (see Figure 8.5).
2	Work, Church, & School same as Chapter 1.
3	Life in Southern Colonies Teacher lecture—brief.
4	Life in Middle Colonies Teacher lecture—brief.
5	Life in the Wilderness Teacher lecture; book talk: *Distant Thunder* (Moore 1991).
6	Government in the English Colonies Teacher lecture; debates (see Figure 8.5).
7	Furs and Farming in New France Teacher lecture—brief.
8	French & English Fight Students read; map study; develop time line, write (see Figure 8.5); book talk and sharing: *The Matchlock Gun* (Edmonds 1991).
9	England Tightens Its Grip Students read.
10	Colonists Become Angry Students read; prioritize value of ways to cause change; compare text & trade book; write (see Figure 8.5); book talk and sharing: *My Brother Sam Is Dead* (Collier & Collier 1974).
11	Liberty or Death Students read; list causes of war, rank order, & defend rankings.
12	New Nation Is Born Students read; discuss Johnny Tremain's change of mind.

Figure 8.5 American Revolution: Suggested Composition Assignments

---

Chapters 1 & 2

Let Johnny Tremain have a dialog with a person of today about the living conditions in the 1700s. Make comparisons.

Write a position paper for living in the 18th century or today.

Compare & contrast women's roles in the 18th century and today, based on reading in *Johnny Tremain*.

Chapter 6

Debate: Develop arguments explaining the points of view of British and colonists. Placards and posters can support either side.

Chapter 8

Thumbnail sketches of important Revolutionary War personalities.

Newspaper articles for *Colonial Times*.

Editorial about British taxation.

Dialog between a colonist and King George III.

List personal freedoms you have and value today. Which of these can be traced to the events of the 1770s? Which were actually fought for in the Revolutionary War?

Chapter 10

Prioritize relative value of various means of gaining one's ends and producing change.

1. Voting
2. Physical force
3. Vigilante (scare) tactics
4. Terrorism
5. Diplomacy

Chapter 12

You have just read *Johnny Tremain*. What part of this story did you react to most strongly? Do you see any connection between this part of the story and your own life?

Reading Aloud

Marques uses the simplest of systems. He reads to his eighth graders books and other sources that are thematically linked to the science topics under consideration. When studying the topic of genetics and genetic engineering, for instance, Marques read Kress's (1996) *Beggar's Ride*. Two hundred years in the future, regular human beings hate and fear the Sleepless and the SuperSleepless, genetically modified humans who are immune to disease and hunger and need no sleep. Marques made other sources available to students that were related to the topic of genetic alteration, including *Dead Water Zone* (Oppel, 1993), about a teenager trying to find his genetically stunted younger brother in the polluted ruins of an American city; *Virus Clans* (Kanaly, 1998), about viruses that evolved billions of years ago on a distant planet and then spread to Earth where they have been directing evolution; and *The Hot Zone* (Preston, 1995), which tells the dramatic and chilling story of an ebola virus outbreak in a suburban Washington, DC, lab.

Combining fiction with current information books, Marques has been able to include young adult literature in nearly all of his units. For example, he used *Buried in Ice: The Mystery of a Lost Arctic Expedition* (Beattie & Geiger, 1992), with its vivid, gripping photographs of mummified explorers found in the Arctic permafrost,

Go to Web Resources for Chapter 8 at *http://www. prenhall.com/brozo*, and look for Read Alouds.

to grab his students' interest in the topic. Isaac Asimov's (1966) *Fantastic Voyage* was read aloud in conjunction with a unit on the systems of the body. His students also listened to and observed Schultz's (1992b) light and informative *Looking Inside the Brain* during this unit.

Don't underestimate the number of texts you can read aloud in the content classroom over the course of a school year taking a mere 15 minutes daily. And read alouds are enjoyable for adolescents, too.

As Marques reads, he asks his students to be active listeners, paying attention not only to plot developments but also to how the ideas in the story relate to those in the text. With this approach, only a single young adult book is needed. Marques reads 15 to 20 minutes daily and is able to complete a book of average length in 2 ½ weeks. During the school year, he often reads as many as 15 books to his classes. Over the same period, he exposes his students to countless other magazine and newspaper articles, picture books and informational books, graphic novels, primary documents, and Web sites.

Like Marques, Courtney reads aloud from a young adult book nearly everyday in her social studies classes. For example, to help put a human face on issues relating to citizenship addressed in sweeping fashion in the textbook, Courtney read Jacqueline Woodson's (2002) novel *Hush*, which chronicles the plight of a family in a protected witness program. As a prelude to reading aloud to students, she identifies good prediction points in the novel where students can speculate on the events described and future scenes they will encounter. By reading aloud for about 10 minutes at the end of a period, Courtney enriches content learning. Moreover, as an added benefit, she has seen how this practice has a soothing effect on her students.

Whole-Class Text

As an alternative to the teacher's reading aloud, the whole class can read or explore common sources together. Bernadette's seventh-grade social studies classes read four primary documents from the U.S. presidential election of 1860, which pitted Stephen Douglas against Abraham Lincoln. Working from a Web site (http://jefferson.village.virginia.edu/vshadow2/newspapers.html), Bernadette made copies of articles and editorials from two newspapers with opposing perspectives on the election. Her students read the original texts from *The New York Tribune* and the *Richmond Enquirer* dated October 29 and November 6, 1860, respectively, a few days before and a few days after Lincoln defeated Douglas. They learned from these original sources that it was actually a four-way race for the presidency with Douglas, a Democratic candidate from the North, a separate Democratic candidate from the South, Lincoln as the Republican nominee, and an individual running for a third party. They compared and contrasted the positions and attitudes of the papers and debated with each other over the issues. These original documents helped Bernadette's students get a feel for how people really felt at that time toward the issues at stake in the election. In particular, they learned the depth of secessionist feelings among Southerners expressed after Lincoln was elected in the editorial in the *Richmond Enquirer* entitled "The Day of Battle Has Arrived."

Multiple Groups and Multiple Texts

A more complex but exciting and powerful management system involves student-directed, cooperative learning groups for reading and sharing multiple sources (Burns, 1998). Earlier, we described how Dora, a ninth-grade science teacher, builds webs for her units to identify salient concepts and subtopics and appropriate print and media for teaching these topics. For her astronomy unit she decided to focus on two of the subtopics, *planets* and *deep space*. She gave groups of four students the following URLs and had them work in teams in the computer lab to learn the material:

- Astronomers Photograph Planet Outside Solar System" (2005, April 16) (**http://www.washingtonpost.com**)
- 'Rocky' Earth-Like Planet Discovered" (2005, June 14) (**http://www. washingtonpost.com**)
- More Trouble for the Hubble" (2005, March 2) *Discover Magazine* (**http:// www.discover.com**)
- Space Telescope Science Institute (**http://stsci.edu/resources/**)

For another group of students she secured four copies of the graphic novel *Dan Dare Pilot of the Future: Marooned on Mercury* (Hampson, 2005).

Dora assigned students in each group particular roles to play in order to ensure everyone's participation. The "idea summarizer" was responsible for putting on paper the key information gleaned from the source; the "vocabulary enricher" looked up and helped define unfamiliar words encountered in the source; the "fact checker" had to find an independent corroborative source for any facts used in the presentation; and the "presenter" was responsible for sharing the key ideas and information learned from studying the source.

In the beginning, Dora carefully modeled each cooperative group assignment and helped clarify confusion through questions and discussions. She devised these cooperative learning group roles because they contribute to students' learning in the manner she desires and with the sources from which she wanted her students to learn. It is important to note that you can create your own cooperative learning group roles, depending on what kinds of learning you want to take place within the groups. (See accompanying Teacher as Learner box.)

Such a system as Dora's is admirably suited to teaching units because a variety of sources, each emphasizing a different aspect of the unit theme, will contribute much to the scope and depth of students' understanding (Elbaum, Schumm, & Vaughn, 1997).

Youth receive a rich, textured look at disciplinary topics when cooperative groups are asked to become experts on information and ideas from different sources and then share with their peers.

Using Multiple Sources as Schema and Interest Builders

Science
A sixth-grade science teacher had her students read Robert Lipsyte's *The Chemo Kid* (1993) as a prelude to a unit on ecology. The story is about two boys who try to stop the pollution of their town's reservoir. The adventures the boys have and the lessons they learn set the stage for the theme of the ecology unit and class discussion by establishing an overall picture of how humans can live and thrive in harmony with nature. In addition, the story gave students a store of unusual, dramatic examples of the interdependence of species, food chains, and habitats, which they then read about in expository form in their science textbooks. Other excellent selections for this topic include Monica Hughes's (1993) *Invitation to the Game*, Mack McDevitt's (1995) *Engines of God*, and Karen Hesse's (1995) *Phoenix Rising*.

Go to Web Resources for Chapter 8 at *http://www. prenhall.com/brozo*, and look for Multiple Texts.

Mathematics
Tenth-grade students were introduced to the study of geometry by reading and exploring Doris Schattschneider's (1990) *Visions of Symmetry: Notebooks, Periodic Drawings, and Related Works of M. C. Escher*. The repetitive patterns in Escher's drawings provided students with excellent models for creating their own repetitive

Teacher as Learner

ASSIGNING COOPERATIVE LEARNING ROLES FOR CONTENT LEARNING

For cooperative groups to function effectively, it is very important to assign roles to students that are unambiguous and contribute positively to the whole group. Debbie created roles for her students that achieved these goals; however, equally effective groups can be formed with alternative roles and assignments. The key is that each individual member makes a contribution that relates to the purpose of the group work and improves the performance of the group overall.

Think about possible roles for individual students in cooperative groups with the following purpose, then list and briefly describe them:

Purpose: Students in math are to find a Web site that explains how to construct a sturdy, weight-bearing house of cards; follow the directions to build one; document the results; and explain the geometrical principles involved.

Role 1: _____

Role 2: _____

Role 3: _____

Role 4: _____

Role 5: _____

Now identify a typical purpose of cooperative learning in your own classroom and list possible roles:

Purpose: _____

_____

_____

Role 1: _____

Role 2: _____

Role 3: _____

Role 4: _____

Role 5: _____

designs. Students read about Escher's descriptions of his drawings—"regular division of the plane." Then they were given the opportunity to find examples of a variety of regular geometric shapes in Escher's works. Students enjoyed finding parallelograms, rhombi, hexagons, rectangles, triangles, and squares in the artist's other-worldly illustrations. These patterns were found on floors, walls, pillars, and even some of Escher's creatures, which seem to grow out of geometric patterns. With these experiences, the 10th graders were much more enthusiastic about continuing their study of geometry.

Students in a senior math class were introduced to probabilities and inferential statistics with the book *Death Qualified: A Mystery of Chaos* (Wilhelm, 1991). Barbara Holloway quits her own law practice to help her father in a murder case. In so doing, she enters a new world of fractals, chaos theory, and computers necessary for developing the case for the modern attorney.

Other good books to use with middle- and upper-grade students in conjunction with math content include Joan Bauer's (1997) *Sticks* and Alan Ritchie's (1991) *Erin McEwan, Your Days Are Numbered*.

Physical Education

Before starting the softball season, a physical education teacher read aloud to his students the interesting sports novel *Striking Out* (Weaver, 1993). Billy Baggs, the central character in the story, possesses almost unbelievable pitching and hitting ability, yet his struggle to find himself and realize his potential while dealing with the hardships of family and farm life nearly cause him to lose everything. The teacher used this particular book because he wanted his students to develop realistic expectations for themselves as ball players and as teenagers. The novel allowed students to become aware of their own strengths inside and outside of sports.

Over the past decade or so, numerous quality fiction and nonfiction trade books for young adults with sports themes and sports characters have become available. For the middle grades and less-able high school reader there is *At the Plate with Mark McGwire* (Christopher, 1999), *Brett Favre* (Dougherty, 1999), *Kobe Bryant: Basketball Big Shot* (Savage, 2000), and *Muhammad Ali: Athlete, Activist, Ambassador* (Duplacey, 1999). Sports books with female protagonists and about women athletes are on the increase as well. Some of the best fictional narratives are *Goalie* (Shreve, 1999) and *Forward Pass* (Dygard, 1999). Information picture books in this same genre include *In These Girls, Hope Is a Muscle* (Blais, 1996), *Winning Ways: A Photohistory of American Women in Sports* (Macy, 1996), and *Venus to the Hoop* (Corbett, 1998).

A group of senior high students who had volunteered to be counselors for summer camp were asked to read *Downriver* (Hobbs, 1991) in their training class. In the book, four 15-year-old Outward Bound trainees, better known among themselves as "hoods in the woods," steal their guide's equipment and raft and attempt to take on the mighty Colorado River on their own. They learn about responsibility the hard way, with disastrous consequences. The seniors read and discussed the book each evening. Although they enjoyed the gripping adventure and the adolescent mischief, the book forced them to look seriously at their role as counselors and served as a focal point for discussions about behavioral problems and health emergencies.

English

In preparation for reading, studying, and doing dramatic interpretations of William Shakespeare's *Hamlet*, Vera had her 12th-grade students read Grant and Mandrake's (1990) comic book version of the play. Lavishly illustrated, this work remains faithful to the story and retains much of the original dialog and narration. Although Vera knew there is no substitute for the actual work, she nonetheless recognized the value of this illustrated comic book for introducing her students to the exciting world and remarkable ideas of *Hamlet*. In this way the book served as a bridge to the original, offering students a story with rich artwork and skillful expressions of Hamlet's anguish and torment.

To create an atmosphere of the late Renaissance as a context for the plays and poems of Shakespeare, Vera provided layered experiences (Nicholson, 2000) using multiple forms of representation, such as music, art, and dance. Students listened to

Comic books and graphic novels are ideal companions to plays, stories, and novels since they provide a visual context, which is especially helpful to striving readers.

The Role of the Teacher Leader

Reading coaches, reading specialists, and curriculum directors can play instrumental roles in supporting disciplinary teachers' efforts to expand text options for students. Given their knowledge of print and nonprint resources, they can point their teaching colleagues in profitable directions for locating books, Web sites, media, and music. They can offer professional development sessions to describe the teaching and learning potential of multiple sources and to deal with practical considerations. They can meet with faculty to discuss feasible ways of implementing practices with multiple texts. They can team up with content teachers to plan and teach lessons and units that infuse multiple sources. They can conduct demonstrations in the classroom of how particular sources might be used most advantageously. Finally, they can encourage and create opportunities for teachers to read and view materials to enrich disciplinary practices.

At the high school where Marco worked as a reading coach he brought the science faculty together to form an after-school club to read, view, and discuss materials that could be used in addition to the textbook. At each meeting, club members brought books, URLs, DVDs, music, or some other source for the others to consider. Depending on length, a film might be viewed in part or in its totality followed by critical dialog about the best ways to incorporate it into classroom instruction as well as the potential obstacles to doing so. Club members gave booktalks of young adult fiction and nonfiction then brainstormed how they might be utilized and with which science topics.

Marco made certain he had something to share at each meeting. For instance, in response to one of the teacher's complaints that many of the print sources discussed in the club were too difficult for her low-achieving students, Marco researched a number of Web sites and found several with simplified and graphic presentations of complex science topics. The club met in the library/media center for that session to access the sites, explore them, and talk about their feasibility. After maneuvering around one site, **www.chem4kids.com,** the teacher was pleasantly surprised by the variety of topics covered and the easy reading level of the texts. With the help of the others, the teacher generated several options for using chem4kids texts with her low-ability readers, including creating booklets with appealing covers and making these available during independent work time. Later, Marco was invited into the teacher's classroom to observe firsthand the success of this approach. He watched as three of the students who would formerly put their heads on the desk or engage in disruptive behavior during individual work time actually read the relevant booklets on the day's topic.

As a teacher leader, Marco was able to convince his colleagues of the value of forming the club and was the force that sustained the group throughout the year. The teachers agreed that what contributed most to their regular participation was the practical and supportive nature of the club. Marco made no demands, but enthusiastically encouraged his peers to give new sources a try and to talk openly about both triumphs and struggles.

compositions both formal and bawdy by Elizabethan-era composers. A couple of members of a troupe of reenactors she had met at the state Renaissance Fair visited the class and got students involved in music, dance, and impromptu drama activities. From various Web sites, Vera projected late Renaissance visual art on the screen and engaged the class in discussion concerning what these pieces could tell them about the attitudes and values of the time period.

Because you know which concepts and information students will eventually encounter, when choosing to read orally from multiple texts, you can easily highlight key passages by reading them with particular emphasis or by reading them again after cueing the students. When multiple sources are read independently or in small groups, you can alert students to these passages before reading. You can also use discussion and demonstrate context strategies for learning terminology that appears in the sources and will show up later in the textbook and as the content is studied more fully.

The principle benefit of using a variety of sources in disciplinary classes is that they elevate student interest (Shiveley & VanFossen, 2001). Texts such as primary documents, young adult literature, graphic novels, and the like engender immediate curiosity often because they are simply an alternative to textbooks. Curiosity can be channeled to motivate youth to read with greater purpose and listen with greater attention. Combining multiple sources with strategies to encourage active participation, including discussion and written responses after daily reading, will build important schemata for more in-depth study of the topic.

Use Multiple Sources to Extend Textbook Ideas

During reading, students can work in small groups to discuss particular issues raised in the textbook and elaborated on in other sources. Students can share what they have found to be particularly informative sections of these sources that support and extend what textbook authors say and what the teacher says. For instance, the teacher and class could read a section of the textbook and then search alternative materials for additional and supporting information, as occurred in the following classroom examples.

History

Eleventh-grade students studying 20th century history used the graphic novel *Persepolis: The Story of a Childhood* (Satrapi, 2004) in conjunction with the textbook to learn more about the rise of Islamic fundamentalism. In this autobiographical story, Satrapi recounts her childhood in Iran during the Islamic Revolution. Tracing the dethroning of the Shah, the rise of fundamentalism, and the war with Iraq through a child's eyes, *Persepolis* gave students an informative overview of Iranian history and culture while serving as a nice point of comparison and contrast for America's own revolutionary roots. As the teacher read the graphic novel, students were asked to listen for passages describing the revolution from the indigenous Iranian people's point of view, a perspective omitted in their textbook treatment.

Science

Kim's seventh-grade science textbook, though of fairly recent vintage, fails to keep pace with the dizzying speed of new developments in space exploration. To keep her students engaged, she supplements the textbook with graphic novels such as *Orbiter* (Ellis & Doran, 2004). In this novel, a space shuttle named *Orbiter* had disappeared 10 years earlier. Then, suddenly it mysteriously returns. The pilot, who hasn't aged a day, is speaking in a tongue no one understands. The authors' science fiction gives Kim's students plenty to ponder as they explore the scientific and cultural merit of manned spaceflight as well as the breathtaking look at the possibilities of the universe. Kim obtained multiple copies of *Orbiter* through a small science teacher grant and has her students work in small groups to read and document similarities and differences between the novel and information about space exploration in the science textbook.

Social Studies

Eighth graders learning about the Age of Exploration in the New World in their social studies textbooks also read in small groups Scott O'Dell's timeless trilogy *The Captive* (1979), *The Feathered Serpent* (1981), and *The Amethyst Ring* (1983), which chronicle the 16th-century world of the Maya, Aztec, and Inca empires, respectively. Information in the textbook was embellished with input from students about the events taking place in their novels. For example, students found passages that helped to explain how and why a mere handful of Spaniards were able to overtake three enormous empires. As we noted earlier, too often the driving human forces behind important historical events are not made clear in textbook accounts. In O'Dell's trilogy, however, the reader is brought face-to-face with the greed and religious zeal that drove many explorers and their followers to fanatical behavior.

Go to Web Resources for Chapter 8 at *http://www. prenhall.com/brozo*, and look for Comics in the Classroom.

Honoring Diversity and Building Competence in the Content Classroom

Gary, an experienced teacher of 14 years, teaches general biology in a high school set in an economically depressed area of an inner city. African Americans and Latinos/Latinas comprise nearly 90% of the student body. Because of the special concerns his students bring to his classroom, Gary has become a resourceful teacher who is constantly searching for new ways to make his instruction more responsive to the needs of his students.

His classroom is an inviting setting for young researchers and scientists. Next to his door in the hall is a large glassed-in display case that he and his students redo with each new 6-week grading period. During a unit on "food chains," for example, the display included the book *Never Cry Wolf* by Farley Mowat (1979), a collage in the shape of a wolf's head composed of pictures of animals that wolves prey upon, a pair of binoculars, and a field book with pencil. The walls of his room are laden with posters, charts, student work, and photographs of field trips Gary and his students have taken over the past few years to such interesting places as the Elk Repopulation Center in Great Smoky Mountains National Park, the Florida Everglades, and the North Carolina Outer Banks. Three large lab tables hold animal specimens in jars, Petri dishes, various artifacts from the natural world (e.g., rocks, grasses, mosses, snake skins, owl pellets, etc.), a large aquarium, and microscopes. Against one wall is a row of eight computers; against another are two large bookshelves—one filled with science-related paperbacks and magazines, the other holding reference and informational books.

Gary's C-Block class had 24 students. The topic for the day's lesson was "Population Crashes," which Gary had projected on a large screen in the front of the room from his computer. After employing a 10-minute PowerPoint presentation that defined and characterized causes and effects of population crashes in the natural world, Gary asked students to work in pairs to seek out as much evidence and as many examples as they could find of such population crashes using the print and nonprint resources available to them. Students were given a recording sheet to document their research.

Tremayne and Elton used a total of four different information sources. They began by thumbing back through the novel *Never Cry Wolf,* which the class had been reading, and wrote down information related to Mowat's description of what happens to the vole population when too many wolves are killed or relocated. They moved from the novel to the Internet and found a site devoted to problems related to overpopulation of humans. Elton remembered something he had seen in a magazine related to human overpopulation and went to the bookshelf, returning with a copy of *Smithsonian.* He and Tremayne looked through the article together and took notes. Finally, the two boys used one of the scientific reference books to look up information on Thomas Malthus—a person Gary mentioned in his presentation—for more leads about population crashes. There was a general biology textbook, but only a couple of students were consulting it for information.

Gary then passed out copies of *Never Cry Wolf* and organized a review of the last chapter read. The review was in a "popcorn" format whereby Gary gave the class the first critical event of the chapter, then waited for other students to stand up and supply a statement about what happened next. Using this approach, the class was able to cover most of the chapter plot within 5 minutes.

Gary then invited volunteers to come to the front of the class and take parts reading the next chapter aloud. In this chapter, a bush pilot and a party of hunters make camp near to where Farley is conducting his research of the wolf pack. He and the hunters have a threatening encounter. Gary took the role of narrator while the others read parts for Farley and members of the hunting party. Students seemed eager to participate and after a couple of pages a new set of students came to the front of the class to continue the read-aloud. Gary was patient with all students and waited until one asked for help with a word before he or a classmate provided it.

At several points in the action, Gary invited class members who were not reading aloud to ask questions of the students who were. This seemed to keep everyone focused on the plot. Student questions were mostly verbatim level. Gary welcomed all of them, however, while modeling higher-level thinking questions.

Gary has a strong desire to help his students develop independent learning skills, so he always includes opportunities for them to explore topics on their own. Gary allows his students to use other resources than the textbook, because, as he says, "That's what researchers do." When information is needed in his classroom, students are used to going to whatever sources are available. Gary knows the textbook is written at a level that's too difficult for many of his students, so he doesn't rely on it. By allowing his class to read about class topics from sources that may be easier for them, they tend to stay on task.

Gary uses novels because he wants his students to be interested in science. He recognizes that if the only way they received science were through a textbook, they would never want to explore science further or become scientists themselves. He is also sensitive to the fact that his students are generally poor readers and the only way they'll get any better is if they get time to read in school. In addition to Farley Mowat's book, Gary read aloud to his class *An American Plague: The True and Terrifying Story of the Yellow Fever Epidemic of 1793* (Murphy, 2004) when studying the role of cells in infectious disease and *The Radioactive Boy Scout : The Frightening True Story of a Whiz Kid and His Homemade Nuclear Reactor* (Silverstein, 2005) when covering a unit on nuclear waste and the environment.

English

Earlier in this chapter, we alluded to a middle school teacher who exploited students' interest in fanfiction (Alvermann & Hagood, 2000) to elevate motivation for writing and increase understanding of story structure. Importing adolescents' personal literacies into classrooms requires a deft hand so that these preferred texts are not stripped of their enjoyment for youth. We need to bear in mind that youth pursue certain literary practices for the simple reason that they are not sanctioned inside of school. Nevertheless, in the hands of caring and knowledgeable teachers, personal and academic literacies can be successfully conjoined.

Kim's seventh-grade English classes had several students who were reading, viewing, and engaging in electronic discussions about anime, Japanese animated comics and video. Kim learned of their interest in anime early in the school year after students shared through My Bag activities (See Chapters 4 and 5). Always on the lookout for ways of tying students' personal interests to school-based activities,

Go to Web Resources for Chapter 8 at *http://www.prenhall.com/brozo*, and look for Anime.

Kim decided to establish a lunchtime club for devotees of anime-related fanfiction. Because some who were interested in anime were in need of improvement in academic literacy, Kim hoped the club would serve as a vehicle for critical reading and creative writing.

One of the anime series the club members wanted to read and write about was *Ranma* $\frac{1}{2}$, created by Takahashi Rumiko-sama (2003). Ranma, when on a training excursion in China, fell into a spring where a girl had drowned and was transformed into a girl. Now every time Ranma splashes cold water on his face he turns into a red-haired girl. Hot water reverses the transformation. So, within the various adventures Ranma experiences, Ranma is sometimes a girl and sometimes a boy. Ranma lives in "Tendo Dojo" with his father and two sisters. Other characters include Akane, handpicked by her father and Ranma's father to be Ranma's wife, and Dr. Tofu.

Club members read from a *Ranma* $\frac{1}{2}$ series comic, talked about the action, and wrote and exchanged episodes related to Ranma. Kim was careful not to turn the club into a substitute for English class, but subtly encouraged students to consider such things as how the *Ranma* $\frac{1}{2}$ anime compared and contrasted with stories from their literature anthology and ways their writing might resemble narrative forms they discussed in class.

Gayle and Toni, two club members who were struggling in Kim's English class, liked to work together to write and illustrate their own *Ranma* $\frac{1}{2}$–inspired comic that featured Nabiki, Ranma's eldest sister. Her character is presented as extremely smart and cunning. She has also turned her interest in taking pictures into a cottage industry, though Nabiki shows her greedy side when bargaining with customers. Gayle did all the artistic work while Toni wrote the text for their episodes of Nabiki. In one, they had her capture Ranma and force him to pose for her camera while cold and hot water are applied to either side of his face, creating a half-boy/half-girl image. Nabiki then sold these unique prints for many thousand yen.

With this particular fanfiction, Kim was able to draw club members into discussion about important narrative elements, such as protagonist, antagonist, conflict, resolution, and theme. And as students like Gayle and Toni felt more confident in their ability to compose a story with essential features, they showed improvement in understanding stories in the literature anthology.

In senior English, Jamal made space in his class for the music his urban students loved—hip-hop. In a unique unit designed to promote an appreciation for the currency of canonical texts in literature, Jamal asked his students to make linkages between the poems and stories they were required to read and hip-hop lyrics they listened to everyday.

Messages in the song and rap lyrics youth listen to daily can provide the background knowledge needed to understand characters and themes in academic texts.

Several pairs of students were formed and given two texts to interpret and analyze. Critical in the analysis were the ways in which the texts shared common themes. Students were given a week to work on the assignment and then make a presentation to the class. Carla and Jarrod were assigned the T. S. Eliot poem "The Wasteland" and Grand Master Flash's "The Message." As they read and reread these texts, important themes began to emerge for them. For instance, they realized that the authors were looking out on their worlds and seeing signs all around of decay and decline; both pieces were apocalyptic visions of death and disease, and both positioned the poet as a messenger or prophet. Jamal knew these kinds of critical and deep connections were made possible by youth who had an affinity with the lived experience of the hip-hop artist and then used this empathy to appreciate other voices with similar messages from disparate cultures and times.

Environmental Science

Every year during Mahmood's unit on hurricanes he connects his ninth graders to primary sources for information and data on the most recent storms to make landfall along our U.S. coasts. Some years yield few significant storms of that type, whereas others have been so cataclysmic they demand extensive study to understand fully their impact on the environment. Such was the case with Hurricane Katrina, in 2005, which transformed the city of New Orleans and surrounding coastal communities into uninhabitable disaster areas.

Mahmood first identifies key topics in the unit using the textbook and science standards then guides his students to helpful Web sites to learn more about these topics. The National Hurricane Center (**http://www.nhc.noaa.gov/**) is one sight he often directs students to for its invaluable maps, data sets, and extensive records of tropical storm activity. For learning more about Katrina, he included URLs with multimedia news clips of on-the-scene reporters and meteorologists; blog sites by those who experienced the hurricane from inside the Louisiana Superdome and then the evacuation ordeal, and New Orleans and Biloxi, Mississippi, newspaper weather reports leading up to the storm's arrival.

Mahmood had his students consult the alternative sources for specific information on Hurricane Katrina after encountering important general information about hurricanes in the textbook. For example, students read in their textbooks about the storm-tracking system of the National Oceanic and Atmospheric Administration (NOAA) then went to the National Hurricane Center site for actual tracking charts of Hurricane Katrina. After studying a chart presented in their textbook with hurricane storm categories, ranked from one to five, and the potential damage each one can cause, Mahmood's students looked at video clips and read news reports of the actual destruction caused by Katrina and read descriptions from bloggers of witnesses to the storm to better appreciate its effects on human lives.

Algebra

During Kim's unit on functions in her advanced algebra class she directed students to some real estate Web sites to apply their new understandings. The sites list a variety of homes for sale in the community with information about the house, a floor plan with room dimensions, and sales price. Students are to determine a functional relationship between a house's floor plan area and its cost. Kim puts students into groups of three and assigns them various questions and problems, such as:

- What function best describes this relationship?
- What other factors affect the sales price of a house?
- What comparisons and conclusions can you make about the additional data that describe the houses?
- Based on your analysis, what should be the current sales price for a fantasy house your group designs (be clear about floor plan, room dimensions, etc.)

Throughout the unit, Kim provides time for groups to meet, access the Web sites, and discuss data gathering and analysis. She asks groups to present what they're learning to the class. They are expected to explain the reasoning, criteria, procedures, and data analyses when presenting their results. Kim points out differences in the groups' functions and encourages questions and challenges over which function best models the relationship.

Go to Web Resources for Chapter 8 at *http://www. prenhall.com/brozo*, and look for The Role of Text in Classroom Learning.

Music

Nina, a 12th-grade music teacher, asked her orchestral class to read *Lohengrin* as they prepared for a performance of the overtures that accompany Wagner's enchanting opera. Much more than a libretto, *Lohengrin*, written by the composer, resembles a novella. Because of its length, the story of *Lohengrin* is well developed and character descriptions are rich. These features make the book ideally suited to instruction in musical interpretation. As the young musicians read the book, they also worked on the music. Cooperative groups were formed on the basis of orchestral sections (strings, woodwinds, percussion instruments, etc.). During each class session, groups were responsible for reflecting on the story, discussing plot and character, and then, based on story interpretations, presenting possible musical interpretations. After whole-class discussions and teacher input, the student musicians attempted to operationalize their interpretations in rehearsals.

Terrence used reading and writing in his music composition class. Every week his inner-city students gathered newspapers and used the headlines for inspiration in their composing. In another example, his class read a book about musical instrument makers of medieval times. The book was filled with illustrations of instruments, some rather exotic, that have long since vanished. The author explained how some contemporary craftspersons were attempting to recreate these extinct instruments. This book inspired the class to create their own instruments. Using junk from garages, closets, attics, and alleys piled in the classroom, students fashioned horns, drums, and stringed instruments. With this motley assemblage, they wrote and performed an original composition. The female students were complaining that they were reading about and hearing compositions only by male composers. Terrence acquired information on and addresses of several contemporary female classical music composers, and his students wrote letters to them. A couple of them wrote back, sending samples of their work on tape and CDs, along with sample scores. The class performed a composition given to them by one of the women and allowed her to listen and watch via a telecommunications hookup.

Terrence keeps several excellent books for adolescents with opera and oratorio themes in his class library. Among them are such picture books as *The Voice That Challenged a Nation: Marian Anderson and the Struggle for Equal Rights* (Freedman, 2005), *Aida* (Price, 1990), *Turandot* (Mayer, 1995), and *Messiah: The Wordbook for the Oratorio* (Handel, Illus. Moser, 1992). Other picture books with classical music themes in Terrence's classroom collection are *Mozart Tonight* (Downing, 1991), *Wolfer: The First Six Years in the Life of Wolfgang Amadeus Mozart* (Weil, 1991), *Ludwig van Beethoven* (Thompson, 1990), *Sleeping Beauty: The Story of the Ballet* (Horosko, 1994), and *Tchaikovsky Discovers America* (Kalman, 1995).

To bring middle and high school students to a better appreciation of jazz and blues music, Terrence also has on his bookshelves *Blind Boone: Piano Prodigy* (Harrah, 2003), *Hip Cat* (London, 1996), *Jazz: My Music, My People* (Monceaux, 1994), and *Satchmo's Blues* (Schroeder, 1996).

Finally, Terrence has made sure to have on hand contemporary books with music themes for students' leisure reading. Among the titles he makes available to his classes are some of the best novels written for today's music-loving youth, including *Fat Kid Rules the World* (Going, 2004), *Tribute to Another Dead Rock Star* (Powell, 1999), *Drive* (Wieler, 2001), *Do Angels Sing the Blues?* (LeMieux, 1999), *The Maestro* (Wynne-Jones, 1996), and *The Rose That Grew from Concrete* (Shakur, 1999).

The volume and variety of young adult books available to the disciplinary teacher today make this text source a readily available addition to any topic of study.

English

Jasmina takes every opportunity to bring real-world reading materials into the classroom so that, through interesting and meaningful activities, her students come to understand how reading needs to be a part of their adult lives. Newspapers, magazines, and various other print sources found in the adult world are used in her daily classroom instruction and made available in the classroom library or reading corner.

A prime example of integrating everyday reading materials into classroom instruction occurred when Jasmina was helping her students understand metaphors. The class grammar book, while a useful reference source, fails to demonstrate authentic applications of rules and form that youth encounter daily. She knew that metaphors are found everywhere—in newspapers, in headlines, advertisements, editorials, and even weather forecasts. Because newspapers are inexpensive, easy to obtain, and contain articles that are generally short and concise, they are an excellent source for figurative language instruction.

Jasmina began by distributing to small groups of students headlines that used metaphorical language, such as "Still Limping, Oil Patch Exits Intensive Care" and "Experts Zero in on Magic Bullet to Kill Cancer Cells." Using a reciprocal teaching strategy (explained in Chapter 3), she modeled a question-asking and question-answering process out loud to demonstrate for students how she interpreted the metaphors in the headlines. For instance, with the first headline, she began by asking "What is an Oil Patch?" Then she dug into the article until she found information that helped her answer the question. The Oil Patch is a group of four states whose net worth and economic stability depend heavily on the production and sale of oil—namely, Louisiana, Oklahoma, Colorado, and Texas.

The next question Jasmina asked was, "In what way could four oil-producing states exit intensive care?" She pointed out that the statement clearly made no sense if interpreted literally, which, by default, made it a metaphor. This question led immediately to her next question, "Who would normally exit, 'limping,' from the intensive care ward?" Students were quick to respond by identifying a sick or injured person who is getting better but is basically still ill or injured. In this way students began to see the similarities between the Oil Patch and a patient just released from intensive care.

At this point, Jasmina asked students working in their groups to come up with an explanation of the metaphor. Most were able to explain that the oil-producing states were in trouble but were in far better financial shape than they were a few years ago, just as the hospitalized person who limps out of intensive care is still in trouble but in better physical condition than not long before.

Jasmina went on to engage students in a discussion of why the author chose to use a metaphorical headline in the first place. To make the article more attractive and "catchy" was one explanation. Another was that the author was "teasing" readers to entice them to read the article. The teacher pointed out that by linking the troubled economies of distant states with something familiar—hospitals, illness—the author was trying to make his subject accessible to more readers.

History

For the study of colonial America and the American Revolution, Angela selected the following teaching goals for her students: (a) to broaden their awareness of what everyday life was like in colonial America from different perspectives, (b) to help them appreciate the diversity of attitudes colonists' had toward the war, and (c) to sensitize them to the tragic consequences war brings its participants. To accomplish these goals, Angela introduced her students to several sources, in addition to the textbook, she found with the help of her school librarian. These sources and descriptions are shown in Figure 8.6.

While students had access to these wonderful sources for study and research, Angela chose to read aloud the young adult book, *My Brother Sam Is Dead* (Collier & Collier, 1974). As students read chapters in their textbook and the various other texts and listened to the trade book, they responded to process guides (discussed in Chapter 3) that were designed to help them see connections across sources, apply their new learning beyond the parameters of the unit, and involve them in dynamic class discussions. In the first guide, (Figure 8.7), students were asked to make inferences about the attitudes of story characters. In this way, students were helped

Figure 8.6 Alternative Texts for a Unit on Colonial America

Terrill, E. T. (2003, November). Did you know?: Various prominent women in early colonial America. *Cobblestone, 24*(8), 24–25. This magazine article describes women of the 17th century who dared to challenge the tradition of early colonial America. The article takes the perspective of a woman and is accompanied by photos of various women in colonial attire. Each of the women described endured hardships during an era when women were not able to voice their opinions.

The TimePage. (2003). *13 originals: Founding the American colonies.* Retrieved June 21, 2005, from http://www.timepage.org/spl/13colony.html#mass. This Web site from TimePage provides information about America's original 13 colonies. Each colony has a brief description and provides links to supplementary history, maps, photos, and important archival information.

Collier, J. L., & Collier, C. (1974). *My brother Sam Is dead.* New York: Scholastic. In this young adult novel, readers learn about the hardships and realities of the Revolutionary War as told by Tim Meeker, a young boy who watches his loyalist father be killed by bandits and his brother Sam, unjustly accused of stealing by his comrades in the colonial army, hanged.

Romero, R. (1997, July 6). Origins and practice of July 4 celebration. *La Prensa,* p. A1. This newspaper article is written from the perspective of a nonstandard English speaker and a non-White-European background. The Hispanic author reviews the colonists' perception of Great Britain and the reasons for coming to America. This background knowledge is used to develop the definition of *freedom,* as it relates to the Fourth of July. Romero helps readers understand the importance of American freedom for all people, not just for one specific group of people.

Mohawk, J. (2003, December 3). Thanksgiving serves up some "old time religion." *Indian Country Today,* p. A5. This newspaper article is written from the perspective of a Native American. Although Americans have been celebrating Thanksgiving for many years, most people do not know the true origin of the First Thanksgiving. This newspaper article from *Indian Country Today* explains how the Home Harvest (English) and one of six ceremonials of thanksgiving (agricultural Indians) created a joint celebration in what is now called the First Thanksgiving.

Loewen, J. W. (1995). *Lies my teacher told me: Everything your American history textbook got wrong.* New York: Touchstone. This nonfiction book is a result of American history textbooks that are unable to make history interesting or memorable. Textbooks tend to omit most of the ambiguity, passion, conflict, and drama from the past. This book puts the truth back into history. The First Thanksgiving and the meaning of the word *settle* are defined.

Levy, E. (2002). *America's funny but true history 1560s–1740s: Cranky colonials.* New York: Scholastic Inc. This comic book features real and factual, yet funny, history about the American colonies. In-depth facts cover the reasons Europeans came to America and why they decided to stay in America. In addition, the perspective of the Native Americans is taken into account as they were already living in America. This comic book specifies ways the Native Americans survived the unruly Europeans.

to understand the various points of view on the war. With another process guide, (Figure 8.8), students were asked to consider the human elements of war—so poignantly brought out in the trade book—by reminding them that the problems and conflicts the revolutionists faced are still real today where other wars are being waged.

Go to Web Resources for Chapter 8 at *http://www. prenhall.com/brozo*, and look for Immigration.

In a study of immigrants to the United States in the early 20th century, Tom read aloud to his juniors from the award-winning book *Letters from Rifka* (Hesse, 1992). Rifka and her Jewish family flee Russia in 1919 to avoid Russian soldiers and a pogrom. Her dream of finding a new, safe world is finally realized when the family arrives in America. Rifka records her journey in her treasured volume of Pushkin poetry, bringing the reader intimately close to her ordeal: humiliating examinations by doctors and soldiers; deadly typhus; separation from family, friends, and homeland; deadly ocean storms; detainment on Ellis Island; and the loss of her beautiful golden hair.

While studying the details and facts of immigration in their textbooks, students in Tom's class were discovering the human drama of immigration through the words

Figure 8.7 Process Guide for *My Brother Sam Is Dead*

Directions: Listed across the page are 9 events or statements from *My Brother Sam Is Dead*. Listed down the left side are the names of characters involved in the story plot. In each box indicate whether that character would agree or disagree with the words stated above. Use the symbols in the key below. You must make some inferences to answer the questions. Be prepared to support your answers with examples from the book.

Key: **A** = Agree **D** = Disagree **X** = Doesn't apply **?** = Not enough info	Children should respect and obey their parents.	Battles of Lexington and Concord.	Men should be free to govern themselves.	Render unto Caesar the things that are Caesar's.	I'm an Englishman but have more say in government as a colonist.	The end justifies the means.	I'm interested in making a living but not in fighting a war.	I'm just against wars.	Declaration of Independence.
Sam Meeker, rebel soldier									
Mr. Meeker, Sam's father									
Mrs. Meeker, Sam's mother									
Tim Meeker, Sam's brother									
Mr. Beacher, minister									
Betsy Read, Sam's girlfriend									
Col. Read, Betsy's father									
Mr. Heron, Meekers' neighbor									
General Putnam									
Captain Betts									

Figure 8.8 Process Guide for *My Brother Sam Is Dead*

"Principle, Sam? You may know principle, Sam, but I know war. Have you ever seen a dear friend lying in the grass with the top of his skull off and his brains sliding out like wet oats? Have you ever looked into the eyes of a man with his throat cut and the blood pouring out between his fingers, knowing that there was nothing you could do, in five minutes he would be dead, yet still trying to beg for grace and not being able because his windpipe was cut in two? Have you ever heard a man shriek when he felt a bayonet go through the middle of his back? I have, Sam, I have. I was at Louisbourg the year before you were born. Oh, it was a great victory. They celebrated it with bonfires all over the colonies. And I carried my best friend's body back to his mother—sewed up in a sack."

Both men had their own principles. Think about what your principles might be about war and the exercise of our freedoms. Immense human sacrifice was made by both sides during the American Revolution. Thomas Paine, a patriot, wrote, "The cause of America is in a great measure the cause of all mankind." What do you think he means by this? Was there another way besides war to achieve the same end? "Could the United States have made its way without all that agony and killing?" ask James and Christopher Collier.

Part I. Pretend you are a United States senator. Indicate whether you would vote yes or no on the suggested imaginary bills on the floor of the United States Senate. Give your reason.

U.S. Senate bill, proposed   *Reason*

_____ The U.S. government should pull out
of the war in Iraq.
_____ The U.S. government should cut spending on
nuclear arms.
_____ The U.S. government should create a fund to
give aid to other countries' rebels or patriots.

Write a bill of your own to be voted on.

in Rifka's diary. Tom had his students trace Rifka's journey on a map of Europe and the United States. Students compared immigration procedures on Ellis Island, as discussed in the textbook, with Rifka's experiences. With so many of his students being recent immigrants themselves, Tom had them recreate their own experiences in the form of a diary or personal travelogue modeled after Rifka's. Students were given regular opportunities to read entries from their diaries to the class.

Mathematics

> Even topics in mathematics can be enriched with numerous young adult books. These books breathe life into the study of facts and figures and increase youths' interest and motivation to learn.

Lori had been struggling to help her geometry students expand their perceptions of geometry and look for real-life parallels to geometric terms, postulates, and theorems. Her efforts accomplished little until she boldly decided to have her class read and discuss novels. She began her search for appropriate literature with some incredulity, but with the help of a local reference librarian she soon discovered several books that appeared ideally suited to teaching geometry, including Abbot's (1884; 1927) *Flatland*, Hinton's (1907) *An Episode in Flatland*, and Dewdney's (1984) *The Planiverse*. She finally chose *Flatland*, a 19th-century British novel of science fiction, as an important tool in trying to humanize students' understanding of geometry.

In *Flatland*, all of the characters are two-dimensional geometric figures that represent different social classes. The first part is essentially a social satire. In the second part, the main character travels to other dimensions to describe the relative merits of different points of view. *Flatland* can be read for its straight geometric descriptions as well as for its social commentary and satire.

Lori found that *Flatland* could be incorporated into her geometry course without ignoring any of the basic material. She tied the book to a unit in the textbook dealing with geometric models of the universe. Class discussion centered on the basic plot: its purpose and social context; details of Flatland, other lands, and their inhabitants; and the story's use of symbolism. In small groups, students were asked to brainstorm solutions to problems in Flatland (not explained by the author) such as rain and snow patterns, locomotion, food, and writing. Then the whole class compared their solutions. As a writing activity, students were asked to select a known person and tell which Flatland class (geometric figure) he or she would be in and why.

Lori's geometry unit was very well received. Many students asked that more novels be used in the class. Lori found her efforts worthwhile because she was able to get to know her students better—how they thought and felt—as a result of the many opportunities to interact during the unit. She also accomplished her goal of humanizing the learning of geometry.

In Latife's physics class, she read aloud during the first grading period *The Uncertainty Principle* (Sommers, 1990). The central character in the story, Kathy, quits the cheerleading squad and takes physics instead. To the dismay of all the boys in class, she excels. For the first time in her life she feels a genuine challenge and begins to dream and plan for a future as a physicist. There are obstacles, of course, among them Kathy's father, who can't accept the idea of sending his daughter to Cal Tech. Latife used this book as a prod, especially for the girls in class, to keep up the work and effort and to accept problems in physics as challenges to be met and overcome.

French

To help a group of first-year students develop an appreciation for the similarities and differences in French and American cultures, Faith had her students read *Mystery of the Metro* (Howard, 1987). In this story, a 16-year-old American girl finds herself alone in France and is forced to deal with all of the challenges of getting by in a foreign country. The story also has a tinge of mystery that makes it even more engaging. As students read the book, Faith had them compare the French styles of eating, transportation, and other customs with the American way of life. Students were also required to research a particular aspect of French culture that presented the main character in the book with problems and report back to the class.

Current Events

Glen's senior class was focusing on the former system of apartheid in South Africa. Resources for the unit included government and United Nations reports, essays by Nelson Mandela, music lyrics by Black South African folk songwriters, and three young adult books. One was the beautifully photographed *Mandela: An Illustrated Autobiography* (Mandela, 1996) accompanied by text that contains an extraordinary amount of detail about his personal life and the history and politics of anti-apartheid. The others were two masterful novels written by Norman Silver. *No Tigers in Africa* (Silver, 1990) tells the story of Selwyn Lewis and his White, racist upbringing in Cape Town, South Africa. When his family moves to England, however, Selwyn's new experiences force him to confront his racism and look within himself to find moral solutions to prejudice. In *An Eye for Color* (Silver, 1991), Basil Kushenovitz narrates interconnecting stories about growing up White and Jewish in Cape Town. About his ambivalent position in a racist culture, Basil says that, like a lizard, "My one eye sees one thing, and my other eye sees something quite different." Basil must try to reconcile his split vision—between his comforts and others' deprivation, between what is expected of a White man and what he himself is willing to become. Glen's goal in having his students read both of Silver's honest and painful novels was to rivet them to the compelling human stories of apartheid, making it possible for them to understand that racist systems leave victims on both sides of the color/culture fence.

Science

Gordy found the ideal novel to use in conjunction with his 10th-grade general biology students' study of molecular processes of life. *The Children Star* (Slonozewski, 1999) features mind-bending genetic engineering of circular and tire-shaped creatures that have evolved triple DNA and exotic amino acids. The sinister side to the plot is that these bizarre life forms plan to overrun a race of humans. Gordy read the novel aloud to his class and exploited it both for its interesting and scientifically sound information about genetics and for its more challenging theme of the dangers of uncontrolled and unregulated manipulation of the genetic code. His students were required to keep a notebook of information gleaned from the novel that related to the biology textbook's treatment of the same topic. Gordy also had his class confront ethical issues of genetic engineering through debates and role-plays.

An eighth-grade teacher captured her students' attention and enthusiasm for learning by using the illustrated informational book *Looking Inside Sports Aerodynamics* (Schultz, 1992a). Filled with outstanding sports figures, from Michael Jordan in basketball to Monica Seles in tennis, this colorful, enjoyable book deals with unseen forces that affect objects in motion. By combining sports and science, the teacher found that students learned the facts of aerodynamics and understood the principles more thoroughly than when the textbook was the sole resource.

In another classroom, Gail taught a unit on the consequences of science and technology through the use of science fiction. Her goal was to promote problem-solving skills and help students clarify values regarding scientific technology. Knowing that science fiction can motivate students to take a greater interest in science (Schmidt, 1996), Gail used *Star Trek: The Next Generation* (Bornholt, 1989) to instigate discussion on controversial issues associated with cloning. In the story, members of the *Enterprise* spaceship, while on a planet populated by original clone settlers, are asked to allow their own tissues to be used to spawn a new generation of clones to replace a line that is malfunctioning. The crew members refuse, but find that their tissues have been stolen while they were rendered unconscious. They return to the planet and destroy their clone look-alikes. The colony claimed that without the new clones they would die out in a few generations.

Given these story events, Gail posed the following question to her students and asked them to take a stand on a values continuum: Did the *Enterprise* crew members have the right to destroy the clones?

Pro-choice.	**Right-to-life**
Do not provide tissue for cloning	Provide tissue for cloning

First, students were asked to write their positions on their own. Then they went to the board and plotted their positions on the values continuum by writing their names along it. This was followed by small-group interaction to crystallize their positions and respond to those of others. The activity concluded with class discussion. Gail has found science fiction to be a rich resource for teaching science because it motivates students to become more active learners and thinkers.

Youth revel in controversies that are often dormant in the class textbook but are made evident to them in alternative sources.

Art

Many students who are not blessed with an artist's hands can learn something of how the artist sees the world through related young adult books (Hurst, 1995; Stover, 1988; Tallman, 1990; Whitin, 1996). Cal, a high school art teacher, began to recognize the connection between good books and art appreciation after reading sleuth books by Gash and Malcolm relating to crimes in the art world. This led him to investigate books for adolescents that would help students who struggle with drawing and painting assignments gain some insights into the way artists see the world and approach compositions. In his search he found several good books and began using them in his art classes. Among students' favorites are *A Single Shard* (Park, 2002), where young people learn about art while grappling with typical adolescent concerns; *Wake up Our Souls: A Celebration of African American Artists* (Bolden, 2005) and *Visions: Stories About Women Artists* (Sills, 1993), both recounting the lives and visions of women who share a commitment to art and creative imagination; and *Andy Warhol, Prince of Pop* (Greenberg & Jordan, 2004), which covers Warhol's childhood and art school years in Pittsburgh, his successful career in commercial art, and his rise in the Pop Art movement.

Cal has read these books aloud to his students, drawing their attention to their central theme: the artist's struggle to capture a vision. In addition, he has found that his students come to care deeply for the engaging characters, both fictional and real, who populate these books, thus learning things from them about artistic expression that Cal himself cannot teach.

Because art is visual, it makes sense to enrich the art class with young adult picture books that have painting and drawing themes. Cal has added to his school studio collection wonderfully illustrated books for his art classes, such as *Redoute: The Man Who Painted Flowers* (Croll, 1996), *A Blue Butterfly: A Story About Claude Monet* (LeTord, 1995), *Leonardo da Vinci* (Stanley, 1996), *Rosa Bonheur* (Turner, 1991), *Pish Posh, Said Hieronymous Bosch* (Willard, 1991), and *The Painter's Cat* (Wooding, 1994).

CASE STUDY REVISITED

Remember Linda, the history teacher? She was preparing a unit on "Immigration to the United States," and we asked you to think of trade book strategies that might be helpful to her as she developed activities for her students. Write your suggestions now.

Linda taught the unit by including a variety of print and visual sources to enliven and personalize the history textbook version. She chose texts and media for their quality representation of the immigrant experience. After an extensive search with the help of her school librarian, she decided to make use of the following sources in her unit: (a) a film about the experiences of immigrant teens today; (b) a nonfiction anthology of writers telling about their immigrant experiences as youth; (c) Web sites with a wealth of information on immigration; and (d) a variety of nonfiction books about American immigrants.

Linda launched the unit with a film entitled *Teens in Between: The Story of Five Immigrant Teens in America (Brodsky, 2002)*. Three female and two male teen immigrants attending Annandale High School in Virginia are featured in this

continued

Before writing your suggestions for Linda in the case study, go to *http://www.pren/hall.com/ brozo*, select Chapter 8, then click on Chapter Review Questions to check your understanding of the material.

film. The recent immigrant youth have similar adjustment issues such as learning a new language, adopting a U.S. teen culture, and balancing between their home and new culture. Yet, their adjustment priorities, strategies, and success levels vary depending on their language skills, family situations, preimmigration experiences, and individual characteristics. They came from Somalia, Egypt, Vietnam, and Honduras for various reasons—political freedom, educational benefits, or economic advancement. Instead of presenting a cookie-cutter portrayal of immigrant teenage struggles, Linda presented this film to her students so they could get an in-depth and realistic look of various immigration experiences for high school teenagers.

Based on the depictions of these four teens, Linda's students were to work from a list of Web sites to conduct Web quests. Web quests (Dodge, 2005) are focused searches designed to avoid endless Internet surfing and ensure students find quickly and efficiently Web-based source material for answering questions and conducting research. (See Chapter 10 for a more complete explanation of Web quests and detailed examples.) Once directed to the sites, students, in teams of three, were to find specific information about the recent history of the countries of origin for the teens in the film and use these data to help explain immigration patterns from these countries. Periodically, student teams were asked to report to the class on their information and analysis. Linda found the following four sites to be especially helpful for this activity:

- Hispanics in the United States: An Insight into Characteristic Groups: **http://www.omhrc.gov/haa/HAA2pg/AboutHAA1a.htm**
- Migration Information Source: **http://www.migrationinformation.org**
- Center for Immigration Studies: **http://www.cis.org/**
- AskAsia: **http://www.askasia.org/**

Throughout the unit Linda read aloud from an outstanding anthology borrowed from the librarian called *First Crossing: Stories About Teen Immigrants* (Gallo & Gallo, 2004). This nonfiction source is comprised of 11 well-known authors who describe the experiences of coming to America as youth. These heartfelt and authentic stories reveal the wide variety of circumstances surrounding individual immigrant experiences. For example, Pam Muñoz Ryan recounts in the book's title story, "First Crossing," the perils of a teen boy being smuggled across the Mexican border. Marie G. Lee's "The Rose of Sharon" tells of a spoiled girl's animosity toward her adoptive parents and her desire to return to Korea to find her birth family. In Jean Davies Okimoto's "My Favorite Chaperone," an immigrant from Kazakhstan shares her relationship with her conservative parents, who rely on her to translate for them but still limit her freedom. Collectively, the underlying theme of these stories is the tension the young people feel caused by the eagerness to cut off ties to the homeland while feeling the need to respect the traditions their parents cannot abandon. The stories from this collection Linda read aloud helped put a very real face on the broad-stroke treatment of immigration found in the history textbook.

To ensure active listening of these stories, Linda engaged students in prereading discussions designed to heighten anticipation and encourage predictions. Afterward, students were asked to write down in a learning log their reactions to what they heard each day: what they liked and did not like, the degree to which the authors' experiences were similar to their own or members of their family, and what overall impressions they had after listening.

As resources for independent research into students' own culture, Linda made available several nonfiction books on topics related to immigration. For example, Muslim students in her class had access to *Coming to America: A Muslim Family's Story* (Wolf, 2003). This big, brightly photographed book profiles Egyptian immigrants living in New York City. The father, Hassan, works nights and worries about not having enough time for his family. His wife, Soad, is a shut-in because of her lack of English. Their three children, however, have adapted to their new country well. Linda's students said the book seemed to be an accurate portrayal of life for new Muslim immigrants while showing a personal and realistic side and not the stereotypes.

Another excellent source, *Growing up Filipino: Stories for Young Adults* (Brainard, 2003), was read by Linda's Filipino students for the life histories of émigrés to the United States. There are more Filipinos living in the United States than most people realize, but finding literature reflective of their experiences is difficult, so Linda was pleased to uncover this source. And Asian American youth in her class had access to Susan Sinnott's (2003) *Extraordinary Asian Americans and Pacific Islanders.* This is a chronicling of the outstanding contributions to the arts, music, business, and government by newly immigrated and older-generation Asian and Pacific Islanders. The book also provides an overview of immigration to the United States and furnishes background information within which to measure the extraordinary accomplishments of these individuals. This resource is accompanied by black-and-white photographs.

Each group was responsible for making a daily oral report summarizing what had been read and learned from the information books. In this way, all students could gain essential content about the immigration experience for different major ethnic groups, especially in a post-9/11 world. As a whole class, students charted the problems each major group of immigrants has faced in American society and the ways in which society has sought to address and solve those problems. Linda's students did not affix blame to any one racial or ethnic group; rather, they recognized that they were all responsible for finding solutions.

Looking Back, Looking Forward

This chapter has been devoted to explaining and describing ideas and practices for teaching disciplinary content with sources in addition to the course textbook. First, we presented a theoretical rationale, specific recommendations, and practical considerations for integrating multiple text sources into the content-area classroom. We have shown that the practical use of a variety of alternative texts can be supported by theories of learning. These texts can help students build on past literacy successes, create interest and motivation, and develop schemata.

In this chapter we provided specific instructional recommendations for (1) developing a unit overview and identifying key themes and concepts within the unit topic, (2) choosing multiple sources to help teach concepts, and (3) teaching with textbooks and other texts. And consistent with the overarching theme of this book, we have presented numerous envisionments of possibilities for using a variety of engaging texts to teach disciplinary content, rather than oversimplified recipes for success.

The inclusion of multiple sources in disciplinary instruction is feasible and has produced elaborate processing of textual information and greater enthusiasm for learning. The probability of success with this approach is enhanced when teachers responsible for content-area subjects look for opportunities to integrate other sources with their textbooks and when the literacy support staff work with these teachers to help bring about such an integration. Moreover, using alternative texts in content classrooms should not be perceived as a device or gimmick to create interest in a topic on Monday that is forgotten by Friday. To use multiple sources alongside textbooks effectively, you need to make long-range plans, carefully considering how each unit's themes and salient concepts will be developed and how the alternative sources can be used to expand upon textbook concepts and information.

Quality texts, once in the hands of youth, will often sell themselves. The key is knowing the sources available for teaching unit themes and concepts. We recommend that you establish and maintain an independent reading program of young adult literature, graphic novels, and other related sources geared to the students and the disciplines you teach. We also strongly urge you to form close alliances with your school and local librarians. Their knowledge of and skills in uncovering print texts and representational media that coincide with the topics you teach will prove invaluable.

The content areas deal with interesting, vital information, but if you rely on textbooks as your sole teaching resource, you may render this information dry and lifeless. Use multiple text sources in conjunction with textbooks to help ensure that students are more actively involved in learning and that the vitality and spirit inherent in the content-area material are kept alive.

In the next chapter, you will discover several sound practices for supporting students in gathering and organizing information and ideas. These study strategies will make it possible for youth to become effective independent readers and learners. This is especially critical in disciplinary classrooms where students are expected to read and learn from multiple sources, classrooms, like those described in this chapter.

References

Alvermann, D., & Hagood, M. (2000). Fandom and critical media literacy. *Journal of Adolescent & Adult Literacy, 43*, 436–446.

Austin, P. (1998). Math books as literature: Which ones measure up? Use of trade books rather than textbooks in schools. *New Advocate, 11*, 119–133.

Baker, L., Afflerbach, P., & Reinking, D. (1995). *Developing engaged readers in school and home communities*. Mahwah, NJ: Lawrence Erlbaum Associates.

Barton, K. C. (2005). Teaching history: Primary sources in history: Breaking through the myths. *Phi Delta Kappan, 86*, 745–751.

Bean, T. (2000). Reading in the content areas: Social constructivist dimensions. In M. Kamil, P. Mosenthal, R. Barr, & P. D. Pearson (Eds.), *Handbook of Reading Research* (Vol. 3). Mahwah, NJ: Lawrence Erlbaum Associates.

Bean, T., Kile, R., & Readence, J. (1996). Using trade books to encourage critical thinking about citizenship in high school social studies. *Social Education, 60*, 227–230.

Bean, T. W., & Moni, K. (2003). Developing students' critical literacy: Exploring identity construction in young adult fiction. *Journal of Adolescent & Adult Literacy, 46*(8), 638—48.

Boyer, P., Clark, C., Kett, J., Salisbury, N., Sitkoff, H., & Woloch, N. (2004). *The enduring vision: A history of the American people* (5th ed.). Boston: Houghton Mifflin.

Brodsky, D. (Producer/Director). (2002). *Teens in Between: The Story of Five Immigrant Teens in America* [Motion picture]. Distributed MHz Networks.

Brown, J., Collins, A., & Duguid, P. (1989). Situated cognition and the culture of learning. *Educational Researcher, 18*, 32–42.

Burns, B. (1998). Changing the classroom climate with literature circles. *Journal of Adolescent & Adult Literacy, 42*, 124–129.

Bushman, J. H., & Haas, K. P. (2001). *Using young adult literature in the English classroom* (3rd ed.). Upper Saddle River, NJ: Merrill Prentice-Hall.

Chandler-Olcott, K., & Mahar, D. (2003). Adolescents' anime-inspired fanfictions: An exploration of multiliteracies. *Journal of Adolescent & Adult Literacy, 46*, 556–566.

Connor, J. J. (2003). "The textbooks never said anything about . . ." Adolescents respond to *The Middle Passage: White Ships/Black Cargo. Journal of Adolescent & Adult Literacy, 47*(3), 240–246.

Dodge, B. (2005). The Web quest page: San Diego State University. Retrieved September 10, 2005, from http://edweb.sdsu.edu/webquest/webquest.html.

Donelson, K., & Nilsen, A. (2004). *Literature for today's young adults* (7th ed.). New York: Allyn & Bacon.

Eisner, E. (1997). Cognition and representation: A way to pursue the American dream? *Phi Delta Kappan, 78*, 348–353.

Elbaum, B., Schumm, J., & Vaughn, S. (1997). Urban middle-elementary students' perceptions of grouping formats for reading instruction. *The Elementary School Journal, 97*, 475–499.

Elkassabany, A., Johnson, C., & Lucas, T. (2000). How do you incorporate history into the English curriculum? *English Journal, 89*, 26–30.

Galda, L., & Liang, L. A. (2003). Literature as experience or looking for facts: Stance in the classroom. *Reading Research Quarterly, 38*(2), 268–275.

Gallo, D., & Gallo, D. (2004). *First crossings: Stories about teen immigration.* Cambridge, MA: Candlewick Press.

George, M., & Stix, A. (2000). Using multilevel young adult literature in middle school American studies. *The Social Studies, 91*, 25–31.

Guthrie, J., & Wigfield, A. (2000). Engagement and motivation in reading. In M. Kamil, P. Mosenthal, R. Barr, & P. D. Pearson (Eds.), *Handbook of Reading Research* (Vol. 3). Mahwah, NJ: Lawrence Erlbaum Associates.

Hammer, L. (2000). The additive effects of semistructured classroom activities on student learning: An application of classroom-based experiential learning techniques. *Journal of Marketing Education, 22*, 25–34.

Hartman, D. (1995). Eight readers reading: Intertextual links of proficient readers reading multiple texts. *Reading Research Quarterly, 30*, 520–561.

Hartwell, D., & Cramer, K. (1994). *The ascent of wonder: The evolution of hard science fiction.* New York: TOR Books.

Hurst, C. (1995). Bringing art into the library. *Teaching Prek–8, 26*, 84–86.

Hynd, C. (1999). Teaching students to think critically using multiple texts in history. *Journal of Adolescent & Adult Literacy, 42*(6), 428–436.

Jacobi-Karna, K. (1995). Music and children's books. *The Reading Teacher, 49*, 264–270.

Jarman, R., & McClune, B. (2001). Use the news: A study of secondary teachers' use of newspapers in the science classroom. *Journal of Biological Education, 35*, 69–74.

Jarman, R., & McClune, B. (2003). Bringing newspaper reports into the classroom: Citizenship and science education. *School Science Review, 84*, 121–129.

Jenkins, H. (1992). *Textual poachers: Television fans and participatory culture.* New York: Routledge.

Jones, P. (2001). Nonfiction: The real stuff. *School Library Journal, 47*, 44–45.

Knabb, M. (2003). Rapping to review: A novel strategy to engage students and summarize course material. *Advances in Physiological Education, 27*, 157–159.

Krashen, S. (1993). *The power of reading.* Englewood, CA: Libraries Unlimited, Inc.

Larimer, R., & Schleicher, L. (1999). *New ways of using authentic materials in the classroom.* Washington, DC: TESOL.

Lawlor, J. M. (2003). My reward: Outstanding student projects based on primary sources. *Social Education, 67*, 405–410.

Lightsey, G. (1996). Using literature to build fifth grade math concepts. *Reading Horizons, 36*, 412–419.

Lombard, R. (1996). Using trade books to teach middle level social studies. *Social Education, 60*, 223–230.

Lott, C., & Wasta, S. (1999). Adding voice and perspective: Children's and young adult literature of the Civil War. *English Journal, 88*, 56–61.

McClune, B., & Jarman, R. (2000). Have I got news for you: Using newspapers in the secondary science classroom. *Media Education Journal, 28*, 10–16.

McDaniel, M., Waddill, P., & Finstad, K. (2000). The effects of text-based interest on attention and recall. *Journal of Educational Psychology, 92*, 492–502.

McMackin, M. (1998). Using narrative picture books to build expository text structure. *Reading Horizons, 39*, 7–20.

McPhail, J., Pierson, J., & Freeman, J. (2000). The role of interest in fostering sixth grade students' identities as competent learners. *Curriculum Inquiry, 30*, 43–70.

Miller-Hewes, K. (1994). Making the connection: Children's books and the visual arts. *School Arts, 94*, 32–38.

Morrell, E., & Duncan-Andrade, J. M. R. (2002). Promoting academic literacy with urban youth through engaging hip-hop culture. *English Journal, 91,* 88–92.

Mui, Y. Q. (2004, December 13). Schools turn to comics as trial balloon novel: Md. program uses genre to encourage reluctant readers. *Washington Post*, B01.

Newman, M. (2005). Rap as literacy: A genre analysis of hip-hop ciphers. *Interdisciplinary Journal for the Study of Discourse, 25*, 399–436.

Nicholson, D. W. (2000). Layers of experience: Forms of representation in a Waldorf school classroom. *Journal of Curriculum Studies, 32*, 575–587.

O'Brien, D., Stewart, R., & Moje, E. (1995). Why content literacy is difficult to infuse into the secondary school: Complexities of curriculum, pedagogy, and school culture. *Reading Research Quarterly, 30*, 442–463.

Pailliotet, A. W. (2003). Integrating media and popular-culture literacy with content reading. In R. C. Richards & M. C. McKenna (Eds.), *Integrating multiple Literacies in k–8 classrooms: Case commentaries and practical applications* (pp. 172–189). Mahwah, NJ: Lawrence Erlbaum.

Pappas, C., & Barry, A. (2001). Examining language to capture scientific understandings. *Science and Children, 38*, 26–29.

Pappas, C., Kiefer, B., & Levstik, L. (1999). *An integrated language perspective in the elementary school* (2nd ed). White Plains, NY: Longman.

Pennac, D. (1994). *Better than life*. Toronto: Coach House.

Royce, C., & Wiley, D. (1996). Children's literature and the teaching of science: Possibilities and cautions. *The Clearinghouse, 70*, 18–23.

Schwarz, G. E. (2002). Graphic novels for multiple literacies. *Journal of Adolescent & Adult Literacy, 46*, 262–265.

Schmidt, G. (1996). Of pulp, substance, and science fiction. *Children's Literature Association Quarterly, 21*, 45–60.

Shiveley, J. M., & VanFossen, P. J. (2001). *Using Internet primary sources to teach critical thinking skills in government, economics, and contemporary world issues*. Westport, CT: Greenwood Press.

Spencer, P. (1994). *What do young adults read next? A reader's guide to fiction for young adults*. Detroit: Gale Research.

Stover, L. (1988, September). What do you mean, we have to read a book for art class? *Art Education*, 8–13.

Sullivan, E. (2001). Some teens prefer the real thing: The case for young adult nonfiction. *English Journal, 90*, 43–47.

Tallman, S. (1990). Cultural literacy. *Arts, 64*, 17–18.

U.S. Department of Education. (2002). *National Assessment of Educational Progress (NAEP), 2001 U.S. history assessment*. Washington, DC: National Center for Education Statistics.

Wade, S. E., & Moje, E. B. (2001). The role of text in classroom learning: Beginning an online dialogue. *Reading online, 5*. Available online at http://www.readingonline.org/articles/ar_index.asp?HREF=/articles/handbook/wade/index.html.

Walker, N., & Bean, T. W. (2002, December). *Sociocultural influences in content area teachers' selection and use of multiple texts*. Paper presented at the 52nd annual National Reading Conference, Miami, FL.

Weiner, S. (2002). Beyond superheroes: Comics get serious. *Library Journal, 127*, 55–58.

Westcott, W., & Spell, J. (1999). Tearing down the wall: Literature and science. *English Journal, 89*, 70–76.

White, R. (2005). Comics in the classroom. Retrieved August 30, 2005, from http://learnnc.org/articles/print/comics0703.

Whitin, P. (1996). Exploring visual responses to literature. *Research in the Teaching of English, 30*, 114–140.

William, C. (2001). Does it really matter? Young people and popular music. *Popular Music, 20*, 223–242.

Young Adult Books and Graphic Novels

Abbot, E. (1927). *Flatland*. Boston: Little, Brown.

Asimov, I. (1966). *Fantastic voyage*. Boston: Houghton Mifflin.

Bauer, J. (1997). *Sticks*. New York: Bantam Books.

Beattie, O., & Geiger, J. (1992). *Buried in ice: The mystery of a lost Arctic expedition*. Toronto: Madison Press Books.

Blais, M. (1996). *In these girls, hope is a muscle*. New York: Warner Books.

Bolden, T. (2005). *Wake up our souls: A celebration of African American artists*. New York: Harry Abrams Inc.

Bornholt, J. (1989). *Star Trek: The next generation*. New York: Dell.

Brainard, C.M. (2003). *Growing up Filipino: Stories for young adults*. Minneapolis: Rebound by Sagebrush.

Campbell-Bartoletti, S. (2005). *Hitler youth: Growing up in Hitler's shadow*. New York: Scholastic.

Carr, F. W. (2003). *Germany's Black Holocaust*. Kearney, ME: Morris Publishing.

Christopher, M. (1999). *At the plate with Mark McGwire*. Boston: Little Brown.

Collier, J. L., & Collier, C. (1974). *My brother Sam is dead*. New York: Scholastic.

Corbett, S. (1998). *Venus to the hoop: A gold medal year in women's basketball*. New York: Anchor Books.

Croll, C. (1996). *Redoute: The man who painted flowers*. New York: Putnam.

Dewdney, A. K. (1984). *The planiverse*. New York: Poseidon Press.

Dougherty, T. (1999). *Brett Favre*. Brookshire, TX: ABDO Publishing Co.

Downing, J. (1991). *Mozart tonight*. New York: Simon & Schuster.

Duplacey, J. (1999). *Muhammad Ali: Athlete, activist, ambassador*. Warwick, CA: Woodside Publishing.

Dygard, T. (1999). *Forward pass*. Minneapolis, MN: Econo-Clad Books.

Edmonds, W. (1991). *The matchlock gun*. New York: Troll.

Ellis, W., & Doran, C. (2004). *Orbiter*. New York: Dc Comics.

Forbes, E. (1945). *Johnny Tremain*. Boston: Houghton Mifflin.

Freedman, K. (2005). *The voice that challenged a nation: Marian Anderson and the struggle for equal rights*. New York: Scholastic.

Going, K. L. (2004). *Fat kid rules the world*. New York: Putnam.

Grant, S., & Mandrake, T. (1990). *William Shakespeare's Hamlet*. New York: Berkley.

Greenberg, J., & Jordan, S. (2004). *Andy Warhol, prince of pop*. New York: Random House Children's Books.

Hampson, F. (2005). *Dan Dare pilot of the future: Marooned on Mercury*. Santa Monica, CA: Titan Books.

Handel, G. F. (1992). *Messiah: The wordbook for the oratorio*. New York: HarperCollins.

Harrah, M. (2003). *Blind Boone: Piano Prodigy*. Minneapolis, MN: Lerner Publishing.

Hesse, K. (1992). *Letters from Rifka*. New York: Henry Holt.

Hesse, K. (1995). *Phoenix rising*. New York: Puffin.

Hinton, C. H. (1907). *An episode in flatland*. London: Swan Sonnenschein.

Hobbs, W. (1991). *Downriver*. New York: Macmillan.

Horosko, M. (1994). *Sleeping beauty: The story of the ballet*. New York: Atheneum.

Howard, E. (1987). *Mystery of the metro*. New York: Random House.

Hughes, M. (1993). *Invitation to the game*. New York: Pocket Books.

Kalman, E. (1995). *Tchaikovsky discovers America*. New York: Scholastic.

Kanaly, M. (1998). *Virus clans*. New York: Ace Books.

Kerrod, R., & Sparrow, G. (2002). *The way the universe works*. New York: Dorling Kindersley Publishing.

Kress, N. (1996). *Beggar's ride*. New York: Tor Books.

LeMieux, A. C. (1999). *Do angels sing the blues?* Minneapolis, MN: Econo-Clad Books.

LeTord, B. (1995). *A blue butterfly: A story about Claude Monet*. New York: Doubleday.

Lipsyte, R. (1993). *The chemo kid*. New York: HarperCollins.

London, J. (1996). *Hip cat*. New York: Chronicle Books.

Macy, S. (1996). *Winning ways: A photohistory of American women in sports*. New York: Henry Holt.

Mandela, N. (1996). *Mandela: An illustrated autobiography*. Boston: Little Brown.

Mayer, M. (1995). *Turandot*. New York: Morrow Avon.

McDevitt, J. (1995). *Engines of God*. New York: Ace Books.

Monceaux, M. (1994). *Jazz: My music, my people*. New York: Alfred Knopf.

Moore, K. (1991). *Distant thunder: A sequel to the Christmas surprise*. Scottsdale, PA: Herald.

Mowat, F. (1979). *Never cry wolf*. New York: Bantam Books.

Murphy, J. (2004). *An American plague: The true and terrifying story of the yellow fever epidemic of 1793*. Boston: Houghton Mifflin.

O'Dell, S. (1979). *The captive*. Boston: Houghton Mifflin.

O'Dell, S. (1981). *The feathered serpent*. Boston: Houghton Mifflin.

O'Dell, S. (1983). *The amethyst ring*. Boston: Houghton Mifflin.

Oppel, K. (1993). *Dead water zone*. Boston: Little Brown.

Park, L. S. (2002). *A single shard*. New York: Scholastic.

Powell, R. (1999). *Tribute to another dead rock star*. New York: Farrar, Straus & Giroux.

Preston, R. (1995). *The hot zone*. New York: Doubleday.

Price, L. (1990). *Aida*. New York: Harcourt Children's Books.

Richter, H. P. (1970). *Friedrich*. New York: Holt, Rinehart & Winston.

Ritchie, A. (1991). *Erin McEwan, your days are numbered*. New York: Random House.

Satrapi, M. (2004). *Persepolis: The story of a childhood*. New York: Random House.

Savage, J. (2000). *Kobe Bryant: Basketball big shot*. Minneapolis, MN: Lerner Publishing Group.

Schattschneider, D. (1990). *Visions of symmetry: Notebooks, periodic drawings, and related works of M. C. Escher*. New York: W. H. Freeman.

Schroeder, A. (1996). *Satchmo's blues*. New York: Doubleday.

Schultz, R. (1992a). *Looking inside sports aerodynamics*. Santa Fe, NM: John Muir.

Schultz, R. (1992b). *Looking inside the brain*. Santa Fe, NM: John Muir.

Shakur, T. (1999). *The rose that grew from concrete*. New York: Simon & Schuster.

Shreve, S. (1999). *Goalie*. Minneapolis, MN: Econo-Clad Books.

Sills, L. (1993). *Visions: Stories about women artists*. Morton Grove, IL: Albert Whitman.

Silver, N. (1990). *No tigers in Africa*. New York: E. P. Dutton.

Silver, N. (1991). *An eye for color*. New York: E. P. Dutton.

Silverstein, K. (2005). *The radioactive boy scout: The frightening true story of a whiz kid and his homemade nuclear reactor*. New York: HarperCollins.

Sinnott, S. (2003). *Extraordinary Asian Americans and Pacific Islanders*. New York: Scholastic Library.

Slonozewski, J. (1999). *The children star*. New York: Tor Books.

Sommers, B. (1990). *The uncertainty principle*. New York: Fawcett.

Spiegelman, A. (1993). *Maus: A survivor's tale*. New York: Pantheon Books.

Stanley, D. (1996). *Leonardo da Vinci*. New York: Morrow.

Takahashi, R. (2003). *Ranma* ½ San Francisco, CA: VIZ Media, LLC.

Thompson, W. (1990). *Ludwig van Beethoven*. New York: Penguin.

Turner, R. M. (1991). *Rosa Bonheur*. Boston: Little Brown.

Weaver, W. (1993). *Striking out*. New York: HarperCollins.

Weil, L. (1991). *Wolfer: The first six years in the life of Wolfgang Amadeus Mozart*. New York: Holiday House.

Wieler, D. (2001). *Drive*. Toronto: Groundwood Books.

Wilhelm, K. (1991). *Death qualified: A mystery of chaos*. New York: St. Martin's Press.

Willard, N. (1991). *Pish posh, said Hieronymous Bosch*. New York: Harcourt Brace.

Wolf, B. (2003). *Coming to America: A Muslim family's story*. New York: Lee and Low.

Wooding, S. (1994). *The painter's cat*. New York: Putnam.

Woodson, J. (2002). *Hush*. New York: Putnam.

Wynne-Jones, T. (1996). *The maestro*. London, UK: Orchard Books.

chapter 9

Learning Strategies

Anticipation Guide

Directions: Read each statement carefully and decide whether you agree or disagree with it, placing a check mark in the appropriate *Before Reading* column. When you have finished reading and studying the chapter, return to the guide and decide whether your anticipations need to be changed by placing a check mark in the appropriate *After Reading* column.

	Before Reading		After Reading	
	Agree	*Disagree*	*Agree*	*Disagree*
1. Research has shown that there is a best strategy for studying.	_____	_____	_____	_____
2. Most adolescents reread and memorize as their method of studying and preparing for exams.	_____	_____	_____	_____
3. The gifted, AP, and college-bound students know how to study.	_____	_____	_____	_____
4. Many students struggle with clarifying what they know and what they do not know.	_____	_____	_____	_____

![Chapter Principle icon]

Chapter Principle: Gather and Organize Print and Nonprint Sources

The research literature has suggested rather consistently that successful independent learners are those who can gather and organize their sources in a task-appropriate and strategic manner (e.g., Zimmerman, 2002). In this chapter we invoke the fifth principle of this text by discussing some teacher-initiated and student-initiated strategies that will enhance students' cognitive and metacognitive processes while they read, solve problems, and study.

*A*s noted by Wilbur McKeachie, a respected expert in strategic learning, the major goal of education should be the development of students' strategies for lifelong learning and problem solving (McKeachie, Pintrich, Smith, & Lin, 1986). We wholeheartedly concur with McKeachie. That is, students should be taught how to become strategic, independent learners so they can thrive within our classrooms and beyond our classrooms. In order to become successful independent learners, students need a wide repertoire of strategies (Ruddell & Unrau, 2004; Simpson, Stahl, & Francis, 2004). At the basic level, *strategies* are the behaviors or actions that students use during learning to make sense out of their texts, monitor their understanding, and clarify what they do not understand. Students typically employ learning strategies when they need to retain material for the purpose of taking a test, writing a paper, participating in class discussion, or any other demonstration of their learning. In addition, students need more elaborative strategies that will help them cope with content-area tasks requiring higher levels of thinking such as when they are asked to organize, synthesize, and critique information from multiple sources.

We know from the research literature that students who use strategies that demand their critical thinking are more likely to do better on their assignments, exams, and papers (Grigg, Daane, Ying, & Campbell, 2003; Winne & Jamieson-Noel, 2002). We also know from numerous studies that many graduating seniors enter college lacking the more sophisticated learning strategies that will assist in their transition from high-school-level tasks to college-level tasks (Peverly, Brobst, Graham, & Shaw, 2003; Simpson & Nist, 2003). If these students, supposedly our best and brightest, are not equipped to be successful independent learners, then we can assume that most secondary-level students need our guidance and strategic instruction.

What, then, should be included in our strategic instruction? Although there is no one answer to that question, the research findings suggest that the strategies we teach students should embed a variety of cognitive and metacognitive processes (Cleary & Zimmerman, 2004; Paris & Paris, 2001; Weinstein, Dierking, Husman, Roska, & Powdrill, 2003; Zimmerman, 2002). These processes include students' abilities to:

1. Select and summarize important ideas
2. Reorganize and elaborate on these ideas
3. Ask questions concerning the significance of targeted information
4. Monitor understanding and "fix-up" situations where understanding is lacking
5. Establish goals and define academic tasks
6. Evaluate plans and reflect on the strategies selected

Such a list implies that no one technique or strategy will work for students in all situations (Zimmerman, 2002). Rather than teaching our students a generic, formulaic approach such as SQ3R, we need to provide instruction that ensures they have the strategies to match the academic tasks and texts they will encounter now and in the future (Simpson et al., 2004).

In this chapter we will address these cognitive and metacognitive processes by examining a variety of strategies and activities, both student-initiated and teacher-initiated, that will build strategic, independent learners across the content areas.

CASE STUDY

Ian is an English teacher who teaches several different classes of gifted students who all plan on attending college. Although most of them are receiving good grades in advanced courses such as chemistry and AP history, Ian knows that these students have mediocre study habits. He has discovered in conversations with his students that they do not read their textbooks, choosing instead to listen carefully in class as the teachers discuss the material. The district coordinator for gifted education has provided Ian with a workbook that contains study tips and memory enhancement exercises, but his students have complained bitterly about the exercises. Ian also feels a certain amount of pressure from the parents who have told him on various occasions that they expect the high school to prepare their children for the rigors of college.

To the Reader:
As you read and work through this chapter on learning strategies, decide what Ian might do to improve his approach with these gifted students. Consider the guidelines and strategies we examine and how Ian might use this information to help his students become more active learners.

Go to *http://www.prenhall.com/brozo*, select Chapter 9, then click on Chapter Objectives to provide a focus for your reading.

Guidelines for Teaching Learning Strategies

In order to develop successful independent learners who have a variety of strategies at their command, we need to acknowledge some basic guidelines drawn from current research and theory. A discussion of these five guidelines follows.

Understand the Importance of Students' Self-Knowledge

The research literature suggests that successful students are those who understand themselves as learners and are aware of their own motivations, beliefs, strengths, and weaknesses (Paris & Paris, 2001; Zimmerman, 2002). When students hold strong, positive views of themselves as learners, they have what Zimmerman (2002) and others have described as strong *self-efficacy*. Rather than attributing academic success to chance or the whims of a teacher, active learners with high self-efficacy ratings attribute what they learn to their own effort and strategy use. Moreover, students with strong self-efficacy are more likely to choose learning strategies and approaches that require them to think critically and elaboratively (Winne & Jamieson-Noel, 2002; Zimmerman, 2002).

In contrast, students with low self-efficacy are more likely to attribute their failures to external factors (e.g., the test was not fair) or to a fixed ability that they cannot change. For example, it is not atypical to hear adolescents say something like this: "I am not good at math and never will be." As a result, these students decide to give up before they even enter the classroom or at the first setback or challenge. Interestingly, you will find that students' self-efficacy varies across the content areas. For example, a student may have a strong sense of self-efficacy in a history course but feel totally overwhelmed or frustrated in an English course that requires her to write critical or creative responses to what she reads (Hofer, 2004).

Another important aspect of students' self-knowledge consists of the beliefs or epistemologies that they have about what constitutes knowledge and learning. Based on the work of Perry (1970) and others, these personal beliefs or theories include students' beliefs about the certainty of knowledge, the organization of knowledge, and the control of knowledge acquisition (Hofer, 2004; Schommer-Atkins, 2002). For example, some students perceive knowledge to be absolute, something handed down by authority that can be acquired quickly, with little effort. In contrast, other students view knowledge acquisition as a tentative, gradual process derived from reason and thought after considerable effort on their parts.

How students define knowledge has a significant impact on how they proceed with their reading and learning in a content area (Hubbard & Simpson, 2003; Hofer, 2004; Schommer-Atkins, 2002). That is, if students believe that reading in biology requires them to focus only on definitions, more than likely they will memorize definitions to words such as *glucose* rather than employ elaborative strategies that involve them in searching for relationships between key concepts (e.g., glucose, insulin, glycogen). Hence, as teachers, it is important for us to know what students believe and to nudge those beliefs from simple to more complex.

Emphasize Task Awareness

Imagine that you are training to run a machine in a factory and you prepare for your job by reading a manual about how to operate it. You read the manual a couple of times, skimming over it before you begin working. Then you are put on the machine and are told to get started. Every few minutes you need to consult the manual; eventually, the machine breaks down, and your boss is at your throat. The reason for your failure? A clear mismatch between the way you trained and the task's demands.

Now imagine that a student is studying for a biology test by using flash cards with the names of the hormones secreted by the endocrine system on one side and their definitions on the other. On the test, students are asked to interpret several diagrams, explaining the relationship between the hormones and their impact on other glands and human behavior. What grade would you predict for this student? Would she pass the test? Was there a match between the way she studied and what she needed to know for the test?

Like the factory worker, this student experienced a mismatch between the strategy and the demands of the task. That is, the biology test required the students to integrate the information about the hormones in the endocrine system. The student, however, focused on rote memorization of definitions rather than the relationships between concepts.

These two examples point out the importance of the principle of *transfer appropriateness*. This principle states that the more appropriate the match between a study process and an academic task, the more easily information can be transferred to long-term memory (Pressley, 2000). When students select strategies that match the tasks they have been assigned, their academic performance will be enhanced. Conversely, many failures or mediocre performances by students can be explained by a mismatch between their perceptions of the task and their teacher's perceptions (Eilam & Aharon, 2003; Zimmerman, 2002).

The implication of this principle is that students must be taught how to analyze the tasks they will encounter in their content-area courses. Tasks, according to Doyle (1983), can be characterized in terms of their products and thinking processes. The products are the papers, projects, lab reports, or tests that students must complete for a course. More important than the product are the thinking processes that students must employ in order to complete the product. For example, if students are assigned a paper for a government class, that paper is the product. If the teacher asks the students to read an editorial by George Will and critique it, the thinking processes for that paper are far more involved than those required for a paper summarizing Will's key ideas. Students must be able to determine and understand the levels of thinking demanded in their academic tasks. More important, they need to be shown that it is acceptable for them to seek information about the nature of their tasks and about other ways they will be held accountable for their learning. With that information, they can make informed decisions about which learning strategy to employ.

Not only should we teach students how to analyze an academic task such as the one required by the government teacher, but we, as teachers, should provide clear and explicit information about what we want students to do and how we want them to do it. By sharing product and process information with our students, we ensure that they will have the task knowledge to make informed strategy decisions.

> When teachers are explicit about the products they assign students and the cognitive and metacognitive processes embedded in those products, students find it easier to learn.

Stress the What, How, When, and Why of Strategy Use

Students need to develop a repertoire of effective strategies and an ability to use the most appropriate ones to match the task demands of the content areas they are reading and studying. In order to do this, students must have three different kinds of strategic knowledge (Paris, Wasik, & Turner, 1991). The first is declarative knowledge or the "what" of a strategy. For example, a student with declarative knowledge of previewing knows that previewing is done before reading and that it involves such steps as reading the introduction and summary. The second kind of strategic knowledge is procedural, or the "how" of a strategy. Strategic learners with declarative and procedural knowledge of the preview strategy could describe the steps for previewing and know how to modify those steps when they encounter different types of texts (e.g., "If the text has no boldface headings, I could read the first sentence of each paragraph.").

In addition to these two types of knowledge, active learners possess conditional knowledge, perhaps the most critical form of strategic knowledge (Paris & Paris, 2001; Zimmerman, 2002). When active learners have conditional knowledge, they know the "when" and "why" to using various strategies. Thus, with the previewing strategy, they know that it may be appropriate to preview only certain texts. They also understand that the time involved in previewing a chapter before they read it is time well spent because it allows them to check the author's organization, set purposes for reading, and divide the reading into meaningful chunks. Students must develop all three kinds of strategic knowledge if they are to transfer the strategies we teach in the classroom to their own reading and learning tasks outside the classroom (Cleary & Zimmerman, 2004; Weinstein et al., 2003).

Take the Time to Develop Students' Strategic Expertise

Pressley (2000) and others have pointed out that students do not quickly transfer or use a new strategy they just have been taught. Most study strategies involve complex processes that cannot be mastered in brief teaching lessons or artificial exercises packaged in workbooks. Admittedly, students may learn the steps of a strategy from such instructional approaches, but they will not gain the conditional and procedural knowledge necessary for them to transfer the strategy to their own tasks. We believe it is critical for any teacher interested in training students to use study strategies to accept this principle; otherwise, the teacher and the class may give up on a strategy, in spite of its potential.

Validated training approaches and models are numerous, but they all agree that instruction should be direct, informed, and explanatory (e.g., Casazza, 2003; Weinstein et al., 2003). In other words, students can be taught to employ a strategy if they receive intensive instruction over a reasonable period of time that is characterized by (1) a description of the strategy and its characteristics, (2) an explanation of why the strategy is important, (3) modeling or demonstrations on how the strategy is used, including the processes involved, (4) explanations as to when and where it is appropriate to apply the strategy, and (5) guidelines for evaluating whether the strategy is working and what to do if it is not. Teachers should also provide students with strategy examples from their content-area textbooks or materials. Strategy examples, especially ones that teachers develop, are important because many students believe that adults never need to study or make an effort to remember an idea. As one way of illustrating the strategy of charting, one of our graduate students shared with her students the chart she had created to learn the different theories of reading. That example was an excellent introduction to her lesson on how to use charts as a means of comparing and contrasting a variety of variables.

The findings from research studies have suggested that it takes at least a few weeks before students begin to feel comfortable with a particular strategy (Hubbard & Simpson, 2003; Simpson et al., 2004). One way teachers have found to facilitate this process is by allowing students to practice the strategy with material that is easy to understand, such as material taken from the newspaper or from a textbook used with younger students. In this way, students avoid overcrowding the cognitive workbench and can focus most of their attention on learning the strategy. Gradually, teachers can increase the difficulty of the material until students demonstrate that

Students will choose to use effective learning strategies if we provide them explicit instruction and numerous practice opportunities using authentic texts and tasks.

they can apply the strategy to their own textbooks. This may take several weeks, but the time is well spent because our ultimate goal is to develop students' strategic expertise and ultimate independence in learning.

Use Content-Area Assignments as an Opportunity to Reinforce Learning Strategies

The topic of homework is often overlooked in teacher education programs. We briefly take up this topic here because we believe that homework, when appropriately designed and assigned, can play an important role in reinforcing students' learning strategies and in encouraging students to read their textbooks. Our data for this discussion do not come from empirical research but rather from anecdotal evidence, interviews with content-area teachers, and our teaching experiences with high school and college students.

Classroom teachers interested in helping students see the connection between how they read and study their textbooks and the course expectations and requirements should assign homework that asks students to integrate particular strategies with the learning of the course content. For example, a biology teacher who wants her students to learn the different glands and hormones in the endocrine system could assign homework requiring them to create a chart to summarize those concepts. In class, the students could brainstorm what information might be contained in the charts (e.g., locations, functions) and examine possible formats. The following day, students could meet in groups to compare and discuss their charts and identify any ambiguous information. The teacher could also give the students a quiz about the endocrine system, allowing them to use their newly created charts. In this way, the teacher receives feedback on how students are progressing in their mastery of the learning strategy simultaneously with information about how well they are learning the course content.

Students frequently perceive homework as an infringement on their time for extracurricular activities, part-time jobs, or recreation. When homework is given judiciously and when it is meaningfully related to the course expectations, there is a greater chance that it will be completed. In turn, students who practice applying strategies to their course content will become competent readers and successful independent learners (Cleary & Zimmerman, 2004; Hadwin, Winne, Stockley, Nesbit, & Woszczyna, 2001).

Based on these five guidelines of effective study strategy instruction, we describe in the next section some basic processes that are important to assisting students in "getting started" in any content area.

Important Basic Processes

Students who are strategic learners understand how their textbooks are organized, how to interpret and record an assignment, how to begin reading their assignments, and how to fix up situations where they are lost or do not understand. As content-area teachers, we cannot assume that students have mastered these four basic processes in the elementary grades.

Knowing the Format and Organization of a Textbook

One basic strategy that students often overlook is the effective use of the textbook. We have known college students who have carried their psychology textbook around for 6 weeks without knowing that there was a glossary at the back or that a list of key terms was included at the end of each chapter. If students can learn how their textbook is organized and capitalize on those features as they read and study, they can increase their concentration, understanding, and remembering.

Louisa, a high school culinary arts teacher, had attended a district workshop where the speaker stressed the importance of introducing the format and organization of textbooks to students. Before the workshop she had assumed, as had many other teachers, that most students take the time to explore their textbooks once they receive them. Like most, she had merely handed out her textbook and assigned the first chapter of reading. Taking part of a class period to explain the "obvious characteristics" of a textbook seemed a bit unnecessary, but she decided to give it a try. She began her discussion by explaining that textbooks contain only the theories, perspectives, and conclusions of certain scholars under contract from a publisher. She then asked the students to read the title page and preface of their textbook to gain information about their authors. The students discovered that three individuals had written their text. After a discussion about the authors, Louisa stressed that the content of all their readings would be filtered through the biases and personal opinions of the authors.

After that brief orientation, which many students found intriguing, Louisa distributed a textbook introduction activity designed to orient her students further to their textbook (see Figure 9.1). In the workshop, Louisa had learned that many students know neither where important textbook parts are located nor how they function. She therefore paired her students and gave them 15 minutes to familiarize themselves with the parts of the textbook through the questions on the activity sheet. Each chapter, as the students soon discovered, had a general introduction; a summary that listed key ideas; and boldfaced headings, subheadings, and italicized words. Louisa closed the period with a discussion of how these aids could help them as they read and studied their first assignment.

Figure 9.1   Getting Acquainted with Your Textbook

Title of textbook _____
Author(s) _____
Copyright date _____ Has the book been revised? _____

1. Read the ***preface*** carefully and completely. Summarize briefly what it says.
2. Find the ***table of contents.*** Answer these questions after studying it:
   a. Are the chapters broken down into many or few subheadings?
   b. Can you list five or six major topics included in the table of contents?
3. Find the ***index.*** On what page does it begin? Name two or three types of information you find there.
4. Find the ***glossary.*** How can it help you?
5. Find the ***appendix.*** What type of information can you find in it?
6. Find one ***bibliography.*** List two authors or titles that interest you.
7. Examine Chapter 1. Check the organizational features available in this textbook:
   a. Introduction _____
   b. Marginal notes _____
   c. Italicized or underlined words _____
   d. Boldfaced headings _____
   e. Pictures _____ Graphs _____ Maps _____ Charts _____
   f. Internal summaries _____ Summary _____
   g. Questions at the end _____

Louisa received positive feedback from her students on this lesson and decided to incorporate it into her beginning-of-the-year routine. We know some school districts insist that all teachers take the time during the first week of school to introduce their textbook with an activity like the one in Figure 9.1. The form can obviously be modified to fit any content-area textbook. What Louisa and many other teachers hope is that students will become critical and savvy consumers of text who will conduct their own "get-acquainted" activities before they begin reading.

Understanding Assignments

As we discussed in the guidelines for effective strategy instruction, if students are to select the most appropriate strategies, they must understand all the nuances of their academic tasks. We, as content-area teachers, can help students in two fundamental ways. First, we must constantly strive to provide students tasks that are explicit and descriptive. One way we can do this is by making sure that our reading assignments contain enough information to make them effective, as described in the accompanying Teacher as Learner box.

Implicit in all the suggestions noted in the Teacher as Learner box is the belief that giving an assignment is more than announcing what pages need to be read. If you want students to read, you must prepare them by making the task as explicit and specific as possible. That same advice applies to other academic tasks as well, such as a writing assignment or a lab experiment.

The second way we can assist students to become independent learners is to provide them questions they should ask themselves about an assignment or task they

Teacher as Learner

CREATING EFFECTIVE READING ASSIGNMENTS

The next time you assign your students to read a text or a selection, make the task more explicit for them by including this information:

1. How should your students read? Should they skim the assignment? Should they read slowly, pausing to study all charts, graphs, or example problems?

2. What should your students focus on when they read? Definitions? Examples? Theories? Functions? Trends? Descriptions? Causes and effects? Comparisons and contrasts? Significant events?

3. How should your students approach a difficult section? Should they use a diagram that explains the concept? Should they refer to their notes from the lab experiment or from the class discussion? Or should they read the chapter summary before they begin reading?

4. How should they break up their reading into smaller chunks?

5. How long should it take them to read the assignment?

6. What will be expected of them once they have read the material? Should they be prepared to write? Participate in a lab experiment? Solve some problems? Discuss?

must complete. For example, the following are general questions that students could use for almost any course:

1. What is the assignment? What am I to produce? What is the purpose of the assignment?

2. What resources should I use? Textbook? Class discussion notes? Computer databases? Outside reading? Videos? Class demonstrations or laboratory experiments?

3. What are the requirements for format, length, or size? Must the assignment be typed? In ink? Stapled?

4. When is the assignment due? Are there any penalties for late work?

5. How will this assignment be evaluated? How much does it count in the total evaluation process?

6. Do I understand all the words that the teacher used to explain the assignment?

Some content-area teachers have posted these six questions on their school's web page in order to help parents as they interact with their children.

The last question is particularly critical because we often use words such as *critique* or *respond creatively* when we give students assignments, assuming that they know what we mean. More often than we would like, students do not understand these words and the processes they embody (Simpson & Nist, 2003).

We know a team of ninth-grade teachers that have these six questions listed on a poster in their classroom in order to encourage students to "get all the information" when they write their assignments in their notebooks. In addition, they encourage students to ask questions about assignments and reinforce them when they do. A serendipitous result of training students to record their assignments in this fashion is often vocal endorsement from the students' parents, who are frequently bewildered by what homework their children should be doing each night. These six questions have reduced students' and parents' bewilderment and frustration.

Previewing

Dominique and Turkessa were preparing to go to a performance of the local symphony. As they were dressing, Turkessa suggested that they read about the composer, Bach, to learn about his life and musical philosophy. Dominique rummaged through their stacks of books in the basement and eventually found the trusty music appreciation text he had used years ago in undergraduate school. He read aloud about Bach as they finished dressing and continued reading to Turkessa as she drove downtown. They arrived at Symphony Hall early and read further from the program about the compositions to be performed that evening. By the time the first note sounded, they had established a context for the music that greatly aided their interpretation and appreciation of what they heard.

This kind of context setting is at the heart of the previewing strategy. Students often seem to begin a reading assignment much like those people who entered Symphony Hall and scurried to find their seats just before the conductor's entrance on the stage. The music rushed over them, but because they did not plan for listening, they may not have known what the composer intended to communicate with his music. Likewise, when students are expected to gain a complete understanding of their text but approach their reading by opening their books to the beginning of the assignment and simply plowing forward, they fail to prepare for the flood of words they encounter and may find themselves in the middle of the chapter unsure about what the author is trying to convey.

To prepare for the reading assignments, students should be taught how to preview. The previewing strategy is a logical follow-up to learning the format and organization

Figure 9.2 Previewing a Driver's Education Chapter

DIRECTIONS: We previewed most of the chapter in class. In order to understand how the chapter is organized, complete the following skeletal outline. You can do this by identifying the author's major headings and subheadings. As you do this activity, be thinking of possible test questions.

Chapter 12: Adverse Conditions

I. Reduced Visibility (1st main topic)
   A. Car windows
   B. Sun glare
   C.
   D. Night
      1. Headlights
      2.
      3.

II. Reduced Traction (2nd main topic)
   A. Wet roads
      1.
      2.
   B. Snow
      1.
      2.
   C.
   D.

FINISH THE CHAPTER'S OUTLINE OR STRUCTURE. THERE ARE A TOTAL OF FOUR MAIN TOPICS IN THIS CHAPTER.

of a textbook because it requires students to know and use those features. As students preview, they read the introductory paragraphs, summaries, topic markers or boldfaced headings, visual aids, summaries, and questions or problems provided by the author. Once students have previewed these text features, they need to take a moment to reflect on this information, allowing the ideas to sink in. By previewing, students should be able to answer questions such as these: (a) What is the chapter about? (b) What are some key terms I will learn? (c) How should I read this chapter and divide up this task?

We know of many teachers who demonstrate the steps of the preview strategy during the first month of school. Gradually, they shift the responsibility to their students to preview their assignments by assigning them to complete a worksheet similar to the one in Figure 9.2. This particular example from a driver's education teacher guides students through the process of identifying key ideas and seeing the relationships between these ideas, an important step in the preview strategy. Content-area teachers can easily modify the example in Figure 9.2 to fit their particular needs and the unique characteristics of their textbooks. For example, a chemistry or physics teacher might wish to emphasize the importance of graphics and example problems.

Why should students preview? As we noted in the guidelines, it is important to discuss with your students the advantages of any strategy so you can counter their initial concerns or doubts. In these discussions, you could stress the fact that previewing provides a meaningful organization of the material to be learned, an important aspect of reading comprehension and fluency (Hartley, 2002). As students read introductory paragraphs and look over headings and subheadings, they will form a mental outline of the major topics and subtopics. This information will provide students with the data they need to make judgments about their readiness to learn the material, the difficulty of the material, and the actions they may need to take to learn the material.

As a strategy, previewing is neither relevant nor appropriate for all texts and tasks. Some texts are not considerately organized, and many literature anthologies do not contain textbook markers or summaries. Hence, students will need to modify the preview strategy (i.e., read the first sentence of each paragraph when there are no textbook markers) or select a more appropriate strategy. Occasionally, some teachers may not want their students to read and study an entire chapter but instead may tell them to memorize specific processes, steps, or formulas. For example, if a chemistry teacher told her class that all they would be required to know from Chapter 3 were the symbols and atomic weights for five specific elements, extensive previewing would not be appropriate. This example points again to the importance of students' knowing what they will be responsible for as a result of reading and studying so that they can employ the most relevant learning strategy (Simpson & Nist, 2003).

Previewing, although not a panacea, certainly will engage students in more active reading and learning. Moreover, previewing is one of the strategies that can be initially introduced by teachers, modeled and reinforced, and then gradually shifted to students for their own responsibility and control.

Fixing Up Difficult Situations

Fix-up strategies are the observable or "in the head" techniques that active learners use when they are trying to increase their understanding of a particular content-area concept (Tovani, 2004). To illustrate the importance of fix-up strategies, read the passage in the accompanying Teacher as Learner box.

Most middle school and high school students have limited fix-up strategies and the ones they do use are usually passive, emphasizing rereading or the rote memorization of information (Tovani, 2004). When grappling with difficult text, the struggling readers in your classroom will just give up and quickly close the textbook, perhaps forever. Teachers, however, can assist students by modeling and demonstrating effective fix-up strategies appropriate to their content area. As explained in Chapter 3, an effective process-modeling session permits students to see that it is normal to experience comprehension difficulties and that even experts must solve these problems with some techniques or strategies.

In addition, throughout the school year teachers can use a variety of other methods to highlight the various fix-up strategies they want their students to use. Angela, a math teacher at a ninth-grade center, begins the year by modeling the fix-up strategies she wants her students to use and then places those strategies on poster board in several parts of the room. She also posts the information on her Web site for students and parents to peruse. One of those Web-based strategies emphasizes the importance of reading word problems with a pencil and paper in hand. A general science teacher at the same school gives his students a bookmark that lists the appropriate fix-up strategies for making sense of the assigned material in his classroom. The options are limitless.

These four basic processes are essential to your students' abilities to become strategic in their content-area learning, whether within the classroom or outside the classroom. In the next section we discuss an extremely important process that provides the foundation for almost every learning strategy or technique: summarization.

Teacher as Learner

FIX-UP STRATEGIES

After reading the following passage, list all the techniques you used or would use to understand what you had read:

> Recent developments in the self-worth theory of achievement motivation attest to the potential heuristic value of maintaining Atkinson's original quadripolar model. In essence, self-worth theory argues that the need for self-acceptance is the highest human priority and that, in reality, the dynamics of school achievement largely reflect attempts to aggrandize and protect self-perceptions of ability. (Covington & Roberts, 1994, p. 161)

Your techniques: _____

_____

What techniques did you include in your list? Some of the more common fix-up strategies include:

1. Rereading the confusing sentence or paragraph

2. Adjusting your reading rate by slowing down or speeding up

3. Reading ahead to see if the information becomes clearer

4. Looking back at previous paragraphs, headings, or introductions to see if the author explains the concept in another way

5. Referring to visual aids provided by the author, such as maps, charts, pictures, or graphs

6. Making a picture in your mind of the concept being discussed

7. Noticing patterns in text structure (macrostructure)

8. Looking for text examples that clarify difficult abstractions

9. Making a connection between the text and your life and your knowledge of the world

10. Checking alternative sources such as textbooks, references, or the Internet

Summarization and Taking Notes from Texts

All of us summarize many times during the course of a day. When you ask your colleague in the hall, "How are you?" and she says, "Fine," she is summarizing—categorizing her collective experiences and feelings and labeling them with a single word. When you ask a fellow student about the weather and he says, "Gloomy," this also is a summary, the selection of a single word that embraces a variety of weather characteristics. Across the content areas, the ability to summarize text is a significant meaning-making process because it provides the foundation for a wide array of other thinking processes such as organizing and synthesizing (Casazza, 2003; Friend, 2000). When students create written summaries, they also are monitoring or checking their level of understanding, an extremely important aspect of becoming strategic, independent learners (Thiede & Anderson, 2003). Unfortunately, many middle and high school students are not adept in summarizing what they have read (Simpson & Nist, 2003; Tovani, 2004). Rather than summarize a concept using their own words, many students resort to memorizing irrelevant details, missing the "big picture" of what they have read or heard during a class discussion.

Fortunately, summarizing has been investigated over a period of time, and researchers have discovered that skilled, fluent readers use certain rules in summarizing (e.g., Brown & Day, 1983; Kintsch & van Dijk, 1978). These rules include:

1. Deleting irrelevant or unimportant information
2. Selecting key idea statements when the author explicitly provides them
3. Collapsing lists and forming categories for those lists of items (e.g., the cause of diabetes rather than glucose, glycogen, and insulin).
4. Integrating the information into a written statement by using invented topic sentences and the first three rules as a guide

When students, especially struggling readers, receive direct, explanatory instruction in these steps, their ability to summarize and comprehend text significantly improves (Brown & Day, 1983; Casazza, 2003; Friend, 2000). As noted in the guidelines at the beginning of the chapter, this instruction should be explicit and occur over time because summarization is a complex process. Casazza (2003) for example, noted from her research that students mastered the first rule of deletion rather quickly, but the other three steps necessitated that she model and provide her students considerable guided practice with easier materials, at first.

Teaching Activities for Summarization

In addition to modeling the steps involved in summarizing, content-area teachers can help their students master the steps with a variety of activities. First, you can provide students examples of summaries that you or former students have composed for a targeted piece of text. By using the overhead projector or a slide to highlight the summary, students see how other individuals might have paraphrased a challenging paragraph or how they linked ideas together. Even more effective is an activity we call "The Good, the Bad, and the Ugly." With this activity you present students three differing summaries for one piece of text—one that is exemplary, one that is satisfactory but lacks some important characteristics (e.g., generalizations), and one that is totally unsatisfactory because it lacks all the characteristics of effective summaries. Without labeling the summaries, you then ask the students to rate the summaries on a scale of one to five, five being the best, and be prepared to discuss their evaluations. These discussions are usually quite animated.

A third way you can assist your students with any complex thinking process such as summarization is to involve them in debriefing sessions with their classmates. During debriefing sessions students work in small groups to compare and analyze their summaries and the content they used for practice. Each group is given three questions to answer and prepare for whole-class discussion: (a) What problems did you have in understanding the content? (b) What problems did you have in using the summarization strategy? and (c) What do you see as the advantages of summarizing?

Figure 9.3 Summary Checklist

> ***To the Student:*** I have checked the areas you need to work on in order to improve your summaries. Please read the checklist carefully and incorporate these suggestions when you revise your summary.
>
> _____1. Your summary represents the author's key ideas. Good work!
>
> _____2. You need to use your own words when summarizing the text.
>
> _____3. Your summary focuses too much on unimportant details.
>
> _____4. Your summary needs to focus more on key ideas and less on details.
>
> _____5. You need to be briefer in your summary.
>
> _____6. You need to be more specific and not so vague with your summary.
>
> _____7. Your summary needs to show the relationships between ideas.

Both the small-group and large-class discussions provide teachers timely, specific feedback on students' growth and progress and excellent opportunities for emphasizing students' procedural and conditional knowledge of summarization.

A fourth practical way you can enhance your students' summarization skills is to provided them concrete, specific feedback on their written products (Butler & Winne, 1995; Simpson et al., 2004). Of course, providing feedback takes considerable time, especially when you see more than 100 students in one day. In order to provide their students quality feedback in an expedient manner, some teachers like to use a checklist. The checklist in Figure 9.3 is similar to one used by Joseph, a consumer economics teacher. He tells us that he can review a class set of summaries in about 15 minutes when he uses a checklist. Gradually and over time, students can be encouraged to use these checklists to evaluate their own summaries.

You, too, can try your hand in evaluating summaries by completing the activity in the Teacher as Learner box.

As you probably determined, Susan's summary was more effective than Derrick's for several reasons. What reasons did you list? Did you note that Susan focused on the overall structure of the section, the four types of pollution and the solutions to water pollution? In contrast, Derrick focused on details with no sense of organization. Did you note that Susan used personal examples and offered a conclusion in her summary? Derrick's summary, in contrast, used only the information provided by the textbook and frequently bordered on plagiarism.

Although Derrick's summary was not as effective as Susan's, he certainly was making strides toward understanding the steps and processes involved in summarization. To help him improve his summary, a teacher could work with him on paraphrasing, noting macrostructures of text (e.g., problem/solution), and using important microstructure features such as connectives (e.g., *on the other hand, however*).

In sum, if you want your students to be able to summarize what they read or hear in your classroom, they will need specific instruction from you, the content-area expert. Asking students to summarize without providing them instruction is just not sufficient. Moreover, it is important to note that summarization is not just a skill that students practice for their teachers. Rather, when students summarize and organize what they have read, they have created important artifacts that they can use to study. Therefore, in the next section we will discuss formats that students can use for their summaries that will allow them to rehearse and study content-area concepts.

In addition to using the four specific teaching suggestions that we just explained, you can enhance your students' skills in text summarization by providing them a variety of formats for their summaries.

Teacher as Learner

EVALUATING TWO DIFFERENT SUMMARIES

Read Susan and Derrick's summaries that they wrote for a selection on water pollution. Decide which is better and why.

Susan's Summary

According to this section of our textbook, there are four sources of water pollution: agriculture, industry, domestic, and other sources such as oil spills. Perhaps the most dangerous source of pollution comes from industry, though oil spills, such as the one in Alaska, have certainly had a large impact on our wildlife and on our economy. Pesticides, fertilizers, and animal waste, the three types of agricultural pollution, are usually not direct but indirect. A notorious example of a pesticide is DDT. There are three kinds of industrial pollution: chemical, thermal, and radiation. The problems associated with radiation seem to be the most severe in that skin cancer and leukemia are possible results of exposure. Organic waste and detergent builders are the main sources of domestic pollution. Both seem to have an adverse effect on our lakes and rivers so that the balance of nature is upset. This section of the chapter ended by discussing some solutions to the problem of water pollution—all of which are costly but very important.

Derrick's Summary

This section of the chapter discussed different kinds of water pollution. Pesticides such as DDT are dangerous to use because they are not biodegradable. Some nitrates are toxic to animals and humans. Nitrates can be reduced to nitrites, which interfere with the transport of oxygen by hemoglobin in the blood. Mercury vapor is highly toxic and can be absorbed through the lungs. There are two types of radiation cell damage, direct and indirect. Detergents and organic wastes can also harm our water sources. Oil spills hurt our aquatic life.

Text Notetaking Formats That Facilitate Students' Studying

Think back to your college experiences and how you dealt with all the textbooks, novels, primary sources, and articles that you were assigned to read. Like most undergraduate and graduate students, you probably developed a system for interacting with that material so you could review and study it later. More than likely, your system involved underlining key ideas and making brief notations in the margin. Because most public school students are not allowed to write in their textbooks, it becomes important to identify formats that allow students to interact with their textbooks.

We examine three such formats that teachers have found useful: sticky notes, foldables, and index cards. All three formats provide students an artifact for their test preparation and encourage them to monitor their understanding or lack thereof. Most teachers have found it useful to demonstrate all three formats and allow students to choose the one they prefer.

Sticky Notes

When students create sticky notes for a content-area reading task, they typically summarize the key ideas from a page and place the sticky note on that page. Some

Figure 9.4 Sticky Note for Genetics

> *Mendel proposed a theory called **particular inheritance**. He said heritable characteristics were controlled by individual units—each plant has 2 for each trait. He called these units "merkmal"—we call them **genes**.*

teachers encourage students to use sticky notes as a way of highlighting a confusing topic or concept that they want clarified during class. The example in Figure 9.4 illustrates a students' sticky note for a genetics unit on inheritance.

If students receive sufficient instruction, they could also place the following on their sticky notes:

1. Examples of important concepts or solutions to problems
2. Steps, important characteristics, functions, trends, significant events or individuals
3. Motifs, themes, character descriptions, conflicts
4. Critiques or critical notes in response to what has been read (e.g., Does the author defend his position about global warming?)

If not instructed otherwise, most students will include only definitions in their summaries and thus, tend to overlook important aspects such as examples, characteristics, functions, trends, or motifs.

Once students have finished a chapter or an assignment, they can then place their sticky notes on a separate piece of paper. You might ask, why not just let the students write those notes on that paper instead of using the sticky notes in the first place? Researchers and practitioners have found that students who take notes on a piece of notebook paper tend to become medieval monks who feel compelled to fill up a page. The use of sticky notes or any such abbreviated format encourages students to think about ideas and reduce them, using their own words (Simpson & Nist, 1990; Tovani, 2004).

Foldables

Foldables (Zike, 1994) are similar to sticky notes in that they are small in size and flexible in their use. However, they differ in that they provide students an opportunity to test themselves, an important aspect of test preparation (King, 1997). As illustrated in Figure 9.5, students fold a piece of construction paper and label a concept or key idea (e.g., *memory processes*) on the front of the paper. Then, the foldable is cut into parts or flaps and these are also labeled (e.g., *encoding, storage,* and *retrieval*). To study the foldable, students read the concept (e.g., memory processes) and then, before lifting the flaps, say aloud the information on the back of each flap. Foldables, like sticky notes, can be adopted to any content area.

Index Cards

As mentioned in Chapter 6, index cards are an efficient and effective way for students to study key vocabulary words and any other content-area concepts. Because they are more portable and durable than notebook paper or slips of paper and because they facilitate self-testing, they are particularly advantageous. As illustrated in Figure 9.6, some students like to place questions on the front of their cards (i.e. what are the three essential parts of a workout?) and answers on the back, whereas other students use the more traditional flashcard format.

Several content-area teachers at a high school in Florida have taught their students how to construct task-specific index cards in order to ensure that their students

Figure 9.5 Foldable for Psychology Unit

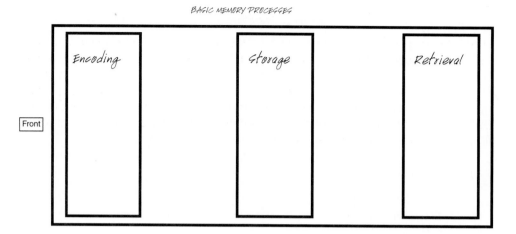

BASIC MEMORY PROCESSES

Front

| Encoding | Storage | Retrieval |

Inside or Back of Foldable

Encoding
a process
changing
physical
scenes or
events into
codes so
they can be
stored

Storaged
to be kept
in memory,
codes must
be organized
or chunked

Retrieval
finding and
using infor-
mation in our
memories is
not always
easy z

Figure 9.6 Index Card for Health and Fitness Unit

Back of Card

1. WARM-UP to prevent injuries, stimulate heart and lungs, increase blood flow, prepare
mentally; varies with the individual; can be done in a variety of ways

2. MAIN CONDITIONING continuous and rhythmic activities such as running, biking, swimming,
walking, aerobic dance; should work at your target heart rate; should modify and vary activities

3. COOL-DOWN tapering off period where you continue working out but at a lower intensity;
walking is good; if you skip this part blood may pool in the muscles or you could become dizzy;
5 minutes is recommended

read and summarize the assigned material. A health and fitness teacher told us that his students now read their assignments and complete the cards, especially after he began giving unannounced pop quizzes where students could use their cards if they brought them to class.

Whatever format your students choose to use to summarize what they have read, it is always useful to provide them models or examples of effective strategies. For example, you might collect the students' foldables or index cards and search for ones that belong to students who are doing well in the course. Then, on the next day, share on an overhead the effective examples so students can modify their strategies accordingly. In sum, if you want your students to be able to summarize what they read in your class, they need specific steps, a format, and feedback. In the next section we address the strategies pertaining to class notes.

Strategies for Taking Class Notes

If you have ever wondered why it is so difficult for your students to take notes during class discussions or during one of your demonstrations of a concept, consider all the prerequisite skills involved in notetaking. Students must be able to:

1. Paraphrase and summarize
2. Select key ideas and discard irrelevant details
3. Establish purposes for listening or observing
4. Identify organizational patterns such as problem-solution or cause-effect
5. Record information quickly using abbreviations and symbols

In addition to these skill prerequisites, students need some prior experiences or background information to make sense of the concepts being discussed or presented during class. In sum, taking class notes is a difficult skill for most middle school and high school students. In fact, many first-year college students have not mastered the skills involved in taking notes from lectures, demonstrations, and discussions (Peverly et al., 2003). Fortunately, this skill can be taught and reinforced across the content areas.

Although most students find it challenging to take useful notes from discussions or demonstrations, content-area teachers can help them master these skills by incorporating several different activities into their daily routine.

We have collected a variety of suggestions from content-area instructors about how they teach notetaking. The following are some of the activities they use:

1. Begin the year with a discussion of your classroom notetaking expectations. Include the why of taking notes, whether you will check notes, how notes will be used, and in what format you would like the notes to be kept (i.e., in a spiral or three-ring notebook).

2. Discuss the qualities of good notes in your course. Include general physical formats, organization, and content. Show examples of your own class notes or previous students' notes via handouts, the overhead projector, a Web page on the computer, or the bulletin board.

3. Model notetaking behaviors by using a framed outline during class. At the beginning of class, distribute a handout with the major points to be covered that day but with ample room for the development of your ideas. Specific cue words could be added for students with learning disabilities (e.g., "The second step of the tennis serve"). Then deliver your presentation and fill in the major points and details on the framed outline using the overhead projector. Require students to add your notes to

their framed outline. Repeat this procedure at least once a week and gradually reduce the cues until you no longer present the notes on the overhead or on the framed outline.

4.   Teach the patterns of organization that are common to your content area (e.g., comparison-contrast, sequence). For example, after discussing the problem-solution organizational format, the building construction teacher could deliver a brief lecture and assign students to note the nature of a problem, the courses of action proposed, and the advantages and disadvantages of the solutions.

5.   Teach and model physical and verbal cues that teachers commonly use during class presentations. Include physical cues such as tone, facial expressions, pace, and gestures. Include verbal cues such as "Now we will consider the second point" or "In summary." Reserve time in class to discuss the students' notes to check if they recorded the important points that were cued.

6.   Teach the common symbols and abbreviations and those unique to your specific content area. For example, students should be taught to use abbreviations such as *ex* to represent examples and = to represent the words *equals* or *equivalent*. Government teachers should teach students to use abbreviations such as *jud* and *leg* to represent the words *judiciary* and *legislation*.

In addition to these activities, it is important for content-area teachers to continually reinforce the usefulness and advantages of taking class notes. Students will not continue to use a strategy unless they see it as effective and worthy of their effort (Paris & Paris, 2001). You can reinforce and reward your students in a variety of ways for taking class notes. We particularly like these four ideas and have found them to be successful with middle school and high school students:

1. Give unannounced quizzes in which students can use their class notes. Make sure that the questions asked pertain to the information and concepts you discussed during the class. Students will quickly learn that it is important to listen and take detailed, organized notes.

2. After some instruction on how to take class notes, collect students' notes without warning, either at the end of the class period or the next day. Evaluate the notes and then discuss them the next day with the students.

3. Have a weekly review of class notes. Ask questions that could be answered by using the notes. Points could be awarded for correct answers. This procedure could also be used at the beginning of each class period.

4. Provide students with class time to review their notes with a partner, especially after an important lesson or before a test or quiz.

In the next section we explain two different formats that students can use to organize their class notes: the split-page notetaking format and the synthesis journal.

The Split-Page Notetaking Format

Some content-area teachers like their students to take class notes in a predictable format such as the split-page format (Palmatier, 1973). With this format, during class students record their notes on the right-hand side of a piece of paper. Later, perhaps as a class assignment, they write on the left-hand side of the paper key idea statements in order to reduce the information and to see the big picture. The notes in Figure 9.7 illustrate how one student used the split-page format in his math class. In addition to writing key idea statements in the left-hand margin, students could be assigned to incorporate key ideas from their textbooks or other sources.

> You will need to model good note-taking procedures and reinforce students on taking notes during class.

Figure 9.7 Sample of Split-Page Notes from a Math Course

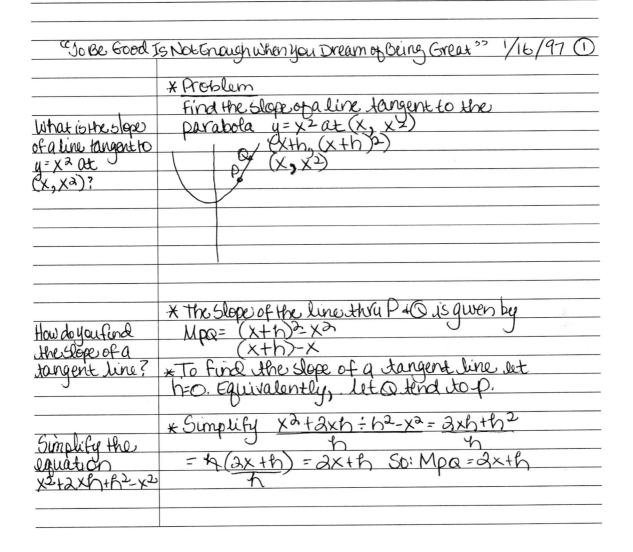

In that way, they can collect and synthesize all the information about a particular concept.

Anthony, a 12th-grade economics teacher, provides his students considerable practice with the split-page format. He begins by asking them to take notes during class in their usual fashion. This assignment provides him and his students with some self-assessment data. Samples of actual notes produced by students are put on the overhead projector and analyzed. Anthony asks the students to consider the note samples relative to the goals of studying, which stimulates discussion of the relevance and transfer appropriateness of notetaking strategies. When he introduces split-page notes, he first describes the format; then, unrehearsed, he creates a set of notes. This gives students a view of Anthony's thoughts and decisions during the notetaking process. In addition, Anthony demonstrates how he would study the notes by covering the right column and using the left-column entries as recall prompts, and vice versa.

The Synthesis Journal as a Notetaking Format

Synthesis journals (Burrell & McAlexander, 1998) are not really journals per se but a format that encourages students to identify, organize, and then synthesize various perspectives on an issue. They are particularly useful for content-area classrooms where discussion predominates. As illustrated in Figure 9.8, when completing a synthesis jour-

Figure 9.8   A Synthesis Journal

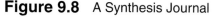

THE AUTHOR SAYS

Drug use in the United States has _not_ decreased, especially among adolescents. He says that alcohol is a Drug and there has been a 15% increase in illegal drinking and driving. He also says that hard drugs like heroin are making a comeback with young people. Finally, the author says binging with alcohol is a real problem.

THE CLASS SAYS

yes, drinking and drugs are more common. Seventh graders are using drugs. Why is alcohol called a Drug? It is legal.

SYNTHESIS

more people are using drugs, especially alcohol. We must learn to take our personal stands on this.

I SAY

I do not use drugs — my friends do not. I do not see the increase, but more classmates are drinking in seventh grade.

THE TEACHER SAYS

Alcohol _is_ a drug. We should learn how to avoid situations where drugs will be used. Many teens have died in car crashes because of alcohol).

nal, students determine and then write in the appropriate place the viewpoints and statements of authors they have read, of their teacher, of their classmates, and finally, their personal viewpoints. The center is reserved for the students to synthesize the viewpoints and then write a generalization. The synthesis journal entry in Figure 9.8 was created by a seventh grader during a unit in his health course about drug use and adolescents.

Synthesis journals obviously have many advantages. Not only do they encourage students to think critically about an issue and synthesize multiple sources, they also stimulate students to identify and explain various perspectives, a problem many middle school and high school students have with their writing (Hynd-Shanahan, Holschuh, & Hubbard, 2004). Moreover, synthesis journals give students a strategy that assists them in taking notes during discussions. Far too often, what the teacher says in class during a discussion becomes more important than what other classmates say about the issue being discussed. In fact, we have observed students' notetaking behaviors during discussions and discovered that they rarely took notes. If they did,

> Synthesis journals are particularly useful in content areas such as music, physical education, or art where teachers rely more on oral presentations to explain their objectives and concepts.

Honoring Diversity and Building Competence in the Content Classroom

Adrian teaches adaptive physical and health education to students in an inner city school in Orlando, Florida. She introduces the synthesis journal by explaining the purpose of the format, stressing that every perspective on a controversial issue deserves consideration and that the synthesis journal recognizes and supports these viewpoints. For a unit on drug abuse and teenagers, Adrian begins by asking the students to read an article from a local newspaper about two well-known high school students, a football player and a cheerleader, who died in a car accident while under the influence of alcohol. She tells them to summarize the article briefly and write it in the "Author Says" section. For students who tend to write too much or have difficulty summarizing key ideas, she suggests that they think about these questions before they start writing: (1) What is the topic of this assignment? (2) What does the author say about the topic? and (3) How does the author explain, support, and defend his or her position on this topic?

The next day in class, Adrian begins the discussion by asking students to share what they have written in their synthesis journals about the author's viewpoint. Before she invites students to share their own perspectives in a class discussion, she asks them to complete the "I Say" corner. Because Adrian reserves the synthesis journal for the more controversial issues in her health course, it does not take much prompting for students to voice their opinions after writing them. Perhaps the most difficult part of the lesson is to stop the discussion so that students will take the time to record what other students believe in the "Class Members Say" section. Adrian leads the discussion but also offers her viewpoints, giving her seventh graders opportunities to fill in the last section—"The Teacher Says."

During the last 15 minutes of class, Adrian asks the students to fill in the middle section, "Synthesis." Because this synthesis was initially difficult for her students, Adrian previously had explained what was meant by a synthesis and then modeled the process for them on an easier topic. In addition, she described how other students had completed their "Synthesis" section on issues they had discussed in her health course. The next day in class, Adrian asks students to share what they have written. For this unit on drugs, she has students meet with their study partners to read each other's entries. Adrian's unit does not end with the synthesis journal, but it certainly starts it in the right direction.

The Role of the Teacher Leader

As a teacher leader in your school, there are a variety of ways in which you can enhance students' strategic learning. An excellent way to begin is to know what is happening beyond the confines of your own classroom. That is, visit other content-area classes, skim other textbooks, and talk to colleagues other than the ones in your department. Do this in order to understand the tasks that students are expected to complete and how you might interact with other content-area teachers to assist students in completing these tasks in an efficient and effective manner. For example, we know of several 10th-grade teachers who share the same students and teach many of the same learning strategies to those students. Hence, those 10th graders learn how to summarize and take class notes from their biology, English, and history teachers. More important, those sophomores are also learning how they might modify their strategies across the content areas.

At the departmental level, there are many ways you can effect change. Some departments have actually devised notetaking systems unique to their own content areas and textbooks. For example, Mark Beaty and Tracy Stephens, science teachers at Winter Park, Florida, teach their ninth graders to use RAW-2, an acronym that represents the steps that students should follow when reading their assignments (i.e., read a section and write two important aspects for that section). In order to create this system, one that students really embrace, those teachers collaborated over many cups of coffee. (Beaty and Stephens, personal communications, 2005)

If your school has a tutoring program, your department could also volunteer to train the tutors in techniques or strategies unique to your content area. For example, tutors would profit greatly from knowing how to teach students to solve problems in content areas such as chemistry, physics, economics, and mathematics.

If your school does not have a tutoring program, you might consult the literature on how to set up a program at your school. Professional organizations such as the International Reading Association have published books and articles on this important topic.

they included only what the teacher said. The synthesis journal validates students' viewpoints as well as the teacher's. Finally, the synthesis journal provides content-area teachers who may use only a few written sources in their classrooms with a strategy for students to use in summarizing and thinking about ideas that have been presented orally during a unit. For example, under the "Author Says" column in Figure 9.8, students could write the ideas and viewpoints presented in a video, film, or class presentation by a guest speaker.

In sum, we should remember that when we ask students to take class notes, they are involved in several critical thinking processes. These processes cannot be mastered in a week or two. We emphasize that if you believe a strategy is worth teaching, students should be given the opportunity to learn it well. More important, students need to develop facility with the strategy so that they can personalize it to the task and the course in a controlled, comfortable manner. In the next section we discuss several additional strategies that will help students become more critical in their thinking and more metacognitively aware.

Strategies and Activities That Encourage Critical Thinking and Metacognitive Awareness

In this section we examine five different strategies or activities that share a common focus of helping students move beyond the memorization level of learning. The first three learning strategies assist students in organizing and synthesizing information from multiple sources and in building their metacognitive awareness. The last two activities encourage students to think critically about information and reflect upon their own performance.

Study Sheets

As we previously noted, students have great difficulty organizing and synthesizing ideas from multiple sources (e.g., Hynd-Shanahan et al., 2004). Thus, when you assign students to write a paper or present a speech using several outside sources, or when you ask them to combine their class notes with the information presented in their textbooks, what they produce will often be mediocre, at best. Moreover, students may inadvertently resort to copying what they have read and listing these "borrowed ideas" without thinking about overall patterns or generalizations. We will discuss a strategy, study sheets, that addresses these difficulties, but remind you that other strategies previously discussed in this chapter or in Chapter 3 (e.g., synthesis journals, mapping, charting) can also assist students.

Study sheets are similar to maps and charts in that they help students summarize and organize ideas from a variety of sources. Akeem, a 10th-grade American history instructor, teaches his students how to create study sheets because he found the strategy extremely helpful when he was a student. He introduces the study sheet strategy during his Civil Rights unit in which students read several different newspaper articles published during the 1950s and 1960s and an excerpt from a recent book by John Lewis. In addition, all his students watch a television documentary about the civil rights movement. Akeem selected these sources carefully so that they illustrated perspectives similar to and different from the ones contained in his students' history textbook.

The beauty of the study sheet strategy is that is can be modified to fit almost any content area.

Darrell, one of Akeem's students, created the study sheet illustrated in Figure 9.9. Notice how Darrell organized the information into smaller categories (e.g., events, groups and their beliefs) and combined ideas from a variety of sources (e.g., documentary, textbook, newspaper articles). Darrell and the other students learned a considerable amount of information merely from the decisions they had to make about the categories and subcategories and their arrangement. Fortunately, Akeem had frontloaded the assignment at the beginning of the year when he told his students that history was not so much about dates and wars as it was a story about people, groups, and significant events. Akeem also made sure his students understood that their history textbook was just one version of the "story" written by several different authors.

Akeem tells us that his students use their study sheets in a variety of ways during the Civil Rights unit—as a resource for class discussions and small-group projects and as a test-preparation strategy for the essay exam that formally closes the unit. Although Akeem personally prefers the study sheet strategy, he also knows that it is important to teach his students a variety of organizing strategies and then orchestrate situations where they can choose the ones they prefer.

Self-Questioning and the Questions/Answers Strategy

We could ask students to answer the questions provided by the authors of our textbooks. Such a task, however, probably does not mesh with the goals and activities of our units of study. Moreover, these text-provided questions do not teach students how to ask their own questions or interrogate the texts they read. Yet, the ability to generate and then answer appropriate questions is essential to becoming metacognitively aware (King, 1997; Weinstein et al., 2003).

Students can learn how to ask thought-provoking questions by using high-utility stems as question starters (King, 1992). The following question stems are useful in most content areas:

1. In my own words, what does this term mean?
2. What are the author's key ideas?

Figure 9.9 Study Sheet on the Civil Rights Movement

Topic: Civil rights movement during the early 1960s	
Leaders	**Groups**
James Farmer: member of CORE, planned Freedom Rides James Meredith: integrated University of Mississippi, March Against Fear Martin Luther King: campaign in Alabama, March on Washington, wins Nobel Peace Prize S. Carmichael: registers voters in Mississippi; suggests the need for Black Power Malcolm X: spokesperson for Black Muslims	CORE SCLC SNCC (changes direction under Carmichael) Black Panthers
Significant Events	**Legislation**
Sit-ins (Greensboro, SC, in 1960) Freedom Riders to Alabama, Mississippi Attempts to integrate universities (Alabama, Mississippi, and James Meredith, Georgia) MLK's campaign in Birmingham, AL (1963) MLK's March on Washington (1963) Explosion in Alabama church that kills four girls (1963) Violence in Selma, Alabama (MLK, Carmichael, and Malcolm X work to register voters in 1965) SNCC launches voter registration in Mississippi (1966) March Against Fear (1966)	*Boynton v. Virginia* Public Order Laws Civil Rights Act of 1964 24th Amendment Voting Rights Act of 1965

These research-validated question stems help students ask meaningful and useful questions about content-area concepts.

3. What is an example of . . . ?

4. How would you use . . . to . . . ?

5. What is a new or different example of . . . ?

6. In my own words, explain why . . . .

7. How does . . . affect . . . ?

8. What are the results or consequences of . . . ?

9. What are the likenesses between . . . and . . . ?

10. How is . . . different from . . . ?

11. What are the advantages of . . . ?

12. What are the disadvantages/limitations of . . . ?

13. What are the functions of . . . ?

14. What are the characteristics of . . . ?

15. Do I agree or disagree with this statement: . . . ?

16. What were the contributions/influences of . . . ?

17. How would you evaluate . . . ?

King found in her research studies that students working in pairs who generated elaborative answers to question stems like those in the preceding list performed better on a content-area objective test than those who did not.

Students have options in organizing and answering their questions about expository text. They could, as did the subjects in King's studies, meet in pairs and quiz each other. They could also write their questions and answers in a format that encourages organizing, synthesizing, and self-testing. One such format is the questions-answers strategy.

Questions-Answers Strategy

Figure 9.10 illustrates how one student used the questions-answers strategy to prepare for a test in an ecology course. His predicted questions focused on information from the assigned readings and from the class discussions. When the questions and answers are written and organized this way, students can test themselves by folding the paper in half and reading the questions aloud. They can also test each other because a permanent written artifact is available for them to share. Because the questions-answers strategy is written, it also can be handed in to teachers for their feedback. For example, by looking at the students' self-generated questions, teachers can determine what misconceptions or difficulties students are encountering with a particular concept.

Questions like the ones in Figure 9.10 do not spout from students' mouths at the first try. In fact, we have found that modeling, coaching, and specific feedback are necessary in teaching students how to ask and answer meaningful questions. Although it may take time to teach this strategy, the results are worth the effort because students learn how to control and monitor their own learning.

Some students prefer writing their question on the front of an index card and their answer on the back.

The Talk-Through

If you have ever verbally rehearsed what you wanted to tell the life insurance agent who kept pestering you with phone calls, you have conducted a talk-through. A talk-through is a study strategy that involves verbal rehearsal of content-area concepts (Simpson, 1994). Many of the learning strategies previously discussed

Figure 9.10   Questions-Answers Strategy in Preparing for a Test

Questions	Answers
1. What is the major source of solid waste? 2. What is the effect of silting on our environment? 3. What causes acid mine drainage? 4. What is the danger of acid mine waste? 5. Why was DDT banned? 6. What chemical compound affects the central nervous system of humans and animals? 7. What is the specific problem associated with thermal pollution? 8. Give an example of a material that is *not* biodegradable.	Agriculture Silting reduces oxygen production and the food supply for fish; also fouls spawning beds of fish.

> ## Honoring Diversity and Building Competence in the Content Classroom
>
> Anna, an algebra teacher, has found that her learning disabled students benefit from using the talk-through strategy in her classes, especially when it comes to internalizing the steps for solving word problems. She begins the school year by teaching the following steps to her students:
>
> 1. Read the problem carefully, underlining key words or phrases.
> 2. Reword the problem using the necessary facts.
> 3. Ask yourself, what problem do I have to solve? What is unknown?
> 4. Translate the reworded problem into an equation.
> 5. Solve the equation.
> 6. Check the answer by substituting the answer in the equation. Ask yourself, Does this answer make sense?
> 7. State the answer to the problem clearly.
>
> Anna posts these seven steps on her Web site. Throughout the first 9 weeks, she provides her own talk-throughs on how to implement the seven steps with sample problems taken from the textbook. However, Anna has added an extra dimension to the talk-through: She uses the chalkboard as a support to her talk-through, sketching situations and setting up equations from the word problems. She has found that the verbal and visual involvement of the talk-through has greatly increased the attention and subsequent learning of her students with learning disabilities.
>
> The following is an example of a talk-through that one of Anna's students, Damien, did at the chalkboard for his classmates:
>
>> This is the problem. "As a chef's assistant in a fancy restaurant, Kendra earns in 1 year a salary of $19,000. This is two-fifths of the head chef's salary. What is the head chef's salary?" First, I will reword the problem. Two-fifths of the head chef's salary is Kendra's salary. I was able to reword the problem because I knew that the word *this* in the second sentence referred to Kendra's salary. I also took out the extra words and reduced the problem to just the necessary facts and words. Second, I will translate these 10 words into symbols and numbers to create an equation. My goal for this problem is to find the chef's salary, which I do not know. Thus, I will represent this unknown with an X (he uses the chalkboard to do this and to reinforce the rest of his talk-through). I do know Kendra's salary: It is $19,000. I also know that two-fifths of the chef's salary, or 2/5 of X or 2/5 times X, is $19,000. Or, stated in another way, 2/5 times $X = $19,000$ or $2/5 (X) = $19,000$. I used the parentheses to stand for "multiplied by." Now I am ready to solve the problem, which is step five of the process.
>
> Although many of the math problems in Anna's class could probably be answered without using the seven steps or the talk-through, she believes that verbal rehearsal on the simple problems will help students later on in the school year with the more demanding problems.

(e.g., synthesis journals) rely on written products. The talk-through, by contrast, involves students in expressing and explaining themselves orally. In fact, the talk-through is very much like teaching, except that the audience is imaginary. We tell students that when they conduct talk-throughs, they should imagine themselves giving a lecture on a topic to an uninformed audience. We urge students with learning difficulties to pace the room, gesture, and talk. We know one student who stood on the top of her desk and delivered her talk-throughs as a way of preparing for her essay exams in history.

Because most of us have used informal talk-throughs to practice delivering important information, it is not surprising to learn that talk-throughs as a learning strategy can improve understanding and remembering of content-area concepts. Simpson's (1994) research demonstrated that students who had been trained to generate talk-throughs performed significantly better on an objective exam (i.e., multiple-choice and true-false) and an essay exam than their counterparts who were not so trained. Even more interesting was the finding that these students predicted more accurately their overall performance on the test and on each item. In other words, the subjects who did talk-throughs were more metacognitively aware of their performance on the exam than their counterparts.

Talk-throughs can be used in any content area, but they must be tailored to the demands of the course. Depending on the course, a talk-through could contain any of the following information:

1. Key ideas, using the student's own words
2. Examples, characteristics, processes, steps, causes, effects, and so on.
3. Personal or creative reactions
4. Summary statement or generalizations
5. Personal applications or examples

> Talk-throughs are especially useful for content areas that emphasize problem solving, processes, steps, or procedures.

Consequently, an effective talk-through in an American history class would probably differ from an effective talk-through in a geometry or physical education course.

We have found from our experiences with the talk-through strategy that it helps to explain to students the steps in developing an effective talk-through. A talk-through like Damien's involves considerable cognitive and metacognitive effort and planning. The following steps, although generic, can be modified according to any content area:

1. Think about the key ideas, trends, issues, and problems. Make sure you are using your own words when you explain them.
2. Organize the key ideas in some way. This can be done on an index card, but be brief because these notes are meant only to prompt your memory.
3. Find a quiet place, close your textbook or class notes, and use your card to deliver your talk-through out loud.
4. After practicing your first talk-through, check your card to make sure you were precise and complete. Ask yourself if you made sense.
5. Find someone to listen to your talk-through. Ask your audience if you made sense.

Because Anna knows that her students will not use the talk-through strategy unless they find it has more benefits than costs (i.e., conditional strategy knowledge), she asks them to generate a list of advantages to the strategy after they have used it several times. The following comments typify what Anna's students and other students have seen as the advantages of the talk-through strategy: (1) Talk-throughs help me determine what

Once students use the talk-through strategy on several different occasions, they see the many advantages it has to offer them.

information I know and what information is still unclear. (2) Talk-throughs improve my understanding of key terms because I am using my own words. (3) Talk-throughs help store information in my long-term memory. (4) Talk-throughs make me more actively involved in my learning. Making these advantages explicit is a necessary part of strategy instruction because students need to know the "why" as well as the "what" and the "how" if they are to adopt new study routines or strategies.

Helping Students Think Critically About Texts

Students do not typically question or challenge what they read, especially their textbooks. Researchers, for example, have found that many high school and college students believe that the ideas in their history textbooks are absolutely true immutable, and nondebatable (Britt & Aglinskas, 2002). In order to feel comfortable challenging texts, students need to interact with a variety of sources on a topic, not just one source. When students encounter multiple texts on an issue or concept, they are more likely to discern differences across the authors, note omissions, and detect the voices of various authors (Hynd-Shanahan et al., 2004; Metzer, Flanagin, & Zwarun, 2003). However, we should stress that providing students multiple sources on a topic, such as evolution or the Vietnam conflict, will not guarantee that students will immediately begin to think critically about texts. Content-area teachers will need to model and guide their students through these critical thinking processes while they are reading.

Mary Beth, a high school instructor who teaches anatomy and kinesiology to juniors, decided to do just that. She began by locating several articles on the Internet concerning dieting and nutrition. One particular article intrigued her because it was written by an individual with a medical degree who was touting a particular diet program and book that could be purchased on the Internet for a considerable sum of money. Moreover, the author offered several statements in the article that contradicted what her students had learned from their textbooks and discussions during class. The second article Mary Beth selected for her students focused on less glamorous but more research-based methods of dieting, such as exercising and using common sense with food choices. The author, however, was not a doctor or researcher.

Students need modeling and guidance when interacting with any written or oral text, especially the ones they encounter on the Internet.

With a third article she located on the Internet, Mary Beth began the mini-unit by introducing the four critical thinking guidelines she wanted to stress: the authority and intent of the author and the accuracy and objectivity of his or her ideas. After modeling and discussing these four guidelines in conjunction with the third article, Mary Beth then informed the students that they, too, would have the opportunity to challenge and question the authors. She placed the students in pairs, giving them their own article to read. Their assignment was to read the article and come to class prepared to teach their partner about their article.

The next day Mary Beth provided the partners 10 minutes to meet and teach each other. After 10 minutes she placed the students in groups of four and distributed the handout titled "Questioning and Challenging the Author" (see Figure 9.11). The groups of four were given 20 minutes to discuss the nine questions. Mary Beth circulated around the room listening to the discussions and guiding their participation, when necessary. She then rang a bell and gave the groups the task of reaching an agreement on how they would "rate the author" (see Part Two in Figure 9.11). The students were also instructed to fill out Part One and to select a spokesperson who would report back to the class.

Needless to say, the students were all actively engaged in the discussion of the articles and in the rating of the authors. And, as Mary Beth hypothesized, two of the groups rated the Internet article by the medical doctor as superior solely on the basis of his "authority." At the end of the hour Mary Beth helped the students debrief the

Figure 9.11   Questioning and Challenging the Author

PART ONE DIRECTIONS: Think about the following questions as you read the article you were assigned. These questions force you to think critically about an author's authority, intent, accuracy, and objectivity. If you think of additional questions that would be useful to you and your group members, write them in the blank lines.

Authority

1. Who is the author or producer of this information?
2. What are the author's qualifications? Are these credentials credible? Are these qualifications sufficient to discuss the content presented in the article?

Intent

3. What is the author trying to say here? What is the message?
4. Did the author explain and support the ideas in a clear fashion? Explain.

Accuracy

5. When was this article written? What do you know about this time period?
6. Can this information be verified by another source? Explain.
7. Is this information consistent with what you already know about the topic? Why or why not?

Objectivity

8. Is there any sort of bias evident in this article? Explain.
9. Is the author's motivation for writing clear to you? What do you think that motivation was?
10. OTHER QUESTIONS:

_____

_____

_____

PART TWO DIRECTIONS: After answering the questions listed above and listening to your peers during the discussion, RATE the author of this article/essay. Complete the grid below so it represents what your group decides. You must reach a consensus and be prepared to defend your rating. Select a spokesperson for your group.

RATE THE AUTHOR

	1	2	3	4	5
	Low		Average		High

Authority

Intent

Accuracy

Objectivity

TOTAL SCORE: _____

experience and discussed how they might use these four guidelines in their own reading, whether it be on the Internet or in magazines or newspapers.

You need not teach anatomy to use these guidelines that encourage students to think critically about what they read. Any content-area teacher can design a similar lesson using the Internet or any source that provides students an alternative viewpoint or an alternative development of an idea.

Encouraging Students to Evaluate and Reflect

Successful independent learners reflect upon the strategies they have employed and evaluate whether these strategies were appropriate for the task and content area (Hubbard & Simpson, 2003; Winne & Jamieson-Noel, 2002). In addition, successful students determine whether their self-selected strategies were appropriate for themselves as learners and make adjustments, when necessary, to remedy the situation and improve their academic performance. Reflecting and evaluating in this manner are highly sophisticated thinking processes that encourage students to be even more metacognitively aware and successful in their independent learning across the content areas (Cleary & Zimmerman, 2004; Zimmerman, 2002). Moreover, when students are engaged in activities that require them to reflect and evaluate, they are less likely to attribute their performance to luck, inherent skill, or "tricky" test questions that the teacher created.

Content-area teachers can employ a variety of activities to encourage their students to reflect and evaluate about their performance. We will examine two of them: the learning log and the self-reflection activity.

Learning Logs

Students write a learning log entry once they have finished taking an exam. In this paragraph, students describe in detail how they read and studied, discuss whether their strategy choices were appropriate, and predict their performance. If you tell students it is important to be honest in writing their entry, you will gain some useful assessment information about them. More important, by thinking about their strategies and whether they were appropriate, your students will realize that they are the ones in control of their academic performance, not you.

Kim, a 10th-grade biology teacher, asked her students to write a learning log entry immediately after they had finished their exam. Then, 2 days later, after discussing the exam during class and going over the answers, Kim asked them to reread their entry. She then assigned her students to write a second entry describing what they had learned about themselves and what they would do differently if they had the opportunity to retake the exam. One student, Jason, wrote the following evaluation paragraphs, labeled before and after. As you read them, think about his strengths and weaknesses as an active learner and what he learned about himself.

Jason's Learning Log Entries

BEFORE: Well, I predict that I will get an A on this test. I have always been smart in science. The test was about what I expected—not too hard, not too easy. I didn't think we would have to diagram the female reproductive cycle— that was a surprise. I studied by skimming the chapters and looking at my notes during homeroom. I probably studied about 10 minutes—science is my thing, so I really did not need to study much. By the way, did we talk in class about the regulation of glucose?

AFTER: Well, I guess I did not do as well as I predicted—I got a D on the test. I missed all the questions on the diagrams. My other science teachers never asked me to label and explain diagrams. I probably should have read the chapters rather than skimming them. I also should have looked at my class notes longer. If I could take the test again, I would certainly study longer, and I would memorize those diagrams you discussed with us in class. Otherwise, if I could take this test over, I probably would not change my strategies that much. I learned from this first test that biology may be different from general science.

What did you learn about Jason? What did you decide his strengths were? His weaknesses? After receiving Jason's evaluation paragraph, Kim hypothesized that Jason was not using active strategies for studying. He was merely skimming or looking at material—very passive strategies. Because Kim requires her students to integrate concepts, Jason's strategies were definitely not appropriate for the thinking processes she emphasizes in her course. Moreover, Jason probably was not listening intently in class because Kim had stressed the importance of studying the diagrams and being able to explain how hormones interact with each other. Kim decided to watch Jason carefully and to work on his definitions of what it means to read and study in a biology course. Kim, however, was not the only individual who gained important information from the learning log entries. Jason and Kim's other students were also gathering important information about themselves as learners in biology.

Although these self-reflection entries in learning logs are intended to help students, teachers can also capitalize on them as opportunities for assessment and diagnosis.

Self-Reflection Activity

In addition to the learning log, content-area teachers can encourage students to evaluate their own strategies and techniques by asking them to participate in a self-reflection activity similar to the one in Figure 9.12. This particular checklist was developed by Nicole, a chemistry teacher, who was concerned about her students and their reactions to the first chemistry exam. Many of her students were dismayed by their mediocre performance and were making comments in class similar to these: "I am just not good in chemistry." "I studied for 8 hours last night and still received a C on the

Figure 9.12 Self-Reflection Activity for Chemistry

Directions: In order to help improve your exam performance, I must know more about the techniques you are using to read and study. Please note that I am interested in how you really studied, not in how you wished you had studied. Be honest as there is no penalty for telling me that you did not read your assignments or did not do any chemistry problems. FILL IN THE BLANKS AND CHECK THE STATEMENTS THAT PERTAIN TO YOU.

YOUR NAME: _____

Estimate the amount of time you spent studying for this exam: _____ (hours/minutes)
When did you begin your serious studying? _____ (the night before, etc.)

I did these things to study for the chemistry exam:
_____ 1. I read my assignments on a daily basis.
_____ 2. After I read a chemistry assignment, I summarized the key ideas on a piece of paper, sticky note, or index card.
_____ 3. I identified the material that I did not understand so I could ask questions in class.
_____ 4. I reviewed my class notes on a daily basis.
_____ 5. I read the lab manual and took the self-check quiz before I did the experiments in lab.
_____ 6. I solved the assigned chemistry problems without looking at the solutions at the back of the book.
_____ 7. I did extra chemistry problems at the end of each chapter.
_____ 8. I did talk-throughs of the key concepts in the chapters.
_____ 9. I quizzed myself or asked someone to quiz me over the key concepts.
_____10. Describe any other methods you used to study. _____
_____

exam." "I am not going to try anymore, because when I study I still fail." Nicole knew these students were not reading and studying appropriately but wanted them to draw that conclusion. Hence, she listed on the checklist all the strategies and techniques that she knew were task appropriate and productive for learning chemistry.

The following day Nicole distributed the checklist and asked her students to complete it. She stressed that the checklist, if done honestly, would help them determine what they needed to do to improve their exam performance. That evening Nicole divided the checklists into categories: students that received an A or B on the exam and students who received a D or F. She then read each checklist and coded the strategies that the students checked so that she could identify the strategies used by the high-performing students and the low-performing students. Although she knew what trends would emerge from this data analysis (e.g., the students who solved all the problems in the workbook were the ones who did well on the exam), she also knew her students would perceive the data from the checklists as extremely credible and useful.

Armed with the data and the trends, Nicole went to class the next day and presented the information to her students on an overhead. In Figure 9.13 you will note the trends that Nicole discussed with her students. As you can see, the students who received an A or B on the first exam were the ones who were reading and studying on a daily basis, solving all the assigned problems, and asking questions during class to clarify concepts. Nicole also found no differences between the high-performing and low-performing students in terms of the amount of time spent studying. As expected, this information about time really surprised her students.

After a discussion of the trends, Nicole asked her students to return to the checklist and circle the strategies and techniques they would be willing to try out for the next exam. This particular step was important because it placed the responsibility

Figure 9.13   Data on Successful Students in Chemistry

The students who received an A or B on the exam

Studied an average of 2 hours for the exam

Began their studying at least 2 days before the exam

Reported an average of 4.8 different strategies

Used these techniques:

(a) They all did extra chemistry problems

(b) They all summarized what they read

(c) They all reviewed their class notes on a daily basis

(d) They all asked questions during class

The students who received a D or F on the exam

Studied an average of 2.8 hours for the exam

Began their studying the night before the exam

Reported an average of 1.7 different strategies

Used these techniques:

(a) They all read their assignments

(b) They did most of the assigned problems

on the students to reflect on the techniques they had been using and to consider the possibility of changing to some more productive ones. Nicole tells us that the time spent on the checklist and the debriefing of the trends from the checklist has proved to be time well spent. During the semester she has observed numerous students making significant changes in their reading and studying behaviors. Because of the success of this lesson, Nicole decided to place the checklist on her Web site as a link for parents so they, too, have a sense of how their children should be reading, studying, and thinking about chemistry.

The procedures that Nicole used with her students in chemistry have been modified slightly and replicated with considerable success in a variety of content-area courses such as physics, biology, history, and art appreciation.

We began this chapter with a comment from Wilbur McKeachie about the goals of education and the importance of emphasizing thinking processes as well as content-area knowledge. We end this chapter by returning to what McKeachie and others have been saying for quite some time: When we build strategic, independent learners, we are building learners for the future.

CASE STUDY REVISITED

Return to the beginning of the chapter, where we described Ian, the English teacher concerned about his gifted students' learning strategies. After reading this chapter, you probably have some ideas about how he could be more creative and effective in his teaching. Take time now to write your suggestions.

As Ian was searching for instructional answers for his gifted students, a situation serendipitously occurred in their AP history class that stimulated considerable discussion and complaining. Most of Ian's students felt that their most recent essay exam in AP history had been unfair and far too demanding. Ian therefore decided to talk to his colleague and running partner who taught the history class. Theo was more than happy to discuss the questions and share some insights with Ian. It seems that the essay questions required students to read and synthesize several written sources about isolationism. Some of the questions asked students to form generalizations and another question asked them to compare and contrast some of the theories.

Armed with this information, Ian went to class the next day and asked his students to evaluate their exam performance by writing an paragraph that addressed several questions (e.g., How long did you study? Describe how you read and studied, What techniques did you use?). That night as he read the students' paragraphs Ian discovered that several of them did not read all the assigned material and that a significant number of them waited until the night before the exam to finish their reading. He also learned that most of the students reported no special techniques or strategies to organize the multiple sources. Ian found his first "hook" for teaching his students more powerful learning strategies—their success in AP history.

The next day he decided to teach his students how to corroborate, an essential higher-level thinking process, by using the charting strategy. Corroboration involves students in comparing and contrasting texts with another source, a process that his students had skipped in their study procedures. Rather than use the history curriculum, Ian decided to introduce the usefulness of charts with the short stories they had been reading in his class. The students selected several characters from

Before writing your suggestions for Ian, go to *http://www.prenhall.com/ brozo*, select Chapter 9, then click on Chapter Review Questions to check your understanding of the material.

continued

the stories and then worked in pairs to compare and contrast them on several different features. Once all the students had completed their charts, Ian then debriefed the experience, stressing the advantages of the chart as a visual organizer and a preparation step for writing.

Two days later Ian followed up the initial charting lesson by explaining to his students that they would be creating another chart in order to compare and contrast historical figures such as Churchill and Wilson. After brainstorming all the possible characteristics that could be used on the vertical axis of their charts (e.g., individual's background, beliefs), Ian placed the students in pairs to work. In order to emphasize the benefits of the charting strategy, the next day Ian gave the students a quick pop quiz over the content in their charts. The students were thrilled to discover that they "aced" the quiz because they had remembered all the information in their charts. This situation provided Ian a perfect opportunity to discuss other ways in which to organize and synthesize ideas.

During the school year, Ian also read a few articles about the teaching of learning strategies in professional publications such as the *Journal of Adolescent & Adult Learning*. From his reading, he realized that he needed to demonstrate for his students how they should modify their reading methods for the different courses they were taking. His students were particularly impressed with his modeling because they had always thought they should read their chemistry assignments in the same way they should read their literature or history assignments.

The first semester has taught Ian many things. Most important, he has realized that students will not be able to transfer study strategies to their own tasks if they do nothing but complete workbook activities.

Looking Back, Looking Forward

Learning strategies should be taught as processes instead of as a series of steps that, when followed, will automatically produce greater learning and retention. We have emphasized the learner as an important part of strategy instruction. Without giving students opportunities to help shape the learning strategies they are being taught, we run the risk of offering them a series of meaningless formulas that have little relevance to their genuine study needs. This has important implications for content-area teachers who want their students to be active rather than passive learners. Your role should be to inform students of each study process and its best possible applications, and then guide them in developing personally meaningful adaptations that transfer to actual study tasks.

We purposely limited our presentation to a few effective research-based strategies and activities because we wanted to reiterate the idea that it takes a great deal of time to develop expertise in using them. We also made it clear that no single text-study strategy will be appropriate for every study need. Consequently, students should be encouraged to learn a few flexible, meaningful study processes so that they can select the most appropriate one for their purposes and tasks.

References

Britt, M. A., & Aglinskas, C. (2002). Improving students' ability to identify and use source information. *Cognition and Instruction, 20,* 485–523.

Brown, A., & Day, J. (1983). Macrorules for summarizing text: The development of expertise. *Journal of Verbal Learning and Verbal Behavior, 22,* 1–14.

Burrell, K. I., & McAlexander, P. J. (1998). Ideas in practice: The synthesis journal. *Journal of Developmental Education, 22,* 20–22, 24, 26, 28, 30.

Butler, D. L., & Winne, P. H. (1995). Feedback and self-regulated learning: A theoretical synthesis. *Review of Educational Research, 65,* 245–281.

Casazza, M. (2003). Using a model of direct instruction to teach summary writing in a college reading class. In N. Stahl & H. Boylan (Eds.), *Teaching developmental reading* (pp. 135–144). Boston: Bedford/St. Martin.

Cleary, T. J., & Zimmerman, B. J. (2004). Self-regulation empowerment program: A school-wide program to enhance self-regulation and self-motivational cycles of learning. *Psychology in the School, 41,* 537–550.

Covington, M. V., & Roberts, B. W. (1994). Self-worth and college achievement: Motivational and personality correlates. In P. R. Pintrich, D. R. Brown, & C. E. Weinstein (Eds.), *Student motivation, cognition, and learning.* Hillsdale, NJ: Lawrence Erlbaum Associates.

Doyle, W. (1983). Academic work. *Review of Educational Research, 53,* 159–199.

Friend, R. (2000). Teaching summarization as a content area reading strategy. *Journal of Adolescent and Adult Literacy, 44,* 32–330.

Grigg, W., Daane, M., Ying, J., & Campbell, J. (2003). *The nation's report card: Reading 2003, National Assessment of Educational Progress.* Washington, DC: National Center for Education Statistics.

Hadwin, A. F., Winne, P. H., Stockley, D. B., Nesbit, J. C., & Woszcyna, C. (2001). Context moderates students' self-reports about how they study. *Journal of Educational Psychology, 93,* 477–488.

Hartley, J. (2002). Designing instructional and informational text. Retrieved June 1, 2005, from http://aectmembers.org/m/research_handbook/Chapters/34.pdf.

Hofer, B. K. (2004). Epistemological understanding as a metacognitive process: Thinking aloud during online searching. *Educational Psychologist, 39,* 43–55.

Hubbard, B. P., & Simpson, M. L. (2003). Developing self-regulated learners: Putting theory into practice. *Reading Research and Instruction, 42,* 62–89.

Hynd-Shanahan, C. R., Holschuh, J., & Hubbard, B. (2004). Thinking like a historian: College students' reading of multiple historical documents. *Journal of Literacy Research, 4,* 238–250.

King, A. (1992). Enhancing peer interaction and learning in the classroom through reciprocal questioning. *American Educational Research Journal, 27,* 664–687.

King, A. (1997). ASK to THINK—TELL WHY: A model of transactive peer tutoring for scaffolding higher level complex learning. *Educational Psychologist, 32,* 221–235.

Kintsch, W., & van Dijk, T. A. (1978). Toward a model of text comprehension and production. *Psychological Review, 85,* 363–394.

McKeachie, W., Pintrich, P. R., Smith, D. A., & Lin, Y. (1986). *Teaching and learning in the college classroom: A review of the research literature.* Ann Arbor: NCRIPTAL, The University of Michigan.

Metzer, M. J., Flanagin, A. J., & Zwarun, L. (2003). College student web use, perceptions of information credibility, and verification behavior. *Computers and Education, 41,* 271–290.

Palmatier, R. A. (1973). A notetaking system for learning. *Journal of Reading, 17,* 36–39.

Paris, S. G., & Paris, A. H. (2001). Classroom applications of research on self-regulated learning. *Educational Psychologist, 36,* 89–101.

Paris, S. G., Wasik, B. A., & Turner, J. C. (1991). The development of strategic readers. In R. Barr, M. L. Kamil, P. B. Mosenthal, & P. D. Pearson (Eds.), *Handbook of reading research* (Vol. II, pp. 609–640). New York: Longman.

Peverly, S., Brobst, K., Graham, M., & Shaw, R. (2003). College students are not good at self-regulation: A study on the relationship of self-regulation, note taking, and test taking. *Journal of Educational Psychology, 95,* 335–346.

Pressley, M. (2000). What should comprehension instruction be the instruction of? In M. Kamil, P. Mosenthal, P. D. Pearson, & R. Barr (Eds.), *Handbook of reading research* (Vol. III, pp. 545–561). Mahwah, NJ: Lawrence Erlbaum Associates.

Ruddell, R., & Unrau, N. (2004). Reading as a meaning-construction process: The reader, the text and the teacher. In R. Ruddell & N. Unrau (Eds.), *Theoretical models and processes of reading* (Vol. 3). Newark, DE: International Reading Association.

Schommer-Atkins, M. (2002, April). Personal epistemology: Conflicts and consensus in an emerging area of inquiry. Paper presented at the American Educational Research Association's Annual Meeting, New Orleans, LA.

Simpson, M. L. (1994). Talk throughs: A strategy for encouraging active learning across the content areas. *Journal of Reading, 38,* 296–304.

Simpson, M. L., & Nist, S. L. (1990). Textbook annotation: An effective and efficient study strategy for college students. *Journal of Reading, 34,* 122–131.

Simpson, M. L., & Nist, S. L. (2003). An update on strategic learning: It's more than textbook reading strategies. In N. Stahl & H. Boylan (Eds.), *Teaching developmental reading* (pp. 157–178). Boston: Bedford/St. Martin.

Simpson, M. L., Stahl, N., & Francis, M. (2004). Reading and learning recommendations for the 21st century. *Journal of Developmental Education, 28,* 2–15.

Thiede, K., & Anderson, M. C. (2003). Summarizing can improve metacomprehension accuracy. *Contemporary Educational Psychology, 28,* 129–161.

Tovani, C. (2004). *Do I really have to teach reading: Content comprehension, grades 6–12.* Portland, ME: Stenhouse Publishers.

Weinstein, C. E., Dierking, D., Husman, J., Roska, L., & Powdrill, L. (2003). The impact of a course in strategic learning on the long-term retention of college students. In N. Stahl & H. Boylan (Eds.), *Teaching developmental reading* (pp. 193–208). Boston: Bedford/St. Martin.

Winne, P. H., & Jamieson-Noel, D. (2002). Exploring students' calibration of self-reports about study tactics and achievement. *Contemporary Educational Psychology, 27,* 551–572.

Zimmerman, B. J. (2002). Becoming a self-regulated learner: An overview. *Theory into Practice, 41,* 64–70.

chapter 10

Expanding Literacy and Content Learning Through Information and Communication Technologies

Anticipation Guide

Directions: Read each statement carefully and decide whether you agree or disagree with it, placing a check mark in the appropriate *Before Reading* column. When you have finished reading and studying the chapter, return to the guide and decide whether your anticipations need to be changed by placing a check mark in the appropriate *After Reading* column.

	Before Reading		After Reading	
	Agree	*Disagree*	*Agree*	*Disagree*
1. ICTs can increase student learning by increasing student engagement.	✓			
2. ICTs are most applicable in technology-rich disciplines like math and science.		✓		
3. Reading and writing are critical skills for taking full advantage of ICT tools.	✓			
4. The Internet can be used to promote higher-level thinking in virtually every discipline.	✓			
5. Word processing is the only computer application supportive of students' literacy growth.		✓		

6. Electronic field trips will be possible
in this decade.

_____ _____ _____ _____

7. Databases and spreadsheets have
limited applicability except in
content areas such as math
and science.

_____ _____ _____ _____

8. Handheld devices such as iPods and
Blackberries are more a nuisance
than an aid to learning.

_____ _____ _____ _____

Chapter Principle: Expand and Generate New Understandings Using Information and Communication Technologies

This principle derives from the belief that information and communication technology (ICT) tools can significantly enhance disciplinary teaching and learning. It acknowledges that ICTs are so much a part of youths' real-world literacy and learning practices that full advantage should be taken of them in secondary classrooms. Further, the principle offers guidance to disciplinary teachers interested in expanding youths' multiliteracy toolkits by exhorting them to explore applications of technology that support students' higher-level thinking, inquiry learning, and critical reading.

Go to *http://www. prenhall.com/brozo,* select Chapter 10, then click on Chapter Objectives to provide a focus for your reading.

*A*s this book attests, becoming sophisticated readers and writers of print is still essential for youth. However, we also believe being print literate is no longer sufficient in a world saturated with digitized media that have become powerful sources of information and tools for communication. Though this chapter focuses on classroom applications of technology, we remind you that in virtually every chapter descriptions can be found of disciplinary teachers taking advantage of digital and media technology to increase student engagement and depth of thinking.

This chapter serves to broaden conceptions of what counts as literacy and extend visions of possible disciplinary practice. We have demonstrated numerous times within these pages that teaching content information and concepts with textbooks as the primary source material is no longer adequate. This is especially true for youth whose everyday lives in the mediasphere involve constructing and reconstructing print and nonprint meanings with sophisticated digital technologies (Alvermann, 2002; Leu, Kinzer, Coiro, & Cammack, 2004). At the same time, recalling our assertions about the complexity and multidimensionality of adolescence, we do not want to leave the impression that digitally mediated literacies are synonymous with young people. The image of the multitasking, imminently "plugged in" adolescent, complete with iPod, Gameboy, and personal computer, is resonant with many young people but certainly not all. Nevertheless, practices that fail to recognize the power of digital media for engaging youth, sustaining attention, and effecting meaningful and critical understandings of content may be leaving many behind (Kamil, 2004; Leander & Sheehy, 2004; Mistler-Jackson & Songer, 2000). Teachers who approach their craft with a thoughtful and inquiring disposition will find numerous ways to acquire and make use of technology tools for enriching learning experiences for youth (Tapscot, 1999), whether they are totally "plugged in" or not.

We begin by presenting the benefits of using ICTs as mediators of content instruction and learning. This is followed by descriptions of actual teachers who employed innovative, technology-based practices that celebrate and extend the multiliteracies of youth.

CASE STUDY

José and his colleagues in the science and math department of a large urban high school received a state-funded technology grant. The grant was designed to be used by teachers of math and science to train their students in the ways in which computer technology could improve learning in those subjects. José received funds to purchase computers, computer software, networked Internet connections, and teacher training in the new uses of computer technology.

In staff development workshops, José discovered a number of exciting applications of computer technology to his biology subject matter. In one workshop session, he and other faculty were asked to think of ways of using the computer to facilitate their students' learning of especially challenging content. José's students seemed most challenged by the sheer volume of detail they were required to learn. For example, for the study of cell types in advanced biology, students had to learn and remember hundreds of facts related to 10 to 20 different cell types. They were having a great deal of difficulty organizing and remembering this information. José had tried to devise study schemes for his students, but they were either too complex or did not provide motivation.

Case studies in this textbook provide an opportunity to apply principles and practices to new contexts.

To the Reader:
As you read and study this chapter, think about José and his goal to help his students organize their biology content more effectively. What computer-based strategies could José use to achieve this goal?

Guidelines for Using Information and Communication Technologies in the Disciplinary Classroom

A report of Internet access in U.S. public schools from 1994 to 2001 (Kleiner & Farris, 2002) documents a 35% increase during that 7-year period to levels of nearly 100% today. This means that virtually all youth—regardless of whether computer technology tools are available in the home, which for over 50% of adolescents are not (U.S. Census Bureau, 2001)—should be able to access ICTs in schools and classrooms. At the same time, at least 31 states require core technical competencies based on national educational standards (Loschert, 2003). These standards serve to further institutionalize the need to weave ICTs into all areas of the secondary school curriculum.

We know, however, that in spite of the prevalence of ICTs in school, taking full advantage of these new teaching and learning tools will depend on disciplinary teachers' interest and willingness to become more tech savvy (Tileston, 2004) and structural supports in schools (Norris & Soloway, 2003). In spite of the omnipresence of technology in schools and everyday life, not everyone is tapping into its educational benefits (Pearson & Young, 2002; Songer, Lee, & Kam, 2002), nor are intermedial practices for critically reading and writing across various digital and nondigital systems as widespread in school as they should be (Pailliotet, Semali, Rodenberg, Giles, & Macaul, 2000; Quesada, Miller, & Armstrong, 2000). For instance, in a study of teachers' technology skills, Newman (2000) found that out of the 30 he interviewed, only a few had experience with more than e-mail and word-processing programs. The stretch from e-mail to the vast and learning-rich potential of the Internet is much easier than some teachers might think (Richardson, 2004). We acknowledge that what may seem like small changes to us are often big changes for content-area teachers by offering guidelines and numerous classroom demonstrations of easy-to-implement, Internet-based practices.

The overriding criterion teachers of adolescents should apply when considering the use of ICTs in their lessons is the extent to which these tools will promote expansive learning and critical thinking. We believe, as others (Kinzer, 2003; Leu & Kinzer, 2000) do, that teachers who create learning contexts where the importance of critical reading and thinking is valued will find appropriate ways to integrate ICTs in support of content learning. The guidelines discussed next should be used to help your decision making about how best to link ICTs to your content-area lessons.

Provide Opportunities for Creative Uses of ICT Tools

Casting aspersions on technology as a tool for learning in schools is akin to heresy in today's high-tech world. We have come to accept the sanguine pronouncements of computer industry spokespersons, bandwagoning policy makers, and well-intentioned educational administrators without challenge (Cuban, 2001; Zhao & Conway, 2001). Yet, as some people in the popular media (Mathews, 2000; Oppenheimer, 2003) and others who develop and study these new technologies (Burbules & Callister, 2000; Leu & Kinzer, 2000; March, 2000) admit, the research basis for grand claims about computers and student learning may yet be quite difficult to defend.

Go to Web Resources for Chapter 10 at *http://www.prenhall.com/brozo,* and look for ICTs and Literacy.

What does seem to be known about the value of ICTs for teaching and learning is that achievement is more likely to rise if schools use them in interesting and creative ways instead of mostly for drill in basic skills (McKenna & Richards, 2003; Wenglinsky, 1998). In fact, using technology for drill, practice, and entertainment was found to depress achievement (Kinzer & Leander, 2003). The idea is that it's not how much time students spend with these technologies but the quality of use that relates to higher achievement.

This guideline also emphasizes that ICTs should be exploited for their unique instructional capabilities and not simply as media for re-presenting predictable worksheet tasks in a visual format. Interesting and creative uses of technology are more likely to enhance learning and develop higher-level thinking skills (Burbules & Callister, 2000). Computers and other electronic media can help students visualize content to be learned in novel ways. For example, virtual reality programs and programs that allow students to work with geometric figures in hyperspace are made possible only through computer-based instructional technology (Marcus, 1995; Winn, 2002). The activities described a bit later in this chapter all emphasize the ways in which technology can be used creatively for engendering higher-level thinking and knowledge acquisition.

> Quality, more so than quantity, of computer time is related to higher student achievement.

Use ICT Tools in Ways That Promote Critical Thinking

With the advent of widespread access to ICT tools in homes and schools, our ideas about literacy have undergone major transformations. We have made clear throughout this book that literacy is no longer viewed solely as the ability to decode and encode printed words. Proponents of new and multiple literacies (Brindley, 2000; Gee, 2003; Lankshear & Knobel, 2003; Luke, 2002) assert that a much broader conception of what it means to be literate encompasses all forms of symbolic communication—those enacted by adolescents and those that influence their lives and learning. This conception must include, of course, information and communication technologies.

Preparing students for a post-typographic world—that is, a world where traditional print literacy is no longer enough—is presented by some (Reinking, McKenna, Labbo, & Kieffer, 1998) as incumbent upon the responsible educator. Post-typographic literacies are seen as vital tools students must have in order to navigate within and "read" our increasingly complex global society (Lankshear & Knobel, 2003; Leu & Kinzer, 2000; Luke, 2002). We agree with the late Brazilian scholar and activist Paulo Freire (1987), who insisted that in order to read the word, we must also be capable of reading the world. Critically reading the world and the word should, therefore, be a vibrant feature of instruction with ICT tools in disciplinary classrooms.

Once again, however, a word of caution is warranted. Hundreds of books on the market today list thousands of opportunities for using information and communication technologies in the classroom. Regarding this glut of books on ICTs, Monke (2001) points out that there is a "disappointing shortage of thoughtful literature devoted to discussing the sobering flip side of opportunity—responsibility" (p. 203). We must never forget that although we may have become excited by and proficient with ICT tools and the different formats they provide for representing meaning (Kress, 1998), we, as teachers, bring a sophisticated and nuanced understanding of our disciplines to these new electronic media—a kind of understanding youth may lack. Therefore, we believe it is our collective responsibility to promote discursive practices while expanding ICT opportunities for adolescents. Consider the astronomer Clifford Stoll's (1999) cautions about technology in science. He says scientists may use computers in their research, but they did not learn science through computers. Computers can yield answers to specific questions but they do not necessarily inspire scientific curiosity or give understanding. To restate our point, then, teachers of adolescents should take advantage of the new and promising benefits of ICTs while enriching and reinforcing students' abilities to think critically about the symbolic forms of meaning displayed and transmitted by electronic media.

Each year, the Internet grows exponentially. This mind-boggling expansion of Web connections has created a greater need than ever before for critical consciousness and critical reading (Salpeter, 2003). Burbules and Callister (2000) describe the opportunity and problems of unrestricted self-expression on the Internet in this way:

Teaching youth media literacy helps them become critical evaluators of the messages they receive daily from electronic and digital sources.

> Participants in this environment often need to read and evaluate so much material, from so many sources, that it becomes impossible to maintain a critical discerning attitude toward it all. The very volume and number of voices has a kind of leveling effect—everything seems to come from the same place and nothing seems much more reliable than anything else. This makes the need to evaluate the value and credibility of what one encounters on the Internet a crucial skill if one is to be an active beneficiary of the available information and interaction. (p. 71)

It is because of the overwhelming proliferation of Web sites and the ease of accessibility and hypertext, or the linking nature of the Internet, that we urge disciplinary teachers in middle and high school to foster in youth a form of critical literacy of the Internet medium itself (Hagood, 2003; Peters & Lankshear, 1996; Salpeter, 2003).

Use ICT Tools in Ways That Promote Authentic Communication

Our best thinking about the most effective ways to increase learning makes it clear that students need ample time to engage in disciplinary activities that have authentic purposes (Brozo, in press). One of the most promising features of computer technology for promoting authentic communication is the Internet. Unlike previous technologies such as television and radio, once thought to have the potential to transform education, the Internet offers teachers and students a blend of communication and retrieval functions within a worldwide framework. More significantly, although the Internet is an electronic network, it nonetheless runs on literacy (Mike, 1997; Schmar-Doblar, 2003). Even for skeptics of computers as learning tools, it is indisputable that reading and writing are essential for electronic navigation, information sharing, and information retrieval (Leu & Kinzer, 2000; Teclehaimanot & Lamb, 2004).

The reading and writing involved in typical computer tasks in secondary schools can provide some of that much needed time for authentic literacy activities (Coiro, 2003). Consider the literacy requirements of a ninth grader's computer research of the rocky planets in our solar system. First, he must read a variety of directions for accessing specific "hits" to review. Next, he must follow additional directions to find texts and other information about the planets of interest. All the while, the student is reading, making critical judgments, and typing key words and phrases to hone his search. There may come a time when students will be able to complete similar tasks with mere voice activation, but for the foreseeable future, reading and writing skills will continue to be a necessity for school-related ICT tasks.

Internet communication should be exploited as a medium for providing an authentic sense of audience for literacy activity. Composition research using that medium has demonstrated its potential for helping students develop audience sensitivity and writing skills (Hawisher & Selfe, 1998). Students who communicate on the Internet are writing for an actual audience of one or perhaps hundreds or thousands. Likewise, students who read Internet communications become part of an audience.

Teachers can take advantage of this experience by helping students develop audience sensitivity with writing assignments on the Internet for various purposes. For example, students can engage in activities as simple as writing personal reactions to a current event on a Web log (blog) and letters to electronic pen pals, and perform more complex communication tasks such as formal inquiries to experts, companies, and organizations and creating home pages and publishing Web-based magazines and newspapers known as *e-zines* (Guzzetti, Campbell, Duke, & Irving, 2003; Knobel & Lankshear, 2002).

> The Internet should be exploited for the instant outlet and audience it provides youth as they further develop their communication skills.

Use ICT Tools in Ways That Increase Student Motivation for and Interest in Purposeful and Meaningful Learning

The strongest advocates for the use of ICTs in teaching and learning claim its most appealing feature is that students are automatically interested in and motivated by computers (Leu et al., 2004). This high level of enthusiasm has given rise to "NetGen" youth (Tapscot, 1998) who represent for Tapscot and others (Howe & Strauss, 2000; Rushkoff, 1996) a desirable model of a new form of consciousness that thrives in the state of chaos found in digital and cyber worlds.

In spite of the cautions against using computers for learning solely on the basis of student interest (Healy, 2000), there is a growing body of research to support the motivating effects of computers when used with students in school-based learning (Leu et al., 2004; Rozell & Gardner, 2000; Sølvberg, 2003). Bridging student motivation with constructive learning is, as we have been repeating throughout this book, the artful task of the content-area teacher. One of our expressed goals in this text is to help teachers develop students who are motivated and engaged learners. If students are more enthusiastic about learning using ICT tools, then disciplinary teachers and students should exploit these tools to whatever extent they can be used to mediate meaningful and critical exploration of content.

Use ICT Tools to Promote Collective Learning and Collaboration

The study of information and communication technologies is now concerned with learning in complex, interactive environments (Winn, 2002). Because these environments are frequently inhabited by more than one person, opportunities for collective learning are ever present. Increasingly sophisticated ICTs are expanding possibilities for collaborative learning unimaginable with earlier technologies. Internet tools designed to facilitate student interaction within a class, school, community, state, nation, and world are becoming easier for teachers to access. It's now possible, for example, to establish virtual relationships between students and distant experts, enabling collaboration mentoring and community building. Disciplinary teachers are taking advantage of these new communication tools by structuring technology-based activities that require frequent, critical, discipline-focused dialog among students' immediate peers as well as others in far-off lands and the broader disciplinary community (Blumenfeld, Fishman, Krajcik, Marx, & Soloway, 2000).

> ICT tools make new forms of collaborative learning possible that bring experts and adolescent learners together from down the hall and around the world.

In the next section of this chapter you will read descriptions of several teachers exploiting the full potential of ICTs for content-area learning. We especially like the approaches and strategies used by these teachers because, in one form or another, the guidelines presented here can be recognized in their practices, which are marked by creativity, opportunities for critical thinking, authentic communication, and engaged and collaborative learning.

Teaching and Learning Strategies Using ICTs Across the Curriculum

In the previous edition of this book, we highlighted four areas of technology we believed would change the face of education in middle and secondary schools in virtually all disciplines: telecommunications, including networking; word processing, including desktop publishing and creating home pages; database management systems; and multimedia. Because some of these ICT applications, such as multimedia, require a fairly high degree of commitment and knowledge, their use has not become as widespread as we anticipated. On the other hand, a growing trend unidentified in earlier editions of this book is the ever-expanding use of personal digital assistants (PDAs) as teaching and learning tools (Lockard & Abrams, 2004; Ray, McFadden, Patterson, & Wright, 2001; Roblyer & Edwards, 2004). In fact, the growing popularity of classroom applications of PDAs has warranted a section on this topic later in the chapter. What has truly amazed us, however, is the unforeseen explosion of teaching and learning possibilities that have resulted from the powerful tool of the Internet. Teachers with limited time and resources who are working to meet content standards have found Internet-based practices easier to integrate into the existing curriculum (Kennedy, 2003).

The Web, a virtually limitless source of information and entertainment, is now being equally exploited as a communications medium. Teachers who have made this discovery are integrating Web logs (blogs), e-zines, and more into disciplinary lessons to facilitate purposeful learning. No longer passive receivers of others' ideas and "spin," youth are now actively contributing their own perspectives and media to dedicated sites they and their teachers design or to online outlets such as Wikipedia, the interactive encyclopedia. All of these digitally mediated communication practices can achieve the goals just outlined for effective teaching with ICTs. We begin, therefore, with descriptions of actual disciplinary practices that come from teachers who have found innovative ways to use the ultimate ICT tool—the Internet.

The Internet—The Ultimate ICT Tool

In this section we will describe several examples of teachers using a host of Internet applications to engage youth in meaningful learning projects. Common to all of these activities is the use of technology for authentic retrieval and communication purposes. In this way, we hope you will see how the Internet can be used to reinforce students' language and literacy skills (Coiro, 2003; Schmar-Dobler, 2003) while building content knowledge and developing critical thinking skills (Blase, 2000; Glazer, 2001; Shiveley & VanFossen, 2001).

Writing Web Logs in English Class

Web logs, or blogs, began as a self-publishing movement for those who wanted to express opinions in an open online forum. Blogs are frequent, chronological publications of thoughts and Web links that often mix what is happening in a person's life and what is happening on the Web. In this way, blogs are a kind of hybrid of a diary and guide sites, with as many unique types of blogs as there are people (Stone, 2002). With the introduction of automated publishing systems, such as Blogger.com, Livejournal.com, and Xanga.com, it became easier for teachers and students to set up their own sites, and, consequently, blogging has now become a powerful communications tool in all the disciplines.

Blogging is the process of writing and publishing to a blog. The uniqueness of blogs as a communication tool is best captured in this description by Kennedy (2003):

> Unlike most Web sites, which generally combine static and dynamic features, a blog is produced with an active writer in mind, one who creates in an online writing space designed to communicate an identity, a personality, and most importantly, a point of view. (p. 11)

Because blogs emphasize publishing and are theoretically accessible to anyone online, they encourage ownership and responsibility of content, heighten youths' sense of audience, and build agency in writing.

Richard is among the growing number of educators starting to explore blogs in his high school English classroom. Using the Web-based blogging tool Livejournal.com, he has developed a class blog to which all student work is exclusively posted. In fact, it has evolved into a totally paperless course, with writing and critiques on the blog. For instance, in journalism, his students work collaboratively to select possible stories from online newspapers to include in the appropriate blog department. These are further vetted by Richard and the department editors until the best stories of the day are selected. Along with the posting of daily stories, students also write about them, expressing their reactions, opinions, and related experiences. This discussion feature of the journalism class blog has been found to be one of the most helpful tools for building writing confidence and editing skills.

In his American literature class, students blog in response to the books and stories they read. Their blog entries include commentary, criticism, and artistic interpretations of important fictional events and images. Because the blog is accessible to the vast audience of the Internet, parents and local writers and poets are invited to join the discussion, forming a book club of cyber proportions. When the class read Sue Monk Kidd's (2002) *The Secret Life of Bees,* Richard was able to entice Kidd to make a virtual appearance at their site, where students asked her questions about the novel and other aspects of being a writer.

Richard is always on the lookout for ways of collaborating with virtual and professional communities. By forging links with one of the local Universities, he now has college journalism and English majors serving as volunteer editors and mentors for the class blogs. This arrangement is mutually beneficial in that the university students learn more about ICT tools while providing general encouragement of these adolescent writers and considered critique of their blogged text.

Though this is the first time Richard has used blogging in his classes, he is already seeing important ways the technology is contributing to students' understanding of writing. Not only are they developing more thoughtful and critical understandings of the news stories and fictional pieces they read, but they are also approaching their own compositions from the stance of a reader. This new positioning in the writing process keeps them ever mindful of the need to express themselves clearly and communicate meaningfully to a broad audience.

Two critical issues should be addressed before leaving the topic of blogging. Be sure to make arrangements with parents and school administration before launching a class blog. Publishing student writing at a digital site open to anyone with Web access means parental permission is needed. Anonymity may need to be preserved by using first names only and avoiding posting personal photographs of students. Teachers can also protect their sites with passwords, though this automatically limits audience. These conditions apply equally to other Web-accessible student publications, such as e-zines (discussed next). Another concern is with server space. Some schools and districts utilize Webmasters to oversee all postings, links, and sites from

Go to Web Resources for Chapter 10 at *http://www. prenhell.com/brozo,* and look for Weblogs in Education.

Blogging and Internet publishing from the classroom require permissions and protections for youths' safety.

The Role of the Teacher Leader

As the capacity of computer technology continues to increase, the size and cost continue to decrease. Fully recognizing the new developments in low-cost handheld personal digital assistants (PDAs), Peter, a high school technology coordinator, decided it was time to take advantage of their ubiquitous computing capabilities in the classroom. PDAs are small enough to fit into backpacks, pockets, and purses, but powerful enough to provide basic computing nearly anywhere one needs it. Accessing PCs, on the other hand, requires students to use computer labs, which are shared among classes and not always available when teachers need them. Or, several students are expected to use a few computers in the classroom, making it difficult for everyone to have adequate monitoring and support time from the teacher.

In spite of the potential benefits of these new and compact ICT tools, Peter knew there could be resistance among some of the faculty to allowing students to do handheld computing, so he met with each department to discuss their concerns and present the many new and exciting teaching and learning opportunities these devices have created.

Each faculty group raised questions about how difficult it would be to monitor students' use of PDAs. Couldn't students simply use them to IM (instant message) each other or play Internet games during class? Peter talked about how teachers in other districts and schools have dealt with similar concerns by holding students accountable for in-class assignments using handhelds as they would with traditional assignments. Teachers also asked him about availability of PDAs and whether all students would have equal access to them. Peter explained that a district technology grant obtained from the state allowed the high school to purchase a set of sophisticated PDAs for each classroom, as well as memory sticks for students to store data. Each student would be issued a handheld device for use while in class. Individual data would be stored on memory sticks for portability to PCs in the school labs and media center or at students' homes.

Teachers in the social studies department were the first to recognize the potential benefits of handhelds. They told Peter how commonplace these devices had already become, and how often they were telling students to put their iPods and Blackberries away during class—now they would actually encourage students to use them for learning! With the teachers' input, it was decided to begin employing PDAs to help students in social studies classes take and organize notes. Teaching effective notetaking was a priority goal for teachers that year, so they were eager to discover how handhelds could help students become better notetakers.

Using a free downloadable from a program called Thought Manager for Teachers, Peter demonstrated how this education resource provides outlines and templates to make it easy to create and organize lesson plans and classroom activities for handhelds. A history teacher, for example, put her lesson notes in the format she wanted her students to adopt and beamed them to each student's PDA. The format resembled the split-page method discussed in Chapter 9. Using this model, students accessed additional notetaking templates in which lecture and class content could be inserted in two columns. Their attempts at organizing information in this way were beamed back and forth among small groups of students for comparison and critique and to the teacher, who projected anonymous samples for the entire class to consider (http://www.handshigh.com/html/tmteachers.html).

Another teacher of history learned how to use the AvantGo software, which provides teachers and students access to a variety of news sources, information about the stock market and financial markets, maps, and weather information. Well-known educational content providers to AvantGo include Scholastic, NASA, and MapQuest. Current events can be examined via the *New York Times*, the *Wall Street Journal*, the *Christian Science Monitor*, the Weather Channel, and many local sources. Using a process known as Web-clipping, students can keep up with current events by clipping a variety of newspaper articles every day. It also allows clipping of primary documents, such as the United States Constitution, the Declaration of Independence, and the Bill of Rights.

With Peter's support, the teacher had his students clip five articles on current events from assigned newspapers to their PDAs. Working in pairs, students went through the articles and selected one to read. Once the article was read, students used the PDAs to write a summary and critique the article using a writing prompt beamed to them by the teacher. The teacher then brought the whole class together for a discussion of the various articles read, an exploration of the points of view the authors of the articles took, and consideration of the implications for current and future events (http://www.avantgo.com).

As the social studies faculty found more and more teaching and learning uses for handhelds, interest in the devices began to grow among teachers in other departments. Peter understood, that as with most technology, teachers must have the professional development opportunities, appropriate software, and administrative support to create a learning environment where PDAs become tools for learning instead of high-tech toys. Consequently, he held special workshops throughout the year on PDA classroom applications and continued to meet with faculty teams and individuals to provide technical assistance. At the same time, he monitored students' attitudes and achievement to ensure learning with handhelds was increasing engagement and improving performance. And he continually searched for and downloaded available free software to increase the range and versatility of PDAs for both teachers and students.

their servers. Once these individuals understand the goals and benefits of creating class blogs they are much more likely to approve them.

"Zinesters" in Science

A relatively new medium for student writing on the Internet is the electronic magazine or e-zine, or just zine (pronounced *zeen*). Zines are electronic publications created by individuals and classes as alternatives to commercial magazines. As independent media they represent the ideas and vision of their creators, called *zinesters* (Guzzetti, et al., 2003). Already there are hundreds of these cyber-creations available on the Web covering every imaginable area of interest, with a growing number designed and composed by young adults (Knoebel & Lankshear, 2002).

Irene's third-block general science class was comprised of 22 freshmen, 12 of whom were receiving special education services and all of whom resided in the inner-city neighborhood around the school. To maximize motivation and engagement, she worked tirelessly to make the learning personally meaningful and relevant to the students' lives and futures. In fact, the inspiration for a science class zine grew out of a project tied to one of the class topics, viral diseases. Working collaboratively with her students, Irene helped them explore the extent of diseases such as AIDS and hepatitis in their own community. The class began their investigation by doing Internet-based searches of local newspapers and conducting phone interviews. With Irene's support, students organized a panel of community volunteers, patients, social workers, and experts to dialog with the class and guests on the relationships between viral diseases and conditions of poverty, malnutrition, poor health care, race, gang violence, teen pregnancy, and other factors. Her students videotaped the panel discussion and later, when they were replaying it, realized they had something quite special and worthy of sharing with a much wider audience. Because theirs was a technology-savvy high school, endowed with state-of-the-art computer labs, high-speed Internet connections, and plenty of innovative software, Irene knew the technology infrastructure would support sophisticated Internet publishing. Her students loved the idea, so they all went to work.

Irene began by assigning the class into teams to tackle different parts of the project. One team focused on the technology; another, the content; and a third, promotional and advertising concerns. The content group operated in much the same way students do when they publish a school newspaper. They wrote informational stories, editorials, event summaries, and public information announcements all based on their work during the study of viral diseases, including, of course, the wealth of information gathered from the panelists. The technology group helped Irene create and design the class zine. Using Adobe PageMaker, they first formatted the zine for regular content, including columns for articles. Next, they experimented with on-screen palettes to find the right logos to drag onto the documents and colors to make the product visually appealing. The advertising group spent time brainstorming a title for the zine and ways of ensuring an audience of potential readers would be aware that it was available. Among all of the interesting titles this group pitched to the rest of the class, "Science in the City" was the one that clicked. The class decided to publish three more editions during the balance of the school year focusing on major units: environmental pollution, human reproduction, and fueling and maintaining the human machine.

With the launching of "Science in the City," Irene's class had a new and entirely deserved sense of pride about their learning. More important, they developed a heightened sense of responsibility and accountability that comes with producing a zine, and improved research skills, writing and spelling skills, and critical thinking skills.

E-zines are ready-made vehicles for using Web-based software to link purposeful writing, visuals, and other digital content with disciplinary topics.

English

Kehus (2000), a high school English teacher, has created a forum on the Internet for youth to publish their work. The Web site allows adolescent writers to submit their completed work for review and possible publication, submit drafts of work for feedback, post messages about their work and the work of others on the site, and exchange points of view about writing with others from around the country. The goals of the Web site are to provide youth an authentic purpose and audience for their writing and create an electronic space for youth to become part of a broad literary community (Leander, 2003; Sinatra, 2000). Those teachers who have created opportunities for youth to publish on and compose for the Internet understand the power of writing for the potentially vast, unseen audience out there looking in on their Cathode ray tubes (CRTs), liquid crystal displays, (LCDs), or handhelds (Knoebel & Lankshear, 2002). Student writers for the Internet are often inspired to write more and to create higher-quality texts. Electronic networks mediating student writing can also help break down, at least on a cyber level, the barriers that keep many of us separated in life: culture, ethnicity, and economics.

Threaded Discussions in Social Studies

A threaded discussion is a form of electronic communication that promotes collaboration and interaction among students by providing a cyber-environment for recording responses and engaging in critical dialog over relevant issues from the content classroom (Nichols, Wood, & Rickelman, 2001; Wolsey, 2004).

Using Microsoft Office FrontPage (Barron & Lyskawa, 1998), Holli and her sixth-grade students carried out a threaded discussion based on opinionnaire statements (White & Johnston, 2001) related to an article on teen alcohol abuse (to refresh your memory of opinionnaires, see Chapter 3). Figure 10.1 presents the opinionnaire statements that were used as prompts for an online threaded discussion as well as excerpts from the online discussion that took place among the students and between Holli and her students.

The first thing we hope you will recognize in the threaded discussion are the rich and considered responses made by students. This was possible because instead of controlling the lesson, computer technology provided a new and creative dimension of communication that made an instructional strategy Holli had been using even more successful.

> Threaded discussions bring teachers and students together electronically to dialog about content-area topics and learn from one another.

WebQuests Across the Curriculum

In Chapter 8 we presented examples of teachers using WebQuests to facilitate their students' meaningful and critical exploration of primary documents. Recall that a WebQuest is an inquiry-based approach to learning that helps students explore essential questions about an issue or topic using Internet tools (Teclehaimanot & Lamb, 2004). We return to this powerful process with information on several additional ways teachers from a range of disciplines have incorporated WebQuests into their classroom practice.

History. Amr's eighth-grade students were surprised to read in their history textbook that thousands of children in the late 19th century and early 20th century were relocated throughout the United States on what were called "orphan trains." This spark of curiosity led Amr to develop a WebQuest around the issue.

Because this was Amr's initial foray into WebQuest teaching, she began by taking advantage of the valuable online resources for teachers designing and adapting WebQuests. At the 42eXplore project site, a Web-based resource for over

Figure 10.1 Excerpts from a Threaded Discussion Based on Opinionnaire Statements

This is an online opinionnaire to be used for an article we will be reading on teen alcohol abuse. All sixth-grade students should post their responses to and explanation for each statement from the opinionnaire. If someone posts a response different from yours, please respond to the sender. Be sure to post any comments, personal opinions, and guesses related to the upcoming article. Once you have read the article, post new responses.

The content frame shows the title of all articles posted to the discussion. When you select a title it will load the corresponding article into this frame.

You should also feel free to:

    * Post a new article and start a new thread

    * Search the articles for a particular word or phrase

Remember also that each article has links to let you continue the thread and navigate the article list. Please post your reactions to the following opinion statements and tell why.

From: Holli   **Date:** 10/14/05   **Time:** 10:15:11 AM
Alcohol must not be really bad for teens otherwise kids in Europe wouldn't be allowed to drink beer and wine just like the adults.

From: Dez   **Date:** 10/14/05   **Time:** 10:47:03 AM
I've heard of that. Don't real young kids get to drink with their parents, like in Italy and France? So maybe if we grew up drinking with our families we wouldn't want to get drunk as teenagers.

From: Truann   **Date:** 10/14/05   **Time:** 1:04:32 PM
I disagree with the statement and with Dez. I think kids who drink probably grow up to be even worse drinkers. Alcohol is a drug that's in your body all the time if you drink every day.

From: Truann   **Date:** 10/15/05   **Time:** 3:01:55 PM
The article agrees with my opinion and not the statement. Teenagers in Europe abuse alcohol just as much as teens do in America. It says that in some countries like Finland and Russia teenagers are the worst drinkers of all.

From: Holli   **Date:** 10/15/05   **Time:** 3:22:41 PM
I remember on a trip I took to Scandinavia a few years ago how surprised I was to see so many young people overdrinking in public. During the summer it stays light well into the evening, as late as 10:00 or 11 PM, so teenagers stay out very late. Do you think teens around the world abuse alcohol because they're trying to act like adults and because of peer pressure?

From: Fareed   **Date:** 10/15/05   **Time:** 3:27:13 PM
Adults abuse alcohol so kids do too. That's what we see so why do adults expect us to be any different?

From: Corinne   **Date:** 10/16/05   **Time:** 8:42:38 AM
I agree with Fareed. How can parents and teachers say don't drink when they drink? I'll bet everyone in this class has beer or wine at home. It's like smoking, too. Parents always tell their kids, "Don't smoke" but then smoke. I think kids won't drink if they have parents who don't drink.

300 popular topics in the disciplines and at all levels, she found a page devoted solely to orphan trains. It provided a description of the topic along with many good Web sites. One site, Orphan Train: The New York–Missouri Connection, created by teachers in New York State, contained resources and suggested activities and projects for students at all grade levels. 42eXplore also had links to existing WebQuests on the topic of orphan trains, which Amr used to help design her own.

Go to Web Resources for Chapter 10 at *http://www.prenhall.com/brozo,* and look for WebQuests.

Using a WebQuest template she found at the 42eXplore site, Amr began with a *project overview* that introduced the WebQuest to her students. She presented this to the entire class using a data projector. The overview was written in an interesting and relevant way so as to spark her eighth graders' imaginations. It included an original photograph of an actual orphan train that captured children's faces pressed to the windows of the cars. She also found an original diary entry by an orphaned girl writing about her fears and anxieties toward meeting her new adopted parents in Illinois. Students were captivated by these primary sources, especially because Amr foreshadowed the fun they would have discovering documents and sources on their own.

The WebQuest template asked next for a description of the task. The guidelines at The WebQuest Taskonomy: A Taxonomy of Tasks at the San Diego State University site were helpful to her because they cautioned against inquiry-based missions that were too ambitious for the participants and time frame. To avoid reducing the power of the quest by merely asking her students to write a report or answer questions, Amr crafted a task that included the following:

- Imagine you are forced to leave an orphanage and take an orphan train to Missouri. Describe in diary form what your experience is like. Use the sites provided as links to sources with background information, photographs, and narratives for writing your diary.

- Based on what you learn about being an orphan in America at that time, describe an alternative way to handle the problem of caring for orphans.

Next, Amr made a variety of Internet-based information resources available to students. You might recall from the information about WebQuests with primary documents in Chapter 8 that we urged teachers to provide students with validated URLs to avoid endless surfing and needlessly wasting time. Amr explored the links to orphan trains from the 42eXplore project site and identified those she considered to be most helpful to completing the task she presented her class. These URLs were posted on the WebQuest.

To facilitate the completion process, Amr also posted step-by-step instructions on the WebQuest. These included where to search for relevant information once in a site, questions to ask themselves while reading or viewing information, and the format and style of the diary and the description tasks. She also embedded helpful learning tips such as reminders to students to organize their notes in the split-page format she had been teaching them that year.

To evaluate her students' WebQuest, Amr designed a rubric that related directly to the task and expectations she spelled out for them. Mindful of her district's social studies standards, she linked satisfactory completion of the quest to three of these standards, particularly the new one that stated *Uses technology to answer questions about history.*

Amr made class time available for the 2-week duration of the WebQuest, and had students make brief presentations on the final day. Other teachers, the principal and his assistants, as well as parents were invited to observe, ask questions, and enjoy refreshments. A ceremony or ritual to bring closure to the WebQuest was recommended in the sources Amr had consulted, and she and her students agreed it was a worthwhile way to bring the project to an end.

Algebra and Contemporary World Events

It is always encouraging for us to learn about teachers who collaborate on units in order for their students to develop deep and connected understandings across subject areas. This was the case with Yuri, an Algebra teacher, and Sherry, a teacher of a course called Contemporary World Events. Both had several of the same 11th graders in their classes and had shown an interest from the beginning of the school

Teacher as Learner
A WebQuest Activity

Using the following WebQuest template, try to sketch out the general features of a WebQuest designed to facilitate other secondary teachers' understanding of content-area literacy.

Project Overview: (How would you introduce a content-area literacy Webquest in a way that would be interesting to your colleagues?)

_____

_____

_____

The Task: (How could you frame the task to promote critical thinking and application instead of asking for answers to questions or a report?)

_____

_____

_____

Internet Sources: (Search the Web for sites and links your colleagues would find helpful in completing the task and list the URLs here.)

_____

_____

_____

Step by Step: (What specific steps could you ask colleagues to take to complete the WebQuest task?)

Step 1:_____

_____

Step 2:_____

_____

Step 3:_____

_____

Step 4:_____

_____

More Steps:

year in linking their curriculum in some way. When Sherry talked with Yuri about her upcoming unit on contemporary presidential politics, he was quick to see the ways they could combine their content through a WebQuest activity. They agreed to focus on one aspect of Sherry's content—the impeachment of former President Bill Clinton—and expand shared activities in the future if things went well.

First, Sherry and Yuri agreed to a WebQuest task that involved political analysis supported by statistics to ensure their students made connections across disciplines. Next, they searched the Internet for appropriate sites. Their efforts uncovered many excellent ones, including those with links to numerous primary sources, such as newspaper articles and the *Congressional Record,* as well as sites with datasets.

Next, Sherry and Yuri generated interesting activities their students could engage in to accomplish the task. For example, students were asked to create an electronic presentation or other display to represent the degree of ideological conservatism and liberalism of the Senate and which senators held relatively unusual views as compared to the Senate as a whole. They were to include numerical analysis in their explanations of the results. Another activity was to determine from the data the extent to which senators' votes were based on party loyalty, and then predict the number of Republican seats in the Senate that would have been needed to remove President Clinton from office. Finally, students were asked to come up with their own question and solution based on information and data from the WebQuest URLs.

Students from both classes were allowed to work together on the quest with partners of their choosing, though they had to submit a description of their separate and shared activities to account for their roles. Mario and Yolanda, students of both teachers, teamed up to fulfill the WebQuest tasks by splitting work according to their areas of strength. Yolanda was strong in algebra, so she was responsible for using the datasets from the site U.S. Senate Votes on Clinton Removal to support generalizations Mario extracted from articles and *Congressional Record* documents. Yolanda was also skillful in computer presentations and turned their answers into an impressive PowerPoint show complete with photographs and short video clips of Clinton, Monica Lewinsky, and important senators. For their own question and solution, Mario thought about exploring the relationship between each senator's vote and how popular the president was in the senator's state. With Yolanda's help they were able to demonstrate a positive correlation between these two variables using available datasets.

Sherry and Yuri's students' feedback on the combined approach to teaching algebra and world events clearly indicated it was a success. They reported that they enjoyed working in teams, liked using the Internet for research, and felt they had developed an appreciation for how algebra and statistics can be used to understand events in everyday life and politics.

Creating a Home Page in Art Class

An ever-increasing number of teachers and students are creating information on the Internet by designing their own home pages, screens on the World Wide Web that identify a particular site. It seems to be a natural progression for students as they become skillful at accessing information on the Web; eventually, they are not satisfied with this activity and want to create their own information. Home page construction seems to support active learning, group problem solving and planning, and interactive teaching (Ryder & Hughes,1997). Students have created various types of home pages, including personal home pages, multimedia newspapers, online portfolios, class supplements, and community resources.

WebQuests create numerous possibilities for interdisciplinary and shared exploration of content-area topics.

A group of students in a high school art class were prompted to develop a home page for other art students after they found it difficult to locate resources on contemporary artists and art movements. The advantage of the Internet over the limited resources available in their school's library became immediately apparent to the students when they initiated their search on the World Wide Web for information about current active artists. Hundreds of relevant sites were identified that included artists' names, biographies, illustrations of their works, and more. The art students decided to design their home page with a collage of photographs of original works they had done. They entitled their home page "The Demon of Curiosity: A 12th Graders' Guide to Modern Art" after a painting by Penck done in the 1980s. The site was designed as a resource for any student wishing to gather information about the current art scene. Students included a brief history of their effort to create the site as well as art autobiographies, links to relevant Internet sites, additional readings about artists and their work, and suggestions of assignments and activities to develop modern painting and sculpting techniques.

> Students from any content classroom can be responsible for creating and maintaining Web sites, thereby linking literacy and content learning.

Other Internet-Based Learning Experiences in the Disciplines

Many technology-based activities and learning experiences teachers in the disciplines craft for students emerge out of their own creative imaginations (Richardson, 2004) and do not fit neatly into any category, such as a threaded discussion, WebQuest, blog, e-zine, or Web page. The following descriptions capture various unique lessons tied to the Internet in which content learning is the focus of the lesson and technology and literacy are the supportive tools.

Math. A seventh-grade math teacher, Milt, designed an Internet-based lesson to help his students understand the concept of tessellation. Milt uses process guides (see Chapter 3) to ensure his students are thinking about content they read in Internet environments at more than surface levels of understanding. The process guide he required his students to complete was based on content from three sites they visited: the Math Forum project of Drexel University, What Is a Tessellation?, and Historical and Geographic Connections.

Recall that process guides present students with suggestions for learning information and concepts. Instead of being confronted with questions, students are typically provided cues about how to think meaningfully about statements or other prompts. Sample guide statements on Milt's guide for tessellations included:

- At the Math Forum site, related to tessellations and infinity, determine whether any regular polygon can tessellate infinitely.
- The site indicates triangles, squares, and hexagons will create regular tessellations; will any other shapes tessellate, too?
- At the What Is a Tessellation? site, there is a discussion of translation and rotation. Look closely at the visual examples of these tessellation processes and be prepared to demonstrate them in class with tiles.
- The Historical and Geographic Connections site provides numerous examples of tessellations in our everyday world (e.g., tiles on our bathroom floors, shapes of flowers and leaves). Look around your house and neighborhood and identify five additional examples of tessellating shapes to share with the class. Be prepared to provide a rationale for your examples.

Milt concluded the Web-based lesson on tessellation with a small-group project in which students were required to create their own tessellations. Students could consult the information and examples at the three sites for inspiration.

Foreign Language. Janette, a Spanish teacher, and her class had been studying the cultures of Spain for several weeks (as described in Newby, Stepich, Lehman, & Russell, 1999). Her students enjoyed reading about the people from different regions of Spain, and she wanted them to have the opportunity to interact directly with Spaniards. As a student herself, Janette had carried on a pen pal relationship with a young girl from Barcelona. She remembered how enjoyable it was to write and receive letters with interesting information and items, such as stamps, coins, and photographs. Eventually the exchange of letters dwindled and then stopped as the girls grew older, but Janette always regretted never being able to meet and speak with her pen pal in person. Janette's knowledge of telecommunications technology helped her decide to arrange for an audio teleconference between her Spanish-class students and students from Spain, which led to establishing an electronic pen pal relationship between the two classes.

After making arrangements with a high school English-language teacher in Seville, Janette and her students prepared questions for their Spanish counterparts. Using a speakerphone from the school's technology center, Janette called the classroom in Seville and the two classes held a 20-minute conversation. The students in Spain got to practice their English, while Janette's students got to practice their conversational Spanish. In the end, everyone seemed to understand each other, and both classes of students were enthusiastic about continuing to interact.

After the teleconference, Janette had her students initiate e-mail conversations with their new pen pal class in Spain. Students were able to practice their writing skills while gaining valuable cultural and language information from their electronic pen pals. Janette felt that the experience had been a success because several of her students continued to correspond with Spanish students months after they were introduced to the long-distance education technologies.

Social Studies. As middle school students in a small community in Alaska began to prepare for their class trip to Disney World in Orlando, Florida, they tried something a little different (Roblyer & Edwards, 2004): They established a computer link with eighth-grade students in Orlando. Using e-mail, students exchanged information, eventually met each other in Orlando, and continued to contact one another after the trip via e-mail. The Alaskan students were mostly native Alaskans, so they were able to share a great deal about their culture and daily lives with the Orlando junior high students while gaining greater facility in letter writing skills and knowledge of telecommunications technology.

Biology. Students in Wisconsin established e-mail links with classrooms all along the migratory route of the whooping crane. Students initiated reports on the movement of the cranes during their migration and created an informational guide to their migration habits.

A group of 10th-grade biology students in Massachusetts used the National Geographic Society's Kids' Net to tap into a national science project. Kids' Net was designed for science classrooms around the country to share in-class science experiments. The students tried various experiments with seeds that had been sent into space aboard the space shuttle to see how space travel had affected them. After collecting data on their experiments, the students sent their results across the country through Kids' Net on the Internet.

Science. Although land-locked, middle graders in Iowa kept track of a U.S. Coast Guard "tall ship" during a training journey using telecommunications technology.

Students gathered updates on its movements and activities through the SAILING forum, which can be accessed through the Internet. The topic was of great interest to the students and included a variety of related learning experiences. Students researched more about the ship. They adopted a sailor or cadet aboard the ship and exchanged e-mail letters and pictures. They read books such as *Mutiny on the Bounty* because the Coast Guard ship was following a route similar to Captain Bligh's. Log sheets were kept, and weekly updates via computer were received. Students learned about time zones, the international date line, and the weather's effects on the seas. They also developed their map-reading skills. Telecommunications technology stimulated and supported the students' exploration of a 20th-century sailing voyage.

Across the Curriculum. For more than a decade classrooms from countries in virtually every part of the globe have been partnering in the Learning Circles Project. The project facilitates cooperation through telecommunications among a small group of classrooms for exploring and seeking solutions to social, environmental, and geopolitical problems (Riel, 1993; Riel & Fulton, 2001). Students discover the varied perspectives their peers in other locations and cultures have on these problems. These multiple perspectives form the basis for testing theories and possible solutions. Internet and multimedia tools give students involved in the collaboratives access to information no single school could possibly acquire. Learning Circles provides students an electronic forum for gaining new knowledge, appreciating diverse points of view, and writing collaboratively with a community of their peers who share an equal commitment to tackling important global issues. The outcome of the project is the publication of jointly authored booklets and papers based on the students' collaborative problem solving. Several Learning Circles projects have taken place over the past few years, including the following:

- Students in Saudi Arabia, along with their partner students in other countries, explored solutions to problems in the Persian Gulf. The students discussed issues such as world dependence on Arabian oil, political freedom, and religious and cultural conflicts.
- West Virginia students have held conferences with prison inmates to discuss a range of social issues. Inmates provide information from their personal life experiences so that students can better understand the origins of crime.
- Students from several urban areas around the country collaborated on studies of homelessness, illiteracy, and substance abuse. Data were compiled and written in a booklet titled "Investigating Society's Problems."
- Students from Belgium worked with collaborating schools in the United States and other industrialized nations on a research project concerned with excessive packaging of goods. They gathered local products and evaluated them from the standpoint of their pricing and their effects on the environment.
- High school students in several cities throughout the country polled the local population on their views of national issues, such as gun control, smoking bans in public places, female presidential candidates, and abortion. Using e-mail, the classes exchanged the data they collected, and all the participating schools shared in an overall analysis of the findings.

Riel and Fulton (2001) found that because students' electronic communication and project publications were part of a discourse for a large networked audience of their peers, they were more fluent, better organized, and more clearly written than compositions produced merely for a grade. Electronically supported collaborative authoring

The Internet connects youth to other students and experts from around the globe engaged in the study of classroom topics.

involving partner students around the world resulted in better use of grammar and syntax as well.

Virtual Field Trips

Experiential learning is one of the most highly valued forms of learning promoted in this book. We believe strongly that when students are given the opportunity to explore content firsthand, they are much more likely to learn information and ideas and commit new learning to memory than they are without direct experience. A common source of frustration among teachers, however, is the lack of resources to make experiential learning through field trips possible. Adding to the problem are increasing liability risks of moving students bodily from the school grounds to the field and back. Undoubtedly, there are countless "Ms. Frizzles" out there who would like nothing more than to hop on a magic bus and journey to some new exotic locale for virtually every topic in the curriculum. Fortunately, this goal is rapidly becoming more achievable through the use of telecommunications technology.

Taking a field trip electronically turns students into "virtual travelers" capable of going to places they could only imagine. Unlike prerecorded video programs of distant places, virtual field trips make it possible for students to interact with other learners, teachers, researchers, scientists, and technicians at remote locations (Mather, 2000). Using two-way voice and video, students communicate with peers and local experts as they explore interesting locations around the world, such as the Guatemalan rain forest or an Antarctic research station. With the development of telerobotics tools it is now possible for students in their classrooms to reserve time on the Hubbell telescope and direct its view of space or control an underwater vehicle as it explores the unique seabed of Monterey Bay.

Science. One of the most exciting electronic field trip projects available to teachers today is the Jason Project. Through a complex network of advanced satellite technology, underwater robotics, two-way audio, and video screens, viewers at participating schools in many locations in the United States and other countries can observe actual exploration sites and participate in the exploration itself. Jason, a remotely operated vehicle for underwater navigation and research from which the project gets its name, has made it possible for students to go on interactive scientific explorations of sites such as the Mediterranean Sea, the Galapagos Islands, and the bottom of Lake Ontario. The project allows students live participation via satellite-delivered images and two-way audio interaction. Teachers and students can pose questions, receive answers, and conduct remote experiments. Special curriculum guides have been developed and can be obtained to help teachers and students study and prepare for each expedition. During Jason's expedition, students and teachers record its progress, communicate through e-mail and real-time video, and participate by completing assignments and experiments.

Go to Web Resources for Chapter 10 at *http://www. prenhall.com/brozo,* and look for Jason Project.

A couple of years ago Jason electronically took students to the most isolated chain of islands in the world to explore "Hawaii: A Living Laboratory." Formed by volcanic activity, the Hawaiian Islands are a unique site for the study of tectonics, ecology, lava flows, steam vents, and much more. Three high school students from Hawaii, Jeff, Maren, and Joe, were chosen to join the Jason expedition team. Better known as student argonauts, these teenagers stayed "wired" for voice and video while in the field with the researchers, so they could communicate with students all over the United States participating in Jason. The student argonauts also kept an electronic field journal accessible to classrooms nationwide. When an eighth grader in North Dakota asked Maren to describe a steam vent, the North Dakotan students watched and listened as Maren trudged cautiously near where vapor plumes rose with force from the volcanic rock. Maren's description of the phenomenon was in the kind of terms adolescents use with one another—plain-speak.

Jason's recent projects include "Mysteries of Earth and Mars," "Disappearing Wetlands," and "Rainforest at the Crossroads." Each of these expeditions is staffed by a team of top scientists and researchers, as well as student hosts who demonstrate for school subscribers real-time math and science learning in an interactive Internet environment.

Across the Curriculum. An increasing number of middle and secondary schools are creating high-tech links with resource-rich museums as a virtual solution for problems associated with conventional field trips. In Wisconsin, for example, a network comprised of interactive television and high-speed data transmission has been put in place that provides collaborative opportunities between students and expert staff at some of the most celebrated and revered shrines of American and world culture. Through two-way voice and video, students access a museum's collections and work directly and in real-time with curators, archivists, and researchers.

In one Wisconsin high school, Waterford Union High, students from nearly all subject areas take advantage of this technology for distance learning. Some of the virtual museum trips Union High students have taken will give you a sense of the promise and possibilities of this new form of cyber travel. A history class visited the Baseball Hall of Fame in Cooperstown, New York, so they could see actual exhibits from the Negro League baseball era and discuss this period in our past with museum staff. An African American studies club journeyed to the Museum of Television and Radio in Los Angeles to learn more about the civil rights movement through its collection of media documentaries. The school jazz ensemble went to New York on several occasions to watch, listen to, and talk jazz with professional musicians at J@zzchool. Art students visited the Indianapolis Museum of Art to learn about the modern art movement and its statement on society and popular culture. Using this information, the students drew and painted their own works, which were critiqued by the museum curators. Finally, life science students took a trip to the Columbus zoo and researched condors.

Virtual museum trips have become a feasible alternative to being there.

Virtual field trips are becoming increasingly popular because of their ease and relatively modest expense. With insurance, travel, safety, chaperone, and time issues forcing many middle and secondary schools to limit or even eliminate conventional field trips, we're likely to see tremendous growth in electronic explorations over the next several years.

Opportunities for electronic communication in the classroom are endless, limited only by the imagination of teachers and students. As many (Pearson & Young, 2002; Richardson, 2004; Salpeter, 2003) point out, the biggest challenge is for teachers to take the first step. We believe that as teachers become more familiar with the benefits of ICTs, an increasing number from all content areas will take advantage of this technology for motivating students to read, write, and exchange meaningful information.

Word Processing for Meaningful Communication

It's difficult to imagine writing for work or recreation without computers. We believe that writing as a conceptual and creative process is facilitated by productivity tools such as word processors. That is why we have included examples of teachers and students using word processing for learning in other sections of this book, such as in Chapter 7. Applications of word-processing programs are becoming increasingly varied.

Students and teachers alike are using word processing for creating imaginative documents, brochures, books, newsletters, and more with desktop publishing programs (Gamble & Easingwood, 2000). Other programs have been developed to facilitate student notetaking.

Desktop Publishing

Desktop publishing software gives teachers and students more powerful formatting capabilities for printed material than regular word-processing programs. Recently, older distinctions between word-processing and desktop publishing software have disappeared as word processors are now including more and more desktop publishing features (Roblyer & Edwards, 2004). With desktop publishing users have a great deal of control and flexibility in the composition and layout of the printed page, including text and graphics. Today many schools are using high-quality desktop publishing software to produce colorful and visually appealing school newspapers and yearbooks, and illustrated material for the classroom.

Mathematics. Sixth-grade students at a middle school in the Southwest planned all of the second semester for a math fair in early May. Not only did individuals and groups work tirelessly on projects to be displayed at the fair, students also worked diligently to make the fair one of the best the school had ever had. Early in the planning stages for the fair, the classes decided to emphasize publicity of the event as a way of increasing participation by the school and the community. Hector, one of the math teachers, aided students in their publicity efforts by introducing them to desktop publishing. Using Microsoft's Publish It! software, Hector taught students how to create a variety of eye-catching and professional communications combining page setup, text format, and graphics elements.

Students first learned how to design their own stationery, blending the school's mascot, an owl, with their own creative arrangement of print and figures. The desktop publishing program made it possible to generate colorful flyers and brochures describing the upcoming math fair. These were mailed in the desktop-generated envelopes to local businesses, churches, and school and community organizations. Additionally, large posters were created and displayed throughout the school and community. With the desktop publishing software, students even discovered the ease of creating a math school newsletter containing updates on the math fair events. The newsletter featured students who had records of high achievement in math, real-world math problems, and a math "puzzler."

The students' advertising campaign paid off. The math fair brought more people to the school to observe, judge, and participate in related activities than any previous math fair. Desktop publishing provided students with an important tool for promoting their event and helped them learn valuable information about using the computer.

Technology-Assisted Outlining and Concept Mapping

Another way to use word processing as a learning tool involves computer-based outlining and concept mapping programs. Outlining and mapping are a couple of the most commonly recommended strategies for organizing textbook and classroom information (Guastello, Beasley, & Sinatra, 2000). That's why we offer suggestions for teaching text organization strategies to students in Chapter 9. As we discuss in that chapter, organizational strategies have been found to be an excellent way to promote active learning (Alexander & Jetton, 2000; Boekaerts, Pintrich, & Zeidner, 2000) and provide students with a record of study for future use, such as in tests, projects, and class discussion (Simpson & Nist, 2001).

Desktop publishing offers students a way of combining fun and purposeful communication with disciplinary content.

Even though students are often urged to incorporate lecture and class information into a unified notetaking format, many will tell you that creating paper-and-pencil outlines or hand-drawn maps can be very inefficient. This is because it is difficult and messy to reorganize, make room for new information, show new relationships, and elaborate on prior information using paper and pencil. Scratch-outs and erasures, changes and additions written in between lines and in margins, drawings, and arrows inevitably force students to recopy everything they've written or to try to learn and study from disorganized notes.

Anderson-Inman and her associates (Anderson-Inman, & Ditson, 1999; Ditson, Kessler, Anderson-Inman, & Mafit, 2001) at the Center for Electronic Studying at the University of Oregon have been investigating ways in which teachers can help students improve their independent study skills by using computer software to record and organize information. Her work has led to the development of computer-based outlining and concept mapping programs designed to make notetaking easier and more efficient for students.

Outlining programs operate similarly to word-processing programs, but the typed text consists of only outline formats. Electronic outlining is an effective form of recording and organizing information from the text and the class (Lin, Strickland, Ray & Denner, 2004) for the following reasons: (1) expandability—students can modify electronic outlines in an infinite number of ways; (2) focusability—program functions such as "hide" and "show" allow students to display particular sections of their outline for concentrated attention; and (3) juxtaposability—electronic outlines allow students to bring together two or more sections from different places in the outline for instant and easy comparisons and for information elaboration. Afterward, the sections can be returned to their original places in the outline.

A variety of concept mapping programs are available to allow users to craft visual representations of ideas and information from text and lecture information depicting content links and concept interrelatedness (Kibum, Turner, & Perez-Quinones, 2004). With the appropriate software, students can use laptops or handhelds with keyboards to design a web that best reflects the organization of the information. The programs allow students to create their own shapes and shading, type in notes, and add connectors with explanations.

Music. Music students in a ninth-grade class created electronic outlines for the topic of historical periods of music (Figure 10.2). The students were taught a five-step process for creating the outline using Inspiration software. First, they went through the primary music textbook and crafted a skeletal outline of the chapter's major headings and subheadings. Second, they summarized textual information using important words and phrases under each heading in the skeletal outline. Third, they read information on the topic in alternative text sources supplied by the teacher and inserted relevant information in the outline. Fourth, class notes from teacher- and peer-led discussions and demonstrations were integrated into the outline. Finally, students restructured the headings and subheadings by adding and consolidating and then rearranged information in the outline to fit the new structure. When their outlines were completed, the music teacher showed students how they could use the outlines to prompt themselves during study and test themselves in anticipation of a test on the content.

As we have demonstrated, word-processing technology offers disciplinary teachers another versatile tool for teaching and learning. Word processors eliminate many of the difficulties associated with editing and producing texts and with sophisticated desktop publishing capabilities, students can integrate word processing with graphics

Electronic notetaking and mapping makes organizing, outlining, and linking information especially easy for youth who have difficulty writing and visualizing relationships.

Go to Web Resources for Chapter 10 at *http://www.prenhall.com/brozo,* and look for Inspiration Software.

Figure 10.2   Electronic Outline for Periods of Music

```
┌─────────────────────────────────────────────────────────────┐
│ □                      Chapter 10                         回目│
├─────────────────────────────────────────────────────────────┤
│                  0 items, 3.9 GB available                    │
├──────────────────────────────┬──────────────────────────────┤
│ Name                         │ Date Modified                 │
├──────────────────────────────┴──────────────────────────────┤
```

I. Ancient Music in Europe
  A. Liturgical music
    1. Chanting
  B. Primitive instruments
    1. Hurdy-gurdy
    2. Crumhorn
    3. Recorders
  C. Basic musical notation

II. Renaissance
  A. Improved musical notation
    1. Similar to current form
  B. The rise of popular music
    1. Peasant songs
    2. Tavern songs
  C. Prominent composers
    1. Michael Pretorius

III. Baroque
  A. Music of the court
  B. Elaborate liturgical music
    1. J.S. Bach
      a. "Jesus Joy to Man's Desire"
  C. Larger ensembles
  D. Development of keyboard instruments
    1. Pianoforte
    2. Organ
    3. Harpsichord

IV. Classical
  A. Large orchestral works
    1. Nonliturgical
  B. Prominent composers
    1. Beethoven
    2. Schubert
    3. Mendelsohn

V. Romantic
  A. Mystical themes from literature/poetry
    1. "Faust"
  B. Moods created with music
    1. Chopin's "Nocturnes"
  C. The Waltz
    1. Strauss
      a. "The Blue Danube Waltz"
  D. Prominent composers
    1. Brahms
    2. Wagner
    3. List

to create professional-looking materials. These materials can serve as vehicles for teaching and honing compositional skills. Finally, when word processing is combined with clever software that allows ideas and information to be logically organized, students are more likely to be active and reflective learners.

Honoring Diversity and Building Competence in the Content Classroom

Patrick was awarded a BellSouth grant that made it possible for him to buy 20 Dell laptops for use by the inclusion students in his classes. He asked for the computers so he could combine technology with the study of U.S. government with the expectation that it would ease the notetaking process for his students with learning disabilities and improve their listening and concentration skills. One of the ways this was accomplished was by teaching students how to make electronic notes from class lectures, discussions, and readings. With Inspiration's diagramming software, Patrick taught his students how to organize course information by mapping content and how to use it as a basis for studying and preparing for debates and tests. Prior to this technology-assisted approach, all of his students and particularly his inclusion students required steady coercion to take longhand notes. Most failed to keep organized or complete notes, despite Patrick's chidings, until the laptops were assigned. Once the special education students caught on to the versatility and ease of the Inspiration format, they never looked back.

Patrick reported that their level of attention in class has increased noticeably, as evidenced by how frequently they now ask clarifying questions, indicating they're becoming more critical listeners, and the quality of the maps they are producing (see Figure 10.3 for an example of a map produced in Patrick's class). More significantly, Patrick's inclusion students have shown overall improvement in their attitudes and achievement.

Figure 10.3   Electronic Notetaking: Map of Branches of Government

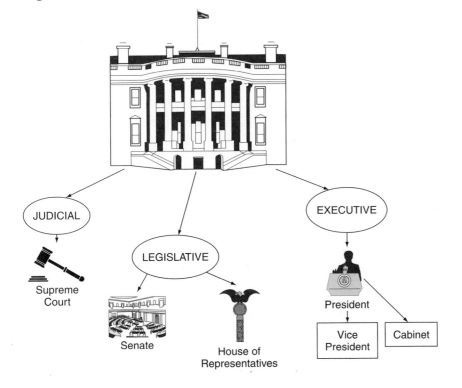

Expanding Learning in Content Classrooms with Databases and Spreadsheets

Databases are extremely versatile computer programs that allow students to collect, organize, and retrieve information. Databases are popular computer applications second only to word-processing programs (Jonassen, Peck, & Wilson, 1999). Similar to phone books, recipe files, and catalogs, databases enable students to find, cross-reference, classify, and sort data and search for specific topics and information quickly and easily. Most libraries store reference materials, including encyclopedias, in databases. The exceptionally large storage requirements for works such as encyclopedias, the complete works of Shakespeare, and world almanacs require the optical storage technologies of CD-ROMs. Similar to audio CDs, CD-ROMs can store hundreds of millions of bits of information. One small CD can hold up to 250,000 pages of information, making it possible to store entire reference works on a single CD, along with an extensive index that allows searchers to access the information within seconds. Using CD-ROMs, students have been able to expand their research skills, improve their ability to organize information, and learn a great deal about a particular topic by authoring their own databases (Turner & Dipinto, 1992). Teachers have found databases excellent ways of developing higher-level thinking skills through questioning (Hancock, Kaput, & Goldsmith, 1992; Merkley, Schmidt, & Allen, 2001).

> Spreadsheets and databases are versatile programs that allow vast amounts and types of information to be organized and easily retrieved for study, tests, and projects.

Spreadsheets are computerized, numerical recordkeeping systems. A spreadsheet is composed of a grid, table, or matrix with columns and rows. Each cell may contain values, formulas, or functions, using either numbers or words. Spreadsheets are used to store, calculate, and present information. Most spreadsheet programs allow the learner to display information in a variety of ways, including graphs and charts. Spreadsheets help users manage numbers in much the same way that word processors help them manage words. In fact, Bozeman (1992) described spreadsheets as a way to "word process numbers" (p. 908). Teachers from a variety of content areas have used spreadsheets to engage and support problem solving and other forms of higher-level thinking. Following are brief descriptions of how databases and spreadsheets have been used by middle and secondary school teachers to improve student motivation and learning in the content classroom.

Social Studies

An eighth-grade social studies teacher had her class compile a database on current events using information from local newspapers about happenings in countries around the world. Each student was assigned 10 newspaper articles per quarter, which were summarized in a database field that included the country, subject, date, title, publication, and student's name. At the end of the year, the class organized their articles into their own encyclopedia containing more than 2,000 newspaper articles. The students developed a convenient retrieval system for accessing articles with key words.

Current Events

Tenth graders engaged in a letter-writing campaign to political prisoners, which grew out of a unit on Amnesty International, and built databases to keep track of their prisoners. They entered such information as the reason for the arrest, the length of the prison term, the current length of imprisonment, the reason for incarceration, health status, and addresses of persons or groups to contact. With the database, they could monitor changes concerning the prisoners, update the record on any prisoner as new information became available, and analyze the information for patterns such as similarities among charges brought against prisoners.

Databases and the Internet

Combining use of the Internet with database systems is an excellent way for teachers to exploit both technologies. Students researching information on the World Wide Web can use a database for organizing and storing information, making study and recall of the information convenient and easy.

Art. An art teacher had his students research information about artists ranging from Leonardo DaVinci to Frida Kahlo. Using a database program, students first created a framework for recording critical information about each artist, including dates of birth and death and the movement he or she represented or defined (Figure 10.4). Students searched Web sites with information about the artists, downloaded and printed what they wanted to retain, and then placed the relevant information in the database. When the databases were completed, students printed them and used them to recall information for class discussion and study for a test.

Kinesiology. Each student in a middle school physical education class was required to maintain a database for the entire school year for recording personal information related to each exercise and athletic activity (Figure 10.5). The purpose of the assignment was to help students learn important information about fitness and muscle development while tying this information to class sports and activities. Students recorded the type of activity (basketball, sit-ups, flag football, etc.), necessary equipment, the type of motion

Figure 10.4   Database of Artists

Artist	Birth	Movement	Death
Leonardo DaVinci	1452	High renaissance	1519
Édouard Manet	1832	Impressionism	1883
Vincent Van Gogh	1853	Impressionism	1890
Salvador Dali	1904	Surrealism	1983
Frida Kahlo	1910	Surrealism	1954
Henri Matisse	1869	Fauvism	1954
George Bellows	1882	Realism	1925
Käthe Kollwitz	1867	Expressionism	1945
Jackson Pollock	1912	Abstractionism	1956
Andy Warhol	1928	Pop art	1987
Mildred Howard	1945	Postmodernism	

Figure 10.5   Database for Personal Exercise and Health

Activity	Equipment	Type of Motion	Muscle Group	Benefits
sit-ups	none	sitting, bending	abdominis	toning stomach
walking	shoes		longus, lateralis	toning, cardiovascular
cycling	bicycle	pedaling	femoris, soleus	toning, cardiovascular
running				
curls				
chin-ups				
push-ups				

required to perform the activity, the primary muscle groups involved, and the cardiovascular and other fitness benefits. Students also made notes on their databases of particularly useful Web sites for acquiring additional information relevant to the activity. Using their direct experience and information from the Internet, the students filled in their databases. Throughout the year, they used their databases to retrieve specific information as needed for class participation and examinations. The teacher often asked students to show the rest of the class an especially helpful Web site and explain how it was used.

Spreadsheets in the Content Classroom

Science. As Earth Day approached, a junior high science teacher had his students develop a spreadsheet assignment for analyzing lunchroom trash (Ramondetta, 1992). Students spent a week organizing trash items into recyclable and nonrecyclable categories, weighing trash samples, and projecting annual waste and costs. Using color pie charts, bar graphs, and grids, students organized and exhibited their findings at the school's Earth Day fair and assembly. Thought-provoking questions were included with the exhibit to help students understand the seriousness of the problem.

In another science class, sixth graders created a spreadsheet to display information concerning relative gravity on Earth and the other planets. The students designed a grid with statistics on all the planets and individual bar graphs comparing Earth with each planet. Feeding the spreadsheet program with the appropriate formulas for calculating relative gravity, students filled in columns with each planet's relative gravity and their body weight on Earth. The program then automatically calculated the students' weights on the other planets. The information was blown up and put on a large chart board to be displayed in class during the study of gravity.

Mathematics. High school math students were given the assignment of calculating the dimensions of the Milky Way. Using a scale model, they plugged their formulas into a spreadsheet that provided a calculation function. This function proved to be critical as students modified their formulas up to the last minute and used the spreadsheet to recalculate all of the new values based on the formula changes. As a result of this project, students developed a much better appreciation for the enormity of space.

Algebra. To better organize and understand nonlinear equations, an algebra teacher had her students develop a spreadsheet (Figure 10.6). The spreadsheet was created as students moved through the text and class material on hyperbolas. As students learned new examples, these were added to the spreadsheet along with additional characteristics and definitional information. When the spreadsheet was completed, the teacher showed her students how to use it to study and prepare for tests she designed based on how the information in the spreadsheet was organized. For example, she asked students to compare and contrast different types of hyperbolas and describe a particular hyperbola based on its critical features.

Database management systems offer teachers and students organized formats for storing and retrieving information. Higher-level thinking skills can be fostered through the use of this computer technology as students comprehend and analyze information to be included in the databases. Furthermore, students can gain short-term and long-term benefit, when they are given responsibility for putting information into the database and creating a record of their study for a later purpose, such as a quiz, test, or class discussion.

Figure 10.6 Spreadsheet for Nonlinear Equations in Algebra

	Intersects itself	Function?	Has a defined range	Has a defined domain	Has an x^2 term	x^2 term + or −	Has a y^2 term	y^2 term + or −	Coefficient of x^2 and y^2 terms are equal
Parabola									
Parabola									
Parabola									
Parabola									
Circle									
Ellipse									
Hyperbola									
Hyperbola									

Hypermedia Tools for Disciplinary Learning

We suggested earlier in this chapter that in spite of the tremendous learning potential of these new digital media, they are not as widely exploited as other ICTs, due, we think, to the ease of applying simpler technologies. *Hypermedia* is a hybrid term that combines *hypertext,* the nonsequential linking of e-based textual information, and *multimedia,* such as photos, video, art, graphics, animation, and audio, to create an interactive computer-mediated experience for participants (Eagleton, 2002; Tolhurst, 1995; Vrasidas, 2002). We endorse applications of hypermedia, also referred to as rich media or interactive online media, in disciplinary classrooms because they enable teachers and students to take an active role in building their own texts, becoming producers and makers of meaning as they choose their own relevant learning path through the Web site. Furthermore, given students' familiarity with electronic images, multimedia and hypermedia presentations in schools, while not yet as popular as other technologies, continue to hold great potential for gaining and holding attention (Jonassen & Land, 2000; McEneaney, 2000; Reinking et al., 1998). Student-developed multimedia, hypermedia, and hypertext projects have also been shown to promote critical literacy (Dillon & Gabbard, 1998; Myers & Beach, 2001), strengthen written and oral communication skills (Browning, 2000; Dillner, 2001), increase motivation, and further creative processes (Hammer & Kellner, 2001; Troxclair, Stephens, Bennett, & Karnes, 1996).

Go to Web Resources for Chapter 10 at *http://www. prenhall.com/brozo,* and look for Hypermedia and Hypertext Software.

With the development of software such as Storyspace (Bolter, Smith, & Joyce, 1990), HyperCard, CD-ROM Bookshelf, HyperStudio (Wagner, 1997–1998), and SuperLink, it is possible to create and use databases containing an enormous amount of multidimensional information (Bolter & Grusin, 2000; Brusilovsky, 2001, De Bra & Calvi, 1998).

Physics

A high school physics teacher had her students create a hypertext database on Nobel Prize winners in physics over the past 10 years. First, using the Internet to establish an initial roster of prize winners, students developed links to news stories, books, scholarly articles, prize winners' university and research centers' home pages, three-dimensional models of prize winners' award-winning work, photos of the physicists, biographical information, and more. When the projects were completed, they were "tested" by other students working through the stacks and links of information in each database on the physicists to determine ease of access and creativity in making connections. In the course of this project, students demonstrated imagination and a great deal of valuable research experience.

History

Dillner (1994) describes the work of an American history teacher who created a hypermedia database for the Bill of Rights. She designed the computer-based lesson to be friendly to even her most inexperienced computer users. When students turned on the classroom computer, a title page with the words "The Bill of Rights" and a graphic of an American flag appeared on screen, while the music of "Yankee Doodle" flowed from the computer speakers. When the song ended, directions appeared on the screen. Using the mouse, students highlighted an arrow at the bottom of the screen and a new page appeared. The new page was a menu with a list of all 10 amendments. Students were asked to highlight an amendment to acquire more information about it. For example, highlighting "Right to Bear Arms" brought on a screen with the amendment title surrounded by five choices (Interpretation, Definition, On Your Own, Examples, Assignments). When students highlighted "Examples," a videotaped clip ran of a student broadcaster and student actors replaying the scene of the day former president Ronald Reagan and his press secretary, James Brady, were shot by John Hinckley. The video was accompanied by audio information about how, since the assassination attempt, James and Sarah Brady have been lobbying against Americans' easy access to handguns. The other choices on each of the amendment screens provided additional media support for learning about the amendments and directing learning of the textbook chapter on the Bill of Rights.

History/Culture

Patterson (2000) had her middle school students use Storyspace (Bolter et al., 1990) to build hypertexts around research they were conducting in American history and culture. For example, during the study of Native Americans, students created biographical webs for Sitting Bull and Sacagawea with links to important related events in history. Students also made Native American poetry webs with links to critical information about Native American culture and history.

For the study of slavery, Patterson developed a joint project with students in Ghana, Africa, to help write a more complete history of the slave trade. The African students began the story with information about how slaves were captured in Africa, while Patterson's middle graders finished the story by describing the slave experience in the southern United States. Based on their research, students then composed hypertext narratives with links to information about slavery.

Science

Some highly motivated junior high students worked together to create a touch-sensitive multimedia kiosk that was installed at a local zoo (Beichner, 1994). Using HyperCard and other hypermedia technology, they designed an information program, working with an on-screen audio recorder, a video tool to operate the videodisc player, color painting and text tools, and a data-linking tool for connecting pieces of information. Hot spots were created on the screen that, when touched by zoo visitors, made it possible to see and hear animals, gather additional information, and even obtain printouts, such as a map and student-generated questions and comments about zoo animals. Students demonstrated great enthusiasm for this project because they saw a real-world connection between their developing technology and science skills and the product of their efforts—the information kiosk for zoo visitors.

Many adolescents become highly engaged readers and learners in disciplinary classrooms when given the opportunity to use ICT tools to manipulate images, text, and sound.

Social Studies

Middle school students, using the tools available in HyperStudio, created a hypermedia presentation on the civil rights movement of the 1960s for a class project during African American History Month. Their research resulted in several hypermedia topics of interest, including music, images (photographs and video), major players, historical background, and more. The program was on display in the school library during February for all students to access. By clicking on a topic of interest, students could read about Rosa Parks, see a video clip of George Wallace, or listen to President John Kennedy make a brief speech.

Hypermedia technology seems to be an ideal way to motivate today's youth to explore information in realistic and multimodal ways. Integrating sights, sounds, texts, graphics, and computers into an overall presentation can be an enriching and memorable learning experience for students in virtually all subject areas (Zahide, Ozden, & Aksu, 2001). Hypermedia and hypertext projects are becoming excellent alternatives to traditional papers and tests as measures of students' overall understanding of a unit or topic. The projects students create can also become part of the classroom collection of resources to be accessed by future students to enrich their learning. As platforms and programs become simpler to navigate, hypermedia as an ICT tool is poised to become even more accessible to disciplinary teachers.

Meaningful Literacy and Learning with Personal Digital Assistants and Handhelds

As stated earlier, the development of classroom applications of personal digital assistants (PDAs) and handhelds has been gaining momentum over the past few years—so much so that teachers from around the country in every discipline have been discovering new ways of employing these devices in school-based contexts (Ravitz & Mergendoller, 2002; Ray, 2001; Rose, 2002; Staudt, 2002).

Handheld computers such as Palms™ and Pocket PCs™ when first introduced in the early 1990s were quickly taken up by the business and medical communities to organize personal and professional information. At about the same time, youth were acquiring experience using handheld devices like Nintendo's Gameboy, cellular phones, and iPods. These interactive technologies are motivating to youth and have made the transition to the PDA format relatively easy for them. Handhelds are now broadly accepted in a variety of educational settings, including secondary content-area classrooms.

The literature on handhelds for instruction and learning suggests a broad range of benefits. Frequently mentioned are their relatively low cost (Holzberg, 2002) and portability (Crawford & Staudt, 1999), which make them an attractive alternative to more expensive laptop and notebook computers (Roland, 2003/2004). This feature has led Staudt (2002) to refer to PDAs as equity computers, as it is economically feasible for schools to make them available to all students. PDAs can be used for notetaking, e-mail, and Web access (Holzberg, 2002), and have been found to increase time on task, test scores, and motivation (Norris & Soloway, 2003). Furthermore, with one-to-one access to handheld computers, integration of technology can occur throughout the school day.

Go to Web Resources for Chapter 10 at *http://www. prenhall.com/brozo*, and look for Handhelds and PDAs.

Another frequently mentioned benefit found in the literature is the potential of handhelds for enhancing collaboration and promoting cooperative learning (Shields & Poftak, 2002; Tinker, Staudt, & Walton, 2002). Synchronization can occur either by docking with a desktop or laptop computer or by beaming information between handhelds. A teacher can store Web pages, assignments, and/or other information on a handheld and then beam them to students, who can beam drafts of and completed work, questions, and self-evaluations back to the teacher or to other students (Perry, 2003). Students who have limited or no access to the Internet can select sites while in the classroom or computer lab, then download information to their handhelds to be read later when they are offline.

Finally, handheld computing has been shown to promote student responsibility and self-directed learning (Regner, 2003). The combination of trusting students with a personal learning device and the implicit accountability in having a single device to store, track, and complete most assignments results in an acknowledgement that students are now responsible for their own learning. Teachers have reported that the use of handhelds increased students' initiative for learning as well as completion of assignments (Vahey & Crawford, 2002).

PDA software applications, much of them available online and free, allow teachers and students to perform a variety of tasks including spreadsheets, concept maps, drawing, simulations, word processing, synchronizing data with desktop or laptop computers, and accessing e-mail and the Internet. These functions allow for a wide range of teaching and learning applications in content classrooms, especially when accessories such as keyboards, cameras, and data collection probes are added (Holzberg, 2002; Thatcher, 2003).

Teacher as Learner

GENERATING APPLICATIONS FOR PDAs IN THE CONTENT AREAS

Most assignments that require students to use PCs can also be accomplished using PDAs. For instance, PDAs can access the Internet for WebQuest activities, researching primary documents, and participating in blogs and discussions. Based on what you've read about PDAs in this section and any personal or professional experiences with handhelds, suggest potential applications for them that will engage learners and expand understandings in the following content-area assignments.

Assignment	Suggested PDA Applications
1. Research the Dred Scott decision in preparation for a court scene role-play.	1.
2. Determine the machines needed to build the great pyramids of Egypt.	2.
3. Identify the symbolism in Shakespeare's *Macbeth*.	3.
4. Find examples of tessellations in nature, architecture, and art.	4.
5. Analyze the possible infringements on civil liberties in the U.S. Patriot Act.	5.

Across the Disciplines

Teachers from across the disciplines are incorporating innovative uses of handhelds into their classroom practices to promote constructivist learning environments (Fryer, 2003). For example:

- Middle school math students in Omaha are asked to make their city a better place with one million dollars to spend. The teacher beams from his PDA to the students' PDAs a checkbook program and deposits a million dollars in each of their accounts. Students use their handhelds to research costs, create charts, and develop budgets for city improvement projects. These plans and charts are exchanged from handheld to handheld and downloaded to a notebook computer to be projected for all to consider.

- High school journalism students working on stories or ideas for stories use handhelds to take notes, get quotes, and take pictures. This information is uploaded to a school newspaper Web site for the editorial team to critique at their weekly meetings. Editors' suggestions posted at the site are downloaded to reporters' PDAs.

- Science students use probes and sensors connected to their handhelds to collect data on water quality in and around San Antonio, Texas. These data are converted into tables and analyzed in reports students send as electronic documents to the water company.

- Students in middle and high schools around the country are using iPods and suters to make podcasts. These online radio shows can be downloaded to an iPod or other portable MP3 player. Podcasts take advantage of the technology youth use in their daily lives and the possibility of reaching a wider audience to increase engagement in reading and learning. A middle school history class's podcast of the American Revolution was filled with humor, catchy tunes, and plenty of critical information. After researching and studying the topic from multiple sources, students developed podcast scripts, including a town crier condemning King George's tyranny. The podcast was recorded and posted on the Internet, making it available, theoretically, to students and teachers anywhere in the world.

> Handheld devices are proving to be an economical and versatile alternative to PCs and laptops for delivering and transmitting a range of digital content.

PDAs and handhelds are expected to continue to decline in cost while increasing in power and versatility. As this occurs their use in secondary disciplinary classrooms is sure to grow. Innovative teachers using handhelds find their own lesson planning and curriculum development becoming more creative and are able to take advantage of countless on-the-spot opportunities for reading, reviewing, research, and writing, as the devices are at every students' immediate disposal (Regner, 2003).

Accessing and Assessing Computer Technology

Because of the rapid developments in computer technology, keeping up with innovations in hardware, software, and related technologies is a daunting task, especially for busy disciplinary teachers. Perhaps the most challenging task for the content-area teacher is the selection of appropriate software. Although ICT tools have the potential to improve teacher effectiveness, this can occur only when quality computer programs are put in the hands of quality teachers. Concerns about quality software are especially critical for those of us promoting the integration of literacy processes within content-area classrooms.

> Although a daunting task, keeping abreast of ICTs for classroom teaching and learning is easier for disciplinary teachers by accessing numerous helpful websites that list and evaluate the best technology tools.

Considering the guidelines described at the opening of this chapter, we recommend that instructional software be selected on the basis of whether it contains meaningful content and can be used for purposeful learning. In addition, software programs should require active participation by the learner and emphasize elaborative and creative thinking instead of repetitive drill. Vigorous efforts have been made over the past 10 years to change the nature of software for students from computerized workbooks to interactive, generative learning tools (Leu & Kinzer, 2000). Therefore, it is important to evaluate closely any computer products that may be potentially useful in your classroom.

One fairly easy way to find out about new developments in ICTs is by exploring the Internet itself. Some of the best sites are designed just for teachers. At these sites information can be found about technology standards, reviews of software, and descriptions of practices using ICTs. A list of organizations and Web sites useful to teachers is shown in Figure 10.7.

Figure 10.7   Organizations and Web Sites on ICTs for Teachers

Association for the Advancement of
Computing in Education (AACE)
P.O. Box 3728
Norfolk, VA 22902
(757) 623-7588; Fax (703) 997-8760
e-mail: info@aace.org
WWW: http://www.aace.org/

Center for Children and Technology
96 Morton St., 7th Floor
New York, NY 10014
(212) 807-4200; Fax (212) 633-8804
e-mail: cct@edc.org
WWW: http://www2.edc.org/cct/cctweb/

Center for Technology in Learning
Sri International
333 Ravenswood Ave.
Menlo Park, CA 93025
(650) 859-2000; Fax (650) 326-5512
e-mail: ctlwebmaster@sri.com
WWW: http://www.sri.com/policy/ctl/

Computer-Using Educators (CUE)
1210 Marina Village Parkway, Suite 100
Alameda, CA 94501
(510) 814-6630; Fax (510) 814-0195
e-mail: cueinc@aol.com
WWW: http://www.cue.org/

Consortium for School Networking
(COSN)
1555 Connecticut Ave. N.W., Suite 200
Washington, DC 20036
(202) 462-9600; Fax (202) 462-9043
e-mail: info@cosn.org
WWW: http://www.cosn.org/

Focus on Technology
National Education Association
1202 16th St. N.W.

Washington, DC 20036
(202) 822-7360
WWW: http://www.nea.org/cet/

Institute for the Transfer of Technology to
Education (ITTE) National School Boards
Association
1680 Duke St.
Alexandria, VA 22314
(703) 838-6722; Fax (703) 683-7590
WWW: http://www.nsba.org/site/
page_micro.asp?trackid=&vid=
35&cid=63&did=195

International Society for Technology in
Education (ISTE)
480 Charnelton St.
Eugene, OR 97403-2626
(800) 336-5191; Fax (541) 302-3778
e-mail: webmaster@iste.org
WWW: http://www.iste.org/

International Technology Education
Association (ITEA)
1914 Association Drive, Suite 201
Reston, VA 20191-1539
(703) 860-2100; Fax (703) 860-0353
e-mail: itea@iris.org
WWW: http://www.iteawww.org/

Office of Educational Technology
U.S. Department of Education
400 Maryland Ave., S.W.
Washington, DC 20202
(800) 872-5327 OR (202) 401-2000;
Fax (202) 401-0689
e-mail: customerservice@inet.ed.gov
WWW: http://www.ed.gov/technology/

CASE STUDY REVISITED

After exploring this chapter, you should now have many new ideas about how to use computer technology in the content classroom for increasing student motivation and active involvement and promoting higher-level thinking. José, the biology teacher who is the focus of this case study, was fortunate enough to discover some of the outstanding instructional applications of computer programs for helping his students better organize, analyze, and study biology information.

José brainstormed with another biology teacher and decided that a database management system held the most promise for helping their students organize a large number of related bits of information. José used the Microsoft Works integrated software package provided with the DOS-based computers purchased through his school's grant.

José introduced his students to the database management system approach to organizing and studying by presenting a database he had completed as an example. José knew that with the students' first exposure, it was critical that the database not be too complex, leading to possible frustration and failure. Wisely, he began with a familiar database of lunch menu items from the previous month, his likes and dislikes, meat and vegetable content, and choice of beverage. First, he projected his database on a large screen using a liquid crystal display (LCD) acquired with grant monies. LCD panels are compact, flat units that fit on top of overhead projectors and allow large groups equal viewing access to computer screen information. After explaining how he constructed his database, he posed several questions to the class, and then had them work in pairs using the database to answer the questions.

José's next step was to have students complete a partially filled-in completed database by using their biology textbooks to fill in the gaps. Again working in pairs, his students then keyed in information related to several different animals, their diets, and their habitats. Several sessions were spent monitoring and coaching the students and demonstrating the desired thinking and computer skills needed to complete the database. Students were encouraged to ask frequent questions of José and their peers as they gained greater facility and confidence in using the process of database construction.

At this stage, José was ready to begin applying the database technology to the study of cell types. As before, he placed a database (this time, blank) on the overhead projector using an LCD panel. Students sat in pairs around a common terminal, with their own blank database on-screen and their textbooks open to the chapter on human cells. José read through the chapter with his students and engaged them in discussion about key terms and descriptions of cell types. As they progressed through the first few pages of the chapter and talked about information they were learning about cells, José demonstrated on the overhead how and where to place critical information in their databases. Finally, essential categories were agreed upon and written into their database grids; these included cell type, shape, function, and location (Figure 10.8). With each subsequent class session, as students read, studied, and engaged in meaningful learning activities related to cells, they were given the opportunity to input relevant information into their databases. At the end of each class session, José engaged students in an exchange of questions

continued

Before writing your suggestions for José in the case study, go to *http://www.pren/hall.com/ brozo,* select Chapter 10, then click on Chapter Review Questions to check your understanding of the material.

CASE STUDY REVISITED (CONTINUED)

about their expanding databases. Students asked questions of each other and of José, as he asked questions of them in a model/elicit format. In this way, José was stimulating critical decision making and higher-level thinking as he prepared his class for a test on the material at the end of their study of the chapter. Through this process, students were able to see how test-like questions were related to their databases and could be answered using information in their grids.

José was proud to report that after his class created, queried, and studied their databases on cells, they scored higher on his chapter test than any previous group. His colleague, who used the same approach, had similar results. Students demonstrated much more enthusiasm for learning the content of the chapter using the computer and reported that they could concentrate and understand the material more easily using a database.

Figure 10.8 José's Class Database

Type of Cell	Shape	Function	Location
astocyte	radiating	supply nutrients	central nervous system (CNS)
basal	cube-like	make new cells	stratum basale
cardiac muscle	branched	pump blood	around heart
erythrocytes	disc	move O_2, remove CO_2	blood plasma
fibroblast	flat	fiber production	connective tissue
keratinocytes	round	strengthen cells	stratum basal
osteoclast	ruffled	bone restoration	bone
sensory neurons	long, thin	impulses to CNS	cell body
simple columnar	columnar	secretion, absorption	digestive tract, glands
simple squamous	flat	diffusion of materials	lungs, blood vessels, kidneys
skeletal muscle	long	movement, posture	bone, skin
smooth muscle	disc	movement	organ walls

Looking Back, Looking Forward

There has been incredibly rapid growth in instructional applications of ICTs over the past couple of editions of this book. We believe the ultimate outcome of this growth is the inevitable use of technology as a teaching and learning tool in an increasing number of middle and secondary schools. We also believe that with this growth comes the need for responsible use of ICTs for meeting the learning needs of adolescents. Consequently, we advocate in this chapter that teachers use ICT tools in meaningful ways to encourage active learning, provide students with opportunities for unique learning experiences, and help them organize and synthesize information across the disciplines. Teachers of today and the future will need to increase their knowledge of classroom applications of ICTs to be wise and purposeful consumers. It is our hope that with this knowledge, teachers will discover ways to make technology tools compatible with the other interactive, prosocial, language-based strategies recommended throughout this book.

In the next and final chapter of this book, additional ICT applications are described for increasing striving readers' engagement in and comprehension of disciplinary content.

References

Alexander, P., & Jetton, T. (2000). Learning from text: A multidimensional and developmental perspective. In M. Kamil, P. Mosenthal, P. D. Pearson, & R. Barr (Eds.), *Handbook of reading research* (Vol. III). Mahwah, NJ: Lawrence Erlbaum Associates.

Alvermann, D. (2002). *Adolescents and literacies in a digital world*. New York: Peter Lang.

Anderson-Inman, L., & Ditson, L. (1999). Computer-based concept mapping: A tool for negotiating meaning. *Learning & Leading with Technology, 26,* 6–13.

Barron, A., & Lyskawa, C. (1998). *Microsoft FrontPage*. Cambridge, MA: International Thompson Publishing.

Beichner, R.J. (1994). Multimedia editing to promote science learning. *Journal of Educational Multimedia and Hypermedia, 3,* 55–70.

Blase, D. W. (2000). A new sort of writing: E-mail in the English classroom. *English Journal, 90,* 47–51.

Blumenfeld, P. C., Fishman, B. J., Krajcik, J. S., Marx, R. W., & Soloway, E. (2000). Creating useable innovations in systemic reform: Scaling up technology-embedded project-based science in urban schools. *Educational Psychologist, 35*(3), 149–164.

Boekaerts, M., Pintich, P., & Zeidner, M. (2000). *Handbook of self-regulation*. San Diego, CA: Academic Press.

Bolter, J. D., & Grusin, R. (2000). *Re-mediation: Understanding new media*. Boston: MIT Press.

Bolter, J. D., Smith, J., & Joyce, M. (1990). *Storyspace*. Cambridge, MA: Eastgate.

Bozeman, W. (1992). Spreadsheets. In G. Bitter (Ed.), *Macmillan encyclopedia of computers*. New York: Macmillan.

Brindley, S. (2000). ICT and literacy, In N. Mamble & N. Easingwood (Eds.): *ICT and literacy: Information and communications technology, media, reading and writing*. London: Continuum.

Browning, T. (2000). Hypermedia design in the English classroom. In D. Hickey & D. Reiss (Eds.), *Learning literature in an era of change: Innovations in teaching.* Sterling, VA: Stylus.

Brozo, W. G. (in press). Authentic contexts for developing language tools in vocational education. In J. Flood, D. Lapp, & Farnan, N. (Eds.), *Content area reading and learning: Instructional strategies*. Mahwah, NJ: Lawrence Erlbaum Associates.

Brusilovsky, P. (2001). Adaptive hypermedia. *User Modeling and User-Adapted Interaction, 11,* 87–110.

Burbules, N., & Callister, T. (2000). *Watch it: The risks and promises of information technologies for education*. Boulder, CO: Westview Press.

Coiro, J. (2003). Reading comprehension on the Internet: Expanding our understanding of reading comprehension to encompass new literacies. *The Reading Teacher, 56,* 458–464.

Crawford, K., & Staudt, C. (1999, Fall). A computer in the palm of their hands. *The Concord Consortium.* Retrieved October 32, 2005, from http://www.concord.org/pubs/1999fall/palm-computer.html.

Cuban, L. (2001). *Oversold and overused: Computers in the classroom*. Cambridge, MA: Harvard University Press.

De Bra, P., & Calvi, L. (1998). AHA! An open adaptive hypermedia architecture. *The New Review of Hypermedia and Multimedia, 4,* 115–139.

Dillner, M. (1994). Using hypermedia to enhance content area instruction. *Journal of Reading, 37,* 260–270.

Dillner, M. (2001, July/August). Using media flexibly to compose and communicate. *Reading Online, 5*(1). Available online at http://www.readingonline.org/articles/ art_index.asp?HREF=/articles/dillner/index./html.

Dillon, A., & Gabbard, R. (1998). Hypermedia as an educational technology: A review of the quantitative research literature on learner comprehension, control, and style. *Review of Educational Research, 68,* 322–349.

Ditson, L. A., Kessler, R., Anderson-Inman, L., & Mafit, D. (2001). *Concept mapping companion*

(2nd ed.). Eugene, OR: The International Society for Technology in Education.

Eagleton, M. B. (2002, July/August). Making text come to life on the computer: Toward an understanding of hypermedia literacy. *Reading Online, 6*(1). Available online at http://www.readingonline.org/articles/art_index.asp?HREF=eagleton2/index.html.

Freire, P. (1987). *Literacy: Reading the word and the world.* South Hadley, MA. Bergin & Garvey.

Fryer, W. A. (2003, January 1). The opportunities and challenges of wireless computing. *Tech Learning.* Retrieved October 10, 2005, from http://www.techlearning.com/db_area/archives/WCE/archives/weswire.html.

Gamble, N., & Easingwood, N. (2000). *ICT and literacy: Information and communications technology, media, reading and writing.* London: Continuum.

Gee, J. P. (2003). *What video games have to teach us about learning and literacy.* New York: Palgrave Macmillan.

Glazer, E. (2001). *Using Internet primary sources to teach critical thinking skills in mathematics.* Westport, CT: Greenwood Press.

Guastello, E. F., Beasley, T. M. & Sinatra, R. C. (2000). Concept mapping effects on science content comprehension of low-achieving inner-city seventh graders. *Remedial & Special Education, 21*(6), 356–364.

Guzzetti, B. J., Campbell, S., Duke, C., & Irving, J. (2003, July/August). Understanding adolescent literacies: A conversation with three zinesters. *Reading Online, 7*(1). Available online at http://www.readingonline.org/newliteracies/lit_index.asp?HREF=guzzetti3/.

Hagood, M. C. (2003). New media and online literacies: No age left behind. *Reading Research Quarterly, 38*(3), 387–395.

Hammer, R., & Kellner, D. (2001, May). Multimedia pedagogy and multicultural education for the new millennium. *Reading Online, 4*(10). Available online at http://www.readingonline.org/newliteracies/lit_index.asp?HREF=/newliteracies/hammer/index.html.

Hancock, C., Kaput, J. J., & Goldsmith, L. T. (1992). Authentic inquiry with data: Critical variables to classroom implementation. *Educational Psychologist, 27,* 337–364.

Hawisher, G., & Selfe, C. (1998). Reflections on computers and composition studies at the century's end. In I. Snyder (Ed.), *Page to screen: Taking literacy into the electronic era.* London: Routledge.

Healy, J. (2000). *Failure to connect: How computers affect our children's minds—for better or worse.* New York: Simon and Schuster.

Holzberg, C. S. (2002, March 15). Getting a handle on handhelds. *Tech Learning.* Retrieved September 28, 2005, from http://www.techlearning.com/db_area/archives/TL/2002/03/handle.html.

Howe, N., & Strauss, W. (2000). *Millenials rising: The next great generation.* New York: Vintage Books.

Jonassen, D. H., & Land, S. (2000). *Theoretical foundations of learning environments.* Mahwah, NJ: Lawrence Erlbaum Erlbaum.

Jonassen, D., Peck, K., & Wilson, B. (1999). *Learning with technology.* Columbus, OH: Merrill.

Kamil, M. (2004). *Reading for the 21st century: Adolescent literacy and learning strategies.* Washington, DC: Alliance for Excellent Education.

Kehus, M. (2000). Opportunities for teenagers to share their writing online. *Journal of Adolescent & Adult Literacy, 44,* 130–134.

Kennedy, K. (2003). Writing with Web logs. *Technology & Learning, 23,* 11–12.

Kibum, K., Turner, S., & Perez-Quinones, E. (2004). *Comparing classroom note taking across multiple platform devices.* Technical Report TR-04-23, Computer Science Virginia Tech. Available online at http://eprints.cs.vt.edu/archives/.

Kidd, S. M. (2002). *The secret life of bees.* New York: Penguin.

Kinzer, C. K. (2003, June). The importance of recognizing the expanding boundaries of literacy. *Reading Online, 6*(10). Available online at http://www.readingonline.org/electronic/elec_index.asp?HREF=/electronic/kinzer/index.html.

Kinzer, C. K., & Leander, K. (2003). Technology and the language arts: Implications of an expanded definition of literacy. In J. Flood, D. Lapp, J. R. Squires, & J. M. Jensen (Eds.), *Handbook of research and teaching the English language arts.* Mahwah, NJ: Lawrence Erlbaum Erlbaum.

Kleiner, A., & Farris, E. (2002, September). *Internet access in U.S. public schools and classrooms: 1994–2001.* Washington, DC: Department of Education, National Center for Education Statistics.

Knobel, M., & Lankshear, C. (2002). Cut, paste, publish: The production and consumption of zines. In D. Alvermann (Ed.), *Adolescents and literacies in a digital world.* New York: Peter Lang.

Kress, G. (1998). Visual and verbal modes of representation in electronically mediated communication: The potentials of new forms of text. In I Snyder (Ed.), Page to screen: Taking literacy into the electronic Rowledge London: Roulade.

Leander, K. M. (2003). Writing travelers' tales on new literacyscapes. *Reading Research Quarterly, 38,* 392–421.

Leander, K. M., & Sheehy, M. (2004). *Spatializing literacy research and practice*. New York: Peter Lang.

Leu, D. J., & Kinzer, C. K. (2000). The convergence of literacy instruction with networked technologies for information and communication. *Reading Research Quarterly, 35*, 108–127.

Leu, D. J., Kinzer, C. K., Coiro, J. L., & Cammack, D. W. (2004). Toward a theory of new literacies emerging from the Internet and other information and communication technologies. In R. Ruddell & N. Unrau (Eds.), *Theoretical Models and Processes of Reading* (5th ed.). Newark, DE: International Reading Association.

Lin, S-Y., Strickland, J., Ray, B., & Denner, P. (2004, Summer). Computer-based concept mapping as a prewriting strategy for middle school students. *Meridian, 7*(2). Available online at http://www.ncsu.edu/meridian/sum2004/.

Lockard, J. & Abrams, P. D. (2004). *Computers for twenty-first century educators* (6th ed.). Boston: Allyn & Bacon.

Loschert, K. (2003). High-tech teaching. *Tomorrow's Teachers, 9*, 2–5.

Luke, C. (2002). Recrafting media and ICT literacies. In D. E. Alvermann (Ed.)., *Adolescents and literacies in a digital world*. New York: Peter Lang.

Marcus, S. (1995). E-meliorating student writing. *Electronic Learning, 14*, 18–19.

Mather, M.A. (2000). Exhibits alive! Museums, Schools, and technology work together. *Technology & learning 21*, 57–62.

Mathews, J. (2000). High-tech heretics. *Washington Post,* May 2, A11.

McEneaney, J. E. (2000, November). Ink to link: A hypertext history in 36 nodes. *Reading Online, 4*(5). Available online at http://www.readingonline.org/articles/art_index.asp?HREF=/articles/mceneaney2/ index.html.

McKenna, M. C., & Richards, J. C. (2003). *Integrating multiple literacies in k–8 classrooms: Cases, commentaries, and practical applications*. Mahwah, NJ: Lawrence Erlbaum Associates.

Merkley, D., Schmidt, D., & Allen, G. (2001). Addressing the English language arts technology standard in a secondary reading methodology course. *Journal of Adolescent & Adult Literacy, 45*, 220–231.

Mike, D. (1997). Internet in the schools: A literacy perspective. *Journal of Adolescent & Adult Literacy, 40*, 4–13.

Mistler-Jackson, M., & Songer, N. B. (2000). Student motivation and Internet technology: Are students empowered to learn science? *Journal of Research in Science Teaching, 37*, 459–479.

Monke, L. (2001). In dreams begin responsibilities. In R. Burniske & L. Monke (Eds.), *Breaking down the digital walls: Learning to teach in a post-modem world*. Albany: State University of New York Press.

Myers, J., & Beach, R. (2001). Hypermedia authoring as critical literacy. *Journal of Adolescent & Adult Literacy, 44*, 538–546.

Newby, T., Stepich, D., Lehman, J., & Russell, J. (1999). *Instructional technology for teaching and learning* (2nd ed.). Englewood Cliffs, NJ: Prentice Hall.

Newman, J. M. (2000). Following the yellow brick road. *Phi Delta Kappan, 81*, 774–779.

Nichols, W. D., Wood, K., & Rickelman, R. (2001). Using technology to engage students in reading and writing. *Middle School Journal, 32*, 45–50.

Norris, C. A., & Soloway, E. M. (2003). The viable alternative: Handhelds. *School Administrator, 60*(4), 26–28.

Oppenheimer, T. (2003). *The flickering mind: The false promise of technology in the classroom and how learning can be saved*. New York: Random House.

Pailliotet, A. W., Semali, L., Rodenberg, R., Giles, J., & Macaul, S. (2000). Intermediality: Bridge to critical media literacy. *The Reading Teacher, 54*, 208–219.

Patterson, N. (2000). Weaving a narrative: From teens to string to hypertext. *Voices from the Middle, 7*, 41–47.

Pearson, G., & Young, A.T. (2002). Technically speaking: Why all Americans need to know more about technology. *The Technology Teacher, 62*, 8–12.

Perry, D. (2003, March). *Handheld computers (PDAs) in schools*. British Educational Communications and Technology Agency. Retrieved October 10, 2005, from http://www.becta.org.uk.

Peters, M., & Lankshear, C. (1996). Critical literacy and digital texts, *Educational Theory, 46,* 51–70.

Quesada, A., Miller, E., & Armstrong, S. (2000). The media literacy imperative. *Technology & Learning, 21*, 49–54.

Ramondetta, J. (1992). Learning from lunchroom trash. *Learning Using Computers, 20*, 59.

Ravitz, J., & Mergendoller, J. (2002). Making the dismal science relevant with projects and handheld computers. *Society for Information Technology and Teacher Education International Conference 2002*(1), 2206.

Ray, B. B. (2001, July/Sept.). PDAs in the classroom: Integration strategies for social studies educators. *Journal of Computers in the Social Studies, 9*(3). Available online at http://www.cssjournal.com/.

Ray, B., McFadden, A., Patterson, S., & Wright, V. (2001, Summer). Personal digital assistants in the middle school classroom: Lessons in hand. Retrieved October 10, 2005, from http://www. ncsu.edu/meridian/sum2001/palm/index.html.

Regner, S. (2003). Handhelds in the classroom: Fad or innovation? Retrieved October 10, 2005, from http://www.loma.k12.ca.us/LPS/text/ Mrs.Regner/portfolio/report_handhelds.pdf.

Reinking, D., McKenna, M., Labbo, L., & Kieffer, R. (1998). *Handbook of literacy and technology: Transformations in a post-typographic world*. Mahwah, NJ: Lawrence Erlbaum Associates.

Richardson, J. (2004, July/August). Content area literacy lessons go high tech. *Reading Online, 8*(1). Available online at http://www.readingonline.org/ articles/art_index.asp?HREF=richardson/index.html.

Riel, M. (1993, April). The writing connection: Global learning circles. Paper presented at the annual meeting of the American Educational Research Association, Atlanta, GA.

Riel, M., & Fulton, K. (2001). The role of technology in supporting learning communities. *Phi Delta Kappan, 82*, 518–523.

Roblyer, M. D., & Edwards, J. (2004). *Integrating educational technology into teaching*. Upper Saddle River, NJ: Merrill/Prentice Hall.

Roland, J. (2003/2004). Getting a handle on handhelds. *Learning and Leading with Technology, 31*(4), 6–11.

Rose, R. (2002). Exploring science education using handheld computers and data collection tools. *World Conference on E-Learning in Corporations, Government, Health, & Higher Education*, 2508–2509.

Rozell, E. J., & Gardner, W. L. (2000). Cognitive, motivation, and affective processes associated with computer related performance: A path analysis. *Computers in Human Behavior, 16*, 199–222.

Rushkoff, D. (1996). *Playing the future: How kids' culture can teach us to thrive in an age of chaos*. New York: HarperCollins.

Ryder, R. J., & Hughes, T. (1997). *Internet for educators*. Upper Saddle River, NJ: Prentice Hall.

Salpeter, J. (2003). Web literacy and critical thinking: A teacher's tool kit. *Technology & Learning, 23*, 4–26.

Schmar-Dobler, E. (2003). Reading on the Internet: The link between literacy and technology. *Journal of Adolescent & Adult Literacy, 47*, 80–85.

Shields, J., & Poftak, A. (2002, February 15). A report card on handheld computing. *Tech Learning*. Retrieved October 10, 2005, from http://techlearning.com//db_area/archives/TL/ 2002/02/handheld. html.

Shiveley, J. M., & VanFossen, P. J. (2001). *Using Internet primary sources to teach critical thinking skills in government, economics, and contemporary world issues*. Westport, CT: Greenwood Press.

Simpson, M. L., & Nist, S. I. (2001). Encouraging active reading at the college level. In M. Pressley & C. Block (Eds.), *Reading comprehension instruction*. New York: Guilford Publications.

Sinatra, R. C. (2000). Teaching learners to think, read, and write more effectively in content subjects. *Clearing House, 73*(5), 266–273.

Sølvberg, A. (2003). Computer-related control beliefs and motivation: A panel study. *Journal of Research on Technology in Education, 35*, 473–487.

Songer, N. B., Lee, H., and Kam, R. (2002). Technology-rich inquiry science in urban classrooms: What are the barriers to inquiry pedagogy? *Journal of Research in Science Teaching, 39*, 128–150.

Staudt, C. (2002). Understanding algebra through handhelds. *Learning and Leading with Technology, 30*(2), 36–38.

Stoll, C. (1999). *Why computers don't belong in the classroom and other reflections by a computer confusion*. New York: Doubleday.

Stone, B. (2002). *Blogging: Genius strategies for instant web content*. Berkeley, CA: New Riders Press.

Tapscot, D. (1998). *Growing up digital: The rise of the Net Generation*. New York: McGraw-Hill.

Tapscot, D. (1999). Educating the Net Generation. *Educational Leadership, 56*, 7–11.

Teclehaimanot, B., & Lamb, A. (2004 March/April). Reading, technology, and inquiry-based learning through literature-rich WebQuests. *Reading Online, 7*. Available online at http://www. readingonline.org/articles/art_index. asp?HREF=teclehaimanot/index.html.

Thatcher, M. (2003, April 15). Software for handhelds. *Tech Learning*. Retrieved October, 10, 2005, from http://www.techlearing.com/db_area/archives/ TL/2003/04/spotlight.html.

Tileston, D. W. (2004). *What every teacher should know about media and technology*. Thousand Oaks, CA: Corwin Press.

Tinker, B., Staudt, C., & Walton, D. (2002). The handheld computer as field guide. *Learning & Leading with Technology, 30*(1), 36–41.

Tolhurst, D. (1995). Hypertext, hypermedia, multimedia defined? *Educational Technology, 35*, 21–26.

Troxclair, D., Stephens, K., Bennett, T., & Karnes, F. (1996). Teaching technology: Multimedia presentations in the classroom. *Gifted Child, 19*, 34–47.

Turner, S. V., & Dipinto, V. M. (1992). Students as hypermedia authors: Themes emerging from a qualitative study. *Journal of Research on Computing in Education, 25,* 187–199.

U.S. Census Bureau. (2001). Home computers and Internet use in the United States: August 2000. Retrieved September 5, 2005, from http://www. census.gov/prod/2001pubs/ p23-207.pdf.

Vahey, P. & Crawford, V. (2002, September). Palm education pioneers program: Final evaluation report. [Report]. SRI International. Retrieved October 7, 2005, from http://www.palmgrants.sri.com.

Vrasidas, C. (2002). A systematic approach for designing hypermedia environments for teaching and learning. *International Journal of Instructional Media, 29,* 13–25.

Wagner, R. (1997–1998). *HyperStudio Workbook.* El Cajon, CA: Roger Wagner Publishing.

Wenglinsky, H. (1998). *Does it compute? The relationship between educational technology and student achievement in mathematics.* Princeton, NJ: Educational Testing Service.

White, B., & Johnston, T. S. (2001). We really do mean it: Implementing language arts standard #3 with opinionnaires. *The Clearing House, 74,* 119–123.

Winn, W. (2002). Current trends in educational technology research: The study of learning environments. *Educational Pscyhology Review, 14,* 331–351.

Wolsey, D. T. (2004, Januray/February). Literature discussion in cyberspace: Young adolescents using threaded discussion groups to talk about books. *Reading Online, 7*(4). Available online at http://www.readingonline.org/articles/ art_index.asp?HREF=wolsey/index.html.

Zahide, Y., Ozden, Y., & Aksu, M. (2001). Comparison of hypermedia learning and traditional instruction on knowledge acquisition and retention. *Journal of Educational Research, 94,* 207–214.

Zhao, Y., & Conway, P. (2001). What's in, what's out— an analysis of state educational technology plans. *Teachers College Record.* Retreived September 20, 2005, from http://www.eusd4kids.org/ edtech/pdf/Wht'sIN.pdf http://www.readingonline. org/newliteracies/lit_ index.asp?HREF=guzzetti3/.

chapter 11

Honoring Diversity and Building Competence: Supporting Striving Adolescent Readers Across the Disciplines

Anticipation Guide

Directions: Read each statement carefully and decide whether you agree or disagree with it, placing a check mark in the appropriate *Before Reading* column. When you have finished reading and studying the chapter, return to the guide and decide whether your anticipations need to be changed by placing a check mark in the appropriate *After Reading* column.

	Before Reading		After Reading	
	Agree	*Disagree*	*Agree*	*Disagree*
1. "At risk" is a term with a specific definition.	____	____	____	____
2. Striving readers have a common set of issues and needs.	____	____	____	____
3. Striving readers deserve a program of basic skills instruction.	____	____	____	____
4. Students of color and in poverty are necessarily at risk of reading failure.	____	____	____	____

5. Striving readers need exposure to engaging and accessible texts in order to improve.

   ____ ____ ____ ____

6. Issues of identity, culture, and self-efficacy should be factored into instructional practices for striving readers.

   ____ ____ ____ ____

Chapter Principle

No single principle applies to this chapter. Our work with striving adolescent readers should be guided by all that we know about effective reading and learning and requires the collective energies and creativity of every teacher who comes into contact with these youth. Consequently, disciplinary practices will make a difference if they connect striving readers' outside-of-school literacies with academic literacies; help them learn to self-assess; keep them engaged in reading, writing, and learning; move them to deeper and more critical levels of understanding of disciplinary content; endow them with the skills to gather and organize multiple sources; and teach them to use ICTs as tools for learning. The test of our principles is met when we use them as guideposts for designing responsive instruction for striving readers and learners.

Go to http://www.
prenhall.com/brozo,
select Chapter 11, then
click on Chapter
Objectives to provide a
focus for your reading.

If we journey back far enough in the history of schooling in America, we come to a time when struggling adolescent readers did not exist. Sure, there were plenty of youth who had limited literacy abilities or could not read at all, but virtually none were allowed or chose to remain in the schools that were available. Most schools did not extend beyond primary or elementary levels. And even with the rise of secondary education in the United States, it was not until the 1940s that high school matriculation rates began to exceed 50% of the eligible adolescent population. For most, schooling went no further than the eighth grade. Consequently, those students who made it to high school were generally regarded as having superior academic abilities and/or came from families that could afford a nonworking teenage son or daughter.

Today, high school attendance is compulsory. Youth from disparate cultures and with wide-ranging ability levels, who would never have had the opportunity for secondary education in years past, comprise the middle and high school student bodies all across America. Meeting the reading and learning needs of this diverse group is no longer an option but a legal mandate and the professional responsibility of all teachers. The right for all students to participate in the regular classroom curriculum is protected by federal legislation (the Individuals with Disabilities Education Act, IDEA), and progress of all students—including those who are English learners, students with disabilities, and students from poverty—must now be documented through requirements of the No Child Left Behind (NCLB) Act.

Legalities and professional responsibilities notwithstanding, evidence abounds that teachers across the United States lack appropriate training and skills in content-area literacy (Barry, 1997; O'Brien, Stewart, & Moje, 1995; Romine, McKenna, & Robinson, 1996). What's more, we have demonstrated in this book that the very nature of content-area literacy is being regularly redefined through emerging technologies (International Reading Association, 2001). Literacy can no longer be thought of as only the effective use of paper, pencil, and books. Students who are literate are also proficient in locating and reading information from digitized sources, and can express themselves using e-mail, word processors, and presentation programs as well as with handwriting. Not only must students be taught the critical literacy skills needed for effective information use, they must be proficient users of rapidly evolving technology while developing the capacity to use yet-unimagined new literacies (International Reading Association, 2001).

When secondary teachers lack understanding of current theories of content literacy and practices to make disciplinary knowledge accessible to all, this may be especially detrimental to striving readers and learners. There are numerous indications that youth of color (Jimenez, 1997; Tatum, 2000, 2005) and those receiving special education services (Fisher, Schumaker, & Deshler, 2002) are not getting adequate training in higher-level literacy skills (Biancarosa & Snow, 2004; Braunger, Donahue, Evans, & Galguera, 2005). Nevertheless, these students can be taught to improve their reading and thinking abilities when knowledge of literacy, language development, and learning strategies is applied to them as it is to other students (Dole, Brown, & Trathen, 1996; Wood & Algozzine, 1994) and, when appropriate, strategies are adapted to meet their unique learning needs (Greenleaf, Jimenez, & Roller, 2002; Pearman, Huang, & Mellblom, 1997).

CASE STUDY

Case studies in this
textbook provide an
opportunity to apply
principles and practices to
new contexts.

Rene is the biracial daughter of an Asian mother and Hispanic father. She is in the 11th grade at a high school in a major urban center in the Midwest. Her school is situated in a community of ethnic and socioeconomic diversity. The school is a large, decaying, fortress-looking building with few windows. Its grounds are littered and unattended. Rene has been in special education classes since the third grade. She recalls with bitterness the experience that seemed to mark her for special services.

> It was the first or second day of school. My mom was real sick, she was having a miscarriage I think. I was really scared. I thought she was going to die. Anyway, the teacher would write a word on the board, erase it, then go around the room and call on someone to say the word and spell it. Well, she finally called on me, but I wasn't paying attention because I was so upset about my mom. I had to stand up...I just couldn't remember the word. The kids started laughing, and the teacher told me to sit down and for not paying attention I had to write the word 50 times. It seems like from that time on I started having a lot of trouble reading, and they put me in special ed.

As an 11th grader, Rene was still in a special reading class. The class included 23 students; all but 2 were youth of color. The classroom was small, cramped, and cluttered. During the winter, the radiators generated stifling heat and clanged uncontrollably. According to the teacher of this special reading class—a former driver's education teacher with four graduate hours in reading coursework from a nearby university—students were suppose to be working on their own in self-paced workbooks and programmed materials. Reading kits with 25-year-old copyright dates and some spelling and phonics books were stacked irregularly on the one small bookcase next to the teacher's desk. Very few of these materials were being used, however. Most of the students either slept, listened to music, or talked quietly. The teacher felt that as long as they weren't disruptive they could do what they wanted. "I'll help the ones who want to help themselves," he commented.

Rene used the time to visit with the only other girl in the class. She commented on her experiences in remedial reading:

> It's a joke. I'm wasting my time in there. Nobody works. We just catch up on what's going on, you know, who's going with who and stuff like that. Mr. Willis hates it too, so he just says, "Don't bother me and I won't bother you." That's cool, but my reading is still bad and I still have to take the test in May like everyone else.

Rene commented on how she gets by in her history, science, and math classes, where reading assignments are given frequently:

> Math's no problem for me. I've always been good in math. History is harder. I sit next to my girlfriend, Stella. She's real smart, she tells me what to do. I don't like that teacher...I never look at him, and he never calls on me.

To the Reader:
When reflecting on this challenging scene of dysfunctional teaching and learning, consider ways in which Mr. Willis's remedial reading class could become a place for meaningful literacy opportunities. How could Rene be reached? How could her reading class be restructured so that it is no longer a waste of time for students like her? Be prepared to write down your ideas and recommendations after reading this chapter.

What Does It Mean to Be a Striving Reader?

We have elected to refer to youth with low-achievement levels in reading as *striving readers* for the following reason. Like all terms and labels, once embedded in the professional vernacular they have a way of reifying expectations and practices for students. Let's consider how this has happened with the thinking that has built up around the popular moniker *at risk*. Throughout our careers we have avoided the proclivity to toss this label around because we believe it inadequately and inappropriately stigmatizes youth (Brozo, 1995; Polakow & Brozo, 1994). The expression *at risk* must always be followed by the question *At risk of what?* A seventh grader of color from a single-parent household in poverty who is a recent immigrant may possess, according to a school district's definition, all of the risk factors of failure, yet we might also ask whether the seventh grader is at risk of unresponsive instruction because the school he attends employs teachers ill-prepared to deal with his needs (Brozo & Brozo, 1994). Flipped completely on its head, *at risk* might become *at promise* when schools and teachers see youth from diverse backgrounds as resources with multilingual and multicultural flexibility and the potential to make great strides given quality instruction.

Seen as "at promise" instead of "at risk" striving readers are more likely to receive instruction that helps them meet their potential.

Similarly, then, if a label must exist, we endorse *striving reader* over those that imply deficit, deficiency, or handicap. This is not because we fail to appreciate the challenges youth who are in need of further development in literacy pose, but to urge a different set of expectations and practices based on language that describes youth in a way that values the strengths they possess, their effort and potential.

Even though the label *striving readers* is a comfortable alternative to other more pejorative ones, it does not describe a single, monolithic condition. Striving readers may all be in need of literacy development but have unique needs, too (Ivey, 1999a). Here are three potentially useful ways of grouping the issues striving readers bring to middle and high school disciplinary classrooms:

- Some striving readers need to learn the cognitive strategies to read independently. With these strategies they may move beyond struggles with comprehension, word recognition and word learning, and fluency.
- Some striving readers harbor strong negative attitudes toward reading. This might have evolved out of a history of reading and writing failure or from being forced to read texts that were too difficult. These attitudes contribute to low self-esteem and low self-efficacy. A defensive shield might come up when confronted with a reading task. The attitudes of these striving readers keep them disengaged from the reading process.
- Some striving readers have lost touch with what books and other material interests them. They need to be surrounded by engaging texts and given the time and space to explore, sample, and experience a range of genres. Their "discourses of desire" need to be honored so as to reacquaint them with the pleasure and rewards associated with reading.

Who Are Striving Readers?

Given the three categories just noted, striving readers represent the diversity of the adolescent population itself. This means youth from *every* socioeconomic group, ethnicity, culture, and gender may be in need of further literacy development. We also know, however, that certain groups are privileged in academic settings because the discourse at home and at school is congruent, whereas others who bring different discourse traditions and patterns to secondary classrooms are more likely to encounter difficulties meeting literacy and learning expectations. The clash of school and home discourses and values seems to place a particularly heavy burden on youth who are recent immigrants and those who may be in poverty.

Even so, reconciling school reading with real-life reading can be challenging for any youth (Alvermann & Hagood, 2000; Bean, Bean, & Bean, 1999; Finders, 1997) and can lead to problems with academic texts and tasks. Adolescents who participate extensively in out-of-school literate activities do so for personally meaningful, identity affirming, and socially functional purposes. They might read the sports page of the newspaper to find out more about a favorite player, rap lyrics in a CD booklet as a guide for writing their own, or exchange e-mails with friends to plan a movie for the weekend. Youths' competence with these real-life literacy tasks may not be valued in or connected to academic settings, resulting in frustration, disengagement, and depressed performance (Primeaux, 2000).

To confound matters, factors that leave readers striving to improve often and necessarily interact, resulting in myriad variations of unique needs (Broaddus & Ivey, 2002). To make this point more vivid, consider the profiles of three different students in the accompanying Teacher as Learner box. These profiles are based on actual youth who participated in a tutorial program supervised by Bill (first author) at his university reading center. Each has a unique reading issue while all find themselves experiencing the same outcome—limited understanding of text.

Valuing striving youths' real-world literacy practices in the classroom may lead to their heightened investment in reading and learning.

Teacher as Learner

Read the brief profiles of three striving readers that follow, and then note the similarities and differences among them in the chart at the end of the box. Finally, make suggestions for disciplinary instructional practices that might facilitate their literacy development and knowledge acquisition.

Donelle

Donelle is a 15-year-old African American. His parents, both professionals, were excellent readers and students in high school, so they are frustrated by their son's poor academic performance and low reading test scores. Donelle has higher than average intelligence and an extensive vocabulary; however, his grades hover in the C/D range, and his state-mandated reading achievement test results places him at about the seventh-grade level. Donelle hates to read novels and textbooks and spends most of his spare time on the computer playing and working out strategies for solving games.

Nguyet

Nguyet, a 13-year-old seventh grader, arrived in the United States from Vietnam 2 years ago with her mother and two brothers. Although her English has improved significantly, she still struggles with reading textbooks and writing papers. Nguyet's ESOL teacher has been trying to build her English vocabulary with daily exercises, and though Nguyet's general word knowledge is increasing,

continued

Teacher as Learner *(continued)*

she is still unable to decode and understand technical vocabulary found in her social studies and science books. She also struggles with English idioms and the figurative language she encounters in her literature anthology.

Clifton

Clifton is a ninth grader living in the foothills of the Smokey Mountains. His parents are on public assistance. Neither finished high school. He works afternoons and nights, sometimes until 10:00 P.M. in his uncle's sawmill. His eighth-grade test scores place him at the fifth-grade level in reading. His teachers say he's inattentive in class though not disruptive. They often find him with his head on the desk, and he refuses to read aloud when called upon. He enjoys looking at magazines about off-road vehicles and is trying to save to buy a dirt bike he can ride on the miles of trails crisscrossing the countryside near his rural home.

Similarities	Differences	Possible Strategies

❭ *What Striving Readers Deserve: Confronting the Challenges*

Striving Readers Deserve the Best Instruction from All Teachers

In bringing secondary teachers to an understanding that language and communication skills are as equally important to teach as the substance of their disciplines, it becomes doubly hard to convince them they are responsible for the literacy development of all their students, not just the ones who "get it." Gary, a high school biology teacher who discovered he had a whopping 15-grade-level spread in one of his classes put it to us this way, "Do you see why we teach to the middle?" He went on to explain that while he had empathy for the very low-ability readers, he had not taken coursework in his graduate program that would allow him to feel competent enough to deal with their issues, and wondered why, as do many teachers in his situation, students with dismal reading skills are allowed to enter and progress through high school in the first place (Brozo & Hargis, 2005).

As experienced university professors in teacher preparation and education programs, we know firsthand the extent of training teachers receive that focuses on practices for youth who are striving readers. And, sadly, that extent is minimal to none. So we could begin with a self-indictment of sorts of the failure of higher education to meet the needs of teachers who must work with these students. Gary found some consolation in fixing blame there. But while reforms are desperately needed in teacher training programs, the issues striving adolescent readers bring to the classroom continue to mount. Gary may be technically correct, yet a refusal, benign or otherwise, to try to address the literacy and learning needs of his striving students would be unacceptable regardless of his self-justifications. With respect to high school biology, Dong's (2002) study of biology teachers demonstrates that when they focused on the academic welfare of striving English learners, creative practices emerged that integrated language and content.

> Disciplinary teachers need more training in effective practices for striving readers.

Striving Readers Deserve Effective Teachers Who Have the Knowledge and Practices to Deal with Their Needs

Striving readers who feel their learning needs are not being met may exhibit a variety of bluffing and off-task behaviors (Brozo, 1990a). Bill (first author of this text) found that many high school striving readers had learned how to "hide out" in disciplinary classrooms in order to avoid exposing their lack of reading competence. See Figure 11.1 for a list of 9 of the most common behaviors reported by striving readers. At first glance, the behaviors may seem contradictory, but the list was developed through sophisticated understanding of the expectations of particular teachers. Sometimes, as Bill found out, it's better for students to invite negative attention, which takes the teacher off task. At other times, it's critical for students to "disappear" in the room to avoid being found out. It's important to note, however, that these behaviors were useful to students only insofar as their teachers failed to see through them. Many teachers are unable to recognize the lengths some striving students might go to in order to keep from laying themselves bare before their peers or engaging in an activity that is painful and unrewarding. At the same time, some teachers have come to tolerate disengagement so long as it isn't disruptive by

Figure 11.1 9 "Hiding Out" Behaviors of Adolescent Striving Readers

- Frequently forgets to bring books and other texts to class
- Feigns attention by looking at teacher and nodding head but is engaging in "mock participation" (Bloome & Green,1984)
- Flags hand and gestures to be called on when knows teacher calls on students thought not to be paying attention
- Frequently puts head on the desk, pretending to be tired or ill
- "Apple polishes" and gives the teacher the impression of being cooperative and concerned
- Sits next to a "with it" student for answers, directions, and help
- Requests urgent need for hall or lavatory pass
- If round-robin oral reading, counts exactly when turn will come and rehearses paragraph or passage as many times as possible before being asked to read
- Simply says "I don't want to read, I'm not feeling well"

allowing striving readers to keep their heads on the desk or sit quietly by themselves. In any case, teachers are unwittingly exacerbating the problem of students hiding out if they lack strategies for addressing this problem.

Gary's complaint that he had not received much information about or practices for working with low-achieving readers in his biology classes was sadly true. This population was given short shrift in both his teacher education program and the professional development sessions provided by his school and district. What Gary and most disciplinary teachers in secondary schools need is well-structured and ongoing training devoted to culturally and individually responsive pedagogy (Vaughn, Klingner, & Bryant, 2001). Administrators, curriculum specialists, and reading coaches should be the instigators and supporters of such professional development (Sturtevant et al., 2006). They should also provide teachers numerous opportunities to collaborate on ways of meeting the literacy needs of striving readers, reflect on and analyze practices with these students, and modify instruction as appropriate. To tell teachers to increase achievement for striving readers without appropriate support is no different than telling students to read better without showing them how. Both need scaffolding for their respective challenges with teaching and texts (Broaddus & Bloodgood, 1999).

> Teachers of striving youth should be provided worthwhile and tangible support in their efforts to practice responsive pedagogy.

Although effective teaching cannot be distilled, bottled, and taken as an elixir, we know that effective middle and secondary disciplinary teachers exhibit certain general characteristics that can serve as guidelines for helping you become a better teacher.

Effective Teachers Collaborate with Students, Teachers, Parents, and Administrators

Many people share an interest in your striving students' reading, writing, and learning development, including, as we demonstrate in subsequent sections, the students themselves. The prospects of students becoming active learners and developing lifelong reading habits greatly increase when all persons concerned—teachers, parents, school administrators—work collaboratively to honor student diversity and build literacy competence. With these collaborative efforts, your teaching effectiveness is sure to increase as well. Following are suggestions for developing collaborative relationships with teachers, parents, administrators, and students.

Let All Interested Groups Know Your Expectations for Reading, Writing, and Learning

To work collaboratively, it isn't necessary to convert others to your approach to teaching, but it is important that they be made aware of the nature of your curriculum and the rationale behind it. Otherwise, suspicion, distrust, and confusion may develop. Before others make judgments about you based on piecemeal or incorrect information, share with them as honestly and as accurately as possible your teaching philosophy and classroom strategies.

Make Sure Striving Students Understand Your Expectations for Them as Readers, Writers, and Learners

Striving students must "revalue" reading and writing as meaningful, functional processes that can be used as vehicles for learning and expanding subject matter knowledge. All the strategies discussed in this book are intended to help you incorporate into your content curriculum learning experiences that demonstrate this revaluing of literacy.

Develop Collaborative Relationships with Students

Rhodes and Dudley-Marling (1988) put it well when they said, "We can teach but we can't force learning; learning is a student's prerogative" (p. 273). Striving students in the middle and upper grades are more likely to choose to learn when they are respected as curricular informants and allowed a hand in determining course topics, materials, learning experiences, projects, and evaluation. Involving students in course decisions will encourage commitment to and cooperation and investment in the learning process. Without students' active complicity in their own education, the chances of expanding their content knowledge, as well as their literacy skills, are greatly diminished (Brozo, 2006).

Develop Collaborative Relationships with Parents

Parents play a vital role in the literacy development and motivation of students, especially striving readers (Bean & Valerio, 1997; Brozo, Valerio, & Salazar, 1996). Teachers and parents can work together to facilitate students' literacy at home (Tice, 2000). Most of the suggestions that teachers make to parents should be reminders of how parents have been supporting literacy at home for generations. When support for literacy at school is provided at home, striving students discover the importance of reading and writing (Moore & Hinchman, 2006; Saravia-Schore & Arvizu, 1992). Parents, in turn, can be useful informants about their students' attitudes, interests, hobbies, and other behavioral and personality insights that the teacher can use when selecting trade books and planning research projects.

> Efforts to facilitate literacy activity in the home can result in improved attitudes and achievement in the classroom.

One of the best ways parents and caregivers can be involved in their adolescent son's or daughter's literacy development is by encouraging and modeling personally meaningful reading. Adolescents who daily catch their parents in the act of reading—whether it's an executive in Los Angeles with the *Wall Street Journal*, a hog farmer in Illinois with the farm report on a computer screen, or a teacher in Florida curled up on the couch with a mystery novel—are likely to develop positive attitudes about reading (DeBruin-Parecki, Paris, & Siedenburg, 1997). Encourage parents to make sure they let their striving adolescents observe them reading, whether from print or digital sources. Instead of ordering and demanding them to read, parents should set an example for their adolescents of the importance and joy of literacy.

Another way to involve parents in the literacy development of their sons and daughters is to encourage them to make a variety of reading material available at home. A student in one of Bill's graduate reading courses told him recently how she had been struggling to get her 12-year-old son to read. She had subscriptions to youth and teen magazines, but he wouldn't read them. She handed him one book after another, only to have each rejected. One day she left Gary Paulsen's *The Haymeadow* (1992) on his bedstand. Later that night she noticed light spilling out from under his bedroom door. To her delight, she found her son engrossed in the book. She almost had to wrestle it from him to get him to go to sleep. The next day a blizzard kept students at home, and he picked up the book on waking and stayed in bed until he was finished. "Man, that was a great book," he said. "Are there any more like that?"

Indeed, there are many more outstanding young adult books that can make the difference between whether or not striving and reluctant youth become lifelong readers. Figure 11.2 presents guidelines adapted from Reed (1988) for helping parents select books for adolescents.

The best way to assist striving youth in developing the reading habit is to be a good role model of an engaged and active reader. As adolescents observe influential adults reading functional and meaningful materials and observe adults' selection processes,

Figure 11.2 A Parents' Guide to Selecting Books for Adolescents

1. Use the book lists and Web sites in Chapters 8 and 11 as guides.
2. Check local bookstores and public and university libraries for the best source of books.
3. Consult librarians, bookstore clerks, university faculty, and teachers who are knowledgeable about young adult books.
4. Become a keen observer of your adolescent's interests, including favorite television shows, hobbies, leisure-time activities, and the kinds of books he or she has read and enjoyed in the past.
5. Consider how well your daughter or son reads when deciding the appropriateness of young adult books.
6. Take a close look at the books to determine whether they match your adolescent's interests.
7. Enroll your son or daughter in a young adult book club, or form one.
8. Be sure the main character in the book approximates the age of your adolescent. Characters who are too young are likely to be poorly received; characters who are a bit older are often preferred.
9. Try to make a variety of books available to your adolescent; then allow her or him to select a favorite one.
10. Don't impose your tastes on your adolescent; use his or her selection to guide you in selecting or purchasing future books.
11. Don't jam the books down your adolescent's throat or lay on a thick, hard sales pitch.
12. Try to increase gradually the literary quality of books.
13. Avoid the tendency to make reading a requirement at home; be patient.
14. Try to gradually induce your adolescent to select young adult books. Help by (a) encouraging regular visits to the public library and bookstore, (b) introducing librarians and clerks who are knowledgeable about young adult books and sensitive to the needs of adolescents, (c) purchasing and sharing annotated bibliographies of young adult books (see the reference guides in Chapter 8), (d) discussing the book your young adult is reading, and (e) suggesting books your young adult might enjoy.

Adapted from *Comics to Classics: A Parent's Guide to Books for Teens and Preteens*, by A. J. S. Reed, 1988, Newark, DE: International Reading Association.

they are likely to imitate this behavior. Teachers and parents can work together to discover what striving readers will enjoy and be capable of reading. Together they can also discuss the importance of parents and caregivers providing thoughtful and sensitive guidance to help striving readers at home increase their reading pleasure and expand their abilities.

Develop Collaborative Relationships with Other Teachers
In Chapter 10 we described how Yuri, an algebra teacher, and Sherry, a history teacher, teamed up on a Web Quest activity. The beneficiaries of their collaboration were 11th graders who learned to apply statistics to current events. This example of cooperative planning between teachers demonstrates the power of collaboration as

an effective way to influence student learning as well as teachers' beliefs about the role of reading and writing in the disciplines.

Another way teachers can support each other to make reading and learning more accessible and engaging for striving youth is by collaborating on thematic units (Gross, 1997; Moore & Hinchman, 2006). For example, an eighth-grade history teacher teamed up with the language arts teacher on a World War I unit. In the language arts classroom, students listened to their teacher read aloud a young adult novel, *No Hero for the Kaiser* (Frank, 1986). In response to the book they kept a log in which they wrote their reactions and how the fiction content related to what they were learning in the history class; used the Internet to research their own family histories to determine who fought in the war; and built spreadsheets relating battles described in their history book to the effects of the battles on the characters in the novel. They engaged in many other literacy experiences designed to integrate the various texts. This support of the history teacher's unit helped striving readers increase their understanding of details and concepts related to World War I and elevate both the students' and the history teacher's enthusiasm for the unit. In this way, the history teacher had time to cover the content he felt was important, while the language arts teacher engaged students in functional and meaningful literacy experiences. In the process, everyone benefited.

Within each of the previous chapters of this book we have described how teacher leaders, such as reading coaches and specialists, can work in tandem with disciplinary teachers to design and employ responsive instructional practices. Chances are your school or district has such an individual. Be sure to introduce yourself to discover what specific services the specialist can offer you to help your striving readers. The reading specialist might be available to work directly with striving students from your class. Coaches and specialists will often team teach with you to develop students' strategies for learning material from multiple texts and class notes. The specialist might conduct demonstration lessons for your students on certain strategies, such as mapping or the survey procedure using your content materials. The reading specialist can also provide you with Web sites, readings, and teaching ideas for inclusion students in your classroom.

Finally, you should develop an effective relationship with your school librarian. Librarians can be invaluable friends and colleagues when you plan units and projects with your striving readers in mind. Librarians are pleased to help you identify relevant resources for upcoming topics. They can provide your class with presentations and demonstrations in using reference material, accessing computer databases, and conducting research. Above all, librarians are often your best link to quality young adult books, youth magazines, and digital sources for striving adolescent readers.

When disciplinary teachers and literacy leaders work together to plan lessons and units, striving readers are the beneficiaries.

Participate in Professional Learning Communities

Throughout this book we have provided scenarios and vignettes of teachers changing their practices and making a significant difference in the academic lives of the students they teach. However, to achieve broad-based support for literacy practices targeted at striving readers, disciplinary teachers need to work in purposeful groups. When teachers work together they are far more likely to solve complex problems and bring about more responsive curriculum for youth who have the greatest need for literacy development. A forum that appears to hold great promise for bringing teachers together has been variously referred to as teacher study groups (Murphy & Lick, 1998), teacher learning teams (Arter, 2001), professional learning communities (DuFour & Eaker, 1998), and peer coaching (Beavers, 2001). We prefer the term *professional learning community* and will describe how it functions and provide examples.

Professional learning communities grew out of the realization that teachers make or break educational innovation. Policy makers can enact the laws, administrators can supply the pressure, staff developers can present the innovative strategies, but teachers make the decision to change or not change the ways they teach. The growing realization among those seeking restructuring of the curriculum, modifications of school policies, or enhancing faculty professionalism is that without teacher support and ownership of the processes involved in making these changes, success will always remain illusive. Professional learning communities comprised primarily of teachers (but extended when appropriate to include as co-partners administrators, parents, and students) who are vested with the responsibility of setting curricular direction are more likely to bring about school improvements (Tichenor & Heins, 2000). Putnam and Borko (2000) assert, "For teachers to be successful in constructing new roles they need opportunities to participate in a professional community that discusses new teacher materials and strategies and that supports the risk taking and struggle entailed in transforming practice" (p. 8).

Professional learning communities have three main purposes (DuFour & Eaker, 1998):

- To help educators implement curricular and instructional innovations
- To engender collaborative planning for school improvement
- To provide educators a forum for studying current research regarding teaching and learning

In professional learning communities teachers themselves ask critical questions about their practice and build a collaborative framework for finding answers. In this way, teachers take control of their learning by actively participating in problem-centered discussions and activities (Crowther, 1998).

Learning communities are comprised of small groups of professionals who agree to research an area of concern, experiment with possible solutions, and meet regularly for a specified period of time to share and reflect upon lessons learned in the classroom. Although there are numerous suggestions for improving the likelihood that professional learning communities will be successful (Murphy, 1999), we found in our own work with teachers in a study group at Foothills High School (Brozo & Hargis, 2005) that the following guidelines were critical:

- *Participants should choose areas of concern that are meaningful to them.* Throughout this book we have been emphasizing the importance of giving students as many opportunities as possible for learning in ways that are personally meaningful to them. We urge this approach because it fits nicely with how learning occurs best in our own adult lives. We found that teacher study-group attendance and involvement remained high when group members were allowed to identify aspects of a school issue that were relevant to them.

  Any number of issues can form the focus of professional learning communities, provided each member of the community or study group has a common reason for joining. For example, teachers in a California middle school formed a study group that included parents to deal with concerns about large numbers of failing ESL students. In a Cincinnati high school teachers came together around the common need to deal more effectively with the educational and social welfare of a growing number of students who were from homeless backgrounds. At Foothills High a teacher study group was established by the principal to respond to problems posed by 30% of the student body reading significantly below grade placement.

Go to Web Resources for Chapter 11 at *http://www.prenhall.com/ brozo,* and look for Professional Learning Communities and Teacher Study Groups.

- *All individuals should participate voluntarily.* Teachers are more likely to get and remain involved in professional learning communities if the first guideline noted is sincerely honored. Once again, lessons from students are instructive here. Adolescents are required to attend school but we cannot force them to read, learn, and stay engaged in classroom activities. Instead, students have to voluntarily decide to involve themselves in the flow of instruction. The chances of their involvement increase significantly if they are offered interesting and personally meaningful learning opportunities. Similarly, teachers who volunteer to become a part of professional learning communities tend to remain actively involved and share their enthusiasm with others in the school (Ross, Rolheiser, & Hogaboam-Gray, 1999).

    The principal of Foothills High School conducted a survey of his faculty to gather information about their perceptions of struggling readers in their classrooms. Based on the results, he invited particular teachers who noted the most serious problems to join in a collective effort to find possible solutions. Not everyone accepted his invitation, but a study group was ultimately formed comprising the librarian, two teachers from English, and one each from special education, biology, business education, and history. Although participation in the professional learning community at Foothills High was voluntary, the principal did create incentives for joining and staying involved. He gave special recognition to group members at faculty and board meetings. He also allowed the teachers to earn staff development points by attending discussions, participating in activities, and documenting new schoolwide reading initiatives and strategies used in their classrooms.

- *Participants should select their own resources for becoming informed and launching new initiatives.* When given the time and support to do so, teacher study groups can demonstrate skill and resourcefulness in identifying appropriate directions and tools for change (Murphy & Lick, 1998). For example, one member of the Foothills High group had recently completed graduate coursework in literacy, the textbooks for which included current chapters and articles pertinent to the focus of their professional learning community. These she disseminated among the members, who read and discussed them. Another member of the group had attended a grant-writing workshop conducted by state department personnel to learn about applying for Reading Excellence Act (REA) monies. She proposed they write a grant that required collaboration with a local university—and that's how we became involved in the reading efforts at Foothills High.

- *Participants should negotiate adequate time for implementation and reflection.* Administrators who are fully committed to the success of professional learning communities know that time is a vital resource. Group members should be able to meet regularly and participants should be allowed time in lieu of other duties, such as faculty meetings, to maximize attendance. At Foothills the principal made arrangements for study-group members to have a full-day retreat to plan and write the REA grant. He also permitted group members to exit whole-staff faculty meetings early to conduct their own sessions.

    Professional learning communities are springing up throughout the country as teachers, administrators, and parents grapple with new and evolving learning concerns for adolescents. Some, like the National Council of Teachers of English (NCTE) Reading Initiatives (Smith & Hudelson, 2001), enjoy official sponsorship by a prominent literacy organization. The Reading Initiative supports teachers and administrators who engage in focused study, conversation, reflection, and problem solving of concerns particular to their school sites by providing participants a 1-year NCTE membership, subscription to an NCTE journal of their choice, and registration to the NCTE annual convention. Others are formed with the help and prodding of university faculty (Tichenor & Heins, 2000). Most, however, are led and monitored by teachers. Regardless of the particular ways in which professional learning communities are formed, they all share a common purpose—to create collegial, supportive school cultures with expressed visions and directions for professional development and school improvement (Marshall, Pritchard, & Gunderson, 2001).

We urge you to get involved in study groups at your school or to form a study group yourself if one doesn't already exist. Raise the idea with your principal and colleagues as an alternative to traditional staff development, which is usually composed of a few days of in-service workshops every year presented by "experts" who may have little appreciation for the particular needs and issues of teachers and students at your site. The funds used to pay for workshop speakers' expenses could be spent on books, journals, computer access, and substitute teachers to cover for study-group participants while they observe programs and strategies in other schools or do off-site materials and information gathering. Start simple to make the prospects more inviting, such as the approach we observed in one of the middle schools we visited, which the teachers called "The Friday Five." Every Friday afternoon five teachers with a common planning period met as a study group for 45 minutes to explore topics related to reading and writing and to support one another's efforts to implement new literacy strategies in their classrooms. The key is that you take control of your own expanding sense of professionalism through inquiry, problem solving, and, most important, peer collaboration.

- *Participants should agree in advance on the kinds of activities the group and each team member should be involved in and hold each other accountable for fulfilling those tasks.* The Foothills High professional learning community members agreed in one of their first team meetings that each session would be taken up with (1) discussing instructional implications of articles and chapters read, (2) proposing reading strategies and efforts designed to leaven the achievement levels of struggling readers and enrich the literate culture of the school as a whole, (3) sharing progress and seeking feedback on classroom strategies, and (4) preparing for the next topic, charge, and/or reading. Between sessions, participants agreed to work on the grant proposal, locate additional relevant books and articles, do the required reading, and try out certain strategies in their classrooms.

- *Participants should report to the entire staff on a regular basis.* Keeping administrators and other faculty fully apprised of developments that grow out of the work of professional learning communities is critical to overall school change. Because team members at Foothills High were responsible for proposing and helping launch literacy initiatives that would eventually require the support of every teacher, open communication was critical. Before submitting their REA grant, members of the study group needed to be certain the project features were feasible, and sensitive to the needs of students in their particular school. Reporting to the entire staff was also meant to

> Research evidence is mounting in favor of teachers charting and implementing their own course for innovation and improvement.

ensure that faculty across all content areas as well as administrators could "buy in" to the initiatives proposed and also helped to gather additional suggestions for improving the ultimate literacy program that would be put into place at Foothills.

Develop Collaborative Relationships with Administrators

In most buildings, school principals, supervisors, and other administrators possess a great deal of decision-making power. Therefore, they can be important allies in your work to find effective practices for striving readers. The extent to which they share their power may depend on how actively you cultivate cooperative relationships with them.

We recommended earlier that to begin, you should make clear your expectations for striving readers within your classroom learning environment. Most administrators are happy to hear of your innovative efforts and are more likely to provide support if they are kept abreast of the reading, writing, and learning strategies you are attempting to incorporate into your classroom for meeting the needs of striving youth. Principals can play an instrumental role in developing and implementing a sustained silent reading or writing program. They can find funds for alternative resources, such as trade books, and can provide the necessary support for book drives, sales, and other plans you devise for finding books and raising money for books. Administrators can help create a supportive environment for teacher collaboration and classroom research. With your cooperation, they can help arrange important and enlightening in-service training and facilitate parent–teacher programs. They can also make critical links to community resources for donations of reading, writing, and other curricular materials.

The more you communicate with administrators about your striving students' instructional needs and growth, the greater the chance that they will appreciate your efforts, understand your concerns, and support your curricular changes.

One last word about collaboration. We do not want to give the impression that students, parents, teachers, and administrators are the only individuals who can contribute to the overall learning and literacy development of your striving adolescent readers. We recommend that you also develop links with other members of the community who can assist you, including local poets, writers, musicians, senior citizens, retired teachers, university student volunteers, and others. Sometimes persistent inquiry can lead to the discovery of some wonderful local resources. Recently, for example, one of our graduate students, an English teacher, while preparing a unit on the Arthurian Legend, found out about a local group of actors known as the Guild of Creative Anachronisms. Several members came into his classroom dressed in Arthurian garb and gave an exciting and informative demonstration on the life, culture, and music during that period and place in history. This strategy enlivened the unit, particularly for his striving readers, and provided his class with a truly unforgettable experience.

> One of the best collaborative roles administrators can play is to provide necessary supports for teachers in their efforts to improve practices with striving readers.

Effective Teachers Employ Innovative Practices That Link Content and Literacy Learning

All of the ideas in this book for expanding reading, writing, and other language processes are suggestions, ways of demonstrating possibilities. These suggestions come from our own work, from research, and most prominently from the exceptional teachers who have developed them and used them successfully. They are to be considered guidelines because, obviously, not all of the suggested strategies and practices will work in your particular setting, not all will work in precisely the ways we describe, and not all will transform your striving readers into sophisticated meaning makers. Effective teachers concerned about the literacy development of striving youth are constantly on the lookout for new ideas, strategies, and practices they can adapt to meet their students' particular needs. This process of modification and adaptation is innovation. In fact, we expect that the strategies we suggest will take on new shapes and forms in the hands of generative teachers.

For example, a 10th-grade music teacher was tutoring three gifted piano students who were also striving readers. She reasoned that if she could link texts related to the musical themes, composers, and compositions her students were studying and performing, reading would be more meaningful and pleasurable for them. Initially she had difficulty finding texts at an appropriate level of difficulty, but then solved this problem by locating Internet sites with pictures, biographies, librettos, letters, and other primary documents that she incorporated into a WebQuest. The students enjoyed the activities in the WebQuest, especially when they discovered they could read with little difficulty the information at the sites. The students also found that the information they acquired about the composers' life histories and the inspiration for their work improved their musical interpretation of the pieces.

> Striving readers can be found in every discipline so will need innovative approaches to developing their literacy skills in every learning context.

In another example, a sixth-grade science teacher wanted to create a language-rich environment in his classroom to entice his striving readers to read more and, he hoped, discover the pleasure of reading about science. By establishing a class library, the teacher could include a variety of science textbooks and information books dealing with many different topics, newspaper articles, science magazines, young adult fiction books with science themes, picture books, biographies of scientists, and URLs with fun science-related experiments and topics. He made a space in the classroom for the library that included an old overstuffed couch, a couple of beanbag chairs, a table with chairs for relaxation reading and personal research, and a couple of computers. Students were given opportunities during nearly every class period to use the class library to work on personal and class projects and to simply read as their science interests dictated. His striving readers found plenty to access in the library and benefited from regular print exposure that helped expand their background knowledge for science topics.

To restate our key point, you do not become an effective teacher by simply following the suggestions of others. Teaching effectiveness will result if you create new strategies based on reframing and expanding existing strategies that are more ideally suited to you, your instructional context, and the needs and interests of your students.

Effective Teachers Understand Literacy Processes

A common concern among the teachers we meet who are trying to face the challenges posed by their striving adolescent readers is expressed in the question "How can I stay abreast of all the new trends and developments in the fields of reading and writing?" In response, we strongly advocate that teachers in every discipline take courses in reading at a local university, enroll in a graduate or certification program, and attend workshops and conferences on reading and writing. Another inevitable answer we must give to this question is that to become aware of current teaching developments in reading and writing practices for striving youth, you must read the professional literature. As we have shown, teacher study groups and professional learning communities can encourage reading and inquiry. We admit, however, that trying to decide what professional literature to read can be a daunting task. Some guidelines follow.

Become a member of the International Reading Association (IRA) and the National Council of Teachers of English (NCTE). As a member of either of these organizations, you will receive a journal that deals with reading and writing issues, concerns, and practical teaching suggestions for adolescent students. Most issues have at least one article or feature devoted to struggling or striving readers. IRA members find the *Journal of Adolescent & Adult Literacy* most helpful for presenting many fresh ideas each month on such topics as teaching vocabulary, writing in the content areas, and using young adult literature. NCTE's *English Journal* and *Voices from the Middle* are also valuable resources for teachers looking for ideas and strategies to facilitate middle and high school students' literacy abilities. Every month, look for articles concerned with striving readers and those discussing practices that might be adapted for them and read them closely. Integrate the ideas and suggestions into your instructional plans, and modify them to meet your striving readers' particular needs. In this way, you will gain regular exposure to the current perspectives on literacy processes and on developing skill at translating ideas and others' suggestions into your own personally meaningful and useful strategies.

These organizations are offering an increasing array of electronic services. The journals just mentioned are available online, eliminating the need for shelving and storage space and allowing archival searches and retrievals. Chat room and threaded discussion opportunities for teachers are other new features of membership. In these cyber-environments teachers pose questions and describe problems, seeking input from kindred spirits. These sites are also sources for detailed explanations of successful educational innovations tried out by teachers working with young adults. IRA has teamed with the Marco Polo foundation to make available fully developed lesson plans that demonstrate how particular strategies featured in their journal articles can be applied in actual classroom contexts.

Go to Web Resources for Chapter 11 at *http://www.prenhall.com/brozo,* and look for IRA Resources for Striving Readers.

Another benefit of membership in IRA and NCTE is the availability of discounted books on a wide range of reading/writing topics, most of which can be purchased only through these professional organizations. New books are added annually. As you peruse the IRA or NCTE catalog, you will find a growing number of publications on topics related to struggling and striving readers. Reading these sources on a regular basis will help to expand your knowledge about literacy processes. It will also provide you with many more strategies for helping striving adolescent readers become more engaged and effective learners in your classroom. These organizations can be contacted at the following addresses:

International Reading Association
800 Barksdale Road
P. O. Box 8139
Newark, DE 19714-8139
www.reading.org

National Council of Teachers of English
1111 Kenyon Road
Urbana, IL 61801
www.ncte.org

Given the staggering number of journals that publish reading and writing articles and the professional texts that appear annually, we suggest that you ease into the current literature in a modest way. Set aside a couple of hours per week to devote to reading journals and books. After reading a journal article or book, jot down notes about the topics on an index card and file the card or create an electronic database that you can consult when you need some ideas for teaching course content with striving readers. As suggested earlier, seek out like-minded colleagues interested in meeting regularly to discuss articles from journals. Like book clubs, these teacher

The Role of the Teacher Leader

Among the various roles of a literacy coach, none is more important than providing leadership and support to schools and staff for meeting the needs of striving readers. This can be accomplished in many ways and through many different activities, such as:

- Using low-stakes tests to determine the overall reading level of all students

- Identifying youth who may be striving readers and assessing them to determine specific strengths, areas that need further development, interests, and instructional strategies that may be effective for them

- Conducting classroom demonstration teaching lessons for content-area teachers using practices that will engage striving readers

- Working with individual and small groups of striving readers in various support contexts, such as peer-led discussion groups and book clubs

- Forming literacy advisory councils comprised of teachers, striving readers, and parents to discuss and recommend programs and practices for these students

- Locating and preparing modified and alternative texts for striving readers for use in disciplinary classrooms

- Partnering with school librarians to find resources to obtain high-interest, accessible texts for striving readers to be added to a library's holdings made and available for individual teacher's classroom collections

- Collaborating with administration to implement school-wide programs, such as sustained silent reading, buddy reading, book drives, and book drops

- Providing professional development opportunities for teachers on strategies and practices for increasing engagement and achievement for striving readers

Let's spotlight a couple of the roles just outlined. A history teacher asked his school's literacy coach to assess one of his students who complained of having difficulty reading the textbook. The coach used an informal reading inventory to determine the student's independent, instructional, and frustration reading levels. The coach also used the inventory to conduct an interactive assessment (Brozo, 1990b). Interactive assessment is a process of trying out strategies with a student to determine their effectiveness for improving comprehension. The coach employed various strategies at each phase of the reading process with inventory passages: before, to activate and build relevant prior knowledge, engender interest and motivation, and set purposes for reading; during, to model and elicit comprehension processes; and after, to extend and apply new understandings. As a result, the literacy coach was able to confirm which strategies had the best potential for helping the student improve his meaning-making skills. Information about the student's overall reading level as well as specific instructional approaches that may be beneficial to him were shared with the history teacher. The coach offered and was asked to demonstrate some of the strategies for the history teacher in the class that had the reader she assessed. Afterward, the literacy coach and history teacher reviewed the strategies and discussed ways they could be incorporated into his instructional plans. The coach also obtained a copy of the teacher's syllabus and volunteered to locate easier readings on the various topics covered. These would be made available to the striving reader in his class as alternatives to the textbook.

study groups can heighten your motivation to read, analyze, and apply new content literacy innovations.

A second common concern, related to the one just discussed, is expressed in the question "How do I determine whether reading strategies are appropriate for my striving students and are based on sound theory and research?" This question, dealing with how to choose appropriate, sound, research-based strategies for teaching reading and writing, is not easily answered. Perhaps the biggest challenge for the concerned professional is to determine the most important criteria related to a research study or methods paper: Is the research based on actual practice in actual school settings with students like mine, or is it based on populations of students and conducted in contexts dissimilar to my own? It is safe to say that because of the mind-boggling number of research studies and reports that continually appear in the professional literature, many teachers including those in higher education, do not always know what information is research based. To confound matters, articles appearing in the same journal often contain conflicting findings. So it is not surprising to find many concerned teachers confused about how best to teach reading and writing in their disciplines.

One way of breaking through the confusing maze of reading research is to begin by defining your personal philosophy about teaching. Your philosophy will be influenced by what you have learned and are learning about reading and writing from coursework, journals, textbooks, other teachers, your students, and, most important, your own classroom research experiences and reflections. Then look for and generate strategies that are consistent with your evolving knowledge about yourself and your students and about the best conditions for teaching and learning. Also, seek support from colleagues by forming study groups that make reading and analyzing the professional literature enjoyable and relevant.

We certainly hope that as your developing philosophy evolves, it encompasses beliefs consistent with the principles that serve as the framework for this book. If your beliefs about language development are similar, then it should be easy for you to modify and adapt the strategies we have offered to help make reading and learning easier for your striving students. Also, as you read about other strategies that may derive from a different philosophical base, you will be better able to decide what, if any, aspects of the strategies can be adapted for your use and what can be left out of your instructional practices.

Effective Teachers Maintain Personal Reading Programs

A strategy we recommend in this book and use each semester to introduce ourselves to a new class of university students and become better acquainted with them is the My Bag activity, discussed in earlier chapters. Because reading is such an important part of our cultural life, our bags always contain numerous books, such as perennial favorites, those we regard as life-altering, and current reads. It often comes as a mild shock, however, to watch our students, particularly those at the graduate level, empty their bags and not a single book can be found among the items. Similarly discouraging is to observe in professional development workshops disciplinary teachers squirming uncomfortably when we ask them how much reading they do in their spare time. "We haven't the time," they often respond. "We're too busy with our required work to read for pleasure."

To be sure, many teachers are avid readers, but there is enough evidence to suggest that a large number of preservice and in-service teachers are not regular or enthusiastic readers and this lack of enthusiasm may be passed on to their students (Applegate & Applegate, 2004; Cardarelli, 1992; Dreher, 2003; Morrison, Jacobs, & Swinyard, 1999). The simple truth is that if teachers aren't reading for pleasure and personal growth, it makes it especially difficult for them to be convincing role models for their striving readers. And it's these students more than anyone else who need highly engaged role models that can motivate them to establish daily personal reading habits in order improve their skills and abilities.

We are not naive; we understand the time constraints placed on secondary school teachers. Teaching often entwines itself around teachers' entire lives, so that outside the classroom they are thinking about their students, their existing methods of instruction, and new ways to improve their instruction, as well as grading papers and preparing lessons. And if that's not enough to occupy teachers' time, many also have a family, children, house chores, and may even be taking additional university courses. Teachers lead incredibly busy lives! Nonetheless, establishing and maintaining a personal reading program may be as integral to your role as a teacher as any other teaching-related activity.

We can reach striving adolescent readers in many ways. Experienced and insightful teachers often discover how to capitalize on subtle teaching moments that are

Teachers of striving youth must be active readers themselves in order to be genuine models of the power of literacy.

not part of a preconceived lesson or curriculum. We know, for instance, that striving learners can be dramatically influenced by teachers who simply show genuine concern for them as individuals with real-world needs and problems. Often, books recommended by a concerned teacher can make a significant difference in the lives of striving readers. These texts may change student's ways of viewing a problem or relationship, their strategies for coping with a personal difficulty, or their interest in knowing more about a topic. It is not uncommon for us to learn from our university students that the books that really moved them as teenagers were recommended by teachers. One student recalled how in seventh grade he was talking with his English teacher, whom he regarded as a friend, about the difficulty he was having in geometry. The teacher suggested that he read the book *The Planiverse* (Dewdney, 1984), which describes life in a two-dimensional world. The student became very excited about the ideas in the book and began approaching his geometry lessons with renewed enthusiasm, which helped him pass the course. Another student recounted how her music teacher, who knew she was pregnant, passed her the book *Spellbound* (McDonald, 2001), which tells the story of single-mother Raven who has aspirations for college but must struggle to finish high school, work, and raise a baby at the same time. It wasn't the book itself that made a difference in her ability to cope, she said, but the fact that her teacher cared enough for her to suggest the book.

Young adult books can obviously play a more direct role in lesson planning and content-area instruction, as demonstrated in Chapter 8. Because of the tremendous influence these books can have on striving readers' lives, we recommend that all teachers become knowledgeable about literature for youth. These texts can be used to stimulate students' interest in the topic of study and help them learn the content information in a more palatable way. Above all, the right book at the right level in adolescent striving readers' hands can introduce them to the pleasure of reading personally and culturally meaningful texts that relate to their needs outside of the classroom. Figure 11.3 is an extensive bibliography of books about young adult literature. Figure 11.4 is a list of print and Web-based resources for identifying culturally diverse young adult texts.

> Stories of teachers introducing youth to books that transform their lives are plentiful but only happen when teachers are familiar with texts to capture striving readers' attention.

To get started on a personal reading program, we suggest you take as little as 15 minutes a day to read. If you are not in the reading habit, a good place to start is with books for youth. Whether a novel, chapter or series book, picture book, informational book, or graphic novel, you'll be able to get through most of them very quickly, often within one to three sittings. Try reading the book before bed. We think you will discover that this kind of teaching preparation is much easier and much more exciting than traditional school-preparation tasks. You will have the pleasure of enjoying quality literature while learning about the power of books for reaching the students in your classroom.

The following list indicates where you can find young adult books for your own reading and for stocking your classroom library:

- Locally owned bookstores and bookstore chains
- Supermarkets, drugstores, and discount department stores
- Used book stores
- Libraries (will often sell duplicate or unused books at a fraction of the original cost)
- Book fairs
- Book clubs (paper and illustrations are often inferior, but the prices are low)
- Garage sales
- Discount book sites on the Internet

Figure 11.3   Bibliography of Literature Resources for Teachers of Youth

Alessio, Amy, and Kevin Scanlon, comp. *Teen Read Week: A Manual for Participation.* ALA, 2002.

Aronson, Marc. *Beyond the Pale: New Essays for a New Era.* Scarecrow, 2003.

Aronson, Marc. "Coming of Age," *Publishers Weekly* (February 11, 2002), 82–86.

Aronson, Marc. *Exploding the Myths: The Truth About Teenagers and Reading.* Scarecrow, 2001.

Bodart, Joni Richards. *Radical Reads: 101 YA Novels on the Edge.* Scarecrow, 2002.

Brenner, Robin. *No Flying, No Tights: A Website Reviewing Graphic Novels for Teens.* http://leep.lis.uiuc.edu/publish/rebrennr/304LE/gn/.

Bromann, Jennifer. *Booktalking That Works.* Neal-Schuman, 2001.

Brozo, William G. *To Be a Boy, To Be a Reader.* International Reading Association, 2002.

Chelton, Mary K., ed. *Excellence in Library Services to Young Adults.* ALA, 2000.

Cart, Michael. *Collection Development: Knowledge & Selection of Materials, A Training Video.* North State Cooperative Library System, 2000.

Cox, Ruth E. *Tantalizing Tidbits for Teens: Quick Booktalks for the Busy High School Specialist.* Linworth, 2002.

Darby, Mary Ann. *Hearing All the Voices: Multicultural Books for Adolescents.* Scarecrow, 2002.

Dresang, Eliza T. *Radical Change: Books for Youth in a Digital Age.* H. W. Wilson, 1999.

Edwards, Kirsten. *Teen Library Events.* Greenwood, 2002.

Edwards, Margaret A. *The Fair Garden and the Swarm of Beasts: The Library and the Young Adult.* ALA, 2002.

Guevara, Anne, and John Sexton. "Extreme Booktalking," *VOYA* (June 2000), 98–101.

Gillespie, J. T. (2000). *Best Books for Young Teen Readers: Grades 7–10.* Westport, CN:Greenwood.

Gillespie, J. T., & Barr, C. (2004). *Best Books for High School Readers.* Westport, CN:Greenwood.

Gillespie, J. T., & Barr, C. (2004). *Best Books for Middle School and Junior High Readers.* Westport, CN: Greenwood.

Halls, Kelly Milner. "Trends in YA Literature," *Kelly Milner. com,* http://www. kellymilnerhalls. com/index.2ts?page5portfolio&catid5279\\&wrtid5392.

Herald, Diana Tixier. *Teen Genreflecting.* Libraries Unlimited, 1997.

Honnold, RoseMary. *101+ Teen Programs That Work.* Neal-Schuman, 2003.

Jones, Patrick. *Connecting Young Adults and Libraries.* Neal-Schuman, 1998.

Jones, Patrick. *A Core Collection for Young Adults.* Neal-Schuman, 2003.

Jones, Patrick. *New Directions for Library Service to Young Adults.* ALA, 2002.

Jones, Patrick. "To the Teen Core," *School Library Journal* (March 1, 2003).

Knowles, Elizabeth. *Reading Rules!: Motivating Teens to Read.* Libraries Unlimited, 2001.

Langemack, Chapple. *The Booktalker's Bible: How to Talk About the Books You Love to Any Audience.* Libraries Unlimited, 2003.

Latest Survey Results," *Smart Girl.* http://www.smartgirl. org/reports/1493716. html.

Lipsyte, Robert. "The Power to Change Young Lives," *New York Times* (April 28, 2003).

Nichols, Mary Anne. *Merchandising Library Materials to Young Adults.* Libraries Unlimited, 2002.

Nilsen, Alleen Pace, and Kenneth L. Donelson. *Literature for Today's Young Adult.* Allyn & Bacon, 2004.

Ohio Library Council. *Oh Ya!: A Manual for Library Staff Who Work with Young Adults.*

Schall, Lucy. *Booktalks Plus: Motivating Teens to Read.* Libraries Unlimited, 2001.

Sullivan, Edward T. *Reaching Reluctant Young Adult Readers.* Scarecrow, 2002.

Vaillancourt, Renée J. *Bare Bones Young Adult Services.* ALA, 2000.

Young Adult Library Services Association. http://www. ala. org/yalsa.

Figure 11.4 Multicultural Literature Resources and Web Links for
Teachers of Youth

Reference Books

Brown, J., Stephens, E., & Salvner, G. (1998). *United in diversity: Using multicultural young adult literature in the classroom*. Urbana, IL: National Council of Teachers of English.

Cai, Mingshui. (2002). *Multicultural literature for children and young adults: Reflections on critical issues*. Westport, CN: Greenwood Press.

Helbig, A. K., & Perkins, A. R. (2000). *Many peoples, one land: A guide to new multicultural literature for children and young adults*. Westport, CN: Greenwood.

Kuharets, O. R. (2001). *Venture into Cultures* (2nd ed.). Chicago: American Library Association.

Kuipers, B. (1995). *American Indian reference and resource books for children and young adults* (2nd ed). Greenwood Village, CO: Libraries Unlimited.

McCaffrey, L. (1998). *Building an ESL collection for young adults*. Westport, CT:Greenwood Press.

Reed, A. (1999). *Multicultural literature anthology*. Reading, MA: Addison-Wesley.

Rochman, H. (1993). *Against borders: Promoting books for a multicultural world*. Chicago, IL: American Library Association.

Roscow, L. (1996). *Light 'n lively reads for ESL, adult and teen readers: A thematic' biography*. Greenwood Village, CO: Libraries Unlimited.

Totten, H., Brown, R., & Garner, C. (1996). *Culturally diverse library collections for youth*. New York: Neal-Schuman.

Valdez, A. (1998). *Using literature to incorporate multicultural education in the intermediate grade school level*. Upper Saddle River, NJ: Prentice Hall.

Willis, A. I. (1998). *Teaching multicultural literature in grades 9–12: Moving beyond the canon*. Norwood, MA: Christopher Gordon.

York, S. (2005). *Ethnic book awards: A directory of multicultural literature for young readers*. Worthington, OH: Linworth Publishing.

Preferred Web Sites

Young Adult Literature: Reference Books and Online Resources
www.neiu.edu/~neiulib/guides/young_adult.html

Multicultural Literature Resources
www.library.cornell.edu/olinuris/ref/multicultural.html

Children's and Young Adult Multicultural Literature
www.lib.lsu.edu/hum/mlk/srs217.html

African American Review: Multicultural Literature for Children and Young Adults
www.findarticles.com/p/articles/mi_m2838/is_n4_v28/ai_16836633

Multicultural Children's Literature: Authorship and Selection Criteria
www.indiana.edu/~reading/ieo/bibs/multicu2.html

Multicultural Reference Books
www.siena.edu/oma/referencebooks.doc

Other Useful Web Sites

Multicultural Literature for Adolescents
http://www.pampetty.com/multiadolescent.htm

Multicultural Literature Resources for Children and Young Adults
http://bullpup.lib.unca.edu/multconf/multcultlit.html

Literacy Matters Web Site/Multicultural Literature Sites/Links
http://www.literacymatters.org/adlit/selecting/multicultural.htm

Adolescent Literature
http://www.indiana.edu/~eric_rec/ieo/bibs/adol-lit.html

continued

Figure 11.4   (continued)

Education World/Multiculturalism
http://www.education-world.com/a_books/books001.html

Multicultural Literature Web Sites/Focus on Pacific Islanders
http://www.uog.edu/coe/paclit/sites.htm

Multicultural Literature for Adolescents/Professional Resources
http://homepages.wmich.edu/~tarboxg/Book_Review_List_on_Adolescence_and_
Adolescent_Lit.html

Multicultural Children's Literature
http://www.lib.msu.edu/corby/education/multicultural.htm

Adolescent Literacy Sites
http://www.elmhurst.edu/library/courses/eng/ENG315.html

Literature of the United States/Multicultural Literature
http://brtom.org/litlinksus.html

The Alliance for the Study and Teaching of Adolescent Literature/Multicultural Literature
http://www.ric.edu/astal/multicultural/

Children's and Young Adult Literature and Culture Links
http://staff.mwsc.edu/~cadden/

Bibliographies on Sensitive Issues
http://www.scils.utgers.edu/~kvander/ChildrenLit/bookssen.html

---

Striving Readers Deserve Special Supports But Not Always Special Settings

Fisher (2001a) and others (Jacobson et al., 2001; Mastropieri et al., 2001) have demonstrated that striving readers are not always best served in pull-out programs and special classes. Cross-age tutoring, reading buddies, and a host of instructional modifications within the content classroom itself may do more to increase engagement and achievement than sequestering youth in homogenous classes of low-ability readers. Cappella and Weinstein (2001) found that most students who enter the ninth grade with reading problems leave high school with reading problems, suggesting two possibilities, both critical of prevailing approaches: (1) that the pervasiveness of the pull-out model may be generally ineffective, and (2) if not in a pull-out program, the literacy issues striving readers bring to secondary schools are not receiving the attention they deserve in spite of the instructional context. The strategies and practices advocated in this chapter emphasize keeping striving readers in content classrooms to ensure they remain a part of the flow of instruction. In this way, they will enjoy the benefits of engaging learning experiences, have regular print encounters, and continue to build disciplinary knowledge.

> To keep striving readers in disciplinary classrooms we need teachers knowledgeable of practices to meet those students' needs.

Striving Readers Deserve More Than a Curriculum of Basic Skills Redux

Striving readers are often penalized. They are usually recycled through a regimen of basic skill instruction that failed to produce reading competence in the first place (Allington, 2006). Basic skills instruction that focuses exclusively on phonics, spelling accuracy, and word attack and requires memorization of rules and performing mechanical routines fails to capitalize on how language is learned best (Ivey & Baker, 2004). Furthermore, skill instruction in an area such as phonics has been shown to be most effective for very young children with diminishing results for students in subsequent grades (National Reading Panel, 2000). When instruction in these skills is embedded in meaningful content-area reading and learning, youth benefit by improving their ability to construct new understandings (NCTE, 2004).

At the same time, we recognize that some adolescents bring remarkably low reading achievement levels to secondary schools. This leaves teachers and administrators grabbing for straws to figure out how to elevate ability to help these students survive in content classrooms and also pass mandated standardized tests. The federal government has recently weighed in on the issue by extending existing NCLB initiatives to include youth reading well-below grade placement in secondary school or, as they are referred to in the legislation, "striving readers." In addition, the U.S. Senate and House have attempted to offer separate bills (Pathways for Success or the PASS Act and Graduation for All) to address the needs of striving readers at the secondary level, though neither has made it to their respective floors for debate and a vote, failing to gain traction in an era of mounting budget deficits. Both the NCLB language and drafts of the congressional bills seem to view adolescent striving readers through a narrow remedial lens. What this is likely to translate into are instructional approaches emphasizing basic skills presumed to have been missed in primary and elementary school. In fact, federal dollars for striving readers are already being targeted toward research studies and projects focused on narrow, highly quantifiable skills, leaving most other possibilities for reaching and improving the abilities and attitudes of these youth undersupported (Moje, 2004). At the same time, publishers are rushing to market phonics and word-attack programs for adolescent striving readers, anticipating that basic skills, remedial approaches will hold sway in middle and high schools once initiatives for youth targeted in the federal legislation are mandated.

Go to Web Resources for Chapter 11 at *http:// www.prenhall. com/ brozo,* and look for Federal Initiatives for Striving Adolescent Readers.

We believe, as others do (Greenleaf, Schoenbach, Cziko, & Mueller, 2001; Ivey, 1999b; Ivey & Baker, 2004), that it should not be assumed that striving readers require inordinate structure and routines to expand their language and literacy abilities. Using reading and writing to help them explore personal interests and satisfy cultural needs can increase their language competence and their engagement in learning. We learned of the power of supporting striving readers through approaches that stress personally meaningful learning from a proprietor of a local magic shop. Dean told us he was diagnosed as learning disabled in the second grade due to his inability to read. Dean recounted how special education and reading teachers bombarded him with daily skills sheets, phonics flash cards, and controlled vocabulary booklets. After several years he experienced very little reading improvement. Just when those teachers were ready to give up on him, his seventh-grade math teacher discovered that Dean was really interested in magic. The teacher gave him books on magic, which Dean struggled through initially but eventually began reading with growing confidence. Soon he was able to apply his increasing reading skills to his school textbooks. Dean went on to graduate from high school and, finally, from the University of Illinois in business. With his degree he opened up his own magic store, which had been operating profitably for several years when we met him.

Striving Readers Deserve to Be Viewed as a Resource

Teachers who value student diversity discover ways of teaching and reaching youth that are personally meaningful and culturally responsive (Moje, 2002). In contrast to an open, diversity-seeking stance is the very definite message that is communicated to students when the teacher and the textbook completely dominate and control instruction. The message is that only the teacher and the textbook can ask the questions, only their questions are worth asking, students cannot learn from one another, and the students' job is to answer questions correctly. A vise-like grip on the curricular controls denies the important contributions each student can make to the construction of knowledge and development of literacy in the classroom. More significantly, it reinforces low self-efficacy in striving readers with a history of learning failure because they learn that their ideas, attitudes, and experiences have little value.

As stated many times in this book, the process of meaning making, whether in reading or writing, depends on an individual's perceptions and is enhanced through students' interaction and collaboration within the social context of the classroom. Youth share many approaches to life and bring to school a store of knowledge, but also hold separate and unique models of reality based on interactions in other discourse communities outside of school, such as family, neighborhood, church, clubs, athletic teams, and so on (Moje et al. 2004). Secondary disciplinary teachers who take advantage of their students as resources structure numerous opportunities for youth to co-construct knowledge through cooperative groups, project teams, student-led discussions, role-plays, and many other forms of informal interaction (Nichols & Miller, 1994).

Furthermore, students' voices regarding curricular content and demonstrations of accomplishment are genuinely considered in order to reinforce the relevancy and meaningfulness of academic literacy and learning (Bomer, 1999). When striving readers see that their input is valued because it helped reshape someone else's perceptions and attitudes about a piece of writing, video, or class activity, their self-efficacy as readers and learners expands.

Unfortunately, the perspectives most directly affected by, but least often consulted about, educational practice are those of students (Cook-Sather, 2002a). We discovered this to be true in our own investigation of students' perspectives of a high school's new reading program (Brozo, 2006). Interviews of a cross-section of the student body, including striving readers, revealed that youth often are mindful of how they are discounted by administrators and teachers when new initiatives are planned and implemented. As a result, the students felt little compunction to contribute to the success of the new school-wide literacy program. Indeed, end-of-year state test results for the school proved disappointing in spite of the reforms, as achievement levels were essentially flat in reading. We concluded that the school might have found more responsive and effective approaches to improving reading and content learning if the individuals for whom the initiatives were intended had been brought into the conversation before and all throughout the year.

To invite striving readers and all students into an open dialog about what they need to become more engaged and increase competence requires viewing them as resources and legitimate members of the school's learning community (Brozo, 2006). Many have shown how students' perspectives can directly improve educational practice by helping teachers better appreciate the lifeworlds of youth and make their teaching more responsive to the experiences and attitudes of students (Cook-Sather, 2002a, 2002b, 2003; Lee, 1999; Wasley, Hampel, & Clark, 1997). Furthermore, when students are taken seriously as a resource, they feel empowered and motivated to participate constructively in their education (Corbett & Wilson, 1995; Heshusius, 1995; Shultz & Cook-Sather, 2001). Finally, Lee (1999) demonstrated that adolescents who are striving readers can be informants to help bring about curricular reforms that support responsive literacy practices. The high school struggling readers he worked with were quite capable of articulating the nature of their learning problems and offering legitimate recommendations for instructional modifications to teachers and administrators.

When striving youth are viewed as stakeholders in their own reading and learning growth, numerous forums can be created to elicit their input.

Striving Readers Deserve Schools with Comprehensive Literacy Programs

Middle and high school teachers have always recognized that adolescents who encounter difficulties in learning can usually attribute their frustrations to major shortcomings in their reading ability (Hock & Deshler, 2003). This means that as students' reading achievement increases, so does their performance in all the subject areas. The relationship between reading scores and overall grade point average has been well documented in findings from the National Assessment of Educational Progress (Donahue, Daane, & Grigg, 2003). Thus, all teachers, regardless of their disciplinary expertise, have a stake in the literacy development of youth (Vacca, 1998). If secondary teachers want good students then they must do what they can to help their students become good readers. This is especially true for striving readers. Helping them become effective learners in content classrooms takes more than the efforts of the reading teacher or literacy coach alone. Every adult with whom striving readers interact during the school day shares responsibility for building positive relationships with them, heightening their engagement for learning, expanding their content knowledge, and leavening their literacy skills.

Striving adolescent readers have made great strides in middle schools and high schools where teachers and administrators have committed themselves to responsive literacy instruction for all students. Just such a commitment has been made by the faculty and administration in schools from New York to Indiana to California and Texas, where effective and exemplary reading programs based on guiding principles similar to those running through this book are in operation. What follows is a description of six comprehensive, school-based reading efforts, including the initiatives that we were a part of at Foothills High School. The main purpose of these program descriptions is to help you (a) appreciate what has been done in real schools to further the literacy growth of all youth, (b) learn how these comprehensive programs accommodate the needs of striving readers, (c) envision possibilities for literacy reform in your own middle or secondary school, and (d) imagine the best role you might play in providing extra supports for striving readers within such programs.

Talent Development High School (TDHS) Ninth-Grade Program

The TDHS program is designed to accelerate achievement of striving learners in high-poverty schools (Balfanz, Legters, & Jordan, 2004; Legters, Balfanz, Jordan, & McPartland, 2002). Though reading and mathematics are the targets for student growth, our discussion here will highlight the reading components of the TDHS program. Students in these programs receive instruction in Ninth-Grade Success Academies, essentially small schools within the larger high school. The academies are located in a separate section of the building and have their own principals. Teachers in the academies have a common planning period to coordinate instructional activities around the needs of the striving ninth-grade readers.

TDHS teachers are provided intensive professional development that is sustained throughout the school year. In addition to receiving 20 to 30 hours of work in reading strategies to accelerate growth and integrating reading across the disciplines, teachers are also given in-class coaching. Along with courses in math, science, and history, students in the academies take a double period of English for the entire year and a course in strategic reading the first semester.

The strategic reading course has four thrusts for expanding striving readers' literacy abilities:

- *Modeling comprehension processes* through read-aloud/think-aloud activities. These are the same approaches to building reading and thinking skills we describe in Chapters 3 and 8. Teachers demonstrate such processes as relating content to prior experience, predicting, using text organization, monitoring understanding, using context for word meanings, and rereading. As teachers

Go to Web Resources for Chapter 11 at *http://www.prenhall.com/brozo*, and look for Schoolwide Literacy Programs.

gradually release responsibility, students take lead roles in modeling these same comprehension processes while interacting with their peers.

- *Providing mini-lessons on literacy strategies* for understanding multiple texts, including fiction, nonfiction, poetry, and plays. Students develop knowledge and skills for constructing meaning from informational and creative prose. These skills are reinforced across the curriculum in each of the academy classes.

- *Working in cooperative learning teams* to practice newly developed skills. Students work together with accessible fiction and nonfiction texts to reinforce vocabulary building, engage in shared reading activities, and improve fluency through repetition. Academy teachers provide discussion guides for each text that help students focus on intended learning goals and literacy strategies.

- *Reading self-selected texts.* Each academy classroom is stocked with high-interest material in a range of genres and possesses centers or stations where students can read along with books on tape.

The TDHS approach has produced highly successful results on standardized tests as compared with control schools not using the program (Balfanz, et al., 2004; Balfanz et al., 2002). This approach to working with striving ninth-grade readers whereby learning takes place within an academy-wide program that focuses on literacy and reinforces literacy practices in all corners of the curriculum has many portable features. A growing number of urban, high-poverty school districts have been able to create smaller schools within larger ones to target particularly needy readers and learners (Bill & Melinda Gates Foundation, 2001; Cushman, 1999; Gregory, 2000; McKinney, Steglich, & Stever-Zeitlin, 2002). First-year classes devoted to building literacy skills for secondary school content texts can be implemented in virtually all high schools. Providing professional development to teachers concerning practices that integrate literacy into disciplinary curricula can also be done provided the commitment is there from district and school leaders.

"Beating the Odds" (BTO) Schools

Langer (2000; 2001) has conducted extensive longitudinal research on the effectiveness of particular middle and high schools in which students have "beaten the odds" that they would fail or achieve at "expected" levels. These urban and near-suburban schools, literally spanning the United States have demographics that might otherwise evoke the indelicate labels of at-risk, poor performing, and low achieving. And yet, because of teacher dedication and a school-wide commitment to excellence, the BTO schools, despite the challenges of serving primarily poor youth and a large percentage of striving readers, have demonstrated better literacy performance on high-stakes tests than comparable schools.

Six distinguishing characteristics of the BTO schools set them apart from their peers. The best schools embody all of the characteristics and each should be viewed as interrelated and mutually supportive of one another.

Feature 1: Students learn skills and knowledge in multiple lesson types. Depending on exhibited needs in particular instructional contexts, youth in the BTO schools receive literacy instruction that is separated, simulated, or integrated. At times, teachers felt it was important to highlight certain aspects of reading and writing in discreet lessons; at other times, language activities were applied to short exercises or analyzed within lesson texts; and in integrated lessons, skills and strategies were employed in the service of student-centered, meaningful learning projects.

Feature 2: Test preparation is integrated into regular instruction. Teachers in the BTO schools make overt for youth the skills and knowledge needed to perform well on high-stakes tests. Instead of reserving special time and units for test preparation, teachers weave activities into daily practice that build striving readers' capacity for meeting the challenges of high-stakes tests. Teachers work together and collaborate with curriculum specialists and literacy coaches to analyze tests and determine best practices and ways these practices can be incorporated into the flow of regular instruction. These practices occur across the curriculum and throughout the school year.

Feature 3: Teachers make connections across instruction, curriculum, and life. Teachers in BTO schools help striving youth make connections within and across content areas and to their everyday lives. Students are taught to see how the skills and knowledge they're acquiring can increase understanding of subject matter in school and be used productively outside of school. Teachers have a voice in planning and implementing professional development opportunities, ensuring what they receive through these experiences can find application to their disciplines, across disciplines, and to the real world.

The research shows that when secondary schools focus on literacy all students benefit, particularly striving readers.

Feature 4: Students learn strategies for doing the work. Students in BTO schools learn that subject matter and how one thinks and communicates about that subject matter are inextricably linked. This vitally important notion should look familiar, because it was laid out in the first chapter of this book and has served as an important underlying premise of virtually all the strategies and practices we have presented. Teachers in BTO schools develop students' metacognitive abilities so as to promote self-monitoring and independence. Students learn what it takes to complete tasks and can communicate the strategies and steps involved in doing so.

Feature 5: Students are expected to be creative thinkers. Teachers in BTO schools take a generative approach to learning, modeling novel applications of skills and knowledge and structuring supportive learning environments so that striving readers can do the same. Students learn to consider events in novels and history from multiple perspectives. They're frequently asked to solve other problems with newly acquired skills and pose new questions to be answered. Above all, striving learners know they have a standing invitation to find connections between classroom-based learning and their real and possible lives at home and in their communities.

Feature 6: Classrooms foster cognitive collaboration. In BTO schools, youth work in supportive teams with their peers and their teachers to share and learn from one another. Teachers value teamwork because they view it as essential to success in students' work and life futures. In learning collaboratives, students play multiple roles, develop empathy for multiple viewpoints, work together to solve problems and generate ideas, and come to value the importance of cognitive and social relationships.

For Langer and the teachers in the BTO schools, the six features represent nothing less than guiding principles for making instruction more responsive to striving readers' needs. The literacy achievement results for students in BTO schools demonstrate the power of suffusing the curriculum with sound, teacher-supported, principled practices.

Winder-Barrow High School, Barrow County, Georgia

In this rural consolidated high school of approximately 1,650 students, a reading program was implemented in 1994 and has since been identified in the state of Georgia as exemplary (Weller & Weller, 1999). Along with this recognition came an $18,000 grant. The state provides funding through its Innovative Program grant in order to support the documentation of the program's effectiveness and the dissemination of information about its positive features to assist other schools in the state that are attempting to implement their own secondary reading programs.

Winder-Barrow High calls its program POWER (Providing Opportunities With Everyday Reading). It targets both reading in the content areas and independent reading. Like many secondary reading initiatives, POWER grew out of a concern over declining test scores on state-mandated standardized achievement measures and teachers' frequent comments that students could not read their course textbooks. The principal lobbied for and received a full-time reading teacher who, along with a couple of subject-area teachers, accompanied him to training seminars in content-area reading. He also paid all teachers in the high school a stipend from staff development funds to attend a summer workshop taught by the teacher facilitators. This approach has been so successful that other teachers who have become expert in the use of reading strategies in their own classrooms now help teach the summer content reading course for all new hires. An advanced course on reading across the curriculum was made available to Winder-Barrow High teachers a couple of years ago, and nearly the entire faculty has taken it.

In addition to content-area reading, the other critical component of POWER is sustained silent reading (see Chapter 8 for a complete description of SSR). Twice weekly during students' 25-minute study hall just after lunch they participate in SSR. The grant helped supply every teacher with reading materials, including young adult novels, paperbacks, magazines, and newspapers to make it easier for students to find something to suit their tastes and ability levels.

Although reading test scores have increased significantly for Winder-Barrow over the past few years, leaving other districts desirous to copy the POWER program, all of the teachers involved in POWER point to its flexibility as the critical component of success. Teachers aren't required to use particular content reading strategies for any number of times per week. Instead, they are urged to make a commitment to teach using the reading strategies of their choosing as derived from their coursework at least twice per week. Virtually the entire staff reports doing so. Importable features of Winder-Barrow High's approach to developing a school-wide reading program include:

- Holding many formal and informal faculty meetings to discuss the importance of reading

- Making research results in the area of secondary content-area reading available to teachers

- Recruiting teacher leaders who believe in the importance of reading at the secondary level

- Allotting funds for groups of teachers to visit other school systems with successful reading programs

- Providing peer coaching and forming teacher collegial groups in support of teachers' efforts to implement reading strategies in their classrooms

- Establishing a reading committee dedicated to expanding the effectiveness of reading initiatives in the school

Take particular note of the features of these programs that can be imported into other school settings to enrich the literate lives of all youth.

Heritage Hills Junior-Senior High School, Lincoln City, Indiana
One of the 2001 winners of the Indiana State Reading Association's and International Reading Association's Exemplary Reading Program Awards, Heritage Hills Junior-Senior High School embraces the idea that the one sure way to improve students' reading abilities is by giving them as much time as possible to engage in sustained print

encounters (Davis, 2001). What we find most admirable about this school is the way in which its principal, faculty, and parents threw their entire support behind the elegant notion that more reading makes better readers (Smith, 1985). This is self-evidently true and is, without exception, endorsed by the entire professional literacy community, yet too few schools provide adolescents a regular forum for "just plain reading." Heritage Hills, however, is one of the few bright examples of the literacy possibilities when real reading is the centerpiece of the curriculum.

But it wasn't always that way. For years, teachers at this rural southern Indiana school held the view about young adults and reading that most at the secondary level hold—it is something you do in elementary school. Once again, declining test scores on the Indiana Statewide Testing for Educational Progress forced faculty and administrators to take a hard look at what was being done in the name of reading for their students. A reading comprehension study group was formed that included teachers, parents, and staff to investigate directions for improvement. Along the way, the group encountered and read *The Power of Reading* (Krashen, 1993) and was so impressed with its message that it decided to put into action three simple yet powerful recommendations:

- Develop a print-rich school environment of authentic reading material.
- Give students numerous formal and informal opportunities to read authentic material.
- Create opportunities for teachers and students to serve as literate role models.

The most prominent feature of the program is 20 to 30 minutes of sustained silent reading (SSR) at the beginning of each day. Referred to as "read-ins," this time is inviolate. Everyone reads, including teachers, administrators, janitors, food handlers, aides, parents, and anyone else who might be in the school building. In this way, students are provided structured time to read independently texts of their choosing while faculty and staff model authentic literate behavior.

As with virtually all other SSR programs, Heritage Hills had to get prepared by stocking classroom libraries. It has taken a few years to build each one, but there is now an average of 300 books per classroom, along with numerous magazines and newspapers. Teachers are given time to travel to bookstores, book fairs, and book sales in the area to enrich their stocks. Once a year seventh graders take a field trip to a local bookstore chain to buy a book of their choosing. Each student is given money from the football concessions fund to use for purchasing books.

Another important aspect of the Heritage Hills program involves students from the Junior-Senior High going once a week to the elementary school to read to children there. This activity heightens the adolescents' sense of responsibility as reading role models and sends a powerful message to kids that athletes and other teens enjoy and value reading.

Heritage Hills has also begun a volunteer summer staff development program called "Journey" that provides reading strategy training. The training has resulted in more teachers employing literacy activities in their subject-area classrooms. Several teachers participate in professional development activities for teachers and administrators from other schools around the state who come to observe the Heritage Hills reading program in action.

The read-ins, role modeling, and literacy across the curriculum efforts have resulted in dramatic increases in student reading achievement as measured on the state test. But, more important, student attitudes toward reading have improved and the entire literate culture of the school and community has changed. Students who had

One way to enlist the participation of all teachers in a school-wide literacy effort is to implement a teacher and student designed sustained silent reading program.

never picked up a book before to read for pleasure are going through 10 to 20 books per year; parents are reporting their teen and preteen sons and daughters spending more time at home reading; and teachers are witnessing an increase in book exchanges among students and more book talk.

Hoover High School, San Diego, California

Unlike Winder-Barrow and Heritage Hills schools, Hoover is an urban high school with a student population that reflects the demographics of most large cities: all qualify for either free or reduced lunch, 96% are ethnic minorities, and 46% are English language learners (Fisher, 2001b). A few years ago Hoover's achievement test scores placed it among the lowest in the state of California, but with the implementation of a school-wide literacy effort, state accountability targets have been met and reading achievement gains continue to be realized. Three initiatives identified by teacher focus groups at Hoover account for the changes in student reading scores: (1) staff development that was focused and required accountability, (2) daily independent reading and regular teacher–student conferences, and (3) block scheduling.

An obvious thread that runs through each of the secondary reading program descriptions thus far is the importance of effective staff development. At Hoover the staff development committee identified particular "reading across the curriculum strategies" all teachers were expected to incorporate into their lessons. These included writing to learn, KWL charts, concept mapping, reciprocal teaching, vocabulary instruction, notetaking techniques, and read-alouds. In-service workshop facilitators presented these strategies at the beginning of the year using examples from a variety of content areas. But instead of assuming exposure was enough, the committee and school administrators provided additional monthly meetings to allow teachers to discuss their challenges and successes in implementing the selected strategies. These meetings were held during the school day to ensure maximum attendance and participation.

To ensure all teachers were making an honest effort to employ the content reading strategies, 10 were randomly chosen and agreed to be observed on three separate unannounced occasions by school administrators. The administrative team prepared well for these observations by attending and participating in all staff development activities and by developing a sophisticated understanding of each of the strategies. Afterward, teachers and administrators met to debrief. Feedback was given and, when appropriate, arrangements were made for individual teachers to receive additional support from their colleagues who had demonstrated expertise in strategy applications. The strength of this approach is that it goes well beyond the traditional approach to staff development, the limitations of which we described earlier in this chapter, by providing scaffolding to teachers in the form of ongoing feedback, modeling, and support.

Another common theme among the secondary reading programs we have described thus far is the provision of sustained silent reading. Hoover High implemented this component of their reading program by doing the following. First, teachers in discussion groups agreed that a "sacred" time for reading should be set aside each day, but were not satisfied with an initial proposal to require SSR time during each English class. In order to make certain the entire faculty was playing a supporting role in the overall reading program, teachers agreed that 20 minutes would be added to the block after lunch, so students and teachers in all classrooms could participate in SSR. This had a potent effect on students, who were able to see their math, chemistry, and even physical education teachers reading. During the first year of SSR a $50,000 library grant was used to purchase books that could be rotated into every teacher's classroom. In addition, teachers were budgeted $500 to acquire extra books for their classroom collections. In the following year, teachers received $800 for such purchases.

An added feature to independent reading time is the teacher–student conference. During SSR, students are called individually to the teacher's desk to chat for 3 to 5 minutes about the particular material they're reading. Students usually give retellings and answer a few general questions. At this time teachers can offer any needed assistance in helping students locate interesting and readable texts. Student responses are summarized either on index cards or in a log. Although the accountability of conferencing raises the stakes a bit for SSR, if conducted in a supportive atmosphere, these sessions need not inhibit students' self-selections nor limit the pleasure that comes with recreational reading.

The third key component Hoover High teachers recognized as contributing to the reading achievement gains made by their students was block scheduling. Four blocks of 90 minutes each comprise a school day. Although not necessarily the norm in American high schools, blocks have been shown to provide teachers with the necessary time to explore topics in more depth than is possible when the day is carved into several brief 45-minute periods (Benton-Kupper, 1999). With 90 minutes, content-area teachers at Hoover were able to work into their daily instruction the required seven critical reading strategies. For example, a science teacher could begin class with a read-aloud, introduce the material with the KWL strategy, demonstrate notetaking and concept mapping with textbook content, and still have time for a lab activity.

The block schedule also helped facilitate professional development. In the past, when workshops were held only after school, teachers who also coached or supervised a club would often have to miss these important sessions. The staff development committee took this into account when it planned content-area reading workshops, deciding instead to schedule them during teachers' planning periods. Once a month for 9 months during teachers' prep time, they attended a 90-minute workshop on content-area strategies. As a result, at the end of the year everyone had been exposed to the same strategic instruction.

> The Hoover High model makes clear that a school-wide literacy emphasis takes a supportive and collaborative relationship among teachers, administrators, and students.

As Fisher (2001b) notes, Hoover's success has been due to sustained professional development and a school structure that accommodates educational innovation. Recognizing what we have been saying throughout this chapter—that student success, especially in challenging urban settings, is contingent upon high-quality teachers—Hoover's principal noted, "Our students don't just need good teachers, they need great teachers who are provided with the right resources to be successful. To improve, we have to support the teachers" (Fisher, 2001b, p. 100).

Foothills High School—Reading Cyclone

Two major components of Foothills High School's reading program, Reading Cyclone, were low-stakes standardized reading achievement testing used as a pre/postmeasure to determine whether or not growth in reading skill had occurred for students and sustained silent reading (Brozo & Hargis, 2005). Achievement testing and SSR are features shared by most of the previously described secondary reading programs. Some additional unique elements that comprised the overall program included (a) in-class demonstration teaching, (b) a textbook readability study, (c) remedial reading tutoring, and (d) the development of curricular readers.

It has been made clear from studies of virtually all reading programs that have demonstrated effectiveness that comprehensive staff development is essential to success (Moore & Hinchman, 2006). Professional learning communities and study groups, peer collaboration, regular feedback sessions, and in-service workshops have been the most common forms of professional development for middle and secondary school faculty implementing new reading initiatives. Not as common are in-class teaching demonstrations conducted by a workshop leader or consultant. Too few in-service workshops presented by an "expert" on one day or one afternoon bring about lasting change because there are few provisions for supporting teachers' sustained efforts to implement literacy and learning innovations. To improve on this approach, the schools described previously have built some form of continuous feedback, support, or even accountability into the process. Foothills accomplished this by requesting us to provide not only two full-day workshops at the beginning of the school year, but then to go into teacher's classrooms throughout the year and conduct lessons using the strategies demonstrated in the workshops.

The strategies for demonstration teaching lessons we provided Foothills teachers were taken right out of this book. For example, we conducted a lesson impression in a 10th-grade history class preparing to read a piece on the Civil War by Stephen Crane. Afterward, during the history teacher's planning period, we met to reflect on the effectiveness of the strategy and discuss ways he might begin to use it himself. During the following week, we worked with the teacher to develop a lesson impression for another Civil War topic and textbook chapter. After observing the lesson, we met again with the teacher to offer feedback and respond to his questions concerning different possibilities for implementing the strategy with other content and making it even more engaging for his 10th graders. Within three or four attempts to employ the strategy, the teacher had reached a level of comfort and confidence with the lesson impression strategy, incorporating it into his instructional repertoire. With in-class modeling and subsequent support of teachers' efforts to apply content reading innovations, we observed many changes in instructional approach.

The comprehensive nature of the secondary literacy programs just described sets them apart from random, uncoordinated approaches typical in most schools. Striving readers stand the best chance of improving their literacy abilities in schools with coordinated and broad-based commitment to initiatives designed to meet the needs of all students. School-wide literacy efforts provide the most effective learning context for striving readers by ensuring that opportunities for meaningful and pleasurable encounters with text are present in every facet of the curriculum. Though outside support in the form of grants and university consultation contributed to each of the programs in varying degrees and can serve as the impetus for such programs, many of the common features of these successful comprehensive literacy initiatives can be incorporated into most middle and high schools provided teachers, staff, and administration have the energy and motivation to do so. The needs of striving readers should provide the motivation; the energy must derive from an inherent sense of dedication to helping all youth maximize their life and career options through literacy.

In the next section of this chapter we present rationales and descriptions of several effective literacy practices for striving readers followed by extended scenarios based on these practices. The scenarios are meant both to provide envisionments of possible practices and to capture the complexities of issues for teachers and striving readers in disciplinary contexts. You will see in these scenarios the diversity of backgrounds and issues striving readers bring to secondary school classrooms, the interrelatedness of potential causes of reading difficulties, and the innovative ways teachers have modified practices to nurture language and literacy development while building content knowledge.

Strategies That Build Reading Competence for Diverse Learners

Sustained Encounters with Diverse Texts

Once children have mastered basic reading skills, the surest road to a richer vocabulary and expanded literacy is wide and sustained reading (Miller, 2002; Yoon, 2002). Unfortunately, many striving readers do not travel down this road. Like any of us who experience failure, striving readers tend to avoid activities they find difficult and that erode self-efficacy. Avoiding reading may bring serious consequences that limit life and career options. Regrettably, this pattern is all too common among minority youth (Larson, Richards, Sims, & Dworkin, 2001), who score lower on achievement tests of traditional print literacy (Gardiner, 2001; Tatum, 2005) and are admitted to colleges in smaller numbers relative to other groups (Ogbu, 1994).

> Striving readers will only improve if they are provided numerous ways to engage with personally meaningful and culturally relevant texts.

It is critical, therefore, that striving readers be given frequent opportunities for sustained encounters with diverse texts in a variety of genres and offering multiple perspectives on real-life experiences (Allington, 2002; Anderson, Wilson, & Fielding, 1988; Cipielewski & Stanovich, 1992; Taylor, Frye, & Maruyama, 1990). Even when innovative teachers expose students to many different texts in their curriculum, others should be self-selected and of high interest to striving youth. Wide independent reading develops fluency, builds vocabulary and knowledge of text structures, and offers readers the experiences they need to read and construct meaning with more challenging texts (Greenleaf, et al., 2001; Kuhn & Stahl, 2003; McQuillan & Au, 2001). And, as we stressed in Chapter 8, text should be broadly viewed to include print, electronic, and visual media.

Through extensive reading of a range of texts, supported by strategy lessons and discussions, readers become familiar with written language structures and text features, develop their vocabularies, and read for meaning more efficiently and effectively (Jensen & Jensen, 2002). Conversations about their reading that focus on the strategies they use and their language knowledge help adolescents build confidence in their reading and become better readers (Goodman & Marek, 1996).

History

Shane, a special education teacher, team teaches a section of 11th-grade American history in the general curriculum with Maria. Five of his students are in her class. Maria is a passionate and knowledgeable historian who has relied over the past several years on instructional practices restricted to lecture and textbook reading. As the number of inclusion students has increased, however, Maria has come to recognize that her teaching approach needs to be modified to ensure the content is accessible and interesting to striving students. Though a newer teacher than Maria, Shane has developed a repertoire of engaging and responsive strategies in order to meet the reading and learning needs of his special learners. Together, they worked to craft a curriculum that included strategies to increase reading engagement and time spent with a variety of texts. This was done primarily to help Shane's inclusion students improve their vocabulary, comprehension, and thinking skills by creating more time in the history block for reading. Much to Maria's delight, these practices helped increase the level of enthusiasm and participation of the more capable readers, too.

For the post–World War I time period, Shane urged Maria to give more attention to the Harlem Renaissance than she had in the past. Four of Shane's five inclusion students in the general education history class were African American, and he wanted to make sure they could find something culturally relevant in the study of this topic

(Bean, 2002). Through Shane's efforts, several texts were made available and time was built in for whole-class read-alouds, small-group sharing, and independent reading. Shane brought to Maria's attention the anthology *Children's Literature of the Harlem Renaissance* (Smith, 2004), from which they identified several high-interest books appropriate for the striving readers in the class.

One outstanding title, *Harlem Stomp! A Cultural History of the Harlem Renaissance* (Hill, 2004), was read aloud to the class. This beautifully illustrated book provided a rich cultural history of the period, capturing the excitement and difficulties of the time. The tone and content grabbed the attention of the entire class, not just Shane's inclusion students.

Twenty minutes of each 90-minute class block was set aside for independent silent reading. All students were allowed to self-select materials. Some went to the Internet for interesting things to read, others used the time to read the textbook. Shane's students were encouraged to take advantage of the young adult books he and Maria brought into the classroom for the unit. Two they found to be outstanding resources for this activity were *The Harlem Renaissance* (Chambers & Wilker, 1997) and *Black Stars of the Harlem Renaissance* (Haskins, Tate, Cox, & Wilkinson, 2002). Both are written at an accessible level for his older striving readers, yet are filled with important historical, cultural, and biographical information about the time. The *Black Stars* became a particular favorite for Shane's students during silent reading because each chapter provided a short biography of a different African American figure, such as Louis Armstrong, W. E. B. DuBois, Marcus Garvey, and Langston Hughes, which even for the slowest reader could be completed in a couple of sessions.

During small-group activities, Shane sat in with his students as they read and discussed texts taken from various sources. For example, in one session his five students were reading and viewing the powerful illustrated book *From Slave Ship to Freedom Road* (Lester & Brown, 1999). The book is comprised of 21 paintings accompanied by a forceful narrative that traces the African American journey from the Middle Passage to post–Civil War emancipation. This book served as a reminder to Shane's students of topics they had covered in Maria's class and helped them put the explosion of art, literature, music, and ideas of the Harlem Renaissance into a meaningful historical context.

Modified Texts in the Content Classroom

Allington (2002) summed up the need to make available to youth modified texts that match their ability levels by saying "you can't learn much from books you can't read" (p. 16). Adolescent striving readers often lack the skills and background knowledge to handle the demands of the complex texts they encounter in middle and high school (Venable, 2003). With inclusion, growing numbers of youth are entering secondary content classrooms with ability levels that do not come close to matching the level of difficulty of the required texts. Earlier in this book we told you about the 10th-grade biology teacher with students reading at the 3rd-grade level in his class. For students with ability gaps this large, who are reading two, three, or more grade levels below their grade placement, engagement with the texts they encounter in their subject-area classes is unrealistic if not impossible. To address this need, it may be necessary to make available modified texts that are accessible and content focused.

Disciplinary teachers tell us the biggest challenge is meeting the reading needs of all students when the ability range is very wide.

Science
Striving readers entering disciplinary classrooms with ability levels far below expectation pose special challenges to most high school teachers. Among these challenges is the fact that most teachers do not have at their immediate disposal texts at a range

of difficulty levels on the same topics of the curriculum. Thandi handled this issue by locating and formatting short readings on the various topics she covered in her ninth-grade general science class and making them available to her striving readers as alternatives to the textbook.

Thandi was quick to realize there was a problem when early in the school year three of her students began feigning sleep during independent study and research time. Her efforts to rouse them produced limited involvement at best and complaints that the work was "too hard." She pulled their files and discovered each one had a history of reading difficulty and was receiving remedial services from the school's literacy coach. After further consultation with the literacy coach, Thandi also learned the students' reading levels were in the fifth-grade range, nearly 4 years below the reported readability level of the class textbook. Finally, Thandi held individual conferences with the three students to discuss their reading and learning concerns and how she might best assist them. To her question about how she could help them, Thandi received the same response from all three: "Give us something easier and fun to read."

Soon into Thandi's search for science materials for her striving readers that were appropriately leveled, she discovered that commercially available products were sparse and did not cover topics relevant to her curriculum. Furthermore, there wasn't any money in the school budget for teachers to purchase supplemental materials. This brought Thandi back to the school literacy coach, who encouraged her to look for sources on the Internet. Within a few hours of searching the Web, Thandi found it offered access to vast amounts of reproducible material on virtually any school-related topic.

For an upcoming unit introducing her ninth graders to basic chemistry, Thandi was able to locate Web sites with easy readings on carbon bonding, the periodic table, and balancing equations. She copied and pasted the readings into a Microsoft Word document and then used the readability feature on the Tools tab to calculate a Flesch-Kincaid difficulty level. To her surprise, even these easy readings required further simplification to ensure the neediest of her striving readers could access the content. With help from the literacy coach, Thandi was able to modify the readings in such a way as to reduce their difficulty while preserving the essential scientific information. She added pronunciation guides for the technical terminology and supported students' understanding of those terms through PowerPoint presentations of the content and other class activities.

During the 90-minute instructional block when students were expected to consult their textbooks for information to solve problems or read and study independently, Thandi allowed her less skillful readers to use the alternative texts as their information source. Thanks to students in her colleague's keyboarding class, these simplified texts were reformatted and given inviting "cool" covers to avoid stigmatizing the less able readers. These texts made it possible for Thandi's striving readers to have print experiences in her classroom while acquiring important information about specific science topics. Once her formerly reluctant students knew they had something they could successfully read in Thandi's classroom, they rarely put their heads on the desk when it was time for independent work.

Embedding Skill Development
in the Context of Authentic Learning

Perhaps the biggest challenge for teachers trying to meet the needs of striving readers at the secondary level is determining the emphasis to place on basic skills and the

Teacher as Learner
SIMPLIFYING TEXTS

Simplifying text takes practice. The key is to make the information more readable while retaining the essential details and concepts. Because disciplinary text is often terminology laden, it's important that students be exposed to these key terms in ways that offer scaffolding for pronunciation and meaning. Following this introduction you will first see a social studies passage on the branches of the United States government. At the 2.3 grade level using the Flesch-Kincaid estimate in Microsoft Word, it is a much simplified version of a middle-school-level text. Sentences have been shortened and unnecessarily long words have been simplified. Notice, however, that the important technical vocabulary words have been left in the passage. These words are highlighted and a guide to pronunciation is provided. Following this passage is another one taken from the same content area about the president of the United States. The Flesch-Kincaid readability estimate is 10.4. Using the readability feature on your computer, simplify the text to at least a fifth-grade level while preserving the key terms. You may want to create a guide to pronunciation.

The Three Branches of Government

When we began as a *nation*, our *leaders* did not want any one person or group to rule. Many of our *leaders* came from *England*. The king of *England* could do anything he wanted. Our *leaders* did not want that for our *nation*. They made sure three groups could help rule. These three groups make up our *government*.

There is the *president* and the people he picks to help him. When you are older you will get to vote for a *president*. There is the *Congress*. This is a group of people we vote for, too. They come from each state. And there is the *Supreme Court*. This is a group of people the *president* picks. These three groups are called *branches*.

Do you like sports? Think of the *president* as one team. Think of the *congress* as another team. Think of the *Supreme Court* as the *referee*.

Key Vocabulary

- nation (na-shun)
- leaders *(lee-derz)*
- England *(Ing-glend)*
- government *(guv-ern-ment)*
- branches *(branch-iz)*
- President *(prez-i-dent)*
- Congress *(kong-griss)*
- Supreme Court *(suh-preem kort)*
- referee *(ref-er-ee)*

The President of the United States

The president is the head of the executive branch of government and generally is viewed as the head of the U. S. government. While he does have significant power, his power is limited by the Constitution. These powers can be categorized into three main areas: head of state, administrative, and legislative. As head of state, the president meets with the leaders of other countries. He has the power to recognize those lands as official countries and to make treaties with them. However, the Senate must approve any treaty before it becomes official. The president also has the power to appoint ambassadors to other countries, with the Senate's approval.

The president is also the official head of the U. S. military. As commander in chief, he can authorize the use of troops overseas without declaring war. To declare war officially, though, he must get the approval of Congress. The president's administrative duties include appointing the heads of each executive branch department. Of course, these appointments are subject to the approval of the Senate. The president also has the power to request the written opinion of the heads of executive branch departments regarding any subject relating to their departments.

Simplified Version

_____

_____

_____

_____

_____

_____

_____

_____

_____

_____

Key Vocabulary

best approaches to use to develop needed skills (Snow, Griffin, & Burns, 2005). It is not uncommon in middle and high schools today, especially in learning-disabled and remedial-reading settings, to find youth with extremely limited vocabulary knowledge and comprehension abilities (Bryant, Goodwin, Bryant, & Higgins, 2003; Mastropieri, Scruggs, & Graetz, 2003; Salinger, 2003). Furthermore, in spite of admonitions and even threats from policy makers that all students learn to read by third grade, some do not and may fail to develop grade-appropriate literacy skills for the demands of middle school and beyond (McCray, Vaughn, & Neal, 2001).

Approaches to teaching "remedial" reading for older students have tended to emphasize learning discreet skills. For instance, graphosyllabic analysis has been recommended as one way to improve reading fluency and spelling (Archer, Gleason, & Vachon, 2003; Bhattacharya & Ehri, 2004). For some, phonics and word-study work may seem to be the most efficient way to address serious reading concerns adolescents bring to secondary classrooms (Blevins, 2001); but instruction in these skills, as with skill instruction of any kind, needs to be considered within the context of authentic literacy practices (Ivey & Baker, 2004) and taught in such a way as to develop independence (Harmon, 2002). Many experienced teachers have witnessed their striving readers demonstrate mastery of discreet skills on worksheets, only to fail to transfer that mastery to naturally occurring text while reading independently (Bomer, 1999; Harmon, 2000). Obviously, skills training is not worth the effort for teachers or students if it doesn't translate into successful meaning making of real texts.

Furthermore, teachers of older striving readers must remain ever mindful of issues of engagement (Guthrie & Davis, 2003) and self-efficacy (Alvermann, 2003). Even if adolescents are lacking the most fundamental of skills, they can't be forced to participate in a program of remediation that doesn't hold their interest or that they perceive as humiliating. In such cases, there is little chance they will persevere long enough for the program to be of any benefit to them. And there is a better chance the program will reinforce their negative attitudes toward reading and themselves as readers. So the question isn't whether seriously striving readers need basic skills or not, it's a question of how they will be apprenticed to acquire and develop the needed skills.

The National Reading Panel found that isolated skill instruction for older students was generally ineffective.

English

Sharmayn wasn't getting answers she felt comfortable with to her questions about how to address the serious needs of her striving readers. Her fellow eighth-grade English colleagues said intensive phonics was the only way two of her students who scored at the third-grade level on an informal reading inventory could ever hope to improve their reading skills. But Sharmayn was dubious. She had become well-acquainted with her striving middle graders and their disaffection for reading the stories, poems, and essays in the class anthology. She wisely reasoned that a skill-and-drill approach could alienate them further from books and print. But what was the alternative? The evidence was clear; the students' demonstrated a significant need for word-attack skills and vocabulary development on the reading inventory. And these issues appeared to be the primary reasons for their limited overall comprehension of the inventory passages as well as the class readings.

At a professional development workshop, Sharmayn had a chance to explain her concerns to the district literacy specialist, who suggested an alternative to programmed and systematic phonics instruction. The specialist agreed with Sharmayn that her eighth graders were not likely to enjoy or stick with an approach that forced them to review basic letter-sound relationships. Instead, she recommended that the needed skills be embedded within meaningful and authentic literacy practices. With interesting and accessible texts Sharmayn's striving readers might come to recognize the value and rewards of learning word-attack skills. Following up via e-mail, Sharmayn wrote to and acquired further specific ideas from the specialist. Soon, she had a coherent set of activities for building word-attack skills ready to try out with her striving readers.

The most important realization for Sharmayn was that her two seriously striving readers were not going to be able to make much if any meaning from the stories, poems, and plays in the literature anthology unless she provided major scaffolding. The students had developed excellent listening skills to compensate for their inability to read most course material, which was a strength on which Sharmayn thought she could build. They also had a rich background of experiences. Carlos was born in Central America, Masood in Sudan. Both had journeyed with their parents as young children to the United States. Both were proud of their culture and continued to celebrate native holidays and traditions with their families.

When the rest of the class was involved in independent reading, Sharmayn used the time to work with Carlos and Masood on building vocabulary and fluency through an apprenticeship approach. Sharmayn, as a knowledgeable and sophisticated role model, provided explicit instruction and created productive opportunities for Carlos and Masood to develop familiarity with and control of critical word-level skills. She worked reciprocally (Alfassi, 2004) by modeling strategies and reading behaviors and then eliciting those same strategies and behaviors from the boys.

Many of the readings in the class literature anthology were too difficult for Carlos and Masood, but some were within their instructional range. To determine this, Sharmayn used a procedure for matching a reader with a text she learned from the literacy specialist (see Figure 11.5 for a complete description of the procedure). She found, for example, that the Robert Frost poem "The Road Not Taken" was comprised of only a

Go to Web Resources for Chapter 11 at *http://www.prenhall. com/brozo,* and look for Apprenticeship Reading.

Figure 11.5 Matching a Reader with a Text

Without testing students using standardized and formal procedures to establish their reading levels, you can determine whether a text is readable or not by following these steps:

1. Determine the readability of a text you plan to use with a student. The simplest way to do this is to use the Flesch-Kincaid readability estimator from the Tools tab in Microsoft Word.

2. Make the best guess you can about for whom the text is most appropriate.

3. Give the text to the student and have him or her read a section without assistance. Obviously, if the student struggles with most of the words, discontinue the use of this text, because it is at the frustration level.

4. While the student is reading, record miscues.

5. When finished, check the miscues to determine how many were related to a failure to decode the cued word. Do not pay attention to repetitions or self-corrections.

6. Tally the total number of words the student was unable to decode or recognize. Divide that number by the total number of words read. Do not count the same word twice. Do not count proper nouns. The percentage you get can be converted to an overall percentage of accurately decoded/recognized words. Use the following chart to determine the reading level of material for a particular student.

Level	% of Word Recognition Miscues	% of Decoded/Recognized Words
Independent	0% – 2%	100% – 98%
Instructional	3% – 5%	97% – 95%
Frustration	6% – higher	94% – below

Definition of Reading Levels

Independent—The level at which a reader can make maximum progress *without* teacher assistance.

Instructional—The level at which a reader can make maximum progress *with* teacher assistance.

Frustration—The level at which a reader cannot make progress *even with* teacher assistance.

few words that were difficult for the boys, making it ideal for the focus of her apprenticeship teaching approach. The ensuing discussion illustrates the productive modeling and eliciting practices Sharmayn employed for developing the boys' word-attack and word-learning strategies.

Sharmayn:	Okay, I'll read the entire poem first like we've done before then we'll go through it together more slowly. (She reads "The Road Not Taken" aloud.) Now, who wants to read from the beginning? Masood?
Masood:	Two roads di...
Sharmayn:	Let's skip that word for now and go back to it after this line and the next one.
Masood:	Okay, Two roads...blank...in a yellow wood, and sorry I could not travel both...
Sharmayn:	Great, okay, let's stop for a minute. Have you ever taken a walk in the woods? You know there are footpaths and sometimes you go down one and then another one might go off from it too.
Carlos:	Yeah, I go walking with my cousin near his house and there's a field with all these trails going through it where you can walk one way or another.
Sharmayn:	Good, see how you can think about what you already know or the things you do that are like what you're reading about? So where is the poet, I mean the person in the poem? What's he doing?
Carlos:	He's in the woods.
Masood:	And there are two roads.
Sharmayn:	Is he going to walk down both roads?
Masood:	No...he says he's sorry he can't take both.
Sharmayn:	Yes, so he's in a yellow wood. Why does he say yellow? (The boys are unsure and shrug their shoulders.) Well, forests and woods can be different colors depending on the season, right? Like in the summer, the woods are usually what color?
Carlos:	Green. Oh, I think I know, it's fall and the leaves have turned yellow.
Sharmayn:	Do you see that, Masood? Here look at this picture. (They turn the page in their literature books to look at a picture of a forest of bright yellow leaves with a road covered in leaves running down the center.) Now, let's take another look at the word in the first line that begins with the letter "d." The first thing I would do to figure it out is look for little parts. I see "di." You know the word from math "divide." What does that mean? What happens when you divide something?
Masood:	To break into two pieces. . .
Sharmayn:	Yes. So this word also has "ver"...
Carlos:	That's ver.
Sharmayn:	And the "ged" gets a soft /j'd/ sound like *aged* or *large*. So let's see if we can say the word now. (Masood and Carlos say diverged along with Sharmayn.) Great! Now, if two roads diverge in the woods what kind of word is "diverge"? I mean, by where it is in the line is it another noun, a verb? As I look at it, it's telling me the roads are doing something, so what kind of words do that?

Masood:	Verbs?
Sharmayn:	Right."Diverge" is a verb...and knowing that can help you figure out what it could mean. Try to do that when you get stumped by a word; see if you can figure out how it's used in the sentence. Okay, so now where do you think the narrator of the poem is? Let's look at the first two lines of the poem for hints again.
Carlos:	He's right there where the two roads come together and you can't go down both at the same time.
Sharmayn:	Excellent. Do you see that, Masood? So what do you think *diverge* means? Is it where two things come together or...
Masood:	Where two things divide or go different ways.
Sharmayn:	Perfect!

Sharmayn went on to review strategies for attacking pronunciations and meanings of unfamiliar words. (See Figure 11.6 for helpful independent word-learning prompts and strategies.) She reminded Carlos and Masood of the steps they went through to figure out the pronunciation and meaning of "diverged." Notice how Sharmayn focused the boys' attention on the various cueing systems for word learning. She modeled the use of graphophonic cues by drawing their attention to the sounds of individual letters and syllables. She demonstrated the utility of syntactic cues by helping the boys figure out the way "diverge" was used in the sentence of the poem or its part of speech. And she invoked the semantic cueing system by asking about the boys' prior knowledge about seasons and forests, relating the prefix "di" to a related word from math, and rereading the couple of lines of the poem to put the word "diverge" in context. As Sharmayn continued the model/elicit process, she had the boys demonstrate these same word-learning strategies with new, unfamiliar vocabulary they came upon in the poem. She made sure they applied the practices she modeled for them and talked out loud about what they did, so as to reinforce their strategic and metacognitive thinking.

To build fluency, Sharmayn ensured Masood and Carlos had multiple opportunities to read and reread familiar text. For instance, after working reciprocally through the entire Robert Frost poem, "The Road Not Taken," she had the boys practice reading it silently, then orally several times until they could get through it without any interruptions or misuces and with appropriate expression. To guide them through oral

Figure 11.6 Independent Word-Learning Prompts and Strategies

> **When striving readers come to an unfamiliar word, have them ask and try to answer the following questions:**
>
> 1. What is the purpose of the word? Does it name something? Show action? Describe something?
> 2. What clues are in the sentence? Is there a common expression, a synonym, a definition, extra description?
> 3. Are there any clues in the sentences before and after the sentence containing the word?
> 4. What things in my life can I connect with the text and the word?
> 5. Can I pronounce the word? Does the pronunciation give me any clues about what the word might mean?
> 6. Does the word have smaller parts? Do they tell me something about the word?
> 7. Is this word so important I need to use the dictionary to look it up?
> 8. If I look up the word in the dictionary, can I say the meaning in a way that makes sense in the text?

reading, Sharmayn took the lead while the boys echoed her words. As fluency further developed, the three read the poem together in choral fashion. Finally, the boys read the poem aloud on their own. Once Carlos and Masood felt totally comfortable with the poem, she invited them to give their oral rendition for the entire class. They particularly enjoyed demonstrating their competence with a reading from the class anthology because it was the same text all of their classmates had to read, too.

Bridging Students' Other Literacies with Academic Literacy

The idea of linking youths' out-of-school literacies with academic literacy has been an overarching theme of this book. In every chapter we have asserted the importance of practices that honor who adolescents are in all their diversity and that demonstrate the value we place on their lifeworlds beyond the classroom walls (Willis, Garcia, Barrera, & Harris, 2003). This is so because of the growing realization that strong teacher–student relationships and respect for individual and cultural identities have a positive effect on learning engagement and achievement (Ancess, 2003; Sturtevant, et al., 2006). We have also learned of the importance of creating spaces in secondary schools for striving readers' everyday literacies so they can showcase and build on their strengths with the print and digital media they use on their own (Knobel, 1998; Morrell, 2002; O'Brien, 2001; 2003).

Self-Contained English

Flashcards and workbooks as the basis for word study was yielding complaints and despondency from Nathan's eighth-grade self-contained English students. This year was the worst of all. His suburban school district had been going through a major demographic shift away from virtually all-White, Euro-American students to a rapidly growing percentage of African American, Latino/a, and Asian American students. Many were new or recent immigrants with strong ties to their native cultures. Nathan's methods, which had served him well for several years, were no longer viable for the new population of youth being placed in his classes. In a word, his pedagogy needed to become more culturally responsive.

An aficionado of popular music himself, Nathan came up with a new idea for doing word studies after talking with his students before class about what they had programmed on their iPods, MP3 players, and other portable music devices. Most were listening to hip-hop, Tejano, or country. He wondered if the lyrics from the songs and raps themselves might serve as the text for learning word families. After getting a few of the most popular titles of tunes from his students, he tracked down the lyrics on the Internet and found they possessed a variety of words that could be studied as families. These words could then be used as models for other similar words in school texts and in their own writing.

The following excerpt highlights how Nathan and his students worked with rap lyrics to engage in word-study practices. You'll see how they created and studied a particular word family, then expanded on the words from the family to generate new words for their individual vocabulary notebooks. Nathan and his class of seven students were sitting at their desks arranged in a circle.

Nathan: All of you should have the sheet with the Snoop Dogg rap lyrics. This rap is called "I Love to Give You Light," compliments of Derek. How many of you know this song? Let's first listen to it and then we'll read the lyrics. (Nathan had downloaded the song from the Internet and played it for the class on his computer.) Okay, now I want you to turn to someone next to you and look at the lyrics for words that have similar sounds or spellings. We're going to try to find some word families in here.

Nathan moved around the interior of the circle to monitor and assist his class. After a few minutes, he invited students to share the words they found that might form word families.

Tori: What about the word "I"—it says that a lot.

James: There are a lot of words that start with /d/, like "Dogg" and "don't."

Nathan: That's possible...good. What else?

Hugo: Me and Casey saw all these words like "block" and "black"...I don't know what you call them. They have the letters "c" and "k" in them.

Nathan: Those are really good. I was looking at those words, too. And did anyone find the words with "ch"? There are quite a few of those, too. Let's see what we can do with those words, the ones with "ch" and the the ones with "ck."

Nathan directed the students to get out their vocabulary notebooks. Each notebook has a personalized cover. Some are collages of magazine images and words. Others have freehand illustrations of symbols. And others are decorated with graffiti. He drew a t-chart on the board and asked students to copy it in their notebooks. At the top of the left column he wrote "ch" and on the right side "ck."

Nathan: Let's read through the rap now together and look for all the words that have either a "ck" or a "ch." Make sure you stop whoever's reading when we find one. I'll start, okay?

Nathan read aloud a few lines and stopped to point out a couple of words that fit in the two word-family categories. He was also stopped after reading another word in the "ch" family. These words were written in the t-chart. He then asked for volunteers to read aloud, going through the same process until he and his students had completed the entire rap and had gathered all the words they could find that fit in the two columns. This is the finished t-chart:

> In the hands of innovative teachers, youth music offers an ideal context for building academic vocabularies.

ch	ck
choir	background
such	Jackers
alchemist	glock
preach	block
church	locked
teachin	black
watchin	
each	
preachin	
reach	
purchase	
Beach	
child	

With the /ch/ words, Nathan and his students identified all of them that had the same sound, as in "such," "preach," "church," and so on. Only two of the words in this column had dissimilar sounds, "choir" with a /kw/ sound and "alchemist" with a /k/ sound. These were put into a separate group. They repeated saying the words aloud, emphasizing the /ch/ sound, and looked at how each word was used in the rap. The same pattern of analysis was used with the /ck/ words. The pronunciation of the /ck/ sound was consistent for words in this column.

Nathan then asked students to work with a partner again and think of new words with the /ch/ and /ck/ sounds. Again, as students worked in pairs, Nathan moved around the circle to facilitate and answer questions. When finished, he called on students to go to the t-chart and add their new words. They also wrote them in their notebooks. In the left column, words such as "catch" "match" "reach" and "bunch" were added. In the right column, new words included "socks" "locker" "backpack" "kick" and "duck."

Finally, Nathan asked student pairs to work together on writing their own rap lyrics that would contain all or some of the new words from the t-chart. Casey read the rap she and Hugo wrote while Hugo kept rhythm on his desk top. It went like this:

I put my *socks* in my *backpack* when I go to school.

I put my backpack in my *locker* or I look like a fool.

I get my *socks* from my backpack when I go to gym.

I gotta *catch* a ball then I *kick* it to him.

Nathan's students never had such fun doing word-study work as when they used song lyrics for analyzing related vocabulary. His students' enthusiasm translated into genuine learning as he noticed their ability to recognize many of the same words in other texts. By eliminating barriers between outside-of-school interests and literacies and classroom practices, Nathan was able to increase engagement in learning and build language competencies for his striving readers.

Cross-Age Tutoring

Research evidence has been growing for the benefits of peer-mediated instruction (Vaughn, et al., 2001). Structuring classroom interaction so that youth have opportunities to learn from and with one another has contributed to higher student engagement in learning and increased teacher satisfaction (Arreaga-Mayer, 1998). Small groups and pairs of students seem to be particularly beneficial arrangements for striving readers, who find it more difficult to learn in whole-class instructional contexts (Elbaum, Schumm, & Vaughn, 1997). One such promising context for accelerating striving readers' literacy development is cross-age tutoring (Jacobson et al., 2001; Smith-D'Arezzo & Kennedy, 2004; Thrope & Wood, 2000). We talked earlier in this chapter about the value of this approach as an alternative to pull-out programs and remedial reading (Fisher, 2001a). In the example that follows, an older and younger striving reader were the beneficiaries of a buddy reading program.

Buddy Reading: A Special Program for Striving Readers

Vince started the 10th grade fully expecting to drop out. Both of his older brothers had left school early, and his sister, who had recently had a baby, was receiving homebound instruction. Carol, the literacy coach working in Vince's school, looked through his file and saw that he was an ideal candidate for the buddy reading program she was launching. While Vince's reading scores were 3 to 4 years below where they should have been for a 16-year-old, he was described by his teachers as "friendly" and even "caring." A repeated theme, however, was that he lacked motivation. Carol saw another possible future for this young teen and recruited him for the cross-age tutoring program as part of an overall plan to improve reading skills for striving youth and keep them in school.

The program Carol put together targeted young men and women like Vince, students at risk of dropping out due to poor academic performance, low ability levels, or difficult home circumstances. She had made arrangements with the elementary school, which was only a short walk across the track field, to host tutorial sessions twice weekly involving second and third graders and high school reading buddies.

After speaking with Vince and several other students individually about participating in the program, and getting commitments from six of them, Carol prepared them for their roles. Vince and the others were in the same third-block study hall, which was an ideal time to run the program. Before meeting their elementary buddies, the high school tutors learned techniques for finding out the children's interests. They were taught simple read-aloud and vocabulary strategies. They learned how to facilitate writing in response to reading, and how to make books. Throughout the training in preparation for tutoring, Carol stressed the need to be encouraging of their younger buddies and help them see that reading and writing can be enjoyable. Above all, Carol hoped that by developing literacy strategies for helping younger, less able readers than themselves, these adolescents would, in fact, expand their own reading and writing skills.

Vince's reading buddy was a second grader by the name of Barry, who was already experiencing difficulties with grade-appropriate reading materials. Vince learned in their first meeting that Barry was almost a neighbor of his. The young boy lived in a housing project just a couple of streets away from Vince's building. Right from the start, Barry told Vince about how much he loved football. He said his father lived in Chicago, and that was the team he wanted to play for when he grew up. Barry also told Vince what he always wanted was his own computer so he could play "cool games."

After spending most of the first tutoring session getting to know one another, Vince read some pages he had practiced from a short biography about Michael Jordan. Before reading, he talked about how much he liked "roundball." As Vince was gathering his materials to leave, Barry asked him when he was coming back, and Vince reassured him he would return in a couple of days. It was a humble start of what was to become an important experience for the two of them.

While some tutors dropped out over the next couple of months, Vince stuck it out and came to enjoy his newfound status as a role model and "expert" reader for his young buddy, Barry. Much of what the two of them read and wrote about had to do with football. Carol found appropriately difficult, high-interest books for them to enjoy together, such as biographies of great Bear's players from the past, such as Dick Butkus, Walter Peyton, Jim McMahon, and the "Fridge" Perry. They kept a scrapbook of the Bears's performance that season, reading newspaper stories and cutting out pictures of their favorite players. Along with these, they wrote captions, statistics, and bits of trivia from players' records.

While cutting out a magazine photo of the Bears's premier running back, Anthony Thomas, better known as the *A-Train*, Barry commented about his powerful physique, wondering out loud how he got so big. Vince thought they could find information on that topic using the Internet. Because the cross-age tutoring sessions were held in the elementary school's media center, computers were available throughout the large, open room. Carol helped get their search started using descriptors such as "football players training," and they found pages of sites concerned with body-building and fitness. What caught Vince's eye, however, were references to performance-enhancement drugs. Carol helped them locate sites with straightforward, objective information about these supplements, which they printed for reading later.

Carol talked with Vince about how he might share this information with Barry, cautioning him not to present it in a way that might inadvertently glorify drug use. Vince assured her he was going to "set him straight about that junk." Under Carol's watchful eye, Vince planned ways he would read, write, and talk about performance-enhancement drugs in the next few sessions. She helped Vince develop strategies for sharing selected content from the book that would help Barry begin to appreciate the drug-free ways of building muscle and stamina for athletic competition.

It was Vince, however, who came up with the idea of a digital activity related to the topic. Aware of Barry's keen interest in computers, he developed a plan for taking a closer look at the characters from popular computer games. His plan was inspired by reading that one of the most common pastimes among many American football players when on the road or during the off-season was playing such games as *True Crime: Streets of LA* (Activision) and *WWF Wrestlemania* (THQ). Typically, the heroes and villains in these games are exaggeratedly muscled in ways that football players and bodybuilders must envy and, perhaps, strive to resemble. Demonstrating once again for Carol his ability to reason critically, Vince saw how these images might influence certain athletes to do whatever it takes, including using drugs, to achieve unusual physiques.

With Carol's help and assistance from the elementary school media specialist, Vince and Barry used the Internet to find pictures of popular computer game figures from *Take No Prisoners* (Red Orb), *The Hulk* (Vivendi-Universal), *Army Men: Sarge's Heroes* (3DO), and *X-Men: Mutant Academy* (Activision). These pictures were then downloaded into Adobe Photoshop so they could be altered. The reading buddies learned how to rework the main characters' physiques, reshaping them in ways that were more proportional to normal muscle development. They displayed their work in a PowerPoint presentation with "before" slides, accompanied by captions warning of the dangers of steroids and other illegal substances for building muscle, and "after" slides with statements about good health, diet, and fitness. Proud of the brief PowerPoint show they had created, Vince and Barry were given special opportunities to share the slides with other students in the cross-age tutoring program. The elementary school's principal was so impressed she made sure the slides were shown to the children during drug awareness events that year.

Carol's buddy reading program offered Vince and Barry the opportunity to establish a positive relationship, increase time spent reading, and develop critical thinking skills. This approach to cross-age tutoring offers striving adolescent readers a context for expanding their skills and motivation while enhancing their self-efficacy through positive role modeling.

CASE STUDY REVISITED

We hope by now you have had a chance to give some thought to Rene's situation. We're sure it became obvious as you read this chapter that a variety of effective practices are possible with striving readers. The fact that Mr. Willis provided very few meaningful literacy experiences for Rene and her classmates is largely inexcusable, we believe, in spite of the less-than-ideal condition of the school and classroom. Here is your chance to suggest ways of transforming Rene's special reading class to make it a more culturally and intellectually responsive environment. Take a moment to write your suggestions now.

We next offer our suggestions for transforming Mr. Willis's classroom. To do so, we describe the outstanding work of a remedial reading teacher who we believe embodies what it means to engage striving adolescent readers in meaningful and personally relevant print experiences.

Carolyn teaches remedial reading in a large suburban high school just outside the boundary of a sprawling city in the mid-Atlantic region. Many of her students are English learners, and all have a history of poor academic achievement. In her classroom she has created a learning environment that supports authentic uses of print. She also regularly demonstrates for students her own comprehension processes, thereby allowing them to observe effective reading and writing strategies. Carolyn believes that development in reading and writing can take place only in contexts where students have frequent opportunities to read and write as meaningful communication.

Youth who enter her classroom are immersed in a language-rich environment characterized by:

- A reading center—a comfortable corner of the classroom crammed with fiction and nonfiction books, magazines, graphic novels and comic books, newspapers, pamphlets, taped stories, high-interest/easy-reading books, two Internet-ready computers, and other print material
- Displays of students' work, including stories, poems, song lyrics, essays, and artwork
- Functional reading and writing spaces, including a message board for exchanging notes and information among students and between Carolyn and her students, lunch menus, part-time job notices, classified ads, and more

Carolyn demonstrates for her students how reading and writing can be functional and enjoyable. For 15 minutes of every class she reads aloud from a young adult book. Students have enjoyed the experience of hearing and discussing books such as *Chaising Vermeer* (Balliett, 2005) about a girl whose mother died but learns to overcome the loss with the help of a wonderful teacher at the lab school she attends in inner-city Chicago; *Who Am I without Him?* (Flake, 2004), a collection of short stories about urban black girls and their feelings and experiences with boys; the National Book Award winner, *Godless* (Hautman, 2005), tells the story of a rebellious adolescent boy who, when forced to participate in a Catholic youth group, starts his own religious sect that gets out of control; and Walter Dean Myers' (2005), *Shooter*, a documentary novel about a school shooting involving three teens who reveal feelings of being outsiders.

Looking Back, Looking Forward

Helping striving adolescent readers develop levels of reading and writing competence necessary for content-area learning is a demanding task. To be successful, a total commitment is required of all teachers with whom striving youth interact during the course of a school day. Growth may not always be as rapid as would be hoped, but is far more likely to occur when secondary teachers, administrators, and support staff dedicate themselves to responsive and culturally sensitive practices for striving readers.

As you reflect on the ideas and practices discussed in this chapter and throughout this book, consider the approaches you might use to meet the needs of striving readers. As you do, remember that these students will need the best of what we know about literacy and youth culture. They will need engaging and meaningful strategies that expand interest, build competence, and promote a sense of agency and independence. They will need highly knowledgeable and skillful teachers as well as comprehensive literacy programs that offer opportunities for encounters with multiple texts and forms of representation throughout the school day. And, perhaps most critically, striving readers will need teachers and school personnel interested in forming close and supportive relationships with them as a context for literacy and learning growth.

References

Alfassi, M. (2004). Reading to learn: Effects of combined strategy instruction on high school students. *The Journal of Educational Research, 97*, 171–184.

Allington, R. L. (2002). You can't learn much from books you can't read. *EducationalLeadership, 60*, 16–19.

Allington, R. L. (2006). *What really matters to struggling readers: Designing research-based programs* (2nd ed). Boston: Allyn & Bacon.

Alvermann, D. (2003). *Seeing themselves as capable and engaged readers: Adolescents and remediated instruction.* Naperville, IL: Learning Point Associates.

Alvermann, D., & Hagood, M. (2000). Fandom and critical media literacy. *Journal of Adolescent & Adult Literacy, 43*, 436–446.

Ancess, J. (2003). *Beating the odds: High schools as communities of practice.* New York: Teachers College Press.

Anderson, R. C., Wilson, P., & Fielding, L. (1988). Growth in reading and how children spend their time outside of school. *Reading Research Quarterly, 23*, 285–303.

Applegate, A. J., & Applegate, M. D. (2004). The Peter effect: Reading habits and attitudes of preservice teachers. *The Reading Teacher, 57*, 554–563.

Archer, A. L., Gleason, M. M., & Vachon, V. L. (2003). Decoding and fluency: Foundation skills for struggling older readers. *Learning Disabilities Quarterly, 26*, 89–102.

Arreaga-Mayer, C. (1998). Increasing active student responding and improving academic performance through classwide peer tutoring intervention in school and clinic, 34, 89–94.

Arter, J. (2001). Learning teams for classroom assessment literacy. *NASSP Bulletin, 85*, 53–65.

Balfanz, R., Legters, N., & Jordan, W. (2004). Catching up: Effect of the talent development ninth-grade instructional interventions in reading and mathematics in high-poverty high schools. *NASSP Bulletin, 88*, 3–30.

Balfanz, R., McPartland, J., & Shaw, A. (2002, April). Re-conceptualizing extra help for high school students in a high standards era. Paper presented at Preparing America's Future: High School Symposium, Washington, DC.

Barry, A. (1997). High school reading programs revisited. *Journal of Adolescent & Adult Literacy, 40*, 524–531.

Bean, T. (2002). Making reading relevant for adolescents. *Educational Leadership, 60*(3), 34–37.

Bean, T., Bean, S., & Bean, K. (1999). Intergenerational conversations and two adolescents' multiple literacies: Implications for redefining content area literacy. *Journal of Adolescent & Adult Literacy, 42*, 438–448.

Bean, T., & Valerio, P. C. (1997). Constructing school success in literacy: The pathway to college entrance for minority students. *Reading Research Quarterly, 32*, 320–327.

Beavers, D. (2001). Professional development: Outside the workshop box. *Principal Leadership, 1*, 43–46.

Benton-Kupper, J. (1999). Can less be more? The quantity versus quality issue of curriculum in a block schedule. *Journal of Research and Development in Education, 32*, 168–177.

Bhattacharya, A., & Ehri, L. C. (2004). Graphosyllabic analysis helps adolescent struggling readers read and spell words. *Journal of Learning Disabilities, 37*, 331–349.

Biancarosa, G., & Snow, C. (2004). *Reading next—A vision for action and research in middle and high school literacy.* New York: Carnegie Corporation.

Bill & Melinda Gates Foundation. (2001). Making the case for small schools. Available online at at: http://www.gatesfoundation.org/NRP/Public/Media/Downloads/ed/evaluation/BMG911SmallScholsBrochure.pdf.

Blevins, W. (2001). *Teaching phonics and word study in the intermediate grades.* New York: Scholastic.

Bloome, D., & Green, J. (1984). Directions in the sociolinguistic study of reading. In P. D. Pearson

(Ed.), *Handbook of reading research* (pp. 395–421). New York: Longman.

Bomer, R. (1999). Conferring with struggling readers: The test of our craft, courage, and hope. *The New Advocate, 12*, 21–38.

Braunger, J., Donahue, D., Evans, K., & Galguera, T. (2005). *Rethinking preparation for content area teaching: The reading apprenticeship approach.* San Francisco, CA: Jossey-Bass.

Broaddus, K., & Bloodgood, J. (1999). "We're supposed to already know how to teach reading": Teacher change to support struggling readers. *Reading Research Quarterly, 34*, 426–451.

Broaddus, K., & Ivey, G. (2002). Taking away the struggle to read in the middle grades. *Middle School Journal, 34*(2). Available online at http://www.nmsa.org/services/msj/mjs_nov2002.htm.

Brozo, W. G. (1990a). Hiding out in secondary classrooms: Coping strategies of unsuccessful readers. *Journal of Reading, 33*, 324–328

Brozo, W. G. (1990b). Learning how at-risk readers learn best: A case for interactive assessment. *Journal of Reading, 33*, 522–527.

Brozo, W. G. (1995). Literacy without "risk": Reconsidering cultural and curricular differentiation in literacy. *State of Reading, 2*, 5–12.

Brozo, W. G. (2006) Tales out of school: Accounting for adolescents in a literacy reform community. *Journal of Adolescent & Adult Literacy.*

Brozo, W. G., & Brozo, C. L. (1994). Literacy assessment in standardized and zero-failure contexts. *Reading and Writing Quarterly, 10*, 189–208.

Brozo, W. G., & Hargis, C. (2005). Taking seriously the idea of reform: One high school's efforts to make reading more responsive to all students. In P. Shannon & J. Edmondson (Eds.), *Reading education policy.* Newark, DE: International Reading Association.

Brozo, W. G., Valerio, P. C., & Salazar, M. (1996). A walk through Gracie's garden: Literacy and cultural explorations in a Mexican American junior high school. *Journal of Adolescent & Adult Literacy, 40*, 164–170.

Bryant, D. P., Goodwin, M., Bryant, B. R., & Higgins, K. (2003). Vocabulary instruction for students with learning disabilities: A review of the research. *Learning Disabilities Quarterly, 26*, 117–129.

Cappella, E., & Weinstein, R. S. (2001). Turning around reading achievement: Predictors of high school students' academic resilience. *Journal of Educational Psychology, 93*, 758–771.

Cardarelli, A. (1992). Teachers under cover: Promoting the personal reading of teachers. *The Reading Teacher, 45*, 664–668.

Cipielewski, J., & Stanovich, K. (1992). Predicting growth in reading ability from children's exposure to print. *Journal of Experimental Child Psychology, 54*, 74–89.

Cook-Sather, A. (2002a). Authorizing students' perspectives: Toward trust, dialogue, and change in education. *Educational Researcher, 31*, 3–14.

Cook-Sather, A. (2002b). Re(in)forming the conversations: Student position, power, and voice in teacher education. *Radical Teacher, 64*, 21–28.

Cook-Sather, A. (2003). Listening to students about learning differences. *Teaching Exceptional Children, 35*, 22–26.

Corbett, H. D., & Wilson, R. L. (1995). Make a difference with, not for, students: A plea for researchers and reformers. *Educational Researcher, 24*, 12–17.

Crowther, S. (1998). Secrets of staff development support. *Educational Leadership, 55*, 75.

Cushman, K. (1999, November). *How small schools increase learning: And what large schools can do about it.* National Association of Elementary School Principals. Available online at http://www.naesp.org/comm/p1199b.htm.

Davis, J. (2001). Heritage Hills tops in school reading. *Indiana Courier Press*, February 11, 1B.

DeBruin-Parecki, A., Paris, S. G., & Siedenburg, J. (1997). Family literacy: Examining practice and issues of effectiveness. *Journal of Adolescent & Adult Literacy, 40*, 596–605.

Dole, J., Brown, K., & Trathen, W. (1996). The effects of strategy instruction on the comprehension performance of at-risk students. *Reading Research Quarterly, 31*, 62–88.

Donahue, P., Daane, M., & Grigg, W. (2003). *The nation's report card: Reading highlights 2003.* Washington, DC: National Center for Education Statistics.

Dong, Y. R. (2002). Integrating language and content: How three biology teachers work with non-English speaking students. *International Journal of Bilingual Education and Bilingualism, 5*, 40–57.

Dreher, M. J. (2003). Motivating teachers to read. *The Reading Teacher, 56*, 338–340.

DuFour, R., & Eaker, R. (1998). *Professional learning communities at work: Best practices for enhancing student achievement.* Bloomington, IN: National Educational Service.

Elbaum, B., Schumm, J., & Vaughn, S. (1997). Urban middle-elementary students' perceptions of grouping formats for reading instruction. *Elementary School Journal, 97*, 475–500.

Finders, M. (1997). *Just girls: Hidden literacies and life in junior high*. New York:Teachers College Press.

Fisher, D. (2001a). Cross age tutoring: Alternatives to the reading resource room for struggling adolescent readers. *Journal of Instructional Psychology, 28,* 234–240.

Fisher, D. (2001b). "We're moving on up": Creating a schoolwide literacy effort in an urban high school. *Journal of Adolescent & Adult Literacy, 45,* 92–101.

Fisher, J., Schumaker, J., & Deshler, D. (2002). Improving the reading comprehension of at-risk adolescents. In C. C. Block & M. Pressley (Eds.), *Comprehension Instruction: Research-based best practices* (pp. 351–364). New York: Guilford.

Gardiner, S. (2001). Ten minutes a day for silent reading. *Educational Leadership, 59,* 32–35.

Goodman, Y. M. & Marek, A. (1996). *Retrospective miscue analysis*. Katonah, NY: Richard C. Owen.

Greenleaf, C., Jimenez, R., & Roller, C. (2002). Reclaiming secondary reading interventions: From limited to rich conceptions, from narrow to broad conversations. *Reading Research Quarterly, 37,* 484–496.

Greenleaf, C., Schoenbach, R., Cziko, C., & Mueller, F. (2001). Apprenticing adolescent readers to academic literacy. *Harvard Educational Review, 71,* 79–129.

Gregory, T. (2000, December). School reform and the no-man's-land of high school size. Available online at http://www.smallschoolsproject.org/articles/download/gregory.pdf.

Gross, P. A. (1997). *Joint curriculum design*. Mahwah, NJ: Erlbaum.

Guthrie, J., & Davis, M. (2003). Motivating struggling readers in middle school through an engagement model of classroom practice. *Reading & Writing Quarterly, 19,*59–85.

Harmon, J. M. (2000). Creating contexts for supporting word meaning constructions: Dialogues with struggling middle school readers. In T. Shannahan & F. V. Rodriguez-Brown (Eds.), *49th Yearbook of the National Reading Conference* (pp. 331–343). Chicago, IL: National Reading Conference.

Harmon, J. M. (2002). Teaching independent word learning strategies to struggling readers. *Journal of Adolescent & Adult Literacy, 45,* 606–615.

Heshusius, L. (1995). Listening to children: "What could we possibly have in common?"From concerns with self to participatory consciousness. *Theory into Practice, 43,*117–123.

Hock, M. F., & Deshler, D. D. (2003). Don't forget the adolescents. *Principal Leadership, 4,* 50–56.

International Reading Association. (2001). *Integrating literacy and technology in the curriculum*.

Retrieved November 5, 2003 from http://www.reading.org/positions/technology.html.

Ivey, G. (1999a). A multicase study in the middle school: Complexities among young adolescent readers. *Reading Research Quarterly, 34,* 172–192.

Ivey, G. (1999b). Reflections on teaching struggling middle school readers. *Journal of Adolescent & Adult Literacy, 42,* 372–381.

Ivey, G. & Baker, M. (2004). Phonics instruction for older students? Just say no. *Educational Leadership, 61,* 35–39.

Jacobson, J., Thrope, L., Fisher, D., Lapp, D., Frey, N., & Flood, J. (2001). Cross-age tutoring: A literacy improvement approach for struggling adolescent readers. *Journal of Adolescent & Adult Literacy, 44,* 528–537.

Jensen, T. L., & Jensen, V. S. (2002). Sustained silent reading and young adult short stories for high school classes. *ALAN Review, 30*(1), 58–60.

Jimenez, R. (1997). The strategic reading abilities and potential of five low-literacy Latina/o readers in middle school. *Reading Research Quarterly, 32,* 224–243.

Knobel, M. (1998). *Everyday literacies: Students, discourse, and social practice*. New York: Peter Lang.

Krashen, S. (1993). *The power of reading*. Englewood, CO: Libraries Unlimited.

Kuhn, M. R., & Stahl, S. A. (2003). Fluency: A review of developmental and remedial practices. *Journal of Educational Psychology, 95,* 3–21.

Langer, J. A. (2000). Excellence in English in middle and high school: How teachers' professional lives support student achievement. *American Educational Research Journal, 37*(2), 397–439.

Langer, J. (2001). Beating the odds: Teaching middle and high school students to read and write well. *American Educational Research Journal, 38,* 837–880.

Larson, R., Richards, M., Sims, B., & Dworkin, J. (2001). How urban African American young adolescents spend their time: Time budgets for location, activities, and companionship. *American Journal of Community Psychology, 29,* 565–597.

Lee, P. W. (1999). In their own voices: An ethnographic study of low-achieving students within the context of school reform. *Urban Education, 34,* 214–244.

Legters, N. E., Balfanz, R., Jordan, W. J., & McPartland, J. M. (2002). *Comprehensive reform for urban high schools: A talent development approach*. New York:Teachers College Press.

Marshall, J., Pritchard, R., & Gunderson, B. (2001). Professional development: What works and what doesn't. *Principal Leadership, 1,* 64–68.

Mastropieri, M. A., Scruggs, T., & Graetz, J. (2003). Reading comprehension instruction for secondary students: Challenges for struggling students and teachers. *Learning Disabilities Quarterly, 26,* 103–116.

Mastropieri, M. A., Scruggs, T., Mohler, L., Beranek, M., Spencer, V., Boon, R., & Talbott, E. (2001). Can middle school students with serious reading difficulties help each other and learn anything? *Learning Disabilities Research, 16,* 18–27.

McCray, A. D., Vaughn, S., & Neal, L. I. (2001). Not all students learn to read by third grade: Middle school students speak out about their reading disabilities. *Journal of Special Education, 35,* 17–30.

McKinney, B., Steglich, D. M., & Stever-Zeitlin, J. A. (2002). *Small schools, big lessons.* Available online at http://www.mckinseyquarterly.com/article_page.asp?ar=1170&L2=33&L3=93.

McQuillan, J., & Au, J. (2001). The effect of print access on reading frequency. *Reading Pscyhology, 22,* 225–248.

Miller, H. M. (2002). The SSR handbook: How to organize and manage a sustained silent reading program. *Journal of Adolescent and Adult Literacy, 45*(5), 434–435.

Moje, E. B. (2002). Re-framing adolescent literacy research for new times: Studying youth as a resource. *Reading Research and Instruction, 41,* 211–228.

Moje, E. B. (2004). Federal adolescent literacy policy: Implication for administration, policy, and the adolescent literacy research community. Paper presented at the Annul Meeting of the National Reading Conference, San Antonio, TX.

Moje, E. B., McIntosh, Ciechanowski, K., Kramer, K., Ellis, L., Carrillo, R., & Collazo, T. (2004). Working toward third space in content area literacy: An examination of everyday funds of knowledge and discourse. *Reading Research Quarterly, 39,* 38–70.

Moore, D. W., & Hinchman, K. A. (2006). *Teaching adolescents who struggle with reading: Practical strategies.* Boston: Allyn & Bacon.

Morrell, E. (2002). Toward a critical pedagogy of popular culture: Literacy development among urban youth. *Journal of Adolescent & Adult Literacy, 45,* 72–77.

Morrison, T. G., Jacobs, J. S., & Swinyard, W. R. (1999). Do teachers who read personally use recommended practices in their classrooms? *Reading Research and Instruction, 38,* 81–100.

Murphy, C. (1999). Use time for faculty study. *Journal of Staff Development, 20,* 20–25.

Murphy, C., & Lick, D. (1998). *Whole-faculty study groups: A powerful way to change schools and enhance learning.* Thousand Oaks, CA: Corwin Press.

National Council of Teachers of English. (2004). *A call to action: What we know about adolescent literacy and ways to support teachers in meeting students' needs.* Urbana, IL: NCTE.

National Reading Panel (2000). *Teaching children to read.* Washington, DC: National Institute of Child Health and Human Development.

Nichols, J. D., & Miller, R. B. (1994). Cooperative learning and student motivation. *Contemporary Educational Psychology, 19,* 167–178.

O'Brien, D. (2001). "At-risk" adolescents: Redefining competence through the multiliteracies of intermediality, visual arts, and representation. *Reading Online, 4*(11). Available online at http://www.readingonline.org/newliteracies/lit_Index. asp?HREF=/newliteracies/Obrien/index. html.

O'Brien, D. (2003, March). Juxtaposing traditional and intermedial literacies to redefine the competence of struggling adolescents. *Reading Online, 6*(7). Available online at http://www.readingonline.org/newliteracies/lit_index.asp?HREF=obrien2/.

O'Brien, D., Stewart, R., & Moje, E. (1995). Why content literacy is difficult to infuse into the secondary school: Complexities of curriculum, pedagogy, and school culture. *Reading Research Quarterly, 30,* 442–463.

Ogbu, J. (1994). Racial stratification and education in the United States: Why inequality persists. *Teachers College Record, 96,* 264–298.

Pearman, E., Huang, A., & Mellblom, C. (1997). The inclusion of all students: Concerns and incentives of educators. *Education and Training in Mental Retardation and Development, 32,* 11–19.

Polakow, V., & Brozo, W. G. (1994). Deconstructing the at-risk discourse: Power, pedagogy, and the politics of inequity: Special section editors' introduction. *The Review of Education, 15,* 217–221.

Primeaux, J. (2000). Focus on research: Shifting perspectives on struggling readers. *Language Arts, 77,* 537–542.

Putnam, R., & Borko, H. (2000). What do new views of knowledge and thinking have to say about research on teacher learning? *Educational Researcher, 29,* 4–15.

Reed, A. J. S. (1988). *Comics to classics: A parent's guide to books for teens and preteens.* Newark, DE: International Reading Association.

Rhodes, L., & Dudley-Marling, C. (1988). *Readers and writers with a difference: A holistic approach to* teaching learning disabled and remedial students*. Portsmouth, NH: Heinemann.

Romine, B., McKenna, M., & Robinson, R. (1996). Reading coursework requirements for middle and high school content area teachers: A U.S. survey. *Journal of Adolescent & Adult Literacy, 40,* 194–200.

Ross, J., Rolheiser, C., & Hogaboam-Gray, A. (1999). Effects of collaborative action research on the knowledge of five Canadian teacher-researchers. *Elementary School Journal, 99,* 255–275.

Salinger, T. (2003). Helping older, struggling readers. *Preventing School Failure, 47,* 79–85.

Saravia-Schore, M., & Arvizu, S. (1992). *Cross-cultural literacy: Ethnographies of communication in multiethnic classrooms.* New York: Garland.

Shultz, J., & Cook-Sather, A. (2001). *In our own words: Students' perspectives on school.* Lanham, MD: Rowman & Littlefield.

Smith, F. (1985). *Reading without nonsense.* New York: Holt, Rinehart & Winston.

Smith-D'Arezzo, W., & Kennedy, B. (2004). Seeing double: Piecing writing together with cross-age partners. *Journal of Adolescent & Adult Literacy, 47,* 390–401.

Smith, K., & Hudelson, S. (2001). The NCTE reading initiative: Politics, pedagogy, and possibilities. *Language Arts, 79,* 29–37.

Snow, K. E., Griffin, P., & Burns, M. S. (2005). *Knowledge to support the teaching of reading: Preparing teachers for a changing world.* San Francisco: Jossey-Bass.

Sturtevant, E., Boyd, F., Brozo, W., Hinchman, K., Alvermann, D., & Moore, D. (2006). *Principled practices for adolescent literacy: A framework for instruction and policy.* Mahwah, NJ: Lawrence Erlbaum Associates.

Tatum, A. (2000). Breaking down barriers that disenfranchise African-American adolescent readers in lower-level tracks. *Journal of Adolescent & Adult Literacy, 44,* 52–64.

Tatum, A. (2005). *Teaching reading to black adolescent males: Closing the achievement gap.* Portland, ME: Stenhouse.

Taylor, B., Frye, B., & Maruyama, G. (1990). Time spent reading and reading growth. *American Educational Research Journal, 27,* 351–362.

Thrope, L., & Wood, K. (2000). Cross-age tutoring for young adolescents. *The Clearing House, 73,* 239–242.

Tice, C. (2000). Enhancing family literacy through collaboration: Program considerations. *Journal of Adolescent & Adult Literacy, 44,* 138–145.

Tichenor, M., & Heins, E. (2000). Study groups: An inquiry-based approach to improving schools. *The Clearing House, 73,* 316–319.

Vacca, R. (1998). Let's not marginalize adolescent literacy. *Journal of Adolescent & Adult Literacy, 41,* 604–609.

Vaughn, S., Klingner, J., & Bryant, D. (2001). Collaborative strategic reading as a means to enhance peer-mediated instruction for reading comprehension and content-area learning. *Remedial and Special Education, 22,* 66–74.

Venable, G. P. (2003). Confronting complex text: Readability lessons from students with language learning disabilities. *Topics in Language Disorders, 23,* 225–240.

Wasley, P. A., Hampel, R. L., & Clark, R. W. (1997). *Kids and school reform.* San Francisco: Jossey-Bass.

Weller, D., & Weller, S. (1999). Secondary school reading: Using the quality principle of continuous improvement to build an exemplary program. *NASSP Bulletin, 83,* 59–68.

Willis, A. I., Garcia, G. E., Barrera, R., & Harris, V. (2003). *Multicultural issues in literacy research and practice.* Mahwah, NJ: Lawrence Erlbaum Associates.

Wood, K., & Algozzine, B. (1994). *Teaching reading to high-risk learners: A unified perspective.* Boston: Allyn & Bacon.

Yoon, J.C. (2002). Three decades of sustained silent reading: A meta-analytic review of the effects of SSR on attitude toward reading. *Reading Improvement, 39*(4), 186–195.

Young Adult Literature and Related Sources

Balliett, B. (2005). *Chaising Vermeer.* New York: Scholastic.

Chambers, V. & Wilker, J. (1997). *The Harlem Renaissance.* New York: Chelsea House.

Dewdney, A. K. (1984), *The planiverse.* New York: Poseidon Press.

Flake, S. (2004). *Who am I without him?* New York: Hyperion.

Frank. R. (1986). *No hero for the Kaiser.* New York: Lothrop, Lee & Shepard.

Haskins, J., Tate, E. E., Cox, C., & Wilkinson, B. (2002). *Black stars of the Harlem Renaissance.* San Francisco, CA: Jossey-Bass.

Hautman, P. (2005). *Godless.* New York: Simon & Schuster.

Hill, L. C. (2004). *Harlem stomp! A cultural history of the Harlem Renaissance.* New York: Little Brown.

Lester, J., & Brown, R. (1999). *From slave ship to freedom road.* New York: Puffin.

Myers, W. D. (2005). *Shooter.* New York: Harpercollins.

McDonald, J. (2001). *Spellbound.* New York: Farrar, Strauss & Giroux.

Paulsen, G. (1992). *The haymeadow.* New York: Dell.

Smith, K. C. (2004). *Children's literature of the Harlem Renaissance.* Bloomington: Indiana University Press.

Name Index

Subject Index